Trübner's Oriental Series

THE INDIAN EMPIRE

T0299787

Trübner's Oriental Series

INDIA: HISTORY, ECONOMY AND SOCIETY
In 11 Volumes

THE INDIAN EMPIRE

ITS PEOPLE, HISTORY, AND PRODUCTS

W W HUNTER

LONDON AND NEW YORK

First published in 1886 by
Trübner & Co Ltd

Reprinted in 2000 by
Routledge
2 Park Square, Milton Park, Abingdon, Oxon, OX14 4RN

Simultaneously published in the USA and Canada by Routledge
711 Third Avenue, New York, NY 10017

Transferred to Digital Printing 2007

Routledge is an imprint of the Taylor & Francis Group

First issued in paperback 2013

The publishers have made every effort to contact authors/copyright holders
of the works reprinted in *Trübner's Oriental Series*.
This has not been possible in every case, however, and we would
welcome correspondence from those individuals/companies
we have been unable to trace.

These reprints are taken from original copies of each book. In many cases
the condition of these originals is not perfect. The publisher has gone to
great lengths to ensure the quality of these reprints, but wishes to point
out that certain characteristics of the original copies will, of necessity, be
apparent in reprints thereof.

British Library Cataloguing in Publication Data
A CIP catalogue record for this book
is available from the British Library

The Indian Empire

ISBN 978-0-415-24495-4 (hbk)
ISBN 978-0-415-86571-5 (pbk)

THE INDIAN EMPIRE:

ITS PEOPLE, HISTORY, AND PRODUCTS.

BY

W. W. HUNTER, C.S.I. C.I.E. LL.D.

SECOND EDITION.

LONDON: TRÜBNER & CO., LUDGATE HILL, 1886.

PREFACE TO THE SECOND EDITION.

THIS book tries to present, within a small compass, an account of India and her people. The materials on which it is based are condensed from my larger works. In 1869, the Government of India directed me to execute a Statistical Survey of its dominions,—a vast enterprise, whose records now make 128 printed volumes, aggregating 60,000 pages. The scale of the operations, although by no means too elaborate for the administrative purposes for which they were designed, necessarily placed their results beyond the reach of the general public. The hundred volumes of *The Statistical Survey* were therefore reduced to a more compendious form as the twelve volumes of *The Imperial Gazetteer of India.* The present book distils into one volume the essence of the whole.

I have elsewhere explained the mechanism by which the materials for the Statistical Survey were collected in each of the 240 Districts, or territorial units, of British India.[1] Without the help of a multitude of ·fellow-workers, the present volume could never have been written. It represents the fruit of a long process of continuous condensation. But in again acknowledging my indebtedness to brethren of my Service in India, I wish to specially commemorate the obligations which I also owe to a friend at home. Mr. J. S. Cotton, late Fellow of Queen's College Oxford, has rendered important aid at many stages of the work.

[1] See Preface to Volume I. of *The Imperial Gazetteer of India.*

Continuous condensation, although convenient to the reader, has its perils for the author. Many Indian topics are still open questions, with regard to which divergences of opinion may fairly exist. In some cases, I have been compelled by brevity to state my conclusions without setting forth the evidence on which they rest, and without any attempt to combat alternative views. In other matters, I have had to content myself with conveying a correct general impression, while omitting the modifying details. For I here endeavour to present an account, which shall be at once original and complete, of a continent inhabited by many more races and nations than Europe, in every stage of human development, from the polyandric tribes and hunting hamlets of the hill jungles, to the most complex commercial communities in the world. When I have had to expose old fables, or to substitute truth for long accepted errors, I clearly show my grounds for doing so. Thus, in setting aside the legend of Mahmúd the Idol-Breaker, I trace back the growth of the myth through the Persian Historians, to the contemporary narrative of Al Biruni (970–1029 A.D.). The calumnies against Jagannáth are corrected by the testimony of three centuries, from 1580, when Abul Fazl wrote, down to the police reports of 1870. Macaulay's somewhat fanciful story of Plassey has been told afresh in the words of Clive's own despatch. The history of Christianity in India is written, for the first time, from original sources and local inquiry.

But almost every period of Indian history forms an arena of controversy. Thus, in the early Sanskrit era, each date is the result of an intricate process of induction ; the chapter on the Scythic inroads has been pieced together from the unfinished researches of the Archæological Survey and from local investigations ; the growth of Hinduism, as the religious and social nexus of the Indian races, is here for the first time written. In attempting to reconstruct Indian history from its original sources in the fewest possible pages, I beg oriental scholars to believe that, although their individual views are not always set forth, they have been respectfully considered. I also pray the English reader to remember that, if he desires a more detailed treatment of the subjects of this volume, he may find it in my larger works.

W. W. H.

March 1886.

TABLE OF CONTENTS.

GENERAL PLAN.

CHAPTER I.

PHYSICAL ASPECTS.

CHAPTER II.

THE POPULATION OF INDIA.

CHAPTER III.

THE NON-ARYAN RACES.

CHAPTER V.

BUDDHISM (543 B.C. TO 1000 A.D.).

CHAPTER VI.

THE GREEKS IN INDIA (327 TO 161 B.C.).

CHAPTER VII.

SCYTHIC INROADS INTO INDIA (126? B.C. TO 544 A.D.).

CHAPTER VIII.

RISE OF HINDUISM (750 TO 1520 A.D.).

CHAPTER X.

EARLY MUHAMMADAN RULERS (711 TO 1526 A.D.).

CHAPTER XI.

THE MUGHAL EMPIRE (1526 TO 1761 A.D.).

CHAPTER XII.

THE MARATHA POWER (1634 TO 1818 A.D.).

CHAPTER XIII.

THE INDIAN VERNACULARS AND THEIR LITERATURE.

b

CHAPTER XIV.

EARLY EUROPEAN SETTLEMENTS (1498 TO 18TH CENTURY A.D.).

CHAPTER XV.

HISTORY OF BRITISH RULE (1757 TO 1885).

CHAPTER XVI.

BRITISH ADMINISTRATION OF INDIA.

CHAPTER XVII.

AGRICULTURE AND PRODUCTS.

CHAPTER XVIII.

MEANS OF COMMUNICATION

CHAPTER XIX.

COMMERCE AND TRADE.

CHAPTER XX.

ARTS AND MANUFACTURES.

CHAPTER XXI.

MINES AND MINERALS.

CHAPTER XXII.

GEOLOGY.

CHAPTER XXIII.

METEOROLOGY.

CHAPTER XXIV.

ZOOLOGY AND BOTANY.

CHAPTER XXV.

VITAL STATISTICS.

APPENDICES.

VOWEL SOUNDS.

a	has the sound of *a* as in	rural.
á	has the sound of *a* as in	far.
e	has the vowel sound in	grey.
i	has the sound of *i* as in	police.
í	has the vowel sound in	pier.
o	has the sound of *o* as in	bone.
u	has the sound of *u* as in	bull.
ú	has the sound of *u* as in	sure.
ai	has the vowel sound in	lyre.

Accents have been used as sparingly as possible ; and omitted in such words or terminals as *pur*, where the Sanskrit family of alphabets takes the short vowel instead of the long Persian one. The accents over *í* and *ú* have often been omitted, to avoid confusing the ordinary English reader, when the collocation of letters naturally gives them a long or open sound. No attempt has been made by the use of dotted consonants to distinguish between the dental and lingual *d*, or to represent similar refinements of Indian pronunciation.

Where the double *oo* is used for *u*, or the double *ee* for *i*, and whenever the above vowel sounds are departed from, the reason is either that the place has obtained a popular fixity of spelling, or that the Government has ordered the adoption of some special form.

I have borne in mind four things—First, that this work is intended for the ordinary English reader. Second, that the twenty-six characters of the English alphabet cannot possibly be made to represent the fifty letters or signs of the Indian alphabets, unless we resort to puzzling un-English devices of typography, such as dots under the consonants, curves above them, or italic letters in the middle of words. Third, that as such devices are unsuitable in a work of general reference, some compromise or sacrifice of scholarly accuracy to popular convenience becomes inevitable. Fourth, that a compromise to be defensible must be successful, and that the spelling of Indian places, while adhering to the Sanskrit vowel sounds, should be as little embarrassing as possible to the European eye.

W. W. H.

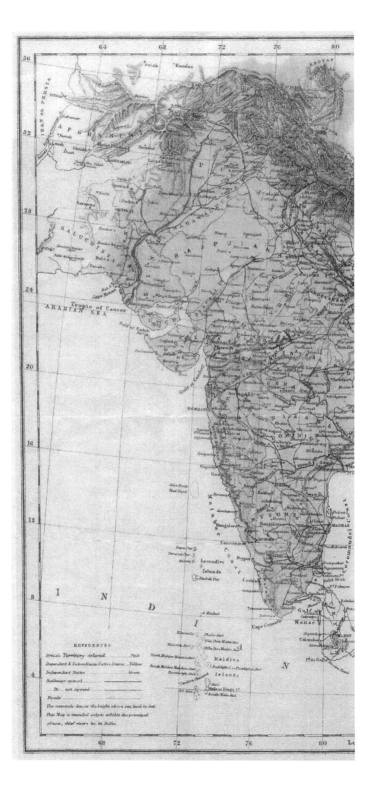

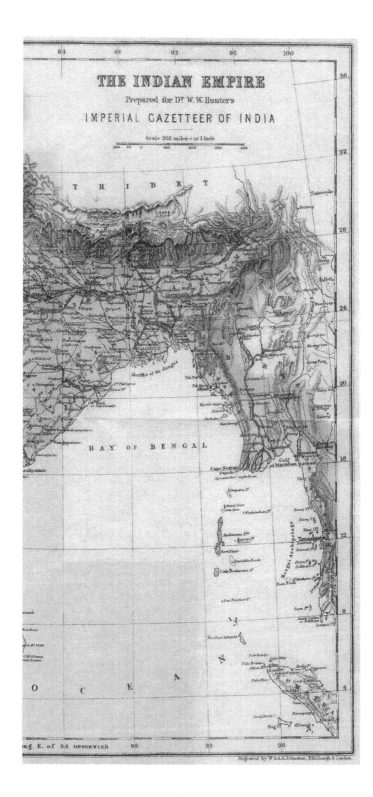

THE INDIAN EMPIRE

Prepared for Dr. W. W. Hunter's

IMPERIAL GAZETTEER OF INDIA

Scale 265 miles — to 1 inch

T H I B E T

BAY OF BENGAL

O C E A N

Long. E. of 84 Greenwich

Engraved by W. & A. K. Johnston, Edinburgh & London.

THE INDIAN EMPIRE.

CHAPTER I.

PHYSICAL ASPECTS.

INDIA forms a great irregular triangle, stretching southwards General
from Mid-Asia into the sea. Its northern base rests upon the outline.
Himálayan ranges; the chief part of its western side is washed
by the Arabian Sea, and the chief part of its eastern side
by the Bay of Bengal. It extends from the eighth to the
thirty-fifth degree of north latitude; that is to say, from the
hottest regions of the equator to far within the temperate zone.
The capital, Calcutta, lies in 88½° E. long.; so that when the
sun sets at six o'clock there, it is just past mid-day in England.

The length of India from north to south, and its greatest Dimen-
breadth from east to west, are both about 1900 miles; but the sions.
triangle tapers with a pear-shaped curve to a point at Cape
Comorin, its southern extremity. To this compact dominion
the English have added, under the name of British Burma, the
strip of country on the eastern shore of the Bay of Bengal.
The whole territory thus described contains close on 1½ millions
of square miles, and over 256 millions of inhabitants. India,
therefore, has an area and a population about equal to the
area and population of the whole of Europe, less Russia. Its
people more than double Gibbon's estimate of 120 millions for
all the races and nations which obeyed Imperial Rome.

This vast Asiatic peninsula has, from a very ancient period, Origin of
been known to the external world by one form or other of the the word
name which it still bears. The early Indians did not them- 'India.'
selves recognise any single designation for their numerous and
diverse races; their nearest approach to a common appellation
for India being Bhárata-varsha, the land of the Bháratas, a
noble warrior tribe which came from the north. But this term,
although afterwards generalized, applied only to the basins
of the Indus and the Ganges, and strictly speaking to only a

A

part of them. The Indus river formed the first great landmark
of nature which arrested the march of the peoples of Central
Asia as they descended upon the plains of the Punjab. That
mighty river impressed itself on the imagination of the ancient
world. To the early comers from the high-lying camping
grounds of inner Asia, it seemed a vast expanse of waters.

Sanskrit, Zend, and Greek forms. They called it in Sanskrit by the word which they gave
to the ocean itself, *Sindhus* (from the root *syand*, 'to flow') :
a name afterwards applied to the ocean-god (Varuna). The
term extended itself to the country around the river, and
in its plural form, *Sindhavas*, to the inhabitants thereof. The
ancient Persians, softening the initial sibilant to an aspirate,
called it *Hendu* in the Zend language : the Greeks, again
softening the initial by omitting the aspirate altogether, derived
from it their *Indikos* and *Indos*. These forms closely correspond to the ancient Persian word *Idhus*, which is used in
the inscriptions of Darius for the dwellers on the Indus. But
the native Indian form (*Sindhus*) was known to the Greeks, as
is proved by the *Sinthos* of the Periplus Maris Erythraei, and
by the distinct statement of Pliny, 'Indus incolis Sindus
appellatus.' Virgil says, 'India mittit ebur.'

Buddhist derivation of 'In-tu.' The eastern nations of Asia, like the western races of
Europe, derived their name for India from the great river of
the Punjab. The Buddhist pilgrims from China, during the
first seven centuries of our era, usually travelled landward to
Hindustán, skirting round the Himálayas, and entering the
holy land of their faith by the north-western frontier of India.
One of the most celebrated of these pious travellers, Hiuen
Tsiang (629–645 A.D.), states that India 'was anciently called
Shin-tu, also Hien-tau ; but now, according to the right
pronunciation, it is called In-tu.' This word in Chinese means
the moon ; and the cradle-land of Buddhism derived its name,
according to the good pilgrim, from its superior glory in the
spiritual firmament, *sicut luna inter minora sidera*. 'Though
there be torches by night and the shining of the stars,' he says,
'how different from the bright (cool) moon ! Just so the
bright connected light of holy men and sages, guiding the
world as the shining of the moon, have made this country
eminent, and so it is called In-tu.'[1] Notwithstanding the
pious philology of the pilgrim, the great river of the Punjab is,
of course, the origin of the Chinese name.

[1] *Si-yu-ki :* Buddhist Records of the Western World ; translated from
the Chinese of Hiuen Tsiang by Samuel Beal. Vol. i. p. 69. Trübner.
1884.

The term Hindustán is derived from the modern Persian form (Hind), and properly applies only to the Punjab and the central basin of the Ganges. It is reproduced, however, with a wider signification in the title of the Queen-Empress, *Kaisar-i-Hind*, the Cæsar, Kaiser, Czar, or Sovereign-paramount of India. *Kaisar-i-Hind.*

India is shut off from the rest of Asia on the north by a vast mountainous region, known in the aggregate as the Himálayas. Among their southern ranges lie the Independent States of Bhután and Nepál : the great table-land of Tibet stretches northward behind: the Native Principality of Kashmír occupies their western corner. At this north-western angle of India (in lat. 36° N., long. 75° E.), an allied mountain system branches southwards. Its lofty offshoots separate India on the west, by the well-marked ranges of the Safed Koh and the Suláimán, from Afghánistán; and by a southern continuation of lower hills (the Hálas, etc.) from Baluchistán. The southernmost part of the western land frontier of India is the river Hab ; and the boundary ends with Cape Monze, at the mouth of its estuary, in lat. 24° 50′ N., long. 66° 43′ E. Still proceeding southwards, India is bounded along the west and south-west by the Arabian Sea and Indian Ocean. Turning northwards from its southern extremity at Cape Comorin (lat. 8° 4′ 20″ N., long. 77° 35′ 35″ E.), the Bay of Bengal forms the main part of its eastern boundary. *Boundaries, on the north, and north-west; on the west; on the east.*

But in the north-east, as in the north-west, India has again a land frontier. The Himálayan ranges at their north-eastern angle (in about lat. 28° N., long. 97° E.) throw off long spurs and chains to the southward. These spurs separate the British Provinces of Assam and Eastern Bengal from Independent Burma. They are known successively as the Abar, Nágá, Patkoi, and Bárel ranges. Turning almost due south in lat. 25°, they culminate in the Blue Mountain, 7100 feet, in lat. 22° 37′ N., long. 93° 10′ E. ; and then stretch southwards under the name of the Arakan Yomas, separating British Burma from Independent Burma, until they again rise into the great mountain of Myin-matin (4700 feet), in 19½ degrees of north latitude. Up to this point, the eastern hill frontier runs in a southerly direction, and follows, generally speaking, the watershed which divides the river systems of Bengal and British Burma (namely, the Brahmaputra, Meghná, Kuladan, etc.) from the Irawadi basin in Independent Burma. But from near the base of the Myin-matin Mountain, the British frontier stretches almost due east in a geographical line, which divides the lower Districts and delta of the Irawadi in British Burma, *Burmese boundary.*

from the middle and upper Districts of that river in Independent Burma. Proceeding south-eastwards from the delta of the Irawadi, a confused succession of little explored ranges separates the British Province of Tenasserim from the Native Kingdom of Siam. The boundary line runs down to Point Victoria at the extremity of Tenasserim (lat. 9° 59′ N., long. 98° 32′ E.), following the direction of the watershed between the rivers of the British territory on the west and of Siam on the east.

Tenasserim boundary.

Physical aspects. The Empire included within these boundaries is rich in varieties of scenery and climate, from the highest mountains in the world, to vast river deltas raised only a few inches above the level of the sea. It forms a continent rather than a country. *The three Regions of India.* But if we could look down on the whole from a balloon, we should find that India consists of three separate and well-defined tracts. The first includes the lofty Himálaya Mountains, which shut it out from the rest of Asia, and which, although for the most part beyond the British frontier, form a most important factor in the physical geography of Northern India. The second region stretches southwards from the base of the Himálayas, and comprises the plains of the great rivers which issue from them. The third region slopes upward again from the southern edge of the river plains, and consists of a high three-sided table-land, buttressed by the Vindhya Mountains on the north, and by the Eastern and Western Gháts which run down the coast on either side of India, till they meet at a point near Cape Comorin. The interior three-sided table-land, thus enclosed, is dotted with peaks and ranges, broken by river valleys, and interspersed by broad level uplands. It comprises the southern half of the peninsula.

First Region— The Himálayas. The first of the three regions is the Himálaya Mountains and their offshoots to the southward. The Himálayas—literally, the 'Abode of Snow,' from the Sanskrit *hima*, frost (Latin, *hiems*, winter), and *álaya*, a house—consist of a system of stupendous ranges, the loftiest in the world. They are the *Emodus* or *Imaus* of the Greek geographers, and extend in the shape of a scimitar, with its edge facing southwards, for a distance of 1500 miles along the northern frontier of India. At the north-eastern angle of that frontier, the Dihang river, the connecting link between the Tsan-pu (Sangpu) of Tibet and the Brahmaputra of Assam, bursts through the main axis of the Himálayas. At the opposite or north-western angle, the Indus in like manner pierces the Himálayas, and turns southwards on its course through the Punjab. The Himálayas, like the Kuen-luen chain, the Tián-shan, and the Hindu Kush, converge towards the Pamír table-land—that central knot whence the great mountain systems of Asia radiate. With the Kuen-luen the Himálayas have a closer connection, as these two mighty ranges form respectively the northern and southern buttresses of the lofty Tibetan plateau. The Himálayas project east and west beyond the Indian frontier. Their total length is about 1750 miles, and their breadth from north to south from 150 to 250 miles.[1]

Regarded merely as a natural frontier separating India from the Tibetan plateau, the Himálayas may be described as a double mountain wall running nearly east and west, with a trough or series of deep valleys beyond. The southernmost of the two walls rises steeply from the plains of India to 20,000 feet, or nearly 4 miles, in height. It culminates in KANCHANJANGA, 28,176 feet, and MOUNT EVEREST, 29,002 feet, the latter being the loftiest measured peak in the world. This outer or southern wall of the Himálayas subsides on the northward into a series of dips or uplands, reported to be 13,000 feet above the level of the sea, beyond which rises the second or inner range of Himálayan peaks. The double Himálayan wall thus formed, then descends into a great trough or line of valleys, in which the Sutlej, the Indus, and the mighty Tsan-pu (Sangpu) gather their waters.

The double Himálayan Wall and Trough beyond.

The Sutlej and the Indus flow westwards, and pierce through the Western Himálayas by separate passes into the Punjab. The Tsan-pu, after a long unexplored course eastwards along the valley of the same name in Tibet, finds its way through the Dihang gorge of the Eastern Himálayas into Assam, where it takes its final name of the Brahmaputra. On the north of the river trough, beyond the double Himálayan wall, rise the Karakoram and Gangri mountains, which form the immediate escarpment of the Tibetan table-land. Behind the Gangris, on the north, the lake-studded plateau of Tibet spreads itself out at a height averaging 15,000 feet. Broadly speaking, the double Himálayan wall rests upon the low-lying plains of India, and descends northward into a river trough beyond which rises the Tibetan plateau. Vast glaciers, one of which is known to be 60 miles in length, slowly move their masses

---

[1] Some geographers hold that the Himálayan system stretches in a continuous chain westwards along the Oxus to 68° E. long. ; and that only an arbitrary line can be drawn between the Himálayan ranges and the elevated regions of Tibet to the north of them.

of ice downwards to the valleys. The higher ranges between India and Tibet are crowned with eternal snow. They rise in a region of unbroken silence, like gigantic frosted fortresses one above the other, till their white towers are lost in the sky.

Himálayan passes. This wild region is in many parts impenetrable to man, and nowhere yields a passage for a modern army. It should be mentioned, however, that the Chinese outposts extend as far as a point only 6000 feet above the Gangetic plain, north of Khatmandu. Indeed, Chinese armies have seriously threatened Khatmandu itself; and Sir David Ochterlony's advance from the plains of Bengal to that city in 1816 is a matter of history. Ancient and well-known trade routes exist, by means of which merchandise from the Punjab finds its way over heights of 18,000 feet into Eastern Túrkistán and Tibet. The Mustagh (Snowy Mount), the Karakoram (Black Mount), and the Chang-chenmo are among the most famous of these passes.

Offshoots of the Himálayas; on east; The Himálayas not only form a double wall along the north of India, but at both their eastern and western extremities send out ranges to the southwards, which protect India's north-eastern and north-western frontiers. On the north-east, those offshoots, under the name of the Nágá and Patkoi mountains, etc., form a barrier between the civilised British Districts and the wild tribes of Upper Burma. The southern continuations of these ranges, known as the Yomas, separate British from Independent Burma, and are crossed by passes, the most historic of which, the An or Aeng, rises to 4517 feet, with gradients of 472 feet to the mile.

and west. On the opposite or north-western frontier of India, the mountainous offshoots run down the entire length of the British boundaries from the Himálayas to the sea. As they proceed southwards, their best marked ranges are in turn known as the Safed Koh, the Suláimán, and the Hála mountains. These massive barriers have peaks of great height, culminating in the Takht-i-Suláimán, or Throne of Solomon, 11,317 feet above the level of the sea. But, as already mentioned, the mountain wall is pierced at the corner where it strikes southwards from the Himálayas by an opening through which the Indus river flows into India. An adjacent opening, the KHAIBAR PASS (3400 feet above sea-level, amid neighbouring heights rising to 6800 feet), with the Kuram Pass on the south of it, the Gwalarí Pass near Dera Ismáil Khán, the Tál Pass debouching near Dera Ghází Khán, and the famous Bolán Pass (5800 feet at top), still farther south, furnish the gateways between India and

The Gateways of India.

Afghánistán. The Hála, Brahui, and Pab mountains form the southern hilly offshoots between India and Baluchistán; but they have a much less elevation than the Safed Koh or the Suláimán.

The Himálayas, while thus standing as a rampart and strong defence around the northern frontier of India, collect and store up water for the tropical plains below. Throughout the summer, vast quantities of water are exhaled from the Indian Ocean. This moisture gathers into vapour, and is borne northward by the monsoon or regular wind, which sets in from the south in the month of June. The monsoon carries the water-laden clouds northwards across India, and thus produces the ' rainy season,' on which agriculture so critically depends. But large quantities of the moisture do not condense or fall as rain in passing over the hot plains. This vast residue is eventually dashed against the Himálayas. Their lofty double walls stop its farther progress northwards, and it either descends in rain on their outer slopes, or is frozen into snow in its attempt to cross their inner heights. Very little gets beyond them ; so that while the southern spurs of the Himálayas receive the largest measured rainfall in the world, and pour it down to the Indian rivers, the great plateau of Tibet on the north of the double Himálayan wall gets scarcely any rainfall.

Himálayan water-supply.

Himálayan rainfall.

At Cherra-Púnjí, where the monsoon first strikes the hills in Assam, 489 inches of rain, according to returns for 25 years ending 1881, fall annually. In one year (1861) as many as 805 inches were reported, of which 366 inches fell in the single month of July. While, therefore, the yearly rainfall in London is about 2 feet, and that of the plains of India from 1 to 6 feet, the rainfall at Cherra-Púnjí is 40 feet, a depth more than is required to float the largest man-of-war ; and in one year, 67 feet of water fell from the sky, or sufficient to drown a three-storied house. The mighty mountains that wall in India on the north form, in fact, a rain-screen which catches the vapour-clouds from the Southern Ocean, and condenses them for the hot Bengal plains. The outer slopes of the Himálayas swell the Indian rivers by their torrents during the rainy season ; their inner ranges and heights store up the rainfall in the shape of snow, and thus form a vast reservoir for the steady supply of the Indian rivers throughout the year.

This heavy rainfall renders the southern slopes of the Himálayas very fertile, wherever there is any depth of tilth. But, on the other hand, the torrents scour away the surface

Himálayan scenery.

soil, and leave most of the mountain-sides bleak and bare. The upper ranges lie under eternal snow; the intermediate heights form arid grey masses; but on the lower slopes, plateaux, and valleys, forests spring up, or give place to a rich though simple cultivation. The temperature falls about $3\frac{1}{3}°$ F. for each thousand feet of elevation; and the vegetation of the Himálayas is divided into three well-marked zones, the tropical, the temperate, and the arctic, as the traveller ascends from the Indian plains. A damp belt of lowland, the *tarái*, stretches along their foot, and is covered with dense, fever-breeding jungle, habitable only by rude tribes and wild beasts. Fertile *dúns* or valleys penetrate their outer margin.

Himálayan vegetation, and forests. In their eastern ranges adjoining the Lieutenant-Governorship of Bengal, where the rainfall is heaviest, the tree-fern flourishes amid a magnificent vegetation. Their western or Punjab ranges are barer. But the rhododendron grows into a forest tree, and large tracts of it are to be found throughout the whole length of the Himálayas. The *deodar* rises in stately masses. Thickets of bamboos, with their graceful light-green foliage, beautify the lower valleys. Higher up, the glistening-grey ilex, mountain oaks with brown young leaves, the Himá-layan cedar, drooping silver-firs, spruces, pines, and the many-hued foliage of the chestnut, walnut, and maple, not to mention a hundred trees of a lower growth hung with bridal veils of clematis in spring, and festooned with crimson virginia-creepers in autumn, form, together with patches of the white medlar blossom, a brilliant contrast to the stretches of scarlet and pink rhododendron. At harvest-time, crops of millet run in red ribands down the hillsides. The branches of the trees are themselves clothed in the damper regions with a luxuriant growth of mosses, ferns, lovely orchids, and flowering creepers. The Himálayas have enriched English parks and hothouses by the *deodar*, the rhododendron, and the orchid; and a great extension in the cultivation of the *deodar* and rhododendron throughout Britain dates from the Himálayan tour in 1848 of Sir Joseph Hooker, now Director of Kew Gardens. The high price of wood on the plains, for railway sleepers and building purposes, has caused many of the hills to be stripped of their forests, so that the rainfall now rushes quickly down their bare slopes, washing away the surface soil, and leaving no tilth in which new woods might grow up. The Forest Department is endeavouring to repair this reckless denudation of the Himálayan woods.

Himálayan cultivation. The hill tribes cultivate barley, oats, and a variety of millets and small grains. Vegetables are also raised on a large scale. The potato, introduced from England, is a favourite crop, and covers many sites formerly under forest.

The hillman clears his potato ground by burning a ring round the stems of the great trees, and then lays out the side of the mountain into terraces. After a few years the bark and leaves drop off the branches, and the forest stands bleached and ruined. Some of the trees rot on the ground, like giants fallen in confused flight; others still remain upright, with white trunks and skeleton arms. In the end, the rank green potato crop marks the spot where a forest has been slain and buried. Several of the ruder hill tribes follow an even more wasteful mode of tillage. Destitute of either ploughs or oxen, they burn down the jungle, and exhaust the soil by a quick succession of crops, raised by the hoe. In a year or two the whole settlement moves off to a fresh patch of jungle, which they clear and exhaust, and then desert in like manner. *Clearing a hill forest.*

Rice is only grown in the Himálayas on ground which has an unfailing command of water—particularly in the damp hot valleys between the successive ranges which roll upwards into the interior. The hillmen practise an ingenious system of irrigation, according to which the slopes are laid out in terraces, and the streams are diverted to a great distance by successive parallel channels along the mountain-side. They also utilize their water-power for mill purposes. Some of them are ignorant of cog-wheels for converting the vertical movement of the mill-wheel into the horizontal movement required for the grinding-stone. They therefore place their mill-wheel flat instead of upright, and lead the water so as to dash with great force on the horizontal paddles. A horizontal rotary movement is thus obtained, and conveyed direct by the axle to the millstone above. *Irrigation and mill-power.*

The chief saleable products of the Himálayas are timber, charcoal, barley, millets, potatoes, other vegetables, honey, jungle products, borax, and several kinds of inferior gems. Strings of ponies and mules straggle with their burdens along the narrow pathways, which are at many places mere ledges cut out of the precipice. The hillmen and their hard-working wives load themselves also with pine stems and conical baskets of grain. The yak-cow and hardy mountain sheep are the favourite beasts of burden in the inner ranges. The little yak-cow, whose bushy tail is manufactured in Europe into lace, patiently toils up the steepest gorges with a heavy burden on her back. The sheep, laden with bags of borax, are driven *Himálayan saleable produce.*

to marts on the outer ranges near the plains, where they are shorn of their wool, and then return into the interior with a load of grain or salt. Hundreds of them, having completed their journey from the upper ranges, are sold for slaughter at a nominal price of perhaps a shilling a-piece, as they are not worth taking back to the inner mountains.

Himálayan animals and tribes. The characteristic animals of the Himálayas include the yak-cow, musk-deer, several kinds of wild sheep and goat, bear, ounce, leopard, and fox ; the eagle, great vultures, pheasants of beautiful varieties, partridges, and other birds. Ethnologically, the Himálayas form the meeting-ground of the Aryan and Turanian races, which in some parts are curiously mingled, although generally distinguishable. The tribes or broken clans of non-Aryan origin number over fifty, with languages, customs, and religious rites more or less distinct. The lifelong labours of Mr. Brian Houghton Hodgson, of the Bengal Civil Service, have done much to illustrate the flora, fauna, and ethnology of the Himálayas ; and no sketch of this region would be complete without a reference to Mr. Hodgson's work.

Second Region of India— The northern River Plains. The wide plains watered by the Himálayan rivers form the second of the three regions into which India is divided. They extend from the Bay of Bengal on the east, to the Afghán frontier and the Arabian Sea on the west, and contain the richest and most densely-crowded Provinces of the Empire. One set of invaders after another have, from pre-historic times, entered by the passes on the north-eastern and north-western frontiers of India. They followed the courses of the rivers, and pushed the earlier comers southwards before them towards the sea. About 150 millions of people now live on and around these river plains in the Provinces known as the Lieutenant-Governorship of Bengal, Assam, the North-Western Provinces, Oudh, the Punjab, Sind, Rájputána and other Native States.

The three River systems of N. India. (1) The Indus, with the Sutlej. (2) The Tsan-pu or Brahma-putra. The vast level tract which thus covers Northern India is watered by three distinct river systems. One of these river systems takes its rise in the hollow trough beyond the Himálayas, and issues through their western ranges upon the Punjab as the Indus and Sutlej. The second of the three river systems also takes its rise beyond the double wall of the Himálayas, not very far from the sources of the Indus and the Sutlej. It turns, however, almost due east instead of west, enters India at the eastern extremity of the Himálayas and becomes the Brahmaputra of Assam and Eastern Bengal. These rivers collect the drainage of the northern slopes of the Himálayas, and convey it, by long, tortuous, and opposite routes, into India. Indeed, the special feature of the Himálayas is that they send down the rainfall from their northern as well as from their southern slopes to the Indian plains. Of the three great rivers of Northern India, the two longest, namely the Indus with its feeder the Sutlej, and the Brahmaputra, take their rise in the trough on the north of the great Himálayan wall. That trough receives the drainage of the inner or northern escarpment of the Himálayas, together with such water-supply as emerges from the outer or southern escarpment of the lofty but almost rainless plateau of Tibet.

The third river system of Northern India receives the drainage of the outer or southern Himálayan slopes, and unites into the mighty stream of the Ganges. In this way, the rainfall, alike from the northern and southern slopes of the Himálayas, and even from the mountain buttresses of the Tibet plateau beyond, pours down upon the plains of India. The long and lofty spur of the outer Himálayas, on which stands Simla, the summer residence of the Government of India, forms the watershed between the river systems of the Indus and Ganges. The drainage from the west of this narrow ridge below the Simla Church flows into the Arabian Sea; while that which starts a few feet off, down the eastern side, eventually reaches the Bay of Bengal. *(3) The Ganges, with the Jumna.*

The INDUS (Sanskrit, *Sindhus;* Ἰνδός, Σινθός) rises in an unexplored region (lat. 32° N., long. 81° E.) on the slopes of the sacred Kailás mountain, the Elysium or Siva's Paradise of ancient Sanskrit literature. The Indus has an elevation of about 16,000 feet at its source in Tibet; a drainage basin of 372,700 square miles; and a total length of over 1800 miles. Shortly after it passes within the Kashmír frontier, it drops to 14,000 feet, and at Leh is only about 11,000 feet above the level of the sea. The rapid stream dashes down ravines and wild mountain valleys, and is subject to tremendous floods. The Indus bursts through the western ranges of the Himálayas by a wonderful gorge near Iskardoh, in North-Western Kashmír—a gorge reported to be 14,000 feet in sheer depth. *The Indus.*

Its great feeder, the SUTLEJ, rises on the southern slopes of the Kailás mountain, also in Tibet. It issues from one of the sacred lakes, the Mánasarowar and Rávana-hráda (the modern Rákhas Tál), famous in Hindu mythology, and still the resort of the Tibetan shepherds. Starting at an elevation of 15,200 feet, the Sutlej passes south-west across the plain of *The Sutlej.*

Gugé, where it has cut through a vast accumulation of deposits by a gully said to be 4000 feet deep, between precipices of alluvial soil. After traversing this plain, the river pierces the Himálayas by a gorge with mountains rising to 20,000 feet on either side. The Sutlej is reported to fall from 10,000 feet above sea-level at Shipki, a Tibetan frontier outpost, to 3000 feet at Rámpur, the capital of a Himálayan State about 60 miles inward from Simla. During this part of its course, the Sutlej runs at the bottom of a deep trough, with precipices and bare mountains which have been denuded of their forests, towering above. Its turbid waters, and their unceasing roar as the river dashes over the rapids, have a gloomy and dis-quieting effect. Sometimes it grinds to powder the huge pines and cedars entrusted to it to float down to the plains. By the time it reaches Biláspur, it has dropped to 1000 feet above sea-level. After entering British territory, the Sutlej receives the waters of the Western Punjab, and falls into the Indus near Mithánkot, after a course of 900 miles.

Lower course of Indus.

A full account of the Indus will be found in the article on that river in volume vii. of *The Imperial Gazetteer of India.* About 800 miles of its course are passed among the Himálayas before it enters British territory, and it flows for about 1000 miles more, south-west, through the British Provinces of the Punjab and Sind. In its upper part it is fordable in many places during the cold weather; but it is liable to sudden freshets, in one of which Ranjít Singh is said to have lost a force, variously stated at from 1200 to 7000 horsemen, while crossing by a ford. A little way above Attock, the Indus receives the Kábul river, which brings down the waters of Northern Afghánistán. The volume of those waters, as repre-sented by the Kábul river, is about equal to the volume of the Indus at the point of junction. At Attock, the Indus has fallen, during a course of 860 miles, from its elevation of 16,000 feet at its source in Tibet to under 2000 feet. These 2000 feet supply its fall during the remaining 940 miles of its course.

The discharge of the Indus, after receiving all its tribu-taries, varies from 40,857 to 446,086 cubic feet per second, according to the season of the year. The enormous mass of water spreads itself over a channel of a quarter of a mile to a mile (or at times much more) in breadth. The effect pro-duced by the evaporation from this fluvial expanse is so marked that, at certain seasons, the thermometer is reported to be 10° F. lower close to its surface than on the surrounding arid plains. The Indus supplies a precious store of water for irrigation works at various points along its course, and forms the great highway of the Southern Punjab and Sind. In its lower course it sends forth distributaries across a wide delta, with Haidarábád (Hyderábád) in Sind as its ancient political capital, and Karáchi (Kurrachee) as its modern port. The silt which it carries down has helped to form the seaboard islands, mud-banks, and shallows, that have cut off the ancient famous emporia around the Gulf of Cambay from modern commerce.

The BRAHMAPUTRA, like the Sutlej, rises near to the sacred lake of Mánasarowar. Indeed, the Indus, the Sutlej, and the Brahmaputra may be said to start from the same water-parting. The Indus rises on the western slope of the Kailás mountain, the Sutlej on its southern, and the Brahmaputra at some distance from its eastern base. The Mariam-la and other saddles connect the more northern Tibetan mountains, to which the Kailás belongs, with the double Himálayan wall on the south. They form an irregular watershed across the trough on the north of the double wall of the Himálayas ; thus, as it were, blocking up the western half of the great Central Asian trench. The Indus flows down a western valley from this transverse watershed ; the Sutlej finds a more direct route to India by a south-western valley. The Brahmaputra, under its Tibetan name of Tsan-pu or Sangpu, has its source in 31° N. lat. and 83° E. long. It flows eastwards down the Tsan-pu valley, passing not very far to the south of Lhasa, the capital of Tibet ; and probably 800 to 900 miles, or about one-half of its total course, are spent in the hollow trough on the north of the Himálayas. This brief account assumes that the Brahmaputra of India is the true continuation of the Sangpu of Tibet. The result of the latest researches into that long mooted question are given under article BRAHMAPUTRA, in volume iii. of *The Imperial Gazetteer of India.*

After receiving several tributaries from the confines of the Chinese Empire, the river twists round a lofty eastern range of the Himálayas, and enters British territory under the name of the DIHANG, near Sadiyá in Assam. It presently receives two confluents, the DIBANG river from the northward, and the Brahmaputra proper from the east (lat. 27° 20′ N., long. 95° 50′ E.). The united stream then takes its well-known appellation of the Brahmaputra, literally the 'Son of Brahma the Creator.' It represents a drainage basin of 361,200 square miles, and its summer discharge at Goálpárá in Assam was

The Tsan-pu or Brahmaputra.

The Kailás watershed.

The Brahmaputra confluents in Assam.

for long computed at 146,188 cubic feet of water per second. Recent measurements have, however, shown that this calculation is below the truth. Observations made near Dibrugarh during the cold weather of 1877–78, returned a mean low-water discharge of 116,484 cubic feet per second for the Brahmaputra at the upper end of the Assam valley, together with 16,945 cubic feet per second for its tributary the SUBANSIRI. Total cold-weather discharge for the united stream, over 133,000 cubic feet per second near Dibrugarh. Several affluents join the Brahmaputra during its course through Assam; and the mean low-water discharge at Goálpárá, in the lower end of the Assam valley, must be in excess of the previous computation at 146,188 cubic feet per second. During the rains the channel rises 30 or 40 feet above its ordinary level, and its flood discharge is estimated at over 500,000 cubic feet per second.

Brahma-putra silt.
The Brahmaputra rolls down the Assam valley in a vast sheet of water, broken by numerous islands, and exhibiting the operations of alluvion and diluvion on a gigantic scale. It is so heavily freighted with silt from the Himálayas, that the least impediment placed in its current causes a deposit, and may give rise to a wide-spreading, almond-shaped mud-bank. Steamers anchoring near the margin for the night sometimes find their sterns aground next morning on an accumulation of silt, caused by their own obstruction to the current. Broad divergent channels split off from the parent stream, and rejoin it after a long separate existence of uncontrollable meandering. By centuries of alluvial deposit, the Brahmaputra has raised its banks and channel in parts of the Assam valley to a higher level than the surrounding country. Beneath either bank lies a low strip of marshy land, which is flooded in the rainy season. Beyond these swamps, the ground begins to rise towards the hills that hem in the valley of Assam on both sides.

The Brahma-putra in Bengal.
After a course of 450 miles south-west down the Assam valley, the Brahmaputra sweeps round the spurs of the Gáro Hills due south towards the sea. It here takes the name of the Jamuná, and for 180 miles rushes across the level plains of Eastern Bengal, till it joins the Ganges at Goálanda (lat. 23° 50′ N., long. 89° 46′ E.). From this point the deltas of the two great river systems of the Ganges and the Brahmaputra unite into one. But before reaching the sea, their combined streams have yet to receive, by way of the CACHAR valley, the drainage of the eastern watershed between Bengal and Burma,

(Jamuná and Meghná.)

under the name of the MEGHNA river, itself a broad and magnificent sheet of water.

The Brahmaputra is famous not only for its vast alluvial deposits, but also for the historical changes which have taken place in its course. One of the islands (the Májulí *char*), which it has created in its channel out of the silt torn away from the distant Himálayas, covers 441 square miles. Every year, thousands of acres of new land are thus formed out of mud and sand; some of them destined to be swept away by the inundations of the following year; others to become the homes of an industrious peasantry or the seats of busy river marts. Such formations give rise to changes in the bed of the river—changes which within a hundred years have completely altered the course of the Brahmaputra through Bengal. In the last century, the stream, on issuing from Assam, bent close round the spurs of the Gáro Hills in a south-easterly direction. This old bed of the Brahmaputra, the only one recognised by Major Rennel in 1765-75, has now been deserted. It retains the ancient name of the Brahmaputra, but during the hot weather it is little more than a series of pools. The modern channel, instead of twisting round the Gáro Hills to the east, bursts straight southwards towards the sea under the name of the Jamuná, and is now separated at places by nearly 100 miles of level land from the main channel in the last century. A floating log thrown up against the bank, a sunk boat, or any smallest obstruction, may cause the deposit of a mud island. Every such silt-bank gives a more or less new direction to the main channel, which in a few years may have eaten its way far across the plain, and dug out for itself a new bed at a distance of several miles. Unlike the Ganges and the Indus, the Brahmaputra is not used for artificial irrigation. But its silt-charged overflow annually replenishes the land. Indeed, the plains of Eastern Bengal watered by the Brahmaputra yield unfailing harvests of rice, mustard, oil-seeds, and the exhausting jute crop, year after year, without any deterioration. The valley of the Brahmaputra in Assam is not less fertile, although inhabited by a less industrious race.

The Brahmaputra is the great high-road of Eastern Bengal and Assam. Its tributaries and bifurcations afford innumerable waterways, almost superseding roads, and at the same time rendering road construction and maintenance very difficult. The main river is navigable by steamers as high up as DIBRUGARH, about 800 miles from the sea; and its broad surface is crowded with country craft of all sizes and rigs, from

Brahmaputra silt-islands.

Great changes in its course.

The Brahmaputra as a high-road.

the dug-out canoe and timber raft to the huge cargo ship, with its high bow and carved stern, its bulged-out belly, and spreading square-sails. The busy emporium of SIRAJGANJ, on the western bank of the Brahmaputra, collects the produce of the Districts for transmission to Calcutta. Fifty thousand native craft, besides steamers, passed Sirájganj in 1876.

Brahma-putra traffic. The downward traffic consists chiefly of tea (to the value of about 1½ million sterling), timber, caoutchouc, and raw cotton, from Assam; with jute, oil-seeds, tobacco, rice, and other grains, from Eastern Bengal. In return for these, Calcutta sends northwards by the Brahmaputra, European piece-goods, salt, and hardware; while Assam imports from the Bengal delta, by the same highway, large quantities of rice (amounting to 14,749 tons in 1883–84) for the labourers on the tea plantations. The total value of the river-borne trade of the Brahmaputra was returned at a little over three millions sterling in 1882–83. But it is impossible to ascertain the whole produce carried by the innumerable native boats on the Brahmaputra. The railway system of India taps the Brahmaputra at Goálanda and Dhubrí; while a network of channels through the Sundarbans supply a cheaper means of water transit for bulky produce across the delta to Calcutta.

The Gangetic river system As the Indus, with its feeder the Sutlej, and the Brahma-putra, convey to India the drainage from the northern or Tibetan slopes of the Himálayas, so the GANGES, with its tributary the Jumna, collects the rainfall from the southern or Indian slopes of the mountain wall, and pours it down upon the plains of Bengal. The Ganges traverses the central part of those plains, and occupies a more prominent place in the history of Indian civilisation than either the Indus in the extreme west, or the Brahmaputra in the extreme east of Hindustán. It passes its whole life to the south of the Himálayas, and for thousands of years has formed an over-ruling factor in the development of the Indian races.

The Ganges issues, under the name of the Bhágírathí, from an ice-cave at the foot of a Himálayan snowbed, 13,800 feet above the sea-level (lat. 30° 56′ 4″ N., long. 79° 6′ 40″ E.). After a course of 1557 miles, it falls by a network of estuaries into the Bay of Bengal. It represents, with its tributaries, an enormous catchment basin, bounded on the north by a section of about 700 miles of the Himálayan ranges, on the south by the Vindhya mountains, and embracing 391,100 square miles. Before attempting a description of the functions performed by the Ganges, it is necessary to form some idea of the mighty masses of water which it collects and distributes. But so many variable elements affect the discharge of rivers, that calculations of their volume must be taken merely as estimates.

At the point where it issues from its snowbed, the infant stream is only 27 feet broad and 15 inches deep, with an elevation of 13,800 feet above sea-level. During the first 180 miles of its course, it drops to an elevation of 1024 feet. At this point, Hardwár, its lowest discharge, in the dry season, is 7000 cubic feet per second. Hitherto the Ganges has been little more than a snow-fed Himálayan stream. During the next thousand miles of its journey, it collects the drainage of its catchment basin, and reaches Rájmahal about 1180 miles from its source. It has here, while still about 400 miles from the sea, a high flood discharge of 1,800,000 cubic feet of water per second, and an ordinary discharge of 207,000 cubic feet; longest duration of flood, about forty days. The maximum discharge of the Mississippi is given at 1,200,000 cubic feet per second.[1] The maximum discharge of the Nile at Cairo is returned at only 362,200 cubic feet; and of the Thames at Staines at 6600 cubic feet of water per second. The Meghná, one of the many outflows of the Ganges, is 20 miles broad near its mouth, with a depth, in the dry season, of 30 feet. But for a distance of about 200 miles, the sea face of Bengal entirely consists of the estuaries of the Ganges, intersected by low islands and promontories, formed out of its silt.

The growth of the Ganges.

Discharge of Ganges.

In forming our ideas with regard to the Ganges, we must begin by dismissing from our minds any lurking comparison of its gigantic stream with the rivers which we are familiar with in England. A single one of its tributaries, the JUMNA, has an independent existence of 860 miles, with a catchment basin of 118,000 square miles, and starts from an elevation at its source of 10,849 feet above sea-level. The Ganges and its principal tributaries are treated of in *The Imperial Gazetteer of India*, in separate articles under their respective names. The following account confines itself to a brief sketch of the work which these Gangetic rivers perform in the plains of Northern India, and of the position which they hold in the thoughts of the people.

The Jumna.

Of all great rivers on the surface of the globe, none can compare in sanctity with the Ganges, or Mother Gangá, as she is affectionately called by devout Hindus. From her source in

Sanctity of the Ganges

---

[1] *Hydraulic Manual*, by Lowis D'A. Jackson, Hydraulic Statistics, Table II. ; Appendix, p. 2 (1875).

B

the Himálayas, to her mouth in the Bay of Bengal, her banks are holy ground. Each point of junction of a tributary with the main stream has its own special claims to sanctity. But the tongue of land at Allahábád, where the Ganges unites with her great sister river the Jumna, is the true *Prayág*, the place of pilgrimage whither hundreds of thousands of devout Hindus repair to wash away their sins in her sanctifying waters. Many of the other holy rivers of India borrow their sanctity from a supposed underground connection with the Ganges. This fond fable recalls the primitive time when the Aryan race was moving southward from the Gangetic plains. It is told not only of first-class rivers of Central and Southern India, like the Narbadá, but also of many minor streams of local sanctity.

Legend of the Ganges. An ancient legend relates how Gangá, the fair daughter of King Himálaya (Himávat) and of his queen the air-nymph Menaka, was persuaded, after long supplication, to shed her purifying influence upon the sinful earth. The icicle-studded cavern from which she issues is the tangled hair of the god Siva. Loving legends hallow each part of her course; and from the names of her tributaries and of the towns along her banks, a whole mythology might be built up. The southern offshoots of the Aryan race not only sanctified their southern rivers by a fabled connection with the holy stream of the north. They also hoped that in the distant future, their rivers would attain an equal sanctity by the diversion of the Ganges' waters through underground channels. Thus, the Bráhmans along the Narbadá maintain that in this evil age of the world (indeed, about the year 1894 A.D.), the sacred character of the Ganges will depart from that polluted stream, and take refuge by an underground passage in their own river.

Gangetic pilgrimages. The estuary of the Ganges is not less sacred than her source. Ságar Island at her mouth is annually visited by a vast concourse of pilgrims, in commemoration of her act of saving grace; when, in order to cleanse the 60,000 damned ones of the house of Ságar, she divided herself into a hundred channels, thus making sure of reaching their remains, and so forming the delta of Bengal. The six years' pilgrimage from her source to her mouth and back again, known as *pradakshina*, is still performed by many; and a few devotees may yet be seen wearily accomplishing the meritorious penance of 'measuring their length' along certain parts of the route. To bathe in the Ganges at the stated festivals washes away guilt, and those who have thus purified themselves carry back bottles of her water to their kindred in far-off provinces.

To die and to be cremated on the river bank, and to have their ashes borne seaward by her stream, is the last wish of millions of Hindus. Even to ejaculate 'Gangá, Gangá,' at the distance of 100 leagues from the river, say her more enthusiastic devotees, may atone for the sins committed during three previous lives.

The Ganges has earned the reverence of the people by centuries of unfailing work done for them. She and her tributaries are the unwearied water-carriers for the densely-peopled provinces of Northern India, and the peasantry reverence the bountiful stream which fertilizes their fields and distributes their produce. None of the other rivers of India comes near to the Ganges in works of beneficence. The Brahmaputra and the Indus have longer streams, as measured by the geographer, but their upper courses lie beyond the great mountain wall in the unknown recesses of the Himálayas. *Work done by the Ganges;*

Not one of the rivers of Southern India is navigable in the proper sense. The Ganges begins to distribute fertility by irrigation as soon as she reaches the plains, within 200 miles of her source, and at the same time her channel becomes in some sort navigable. Thenceforward she rolls majestically down to the sea in a bountiful stream, which never becomes a merely destructive torrent in the rains, and never dwindles away in the hottest summer. Tapped by canals, she distributes millions of cubic feet of water every hour in irrigation ; but her diminished volume is promptly recruited by great tributaries, and the wide area of her catchment basin renders her stream inexhaustible in the service of man. Embankments are in but few places required to restrain her inundations, for the alluvial silt which she spills over her banks affords in most parts a top-dressing of inexhaustible fertility. If one crop be drowned by the flood, the peasant comforts himself with the thought that the next crop from his silt-manured fields will abundantly requite him. The function of the Ganges as a land-maker on a great scale will be explained hereafter. *The water-carrier and fertilizer of Bengal.*

The Ganges has also played a pre-eminent part in the commercial development of Northern India. Until the opening of the railway system, 1855 to 1870, her magnificent stream formed almost the sole channel of traffic between Upper India and the seaboard. The products not only of the river plains, but even the cotton of the Central Provinces, were formerly brought by this route to Calcutta. Notwithstanding the revolution caused by the railways, the heavier and more *The Ganges the great highway of Bengal.*

bulky staples are still conveyed by the river, and the Ganges may yet rank as one of the greatest waterways in the world.

Traffic on the Ganges.

The upward and downward trade of the interior with Calcutta alone, by the Gangetic channels, was valued in 1881 at over 20 millions sterling. This is exclusive of the sea-borne commerce. At Bámangháta, on one of the canals east of Calcutta, 178,627 cargo boats were registered in 1876–77; at Húglí, a river-side station on a single one of the many Gangetic mouths, 124,357; and at Patná, 550 miles from the mouth of the river, the number of cargo boats entered in the register was 61,571. The port of Calcutta is itself one of the world's greatest emporia for sea and river borne commerce. Its total exports and imports landward and seaward amounted in 1881 to about 140 millions sterling.

Not diminished by the railway.

Articles of European commerce, such as wheat, indigo, cotton, opium, and saltpetre, prefer the railway; so also do the imports of Manchester piece-goods. But if we take into account the vast development in the export trade of oil-seeds, rice, etc., still carried by the river, and the growing interchange of food-grains between various parts of the country, it seems probable that the actual amount of traffic on the Ganges has increased rather than diminished since the opening of the railways. At well-chosen points along her course, the iron lines touch the banks, and these river-side stations form centres for collecting and distributing the produce of the surrounding country. The Ganges, therefore, is not merely a rival, but a feeder, of the railway. Her ancient cities, such as ALLAHABAD, BENARES, and PATNA, have thus been able to preserve their former importance; while fishing villages like SAHIBGANJ and GOALANDA have been raised into thriving river marts.

The great Gangetic cities.

For, unlike the Indus and the Brahmaputra, the Ganges is a river of great historic cities. CALCUTTA, PATNA, and BENARES are built on her banks; AGRA and DELHI on those of her tributary, the Jumna; and ALLAHABAD on the tongue of land where the two sister streams unite. Many millions of human beings live by commerce along her margin. Calcutta, with its suburbs on both sides of the river, contains a population of over $\frac{3}{4}$ of a million. It has a municipal revenue of £270,000 to £290,000; a sea-borne and coasting commerce of about 65 millions sterling, with a landward trade of 75 millions sterling. These figures vary from year to year, but show a steady increase. Calcutta lies on the HUGLI, the most westerly of the mouths by which the Ganges enters the sea. To the eastwards stretches the delta, till it is hemmed

Calcutta.

in on the other side by the MEGHNA, the most easterly of the
mouths of the Ganges; or rather the vast estuary by which
the combined waters of the Brahmaputra and Gangetic river
systems find their way into the Bay of Bengal.

In order, therefore, to understand the plains of Northern The part
India, we must have a clear idea of the part played by the played by
the great
great rivers; for the rivers first create the land, then fertilize rivers.
it, and finally distribute its produce. The plains of Bengal
were in many parts upheaved by volcanic forces, or deposited
in an aqueous era, before the present race of man appeared.
But in other parts they have been formed out of the silt which the
rivers bring down from the mountains; and at this day we may
stand by and watch the ancient process of land-making go on.

A great Indian river like the Ganges has three distinct Three
stages in its career from the Himálayas to the sea. In stages in
the life of
the first stage of its course, it dashes down the Himálayas, a river.
cutting out for itself deep gullies in the solid rock, ploughing First
up glens between the mountains, and denuding the hillsides stage;
of their soil. In wading over the Sutlej feeders among the
hills in the rainy season, the ankles are sore from the pebbles
which the stream carries with it; while even in the hot weather,
the rushing sand and gravel cause a prickly sensation across
the feet.

The second stage in the life of an Indian river begins at the Second
point where it emerges from the mountains upon the plains. stage.
It then runs peacefully along the valleys, searching out
for itself the lowest levels. It receives the drainage and
mud of the country on both sides, absorbs tributaries, and
rolls forward with an ever-increasing volume of water and
silt. Every torrent from the Himálayas brings its separate
contribution of new soil, which it has torn from the rocks or
eroded from its banks. This process repeats itself throughout more than ten thousand miles; that is to say, down the
course of each tributary from the Himálayas or Vindhyas,
and across the plains of Northern India. During the second
stage of the life of a Bengal river, therefore, it forms a great
open drain, which gradually deepens itself by erosion of its
channel. As its bed thus sinks lower and lower, it draws off
the water from swamps or lakes in the surrounding country.
Dry land takes the place of fens; and in this way the physical
configuration of Northern India has been greatly altered, even
since the Greek descriptions 2000 years ago.

As long as the force of the current is maintained by a

First and second stages of a great river, as a silt-collector.

sufficient fall per mile, the river carries forward the silt thus supplied, and adds to it fresh contributions from its banks. Each river acquires a character of its own as it advances, a character which tells the story of its early life. Thus, the Indus is loaded with silt of a brown hue ; the Chenáb has a reddish tinge ; while the Sutlej is of a paler colour. The exact amount of fall required per mile depends upon the specific gravity of the silt which it carries. At a comparatively early stage, the current drops the heavy particles of rock or sand which it has torn from the Himálayan precipices. But a fall of 5 inches per mile suffices to hold in suspension the great body of the silt, and to add further accretions in passing through alluvial plains. The average fall of the Ganges between Benares and the delta-head (about 461 miles) is nearly 5 inches per mile. In its upper course its average declivity is much greater, and suffices to bear along and pulverize the heavier spoils torn from the Himálayas.

Loss of carrying power.

By the time the Ganges reaches its delta in Lower Bengal (Colgong to Calcutta), its average fall per mile has dropped to 4 inches. From Calcutta to the sea the fall varies in the numerous distributaries of the parent stream, according to the tide, from 1 to 2 inches. In the delta the current seldom suffices to carry the burden of its silt, except during the rains, and so deposits it.[1]

Third stage of an Indian river, as a land-maker.

In Lower Bengal, therefore, the Ganges enters on the third stage of its life. Finding its speed checked by the equal level of the plains, and its bed raised by the deposit of its own silt, it splits out into channels, like a jet of water suddenly obstructed by the finger, or a jar of liquid dashed on the ground. Each of the new streams thus created throws out in turn its own set of distributaries to right and left. The country which their many offshoots enclose and intersect forms

[1] The following facts may be useful to observers in Bengal who wish to study the most interesting feature of the country in which they live, namely the rivers. Ten inches per mile is considered to be the fall which a navigable river should not exceed. The average fall of the Ganges from the point where it unites with the Jumna at Allahábád to Benares (139 miles), is 6 inches per mile ; from Benares to Colgong (326 miles), 5 inches per mile ; from Colgong to the delta-head, where the Bhágírathí strikes off (about 135 miles), 4 inches per mile ; from the delta-head to Calcutta (about 200 miles), also 4 inches per mile ; from Calcutta to the sea *viâ* the Húglí (about 80 miles), 1 to 2 inches per mile, according to the tide. The fall of the Nile from the first Cataract to Cairo (555 miles), is 6½ inches per mile ; from Cairo to the sea, it is very much less. The fall of the Missis-sippi for the first hundred miles from its mouth, is 1·80 inch per mile ; for the second hundred miles, 2 inches ; for the third hundred, 2·30

the delta of Bengal. The present delta of the Ganges may be The delta
taken to commence at a point 1231 miles from its source, of Bengal.
and 326 from the sea by its longest channel. At that point
the head-waters of the Húglí break off, under the name
of the Bhágírathí, from the parent channel, and make their
way south to the sea. The main volume of the Ganges pursues
its course to the south-east, and a great triangle of land, with
its southern base on the Bay of Bengal, is thus enclosed.

Between the Húglí on the west and the main channel on The
the east, a succession of offshoots strike southward from the deltaic
distribu-
Ganges. The network of streams struggle slowly seaward taries;
over the level delta. Their currents are no longer able, by
reason of their diminished speed, to carry along the silt or
sand which the more rapid parent river has brought down
from Northern India. They accordingly drop their burden of
silt in their channels or along their margins, producing how they
almond-shaped islands, and by degrees raising their banks raise their
banks
and channels above the surrounding plains. When they spill above sur-
over in time of flood, the largest amount of silt is deposited rounding
country.
on their banks, or near them on the inland side. In this way
not only their beds, but also the lands along their banks, are
gradually raised.

SECTION OF A DELTAIC CHANNEL OF THE GANGES.

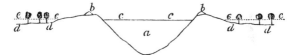

a. The river channel; *b b* the two banks raised by successive deposits of silt from the
spill-water in time of flood; *c c.* the surface of the water when not in flood; *d d.* the low-
lying swamps stretching away from either bank, into which the river flows when it spills
over its banks in time of flood; *e e.* the dotted lines represent the ordinary level of the
river surface.

inches; for the fourth hundred, 2·57 inches; and for the whole section
of 855 miles from the mouth to Memphis, the average fall is given as 4½
inches to the mile.

The following table, calculated by Mr. David Stevenson (*Canal and
River Engineering*, p. 315), shows the silt-carrying power of rivers at various
velocities :—

Inches per Second.		Mile per Hour.	
3	=	0·170	will just begin to work on fine clay.
6	=	0·340	will lift fine sand.
8	=	0 4545	will lift sand as coarse as linseed.
12	=	0·6819	will sweep along fine gravel.
24	=	1·3638	will roll along rounded pebbles 1 inch in diameter.
36	=	2·045	will sweep along slippery angular stones of the size of an egg.

Delta rivers build themselves up into high-level canals.   The rivers of a delta thus build themselves up, as it were, into high-level canals, which in the rainy season overflow their banks and leave their silt upon the low country on either side. Thousands of square miles in Lower Bengal receive in this way each summer a top-dressing of new soil, carried free of cost for more than a thousand miles by the river currents from Northern India or the still more distant Himálayas—-a system of natural manuring which yields a constant succession of rich crops.

Junction of Ganges, Brahmaputra, and Meghná.   At Goálanda, about half-way between the delta-head and the sea, the Ganges unites with the main stream of the Brahmaputra, and farther down with the Meghná. Their combined waters exhibit deltaic operations on the most gigantic scale. They represent the drainage collected by the two vast river systems of the Ganges and the Brahmaputra, from an aggregate catchment basin of 752,000 square miles on both sides of the Himálayas, together with the rainfall poured into the Meghná from the eastern Burmese watershed.

Their combined delta.   The forces thus brought into play defy the control even of modern engineering. As the vast network of rivers creeps farther down the delta, they become more and more sluggish, and raise their beds still higher above the adjacent flats. Each set of channels has a depressed tract or swamp on either side, so that the lowest levels in a delta lie about half-way between the rivers. The stream constantly overflows into these depressed tracts, and gradually fills them up with its silt. The water which rushes from the river into the swamps has sometimes the colour of pea-soup, from the quantity of silt which it carries. When it has stood a few days in the swamps, and the river flood subsides, the water flows back from the swamps into the river channel; but it has dropped all its silt, and is of a clear dark-brown hue. The silt remains in the swamp, and by degrees fills it up, thus slowly creating new land. The muddy foliage of the trees which have been submerged bears witness to the fresh deposit. As we shall presently see, buried roots and decayed stumps are found at great depths; while nearer the top the excavator comes upon the remains of old tanks, broken pottery, and other traces of human habitations, which within historic times were above the ground.

Deltaic swamps,

how filled up by silt.

Last scene in the life of an Indian river.   The last scene in the life of an Indian river is a wilderness of forest and swamp· at the end of the delta, amid whose malarious solitude the network of tidal creeks merges into the sea. Here all the secrets of land-making stand disclosed. The river channels, finally checked by the dead weight of the sea, deposit most of their remaining silt, which emerges from the estuary as banks or blunted headlands. The ocean currents also find themselves impeded by the outflow from the rivers, and in their turn drop the burden of sand which they sweep along the coast. The two causes combine to build up breakwaters of mingled sand and mud along the foreshore. In this way, while the solid earth gradually grows outward into the sea, owing to the deposits of river silt; peninsulas and islands are formed around the river mouths from the sand dropped by the ocean currents ; and a double process of land-making goes on. *Land-making in the estuary.*

The great Indian rivers, therefore, have not only supplied new solid ground by draining off the water from neighbouring lakes and marshes in their upper courses, and by depositing islands in their beds lower down. They are also constantly filling up the low-lying tracts or swamps in their deltas, and are forming banks and capes and masses of low-lying land at their mouths. Indeed, they slowly construct their entire deltas by driving back the sea. Lower Egypt was thus 'the gift of the Nile,' according to her priests in the age of Herodotus; and the vast Province of Lower Bengal is in the strictest scientific sense the gift of the Ganges, the Brahmaputra, and the Meghná. The deltas of these three river systems are in modern times united into one, but three distinct delta-heads are observable. The delta-head of the Brahmaputra commences near the bend where the river now twists due south round the Gáro Hills, 220 miles from the sea as the crow flies. The present delta-head of the Ganges begins at the point where the Bhágírathí breaks southward from the main channel, also about 220 miles in a direct line from the sea. The delta of the Meghná, which represents the heavy southern rainfall of the Khási Hills together with the western drainage of the watershed between Bengal and Independent Burma, commences in Sylhet District. *Egypt, the 'Gift of the Nile.'* *Bengal, the 'Gift of the Ganges.'*

The three deltas, instead of each forming a triangle like the Greek Δ, unite to make an irregular parallelogram, running inland 220 miles from the coast, with an average breadth also of about 220 miles. This vast alluvial basin of say 50,000 square miles was once covered with the sea, and it has been slowly filled up to the height of at least 400 feet by the deposits which the rivers have brought down. In other words, the united river systems of the Ganges, Brahmaputra, and Meghná have torn away from the Himálayas and North-eastern Bengal enough earth to build up a lofty island, with an area of 50,000 square miles, and a height of 400 feet. *Size of the Bengal delta.*

Successive depressions of the delta.   Care has been taken not to overstate the work performed by the Bengal rivers. Borings have been carried down to 481 feet at Calcutta, but the auger broke at that depth, and it is impossible to say how much farther the alluvial deposits may go. There seem to have been successive eras of vegetation, followed by repeated depressions of the surface. These successive eras of vegetation now form layers of stumps of trees, peat-beds, and carbonized wood. Passing below traces of recently submerged forests, a well-marked peat-bed is found in excavations around Calcutta at a depth varying from 20 to 30 feet; and decayed wood, with pieces of fine coal, such as occur in mountain streams, has been met with at a depth of 392 feet. Fossilized remains of animal life have been brought up from 372 feet below the present surface. The footnote[1] illustrates the successive layers of the vast and lofty island, so to speak, which the rivers have built up—an island with an area of 50,000 square miles, and 400 feet high from its foundation, although at places only a few inches above sea-level.

Its subterranean structure.   [1] 'Abstract Report of Proceedings of Committee appointed to superintend the Borings at Fort-William, December 1835 to April 1840.' 'After penetrating through the surface soil to a depth of about 10 feet, a stratum of stiff blue clay, 15 feet in thickness, was met with. Underlying this was a light-coloured sandy clay, which became gradually darker in colour from the admixture of vegetable matter, till it passed into a bed of peat, at a distance of about 30 feet from the surface. Beds of clay and variegated sand, intermixed with *kankar*, mica, and small pebbles, alternated to a depth of 120 feet, when the sand became loose and almost semi-fluid in its texture. At 152 feet, the quicksand became darker in colour and coarser in grain, intermixed with red water-worn nodules of hydrated oxide of iron, resembling to a certain extent the laterite of South India. At 159 feet, a stiff clay with yellow veins occurred, altering at 163 feet remarkably in colour and substance, and becoming dark, friable, and apparently containing much vegetable and ferruginous matter. A fine sand succeeded at 170 feet, and this gradually became coarser, and mixed with fragments of quartz and felspar, to a depth of 180 feet. At 196 feet, clay impregnated with iron was passed through; and at 221 feet sand recurred, containing fragments of limestone with nodules of *kankar* and pieces of quartz and felspar; the same stratum continued to 340 feet; and at 350 feet a fossil bone, conjectured to be the humerus of a dog, was extracted. At 360 feet, a piece of supposed tortoiseshell was found, and subsequently several pieces of the same substance were obtained. At 372 feet, another fossil bone was discovered, but it could not be identified, from its being torn and broken by the borer. At 392 feet, a few pieces of fine coal, such as are found in the beds of mountain streams, with some fragments of decayed wood, were picked out of the sand, and at 400 feet a piece of limestone was brought up. From 400 to 481 feet, fine sand, like that of the seashore, intermixed largely with shingle composed of fragments of primary rocks, quartz, felzpar, mica, slate, and limestone, prevailed, and in this stratum the bore has been terminated.'

It should be remembered, however, that the rivers have been aided in their work by the sand deposited by the ocean currents. But, on the other hand, the alluvial deposits of the Ganges and Brahmaputra commence far to the north of the present delta-head, and have a total area greatly exceeding the 50,000 square miles mentioned in a former paragraph. The Brahmaputra has covered with thick alluvium the valley of Assam ; its confluent, the Meghná, or rather the upper waters which ultimately form the Meghná, have done the same fertilizing task for the valleys of Cachar and Sylhet ; while the Ganges, with its mighty feeders, has prepared for the uses of man thousands of square miles of land in the broad hollow between the Himálayas and the Vindhyas, far to the north-west of its present delta. A large quantity of the finest and lightest silt, moreover, is carried out to sea, and discolours the Bay of Bengal 150 miles from the shore. The plains of Bengal are truly the gift of the great rivers. *Upper Bengal 'finished' by river silt.*

Several attempts have been made to estimate the time which the Ganges and Brahmaputra must have required for accomplishing their gigantic task. The borings already cited, together with an admirable account by Colonel Baird Smith in the *Calcutta Journal of Natural History*,[1] and the Rev. Mr. Everest's calculations, form the chief materials for such an estimate. Sir Charles Lyell [2] accepts Mr. Everest's calculation, made half a century ago, that the Ganges discharges 6368 millions of cubic feet of silt per annum at Gházípur. *Amount of silt brought down.*

This would alone suffice to supply 355 millions of tons a year, or nearly the weight of 60 replicas of the Great Pyramid. ' It is scarcely possible,' he says, ' to present any picture to the mind which will convey an adequate conception of the mighty scale of this operation, so tranquilly and almost insensibly carried on by the Ganges.' About 96 per cent. of the whole deposits are brought down during the four months of the rainy season, or as much as could be carried by 240,000 ships, each of 1400 tons burthen. The work thus done in that season may be realized if we suppose that a daily succession of fleets, each of two thousand great ships, sailed down the river during the four months, and that each ship of the daily 2000 vessels deposited a freight of 1400 tons of mud every morning into the estuary. *Ganges silt at Gházípur.*

---

[1] Vol. i. p. 324. The other authorities, chiefly from the *Journal* of the Bengal Asiatic Society, are fully quoted in the *Geology of India*, by Messrs. Medlicott and Blanford, vol. i. pp. 396 *et seq.* (Calcutta Government Press, 1879).

[2] *Principles of Geology*, vol. i. pp. 478 *et seq.* (1875).

Estimated silt of united river system at the delta.

But the Ganges at Gházípur is only a single feeder of the mighty mass of waters which have formed the delta of Bengal. The Ganges, after leaving Gházípur, receives many of its principal tributaries, such as the GOGRA, the SON, the GANDAK, and the KUSI. It then unites with the Brahmaputra, and finally with the Meghná, and the total mass of mud brought down by these combined river systems is estimated by Sir Charles Lyell to be at least six or seven times as much as that discharged by the Ganges alone at Gházípur. We have therefore, at the lowest estimate, about 40,000 millions of cubic feet of solid matter spread over the delta, or deposited at the river mouths, or carried out to sea, each year; according to Sir Charles Lyell, five times as much as is conveyed by the Mississippi to its delta and the Gulf of Mexico. The silt borne along during the rainy season alone represents the work which a daily succession of fleets, each of 13,000 ships a-piece, sailing down the Ganges during the four rainy months would perform, if each ship of the daily 13,000 vessels discharged a freight of 1400 tons a-piece each morning into the Bay of Bengal. This vast accumulation of silt takes place every rainy season in the delta or around the mouths of the Ganges; and the process, modified by volcanic upheavals and depressions of the delta, has been going on during uncounted thousands of years.

Time required by rivers to construct the delta.

General Strachey took the area of the delta and coast-line within influence of the deposits at 65,000 square miles, and estimated that the rivers would require 45·3 years to raise it by 1 foot, even by their enormous deposit of 40,000 millions of cubic feet of solid earth per annum. The rivers must have been at work 13,600 years in building up the delta 300 feet. But borings have brought up fluvial deposits from a depth of at least 400 feet. The present delta forms, moreover, but a very small part of the vast alluvial area which the rivers have constructed in the great dip between the Himálayas and the Vindhyan mountains. The more closely we scrutinize the various elements in such estimates, the more vividly do we realize ourselves in the presence of an almost immeasurable labour carried on during an almost immeasurable past.

River irrigation.

The land which the great Indian rivers thus create, they also fertilize. In the lower parts of their course we have seen how their overflow affords a natural system of irrigation and manuring. In the higher parts, man has to step in, and to bring their water by canals to his fields. Some idea of the enormous irrigation enterprises of Northern India may be obtained in the four articles in *The Imperial Gazetteer* on the

Ganges and Jumna canals. The Ganges Canal had, in 1883, a length of 445 miles, with 3428 miles of distributaries; an irrigated area of 856,035 acres (including both autumn and spring crops); and a revenue of £279,449, on a total outlay of 2¾ millions sterling (£2,767,538 to 1883). The Lower Ganges Canal will bring under irrigation nearly 1¼ million acres (including both autumn and spring crops). It has already (1882–83) a main channel of 556 miles, with 1991 miles of distributaries; an irrigated area of 606,017 acres; and a clear revenue of £107,000, or 4·13 per cent. on the total outlay up to 1883 (£2,589,624). The Eastern Jumna Canal has a length of 130 miles, with 618 miles of main distributaries. In 1883, the total distributaries aggregated nearly 900 miles, with an irrigated area of 240,233 acres; and a revenue of £82,665, or 28·4 per cent. on the total outlay to that year (£290,839). The Western Jumna Canal measures 433 miles, with an aggregate of 259 miles of distributing channels, besides private watercourses, irrigating an area of 374,243 acres; with a revenue of £74,606, or 8·4 per cent. on a capital outlay to 1883 of £884,952. The four Ganges and Jumna Canals, therefore, already irrigate an aggregate area of over two million acres, and will eventually irrigate over three millions. Among many other irrigation enterprises in Upper India are the Agra, Bári Doáb, Rohilkhand and Bijnor, Betwá, and the Sutlej-Chenab and Indus Inundation Canals.

The Indian rivers form, moreover, as we have seen, the great highways of the country. They supply cheap transit for the collection, distribution, and export of the agricultural staples. What the arteries are to the living body, the rivers are to the plains of Bengal. But the very potency of their energy some- times causes terrible calamities. Scarcely a year passes without floods, which sweep off cattle and grain stores and the thatched cottages, with anxious families perched on their roofs. *The Rivers as high-ways.*

The Rivers as de-stroyers.

In their upper courses, where their water is carried by canals to the fields, the rich irrigated lands breed fever, and are in places rendered sterile by a saline crust called *reh.* Farther down, the uncontrollable rivers wriggle across the face of the country, deserting their old beds, and searching out new channels for themselves, sometimes at a distance of many miles. Their old banks, clothed with trees and dotted along their route with villages, run like high ridges through the level rice-fields, and mark the deserted course of the river.

It has been shown how the Brahmaputra deserted its main channel of the last century, and now rushes to the sea by a

Changes of river-beds.

new course, far to the westwards. Such changes are on so vast a scale, and the eroding power of the current is so irresistible, that it is perilous to build large or permanent structures on the margin. The ancient sacred stream of the Ganges is now a dead river, which ran through the Districts of Húglí and the 24 Parganás. Its course is marked by a line of tanks and muddy pools, with temples, shrines, and burning *gháts* along high banks overlooking its deserted bed.

Deserted river-capitals.

Many decayed or ruined cities attest the alterations in river-beds within historic times. In our own days, the Ganges passed close under Rájmahal, and that town, once the Muhammadan capital of Bengal, was (1850–55) selected as the spot where the railway should tap the river system. The Ganges has now turned away in a different direction, and left the town high and dry, 7 miles from the bank. In 1787–88, the TISTA, a great river of Northern Bengal, broke away from its ancient bed. The ATRAI, or the old channel, by which the Tístá waters found their way into the Ganges, has dwindled into a petty stream, which, in the dry weather, just suffices for boats of 2 tons burthen; while the Tístá has branched to the eastwards, and now pours into the Brahmaputra. In 1870, the RAVI, one of the Five Rivers of the Punjab, carried away the famous shrine of the Sikhs near DERA NANAK, and still threatens the town.

If we go back to a more remote period, we find that the whole ancient geography of India is obscured by changes in the courses of the rivers. Thus, Hastinápur, the Gangetic capital of the Pándavas, in the Mahábhárata, is with difficulty identified in a dried-up bed of the Ganges, 57 miles north-east of the present Delhi. The once splendid capital of KANAUJ, which also lay upon the Ganges, now moulders in desolation 4 miles away from the modern river-bank. The remnant of its inhabitants live for the most part in huts built up against the ancient walls.

A similar fate on a small scale has befallen Kushtiá, the river terminus of the Eastern Bengal Railway. The channel silted up (1860–70), and the terminus had to be removed to Goálanda, farther down the river. On the HUGLI river[1] a succession of emporia and river-capitals have been ruined from the same cause, and engineering efforts are required to secure the permanence of CALCUTTA as a great port.

The *bore*

An idea of the forces at work may be derived from a single well-known phenomenon of the Húglí and the Meghná, the *bore*. The tide advances up their broad estuaries until checked

[1] See article HUGLI RIVER, *The Imperial Gazetteer of India.*

by a rapid contraction of the channel. The obstructed influx, no longer able to spread itself out, rises into a wall of waters from 5 to 30 feet in height, which rushes onwards at a rate nearly double that of a stage-coach. Rennel stated that the Húglí *bore* ran from Húglí Point to Húglí Town, a distance of about 70 miles, in four hours. The native boatmen fly from the bank (against which their craft would otherwise be dashed) into the broad mid-channel when they hear its approaching roar. The *bore* of the Meghná is so 'terrific and dangerous' that no boat will venture down certain of the channels at spring-tide.

The Indian rivers not only desert the cities on their banks, Hamlets but they sometimes tear them away. Many a hamlet and torn away. rice-field and ancient grove of trees is remorselessly eaten up each autumn by the current. A Bengal proprietor has often to look on helplessly while his estate is being swept away, or converted into the bed of a broad, deep river. An important branch of Indian legislation deals with the proprietary changes thus caused by alluvion and diluvion.

The rivers have a tendency to straighten themselves out. River- Their course consists of a series of bends, in each of which the windings. current sets against one bank, which it undermines ; while it leaves still water on the other bank, in which new deposits of land take place. By degrees these twists become sharper and sharper, until the intervening land is almost worn away, leaving only a narrow tongue between the bends. The river finally bursts through the slender strip of soil, or a canal is cut across it by human agency, and direct communication is thus established between points formerly many miles distant by the windings of the river. This process of eating away soil from the one bank, against which the current sets, and depositing silt in the still water along the other bank, is constantly at work. Even in their quiet moods, therefore, the rivers steadily steal land from the old owners, and give it to new ones.

During the rains these forces work with uncontrollable fury. A railway We have mentioned that the first terminus of the Eastern Bengal terminus Railway at Kushtiá had been partially deserted by the Ganges. away. Its new terminus at Goálanda has suffered from an opposite but equally disastrous accident. Up to 1875, the Goálanda station stood upon a massive embankment near the water's edge, protected by masonry spurs running out to the river. About £130,000 had been spent upon these protective works, and it was hoped that engineering skill had conquered the violence of the Gangetic floods. But in August 1875, the solid masonry spurs, the railway station, and the magistrate's court, were all swept away; and deep water covered their site. A new Goálanda terminus had to be erected two miles inland from the former river-bank. Higher up the Ganges, fluvial changes on so great a scale have been encountered at the river-crossing, where the Northern Bengal Railway begins and the Eastern Bengal Railway ends, that no costly or permanent terminus has yet been attempted. Throughout the long courses of the Ganges and Brahmaputra, the mighty currents each autumn undermine and then rend away many thousand acres of solid land. They afterwards deposit their spoil in their channels farther down, and thus, as has been shown, leave high and dry in ruin many an ancient city on their banks.

Poetry of Indian river-names.   Their work, however, is on the whole beneficent; and a poem of Ossian might be made out of the names which the Indian peasant applies to his beloved rivers. Thus, we have the Goddess of Flowing Speech (*Saraswati*), or, according to another derivation, the River of Pools; the Streak of Gold (*Suvarna-rekhá*); the Glancing Waters (*Chitra*); the Dark Channel (*Kála-nadí*), or the Queen of Death (*Kálí-nadí*); the Sinless One (*Pápagíní = Pápahíní*); the Arrowy (*Sharavati*); the Golden (*Suvarnamati*); the Stream at which the Deer Drinks (*Haringháta*); the Forest Hope (*Banás*); the Old Twister (*Burabalang*); besides more common names, such as the All-Destroyer, the Forest King, the Lord of Strength, the Silver Waters, and the Flooder.

Crops of the river plains.   Throughout the river plains of Northern India, two harvests, and in some Provinces three, are reaped each year. These crops are not necessarily taken from the same land; but in most Districts the best situated fields yield two harvests within the twelve months. In Lower Bengal, pease, pulses, oil-seeds, *The three harvests of the year.* and green crops of various sorts, are reaped in spring; the early rice crops in September; and the great rice harvest of the year in November and December. Before the last has been gathered in, it is time to prepare the ground for the spring crops, and the husbandman knows no rest except during the hot weeks of May, when he is anxiously waiting for the rains. Such is the course of agriculture in Lower Bengal. But it *Rice.* should always be remembered that rice is the staple crop in a limited area of India, and that it forms the everyday food of only about 70 millions, or under one-third of the population. It has been estimated that, in the absence of irrigation, the rice crop requires an annual rainfall of at least 36 inches; and an

Indian District requires an average fall of not less than 40 to 60 inches in order to grow rice as its staple crop. A line might almost be drawn across Behar, to the north of which rice ceases to be the staple food of the people; its place being taken by millets, and in a less degree by wheat. There are, indeed, rice-growing tracts in well-watered or low-lying Districts of Northern India, and in the river valleys or deltas and level strips around the southern coast. But speaking generally, throughout North-Western, Central, and Southern India (except in the coast strip), rice is consumed only by the richer classes.

The products of each Province are carefully enumerated in the separate provincial articles in *The Imperial Gazetteer of India*, and an account of the most important will be found under the heading of Agriculture in the present volume. They are here referred to only so far as is necessary to give a general idea of the scenery of the river plains. Along the upper and middle courses of the Bengal rivers, the country rises gently from their banks in fertile undulations, dotted with mud villages and adorned with noble trees. Mango groves scent the air with their blossom in spring, and yield their abundant fruit in summer. The spreading banyan, with its colonnades of hanging roots; the stately *pipal*, with its green masses of foliage; the wild cotton-tree, glowing while still leafless with heavy crimson flowers; the tall, daintily-shaped tamarind, and the quick-growing *bábul*, rear their heads above the crop fields. As the rivers approach the coast, the palm-trees take possession of the scene. The ordinary landscape in the delta is a flat stretch of rice-fields, fringed round with an evergreen border of bamboos, cocoa-nuts, date-trees, areca, and other coronetted palms. This densely-peopled tract seems at first sight bare of villages, for each hamlet is hidden away amid its own grove of plantains and wealth-giving trees. The bamboo and cocoa-nut play a conspicuous part in the industrial life of the people; and the numerous products derived from them, including rope, oil, food, fodder, fuel, and timber, have been dwelt on with admiration by many writers.

The crops also change as we sail down the rivers. In the north, the principal grains are wheat, barley, Indian corn, and a variety of millets, such as *joár* (Sorghum vulgare) and *bájra* (Pennisetum typhoideum). In the delta, on the other hand, rice is the staple crop, and the universal diet. In a single District, Rangpur, there are 295 separate kinds of rice known to the peasant,[1] who has learned to grow his favourite

Marginal notes: Scenery of the river plains. In North Western Bengal. In the delta. Crops of North-Western Bengal; of the delta.

---

[1] *Statistical Account of Bengal*, vol. vii. pp. 234–237.

crop in every locality, from the comparatively dry ground, which yields the *áman* harvest, to the swamps 12 feet deep, on the surface of whose waters the rice ears may be seen struggling upwards for air. Sugar-cane, oil-seeds, flax, mustard, sesamum, palma-christi, cotton, tobacco, indigo, safflower and other dyes, ginger, coriander, red pepper, capsicum, cummin, and precious spices, are grown both in the Upper Provinces, and in the moister valleys and delta of Lower Bengal.

Drugs, fibres, oil-seeds, etc.   A whole pharmacopœia of medicines, from the well-known aloe and castor - oil, to obscure but valuable febrifuges, is derived from shrubs, herbs, and roots.   Resins, gums, varnishes, india-rubber, perfume-oils, and a hundred articles of commerce or luxury, are obtained from the fields and the forests.   Vegetables, both indigenous and imported from Europe, largely enter into the food of the people.   The melon and huge yellow pumpkin spread themselves over the thatched roofs ; fields of potato, *brinjal,* and yams are attached to the homesteads.   The tea-plant is reared on the hilly ranges which skirt the plains both in the North-West and in Assam ; the opium poppy about half-way down the Ganges, around Benares and in Behar ; the silkworm mulberry still farther down in Lower Bengal ; while the jute fibre is essentially a crop of the delta, and would exhaust any soil not fertilized by river floods.

Jungle products.   Even the jungles yield the costly lac and the *tasar* silk cocoons. The *mahuá,* also a gift of the jungle, produces the fleshy flowers which form a staple article of food in many districts, and when distilled supply a cheap spirit.   The *sál, sissu, tún,* and many other indigenous trees yield excellent timber. Flowering creepers, of gigantic size and gorgeous colours, festoon the jungle ; while each tank bears its own beautiful crop of the lotus and water-lily.   Nearly every vegetable product which feeds and clothes a people, or enables it to trade with foreign countries, abounds.

Third Region of India— The Southern Tableland.   Having described the leading features of the Himálayas on the north, and of the great river plains at their base, we come now to the third division of India, namely, the three-sided table-land which covers the southern half or more strictly peninsular portion of India.   This tract, known in ancient times as the Deccan (Dakshin), literally *The South,* comprised, in its widest application, the CENTRAL PROVINCES, BERAR, MADRAS, BOMBAY, MYSORE, with the Native Territories of the Nizám, Sindhia, Holkar, and other Feudatory chiefs.   It had in 1881 an aggregate population of about 100 millions.   For the sake of easy remembrance, therefore, we may take the inhabitants of the river plains in the north at about 150 millions, and the inhabitants of the southern table-land at 100 millions.

The Deccan, in its local acceptation, is restricted to the high inland tract between the Narbadá (Nerbudda) and the Kistna rivers; but the term is also loosely used to include the whole country south of the Vindhyas as far as Cape Comorin. Taken in this wide sense, it slopes up from the southern edge of the Gangetic plains. Three ranges of hills support its northern, its eastern, and its western side, the two latter meeting at a sharp angle near Cape Comorin. *The Deccan;* *Its three supporting mountain walls.*

The northern side is buttressed by confused ranges, with a general direction of east to west, popularly known in the aggregate as the Vindhya mountains. The Vindhyas, however, are made up of several distinct hill systems. Two sacred peaks stand as outposts in the extreme east and west, with a succession rather than a series of ranges stretching 800 miles between. At the western extremity, Mount Abu, famous for its exquisite Jain temples, rises, as a solitary outlier of the Aravalli hills, 5653 feet above the Rájputána plains, like an island out of the sea. Beyond the southern limits of that plain, the Vindhya range of modern geography runs almost due east from Gujarát, forming the northern wall of the Narbadá valley. The Sátpura mountains stretch, also east and west, to the south of the Narbadá river, and form the watershed between it and the Tápti. Towards the heart of India, the eastern extremities of the Vindhyas and Sátpuras end in the highlands of the Central Provinces. Passing still east, the hill system finds a continuation in the Káimur range and its congeners. These in their turn end in the outlying peaks and spurs that mark the western boundary of Lower Bengal, and abut on the old course of the Ganges under the name of the Rájmahál hills. On the extreme east, Mount Parasnáth—like Mount Abu on the extreme west, sacred to Jain rites—rises to 4479 feet above the Gangetic plain. *The Vindhya mountains;* *their various ranges;*

The various ranges of the Vindhyas, from 1500 to over 4000 feet high, form, as it were, the northern wall and buttresses which support the central table-land. But in this sense the Vindhyas must be taken as a loose convenient generalization for the congeries of mountains and table-lands between the Gangetic plains and the Narbadá valley. Now pierced by road and railway, they stood in former times as a barrier of mountain and jungle between Northern and Southern India, and formed one of the main difficulties in welding the *the ancient barrier between Northern and Southern India.*

whole into an empire.   They consist of vast masses of forests, ridges, and peaks, broken by cultivated tracts of the rich cotton-bearing black soil, exquisite river valleys, and high-lying grassy plains.

The Ghâts.   The other two sides of the elevated southern triangle are known as the Eastern and Western GHATS.   These ranges start southwards from the eastern and western extremities of the Vindhyas, and run along the eastern and western coasts *Eastern* of India.   The Eastern Ghâts stretch in fragmentary spurs *Ghâts.* and ridges down the Madras Presidency, receding inland and leaving broad level tracts between their base and the coast. *Western* The Western Ghâts form the great sea wall of the Bombay *Ghâts.* Presidency, with a comparatively narrow strip between them and the shore.   Some of them rise in magnificent precipices and headlands out of the ocean, and truly look like colossal 'landing-stairs' (*ghâts*) from the sea.   The Eastern or Madras Ghâts recede upwards to an average elevation of 1500 feet. *The up-* The Western or Bombay Ghâts ascend more abruptly from the *heaved* sea to an average height of about 3000 feet, with peaks up to *southern* *angle.* 4700, along the coast; rising to 7000 feet and even 8760 feet in the upheaved angle where they unite with the Eastern Ghâts, towards their southern extremity.

The cen- The inner triangular plateau thus enclosed lies from 1000 to *tral trian-* 3000 feet above the level of the sea.   But it is dotted with *gular* *plateau.* peaks and seamed with ranges exceeding 4000 feet in height. Its best known hills are the Nîlgiris (Blue Mountains), with the summer capital of Madras, Utakamand, over 7000 feet above the sea.   Their highest point is Dodábetta peak, 8760 feet, in the upheaved southern angle.   The interior plateau is *Passes* approached by several famous passes from the level coast-strip *from the* on the western side.   The Bhor-Ghât, for example, ascends a *coast; the* *Bhor-Ghât* tremendous ravine about 40 miles south-east of Bombay city, to a height of 2027 feet.   In ancient times it was regarded as the key to the Deccan, and could be held by a small band against any army attempting to penetrate from the coast.   A celebrated military road was constructed by the British up this pass, and practically gave the command of the interior to the then rising port of Bombay.   A railway line has now been carried up the gorge, twisting round the shoulders of mountains, tunnelling through intervening crags, and clinging along narrow ledges to the face of the precipice.   At one point the zigzag is so sharp as to render a circuitous turn impossible, and the trains have to stop and reverse their direction on a levelled terrace.   The Thall Ghât (1912 feet), to the north-east of Bombay, has in like manner been scaled both by road and the and railway. Another celebrated pass, farther down the coast, Ghát. connects the military centre of Belgáum with the little port of Vengurla.

These 'landing-stairs' from the sea to the interior present scenes of rugged grandeur. The trap rocks stand out, after ages of denudation, like circular fortresses flanked by round Hill forts. towers and crowned with nature's citadels, from the mass of hills behind; natural fastnesses, which in the Marátha times were rendered impregnable by military art. In the south of Bombay, the passes climb up from the sea through thick forests, the haunt of the tiger and the mighty bison. Still farther down the coast, the western mountain wall dips deep into the Palghát valley—a remarkable gap, 20 miles broad, The Pal- and leading by an easy route, only 1000 feet in height, from ghát Pass. the seaboard to the interior. A third railway and military road penetrate by this passage from Beypur, and cross the peninsula to Madras. A fourth railway starts inland from the coast at the Portuguese Settlement of Goa.

On the eastern side of India, the Gháts form a series of The rivers spurs and buttresses for the elevated inner plateau rather of the than a continuous mountain wall. They are traversed by a plateau; number of broad and easy passages from the Madras coast. Through these openings, the rainfall of the southern half of the inner plateau reaches the sea. The drainage from the northern or Vindhyan edge of the three-sided table-land falls into the Ganges. The Narbadá (Nerbudda) and Tápti carry the rainfall of the southern slopes of the Vindhyas and of the Sátpura Hills, by two almost parallel lines, into the Gulf of Cambay. But from Surat, in lat. 21° 28′, to Cape Comorin, in lat. 8° 4′, no great river succeeds in piercing the Western Gháts, no exit or in reaching the Bombay coast from the interior table-land. wards;

The Western Gháts form, in fact, a lofty unbroken barrier between the waters of the central plateau and the Indian Ocean. The drainage has therefore to make its way across its drain-India to the eastwards, now foaming and twisting sharply age east-wards. round projecting ranges, then tumbling down ravines, roaring through rapids, or rushing along valleys, until the rain which the Bombay sea-breeze has dropped on the ridges of the Western Gháts finally falls into the Bay of Bengal. In this way, the three great rivers of the Madras Presidency, viz. the Godávari, the Kistna (Krishna), and the Káveri (Cauvery), rise in the mountains overhanging the Bombay coast, and traverse the whole breadth of the central table-land before they reach the sea on the eastern shores of India.

Historical signifi-cance of the Eastern and West-ern Gháts;   The physical geography and the political destiny of the two sides of the Indian peninsula have been determined by the characteristics of the mountain ranges on either coast.   On the east, the Madras country is comparatively open, and was always accessible to the spread of civilisation.   On the east, therefore, the ancient dynasties of Southern India fixed their capitals. Along the west, only a narrow strip of lowland intervenes between the barrier range and the Bombay seaboard.   This western tract long remained apart from the civilisation of the eastern coast.   To our own day, one of its ruling races, the Nairs, retain land tenures and social customs, such as poly-andry, which mark a much ruder stage of human advancement than Hinduism, and which in other parts of India only linger among isolated hill tribes.   On the other hand, the people and of the rainfall.   of this western or Bombay coast enjoy a bountiful rainfall, unknown in the inner plateau and the east.   The monsoon dashes its rain-laden clouds against the Western Gháts, and pours from 100 to 200 inches of rain upon their maritime slopes from Khándesh down to Malabár.   By the time the monsoon has crossed the Western Gháts, it has dropped the greater part of its aqueous burden ; and central Districts, such as Bangalore, obtain only about 35 inches.   The eastern coast also receives a monsoon of its own ; but, except in the neigh-bourhood of the sea, the rainfall throughout the Madras Presidency is scanty, seldom exceeding 40 inches in the year. The deltas of the three great rivers along the Madras coast form, however, tracts of inexhaustible fertility ; and much is done by irrigation to husband and utilize both the local rainfall and the accumulated waters which the rivers bring down.

The Four Forest Regions of Southern India.   The ancient Sanskrit poets speak of Southern India as buried under forests.   But much of the forest land has gradually been denuded by the axe of the cultivator, or in consequence of the deterioration produced by unchecked fires and the grazing of innumerable herds of cattle, sheep, and goats.   Roughly speaking, Southern India consists of four forest regions—First, the Western Gháts and the plains of the Konkan, Malabár, and Travancore between them and the sea ; second, the Karnátik, with the Eastern Gháts, occupying the lands along the Coromandel coast and the outer slopes of the hill ranges behind them ; third, the Deccan, comprising the high plateaux of Haidarábád, the Ceded Districts, Mysore,

Coimbatore, and Salem; fourth, the forests of the Northern
Circars in the Madras Presidency.

Each of these Districts has its own peculiar vegetation. Forests of
That of the first region, or Western Gháts, largely consists of Western
virgin forests of huge trees, with an infinite variety of smaller
Gháts.
shrubs, epiphytic and parasitic plants, and lianas or tangled
creepers which bind together even the giants of the forest.
The king of these forests is the teak (Tectona grandis,
Linn.). This prince of timber is now found in the greatest
abundance in the forests of Kánara, in the Wynád, and in
the Anamalai Hills of Coimbatore and Cochin. The *pún*
tree (Calophyllum inophyllum, *Linn.*) is more especially found
in the southernmost forests of Travancore and Tinnevelli, where
tall straight stems, fit for the spars and masts of seagoing ships,
are procured. The jack fruit (Artocarpus integrifolia, *Linn.*)
and its more common relation the *aini* (Artocarpus hirsuta,
Lam.), furnish a pretty yellow-coloured timber; the blackwood
(Dalbergia latifolia, *Roxb.*) yields huge logs excellent for carved
furniture. The Terminalias (T. tomentosa and T. paniculata,
W. and A.) with the benteak (Lagerstrœmia microcarpa, *Wight.*)
supply strong wood suitable for the well-built houses of the
prosperous population of Malabár and Travancore. The
dammer tree or Indian copal (Vateria indica, *Linn.*) yields its
useful resin. The ground vegetation supplies one of the most
valuable of Indian exports, the cardamom. To enumerate all
the important trees and products of the Western Gháts would,
however, be impossible.

In the Karnátik region, the forests rarely consist of large Forests of
timber, in consequence of the drier climate and the shorter Eastern
monsoon rains. Nor are they of a wide area. Most of the Karnátik.
Gháts and
forests consist of what is known as 'Evergreen Scrub,' in which
the prominent trees are the Eugenia jambolana, *Lam.*, Mimusops
indica, *Linn.*, and the strychnine (Strychnos nux-vomica, *Linn.*).
On the slopes of the hills deciduous forest appears with teak,
Terminalias, Anogeissus, and occasional red sanders.

The Deccan region, which gets a share of both monsoons Forests
(namely the monsoon from the south-west from June to Sep- of the
tember, and that from the north - east from September to Deccan.
January), has still some large areas covered with fine forest,
and yielding good timber. Chief among these areas are the
Nallamalai Hills of Karnul, the Pálkonda Hills of Cuddapah,
the Collegal Hills of Coimbatore, and the Shevaroy and
Javadi ranges of Salem and North Arcot. In the Nallamalai
Hills, *bijasál* (Pterocarpus Marsupium, *Roxb.*) and *sáj* (Ter-

minalia tomentosa, *W. and A.*) are the prevailing timbers; the valuable red sanders-wood (Pterocarpus santalinus, *Linn.*) has its home in the Pálkonda and adjoining ranges of Cuddapah, while the growth on the hills of Coimbatore includes the precious sandal-wood (Santalum album, *Linn.*). In the drier country of Bellary and Penukonda, the chief tree is the *anjan* (Hardwickia binata, *Roxb.*), furnishing the hardest and heaviest of Indian woods.

Forests of Northern Madras.

The fourth forest region is that of the Northern Circars. It stretches from the Kistna river up to the Chilka lake, and includes fine forests of almost untouched *sál* (Shorea robusta, *Gaert.*), the iron-wood (Xylia dolabriformis, *Benth.*), the satin-wood (Chloroxylon Swietenia, *D.C.*), and many other timbers of value.

Scenery of southern hill country.

In wild tropical beauty nothing can surpass the luxuriance of an untouched Coorg forest, as viewed from one of the peaks of the Western Gháts. A waving descent of green, broken into terraces of varying heights, slopes downward on every side. North and south run parallel ranges of mountains, wooded almost to the summit; while to the west, thousands of feet below, the view is bounded by the blue line of the Arabian Sea. Wild animals of many kinds breed in the jungle, and haunt the grassy glades. The elephant, the tiger, and the leopard, the mighty bison, the stately *sámbhar* deer, and the jungle sheep, with a variety of smaller game, afford adventure to the sportsman. During the rains magnificent cataracts dash over the precipices. The Gersappa falls, in the Western Gháts, have a descent of 830 feet.

Crops of Southern India.

In the valleys, and upon the elevated plains of the central plateau, tillage is driving back the jungle to the hilly recesses, and fields of wheat and many kinds of smaller grain or millets, tobacco, cotton, sugar-cane, and pulses, spread over the open country. The black soil of Southern India, formed from the detritus of the trap mountains, is proverbial for its fertility; while the level strip between the Western Gháts and the sea rivals even Lower Bengal in its fruit-bearing palms, rice harvests, and rich succession of crops. The deltas of the rivers which issue from the Eastern Gháts are celebrated as rice-bearing tracts. But the interior of the table-land is liable to droughts. The cultivators here contend against the calamities of nature by varied systems of irrigation—by means of which they store the rain brought during a few months by the monsoon, and husband it for use throughout the whole year. Great tanks or lakes, formed by damming up the valleys, are a striking feature of Southern India. The food of the common people consists chiefly of small grains, such as *joár*, *bájra*, and *rágí*. The great export is cotton, with wheat from the northern Districts of the table-land. The pepper trade of Malabár dates from far beyond the age of Sindbad the Sailor, and reaches back to Roman times. Cardamoms, spices of various sorts, dyes, and many medicinal drugs, are also grown.

It is on the interior table-land, and among the hilly spurs Minerals; which project from it, that the mineral wealth of India lies hid. Coal-mining now forms a great industry on the Coal, north-eastern side of the table-land, in Bengal; and also in Lime, Iron. the Central Provinces. Beds of iron-ore and limestone have been worked in several places, and hold out a possibility of a new era of enterprise to India in the future. Many districts are rich in building stone, marble, and the easily-worked laterite. Copper and other metals exist in small quantities. Golconda was long famous as the central mart for the produce of the diamond districts, which now yield little more than a bare living to the workers. Gold dust has from very ancient times been washed out of the river-beds; and quartz-crushing for gold is being attempted on scientific principles in Madras and Mysore.

We have now briefly surveyed the three regions of India. Recapitu- The first, or the Himálayan, lies for the most part beyond the the Three British frontier; but a knowledge of it supplies the key to Regions of the climatic and social conditions of India. The second India. region, or the River Plains in the north, formed the theatre of the ancient race movements which shaped the civilisation and political destinies of the whole Indian peninsula. The third region, or the Triangular Table-land in the south, has a character quite distinct from either of the other two divisions, and a population which is now working out a separate develop- ment of its own. Broadly speaking, the Himálayas are Their peopled by Turanian tribes, although to a large extent ruled races and lan- by Aryan immigrants. The great River Plains of Bengal are guages. still the possession of the Indo-Aryan race. The Triangular Table-land has formed an arena for a long struggle between the Aryan civilisation from the north, and what is known as the Dravidian stock in the south.

To this vast Empire the English have added BRITISH British BURMA, consisting of the lower valley of the Irawadi (Irra- Burma waddy) with its delta, and a long flat strip stretching down the eastern side of the Bay of Bengal. Between the narrow maritime tract and the Irawadi valley runs a backbone of lofty ranges. These ranges, known as the Yoma (Roma) mountains, are covered with dense forests, and separate the Irawadi valley from the strip of coast. The Yoma ranges have *Its valleys* peaks exceeding 4000 feet, and culminate in the Blue *and moun-* Mountain, 7100 feet. They are crossed by passes, one of *tains ;* which, the An or Aeng, rises to 4517 feet above the sea-level. A thousand creeks indent the seaboard ; and the whole of the level country, both on the coast and in the Irawadi valley, forms one vast rice-field. The rivers float down an abundant *Its pro-* supply of teak and bamboos from the north. Tobacco, of *ducts.* an excellent quality, supplies the cigars which all Burmese (men, women, and children) smoke, and affords an industrial product of increasing value. Arakan and Pegu, or the Provinces of the coast strip, and also the Irawadi valley, *Tenas-* contain mineral oil-springs. Tenasserim forms a long narrow *serim.* maritime Province, running southward from the mouths of the Irawadi to Point Victoria, where the British territory adjoins Siam. Tenasserim is rich in tin mines, and contains iron-ores equal to the finest Swedish ; besides gold and copper in smaller quantities, and a very pure limestone. Rice and timber form the staple exports of Burma ; and rice is also the universal food of the people. British Burma, including Tenasserim, has an area of over 87,000 square miles ; and a population, in 1881, of $3\frac{3}{4}$ million persons. It is fortunate in still possessing wide areas of yet uncultivated land to meet the wants of its rapidly increasing people.[1]

Annexa- Since these sheets went to press, the persistent misconduct *tion of* of King Thebau in Upper Burma, his obstinate denial of *Upper* *Burma,* justice, and his frustration of Lord Dufferin's earnest endea- *1886.* vours to arrive at a conciliatory settlement, compelled the British Government to send an expedition against him. A force under General Prendergast advanced up the Irawadi valley with little opposition, and occupied Mandalay. King Thebau surrendered, and was removed to honourable confine- ment in British India. His territories were annexed to the British Empire, by Lord Dufferin's Proclamation, on the 1st of January 1886.

[1] *Vide post,* pp. 47, 50.

CHAPTER II.

THE PEOPLE.

THE POPULATION OF INDIA, with British Burma, amounted General
in 1881 to 256 millions, or, as already mentioned, more than survey of
double the number which Gibbon estimated for the Roman thePeople.
Empire in the height of its power. But the English Government has respected the possessions of native chiefs, and one-
third of the country still remains in the hands of its hereditary
rulers. Their subjects make about one-fifth of the whole Indian
people. The British territories, therefore, comprise only two-
thirds of the area of India, and about four-fifths of its inhabitants.

The native princes govern their States with the help of The Feu-
certain English officers, whom the Viceroy stations in native datory
territory. Some of the Chiefs reign almost as independent Chiefs.
sovereigns; others require more assistance, or a stricter
control. They form a magnificent body of feudatory rulers,
possessed of revenues and armies of their own. The more Their
important of these princes exercise the power of life and death various
over their subjects ; but the authority of each is limited by usage, powers.
or by treaties or engagements, acknowledging their subordination
to the British Government. That Government, as Suzerain
in India, does not allow its feudatories to make war upon
each other, or to have any relations with foreign States. It
interferes when any chief misgoverns his people; rebukes, and
if needful removes, the oppressor; protects the weak; and
firmly imposes peace upon all.

The British possessions are distributed into twelve govern- British
ments, each with a separate head; but all of them under the India—the
orders of the supreme Government of India, consisting of Twelve
the Governor-General in Council. The Governor-General, Provinces,
who also bears the title of Viceroy, holds his court and
government at Calcutta in the cold weather, and during
summer at Simla, an outer spur of the Himálayas, 7000 feet
above the level of the sea. The Viceroy of India, and the
Governors of Madras and Bombay, are usually British statesmen appointed in England by the Queen. The heads of how
the other ten Provinces are selected for their merit from the governed.

Anglo-Indian services, and are nominated by the Viceroy,
subject in the case of the Lieutenant - Governorships to
approval by the Secretary of State.

Census of 1881 and of 1872.   The Census of 1881 returned a population of 256,396,646
souls for all India. The following tables give an abstract of
the area and population of each of the British Provinces, and

THE TWELVE GOVERNMENTS OR PROVINCES OF
BRITISH INDIA, IN 1881.

NAME OF PROVINCE (Exclusive of the Native States attached to it).	Area in Square Miles.	Total Population.	Number of Persons per Square Mile.
1. Government of Madras,[1] . . .	141,001	31,170,631	221
2. Government of Bombay, with Sind, .	124,122	16,454,414	133
3. Lieutenant-Governorship of Bengal,[2] .	150,588	66,691,456	443
4. Lieutenant-Governorship of the Punjab,	106,632	18,850,437	177
5. Lieutenant-Governorship of the North-Western Provinces, . . .	106,111	44,107,869	416
6. Chief-Commissionership of Oudh,[3]			
7. Chief-Commissionership of the Central Provinces, ...	84,445	9,838,791	117
8. Chief - Commissionership of British Burma, ...	87,220	3,736,771	43
9. Chief-Commissionership of Assam,[4] .	46,341	4,881,426	105
10. Commissionership of Berar,[5] .	17,711	2,672,673	151
11. Commissionership of Ajmere, . .	2,711	460,722	170
12. Commissionership of Coorg, . .	1,583	178,302	113
Total for British India,[6] . .	868,465	199,043,492	229

[1] Including the three petty States of Pudukota, Banganapalli, and Sandhúr.

[2] Exclusive of 5976 square miles of unsurveyed and half-submerged Sundarbans along the sea face of the Bay of Bengal. The Imperial Census Report
does not distinguish between the Feudatory States and British territory in the
returns for Bengal. The figures given above are taken from the Provincial
Census Report, and refer to British territory only. The area and population
of the Native States of Bengal are shown in the table on the next page.

[3] Oudh has been incorporated, since 1877, with the North-Western Provinces. The Lieutenant-Governor of the North-Western Provinces is also
Chief-Commissioner of Oudh.

[4] Assam was separated from the Lieutenant-Governorship of Bengal in 1874,
and erected into a Chief-Commissionership. The area includes an estimate
for the unsurveyed tracts in the Cachar, Nágá, and Lakhimpur Hills.

[5] Berar consists of the six 'Assigned Districts' made over to the British
administration by the Nizám of Haidarábád for the maintenance of the
Haidarábád Contingent, which he was bound by treaty to maintain, and in
discharge of other obligations.

[6] These figures are exclusive of the population of the British Settlement of
Aden in Arabia (34,860), and of the Andaman Islands in the Bay of Bengal
(14,628). These places have not been included in the tables of the Imperial
Census Report, as being outside the geographical limits of India.

groups of Native States, together with the French and
Portuguese possessions in India. The population in 1872
was as follows :—British India, 186 millions ; Feudatory States,
over 54 millions; French and Portuguese possessions, nearly
¾ of a million ; total for all India, 240,931,521 in 1872.

THE THIRTEEN GROUPS OF NATIVE STATES FORMING FEUDATORY INDIA, IN 1881.

	NAME OF STATE.	Total Area in Square Miles.	Total Population.	Number of Persons per Square Mile.
Under the Governor-General in Council.	1. Rájputána, ...	129,750	10,268,392	79
	2. Haidarábád (Nizám's Dominions)	71,771	9,845,594	137
	3. Central Indian Agency and Bundelkhand, ...	75,079	9,261,907	123
	4. Baroda, ...	8,570	2,185,005	255
	5. Mysore,[1]	24,723	4,186,188	169
	6. Kashmír,[2]	80,900	1,534,972	19
	7. Manipur, ...	8,000	221,070	27
Under the Local Governments.	8. Native States under Bombay Government, ...	73,753	6,941,249	94
	9. Native States under Madras Government, ...	8,091	3,001,436	370
	10. Native States under Bengal Government, ...	36,634	2,845,405	78
	11. Native States under Punjab Government, ...	35,817	3,861,683	108
	12. Native States under North-Western Provinces, . .	5,125	741,750	145
	13. Native States under Central Provinces, ...	28,834	1,709,720	59
	Total for Feudatory India, .	587,047	56,604,371	96

If to the foregoing figures we add the French and Portuguese possessions, we obtain the total for all India. Thus—

ALL INDIA, INCLUDING BRITISH BURMA.
(Based chiefly on the Census of 1881.)

	Area in Square Miles.	Population.	Number of Persons per Square Mile.
British India, ...	868,465	199,043,492	229
Feudatory India, . . .	587,047	56,604,371	96
Portuguese Settlements, . .	2,365	475,172	201
French Settlements, . . .	203	273,611	135
Total for all India, including British Burma, . .	1,458,080	256,396,646	176

[1] Mysore was under direct British administration from 1830 to 1881, when
it was restored to native rule on its young chief attaining his majority.

[2] The Kashmír figures relate to the year 1873.

Density of
the popu-
lation,

British India, therefore, supports a population much more than twice as dense as that of the Native States. If we exclude the outlying and lately-acquired Provinces of British Burma and Assam, the proportion is nearly three-fold, or 260 persons to the square mile. How thick this population is, may be realized from the fact that France had in 1876 only

compared
with
France and
England.

180 people to the square mile; while even in crowded England, wherever the density approaches 200 to the square mile it ceases to be a rural population, and has to live, to a greater or less extent, by manufactures, mining, or city industries.[1] Throughout large areas of Bengal, two persons have to live on the proceeds of each cultivated acre, or 1280 persons to each cultivated square mile. The Famine Commissioners reported in 1880, that over 6 millions of the peasant holdings of Bengal, or two-thirds of the whole, averaged from 2 to 3 acres a-piece. Allowing only four persons to the holding, for men, women, and children, this represents a population of 24 millions struggling to live off 15 million acres, or a little over half an acre a-piece.

Absence
of large
towns.

Unlike England, India has few large towns, and no great manufacturing centres. Thus, in England and Wales 42 per cent., or nearly one-half of the population in 1871, lived in towns with upwards of 20,000 inhabitants, while in British India only 4½ per cent., or not one-twentieth of the people,

Population
entirely
rural.

live in such towns. India, therefore, is almost entirely a rural country; and many of the so-called towns are mere groups of villages, in the midst of which the cattle are driven a-field, and ploughing and reaping go on. Calcutta itself has grown out of a cluster of hamlets on the bank of the Húgli; and the term 'municipality,' which in Europe is only applied to towns, often means in India a 'rural union,' or collection of home-steads for the purposes of local government.

Over-
crowded
Districts.

We see, therefore, in India, a dense population of husband-men. Wherever their numbers exceed 1 to the acre, or 640 to the square mile,—excepting in suburban districts or in irrigated tracts,—the struggle for existence becomes hard. At half an acre a-piece that struggle is terribly hard. In such Districts, a good harvest yields just sufficient food for the people; and thousands of lives depend each autumn on a few inches more or less of rainfall. The Government may, by great efforts, feed the starving in time of actual famine; but it cannot stop the yearly work of disease and death among a steadily underfed people. In these overcrowded tracts the

[1] Report on the Census of England and Wales for 1871.

population reaches the stationary stage. For example, in Allahábád District during twenty years, the inhabitants increased
by only 6 persons in 10,000 each year. During the nine
years from 1872 to 1881, the annual increase was 8 persons
in 10,000. In still more densely-peopled localities upon the
line of railway, facilities for migration have drained off the
excessive population, and their total number in 1872 was
less than it had been twenty years before. On the other hand,
in thinly-peopled Provinces the inhabitants quickly multiply. Under-
Thus, when we obtained the District of Amherst in 1824 from peopled
the king of Burma, it had been depopulated by savage native Provinces.
wars. The British established their firm rule; people began
to flock in; and by 1829 there were 70,000 inhabitants. In
fifty years the population had increased by more than four-
fold, or to 301,086 in 1881.

In some parts of India, therefore, there are more husband- The 'im-
men than the land can feed; in other parts, vast tracts of fertile mobile'
soil still await the cultivator. In England the people would peasant.
move freely from the over-populated districts to the thinly-
inhabited ones; but in India the peasant clings to his hereditary homestead long after his family has outgrown his fields.
If the Indian races will only learn to migrate to tracts where
spare land still abounds, they will do more than the utmost
efforts of Government can accomplish to prevent famines.

The facts disclosed by the Census in 1872 and 1881 prove, Move-
indeed, that the Indian peasant has lost something of his ments of
old immobility. The general tendency of the population the people.
in Bengal is south and east to the newly-formed delta, and
north-east to the thinly-peopled valleys of Assam. In 1881,
it was ascertained that out of a specified population of 247
millions, nearly 6½ millions were living in Provinces in which
they had not been born. But the clinging of the people to
their old villages in spite of hardship and famine still forms
a most difficult problem in India.

Throughout many of the hill and border tracts, land is so
plentiful that it yields no rent. Any one may settle on a patch
which he clears of jungle, exhausts the soil by a rapid succession The
of crops, and then leaves it to relapse into forest. In such tracts nomadic
no rent is charged; but each family of wandering husbandmen of hus-
pays a poll-tax to the chief, or to the Government under whose bandry.
protection it dwells. As the inhabitants increase, this nomadic
system of cultivation gives place to regular tillage. Throughout British Burma we see both methods at work side by side;
while on the thickly-peopled plains of India the 'wandering

husbandmen' have long since disappeared, and each household remains rooted to the same plot of ground during generations.

Labour and land in the last century ; In some parts of India, this change in the relation of the people to the land has taken place before our own eyes. Thus, in Bengal there was in the last century more cultivable land than there were husbandmen to till it. A hundred years of British rule has reversed the ratio ; and there are now, in some Districts, more people than there is land for them to till. This change has produced a silent revolution in the rural economy of the Province. When the English obtained Bengal in the last century, they found in many Districts two distinct rates of rent current for the same classes of soil. The higher rate was paid by the *tháni ráyats,* literally ' stationary ' tenants, who had their houses in the hamlet, and formed the permanent body of cultivators. These tenants would bear a great deal of extortion rather than forsake the lands on which they had expended labour and capital in digging tanks, cutting irrigation channels, and building homesteads. They were oppressed accordingly ; and while they had a right of occupation in their holdings, so long as they paid the rent, the very highest rates were squeezed out of them. The temporary or wandering cultivators, *paikhást ráyats,* were those who had not their homes in the village, and who could therefore leave it whenever they pleased. They had no right of occupancy in their fields ; but on the other hand, the landlord could not obtain so high a rent from them, as there was plenty of spare land in adjoining villages to which they could retire in case of oppression. The landlords were at that time competing for tenants ; and one of the commonest complaints which they brought before the Company's officials was a charge against a neighbouring proprietor of ' enticing away their cultivators ' by low rates of rent.

and at the present day. This state of things is now reversed in most parts of Bengal. The landlords have no longer to compete for tenants. It is the husbandmen who have to compete with one another for land. There are still two rates of rent. But the lower rates are now paid by the ' stationary ' tenants, who possess occupancy rights ; while the higher or rack-rents are paid by the other class, who do not possess occupancy rights. In ancient India, the eponymous hero, or original village founder, was the man who cut down the jungle. In modern India, special legislation and a Forest Department are required to preserve the trees which remain. Not only has the country been stripped of its woodlands, but in many

Districts the pastures have been brought under the plough, to the detriment of the cattle. The people can no longer afford to leave sufficient land fallow, or under grass, for their oxen and cows.

It will be readily understood that in a country where, almost Serfdom down to the present day, there was more land than there in India. were people to till it, a high value was set upon the cultivating class. In tracts where the nomadic system of husbandry survives, no family is permitted by the native chief to quit his territory. For each household there pays a poll-tax. In many parts of India, we found the lower classes attached to the soil in a manner which could scarcely be distinguished from prædial slavery. In spite of our legislative enactments, this system lingered on during nearly a century of British rule. Our early officers in South-Eastern Bengal, especially in the great island of Sandwíp, almost raised a rebellion by their attempts to liberate the slaves. Indeed, in certain tracts where we found the population very depressed, as in Behar, the courts have in our own day occasionally brought to light the survival of serfdom. A feeling still survives in the minds of some British officers against migrations of the people from their own Districts to adjoining ones, or to Native States.

If we except the newly-annexed Provinces of Burma Unequal and Assam, the population of British India is nearly three pressure of times more dense than the population of Feudatory India. tion on the This great disproportion cannot be altogether explained by land. differences in the natural capabilities of the soil. It would be for the advantage of the people that they should spread themselves over the whole country, and so equalize the pressure throughout. The Feudatory States lie interspersed among British territory, and no costly migration by sea is involved. That the people do not thus spread themselves out, but crowd together within our Provinces, is partly due to their belief that, on the whole, they are less liable to oppression under British rule than under native chiefs. But any outward movement of the population, even from the most densely-peopled English Districts, would probably be regarded with pain by the local officers. Indeed, the occasional exodus of a few cultivators from the overcrowded Province of Behar into the thinly-peopled frontier State of Nepál, has formed a subject of sensitive self-reproach. In proportion as we can enforce good government under the native chiefs of India, we should hope to see a gradual movement of the people into the Feudatory States. There is plenty of land in India for the whole population. What is required is not the diminution of the people, but their more equal distribution.

Census of 1881.

The Census, taken in February 1881, shows an increase of 15½ millions for all India, or 6·4 per cent., during the nine years since 1872. But this general statement gives but an imperfect insight into the local increment of the people. For while in the southern Provinces, which suffered most from the famine of 1877–78, the numbers have stood still, or even receded,

Increase of the people.

an enormous increase has taken place in the less thickly-peopled tracts. Thus, the British Presidency of Madras shows a diminution of 1·4 per cent.; while the Native State of Mysore, which felt the full effects of the long-continued dearth of 1876–79, had 17 per cent. fewer inhabitants in 1881 than in 1872. The Bengal population has increased by 11 per cent. in the nine years, notwithstanding the milder scarcity of 1874. But the great increase is in the outlying, under-peopled Districts of India, where the pressure of the inhabitants on the soil has not yet begun to be felt, and where thousands of acres still await the cultivator. In Assam the increase (1872–81) has been 19 per cent.—largely due to immigration; in the Central Provinces, with their Feudatory States and tracts of unreclaimed jungle, 25 per cent.; in Berar (adjoining them), 20 per cent.; while in Burma—which, most of all the British Provinces, stands in need of inhabitants—the nine years have added 36 per cent. to the population, equivalent to doubling the people in about twenty-five years.

The following table compares the results of the Census of 1872 with those of the Census of 1881. It should be borne in mind, however, that the Census of 1872 was not a synchronous one; and that in some of the Native States the returns of 1872 were estimates rather than actual enumerations.[1]

POPULATION OF INDIA IN 1872 AND 1881.

	In 1872.	In 1881.	Increase.	Per-centage.
British Provinces, . .	186,041,191	199,043,492	13,002,301	6·99
Feudatory States, . .	54,211,158	56,604,371	2,393,213	4·41
French and Portuguese Possessions, . . .	679,172	748,783	69,611	10·25
	240,931,521	256,396,646	15,465,125	6·42

[1] The figures for 1872 in the above table are taken from the finally revised statements, after allowing for transfers of territory and the restoration of Mysore to Native rule. How far the increase in the French and

THE ETHNICAL HISTORY OF INDIA.—The statistical elucida- Ethno-
tion of the races and Provinces of India can only be effected logy.
by tabular forms. At the end of this volume, therefore, will be
found a series of ten statements dealing with the various aspects
of the Indian population.[1] The briefest summary of the
ethnological elements which compose that population is all
that can be here attempted.

European writers formerly divided the Indian population into Four-fold
two races—the Hindus and the Muhammadans. But when we division
look more closely at the people, we find that they consist of four People.
well-marked elements. These are, first, the recognised non- (1) Non-
Aryan Tribes, called the Aborigines, and their half-Hinduized Aryans.
descendants, numbering over $17\frac{1}{2}$ millions in British India
in 1872. Second, the comparatively pure offspring of the (2) Aryans.
Aryan or Sanskrit-speaking Race (the Bráhmans and Rájputs), about 16 millions in 1872. Third, the great Mixed
Population, known as the Hindus, which has grown out (3) Mixed
of the Aryan and non-Aryan elements (chiefly from the Hindus.
latter), 111 millions in 1872. Fourth, the Muhammadans, (4) Mu-
41 millions. These made up the 186 millions of people under hamma-
British rule in 1872. The same four-fold division applied to dans.
the population of the 54 millions in Feudatory India in 1872,
but we do not know the numbers of the different classes.

The figures for 1872 are reproduced in the last paragraph,
as the Census of 1881 adopted a different classification, which

Portuguese Possessions is due to more accurate enumeration in 1881, cannot
be exactly ascertained.

[1] Viz.—Table   I. Area, villages, houses, and population, etc., in each
                      Province of British India in 1881.
            ,,   II. Distribution into town and country, or 'towns and
                      villages in British India.'
            ,,   III. Cultivated, cultivable, and uncultivable land in
                      Provinces for which returns exist.
            ,,   IV. Population of British India classified according to age
                      and sex.
            ,,   V. Population of British India classified according to
                      religion.
            ,,   VI. Asiatic non-Indian population of British India classi-
                      fied according to birth-place.
            ,,   VII. Non-Asiatic population of British India classified
                      according to birth-place.
            ,, VIII. Town population of India, being a list of the 149
                      towns of British India, of which the population
                      exceeds 20,000.
            ,,   IX. Population of British India according to education.
            ,,   X. Population of British India, classified according to
                      caste, sect, and nationality.

does not so clearly disclose the ethnical elements of the people. This difference will be more fully explained in the next chapter.

According to the Census of 1881, the comparatively pure descendants of the Aryan race (the Bráhmans and Rájputs) still numbered 16 millions in British India; the mixed population, including lower caste Hindus, Aboriginal Tribes, and Christians, 138 millions; and the Muhammadans, 45 millions. These make up the 199 millions in British India in 1881. In the Feudatory States there appear to have been $5\frac{1}{4}$ millions of Bráhmans and Rájputs; $46\frac{1}{4}$ millions of lower caste Hindus and Aboriginal Tribes; and 5 millions of Muhammadans,—making up the $56\frac{1}{2}$ millions in Feudatory India in 1881. The aboriginal element of the population was chiefly returned as low-caste Hindus. Only $4\frac{3}{4}$ millions were separately registered as non-Aryans, or Aborigines in British India; and $1\frac{3}{4}$ millions in the Feudatory States; making $6\frac{1}{2}$ millions for all India in 1881.

Plan of this volume in dealing with the Indian Races and their history.   The following chapters first treat of each of these four classes separately, namely the non-Aryan or so-called aboriginal tribes; the Aryan immigrants from the north; the mixed population or Hindus; and the Muhammadans. These are the four elements which make up the present population. Their history, as a loosely-connected whole, after they had been pounded together in the mortar of Muhammadan conquest, will next be traced. A narrative of the events by which the English nation became answerable for the welfare of this vast section of the human family, will follow. Finally, it will be shown how the British Government is trying to discharge its solemn responsibility, and the administrative mechanism will be explained which has knit together the discordant races of India into a great pacific Empire.

The two races of pre-historic India.   Our earliest glimpses of India disclose two races struggling for the soil. The one was a fair-skinned people, which had lately entered by the north-western passes ; a people of ARYAN, literally ' noble,' lineage, speaking a stately language, worshipping friendly and powerful gods. The other was a race of a lower type, who had long dwelt in the land, and whom the lordly new-comers drove back before them into the mountains, or reduced to servitude on the plains. The comparatively pure descendants of these two races were in 1872 nearly equal in numbers, total $33\frac{1}{2}$ millions; the intermediate castes, sprung chiefly from the ruder stock, make up the mass of the present Indian population.

CHAPTER III.

THE NON-ARYAN RACES.

THE present chapter treats of the lower tribes, an obscure people, who, in the absence of a race-name of their own, may be called the non-Aryans or Aborigines. They have left no written records; indeed, the use of letters, or of any simplest hieroglyphs, was to them unknown. The sole works of their hands which have come down to us are rude stone circles, and the upright slabs and mounds, beneath which, like the primitive peoples of Europe, they buried their dead. From these we only discover that, at some far-distant but unfixed period, they knew how to make round pots of hard, thin earthenware, not inelegant in shape; that they fought with iron weapons, and wore ornaments of copper and gold. Coins of Imperial Rome have been dug up from their graves. Still earlier remains prove that, long before their advent, India was peopled as far as the depths of the Central Provinces, by tribes unacquainted with the metals, who hunted and warred with polished flint axes and other deftly-wrought implements of stone, similar to those found in Northern Europe. And even these were the successors of yet ruder beings, who have left their agate knives and rough flint weapons in the Narbadá valley. In front of this far-stretching background of the early Metal and Stone Ages, we see the so-called Aborigines being beaten down by the newly-arrived Aryan race.

The struggle is commemorated by the two names which the victors gave to the early tribes, namely, the Dasyus, or 'enemies,' and the Dásas, or 'slaves.' The new-comers from the north prided themselves on their fair complexion, and their Sanskrit word for 'colour' (*varna*) came to mean 'race' or 'caste.' Their earliest poets, 3000 years ago, praised in the Rig-Veda their bright gods, who, 'slaying the Dasyus, protected the *Aryan colour;*' who 'subjected the black-skin to the Aryan man.' They tell us of their 'stormy deities, who rush on like furious bulls and scatter the black-skin.' The sacrificer gave thanks to his god for 'dispersing the slave bands of black descent,'

Side notes: ARYANS or Aborigines. Kistvaen-builders. Flint weapons. The Non-Aryans as described by the Aryans. The 'Black-skin.'

and for sweeping away 'the vile Dasyan colour.' Moreover, the Aryan, with his finely-formed features, loathed the squat Mongolian faces of the Aborigines. One Vedic singer speaks

Flat-nosed. of them as 'noseless' or flat-nosed, while another praises his own 'beautiful-nosed' gods. Indeed, the Vedic hymns abound in scornful epithets for the primitive tribes, as 'disturbers of

Raw-eaters. sacrifices,' 'gross feeders on flesh,' 'raw-eaters,' 'lawless,' 'not-sacrificing,' 'without gods,' and 'without rites.' As time went on, and these rude tribes were driven back into the forest, they were painted in still more hideous shapes, till they became

The 'Demons' of the Aryan race. the 'monsters' and 'demons' of the Aryan poet and priest. Their race-name Dasyu, 'enemy,' thus grew to signify a devil, as the old Teutonic word for enemy (still used in that sense in the German *feind*) has become the English 'fiend.'

More civilised non-Aryan tribes. Nevertheless, all of them could not have been savages. We hear of wealthy Dasyus, and even the Vedic hymns speak of their 'seven castles' and 'ninety forts.' In later Sanskrit literature, the Aryans make alliance with aboriginal princes ; and when history at length dawns on the scene, we find some of the most powerful kingdoms of India ruled by dynasties of non-Aryan descent. Nor were they devoid of religious rites, or of cravings after a future life. 'They adorn,' says an ancient Sanskrit treatise,[1] 'the bodies of their dead with gifts, with raiment, with ornaments; imagining that thereby they shall attain the world to come.' These ornaments are the bits of bronze, copper, and gold which we now dig up from beneath their rude stone monuments. In the Sanskrit epic which narrates the advance of the Aryans into Southern India, a non-Aryan chief describes his race as 'of fearful swiftness, unyielding in battle, in colour like a dark-blue cloud.'[2]

The non-Aryans as they are. Let us now examine these primitive peoples, not as portrayed by their enemies 3000 years ago, but as they exist at the present day. Thrust back by the Aryans from the plains, they have lain hidden away in the recesses of the mountains, like the remains of extinct animals which palæontologists find in hill caves. India thus forms a great museum of races, in which we can study man from his lowest to his highest stages of culture. The specimens are not fossils or dry bones, but living communities, to whose widely-diverse conditions we have to adapt our administration and our laws.

---

[1] *Chandogya Upanishad,* viii. 8. 5 ; Muir's *Sanskrit Texts,* ii. 396 (1874).

[2] Rámáyana (ed. Gorresio), iii. 28. 18.

Among the rudest fragments of mankind are the isolated The Andaman islanders in the Bay of Bengal. The old Arab and Andaman islanders. European voyagers described them as dog-faced man-eaters. The English officers sent to the islands in 1855 to establish a Settlement, found themselves surrounded by naked cannibals of a ferocious type ; who daubed themselves when festive with red earth, and mourned in a suit of olive-coloured mud. They used a noise like *crying* to express friendship or joy ; bore only names of common gender, which they received before birth, and which therefore had to be applicable to either sex ; and their sole conception of a god was an evil spirit, who spread disease. For five years they repulsed every effort at intercourse with showers of arrows ; but our officers slowly brought them to a better frame of mind by building sheds for them near the British Settlement, where these poor beings might find shelter from the tropical rains, and receive medicines and food.

The Anamalai Hills, in Southern Madras, form the refuge Anamalai of a whole series of broken tribes. Five hamlets of long-haired, hillmen. wild-looking Puliars were found living on jungle products, mice, or any small animals they could catch; and worshipping demons. The Mundavers shrink from contact with the outside world, and possessed no fixed dwellings, but wandered over the innermost hills with their cattle, sheltering themselves under little leaf sheds, and seldom remaining in one spot more than a year. The thick-lipped, small-bodied Kaders, 'Lords of the Hills,' are a remnant of a higher race. These hills, now almost uninhabited, abound in the great stone monuments (kistvaens and dolmens) which the primitive tribes erected over their dead. The Nairs, or aborigines of South-Western India, still The Nairs. practise polyandry, according to which one woman is the wife of several husbands, and a man's property descends not to his own but to his sister's children. This system also appears among the Himálayan tribes.

In the Central Provinces, the aboriginal races form a large Non-proportion of the population. In certain Districts, as in the Aryan tribes State of Bastár, they amounted in 1872 to three-fifths of the of the inhabitants. Their most important race, the Gonds, have made Central some advances in civilisation; but the wilder tribes still cling Provinces. to the forest, and live by the chase. Some of them are Gonds. reported to have used, within our own times, flint points for their arrows. The Máriás wield bows of great strength, which they hold with their feet while they draw the string with both hands. A still wilder tribe, the Márís, fled from their grass-built

Tax-gathering among the Máris. huts on the approach of a stranger. Once a year a messenger came to them from the local Rájá to take their tribute, which consisted chiefly of jungle products. He did not, however, enter their hamlets, but beat a drum outside, and then hid himself. The shy Máris crept forth, placed what they had to give in an appointed spot, and ran back into their retreats.

The Juángs or 'Leaf-wearers' of Orissa Hill States; Farther to the north-east, in the Tributary States of Orissa, there is a poor tribe, 10,000 in 1872, of Juángs or Patuas, literally the 'leaf-wearers,' whose women wore no clothes. The only covering on the females consisted of a few strings of beads round the waist, with a bunch of leaves tied before and behind. clothed by Government. Those under British influence were, in 1871, clothed by order of the Government, and their Chief was persuaded to do the same work for others. The English officer called together the clan, and after a speech, handed out strips of cotton for the women to put on. They then passed in single file, to the number of 1900, before him, made obeisance to him, and were afterwards marked on the forehead with vermilion, as a sign of their entering into civilised society. Finally, they gathered the bunches of leaves which had formed their sole clothing into a heap, and set fire to it. It is reported, however, that many of the Juáng women have since relapsed to their foliage attire.

A relic of the Stone Age. This leaf-wearing tribe had no knowledge of the metals till quite lately, when foreigners came among them; and no word existed in their own language for iron or any other metal. But their country abounds in flint weapons, so that the Juángs Juáng dwellings. form a remnant to our own day of the Stone Age. 'Their huts,' writes the officer who knows them best, 'are among the smallest that human beings ever deliberately constructed as dwellings. They measure about 6 feet by 8. The head of the family and all the females huddle together in this one shell, not much larger than a dog-kennel.' The boys and the young men of the village live in a building apart by themselves; and this custom of having a common abode for the whole male youth of the hamlet is found among many aboriginal tribes in distant parts of India.

Himálayan tribes. Proceeding to the northern boundary of India, we find the slopes and spurs of the Himálayas peopled by a great variety of rude tribes. Some of the Assam hillmen have no word for expressing distance by miles nor any land measure, but reckon the length of a journey by the number of quids of tobacco or betel-leaf which they chew upon the way. As a rule, they are fierce, black, undersized, and ill-fed. They eked out a wretched subsistence by plundering the more civilised hamlets of the Assam valley; a means of livelihood which they have but slowly given up under British rule. Some of the wildest of them, like the independent Abars, are now engaged as a sort of irregular police, to keep the peace of the border, in return for a yearly gift of cloth, hoes, and grain. Their very names bear witness to their former wild life. One tribe, the Akas of Assam, is divided into two clans, known respectively as 'The eaters of a thousand hearths,' and 'The thieves who lurk in the cotton-field.' *Akas of Assam.*

Many of the aboriginal tribes, therefore, remain in the same early stage of human progress as that ascribed to them by the Vedic poets more than 3000 years ago. But others have made great advances, and form communities of a well-developed type. It must here suffice to briefly describe two such races; the Santáls and the Kandhs who inhabit the north-eastern edge of the central plateau. The Santáls have their home among the hills which abut on the Ganges in Lower Bengal. The Kandhs live 150 to 350 miles to the south, among the highlands which look down upon the Orissa delta and Madras coast. *More advanced non-Aryan tribes.*

The Santáls dwell in villages in the jungles or among the mountains, apart from the people of the plains. They numbered about a million in 1872, and give their name to a large District, the SANTAL PARGANAS, 140 miles north-west of Calcutta. Although still clinging to many customs of a hunting forest tribe, they have learned the use of the plough, and settled down into skilful husbandmen. Each hamlet is governed by its own head-man, who is supposed to be a descendant of the original founder of the village, and who is assisted by a deputy head-man and a watchman. The boys of the hamlet have their separate officers, and are strictly controlled by their own head and his deputy till they enter the married state. The Santáls know not the cruel distinctions of Hindu caste, but trace their tribes, usually numbering seven, to the seven sons of the first parents. The whole village feasts, hunts, and worships together; and the Santál had to take his wife, not from his own tribe, but from one of the six others. So strong is the bond of race, that expulsion from the tribe was the only Santál punishment. A heinous criminal was cut off from 'fire and water' in the village, and sent forth alone into the jungle. Minor offences were forgiven upon a public reconciliation with the tribe; to effect which the guilty one provided a feast, with much rice-beer, for his clansmen. *The Santáls.* *Santál village government.* *No castes, but strong tribal feeling.*

The six Santál ceremonies. The chief ceremonies in a Santál's life, six in number, vary in different parts of the country, but are all based upon this strong feeling of kinship. The first is the admission of the newly-born child into the family,—a secret rite, one act of which consists in the father placing his hand on the infant's head and repeating the name of the ancestral deity. The second, the admission of the child into the tribe, is celebrated three or five days after birth,—a more public ceremony, at which the child's head is shaved, and the clansmen drink beer. The third ceremony, or admission into the race, takes place about the fifth year; when all friends, whatever may be their tribe, are invited to a feast, and the child is marked on his right arm with the Santál spots. The fourth consists of the union of his own Santál marriages. tribe with another by marriage, which does not take place till the young people can choose for themselves. At the end of the ceremony, the girl's clanswomen pound burning charcoal with the household pestle, in token of the breaking up of her former family ties, and then extinguish it with water, to signify the separation of the bride from her clan. The Santáls respect their women, and seldom or never take a second wife, except for the purpose of obtaining an heir. The fifth ceremony consists of the dismissal of the Santál from the race, by the solemn burning of his body after death. The sixth is the reunion of the dead with the fathers, by floating three fragments of the skull down the Dámodar river (if possible), the sacred stream of the race.

Santál religion. The Santál had no conception of bright and friendly gods, such as the Vedic singers worshipped. Still less could he imagine one omnipotent and beneficent Deity, who watches over mankind. Hunted and driven back before the Hindus and Muhammadans, he did not understand how a Being could be more powerful than himself without wishing to harm him. 'What,' said a Santál to an eloquent missionary, who had been discoursing on the Christian God—'what if that strong One should eat me?' Nevertheless, the earth swarms with spirits and demons, whose ill-will he tries to avert. His religion consists of nature-worship, and offerings to the ghosts of his ancestors; and his rites are more numerous even than those of Race-god; Tribe- god; Family- god; Demons. the Hindus. First, the Race-god; next, the Tribe-god of each of the seven clans; then the Family-god, requires in turn his oblation. But besides these, there are the spirits of his forefathers, river-spirits, forest-spirits, well-demons, mountain-demons, and a mighty host of unseen beings, whom he must keep in good humour. He seems also to have borrowed from the Hindus some rites of sun-worship. But his own gods dwell chiefly in the ancient *sál* trees which shade his hamlets. Them he propitiates by offerings of blood ; with goats, cocks, and chickens. If the sacrificer cannot afford an animal, it is with a red flower, or a red fruit, that he draws near to his gods. In some hamlets, the people dance round every tree, so that they may not by evil chance miss the one in which the village-spirits happen to be dwelling.

Until nearly the end of the last century, the Santáls were the pests of the neighbouring plains. Regularly after the December harvest, they sallied forth from their mountains, plundered the lowlands, levied black-mail, and then retired with their spoil to their jungles. But in 1789, the British Government granted the proprietary right in the soil to the landholders of Bengal under the arrangements which four years later became the Permanent Settlement. Forthwith every landholder tried to increase the cultivated area on his estate, now become his own property. The Santáls and other wild tribes were tempted to issue from their fastnesses by high wages or rent-free farms. ' Every proprietor,' said a London newspaper, the *Morning Chronicle*, in 1792, ' is collecting husbandmen from the hills to improve his lowlands.' The English officers found they had a new race to deal with, and gradually won the highlanders to peaceful habits by grants of land and ' exemption from all taxes.' They were allowed to settle disputes ' among themselves by their own customs,' and they were used as a sort of frontier police, being paid to deliver up any of their own people who committed violent crimes. Such criminals, after being found guilty by their countrymen, were handed over for punishment to the English judge. The Santáls gained confidence in us by degrees, and came down in great numbers within the fence of stone pillars, which the British officers set up in 1832 to mark off the country of the hill people from the plains.

The Hindu money-lender soon made his appearance in their settlements, and the simple hillmen learned the new luxury of borrowing. Our laws were gradually applied to them, and before the middle of this century most of the Santál hamlets were plunged in debt. Their strong love of kindred prevented them from running away, and the Hindu usurers reduced them to a state of practical slavery, by threatening the terrors of a distant jail. In 1848, three whole villages threw up their clearings, and fled in despair to the jungle. In June 1855, the southern Santáls started in a body, 30,000 strong, with their bows and arrows, to walk 140 miles to Calcutta and

The Santáls under British rule.

They come forth from the hills.

The Santáls sink into debt to the Hindus.

lay their condition before the Governor-General. At first they were orderly; but the way was long, and they had to live.

Santál rising, 1855.

Robberies took place; quarrels broke out between them and the police; and within a week they were in armed rebellion. The rising was put down, not without mournful bloodshed; and their wrongs were carefully inquired into. A very simple form of administration was introduced, according to which their village head-men were brought into direct contact with the English officer in charge of the District, and acted as the representatives of the people. Our system of justice and government has been adapted to their primitive needs, and the Santáls have for years been among the most prosperous of the Indian races.

The Kandhs or Kondhs.

The Kandhs, literally 'The Mountaineers,' a tribe about 100,000 strong in 1872, inhabit the steep and forest-covered ranges which rise inland from the Orissa delta, and the Madras Districts of Ganjám and Vizagapatam. They form one of a group of non-Aryan races who still occupy the position assigned to them by the Greek geographers 1500 years ago. Before that early date, they had been pushed backwards by the advancing Aryans from the fertile delta which lies between the mountains and the sea. One section of the Kandhs was completely

Breaking up of the race.

broken up, and has sunk into landless low-castes among the Aryan or Hindu communities at the foot of the hills. Another section stood its ground more firmly, and became a peasant militia, holding grants of land from the Hindu chiefs in return for military service. A third section fell back into the fastnesses of the mountains, and was recognised as a wild but free race. It is of this last section that the present chapter treats.

Kandh patri-archal govern-ment.

The Kandh idea of government is purely patriarchal. The family is strictly ruled by the father. The grown-up sons have no property during his life, but live in his house with their wives and children, and all share the common meal prepared by the grandmother. The clan consists of a number of families, sprung from a common father; and the tribe is made up in like manner from a number of clans who claim descent from the same ancestor. The head of the tribe is usually the eldest son of the patriarchal family; but if he be not fit for the post he is set aside, and an uncle or a younger brother appointed. He enters on no undertaking without calling together the heads of clans, who in their turn consult the heads of families.

Kandh wars and punish-ments.

According to the Kandh theory of existence, a state of war might lawfully be presumed against all neighbours with

whom no express agreement had been made to the contrary.
Murders were punished by blood-revenge, the kinsmen within Blood-
a certain degree being one and all bound to kill the slayer, revenge.
unless appeased by a payment of grain or cattle. The man
who wounded another had to maintain the sufferer until he
recovered from his hurt. A stolen article must be returned,
or its equivalent paid; but the Kandh twice convicted of
theft was driven forth from his tribe, the greatest punishment known to the race. Disputes were settled by combat,
or by the ordeal of boiling oil or heated iron, or by taking a
solemn oath on an ant-hill, or on a tiger's claw, or a lizard's
skin. When a house-father died, leaving no sons, his land was
parcelled out among the other male heads of the village; for
no woman, nor indeed any Kandh, was allowed to hold land
who could not with his own hand defend it.

The Kandh system of tillage represented a stage half-way Kandh
between the migratory cultivation of the ruder non-Aryan agricul-
tribes and the settled agriculture of the Hindus. They did ture.
not, on the one hand, merely burn down a patch in the
jungle, take a few crops off it, and then move on to fresh
clearings. Nor, on the other hand, did they go on cultivating
the same fields from father to son. When their lands showed
signs of exhaustion, they deserted them; and it was a rule in
some of their settlements to change their village sites once
in fourteen years. Caste is unknown; and, as among the
Santáls, marriage between relations, or even within the same
tribe, is forbidden. A Kandh wedding consisted of forcibly Kandh
carrying off the bride in the middle of a feast. The boy's marriages
father paid a price for the girl, and usually chose a strong ture.'
one, several years older than his son. In this way, Kandh
maidens were married about fourteen, Kandh boys about ten.
The bride remained as a servant in her new father-in-law's house
till her boy-husband grew old enough to live with her. She
generally acquired a great influence over him; and a Kandh
may not marry a second wife during the life of his first one,
except with her consent.

The Kandh engaged only in husbandry and war, and despised Serfs of
all other work. But attached to each village was a row of hovels the Kandh
inhabited by a lower race, who were not allowed to hold land, village.
to go forth to battle, or to join in the village worship. These
poor people did the dirty work of the hamlet, and supplied
families of hereditary weavers, blacksmiths, potters, herds-
men, and distillers. They were kindly treated, and a portion of
each feast was left for them. But they could never rise in the

social scale. No Kandh could engage in their work without degradation, nor eat food prepared by their hands. They can give no account of their origin, but are supposed to be the remnants of a ruder race whom the Kandhs found in possession of the hills when they themselves were pushed backwards by the Aryans from the plains.

Kandh human sacrifices. The Kandhs, like the Santáls, have many deities, race-gods, tribe-gods, family-gods, and a multitude of malignant spirits and demons. But their great divinity is the Earth-god, who represents the productive energy of nature. Twice each year, at sowing-time and at harvest, and in all seasons of special calamity, the Earth-god required a human sacrifice (*meriah*). The duty of providing the victims rested with the lower race attached to the Kandh village. Brahmáns and Kandhs were the only classes exempted from sacrifice, and an ancient rule ordained **The victims.** that the offering *must be bought with a price.* Men of the lower race kidnapped the victims from the plains, and a thriving Kandh village usually kept a small stock in reserve, 'to meet sudden demands for atonement.' The victim, on being brought to the hamlet, was welcomed at every threshold, daintily fed, and kindly treated till the fatal day arrived. He **The sacrifice.** was then solemnly sacrificed to the Earth-god, the Kandhs shouting in his dying ear, 'We bought you with a price; no sin rests with us!' His flesh and blood were distributed among the village lands.

The Kandhs under British rule. In 1835, the Kandhs passed under our rule, and these rites had to cease. The proud Kandh spirit shrank from compulsion; but after many tribal councils, they agreed to give up their stock of victims as a valuable present to their new suzerain. Care was taken that they should not procure fresh ones. The **Human sacrifices abolished.** kidnapping of victims for human sacrifice was declared a capital offence; and their priests were led to discover that goats or buffaloes did quite as well for the Earth-god under British rule as human sacrifices. Until 1835, they consisted of separate tribes, always at war with each other and with the world. But under able English administrators (especially Campbell, Macpherson, and Cadenhead), human sacrifices were abolished, and the Kandhs were formed into a united and peaceful race (1837–45). The British officer removed their old necessity for tribal wars and family blood-feuds by setting himself up as a central authority. He adjusted their inter-tribal disputes, **The race won over to peaceful industry.** and punished heinous crimes. Lieutenant Charters Macpherson, in particular, won over the more troublesome clans to quiet industry, by grants of jungle tracts, of little use to us, but a paradise to them, and where he could keep them well under his eye. He made the chiefs vain of carrying out his orders by small presents of cattle, honorific dresses, and titles. He enlisted the whole race on his side by picking out their best men for the police ; and drew the tribes into amicable relations among themselves by means of hill-fairs. He constructed roads, and taught the Kandhs to trade, with a view to 'drawing them from their fastnesses into friendly contact with other men.' The race has prospered and multiplied under British rule.

Whence came these primitive peoples, whom the Aryan invaders found in the land more than 3000 years ago, and who are still scattered over India, the fragments of a pre-historic world? Written annals they do not possess. Their oral traditions tell us little ; but such hints as they yield, feebly point to the north. They seem to preserve dim memories of a time when their tribes dwelt under the shadow of mightier hill ranges than any to be found on the south of the river plains of Bengal. 'The Great Mountain' is the race-god of the Santáls, and an object of worship among other tribes. Indeed, the Gonds, who numbered 1½ million in the heart of Central India in 1872, have a legend that they were created at the foot of Dewálagiri peak in the Himálayas. Till lately, they buried their dead with the feet turned northwards, so as to be ready to start again for their ancient home in the north. *Origin of the non-Aryan tribes.* *Non-Aryan traditions.*

But the language of the non-Aryan races, that record of a nation's past more enduring than rock-inscriptions or tables of brass, is being slowly made to tell the secret of their origin. It already indicates that the early peoples of India belonged to three great stocks, known as the Tibeto-Burman, the Kolarian, and the Dravidian. *Non-Aryan speech.* *The three non-Aryan stocks.*

The first stock, or Tibeto-Burman tribes, cling to the skirts of the Himálayas and their north-eastern offshoots. They crossed over into India by the north-eastern passes, and in some pre-historic time had dwelt in Central Asia, side by side with the forefathers of the Mongolians and the Chinese. Several of the hill languages in Eastern Bengal preserve Chinese terms, others contain Mongolian. Thus, the Nágás in Assam still use words for *three* and *water* which might almost be understood in the streets of Canton.[1] *(1) The Tibeto-Burmans.*

---

[1] The following are the twenty principal languages of the Tibeto-Burman group :—(1) Cachari or Bodo, (2) Gáro, (3) Tipura or Mrung, (4) Tibetan or Bhutiá, (5) Gurung, (6) Murmi, (7) Newar, (8) Lepchá, (9) Miri, (10) Aka, (11) Mishmi dialects, (12) Dhimal, (13) Kanáwari dialects, (14) Míkír, (15) Singpho, (16) Nágá dialects, (17) Kuki dialects, (18) Burmese,

(2) The Kolarians

The Kolarians, the second of the three non-Aryan stocks, appear also to have entered Bengal by the north-eastern passes. They dwell chiefly in the north, and along the north-eastern edge, of the three-sided table-land which covers the southern half of

(3) The Dravidians.

India. The Dravidians, or third stock, seem, generally speaking, on the other hand, to have found their way into the Punjab by the north-western passes. They now inhabit the southern part of the three-sided table-land, as far down as Cape Comorin, the southernmost point of India. It appears as if the two streams, namely the Kolarian tribes from the north-east and the

Their convergence in Central India.

Dravidians from the north-west, had converged and crossed each other in Central India. The Dravidians proved the stronger, broke up the Kolarians, and thrust aside their fragments to east and west. The Dravidians then rushed forward in a mighty body to the south.

The Kolarians broken up.

It thus came to pass that while the Dravidians formed a vast mass in Southern India, the Kolarians survived only as isolated tribes, so scattered as to soon forget their common

---

(19) Khyeng, and (20) Manipuri. ' It is impossible,' writes Mr. Brandreth, ' to give even an approximate number of the speakers included in this group, as many of the languages are either across the frontier or only project a short distance into our own territory. The languages included in this group have not, with perhaps one or two exceptions, both a cerebral and dental row of consonants, like the South-Indian languages ; some of them have aspirated forms of the surds, but not of the sonants ; others have aspirated forms of both. All the twenty dialects have words in common, especially numerals and pronouns, and also some resemblances of grammar. In comparing the resembling words, the differences between them consist often less in any modification of the root-syllable than in various additions to the root. Thus in Burmese we have *na*, "ear ;" Tibetan, *rna-ba* ; Magar, *na-kep* : Newar, *nai-pong* ; Dhimal, *na-hathong* ; Kiranti dialects, *na-pro, na-rék, na-phak* ; Nágá languages, *te-na-ro, te-na-rang* ; Manipuri, *na-kong* ; Kupui, *ka-na* ; Sak, *aka-na* ; Karen, *na-khu* ; and so on. It can hardly be doubted that such additions as these to monosyllabic roots are principally determinative syllables for the purpose of distinguishing between what would otherwise have been monosyllabic words having the same sound. These determinatives are generally affixed in the languages of Nepál and in the Dhimal language ; prefixed in the Lepchá language, and in the languages of Assam, of Manipur, and of the Chittagong and Arakan Hills. Words are also distinguished by difference of tone. The tones are generally of two kinds, described as the abrupt or short, and the pausing or heavy. It has been remarked that those languages which are most given to adding other syllables to the root make the least use of the tones, and, *vice versa*, where the tones most prevail the least recourse is had to determinative syllables.' — This and the following quotations, from Mr. E. L. Brandreth, are condensed from his valuable paper in the *Journal of the Royal Asiatic Society*, New Series, vol. x. (1877), pp. 1-32.

origin. We have seen one of the largest of the Kolarian races, the Santáls, dwelling on the extreme eastern edge of the three-sided table-land, where it slopes down into the Gangetic valley. The Kurkus, a broken Kolarian tribe, inhabit a patch of country about 400 miles to the west. They have for perhaps thousands of years been cut off from the Santáls by mountains and pathless forests, and by intervening races of the Dravidian and Aryan stocks. The Kurkus and Santáls have no tradition of a common origin; yet at this day the Kurkus speak a language which is little else than a dialect of Santáli. The Savars, once a great Kolarian tribe, mentioned by Pliny and Ptolemy, are now a poor wandering race of woodcutters in Northern Madras and Orissa. Yet fragments of them have lately been found deep in Central India, and as far west as Rájputána on the other side. The Juángs are an isolated non-Aryan remnant among an Aryan and Uriya-speaking population. They have forgotten, and disclaim, any connection with the Hos or other Kolarian tribes. Nevertheless, their common origin is attested by a number of Kolarian words which they have unconsciously preserved.[1]

The compact Dravidians in the south, although in after-days

Scattered Kolarian fragments.

---

[1] The nine principal languages of the Kolarian group are—(1) the Santál, (2) Mundári, (3) Ho, (4) Bhumij, (5) Korwa, (6) Kharria, (7) Juáng, (8) Kurku, and perhaps (9) the Savar. Some of them, however, are separated only by dialectical differences. 'The Kolarian group of languages,' writes Mr. Brandreth, 'has both the cerebral and dental row of letters, and also aspirated forms, which last, according to Caldwell, did not belong to early Dravidian. There is also a set of four sounds, which are perhaps peculiar to Santáli, called by Skrefsrud semi-consonants, and which, when followed by a vowel, are changed respectively into g, j, d, and b. Gender of nouns is animate and inanimate, and is distinguished by difference of pronouns, by difference of suffix of a qualifying noun in the genitive relation, and by the gender being denoted by the verb. As instances of the genitive suffix, we have in Santáli *in-ren hopon* "my son,",but *in-ak orak* "my house." There is no distinction of sex in the pronouns, but of the animate and inanimate gender. The dialects generally agree in using a short form of the third personal pronoun suffixed to denote the number, dual and plural, of the noun, and short forms of all the personal pronouns are added to the verb in certain positions to express both number and person, both as regards the subject and object, if of the animate gender; the inanimate gender being indicated by the omission of these suffixes. No other group of languages, apparently, has such a logical classification of its nouns as that shown by the genders of both the South Indian groups. The genitive in the Kolarian group of the full personal pronouns is used for the posses-sive pronoun, which again takes all the post-positions, the genitive relation being thus indicated by the genitive suffix twice repeated. The Kolarian languages generally express grammatical relations by suffixes, and add the post-positions directly to the root, without the intervention of an

E

The compact Dravidians of Southern India.

subdued by the higher civilisation of the Aryan race which pressed in among them, were never thus broken into fragments.[1] Their pure descendants consist, indeed, of small and scattered tribes ; but they have given their language to 28 millions of people in Southern India. A theory has been started that some of the islands in the distant Pacific Ocean were peopled either from the Dravidian settlements in India, or from an earlier common source. Bishop Caldwell points out that the aboriginal tribes in Southern and Western Australia use almost the same words for *I, thou, he, we, you,* etc., as the Dravidian fishermen on the Madras coast ; and resemble in other ways the Madras hill tribes, as in the use of their national weapon, the boomerang. The civilisation and literature which the Dravidians developed in Southern India will be described in a later chapter on the Indian vernaculars.

Their offshoots beyond sea (?)

oblique form or genitive or other suffix. They agree with the Dravidian in having inclusive and exclusive forms for the plural of the first personal pronoun, in using a relative participle instead of a relative pronoun, in the position of the governing word, and in the possession of a true causal form of the verb. They have a dual, which the Dravidians have not, but they have no negative voice. Counting is by twenties, instead of by tens, as in the Dravidian. The Santáli verb, according to Skrefsrud, has 23 tenses, and for every tense two forms of the participle and a gerund.'

[1] Bishop Caldwell recognises twelve distinct Dravidian languages :—
(1) Tamil, (2) Malayálam, (3) Telugu, (4) Kanarese, (5) Tulu, (6) Kudugu, (7) Toda, (8) Kota, (9) Gond, (10) Kandh, (11) Uráon, (12) Rájmahal. ' In the Dravidian group,' writes Mr. Brandreth, 'there is a rational and an irrational gender of the nouns, which is distinguished in the plural of the nouns, and sometimes in the singular also, by affixes which appear to be fragmentary pronouns, by corresponding pronouns, and by the agreement of the verb with the noun, the gender of the verb being expressed by the pronominal suffixes. To give an instance of verbal gender, we have in Tamil, from the root *sey,* "to do," *seyd-an,* "he (rational) did ; " *seyd-ál,* "she (rational) did ; " *seyd-adu,* "it (irrational) did ; " *seyd-ar,* "they (the rationals) did ; " *seyd-a,* "they (the irrationals) did ; " the full pronouns being *avan,* "he ; " *aval,* "she ; " *adu,* "it ; " *avar,* "they ; " *avei,* "they." This distinction of gender, though it exists in most of the Dravidian languages, is not always carried out to the extent that it is in Tamil. In Telugu, Gond, and Kandh, it is preserved in the plural, but in the singular the feminine rational is merged in the irrational gender. In Gond, the gender is further marked by the noun in the genitive relation taking a different suffix, according to the number and gender of the noun on which it depends. In Uráon, the feminine rational is entirely merged in the irrational gender, with the exception of the pronoun, which preserves the distinction between rationals and irrationals in the plural ; thus, *as,* "he," referring to a god or a man ; *ad,* "she " or "it," referring to a woman or an irrational object ; but *ar,* "they," applies to both men and women ; *abra,* "they," to irrationals only. The rational gender, besides human beings, includes the celestial and infernal deities ; and it is further

The following is a list of 142 of the principal non-Aryan List of
languages and dialects, prepared by Mr. Brandreth for the Royal non-Aryan
Asiatic Society in 1877, and classified according to their gram-languages.
matical structure. Mr. Robert Cust has also arranged them in guages.
another convenient form, according to their geographical habitat.

TABLE OF THE NON-ARYAN LANGUAGES OF INDIA.[1]

DRAVIDIAN GROUP.	Dravidian Group—*continued.*
Tamil.	*Yerukala.*
Malayálam.	*Gadaba* (Kolarian ?).
Telugu.	
{ Kanarese.	KOLARIAN GROUP.
{ Badaga.	
Tulu.	Santáli.
Kudugu or Coorg.	{ Mundári.
Toda.	{ Ho or Larka Kol.
Kota.	{ Bhumij.
Gond dialects.	Korwa.
{ *Mahádeo.*	Kharria.
{ *Ráj.*	Juáng.
{ *Maria.*	{ Kuri.
Kandh or Ku.	{ Kurku.
Uráon or Dhangar.	Mehto.
Rájmahalí or Máler.	Savara.
Miscellaneous Dialects.	
{ *Naikude.*	TIBETO-BURMAN GROUP.
{ *Kolami.*	I. { Káchárí or Bodo.
{ *Keikádi.*	{ Mech.
	{ Hojai.

sub-divided, in some of the languages, but in the singular only, into
masculine and feminine. The grammatical relations in the Dravidian are
generally expressed by suffixes. Many nouns have an oblique form, which
is a remarkable characteristic of the Dravidian group; still, with the
majority of nouns, the post-positions are added directly to the nominative
form. Other features of this group are—the frequent use of formatives to
specialize the meaning of the root; the absence of relative pronouns and
the use instead of a relative participle, which is usually formed from the
ordinary participle by the same suffix as that which Dr. Caldwell considers
as the oldest sign of the genitive relation; the adjective preceding the
substantive; of two substantives, the determining preceding the determined;
and the verb being the last member of the sentence. There is no true
dual in the Dravidian languages. In the Dravidian languages there are
two forms of the plural of the pronoun of the first person, one including,
the other excluding, the person addressed. As regards the verbs, there is
a negative voice, but no passive voice, and there is a causal form.' Bishop
Caldwell's second edition of his great work, the *Comparative Grammar of
the Dravidian Languages* (Trübner, 1875), forms in itself an epoch in that
department of human knowledge. Mr. Beames' *Comparative Grammar
of the Modern Aryan Languages of India* (Trübner, 1872) has laid the
foundation for the accurate study of North Indian speech. Colonel
Dalton's *Ethnology of Bengal* (Calcutta, 1872), and Sir George Campbell's
Specimens of the Languages of India (Bengal Secretariat Press, 1874), have
also shed new and valuable light on the questions involved.

[1] Brackets refer to dialects that are very closely related ; ✝ to languages
beyond the circle of the Indian languages. (*See list above and on next page.*)

Tibeto-Burman Group—*continued.*

Gáro.
Páni-Koch.
Deori-Chutia.
Tipura or Mrung.
II. (Tibetan or Bhutiá.
　　{ Sarpa.
　　(Lhopa or Bhutáni.
Changlo.
Twang.
III. (Gurung.
　　{ Murmi.
Tháksya.
　　{ Newar.
　　(Pahri.
Magar.
IV. Lepchá.
V. Daphlá.
Miri.
Abar.
Bhutiá of Lo.
VI. Aka.
VII. Mishmi dialects.
　　Chulikata.
　　Taying or *Digaru.*
　　Mijhu.
VIII. Dhimal.
IX. Kanáwari dialects.
　　(*Milchan.*
　　{ *Tibarskad.*
　　(*Sumchu.*
X. (Kiranti.
　　{ Limbu.
Sunwár.
Brámu.
Chepang.
Váyu.
Kusunda.
XI. Nágá dialects.
　　Namsang or *Jáipuria.*
　　{ *Banpárá* or *Joboka.*
　　{ *Mithan.*
　　{ *Tablung.*
　　(*Mulung.*
XII. Nágá dialects.
　　Khari.
　　{ *Naugáon.*
　　(*Tengsa.*
　　Lhota.
XIII. Nágá dialects.
　　Angámi.
　　Rengma.
　　{ *Arung.*
　　(*Kutcha.*
　　Liyang or *Kareng.*
Marám.
XIV. Míkir.
XV. (Singpho.
　　(Jili.
XVI. Burmese.
XVII. Kuki dialects.
　　Khyeng.

Tibeto-Burman Group—*continued.*

(*Thado.*
{ *Lushai.*
(*Hallami.*
Manipuri.
{ Maring.
(Khoibu.
Kupui.
Tangkhul.
Luhupa.
Khungui.
Phadang.
Champhung.
Kupome.
Takaimi.
Andro and Sengmai.
Chairel.
Anal and Namfau.
XVIII. (Kumi.
　　(Kami.
Mru.
{ Banjogi or Lungkhe.
(Pankho.
Shendu or Poi.
Sak.
Kyau.
XIX. Karen dialects.
　　Sgau.
　　Bghai.
　　Red Karen.
　　Pwo.
　　Taru.
　　Mopgha.
　　Kay or *Gaikho.*
　　Taungthu.
　　†Lísaw.
　　†Gyarung.
　　†Takpa.
　　†Manyak.
　　†Thochu.
　　†Horpa.

KHASI.

Khási.

TAI.

(Siamese or Thai.
| Lao.
{ Shan.
| Ahom.
| Khamti.
(Aiton.
†Tai Mow or Chinese Shan.

MON-ANAM.

Mon.
†Kambojan.
†Anamese.
†Paloung.

We discern, therefore, long before the dawn of history, Recapitu-
masses of men moving uneasily over India, and violently lation—
pushing in among still earlier tribes.   They crossed the snows Aryan
of the Himálayas, and plunged into the tropical forests in races.
search of new homes.   Of these ancient races, fragments now
exist almost in exactly the same stage of human progress as
they were described by Vedic poets more than 3000 years ago.
Some are dying out, such as the Andaman islanders, among
whom in 1869 only one family had as many as three children.
Others are increasing like the Santáls, who have doubled
themselves under British rule.   But they all require special
and anxious care in adapting our complex administration to
their primitive condition and needs.   Taken as a whole, and
including certain half-Hinduized branches, they numbered
17,627,758 in 1872, then about equal to three-quarters of the
population of England and Wales.   But while the bolder or
more isolated of the aboriginal races have thus kept themselves apart, by far the greater portion submitted in ancient
times to the Aryan invaders, and now make up the mass of
the Hindus.

The following table shows the distribution of the aboriginal Distribu-
tribes throughout British India in 1872.   But many live in tion of
aborigines
Native States, not included in this enumeration; and the in India
Madras Census of 1872 did not distinguish aborigines from in 1872.
low-caste Hindus.   Their total number throughout all India
(British and Feudatory) probably exceeded 20 millions in
1872.

Aboriginal Tribes and Semi-Hinduized Aborigines in 1872.

(Madras Presidency and the Feudatory States not included.)

Bengal, ...	11,116,883
Assam, ...	1,490,888
North-Western Provinces, . .	377,674
Oudh, ...	90,490
Punjab, ...	959,720
Central Provinces, . . .	1,669,835
Berar, ...	163,059
Coorg, ...	42,516
British Burma, . . .	1,004,991
Bombay, ...	711,702
	17,627,758

As already stated, the Census of 1881 adopted a classification Aborigines
which fails to clearly distinguish the aboriginal elements in the in 1881.
Indian population.   In the North-Western Provinces, Oudh,

and the Punjab, which returned an aggregate of nearly $1\frac{1}{2}$ millions of aboriginal or non-Aryan castes or tribes in 1872, no separate return of the aboriginal or non-Aryan element was made in 1881. It is merged by the enumerators in the returns of the Hindu low-castes. The same process has affected the returns of other Provinces. In Madras, for example, 27 castes formerly included in the list of aboriginal tribes, were transferred to the Hindu section of the population. In Bengal, the Census officers explain that the non-registration of the aboriginal element is in some cases due to 'radical differences in the system upon which the castes, and especially the sub-divisions of castes, were classified in 1872 and in 1881.' In the North-Western Provinces and Oudh, the special officer states that his system of classification ' is not compatible with the modern doctrine which divides the population of India into Aryan and aboriginal.'

Under these circumstances it would be misleading to attempt a comparison between the returns of the aboriginal or non-Aryan population in 1872 and in 1881. On the one hand, there can be no doubt that the aboriginal castes and tribes are, in many parts of the country, tending towards Hinduism ; and that many of them, as they rise in the scale of civilisation, lose their identity in the Hindu community. On the other hand, it is evident that the decreased returns of the aboriginal tribes and castes in 1881 are not entirely, or indeed chiefly, due to this process. It would be erroneous, therefore, to infer that the balance of $12\frac{3}{4}$ millions between the $17\frac{1}{2}$ millions of aborigines returned for British India in 1872 and the $4\frac{3}{4}$ millions nominally returned in 1881, had become Hindus.

A Hinduizing process is going on both among the aboriginal low castes in Hindu Provinces, and among the aboriginal tribes who border on such Provinces. But the apparent disappearance of nearly 13 millions of aborigines between 1872 and 1881 is due, not so much to this Hinduizing process, as to differences in the system of classification and registration adopted by the Census officers. That the disappearance of the Indian aborigines is apparent and not real, can be proved. The birth-rate among some of the aboriginal races is unusually high ; and, with exceptions, the aboriginal tribes and castes are numerically increasing, although they are partially merging their separate identity in the Hindu community.

In Bengal and Assam, the aboriginal races are divided into

Side notes:

Not separately returned.

No common data for 1872 and 1881.

Hinduizing tendencies.

nearly 60 distinct tribes.[1] In the North-Western Provinces, *Their principal races in 1872.* In the Central Provinces they numbered $1\frac{3}{4}$ millions (1872); the ancient race of Gonds, who ruled the central table-land before the rise of the Maráthás, alone amounting to $1\frac{1}{2}$ millions. In British Burma, the Karens, whose traditions have a singularly Jewish tinge, numbered 330,000 in 1872, and 518,294 in 1881.

In Oudh, the nationality of the aboriginal tribes has been *Crushed tribes.* buried beneath waves of Rájput and Muhammadan invaders. For example, the Bhars, formerly the monarchs of the centre and east of that Province, and the traditional fort-builders to whom all ruins are popularly assigned, were stamped out by Ibráhím Shárki of Jaunpur, in the 15th century. The Gaulis or ancient ruling race of the Central Provinces, the Ahams of Assam, and the Gonds, Chandels, and Bundelas of Bundelkhand,[2] are other instances of crushed races. In centres of the Aryan civilisation, the aboriginal peoples have been pounded down in the mortar of Hinduism, into the low-castes and out-castes on which the social fabric of India rests. A few of them, how- *Gipsy* ever, still preserve their ethnical identity as wandering tribes *clans.* of jugglers, basket-weavers, and fortune-tellers. Thus, the Náts, Bediyas, and other gipsy clans are recognised to this day as distinct from the surrounding Hindu population.

The aboriginal races on the plains have supplied the *Aboriginal* hereditary criminal classes, alike under the Hindus, the *criminal tribes on* Muhammadans, and the British. Formerly organized robber *the plains.* communities, they have, under the stricter police of our days, sunk into petty pilferers. But their existence is still recognised by the Criminal Tribes Act, passed so lately as 1871, and still enforced within certain localities of Oudh and Northern India.

The non-Aryan hill races, who appear from Vedic times down- *Predatory* wards as marauders, have at length ceased to be a disturbing *hill races.* element in India. But many of them figure as predatory clans in Muhammadan and early British history. They sallied forth from their mountains at the end of the autumn harvest, pillaged and burned the lowland villages, and retired to their fastnesses laden with the booty of the plains. The measures

---

[1] Among them may be noted the Santáls, 850,000 under direct British administration, total about a million in 1872; Kols, 300,000; Uráons or Dhangars, 200,000; and Mundas, 175,000—within British territory. In Assam—Cacharís, 200,000; Khásis, 95,000. These figures all refer to 1872.

[2] See for the origin of the Bundelas, Mr. J. Beames' *Races of the North-Western Provinces*, vol. i. p. 45, etc. (1869).

by which these wild races have been reclaimed, form some of
the most honourable episodes of Anglo-Indian rule. Cleveland's Hill-Rangers in the last century, and the Bhíls and
Mhairs in more recent times, are well-known examples of how
marauding races may be turned into peaceful cultivators and
loyal soldiers. An equally salutary transformation has taken
place in many a remote forest and hill tract of India. The
firm order of British rule has rendered their old plundering
life no longer a possible one, and at the same time has opened
up to them new outlets for their energies. A similar vigilance
is now being extended to the predatory tribes in the Native
States. The reclamation of the wild Moghias of Central India,
and their settlement into agricultural communities, has been
effected by British officers within the past five years.

Character
of the
non-Aryan
tribes.

The hill and forest tribes differ in character from the
tamer population of the plains. Their truthfulness, sturdy
loyalty, and a certain joyous bravery, almost amounting to
playfulness, appeal in a special manner to the English mind.
There is scarcely a single administrator who has ruled over
them for any length of time without finding his heart drawn
to them, and leaving on record his belief in their capabilities
for good. Lest the traditional tenderness of the Indian Civil
Service to the people should weaken the testimony of such
witnesses, it may be safe to quote only the words of soldiers
with reference to the tribes with which each was specially
acquainted.

The non-
Aryan hill
tribes as
soldiers.

'They are faithful, truthful, and attached to their superiors,'
writes General Briggs; 'ready at all times to lay down their
lives for those they serve, and remarkable for their indomitable courage. These qualities have always been displayed
in our service. The aborigines of the Karnatik were the
sepoys of Clive and of Coote. A few companies of the same
stock joined the former great captain from Bombay, and
helped to fight the battle of Plassey in Bengal, which laid the
foundation of our Indian Empire. They have since distinguished themselves in the corps of pioneers and engineers,
not only in India, but in Ava, in Afghánistán, and in the
celebrated defence of Jalálábád. An unjust prejudice against
them grew up in the native armies of Madras and Bombay,
produced by the feelings of contempt for them existing among
the Hindu and Muhammadan troops. They have no prejudices themselves; are always ready to serve abroad and embark
on board ship; and I believe no instance of mutiny has ever
occurred among them.' Since General Briggs wrote these

sentences, the non-Aryan hill races have supplied some of the bravest and most valued of our Indian regiments, particularly the gallant little Gúrkhas.

Colonel Dixon's report, published by the Court of Directors, portrays the character of the Mhair tribes with admirable minuteness. He dilates on their 'fidelity, truth, and honesty,' their determined valour, their simple loyalty, and an extreme and almost touching devotion when put upon their honour. Strong as is the bond of kindred among the Mhairs, he vouches for their fidelity in guarding even their own relatives as prisoners when formally entrusted to their care. For centuries they had been known only as exterminators; but beneath the considerate handling of one Englishman, who honestly set about understanding them, they became peaceful subjects and well-disciplined soldiers. *Colonel Dixon on the Mhairs.*

Sir James Outram, when a very young man, did the same good work for the Bhíls of KHANDESH. He made their chiefs his hunting companions, formed the wilder spirits into a Bhíl battalion, and laid the basis for the reclamation of this formerly intractable race. (See also THE DANGS, *Imperial Gazetteer of India.*) *Outram's work among the Bhíls.*

Every military man who has had anything to do with the aboriginal races acknowledges, that once they admit a claim on their allegiance, nothing tempts them to a treacherous or disloyal act. 'The fidelity to their acknowledged chief,' wrote Captain Hunter, 'is very remarkable; and so strong is their attachment, that in no situation or condition, however desperate, can they be induced to betray him. If old and decrepit, they will convey him from place to place, to save him from his enemies.' Their obedience to recognised authority is absolute; and Colonel Tod relates how the wife of an absent chieftain procured for a British messenger safe-conduct and hospitality through the densest forests by giving him one of her husband's arrows as a token. The very officers who have had to act most sharply against them speak most strongly, and often not without a noble regret and self-reproach, in their favour. 'It was not war,' Major Vincent Jervis writes of the operations against the Santáls in 1855. 'They did not understand yielding; as long as their national drums beat, the whole party would stand, and allow themselves to be shot down. They were the most truthful set of men I ever met.' *Fidelity of the hill races.*

We have seen that India may be divided into three regions— the Himálayas on the north, the great River Plains that stretch *Ethnical distribution of Indian races.*

southward from their foot, and the Three-sided Table-land which slopes upwards again from the River Plains, and covers the whole southern half of India. Two of these regions, the Himálayas on the north, and the Three-sided Table-land in the south, still afford retreats to the non-Aryan tribes. The third region, or the great River Plains, became in very ancient times the theatre on which a nobler race worked out its civilisation.

CHAPTER IV.

THE ARYANS IN ANCIENT INDIA.

THIS nobler race belonged to the ARYAN or Indo-Germanic THE stock, from which the Bráhman, the Rájput, and the English- ARYAN STOCK. man alike descend. Its earliest home, visible to history, was in Central Asia. From that common camping-ground, certain branches of the race started for the east, others for the west. One of the western offshoots founded the Persian kingdom; another built Athens and Lacedæmon, and became the Hellenic nation; a third went on to Italy, and reared the City on the Its Seven Hills, which grew into Imperial Rome. A distant European branches. colony of the same race excavated the silver-ores of pre-historic Spain; and when we first catch a sight of ancient England, we see an Aryan settlement fishing in wattle canoes, and working the tin mines of Cornwall. Meanwhile, other Its branches of the Aryan stock had gone forth from the primitive Eastern home in Central Asia to the east. Powerful bands found their branches. way through the passes of the Himálayas into the Punjab, and spread themselves, chiefly as Bráhmans and Rájputs, over India.

We know little regarding these Aryan tribes in their early The camping-ground in Central Asia. From words preserved in Aryans in the languages of their long-separated descendants in Europe their primitive and India, scholars infer that they roamed over the grassy home. steppes with their cattle, making long halts to rear crops of grain. They had tamed most of the domestic animals; were acquainted with a hard metal, probably iron,[1] and silver;[2] understood the arts of weaving and sewing; wore clothes; and ate cooked food. They lived the hardy life of the temperate zone, and the feeling of cold seems to be one of the earliest common remembrances of the eastern and the western branches of the race. Ages afterwards, when the Vedic singers in hot

---

[1] Sanskrit, *ayas*, iron or, in a more general sense, metal, including gold but not copper in Sanskrit; Latin, *aes, aeris*, copper, bronze; Gothic, *ais, eisam;* old German, *er*, iron; modern German, *eisen*.

[2] Sanskrit, *kharjura*, silver; Latin, *argentum;* Greek, ἄργυρος, ἀργύριον.

India prayed for long life, they still asked for 'a hundred *winters.*' To this day the November rice in the tropical delta of the Ganges is called the *haimántik* (cf. Latin *hiems*) or crop of the 'snowy' season.

The forefathers of the Greek and the Roman, of the Englishman and the Hindu, dwelt together in Asia, spoke the same tongue, worshipped the same gods. The languages of Europe and India, although at first sight they seem wide apart, are merely different growths from the original Aryan speech. This is especially true of the common words of family life. The names for *father, mother, brother, sister,* and *widow* (Sanskrit, *vidhavá*), are the same in most of the Aryan languages, whether spoken on the banks of the Ganges, of the Tiber, or of the Thames. Thus the word *daughter* (Sanskrit, *duhitri*), which occurs in nearly all of them, has been derived from the Sanskrit root *duh,* 'milk,' and preserves the memory of the time when the daughter was the little milkmaid in the primitive Aryan household.

European and Indian languages merely varieties of Aryan speech.

Indo-European words. The words preserved alike by the European and Indian branches of the Aryan race, as heirlooms of their common home in Western Central Asia, include most of the terms required by a pastoral people who had already settled down to the cultivation of the more easily reared crops. Their domesticated animals are represented by names derived from the same root, for cattle, sheep, wool, goats, swine, dogs, horses, ducks, geese; also mice; their agricultural life, by cognate words for corn (although the particular species of the cereal varied), flax or hemp, ploughing and grinding; their implements, by cognate terms for copper or iron, cart or waggon, boat, helm; their household economy and industries, by words from the same roots for sewing and weaving, house, garden, yard; also for a place of refuge, the division of the year into lunar months, and several of the numerals.

Common origin of European and Indian religions. The ancient religions of Europe and India had a similar origin. They were to some extent made up of the sacred stories or myths which our common ancestors had learned while dwelling together in Central Asia. Certain of the Vedic gods were also the gods of Greece and Rome; and the Deity is still adored by names derived from the same old Aryan root (*div,* to shine, hence The Bright One, the Indian *Deva,* Latin *Deus,* or Divinity), by Bráhmans in Calcutta, by the Protestant clergy of England, and by Catholic priests in Peru.

The Indo-Aryans on the march, The Vedic hymns exhibit the Indian branch of the Aryans on their march to the south-east, and in their new homes.

The earliest songs disclose the race still to the north of the Khaibar Pass, in Kábul; the latest ones bring them as far as the Ganges. Their victorious advance eastwards through the intermediate tract can be traced in the Vedic writings almost step by step. One of their famous settlements lay between the two sacred rivers, the Saraswatí, supposed to be the modern Sarsutí near Thánesar in the Punjab, and the Drishad-vatí, or Ghaggar, a day's march from it. This fertile strip of land, not more than 60 miles long by 20 broad, was fondly remembered by the Indo-Aryans as their Holy Land (*Brahmá-vartta*), 'fashioned of God, and chosen by the Creator.' As their numbers increased, they pushed eastwards along the base of the Himálayas, into what they afterwards called the Land of the Sacred Singers (*Brahmarshi-desha*). Their settlements included by degrees the five rivers of the Punjab, together with the upper course of the Jumna and perhaps of the Ganges. *and in their new settle-ments.*

Here the Vedic hymns were composed; and the steady supply of water led the Aryans to settle down from their old state of wandering pastoral tribes into communities of husbandmen. Their Vedic poets praised the rivers which enabled them to make this great change—perhaps the most important step in the progress of a race. ' May the Indus,' they sang, ' the far-famed giver of wealth, hear us; (fertilizing our) broad fields with water.' The Himálayas, through whose offshoots they had reached India, and at whose southern base they long dwelt, made a lasting impression on their memory. The Vedic singer praised ' Him whose greatness the snowy ranges, and the sea, and the aerial river declare.' In all its long wanderings through India, the Aryan race never forgot its northern home. There dwelt its gods and holy singers; and there eloquence descended from heaven among men; while beyond the mountain-wall lay the paradise of deities and heroes, where the kind and the brave for ever repose. *Function of the Rivers.* *Recollec-tions of their northern home.*

The Rig-Veda forms the great literary memorial of the early Aryan settlements in the Punjab. The age of this venerable hymnal is unknown. The Hindus believe, without evidence, that it existed ' from before all time,' or at least from 3101 years B.C., nearly 5000 years ago. European scholars have inferred from astronomical dates that its composition was going on about 1400 B.C. But these dates are themselves given in writings of modern origin, and might have been calculated backwards. We know, however, that the Vedic religion had been at work long before the rise of Buddhism in the 6th century B.C. The antiquity of the Rig-Veda, although *The Rig-Veda.* *Insufficient evidence for its sup-posed dates, 3101 B.C. (?) 1400 B.C. (?)*

not to be dogmatically expressed in figures, is abundantly established. The earlier hymns exhibit the Aryans on the north-
western frontiers of India, just starting on their long journey.

Neverthe-
less of
great anti-
quity.

Before the embassy of the Greek Megasthenes, at the end of
the 4th century B.C., they had spread at least to the verge of
the Gangetic delta, 1500 miles distant. At the time of the
Periplus, *circ.* 70 A.D., the southernmost point of India was
apparently a seat of their worship. A temple to the queen of
the god Siva stood on Cape Comorin, before the end of the first
Christian century ; and the inferences of European scholarship
point to the composition of at least some of the Vedic psalms
at a period not later than twelve to sixteen centuries before the
commencement of our era.

Inspira-
tion of the
Veda.

The Bráhmans declare that the Vedic hymns were directly
inspired by God. Indeed, in our own times, the young Theistic
Church of Bengal, which rejects Bráhmanical teaching, was
split into two sects on the question of the divine authority
of the Veda. The hymns seem to have been composed by
certain families of Rishis or psalmists, some of whose names

The Rig-
Veda ;
1017
hymns,
10,580
verses.

are preserved. The Rig-Veda is a very old collection of 1017
of these short lyrical poems, chiefly addressed to the gods,
and containing 10,580 verses. They show us the Aryans on
the banks of the Indus, divided into various tribes, sometimes at war with each other, sometimes united against the

Caste not
known to
Rig-Veda,

'black-skinned' aborigines. Caste, in its later sense, is
unknown. Each father of a family is the priest of his own
household. The chieftain acts as father and priest to the tribe;
but at the greater festivals he chooses some one specially learned
in holy offerings to conduct the sacrifice in the name of the
people. The chief, although hereditary, seems to have been partly
elected; and his title of Vis-pati, 'Lord of the Settlers,' survives
in the old Persian Vis-paiti, and as the Lithuanian Wiéz-patis
in central Europe at this day. Women enjoyed a high position,
and some of the most beautiful hymns were composed by
ladies and queens. Marriage was held sacred. Husband and
wife were both 'rulers of the house' (*dampatí*) ; and drew

nor
widow-
burning.

near to the gods together in prayer. The burning of widows
on the husbands' funeral pile was unknown ; and the verses
in the Veda which the Bráhmans afterwards distorted into a
sanction for the practice, have the very opposite meaning.
'Rise, woman,' says the sacred text to the mourner ; 'come to
the world of life. Come to us. Thou hast fulfilled thy duties
as a wife to thy husband.'

The Aryan tribes in the Veda are acquainted with most of

the metals. They have blacksmiths, coppersmiths, and gold- Aryan
smiths among them, besides carpenters, barbers, and other civilisation
artisans. They fight from chariots, and freely use the horse, Veda.
although not yet the elephant, in war. They have settled
down as husbandmen, till their fields with the plough, and live
in villages or towns. But they also cling to their old wandering life, with their herds and 'cattle-pens.' Cattle, indeed, still
form their chief wealth—the coin (Latin, *pecunia*) in which
payments or fines are made; and one of their words for war
literally means 'a desire for cows.' They have learned to
build 'ships,' perhaps large river-boats; and have seen or heard
something of the sea. Unlike the modern Hindus, the Aryans
of the Veda ate beef; used a fermented liquor or beer, made
from the *soma* plant; and offered the same strong meat and
drink to their gods. Thus the stout Aryans spread eastwards Spread of
through Northern India; pushed on from behind by later the Aryans
arrivals of their own stock; and driving before them, or eastwards.
reducing to bondage, the earlier 'black-skinned' races. They
marched in whole communities from one river valley to
another; each house-father a warrior, husbandman, and priest;
with his wife, and his little ones, and cattle.

These free-hearted tribes had a great trust in themselves The gods
and in their gods. Like other conquering races, they believed of the
that both themselves and their deities were altogether superior Veda.
to the people of the land and to their poor, rude objects of
worship. Indeed, this noble self-confidence is a great aid to
the success of a nation. Their divinities—*devas*, literally 'The
Shining Ones,' from the Sanskrit root *div*, 'to shine'—were the
great powers of nature. They adored the Father-heaven,
Dyaush-pitar in Sanskrit, the *Dies-piter* or *Jupiter* of Rome,
the *Zeus* of Greece, the Low German *Duus*, and, through
the old French god-demon, *Dus-ius*, probably the *Deuce* of
English slang; together with Mother-Earth; and the Encompassing Sky, *Varuna* in Sanskrit, *Uranus* in Latin, *Ouranos*
in Greek. The Sárameyas, or two children of Indra's watch-
dog, the messengers of death, have been compared with the
Greek Hermeias, the conductor of the dead. Such common
ideas and names penetrate deeply into the mythology of the
ancient world, although they have sometimes been exaggerated.
Jupiter *Feretrius*, for whom the Romans invented conflicting
derivations, may be really the *Vritra-han*, or destroyer of the
old Aryan demon Vritra. On the coins of the Republic, Juno
Sospita is represented with a skin and horns over her. General
Cunningham suggests that her epithet represents the Sanskrit

Saspatní (*Sasí*), a name for the moon, so called from the marks on the moon being supposed to resemble a hare (*sasa*).

Influence of the rainy season on Aryan mythology. Indra, or the Aqueous Vapour that brought the precious rain on which plenty or famine depended each autumn, received the largest number of hymns. By degrees, as the settlers realized more and more keenly the importance of the periodical rains to their new life as husbandmen, he became the chief of the Vedic gods. 'The gods do not reach unto thee, O Indra, or men; thou overcomest all creatures in strength.' Agni, the God of Fire (Latin, *igni-s*), ranks next to Indra in the number of hymns in his honour as the friend of man, the guide of the people, the lord and giver of wealth.

Indra and Agni. Judging, indeed, from the preponderance of the invocations to Agni, and from the position which the corresponding deity holds in Iranian mythology, it would appear as if Agni and not Indra had been the chief god of the race, while the Indian and old Persian branches still dwelt together. Among the cold heights and on the uplands of Central Asia, to the north-west of the Himálayas, Heat was the great factor of fertility, the giver of human comfort, and the ripener of the crops. When the eastern offshoots of the Aryans descended upon the plains of India, they found, as they advanced southward, that heat was an element of productiveness which might be taken for granted, a constant factor in the husbandry **Moisture *v.* Heat.** of the Indus and Jumna valleys. Here it was upon moisture rather than on heat that their harvest depended. To the right of their line of march across the five rivers of the Punjab, a rather narrow tract stretched to the foot of the Himálayas, with an ample rainfall, now averaging 35 inches a year. But on the broad plains to their left, the water-supply was less abundant and more capricious. At the present day the tract immediately to the south of the Aryan route receives only 20 to 30 inches per annum, diminishing through successive belts of rainfall down to 10 inches.

Agni gives place to Indra. As the Aryan immigrants spread south, therefore, it was no longer so necessary to pray for heat, and it became more necessary to pray for moisture. Agni, the heat-giving god, without being discredited, became less important, and receded in favour of Indra, the rain-bringing deity. In the settlements of the Punjab, Indra thus advanced to the first place among **Indra, the rain-bringer.** the Vedic divinities. He is the cloud compeller, dropping bountiful showers, filling the dried-up rivers from the Himálayas and bringing the rain-storms. His voice is the thunder; with his spear of lightning he smites open the black clouds, and rends the black bodies of the demons who have drunk up the wished-for rains. He makes the sun to shine forth again. ' I will sing of the victories of Indra, of the victories won by the God of the Spear,' chanted the Rig-Vedic psalmist. ' On the mountains he smote the demon of drought (Ahi) ; he poured out the waters and let the river flow from the mountains : like calves to cows, so do the waters hasten to the sea.' ' Thou hast broken open the rain-prisons[1] rich in cattle. The bonds of the streams hast thou burnt asunder.'[2]

As the Aryans pushed forward into the middle and lower Indra gives valley of the Ganges, they found themselves in a region of place to the Triad, copious rainfall brought by the unfailing monsoons. The rain-storms of Indra thus became less important. His waterspouts, although well worth praying for in the Punjab, evidently belonged to an inferior grade of divine energy than that which presided over the irresistible, majestically ordered advance of the periodical rains in Bengal. Indra, the Cloud-Compeller, shared in his turn the fate of Agni, the God of Heat, and gave way to three deities on a scale commensurate with the vaster of Brahmá, forces of nature in the Lower Gangetic valley. We shall see how Vishnu, Siva. the abstract but potent conception of Divine energy embodied in the Bráhmanical Triad of the Creator, Preserver, and Destroyer took the place alike of Agni and of Indra, and of the other Vedic gods. But, meanwhile, Indra, the Giver of Rain, was the most important deity to the Aryan settlers in the Punjab. He stands forth in the Veda as the foremost Shining One.

The Maruts were the Vedic Storm Gods, 'who make the Other rocks to tremble, who tear in pieces the forest.' Ushas, 'the Vedic gods. High-born Dawn' (Greek, *Eos*), 'shines upon us like a young wife, rousing every living being to go forth to his work.' The Aswins, or ' Fleet Outriders' of the Dawn, are the first rays of sunrise, 'Lords of Lustre.' The Solar Orb (Súrjya, Savitri), the Wind (Váyu), the Sunshine or Friendly Day (Mitra), the animating fermented juice of the Sacrificial Plant (Soma), and many other Shining Ones, are invoked in the Veda ; in all, about thirty-three gods, 'who are eleven in heaven, eleven on earth, and eleven dwelling in glory in mid-air.'

The terrible blood-drinking deities of modern Hinduism are

---

[1] Literally, ' Thou hast broken the cave of Vritra,' the demon who imprisons the rain and causes drought, with whom Indra is constantly waging victorious war.

[2] The Rig-Vedic attributes of Indra are well summarized by Professor Max Duncker, *Ancient History of India*, pp. 47–49 (ed. 1881), following Roth and Benfey ; and are detailed with completeness by Muir, 'Sanskrit Texts,' pp. 76–139, vol. v. (1872).

F

The blood-loving deities of Hinduism scarcely known in the Veda. scarcely known in the Veda. Buffaloes are indeed offered; and one hymn points to a symbolism based on human sacrifices, an early practice apparently extinct before the time of the Vedic singers. The great Horse-Sacrifice (Aswamedha) seems, in some of its aspects, a substitution for the flesh and blood of a man. But, as a whole, the hymns are addressed to bright, friendly gods. Rudra, who was destined to become the Siva of the Hindus, and the third person or Destroyer in their Triad, is only the god of Roaring Tempests in the Veda. Vishnu, the second person or Preserver in the Hindu Triad, is but slightly known to the Vedic singers as the deity of the Shining Firmament; while Brahmá, the first person, or Creator, has no separate existence in their simple hymns. The names of the dreadful Mahádeva, Dúrga, Káli, and of the gentler but intensely human Krishna and Ráma, are alike unknown.

Attitude of the Vedic singer to his gods. The Aryan settlers lived on excellent terms with their bright gods. They asked for protection with an assured conviction that it would be granted. 'Give me cows, or land, or long life, in return for this hymn or offering;' 'slay my enemy, scatter the black-skin, and I will sacrifice to thee,'—such is the ordinary frame of mind of the singer to his gods. But, at the same time, he was deeply stirred by the glory and mystery of the earth and the heavens. Indeed, the majesty of nature so filled his mind, that when he praises any one of his Shining Gods he can think of none other for the time being, and adores him as the Supreme Ruler. Verses of the Veda may be quoted declaring each of the greater deities to be the One Supreme: 'Neither gods nor men reach unto thee, O Indra;' Soma is 'king of heaven and earth, the conqueror of all.' To Varuna also it is said, 'Thou art lord of all, of heaven and earth; thou art king of all those who are gods, and of all those who are men.' Agni is likewise addressed as the mightiest and as the most beloved of the gods: 'No one can approach thy darting, strong, terrible flames: burn thou the evil spirits, and every enemy.' The more spiritual of the Vedic singers, therefore, may be said to have worshipped One God, although not One Alone.

Higher conceptions of the Deity in the Veda. Some beautiful souls among them were filled not only with the splendours of the visible universe, but with the deeper mysteries of the Unseen, and the powerlessness of man to search out God.

A Vedic hymn. 'In the beginning there arose the Golden Child. He was the one born lord of all that is. He established the earth and this sky. Who is the God to whom we shall offer our sacrifice?

'He who gives life, he who gives strength; whose command all the Bright Gods revere; whose shadow is immortality, whose shadow is death. Who is the God to whom we shall offer our sacrifice?

'He who, through his power, is the one king of the breathing and awakening world. He who governs all, man and beast. Who is the God to whom we shall offer our sacrifice?

'He through whom the sky is bright and the earth firm; he through whom the heaven was established, nay, the highest heaven; he who measured out the light and the air. Who is the God to whom we shall offer our sacrifice?

'He who by his might looked even over the water-clouds; he who alone is God above all gods. Who is the God to whom we shall offer our sacrifice?'[1]

The yearning for rest in God, that desire for the wings of a dove, so as to fly away and be at rest, with which noble hearts have ached in all ages, breathes in several exquisite hymns of the Rig-Veda: 'Where there is eternal light, in the world where the sun is placed,—in that immortal, imperishable world, place me, O Soma! Where life is free, in the third heaven of heavens, where the worlds are radiant,—there make me immortal! Where there is happiness and delight, where joy and pleasure reside, where our desires are attained,—there make me immortal.'[2] *'The Better Land.'*

Nor was the sense of sin, and the need of pardon, absent from the minds of these ancient psalmists. As a rule, an honourable understanding seems to have existed between the Vedic sacrificer and his bright god: the god being equitably pledged to the fulfilment of the sacrificer's prayer in return for the offering, although the wisest might leave it to Indra himself to decide what was best to bestow. But even the cheerful worshippers of the Veda at times felt deeply the sinfulness of sin, and the fear of the sins of the father being visited upon the children. 'What great sin is it, O Varuna,' says a hymn of the Rig-Veda, 'for which thou seekest to slay thy worshipper and friend?' 'Absolve us from the sins of our fathers and from those which we committed in our own persons.' 'It was not our own doing that led us astray, O Varuna, it was *The sense of sin and need of forgiveness.*

---

[1] Rig-Veda, x. 121; translated by Prof. Max Müller, *Hist. Anc. Sansk. Lit.* p. 569; *Chips*, vol. i. p. 29 (ed. 1867).

[2] Rig-Veda, ix. 113. 7, Max Müller's translation.

necessity (or temptation); wine, anger, dice, or thoughtlessness.
The stronger perverts the weaker.   Even sleep bringeth sin.'[1]
'Through want of strength, thou strong and bright god,' says
another hymn to Varuna, 'have I gone wrong : have mercy,
almighty, have mercy. I go along trembling like a cloud driven
before the wind : have mercy, almighty, have mercy. Through
want of power (to do right) have I transgressed, O bright and
mighty god : have mercy, almighty, have mercy. Whenever we
men, O Varuna, commit an offence before the heavenly host,
whenever we break the law through thoughtlessness, have
mercy, almighty, have mercy.'[2]

Prayers for pardon.

The very ancient Aryans in Central Asia buried their dead,
although cremation seems also to have been resorted to.   In
Iran the custom of burial eventually gave place to that of
exposing the corpse on a mountain to the birds of heaven ;
a custom still practised in the Pársí Towers of Silence at
Bombay and elsewhere. We have seen that Agni, god of
heat, appears to have been the chief deity of the Aryan race
in Iran ; and fire was regarded by the ancient Persian as too
sacred an element to be polluted by a human corpse. The
Aryan settlers in India for a time retained the custom of
burial. 'Let me not, O Varuna, go to the house of clay,'
says one hymn of the Rig-Veda.[3] 'O earth, be not too narrow
for him,' says another hymn, 'cover him like the mother who
folds her son in her garment.'[4] But in time the Indo-Aryans
substituted the fire for the grave ; and the burning of the corpse
became a distinctive feature of the race, as contrasted with
the ruder and more primitive peoples whom they found in the
Punjab.

Primitive Aryan burial.

While the aboriginal tribes buried their dead under rude
stone monuments, the Aryan—alike in India, in Greece, and
in Italy—made use of the funeral-pyre as the most solemn
method of disposing of the mortal part of man. As the Indo-
Aryan derived his natural birth from his parents ; and a partial
regeneration, or second birth, from the performance of his
religious duties ; so the fire, by setting free the soul from the
body, completed the third or heavenly birth.   His friends

Burning of the dead.

[1] Rig-Veda, vii. 86 ; translated in Muir's 'Sanskrit Texts,' vol. v. p. 66
(1872).

[2] Rig-Veda, vii. 89.   Max Müller's beautiful translation is reproduced
by Professor Duncker, *Ancient History of India*, p. 53 (1881).   See also
Muir's translation, 'Sanskrit Texts,' vol. v. p. 67 (1872).

[3] Rig-Veda, vii. 89. 1.   Muir's 'Sanskrit Texts,' vol. v. p. 67 (1872).

[4] Rig-Veda, x. 18.   Roth's rendering in Duncker, *Ancient History of
India*, p. 63 (1881).

stood round the pyre as round a natal bed, and commanded his eye to go to the sun, his breath to the wind, his limbs to the earth, the water and plants whence they had been derived. But ‘as for his unborn part, do thou, Lord (Agni), quicken it with thy heat; let thy flame and thy brightness quicken it; convey it to the world of the righteous.’

For the lonely journey of the soul after its separation from the body, the Aryans, both in Asia and Europe, provided faithful guides (the *Sârameyas* in Sanskrit, *Hermeias* in Greek). According to the Zend or old Aryan legend in Persia, Yama was a monarch in the old time, when sorrow and sickness were unknown. By degrees sin and disease crept into the world; the slow necessity of death hastened its step; and the old king retired, with a chosen band, from the polluted earth into a better country, where he still reigns. The Indian version of the story makes Yama to be the first man who passed through death into immortality. Having discovered the way to the other world, he leads men thither. He became the nekropompos, or guide of the Aryan dead. Meanwhile his two dogs (*Sârameyas*)—‘black and spotted,’ ‘broad of nostril,’ and ‘with a hunger never to be satisfied’—wander as his messengers among men. ‘Worship with an offering King Yama, the Assembler of Men, who departed to the mighty waters, who found out the road for many.’[1] Aryan legend of King Yama, or Death.

Several exquisite hymns bid farewell to the dead :—‘Depart thou, depart thou by the ancient paths to the place whither our fathers have departed. Meet with the Ancient Ones; meet with the Lord of Death. Throwing off thine imperfections, go to thy home. Become united with a body; clothe thyself in a shining form.’ ‘Let him depart to those for whom flow the rivers of nectar. Let him depart to those who, through meditation, have obtained the victory; who, by fixing their thoughts on the unseen, have gone to heaven. Let him depart to the mighty in battle, to the heroes who have laid down their lives for others, to those who have bestowed their goods on the poor.’ The doctrine of transmigration was unknown. The circle round the funeral-pile sang with a firm assurance that their friend went direct to a state of blessedness and reunion with the loved ones who had gone before. ‘Do thou conduct The Vedic farewell to the dead.

---

[1] Rig-Veda, x. 14. I. See Dr. John Muir's ‘Sanskrit Texts,’ and his essay on ‘Yama,’ *Journal of the Royal Asiatic Society*, part ii., 1865, whence many of the above quotations are derived. See also Max Müller's essay on the ‘Funeral Rites of the Bráhmans,’ on which the following paragraph is chiefly based.

us to heaven,' says a hymn of the later Atharva-Veda ; 'let us be with our wives and children.' 'In heaven, where our friends dwell in bliss,—having left behind the infirmities of the body, free from lameness, free from crookedness of limb,—there let us behold our parents and our children.' 'May the water-shedding spirits bear thee upwards, cooling thee with their swift motion through the air, and sprinkling thee with dew.' 'Bear him, carry him ; let him, with all his faculties complete, go to the world of the righteous. Crossing the dark valley which spreadeth boundless around him, let the unborn soul ascend to heaven. Wash the feet of him who is stained with sin ; let him go upwards with cleansed feet. Crossing the gloom, gazing with wonder in many directions, let the unborn soul go up to heaven.'

The hymns of the Rig-Veda were composed, as we have seen, by the Aryans in their colonies along the Indus, and on their march eastwards towards the Jumna and upper Ganges. The growing numbers of the settlers, and the arrival of fresh Aryan tribes from behind, still compelled them to advance. From ' The Land of the Sacred Singers,' in the Eastern Punjab (*Brahmarshi-desha, ante,* p. 77), Manu describes them as spreading through ' The Middle Land' (*Madhya-desha*). This comprised the river system of the Ganges as far east as Oudh and Allahábád, with the Himálayas as its northern, and the Vindhya ranges as its southern boundary.

The Ganges is only twice mentioned, and without special emphasis, in the Rig-Veda. The conquest of the Middle Land seems, therefore, not to have commenced till the close of the Rig-Vedic era. It must have been the work of many genera-tions, and it will be referred to when we come to examine the historical significance of the two great Sanskrit epics. Between the time when the Aryans descended from Central Asia upon the plains of the Indus and the age when they passed the Ganges, they had conquered many of the aboriginal races, left others behind on their route, and had begun to wage inter-tribal wars among themselves, under rival Aryan heroes and rival Vedic priests.

During this advance, the simple faith of the Rig-Vedic singers was first adorned with stately rites, and then extinguished beneath them. The race progressed from a loose confederacy of tribes into several well-knit nations, each bound together by the strong central force of kingly power, directed by a powerful priesthood, and organized on a firm basis of caste.

Whence arose this new constitution of the Aryan tribes into

nations, with castes, priests, and kings? We have seen that *The Aryan tribes organized into kingdoms.* although in their earlier colonies on the Indus each father was priest in his family, yet the Chieftain, or Lord of the Settlers, called in some man specially learned in holy offerings to conduct the greater tribal sacrifices. Such men were highly honoured, and the famous quarrel which runs throughout the whole Veda sprang from the claims of two rival sages, Vasishtha and Viswámitra, to perform one of these ceremonies. The art of writing was unknown, and the hymns and sacrificial formulæ had to be handed down by word of mouth from father to son.

It thus came to pass that the families who knew these *Origin of priestly families.* holy words by heart became the hereditary owners of the liturgies required at the most solemn offerings to the gods. Members of such households were chosen again and again to conduct the tribal sacrifices, to chant the battle-hymn, to implore the divine aid, or to pray away the divine wrath. Even the early Rig-Veda recognises the importance of these sacrifices. ' That king,' says a verse, ' before whom marches the priest, he alone dwells well established in his own house ; to him the people bow down. The king who gives wealth to the priest, he will conquer; him the gods will protect.' The tribesmen first hoped, then believed, that a hymn or prayer which had once acted successfully, and been followed by victory, would again produce the same results. The hymns became a valuable family property for those who had composed or learned them. The Rig-Veda tells how the prayer of Vasishtha prevailed ' in the battle of the ten kings,' and how that of Viswámitra ' preserves the tribe of the Bhárats.' The potent prayer was termed *brahman* (from the root *brih = vrih*, to increase), and he who offered it, *bráhman*. Woe to him who despised either ! ' Whosoever,' says the Rig-Veda, ' scoffs at the prayer which we have made, may hot plagues come upon him, may the sky burn up that hater of Bráhmans.' [1]

Certain families thus came to have not only a hereditary *Growing numbers of priests.* claim to conduct the great sacrifices, but also the exclusive knowledge of the ancient hymns, or at any rate of the traditions which explained their symbolical meaning. They naturally tried to render the ceremonies solemn and imposing. By degrees a vast array of ministrants grew up around each of the greater sacrifices. There were first the officiating priests and

---

[1] The following pages are largely indebted to Professor Weber's *History of Indian Literature* (Trübner, 1878), —a debt very gratefully acknowledged.

their assistants, who prepared the sacrificial ground, dressed the altar, slew the victims, and poured out the libations; second, the chanters of the Vedic hymns; third, the reciters of other parts of the service; fourth, the superior priests, who watched over the whole, and corrected mistakes.

The four Vedas. The entire service was derived from the Veda, or ' inspired knowledge,' an old Aryan word which appears in the Latin *vid-ere*, 'to see or perceive;' in the Greek *feido* of Homer, and *oida*, ' I know;' in the Old English, *I wit;* in the modern *(1) The Rig-Veda.* German and English, *wissen, wisdom*, etc. The Rig-Veda exhibits the hymns in their simplest form, arranged in ten 'circles,' according to the families of their composers, the Rishis. Some of the hymns are named after individual minstrels.

But as the sacrifices grew more elaborate, the hymns were also arranged in four collections (*sanhitás*) or service-books *(2) The Sáma-Veda.* for the ministering priests. Thus, the second, or Sáma-Veda, was made up of extracts from the Rig-Vedic hymns used at the Soma sacrifice. Some of its verses stamp themselves, by their antiquated grammatical forms, as older than their render- *(3) The Yajur-Veda;* ing in the Rig-Veda itself. The third, or Yajur-Veda, consists not only of Rig-Vedic verses, but also of prose sentences, to be used at the sacrifices of the New and Full Moon; and at the Great Horse Sacrifice, when 609 animals of various kinds were offered, perhaps in substitution for the earlier Man Sacrifice, *its (a) Black and (b) White editions.* which is also mentioned in the Yajur-Veda. The Yajur-Veda is divided into two editions, the Black and the White Yajur; both belonging to a more modern period than either the Rig or the Sáma Vedas, and composed after the Aryans had spread far to the east of the Indus.

(4) The Atharva-Veda. The fourth, or Atharva-Veda, was compiled from the least ancient hymns of the Rig-Veda in the tenth book; and from the still later songs of the Bráhmans, after they had established their priestly power. It supplies the connecting link between the simple Aryan worship of the Shining Ones exhibited in the Rig-Veda, and the complex Bráhmanical system which followed. It was only allowed to rank as part of the Veda after a long struggle.

The four Vedas become insufficient. The four Vedas thus described, namely, the Rig-Veda, the Sáma, the Yajur, and the Atharva, formed an immense body of sacrificial poetry. But as the priests grew in number and power, they went on elaborating their ceremonies, until even the four Vedas became insufficient guides for them. They *The Bráh-manas compiled.* accordingly compiled prose treatises, called Bráhmanas, attached to each of the four Vedas, in order to more fully explain the

functions of the officiating priests. Thus the Bráhmana of the
Rig-Veda deals with the duties of the Reciter of the Hymns
(*hotar*); the Bráhmana of the Sáma-Veda, with those of the
Singer at the Soma sacrifice (*udgátar*); the Bráhmana of the
Yajur-Veda, with those of the actual performer of the Sacrifice
(*adhvaryu*); while the Bráhmana of the Atharva-Veda is a
medley of legends and speculations, having but little direct
connection with the Veda whose name it bears. All the *Sruti*, or
Bráhmanas, indeed, besides explaining the ritual, lay down Revealed
religious precepts and dogmas. Like the four Vedas, they Truth.
are held to be the very Word of God. The Vedas and the
Bráhmanas form the Revealed Scriptures (*sruti*) of the Hindus;
the Vedas supplying their divinely-inspired psalms, and the
Bráhmanas their divinely-inspired theology or body of doctrine.

Even this ample literature did not suffice. The priests The Sútras
accordingly composed a number of new works, called Sútras, or Sacred
which elaborated still further their system of sacrifice, and Traditions;
which asserted still more strongly their own claims as a separate
and superior caste. They alleged that these Sútras, although
not directly revealed by God, were founded on the inspired
Vedas and Bráhmanas, and that they had therefore a divine
authority as sacred traditions (*smriti*). The Sútras, literally, *Smriti;*
'strings' of aphorisms, were composed in the form of short not
sentences, for the sake of brevity, and in order that their vast 'revealed.'
number might be the better remembered in an age when writing
was little practised, or unknown. Some of them, such as their
the Kalpa-Sútras, deal with the ritual and sacrifices; others, subject-
like the 'Household' or Grihya-Sútras, prescribe the ceremonies matter.
at birth, marriage, and death; a still larger class of Sútras treat
of the doctrines, duties, and privileges of the priests. The
Sútras thus became the foundation of the whole legislation and
philosophy of the Bráhmans in later times. They exhibit the The
Bráhmans no longer as the individual sacrificers of the Vedic Bráhman
caste fully
period, but as a powerful hereditary caste, claiming supremacy formed.
alike over king and people.

Meanwhile, other castes had been gradually formed. As Growth
the Aryans moved eastwards from the Indus, some of the of the
warrior
warriors were more fortunate than others, or received larger caste
shares of the conquered lands. Such families had not to till (Kshat-
their fields with their own hands, but could leave that work triyas).
to be done by the aboriginal races whom they subdued. In
this way there grew up a class of warriors, freed from the
labour of husbandry, who surrounded the chief or king, and
were always ready for battle. It seems likely that these kinsmen

and companions of the king formed an important class among the early Aryan tribes in India, as they certainly did among the mediæval branches of the race in Europe, and still do at the petty courts of India.   Their old Sanskrit names, *Kshattriya, Rájanya,* and *Rájbansi,* mean 'connected with the royal power,' or ' of the royal line ; ' their usual modern name *Rájput* means ' of royal descent.'   In process of time, when the Aryans settled down, not as mere fighting clans, but as powerful nations, in the Middle Land along the Jumna and Ganges, this warrior class grew in numbers and in power. The black races had been reduced to serfdom, or driven back towards the Himálayas and the Vindhyas, on the north and on the south of the central tract.   The incessant fighting, which had formed the common lot of the tribes on their actual migration eastwards from the Indus, now ceased.

The cultivating caste (Vaisyas).   A section of the people accordingly laid aside their arms, and, devoting themselves to agriculture or other peaceful pursuits, became the *Vaisyas.*   The sultry heats of the Middle Land must have abated their old northern energy, and inclined them to repose.   Those who, from family ties or from personal inclination, preferred a soldier's life, had to go beyond the frontier to find an enemy.   Distant expeditions of this sort could be undertaken much less conveniently by the husbandman than in the ancient time, when his fields lay on the very border of the enemy's country, and had just been wrested from it.   Such expeditions required and probably developed a military class ; endowed with lands, and with serfs to till the soil during the master's absence at the wars.   The old companions and kinsmen of the king formed a nucleus round which gathered the more daring spirits.   They became in time a distinct military caste.

The four castes :
(1) Bráhmans,
(2) Kshattriyas,
(3) Vaisyas,
   The Aryans on the Ganges, in the ' Middle Land,' thus found themselves divided into three classes—first, the priests, or Bráhmans ; second, the warriors and king's companions, called in ancient times Kshattriyas, at the present day Rájputs ; third, the husbandmen, or agricultural settlers, who retained the old name of Vaisyas, from the root *vis,* which in the Vedic period had included the whole ' people.'   These three classes gradually became separate castes ; intermarriage between them was forbidden, and each kept more and more strictly to its hereditary employment.   But they were all recognised as belonging to ' Twice-born,' or Aryan race ; they were all present at the great national sacrifices ; and all worshipped the same Bright Gods.

(4) Súdras.   Beneath them was a fourth or servile class, called Súdras, the

remnants of the vanquished aboriginal tribes whose lives had been spared. These were 'the slave-bands of black descent,' the Dásas of the Veda. They were distinguished from their 'Twice-born' Aryan conquerors as being only 'Once-born,' and by many contemptuous epithets. They were not allowed to be present at the great national sacrifices, or at the feasts which followed them. They could never rise out of their servile condition ; and to them was assigned the severest toil in the fields, and all the hard and dirty work of the village community.

Of the four Indian castes, three had a tendency to increase. As the Aryan conquests spread, more aboriginal tribes were reduced to serfdom, as Súdras. The warriors, or Kshattriyas, would constantly receive additions from wealthy or enterprising members of the cultivating class. When an expedition or migration went forth to subdue new territory, the whole colonists would for a time lead a military life, and their sons would probably all regard themselves as Kshattriyas. In ancient times, entire tribes, and at the present day the mass of the population throughout large tracts, thus claim to be of the warrior or Rájput caste. Moreover, the kings and fighting-men of aboriginal races who, without being conquered by the Aryans, entered into alliance with them, would probably assume for themselves the warrior or Kshattriya rank. We see this process going on at the present day among many of the aboriginal peoples. The Bráhmans, in their turn, appear at first to have received into their body distinguished families of Kshattriya descent. In later times, too, we find that sections of aboriginal races were also 'manufactured' wholesale into Bráhmans. Unmistakeable cases of such 'manufactures' or ethnical syncretisms are recorded; and besides the upper-class agricultural Bráhmans, there are throughout India many local castes of Bráhmans who follow the humble callings of fishermen, blacksmiths, ploughmen, and potato-growers.[1]

The Bráh-mans, Kshat-triyas, and Súdras increase.

The Vaisya or cultivating caste did not tend, in this manner, to increase. No one felt ambitious to win his way into it, except perhaps the enslaved Súdras, to whom any change of condition was forbidden. The Vaisyas themselves tended in early times to rise into the more honourable warrior class ; and at a later period, to be mingled with the labouring multitude of Súdras, or with the castes of mixed descent. In many Provinces they have now almost disappeared as a distinct caste. In ancient India, as at the present day, the three conspicuous castes were (1) the priests and (2) warriors of

The Vaisyas diminish.

[1] See Hunter's *Orissa*, vol. i. pp. 239-264 (1872).

Aryan birth, and (3) the serfs or Súdras, the remnants of
earlier races. The Súdras had no rights ; and, once conquered, ceased to struggle against their fate. But a long
contest raged between the priests and warriors for the chief
place in the Aryan commonwealth.

Struggle
between
priestly
and
warrior
castes.
In order to understand this contest, we must go back to
the time when the priests and warriors were simply fellow-
tribesmen. The Bráhman caste seems to have grown out of
the families of Rishis who composed the Vedic hymns, or
who were chosen to conduct the great tribal sacrifices. In
after-times, the whole Bráhman population of India pretended
to trace their descent from the Seven Rishis, heads of the
seven priestly families to whom the Vedic hymns were
assigned. But the composers of the Vedic hymns were
sometimes kings or distinguished warriors rather than priests ;
indeed, the Veda itself speaks of these royal Rishis (*Rájarshis*).

Rising
pretension
of the
Bráhmans.
When the Bráhmans put forward their claim to the highest
rank, the warriors or Kshattriyas were slow to admit it ; and
when the Bráhmans went a step further, and declared that only
members of their families could be priests, or gain admission
into the priestly caste, the warriors seem to have disputed
their pretensions. In later ages, the Bráhmans, having the
exclusive keeping of the sacred writings, effaced from them, as
far as possible, all traces of their struggle with the Kshattriyas.
The Bráhmans taught that their caste had come forth from the
mouth of God, divinely ordained to the priesthood from the
beginning of time. Nevertheless, the Vedic and Sanskrit texts
record a long contest, perhaps representing a difference in race
or separate waves of Aryan migrations.

Viswá-
mitra and
Vasishtha
The quarrel between the two sages Viswámitra and Vasishtha, which, as has been mentioned, runs through the whole
Veda, is typical of this struggle. Viswámitra stands as a
representative of the royal-warrior rank, who claims to perform
a great public sacrifice. The white-robed Vasishtha represents
the Bráhmans or hereditary priesthood, and opposes the
warrior's claim. In the end, Viswámitra established his title to
conduct the sacrifice ; but the Bráhmans explain this by saying
that his virtues and austerities won admission for him into
the priestly family of Bhrigu. He thus became a Bráhman,
and could lawfully fill the priestly office. Viswámitra serves as
a typical link, not only between the priestly and the worldly
castes, but also between the sacred and the profane sciences.
He was the legendary founder of the art of war, and his equally
legendary son Susruta is quoted as the earliest authority on

Indian medicine. These two sciences of war and medicine, together with music and architecture, form *upa-Vedas*, or supplementary sections of the divinely-inspired knowledge of the Bráhmans.

Another famous royal Rishi, Vítahavya, ' attained the condition of Bráhmanhood, venerated by mankind,' by a word of the saintly Bhrigu. Parasu-Ráma, the Divine Champion of the Bráhmans, was of warrior descent by his mother's side. Manu, their legislator, sprang from the warrior caste ; and his father is expressly called ' the seed of all the Kshattriyas.' But when the Bráhmans had firmly established their supremacy, they became reluctant to allow the possibility of even princes finding an entrance into their sacred order. King Ganaka was more learned than all the Bráhmans at his court, and performed terrible penances to attain to Bráhmanhood. Yet the legends leave it doubtful whether he gained his desire. The still more holy, but probably later, Matanga, wore his body to skin and bone by a thousand years of austerities, and was held up from falling by the hand of the god Indra himself. Nevertheless, he could not attain to Bráhmanhood. Gautama Buddha, who in the 6th century before Christ overthrew the Bráhman supremacy, and founded a new religion, was a prince of warrior descent ; perhaps born in too late an age to be adopted into, and utilized by, the Bráhman caste.

Other cases of Kshattriyas attaining to Bráhmanhood.

Among some of the Aryan tribes the priests apparently failed to establish themselves as an exclusive order. Indeed, the four castes, and especially the Bráhman caste, seem only to have obtained their full development amid the plenty of the Middle Land (*Madhya-desha*), watered by the Jumna and the Ganges. The early Aryan settlements to the west of the Indus long remained outside the caste system ; the later Aryan offshoots to the south and east of the Middle Land only partially carried that system with them. But in the Middle Land itself, with Delhi as its western capital, and the great cities of Ajodhya (Oudh) and Benares on its eastern frontier, the Bráhmans grew by degrees into a compact, learned, and supremely influential body, the makers of Sanskrit literature. Their language, their religion, and their laws, became .in after times the standards aimed at throughout all India. They naturally denounced all who did not submit to their pretensions, and they stigmatized the other Aryan settlements who had not accepted their caste system as lapsed tribes or outcasts (*Vrishalas*). Among the lists of such fallen races we read the name afterwards applied to the Ionians or Greeks (*Yavanas*). The Bráhmans of the Middle

The ' Middle Land,' the focus of Bráhmanism.

Aryan tribes beyond the Bráhmanical pale.

Land had not only to enforce their supremacy over the powerful warriors of their own kingdoms; they had also to extend it among the outlying Aryan tribes who had never fully accepted their caste system.   This must have been a slow work of ages, and it seems to have led to bitter feuds.

Bráhman discomfitures.

There were moments of defeat, indeed, when Bráhman leaders acknowledged the superiority of the warrior caste. 'None is greater,' says the Brihad Aranyaka Upanishad, 'than the Kshattriya ; therefore the Bráhman, under the Kshattriya, worships at the royal sacrifice (*rájasúya*).'[1]   It seems likely that numbers of the Vaisyas or cultivators would take part with the Kshattriyas, and be admitted into their caste. That the contest was not a bloodless one is attested by many legends, especially that of Parasu-Ráma, or 'Ráma of the Axe.'   This hero, who was divinely honoured as the sixth Incarnation of Vishnu, appeared on the scene after alternate massacres by Bráhmans and Kshattriyas had taken place. He fought on the Bráhman side, and covered India with the carcases of the warrior caste.   'Thrice seven times,' says the Sanskrit epic, 'did he clear the earth of the Kshattriyas,' and so ended in favour of the Bráhmans the long struggle.

The Bráhman supremacy established.

It is vain to search into the exact historical value of such legends.   They suffice to indicate an opposition among the early Aryan kingdoms to the claims of the Bráhmans, and the mingled measures of conciliation and force by which that opposition was overcome.   The Bráhman caste, having established its power, made a wise use of it.   From the ancient Vedic times its leaders recognised that if they were to exercise spiritual supremacy, they must renounce earthly pomp.   In arrogating the priestly function, they gave up all claim to the royal office.   They were divinely appointed to be the guides of nations and the counsellors of kings, but they could not be kings themselves.   As the duty of the Súdra was to serve, of the Vaisya to till the ground and follow middle-class trades or crafts, so the business of the Kshattriya was with

They make a wise use of it.

---

[1] It is easy to exaggerate the significance of this passage, and dangerous to generalize from it.   The author has to thank Prof. Cowell and the late Dr. John Muir for notes upon its precise application.   Weber, *Hist. Ind. Lit.* p. 54 (1878), describes the *rájasúya* as 'the consecration of the king.' The author takes this opportunity of expressing his many obligations to Dr. John Muir, his first teacher in Sanskrit.   Dr. Muir, after an honourable career in the Bengal Civil Service, devoted the second half of his life to the study of ancient Indian literature ; and his five volumes of *Original Sanskrit Texts* form one of the most valuable and most permanent contributions to Oriental learning made in our time.

the public enemy, and that of the Bráhmans with the national gods.

While the Bráhman leaders thus organized the occupations of the commonwealth, they also laid down strict rules for their own caste. They felt that as their functions were mysterious and above the reach of other men, so also must be their lives. Each day brought its hourly routine of ceremonies, studies, and duties. Their whole life was mapped out into four clearly-defined stages of discipline. For their existence, in its full religious significance, commenced not at birth, but on being invested at the close of childhood with the sacred thread of the Twice-Born. Their youth and early manhood were to be spent in learning by heart from some Bráhman sage the inspired Scriptures, tending the sacred fire, and serving their preceptor. Having completed his long studies, the young Bráhman entered on the second stage of his life, as a householder. He married and commenced a course of family duties. When he had reared a family, and gained a practical knowledge of the world, he retired into the forest as a recluse, for the third period of his existence ; feeding on roots or fruits, and practising his religious rites with increased devotion. The fourth stage was that of the ascetic or religious mendicant, wholly withdrawn from earthly affairs, and striving to attain a condition of mind which, heedless of the joys, or pains, or wants of the body, is intent only on its final absorption into the deity. The Bráhman, in this fourth stage of his life, ate nothing but what was given to him unasked, and abode not more than one day in any village, lest the vanities of the world should find entrance into his heart. Throughout his whole existence, he practised a strict temperance ; drinking no wine, using a simple diet, curbing the desires, shut off from the tumults of war, and his thoughts fixed on study and contemplation. ' What is this world ? ' says a Bráhman sage. ' It is even as the bough of a tree, on which a bird rests for a night, and in the morning flies away.'

It may be objected that so severe a life of discipline could never be led by any large class of men. And no doubt there have been at all times worldly Bráhmans ; indeed, the struggle for existence in modern times has compelled the great majority of the Bráhmans to betake themselves to secular pursuits. But the whole body of Sanskrit literature bears witness to the fact that this ideal life was constantly before their eyes, and that it served to the whole caste as a high standard in its two really essential features of self-culture and self-restraint.

[Side notes:] Four stages of a Bráhman's life.

First stage: The Learner (*brahma-chári*).

(2) The House-holder (*grihas-tha*).

(3) The Forest-Recluse (*vána-prastha*).

(4) The Ascetic (*san-yási*).

Bráhman ideal of life.

Incidents in the history of Buddha, in the 6th century before Christ, show that numbers of Bráhmans at that time lived according to this rule of life. Three hundred years later, the Greek ambassador, Megasthenes, found the Bráhmans discoursing in their groves, chiefly on life and death. The Chinese travellers, down to the 10th century A.D., attest the survival of the Bráhmanical pattern of the religious life. The whole monastic system of India, and those vast religious revivals which have given birth to the modern sects of Hinduism, are based on the same withdrawal from worldly affairs. At this day, Bráhman colleges, called *tols*, are carried on without fees on the old model, at Nadiyá in Bengal, and elsewhere. The modern visitor to these retreats can testify to the stringent self-discipline, and to the devotion to learning for its own sake, often protracted till past middle-life, and sometimes by grey-haired students.

Bráhman rule of life.

The Bráhmans, therefore, were a body of men who, in an early stage of this world's history, bound themselves by a rule of life the essential precepts of which were self-culture and self-restraint. As they married within their own caste, begat children only during their prime, and were not liable to lose the finest of their youth in war, they transmitted their best qualities in an ever-increasing measure to their descendants.

Its hereditary results on the caste.

The Bráhmans of the present day are the result of nearly 3000 years of hereditary education and self-restraint; and they have evolved a type of mankind quite distinct from the surrounding population. Even the passing traveller in India marks them out, alike from the bronze-cheeked, large-limbed, leisure-loving Rájput or warrior caste of Aryan descent; and from the dark-skinned, flat-nosed, thick-lipped low-castes of non-Aryan origin, with their short bodies and bullet heads. The Bráhman

The Bráhman type.

stands apart from both; tall and slim, with finely modelled lips and nose, fair complexion, high forehead, and somewhat cocoa-nut shaped skull—the man of self-centred refinement. He is an example of a class becoming the ruling power in a country, not by force of arms, but by the vigour of hereditary culture and temperance. One race has swept across India after another, dynasties have risen and fallen, religions have spread themselves over the land and disappeared. But since the dawn of history, the Bráhman has calmly ruled; swaying the minds and receiving the homage of the people, and accepted by foreign nations as the highest type of Indian mankind.

The paramount position which the Bráhmans won, resulted, in no small measure, from the benefits which they bestowed.

For their own Aryan countrymen, they developed a noble The work done by the Bráh-mans for India. language and literature. The Bráhmans were not only the priests and philosophers. They were also the lawgivers, the statesmen, the administrators, the men of science, and the poets of their race. Their influence on the aboriginal peoples, the hill and forest races of India, was not less important. To these rude remnants of the flint and bronze ages they brought in ancient times a knowledge of the metals and of the gods. Within the historical period, the Bráhmans have incorporated the mass of the backward races into the social and religious organization of Hinduism. A system of worship is a great comfort to a tropical people, hemmed in by the uncontrolled forces of nature, as it teaches them how to propitiate those mysterious powers, and so tends to liberate their minds from the terrors of the unseen.

The reflective life of the Middle Land (*Madhya-desha*) led Bráhman theology. the Bráhmans to see that the old gods of the Veda were in reality not supreme beings, but poetic fictions. For when they came to think the matter out, they found that the sun, the aqueous vapour, the encompassing sky, the wind, and the dawn, could not each be separate and supreme creators, but must have all proceeded from one First Cause. They did not shock the religious sense of the less speculative castes by any public rejection of the Vedic deities. They accepted the old Its esoteric and exo-teric sides. 'Shining Ones' of the Veda as beautiful manifestations of the divine power, and continued to decorously conduct the sacrifices in their honour. But among their own caste, the Bráhmans distinctly enunciated the unity of God. To the Veda, the Bráhmanas, and the Sútras, they added a vast body of theo-logical literature, composed at intervals between 800 B.C. and 1000 A.D. The Upanishads, meaning, according to their great Bráhman expounder, 'The Science of God,' and His 'identity with the soul;' the Aranyakas, or 'Tracts for the Forest-Recluse;' and the much later Puránas, or 'Traditions from of Old,'—contain mystic and beautiful doctrines inculcating the unity of God and the immortality of the soul, mingled with less noble dogmas, popular tales, and superstitions. The mass of the people were left to believe in four castes, four Vedas, and many deities. But the higher thinkers among the Bráhmans recognised that in the beginning there was but one caste, one Veda, and one God.

The old 'Shining Ones' of the Vedic singers were, indeed, Rise of the post-Vedic gods. no longer suitable deities, either for the life which the Aryans led after they advanced into Southern Bengal, or for the country

in which they lived. The Vedic gods were the good ' friends '
of the free-hearted warring tribes in Northern India, settled
The vast on the banks of fordable streams or of not overpowering rivers.
forces of
nature, In Central and South-Eastern Bengal, the Bráhmans required
deities whose nature and attributes would satisfy profoundly
reflective minds, and at the same time would be commensurate
with the stupendous forces of nature amid which they dwelt. The
storm-gods (*Maruts*) of the Veda might suffice to raise the
dust-whirlwinds of the Punjab, but they were evidently deities
on a smaller scale than those which wielded the irresistible
cyclones of Bengal. The rivers, too, had ceased to be merely
bountiful givers of wealth, as in the north. Their accumulated
in Bengal. waters came down in floods, which buried cities and drowned
provinces; wrenching away the villages on their banks, destroying and reproducing the land with an equal balance. The
High-born Dawn, the Genial Sun, the Friendly Day, and the
kindly but confused old groups of Vedic deities, accordingly
gave place to the conception of one god in his three solemn
manifestations as Brahmá the Creator, Vishnu the Preserver,
and Siva the Destroyer and Reproducer.

The Hindu Each of these highly elaborated gods had his prototype
Triad :
among the Vedic deities; and they remain to this hour the
Brahmá ; three persons of the Hindu Triad. Brahmá, the Creator, was
too abstract an idea to be a popular god ; and in a journey
through India, the traveller comes on only one great seat of
his worship at the present day, on the margin of the sacred
lake PUSHKARA, near Ajmere. A single day of Brahmá is
Vishnu ; 2160 millions of man's years. Vishnu, the Preserver, was a more
useful and practical deity. In his ten incarnations, especially
in his seventh and eighth, as Ráma and Krishna, under many
names and in varied forms, he took the place of the bright
Siva. Vedic gods. Siva, the third person of the Triad, embodied,
as Destroyer and Reproducer, the profound Bráhmanical conception of death as a change of state and an entry into new life.
He thus obtained, on the one hand, the special reverence of the
mystic and philosophic sects among the Bráhmans ; while, on
the other, his terrible aspects associated him alike with the
Rudra, or ' God of Roaring Tempests ' of the Veda, and with
the blood-loving deities of the non-Aryan tribes. Vishnu and
Siva, in their diverse male and female shapes, now form, for
practical purposes, the gods of the Hindu population.

Bráhman The truth is, that the Aryans in India worshipped—first, as
philoso-
phy. they feared ; then, as they admired ; and finally, as they reasoned.
Their earliest Vedic gods were the stupendous phenomena of

the visible world; these deities became divine heroes in the epic legends; and they were spiritualized into abstractions by the philosophical schools. From the Vedic era downward—that is to say, during a period which cannot be estimated at less than 3000 years—the Bráhmans have slowly elaborated the forces and splendid manifestations of nature into a harmonious godhead, and constructed a system of belief and worship for the Indian people. They also pondered deeply on the mysteries of life. Whence arose this fabric of the visible world, and whence came we ourselves—we who with conscious minds look out upon it? It is to these questions that philosophy has, among all races, owed her birth; and the Bráhmans arranged their widely diverse answers to them in six great systems or *darsanas*, literally 'mirrors of knowledge.'

The present sketch can only touch upon the vast body of speculation which thus grew up, at least 500 years before Christ. The universal insoluble problems of thought and being, of mind and matter, and of soul as apart from both, of the origin of evil, of the *summum bonum* of life, of necessity and freewill, and of the relations of the Creator to the creature, are in the six schools of Bráhmanical philosophy endlessly discussed. *The six darsanas or schools;*

The Sánkhya system of the sage Kapila explains the visible world by assuming the existence of a primordial matter from all eternity, out of which the universe has, by successive stages, evolved itself. The Yoga school of Patanjali assumes the existence of a primordial soul, anterior to the primeval matter, and holds that from the union of the two the spirit of life (*mahán-átmá*) arose. The two Vedanta schools ascribe the visible world to a divine act of creation, and assume an omnipotent god as the cause of the existence, the continuance, and the dissolution of the universe. The Nyáya or logical school of Gautama enunciates the method of arriving at truth, and lays special stress on the sensations as the source of knowledge. It is usually classed together with the sixth school, the Vaiseshika, founded by the sage Kanáda, which teaches the existence of a transient world composed of eternal atoms. All the six schools had the same starting-point, *ex nihilo nihil fit.* Their sages, as a rule, struggled towards the same end, namely the liberation of the human soul from the necessity of existence and from the chain of future births, by its absorption into the Supreme Soul, or primordial Essence of the universe.[1] *(1) The Sánkhya; (2) The Yoga; (3, 4) The Vedantas; (5) The Nyáya; (6) The Vaiseshika.*

[1] Any attempt to fuse into a few lines the vast conflicting masses of Hindu philosophical doctrines must be unsatisfactory. Objections may be taken to compressing the sub-divisions and branching doctrines of each

Summary of Bráhman religion.   The Bráhmans, therefore, treated philosophy as a branch of religion. Now the universal functions of religion are to lay down a rule of conduct for this life, and to supply some guide to the next. The Bráhman solutions to the problems of practical religion, were self-discipline, alms, sacrifice to and contemplation of the deity. But besides the practical questions of the spiritual life, religion has also intellectual problems, such as the compatibility of evil with the goodness of God, and the unequal distribution of happiness and misery in this life. Bráhman philosophy exhausted the possible solutions of these difficulties, and of most of the other great problems which have since perplexed Greek and Roman sage, mediæval schoolman, and modern man of science. The various hypotheses of Creation, Arrangement, and Development were each elaborated; and the views of physiologists at the present day are a return, with new lights, to the evolution theory of Kapila. His Sánkhya system is held by Weber to be the oldest of the six Bráhman schools, and certainly dates from not later than 500 B.C. The works on Religion published in the native languages in India in 1877 numbered 1192, besides 56 on Mental and Moral Philosophy. In 1882, the totals had risen to 1545 on Religion, and 153 on Mental and Moral Philosophy.

Bráhman science.   The Bráhmans had also a circle of sciences of their own. The Science of Language, indeed, had been reduced in India to fundamental principles at a time when the grammarians of the West still treated it on the basis of accidental resemblances; and modern philology dates from the study of Sanskrit by European scholars. Pánini was the architect of Sanskrit grammar; but a long succession of grammarians must have laboured before he reared his enduring fabric. The date of Pánini has been assigned by his learned editor Böhtlink to about 350 B.C. Weber, reasoning from a statement made (long afterwards) by the Chinese pilgrim Hiuen Tsiang, suggests that it may have been later. The grammar of Pánini stands supreme among the grammars of the world, alike for its precision of statement, and for its thorough analysis of the roots of the language and of the formative principles of words. By employing an algebraic terminology it attains a sharp succinctness unrivalled in brevity, but at times enigmatical. It arranges, in logical harmony, the whole phenomena

Sanskrit grammar.

Pánini.

school into a single sentence. But space forbids a more lengthy disquisition. The foregoing paragraphs endeavour to fairly condense the accounts which H. H. Wilson, Albrecht Weber, Professor Dowson, and the Rev. K. M. Banarjí give of the Six *Darsanas* or Schools.

which the Sanskrit language presents, and stands forth as one of the most splendid achievements of human invention and industry. So elaborate is the structure, that doubts have arisen whether its complex rules of formation and phonetic change, its polysyllabic derivatives, its ten conjugations with their multiform aorists and long array of tenses, could ever have been the spoken language of a people. This question will be discussed in the chapter on the modern vernaculars of India.

It is certain that a divergence had taken place before the time of Pánini (350 B.C.), and that the spoken language, or *Prákrita-bháshá,* had already assumed simpler forms by the assimilation of consonants and the curtailment of terminals. The *Samskrita-bháshá,* literally, the 'perfected speech,' which Pánini stereotyped by his grammar, developed the old Aryan tendency to accumulations of consonants, with an undiminished, or perhaps an increased, array of inflections. In this highly elaborated Sanskrit the Bráhmans wrote. It became the literary language of India,—isolated from the spoken dialects, but prescribed as the vehicle for philosophy, science, and all poetry of serious aim or epic dignity. As the Aryan race mingled with the previous inhabitants of the land, the spoken Prákrits adopted words of non-Aryan origin and severed themselves from Sanskrit, which for at least 2000 years has been unintelligible to the common people of India. The old synthetic spoken dialects, or Prákrits, underwent the same decay as Latin did, into analytic vernaculars, and about the same time. The noble parent languages, alike in India and in Italy, died; but they gave birth to families of vernaculars which can never die. *[margin: Sanskrit and Prákrit speech.]*

An intermediate stage of the process can be traced in the Hindu drama, in which persons of good birth speak in Prákritized Sanskrit, and the low-castes in a *bháshá,* or patois, between the old Prákrit and the modern dialects. It is chiefly under the popularizing influences of British rule that the Indian vernaculars have become literary languages. Until the last century, Sanskrit, although as dead as Latin so far as the mass of the people were concerned, was the vehicle for all intellectual and artistic effort among the Hindus, their local ballads and the writings of religious reformers excepted. In addition, therefore, to other sources of influence, the Bráhmans were the interpreters of a national literature written in a language unknown to the people.

The priceless inheritance thus committed to their charge they handed down, to a great extent, by word of mouth. Partly *[margin: Sanskrit manuscripts.]*

No very
ancient
Indian
MSS.

from this cause, but chiefly owing to the destructive climate of India, no Sanskrit manuscripts of remote antiquity exist. A fairly continuous series of inscriptions on rocks, pillars, and copper-plates, enable us to trace back the Indian alphabets to the 3rd century B.C.   But the more ancient of existing Sanskrit manuscripts are only four hundred years old, very few have an age exceeding five centuries, and only two date as far back as 1132 and 1008 A.D.[1]   The earliest Indian MS.

1008 A.D.

(1008 A.D.) comes from the cold, dry highlands of Nepál.[2]   In Kashmír, birch-bark was extensively used : a substitute for paper also employed in India before 500 A.D., and still surviving in the amulets with verses on them which hang round the neck of Hindus.[3]   Indeed, birch-bark is to this day used by some native merchants in the Simla Hills for their account books.

Palm-leaf
MSS. of
Japan.

The palm-leaf was, however, the chief writing material in ancient and mediæval India.   Two Sanskrit manuscripts on this substance have been preserved in the Monastery of Horiûzi in Japan since the year 609 A.D.   It seems probable that these two strips of palm-leaf were previously the property of a

520 A.D. ?

Buddhist monk who migrated from India to China in 520 A.D.[4] At any rate, they cannot date later than the first half of the 6th century ; and they are the oldest Sanskrit manuscripts yet discovered.   They were photographed in the *Anecdota Oxoniensia*, 1884.

The
Indian
Alphabets.

With regard to the origin of the Indian alphabets, the evidence is still too undigested to safely permit of cursory statement.   Of the two characters in which the Asoka inscriptions were written (250 A.D.), the northern variety, or Ariano-Páli, is now admitted to be of Phœnician, or at any rate of non-Indian,

---

[1] Footnote 198a to Weber's *Hist. Ind. Lit.* p. 182 (1878), quoting the report of Rájendrá Lálá Mitra (1874), and Dr. Rost's letter (1875).   Mr. R. Cust, in a note for *The Imperial Gazetteer of India*, assigns the year 883 A.D. as the date of the earliest existing Sanskrit MS. at Cambridge.   But this remains doubtful.   For very interesting information regarding the age of Indian MSS. see the official reports of the Search for Sanskrit Manuscripts in Bengal, Bombay, and Madras ; particularly Dr. G. Bühler's (extra number of the *Journal of the Bombay Branch of the Royal Asiatic Society*, No. xxxiv.A, vol. xii. 1877), and Professor P. Peterson's (extra numbers of the same Journal, xli. 1883, and xliv. 1884).

[2] The present author has printed and sent to the India Office Library, for public reference, a catalogue of the 332 Sanskrit Buddhist MSS. collected by Mr. B. H. Hodgson in Nepál.

[3] Dr. Bühler's *Tour in Search for Sanskrit MSS.*, *Journal Bombay Asiatic Society*, xxxiv.A, p. 29, and footnote.   1877.

[4] *Anecdota Oxoniensia*, Aryan Series, p. 64, vol. i. Part III. (1884.)   See also Part I. of the volume, and pp. 3, 4 of Part III.

parentage. The southern variety, or Indo-Páli, is believed by some scholars to be of Western origin, while others hold it to be an independent Indian alphabet. An attempt has even been made to trace back its letters to an indigenous system of picture-writing, or hieroglyphs, in pre-historic India.[1] Quintus Curtius mentions that the Indians wrote on leaves in the time of Alexander (326 B.C.).[2] They do so to this hour. Few, if any, Indian manuscripts on paper belong to a period anterior to the 16th century A.D. The earliest Indian writings are on copper or stone; the mediæval ones generally on strips of palm-leaves. General Cunningham possesses a short inscription, written with ink in the inside of a lid made of soapstone, dating from the time of Asoka, or 256 B.C. The introduction of paper as a writing material may be studied in the interesting collection of Sanskrit manuscripts at the Deccan College, Poona.

Sanskrit literature was the more easily transmitted by word of mouth, from the circumstance that it was almost entirely written in verse. A prose style, simple and compact, had grown up during the early age following that of the Vedic hymns. But Sanskrit literature begins with the later, although still ancient, stage of Aryan development, which superseded the Vedic gods by the Bráhmanical Triad of Brahmá, Vishnu, and Siva. When Sanskrit appears definitively on the scene in the centuries preceding the birth of Christ, it adopted once and for all a rhythmic versification alike for poetry, philosophy, science, law, and religion, with the exception of the Beast Fables and the almost algebraic strings of aphorisms in the Sútras. The Buddhist legends adhered more closely to the spoken dialects of ancient India, *prákrita-bháshá ;* and they also have retained a prose style. But in classical Sanskrit literature, prose became an arrested development; the *sloka* or verse reigned supreme; and nothing can be clumsier than the attempts at prose in later Sanskrit romances and commentaries. Prose-

Sanskrit writings almost entirely in verse.

Prose, a forgotten art.

---

[1] By General Cunningham, *Corpus Inscriptionum Indicarum*, pp. 52 *et seq.* The attempt cannot be pronounced successful. Dr. Burnell's *Palæography of Southern India* exhibits the successive developments of the Indian alphabet. For the growth of the Indian dialects, see Mr. Beames' *Comparative Grammar of the Modern Aryan Languages of India ;* Dr. Rudolph Hœrnle's *Comparative Grammar of the Gaudian Languages ;* two excellent papers, by Mr. E. L. Brandreth, on the Gaudian Languages, in the *Journ. Roy. As. Soc.*, vols. xi. xii.; and Mr. R. N. Cust's *Linguistic and Oriental Essays*, pp. 144–171, Trübner, 1880. For a compendious view of the Indian alphabets, see Faulmann's *Buch der Schrift*, 119–158, Vienna, 1880.

[2] *Alexander in India*, lib. viii. cap. 9, v. 15.

writing was practically a lost art in India during eighteen hundred years.

Sanskrit diction- aries.

Sanskrit dictionaries are a more modern product than Sanskrit grammars. The oldest Indian lexicographer whose work survives, Amara-Sinha, ranked among the 'nine gems' at the court of Vikramáditya, one of several monarchs of the same name—assigned to various periods from 56 B.C. to 1050 A.D. The particular Vikramáditya under whom the 'nine gems' are said to have flourished, appears from evidence in Hiuen Tsiang's travels to have lived about 500 to 550 A.D. A well-known memorial verse makes Amara-Sinha a contemporary of Varáha-Mihira, the astronomer, 504 A.D. The other Sanskrit lexicons which have come down belong to the 11th, 12th, and subsequent centuries A.D. Those centuries, indeed, seem to

The Amara- kosha, 550 A.D. ?

mark an era of industry in Sanskrit dictionary - making ; and there is little inherent evidence in Amara - Sinha's work (the Amara-kosha) to show that, in its present form, it was separated from them by any wide interval. The number of works on language published in 1877 in the Indian tongues, was 604 ; and in 1882, 738.

Bráhman astronomy.

The astronomy of the Bráhmans has formed alternately the subject of excessive admiration and of misplaced contempt. The truth is, that there are three periods of Sanskrit astronomy

Indepen- dent period, to 500 B.C.

(*Jyoti-sástra*). The first period belongs to Vedic times, and has left a moderate store of independent observations and inferences worked out by the Bráhmans. The Vedic poets had arrived at a tolerably correct calculation of the solar year ; which they divided into 360 days, with an intercalary month every five years. They were also acquainted with the phases of the moon ; they divided her pathway through the heavens into 27 or 28 lunar mansions ; and they had made observations of a few of the fixed stars. The order in which the lunar mansions are enumerated is one which must have been established 'somewhere between 1472 and 536 B.C.' (Weber). The planets were also an independent, although a later discovery, bordering on the Vedic period. At first seven, afterwards nine in number, they bear names of Indian origin ; and the generic term for planet, *graha*, the seizer, had its source in primitive Sanskrit astrology. The planets are mentioned for the first time, perhaps, in the Taittiríya-Aryanaka. The Laws of Manu, however, are silent regarding them ; but their worship is inculcated in the later code of Yájnavalkya. The zodiacal signs and the Jyotisha, or so-called Vedic Calendar,—with its solstitial points referring to 1181 B.C., or to a period still more remote,—seem to have

parentage. The southern variety, or Indo-Páli, is believed by some scholars to be of Western origin, while others hold it to be an independent Indian alphabet. An attempt has even been made to trace back its letters to an indigenous system of picture-writing, or hieroglyphs, in pre-historic India.[1] Quintus Curtius mentions that the Indians wrote on leaves in the time of Alexander (326 B.C.).[2] They do so to this hour. Few, if any, Indian manuscripts on paper belong to a period anterior to the 16th century A.D. The earliest Indian writings are on copper or stone; the mediæval ones generally on strips of palm-leaves. General Cunningham possesses a short inscription, written with ink in the inside of a lid made of soapstone, dating from the time of Asoka, or 256 B.C. The introduction of paper as a writing material may be studied in the interesting collection of Sanskrit manuscripts at the Deccan College, Poona.

Sanskrit literature was the more easily transmitted by word of mouth, from the circumstance that it was almost entirely written in verse. A prose style, simple and compact, had grown up during the early age following that of the Vedic hymns. But Sanskrit literature begins with the later, although still ancient, stage of Aryan development, which superseded the Vedic gods by the Bráhmanical Triad of Brahmá, Vishnu, and Siva. When Sanskrit appears definitively on the scene in the centuries preceding the birth of Christ, it adopted once and for all a rhythmic versification alike for poetry, philosophy, science, law, and religion, with the exception of the Beast Fables and the almost algebraic strings of aphorisms in the Sútras. The Buddhist legends adhered more closely to the spoken dialects of ancient India, *prákrita-bháshá;* and they also have retained a prose style. But in classical Sanskrit literature, prose became an arrested development; the *sloka* or verse reigned supreme; and nothing can be clumsier than the attempts at prose in later Sanskrit romances and commentaries. Prose-

Sanskrit writings almost entirely in verse.

Prose, a forgotten art.

---

[1] By General Cunningham, *Corpus Inscriptionum Indicarum,* pp. 52 *et seq.* The attempt cannot be pronounced successful. Dr. Burnell's *Palæography of Southern India* exhibits the successive developments of the Indian alphabet. For the growth of the Indian dialects, see Mr. Beames' *Comparative Grammar of the Modern Aryan Languages of India;* Dr. Rudolph Hœrnle's *Comparative Grammar of the Gaudian Languages;* two excellent papers, by Mr. E. L. Brandreth, on the Gaudian Languages, in the *Journ. Roy. As. Soc.,* vols. xi. xii.; and Mr. R. N. Cust's *Linguistic and Oriental Essays,* pp. 144-171, Trübner, 1880. For a compendious view of the Indian alphabets, see Faulmann's *Buch der Schrift,* 119-158, Vienna, 1880.

[2] *Alexander in India,* lib. viii. cap. 9, v. 15.

of De la Hire, published in 1702, before the French accepted the Newtonian Astronomy. The Rájá left, as a monument of
Rájá ot Jaipur's observatories, 1728.
his skill, lists of stars collated by himself, known as the Tij Muhammad Sháhi, or Tables of Muhammad Sháh, the Emperor of Delhi, by whose command he undertook the reformation of the Indian Calendar. His observatory at Benares survives to this day; and elsewhere, his huge astronomical structures testify, by their ruins, to the ambitious character of his observations. Nevertheless, Hindu astronomy steadily declined. From Vedic times it had linked omens and portents with the study of the heavens. Under the Muhammadan dynasties it degenerated into a tool of trade in the hands of almanac-makers, genealogists, astrologers, and charlatans. It is doubtful how far even Rájá Jai Singh's observations were conducted by native astronomers. It is certain that the Catholic missionaries contributed greatly to his reputation; and that since the sixteenth century the astronomy of the Hindus, as of the Chinese, is deeply indebted to the science of the Jesuits.

Bráhman mathematics.
In algebra and arithmetic, the Bráhmans attained to a high degree of proficiency independent of Western aid. To them we owe the invention of the numerical symbols on the decimal system; the Indian figures 1 to 9 being abbreviated forms of the initial letters of the numerals themselves,[1] and the zero, or 0, representing the first letter of the Sanskrit word for empty (*súnya*). The correspondence of the numeral figures with the initial letters of their Indian names, can be clearly traced in the Lúndi character, a cursive form of writing still used in the Punjab, especially among the hereditary trading castes. The Arabs borrowed these figures from the Hindus, called them the 'Indian cyphers,' and transmitted them to Europe. The Arabian mathematicians, indeed, frequently extol the learning of the Indians; and the Sanskrit term for the apex of a planet's orbit seems to have passed into the Latin translations of the Arabic astronomers.[2] The works on mathematics and mechanical science, published in the native languages in India in 1877, numbered 89; and, in 1882, 166.

Bráhman medicine.
The medical science of the Bráhmans was also an independent development. The national astronomy and the national medicine of India alike derived their first impulses from the exigencies of the national worship. Observations of the

---

[1] Dr. Burnell, however, questioned this generally accepted view, and suggested that the old cave numerals of India are themselves of Greek origin.

[2] The Sanskrit *uccha* has become the *aux* (gen. *augis*) of the Latin translators (Reinaud, p. 525; Weber, p. 257).

heavenly bodies were required to fix the dates of the recurring festivals ; anatomical knowledge took its origin in the dissection of the victim at the sacrifice, with a view to dedicating the different parts to the proper gods. The Hindus ranked their Its inde- medical science as an *upa-veda*, or a supplementary revelation, pendent under the title of Ayur-Veda, and ascribed it to the gods. develop- ment, 4th But their earliest medical authorities belong to the Sútra century period, or later scholastic development, of the Yájur-Veda. B.C. to 8th century The specific diseases whose names occur in Pánini's Grammar A.D. : indicate that medical studies had made progress before his time (350 B.C.). The chapter on the human body in the earliest Sanskrit dictionary, the Amara-kosha (*circ.* 550 A.D.), presupposes a systematic cultivation of the science. The works of the great Indian physicians, Charaka and Susruta, were translated into Arabic not later than the 8th century.

Unlike the astronomical treatises of the Bráhmans, the The basis Hindu medical works never refer to the Yavanas, or Greeks, of Arabic and as authorities ; and, with one doubtful exception, they con- European tain no names which point to a foreign origin. The chief seat medicine. of the science was at Benares, far to the east of Greek influence in India. Indeed, Indian pharmacy employed the weights and measures of Provinces still farther to the south-east, namely, Magadha and Kalinga. Arabic medicine was founded on the translations from the Sanskrit treatises, made by command of the Kaliphs of Bagdad, 750–960 A.D. European medicine, down to the 17th century, was based upon the Arabic ; and the name of the Indian physician Charaka repeatedly occurs in the Latin translations of Avicenna (Ibn Sina), Rhazes (Al Rasi), and Serapion (Ibn Serabi).

Indian medicine dealt with the whole area of the science. Scope of It described the structure of the body, its organs, ligaments, Indian medicine. muscles, vessels, and tissues. The *materia medica* of the Hindus embraces a vast collection of drugs belonging to the mineral, vegetable, and animal kingdoms, many of which have been adopted by European physicians. Their pharmacy contained ingenious processes of preparation, with elaborate directions for the administration and classification of medicines. Much attention was devoted to hygiene, to the regimen of the body, and to diet.

The surgery of the ancient Indian physicians appears to Indian have been bold and skilful. They conducted amputations, surgery. arresting the bleeding by pressure, a cup-shaped bandage, and boiling oil. They practised lithotomy ; performed operations in the abdomen and uterus ; cured hernia, fistula, piles ; set broken bones and dislocations; and were dexterous in the extraction of foreign substances from the body. A special branch of surgery was devoted to rhinoplasty, or operations for improving deformed ears and noses, and forming new ones; a useful operation in a country where mutilation formed part of the judicial system, and one which European surgeons have borrowed. It is practised with much success in the Residency Hospital at Indore, Holkar's capital; as jealous husbands in Native States still resort, in spite of more humane laws, to their ancient remedy against a suspected or unfaithful wife. This consists in throwing the woman violently down on the ground and slashing off her nose.

Nose-making.

The ancient Indian surgeons also mention a cure for neuralgia, analogous to the modern cutting of the fifth nerve above the eyebrow. They devoted great care to the making of surgical instruments, and to the training of students by means of operations performed on wax spread out on a board, or on the tissues and cells of the vegetable kingdom, and upon dead animals. They were expert in midwifery, not shrinking from the most critical operations; and in the diseases of women and children. Their practice of physic embraced the classification, causes, symptoms, and treatment of diseases, —diagnosis and prognosis. The maladies thus dealt with have been arranged into 10 classes, namely—those affecting (1) the humours; (2) the general system, including fevers; (3 to 9) the several organs and parts of the body; and (10) trivial complaints. Considerable advances were also made in veterinary science, and monographs exist on the diseases of horses and elephants.

Operation for neuralgia.

Veterinary surgery.

The best era of Indian medicine was contemporary with the ascendancy of Buddhism (250 B.C. to 750 A.D.), and did not long survive it. The science was studied in the chief centres of Buddhist civilisation, such as the great monastic university of Nalanda, near Gayá. The ancient Bráhmans may have derived the rudiments of anatomy from the dissection of the sacrifice; but the public hospitals which the Buddhist princes established in every city were probably the true schools of Indian medicine. A large number of cases were collected in them for continuous observation and treatment; and they supplied opportunities for the study of disease similar to those which the Greek physicians obtained at their hospital camps around the mineral springs. Hippokrates was a priest-physician, indeed the descendant of a line of priest-physicians, practising at such a spring; and Charaka was in many ways his Indian

Best age of Indian medicine, 250 B.C. to 750 A.D.

Buddhist public hospitals.

counterpart. To the present day, works on Hindu medicine frequently commence their sections with the words, ' Charaka says.' This half-mythical authority, and Susruta, furnish the types of the ancient Indian physician, and probably belong, so far as they were real personages, to about the commencement of the Christian era. Both appear as Bráhmans; Susruta being, according to tradition, the son of the sage Viswámitra (p. 92); and Charaka, of another ' Veda-learned Muni.'

As Buddhism passed into modern Hinduism (750–1000 A.D.), and the shackles of caste were reimposed with an iron rigour, the Bráhmans more scrupulously avoided contact with blood or morbid matter. They withdrew from the medical profession, and left it entirely in the hands of the Vaidyas; a lower caste, sprung from a Bráhman father and a mother of the Vaisya or cultivating class. These in their turn shrank more and more from touching dead bodies, and from those ancient operations on ' the carcase of a bullock,' etc., by which alone surgical skill could be acquired. The abolition of the public hospitals, on the downfall of Buddhism, must also have proved a great loss to Indian medicine. The series of Muhammadan conquests, commencing about 1000 A.D., brought in a new school of foreign physicians, who derived their knowledge from the Arabic translations of the Sanskrit medical works of the best period. These Musalmán doctors or *hakíms* monopolized the patronage of the Muhammadan princes and nobles of India. The decline of Hindu medicine went on until it has sunk into the hands of the village *kabiráj*, whose knowledge consists of jumbled fragments of the Sanskrit texts, and a by no means contemptible pharmacopœia; supplemented by spells, fasts, and quackery. While the dissection of the human body under Vesalius and Fabricius was giving birth to modern medicine in the 17th century, the best of the Hindu physicians were working upon the recollections of a long past age without any new lights.

On the establishment of medical colleges in India by the British Government, in the middle of the present century, the Muhammadan youth took advantage of them in disproportionately large numbers. But the Bráhmans and intellectual classes of the Hindus soon realized that those colleges were the doors to an honourable and a lucrative career. Having accepted the change, they strove with their characteristic industry and acuteness to place themselves at the head of it. In 1879, of the 1661 pupils in British medical schools throughout India, 950 were Hindus and 284 were

Revival of medicine in India.

Muhammadans, while the remaining 427 included Christians, Pársís, and all others. Of three Indian youths studying medicine at the University of Edinburgh during the same year, one belonged to the Káyasth or Hindu writer caste, another to the Vaidya or hereditary physician caste, and the third was a Bráhman. The number of medical works published in the native languages of India in 1877 amounted to 130; and in 1882 to 212, besides 87 on natural science, not including mathematics and mechanics.[1]

Hindu art of war.

The Bráhmans regarded not only medicine, but also the arts of war, music, and architecture as *upa-vedas,* or supplementary parts of their divinely-inspired knowledge. Viswámitra, the Vedic sage of royal warrior birth, who in the end attained to Bráhmanhood (p. 92), was the first teacher of the art of war (*dhanur-veda*). The Sanskrit epics prove that strategy had attained to the position of a recognised science before the birth of Christ, and the later Agni Purána devotes long sections to its systematic treatment.

Indian music.

The Indian art of music (*gándharva-veda*) was destined to exercise a wider influence. A regular system of notation had been worked out before the age of Pánini (350 B.C.), and the seven notes were designated by their initial letters. This notation passed from the Bráhmans through the Persians to Arabia, and was thence introduced into European music by Guido d'Arezzo at the beginning of the 11th century.[2] Some, indeed, suppose that our modern word *gamut* comes not from the Greek letter gamma, but from the Indian *gáma* (in Prákrit; in Sanskrit, *gráma*), literally 'a musical scale.'

Hindu music, after a period of excessive elaboration, sank under the Muhammadans into a state of arrested development. Of the 36 chief musicians in the time of Akbar, only 5 were Hindus. Not content with tones and semi-tones, the Indian

[1] For monographs on this interesting branch of Indian science, see the articles of Dr. E. Haas, 'Ueber die Ursprünge der Indischen Medizin, mit besonderem Bezug auf Susruta,' and 'Hippokrates und die Indische Medizin des Mittelalters,' *Zeitschrift der Deutschen Morgenländischen Gesellschaft* for 1876, p. 617, and 1877, p. 647; the 'Indische Medicin, Karaka,' of Professor Roth in the *Zeitschrift der Deutschen Morgenländischen Gesellschaft* for 1872, p. 441; the *Review of the History of Medicine among the Asiatics,* by T. A. Wise, M.D., 2 vols., 1867; H. H. Wilson's little essay, *Works,* iii. 269 (ed. 1864); the excellent summary in Weber's *History of Indian Literature,* Trübner, 1878; and Dr. Watts' *Dict. Economic Products of India* (Calcutta, 1885).

[2] Von Bohlen, *Das Alte Indien,* ii. 195 (1830); Benfey's *Indien* (Ersch & Gruber's *Encyclopædie,* xvii., 1840); quoted by Weber, *Hist. Ind. Lit.,* p. 272, footnote 315 (1878).

musicians employ a more minute sub-division, together with a number of sonal modifications, which the Western ear neither recognises nor enjoys. Thus they divide the octave into 22 sub-tones, instead of the 12 tones and semi-tones of the European scale. This is one of several fundamental differences, but it alone suffices to render Indian music barbaric to us; giving it the effect of a Scotch ballad in a minor key, sung intentionally a little out of tune.

Melodies which the Indian composer pronounces to be Its peculithe perfection of harmony, and which have for ages touched arities. the hearts and fired the imagination of Indian audiences, are condemned as discord by the European critic. The Hindu ear has been trained to recognise modifications of sound which the European ear refuses to take pleasure in. Our ears, on the other hand, have been taught to expect harmonic combinations for which Indian music substitutes different combinations of its own. The Indian musician declines altogether to be judged by the few simple Hindu airs which the English ear can appreciate. It is, indeed, impossible to adequately represent the Indian system by the European notation; and the full range of its effects can only be rendered by Indian instruments—a vast collection of sound - producers, slowly elaborated during 2000 years to suit the special requirements of Hindu music. The complicated structure of its musical modes (*rágs*) rests upon three separate systems, one of which consists of five, another of six, and the other of seven notes. It preserves in a living state some of the early forms which puzzle the student of Greek music, side by side with the most complicated developments.

Patriotic Hindus have of late endeavoured to bring about Revival of a musical revival upon the old Sanskrit basis. Within the Hindu music. past fifteen years, Rájá Sir Surendra Mohan Tagore of Calcutta has published a series of interesting works on Indian music in the English tongue, adopting as far as possible the European notation. He has organized an orchestra to illustrate the art; and presented complete collections of Hindu instruments to the Conservatoire at Paris, and to other institutions in Europe. One of the earliest subjects which the new movement took as its theme, was the celebration of the Queen of England and her ancestors, in a Sanskrit volume entitled the Victoria-Gítika (Calcutta, 1875). No Englishman has yet brought an adequate acquaintance with the *technique* of Indian instrumentation to the study of Hindu music. The art still awaits investigation by some eminent

Western professor; and the contempt with which Europeans in India regard it, merely proves their ignorance of the system on which Hindu music is built up.

Indian architec-ture.

Indian architecture (*artha-sástra*[1]), although also ranked as an *upa-veda* or supplementary part of inspired learning, derived its development from Buddhist rather than from Bráhmanical impulses. A brick altar sufficed for the Vedic ritual. The Buddhists were the great stone-builders of India. Their monasteries and shrines exhibit the history of the art during twenty-two centuries, from the earliest cave structures and rock-temples, to the latest Jain erections, dazzling in stucco and overcrowded with ornament. It seems not improbable that the churches of Europe owe their steeples to the Buddhist

Greco-Bactrian and

topes. The Greco-Bactrian kingdom profoundly influenced architecture and sculpture in Northern India ; the Musalmán conquerors brought in new forms and requirements of their own. Nevertheless, Hindu art powerfully asserted itself in the imperial works of the Mughals, and has left memorials which extort the admiration and astonishment of our age.

Muham-madan influences.

The Hindu builders derived from the Muhammadans a lightness of structure which they did not formerly possess. The Hindu palace-architecture of Gwalior, the Indian-Muham-madan mosques and mausoleums of Agra and Delhi, with several of the older Hindu temples of Southern India, stand unrivalled for grace of outline and elaborate wealth of orna-ment. The Táj-Mahal at Agra justifies Heber's exclamation, that its builders had designed like Titans, and finished like jewellers. The open-carved marble windows and screens at Ahmadábád furnish examples of the skilful ornamentation which beautifies every Indian building, from the cave monas-teries of the Buddhist period downward. They also show with what plasticity the Hindu architects adapted their Indian ornamentation to the structural requirements of the Muham-madan mosque.

Indian decorative art.

English decorative art in our day has borrowed largely from Indian forms and patterns. The exquisite scrolls on the rock-temples at Karli and Ajanta, the delicate marble tracery and flat wood-carving of Western India, the har-monious blending of forms and colours in the fabrics of Kashmír, have contributed to the restoration of taste in England. Indian art-work, when faithful to native designs, still obtains the highest honours at the international exhibitions of Europe. In pictorial art, the Hindus never

[1] Specifically, *nirmána-silpam*, or *nirmána-vidyá*.

made much progress, except in miniature-painting, for which Indian
perspective is not required. But some of the book-illustrations, painting.
executed in India under Persian impulses, are full of spirit
and beauty. The Royal library at Windsor contains the finest
existing examples in this by-path of art. The noble manuscript
of the *Sháh Jahán Námah*, purchased in Oudh for £1200 in the
last century, and now in possession of Her Majesty, will itself
amply repay a visit. The specimens at the South Kensington
Museum do not adequately represent Indian painting (1882).
But they are almost everything that could be desired as
regards Indian ornamental design, including Persian book-
binding, and several of the minor arts.

While the Bráhmans claimed religion, theology, and philo- Bráhman
sophy as their special domain, and the chief sciences and arts law.
as supplementary sections of their divinely-inspired knowledge,
they secured their social supremacy by codes of law. Their
earliest Dharma-sástras, or legal treatises, belong to the Grihyá- Grihyá-
Sútra period, a scholastic outgrowth from the Veda. But their 500 B.C.(?).
two great digests, upon which the fabric of Hindu jurisprudence
has been built up, are of later date. The first of these, the
code of Manu, is separated from the Vedic era by a series of The code
Bráhmanical developments, of which we possess only a few of of Manu.
the intermediate links. It is a compilation of the customary
law, current probably about the 5th century B.C., and exhibits
the social organization which the Bráhmans, after their
successful struggle for the supremacy, had established in the
Middle Land of Bengal. The Bráhmans, indeed, claim for
their laws a divine origin, and ascribe them to the first Manu
or Aryan man, 30 millions of years ago. But as a matter of
fact, the laws of Manu are the result of a series of attempts
to codify the usages of some not very extensive centre of
Bráhmanism in Northern India. They form a metrical digest of
local customs, condensed by degrees from a legendary mass of
100,000 couplets (*slokas*) into 2685. They may possibly have
been reduced to a written code with a view to securing the
system of caste against the popular movement of Buddhism ;
and they seem designed to secure a rigid fixity for the
privileges of the Bráhmans.

The date of the code of Manu has formed a favourite The age of
subject for speculation from the appearance of Sir William Manu.
Jones' translation [1] downwards. The history of those speculations is typical of the modernizing process which scholarship

---

[1] Calcutta, 1794 ; followed by Hüttner's translation into German, 1797.

has applied to the old pretensions of Indian literature. The present writer has refrained from anything approaching to dogmatic assertion in regard to the dates assigned to Vedic and Sanskrit works ; as such assertions would involve disquisitions quite beyond the scope of this volume.

Date of Manu?

It may, therefore, be well to take the code of Manu as a single instance of the uncertainty which attaches to the date of one of the best known of Indian treatises. Sir William Jones accepted for it a fabulous antiquity of 1250 to 500 B.C. Schlegel was confident that it could not be later than 1000 B.C. Professor Monier Williams puts it at 500 B.C., and Johaentgen

Older prose code 500-200 B.C. (?).

assigns 350 B.C. as the lowest possible date. Dr. Burnell, in his posthumous edition of the code,[1] discusses the question with admirable learning, and his conclusions must, for the present, be accepted as authoritative. As indicated in a recent paragraph, the code of Manu, or Mánava-Dharmasástra, is not in its existing metrical form an original treatise, but a versified recension of an older prose code. In its earlier shape it belonged to the Sútra period, probably extending from the

Present metrical code 100-500 A.D.

sixth to the second century B.C. Dr. Burnell's investigations show that our present code of Manu was a popular work intended for princes or Rájás, and their officials, rather than a technical treatise for the Bráhmans. They also prove that the present code must have been compiled between 100 and

Probably 500 A.D.

500 A.D. ; and they indicate the latter date as the most probable one, viz. 500 A.D. ' It thus appears,' concludes Dr. Burnell, 'that the text belongs to an outgrowth of the Bráhmanical literature, which was intended for the benefit of the kings, when the Bráhmanical civilisation had begun to extend itself over the south of India.'[2]

Code of Yájna-valkya.

The second great code of the Hindus, called after Yájna-valkya, belongs to a period when Buddhism had established itself, and probably to a territory where it was beginning to succumb to the Bráhmanical reaction. It represents the Bráhmanical side of the great controversy (although a section of it deals with the organization of Buddhist monasteries),

6th century A.D. ?

refers to the execution of deeds on metal plates, and altogether marks an advance in legal precision. It refers more especially to the customs and state of society in the kingdom of Míthila, now the Tirhút and Purniyá Districts, after the Aryans had securely settled themselves in the Gangetic Provinces to the

---

[1] *The Ordinances of Manu,* by the late Arthur Coke Burnell, Ph.D., C.I.E., of the Madras Civil Service. Trübner. 1884. Pp. xv.-xlvii.

[2] *Idem,* xxvii.

east and south-east of their old Middle Land of Bengal. The Miták-
Mitákshará commentary of the law which bears the name of shará.
Yájnavalkya is in force over almost all India except Lower
Bengal Proper; and the Hindus, as a whole, allow to
Yájnavalkya an authority only second to that of Manu.
Yájnavalkya's code was compiled apparently not later than the
6th or 7th century A.D. It is right again to mention that much
earlier periods have been assigned both to Manu and Yájnavalkya than those adopted here. Duncker still accepts the
old date of 600 B.C. as that at which Manu's code 'must have
been put together and written down.'[1]

These codes deal with Hindu law in three branches, Scope of
namely—(1) domestic and civil rights and duties; (2) the Hindu
administration of justice; (3) purification and penance. They law.
stereotyped the unwritten usages which regulated the family
life and social organization of the old Aryan communities in
the Middle Land of Bengal. They did not pretend to supply
a body of law for all the numerous races of India, but only
for Hindu communities of the Bráhmanical type. It is doubtful whether they correctly represented the actual customary
law even among the Hindu communities in the Middle Land
of the Ganges. For they were evidently designed to assert and
maintain the special privileges of the Bráhmans. This they
effected by a rigid demarcation of the employments of the
people, each caste or division of a caste having its own hereditary
occupation assigned to it; by stringent rules against the inter- Its rigid
mingling of the castes in marriage; by forbidding the higher caste
castes, under severe penalties, to eat or drink or hold social system.
intercourse with the lower; and by punishing the lower castes
with cruel penances, for defiling by their touch the higher
castes, or in any way infringing their privileges.

They exhibit the Hindu community in the four ancient Legal
classes of priests, warriors, cultivators, and serfs (*súdras*). division of
But they disclose that this old Aryan classification failed to the people.
represent the actual facts even among the Aryan communities
in Northern India. They admit that the mass of the people
did not belong to any one of the four castes, and they
very inadequately ascribe it to concubinage or illicit connections. The ancient Bráhmanical communities in Northern
India, as revealed by the codes, consisted—First, of an Aryan The actual
element divided into priests, warriors, and cultivators, all of division of
whom bore the proud title of the Twice-Born, and wore the the people.
sacred thread. Second, the subjugated races, 'the once-born'

[1] *Ancient History of India*, by Professor Max Duncker, p. 195, ed. 1881.

Súdras.   Third, a vast residue termed the Varna-sankara, literally the 'mingled colours;' a great but uncertain number of castes, exceeding 300, to whom was assigned a mixed descent from the four recognised classes.   The first British Census of India, in 1872, proved that the same division remains the fundamental one of the Hindu community to this day.

Growth of Hindu law.   As the Bráhmans spread their influence eastwards and southwards from the Middle Land of Bengal, they carried their codes with them.   The number of their sacred law-books (Dharma-sástras) amounted to at least fifty-six, and separate schools of Hindu law sprang up.   Thus the Dáya-bhága version of the Law of Inheritance prevails in Bengal; while the Mitákshará commentary on Yájnavalkya is current in Madras and throughout Southern and Western India.   But all modern recensions of Hindu law rest upon the two codes of Manu or of Yájnavalkya; and these codes, as we have seen, only recorded the usages of certain Bráhmanical centres in the north, and perhaps did not fairly record even them.

As the Bráhmans gradually moulded the population of India into Hinduism, such codes proved too narrow a basis for dealing with the rights, duties, and social organization of the people.

Based on customary law.   Later Hindu legislators accordingly inculcated the recognition of the local usages or land-law of each part of the country, and of each class or tribe.   While binding together, and preserving the historical unity of, the Aryan twice-born castes by systems of law founded on their ancient codes, they made provision for the customs and diverse stages of civilisation of the ruder peoples of India, over whom they established their ascendency.   By such provisions, alike in religion and in law, the Bráhmans incorporated the Indian races into that loosely coherent mass known as the Hindu population.

Plasticity of Hinduism.   It is to this plastic element that Hinduism owes its success; and it is an element which English administrators have sometimes overlooked.   The races of British India exhibit many stages of domestic institutions, from the polyandry of the Nairs to the polygamy of the Kulin Bráhmans.   The structure of their rural organization varies, from the nomadic husbandry of the hillmen, to the long chain of tenures which in Bengal descends from the landlord through a series of middle-men to the actual tiller of the soil.   Every stage in industrial progress is represented; from the hunting tribes of the central plateau to the rigid trade-guilds of Gujarát.   The Hindu legislators recognised that each of these diverse stages of social development had its own usages and unwritten law.   Even

the code of Manu acknowledged custom as a source of law, Incor-
and admitted its binding force when not opposed to express law. poration
Vrihaspati says, 'The laws (*dharma*) practised by the various customs
countries, castes, and tribes, they are to be preserved; other- into
wise the people are agitated.' Devala says, 'What gods there Hinduism.
are in any country, . . . and whatsoever be the custom and
law anywhere, they are not to be despised there; the law there
is such.' Varáha-Mihira says, 'The custom of the country is
first to be considered; what is the rule in each country, that
is to be done.' A learned English judge in Southern India
thus summed up the texts : ' By custom only can the Dharma-
sástra [Hindu law] be the rule of others than Bráhmans [only
one-thirtieth of the population of Madras]; and even in the
case of Bráhmans it is very often superseded by custom.'[1]

The English, on assuming the government of India, wisely Perils of
declared that they would administer justice according to the modern
customs of the people. But our High Courts enforce the codifica-
Bráhmanical codes with a comprehensiveness and precision tion.
unknown in ancient India. Thus in Bengal, the non-Hindu
custom of *sagai*, by which deserted or divorced wives among
the lower castes marry again, was lately tried according to
'the spirit of Hindu law;' while in Madras, judges have
pointed out a serious divergence between the Hindu law as
now administered, and the actual usages of the people. Those
usages are unwritten and uncertain. The Hindu law is printed
in many accessible forms;[2] and Hindu barristers are ever
pressing its principles upon our courts. The Hindu law is
apt to be applied to non-Hindu, or semi-Hindu, customs.

Efforts at comprehensive codification in British India are
thus surrounded by special difficulties. For it would be im-
proper to give the fixity of a code to all the unwritten half-
fluid usages current among the 300 unhomogeneous castes
of Hindus ; while it might be fraught with future injustice
to exclude any of them. Each age has the gift of adjusting

---

[1] Dr. Burnell's *Dáya-vibhágha*, Introd. p. xv. See also *Hindu Law
as administered by the High Court of Judicature at Madras*, by J. Nelson,
M.A., District Judge of Cuddapah, chaps. iii. and iv. (Madras, 1877);
and *Journal Roy. As. Soc.*, pp. 208-236 (April 1881).

[2] For the latest treatment of Hindu law from the philosophical, scholarly,
and practical points of view, see the third edition of West and Bühler's
Digest of the Hindu Law of Inheritance, Partition, and Adoption. 2 vols.
Bombay 1884. From the writings of Mayne, Burnell, and Nelson in
Madras, and those of the Honourable Raymond West and Dr. Bühler
in Bombay, a new and more just conception of the character of Hindu law
and of its relations to Indian custom may be said to date.

Codes *versus* survival of fittest customs.   its institutions to its actual wants, especially among tribes whose customs have not been reduced to written law.   Many of those customs will, if left to themselves, die out.   Others of them, which prove suited to the new social developments under British rule, will live.   A code should stereotype the survival of the fittest ; but the process of natural selection must be the work of time, and not an act of conscious legislation.

Restricted scope of Indian codification.   This has been recognised from time to time by the ablest of Anglo-Indian codifiers.   They restrict the word code to the systematic arrangement of the rules relating to some well-marked section of juristic rights, or to some executive department of the administration of justice.   'In its larger sense,' write the Indian Law Commissioners in 1879, 'of a general assemblage of all the laws of a community, no attempt has yet been made in this country to satisfy the conception of a code.   The time for its realization has manifestly not arrived.'   The number of works on Law, published in the native languages of India in 1877, was 165 ; and in 1882, 181, besides 157 in English ; total, 338 works on law published in India in 1882.

Secular literature of the Hindus.   The Bráhmans were not merely the depositaries of the sacred books, the philosophy, the science, and the laws of the ancient Hindu commonwealth ; they were also the creators and custodians of its secular literature.   They had a practical monopoly of Vedic learning, and their policy was to trace back every branch of knowledge and of intellectual effort to the Veda.   In this policy they were aided by the divergence which, as we have seen, arose at a very early date between the written and spoken languages of India.   Sanskrit literature, apart from religion, philosophy, and law, consists mainly of two great epics, the drama, and a vast body of legendary, erotic, and mystical poetry.

Its chief branches.

The Mahá-bhárata ;   The venerable epic of the Mahábhárata ranks first.   The orthodox legend ascribes it to the sage Vyása, who, according to Bráhman chronology, compiled the inspired hymns into the four Vedas, nearly five thousand years ago (3101 B.C.).   But one beauty of Sanskrit is that every word discloses its ancient origin in spite of mediæval fictions, and Vyása means simply the 'arranger,' from the verb 'to fit together.'   No fewer than twenty-eight Vyásas, incarnations of Brahma and Vishnu, came down in successive astronomical eras to arrange and promulgate the Vedas on earth.   Many of the legends in the Mahábhárata are of Vedic antiquity, and the main story deals with a period assigned, in the absence of conclusive evidence, to about 1200 B.C. ; and certainly long anterior to the time of Buddha, 543 B.C. But its compilation into its present form seems to have taken place many centuries later.

Pánini (350 B.C.) makes no clear reference to it. The in- Its date ; quisitive Greek ambassador and historian, Megasthenes, does not appear to have heard of it during his stay in India, 300 B.C. Dion Chrysostomos supplies the earliest external evidence of the existence of the Mahábhárata, *circ.* 75 A.D. The arrangement of its vast mass of legends must probably have covered a long period. Indeed, the present poem bears traces of three separate eras of compilation ; during which its collection of primitive folk-tales grew from 8800 *slokas* Its or couplets, into a cyclopædia of Indian mythology and growth. legendary lore extending over eighteen books and 220,000 lines. The twenty-four books of Homer's *Iliad* comprise only 15,693 lines ; the twelve books of Virgil's *Æneid*, only 9868.

The central story of the Mahábhárata occupies scarcely Central one-fourth of the whole, or about 50,000 lines. It narrates story of a pre-historic struggle between two families of the Lunar bhárata. race for a patch of country near Delhi. These families, alike descended from the royal Bharata, consisted of two brotherhoods, cousins to each other, and both brought up under the same roof. The five Pándavas were the miraculously born sons of King Pándu, who, smitten by a curse, resigned the sovereignty to his brother Dhrita-ráshtra, and retired to a hermitage in the Himálayas, where he died. The ruins of his capital, Hastinápura, or the 'Elephant City,' are pointed out beside a deserted bed of the Ganges, 57 miles north-east of Delhi, at this day. His brother Dhrita-ráshtra ruled in his stead, and to him one hundred sons were born, who took the name of the Kauravas from an ancestor, Kuru. Dhrita-ráshtra acted as a faithful guardian to his five nephews, the Pándavas, and chose the eldest of them as heir to the family kingdom. His own sons resented this act of supersession ; and so arose the quarrel between the hundred Kauravas and the five Pándavas which forms the main story of the Mahábhárata. The nucleus of the legend probably belongs to the period when the Aryan immigrants were settling in the upper part of the triangle 12th cenof territory between the Jumna and the Ganges, and before tury B.C. they had made any considerable advances beyond the latter river. It is not unreasonable to assign this period to about the 12th century B.C.

The hundred Kauravas forced their father to send away their Its outline.

five Pándava cousins into the forest. The Kauravas then burned
down the woodland hut in which the five Pándavas dwelt. The
five escaped, however, and wandered in the disguise of Bráhmans to the court of King Draupada, who had proclaimed a
swayam-vara, or maiden's-choice,—a tournament at which his
daughter would take the victor as her husband. Arjuna, one
of the Pándavas, bent the mighty bow which had defied the
strength of all the rival chiefs, and so obtained the fair princess,
Draupadí, who became the common wife of the five brethren.
Their uncle, the good Dhrita-ráshtra, recalled them to his
capital, and gave them one-half of the family territory towards
the Jumna, reserving the other half for his own sons.

The Pándava brethren hived off to their new settlement,
Indra-prastha, afterwards Delhi ; clearing the jungle, and
driving out the Nágas or forest-races. For a time peace
reigned ; but the Kauravas tempted Yudishthira, 'firm in
fight,' the eldest of the Pándavas, to a gambling match, at
Gambling which he lost his kingdom, his brothers, himself, and last of
matches. all, his wife. Their father, however, forced his sons to restore
their wicked gains to their cousins. But Yudishthira was
again seduced by the Kauravas to stake his kingdom at dice,
again lost it, and had to retire with his wife and brethren
into exile for twelve years. Their banishment ended, the five
Pándavas returned at the head of an army to win back their
Final kingdom. Many battles followed. Other Aryan tribes between
overthrow the Jumna and the Ganges, together with their gods and divine
of the 100 heroes, joined in the struggle, until at last all the hundred
Kauravas. Kauravas were slain, and of the friends and kindred of the
Pándavas only the five brethren remained.

Reign of   Their uncle, Dhrita-ráshtra, made over to them the whole
the five kingdom ; and for a long time the Pándavas ruled gloriously,
Pándavas. celebrating the *aswa-medha,* or 'great horse sacrifice,' in token
of their holding imperial sway. But their uncle, old and blind,
ever taunted them with the slaughter of his hundred sons,
until at last he crept away with his few surviving ministers,
his aged wife, and his sister-in-law the mother of the Pándavas,
to a hermitage, where the worn-out band perished in a forest
fire. The five brethren, smitten by remorse, gave up their
kingdom ; and taking their wife, Draupadí, and a faithful dog,
Their pil- they departed to the Himálayas to seek the heaven of Indra
grimage to on Mount Meru. One by one the sorrowful pilgrims died upon
heaven. the road, until only the eldest brother, Yudishthira, and the
dog reached the gate of heaven. Indra invited him to enter,
but he refused if his lost wife and brethren were not also

admitted. The prayer was granted, but he still declined unless his faithful dog might come in with him. This could not be allowed, and Yudishthira, after a glimpse of heaven, was thrust down to hell, where he found many of his old comrades in anguish. He resolved to share their sufferings rather than enjoy paradise alone. But having triumphed in this crowning trial, the whole scene was revealed to be *máyá* or illusion, and the reunited band entered into heaven, where they rest for ever with Indra.

Even this story, which forms merely the nucleus of the Mahábhárata, is the collective growth of far-distant ages. For example, the two last books, the 17th and 18th, which narrate 'the Great Journey' and 'the Ascent to Heaven,' are the product of a very different epoch of thought from the early ones, which portray the actual life of courts and camps in ancient India. The *swayam-vara* or husband-choosing of Draupadí is a genuine relic of the tournament age of Aryan chivalry. Her position as the common wife of the five brethren preserves a trace of even more primitive institutions —institutions still represented by the polyandry of the Nairs and Himálayan tribes, and by domestic customs which are survivals of polyandry among the Hinduized low-castes all over India. Thus, in the Punjab, among Ját families too poor to bear the marriage expenses of all the males, the wife of the eldest son has sometimes to accept her brothers-in-law as joint husbands. The polyandry of the Ghakkars, the brave people of Ráwal Pindi District, was one of their characteristics which specially struck the advancing Muhammadans in 1008 A.D. The Kárakat Vellálars of Madura, at the opposite extremity of the peninsula, no longer practise polyandry; but they preserve a trace of it in their condonement of cohabitation with the husband's kindred, while adultery outside the husband's family entails expulsion from caste. *Slow growth of the central story. The polyandry of Draupadí.*

Such customs became abhorrent to the Bráhmans. The Bráhmans justify Draupadí's position, however, on the ground that as the five Pándava brethren were divinely begotten emanations from one deity, they formed in reality only one person, and could be lawfully married to the same woman. No such afterthought was required to uphold the honour of Draupadí in the age when the legend took its rise. Throughout the whole Mahábhárata she figures as the type of a high-born princess, and a chaste, brave, and faithful wife. She shares in every sorrow and triumph of the five brethren; bears a son to each; and finally enters with the true-hearted band into the glory of Indra. Her husbands take a terrible vengeance on insult offered to her, and seem quite unaware that a later age would deem her position one which required explanation.[1]

The rest of the Mahá-bhárata.
The struggle for the kingdom of Hastinápura forms, however, only a fourth of the Mahábhárata. The remainder consists of later additions. Some of these are legends of the early Aryan settlements in the Middle Land of Bengal, tacked on to the central story; others are mythological episodes, theological discourses, and philosophic disquisitions, intended to teach the military caste its duties, especially its duty of reverence to the Bráhmans. Taken as a whole, the Mahábhárata may be said to form the cyclopædia of the Heroic Age in Northern India, with the struggle of the Pándavas and Kauravas as its original nucleus; and the submission of the military power to priestly domination as its later didactic design.

The Rámáyana.
The second great Indian epic, the Rámáyana, recounts the advance of the Aryans into Southern India. Unlike the Mahábhárata, its composition is assigned not to a compiler (*vyása*) in the abstract, but to a named poet, Válmíki. On the other hand, the personages and episodes of the Rámáyana have an abstract or mythological character, which contrasts with the matter-of-fact stories of the Mahábhárata. The heroine of the Rámáyana, Sítá, is literally the ' field-furrow,' to whom the Vedic hymns and early Aryan ritual paid divine honour.

Its allegorical character.
She represents Aryan husbandry, and has to be defended against the raids of the aborigines by the hero Ráma, an incarnation of the Aryan deity Vishnu, and born of his divine nectar. Ráma is regarded by Weber as the analogue of Balaráma, the ' Ploughbearer' (*halabhrit*). From this abstract point of view, the Rámáyana exhibits the progress of Aryan plough-husbandry among the mountains and forests of Central and Southern India; and the perils of the agricultural settlers from the non-ploughing nomadic cultivators and hunting tribes.

Its central idea
The abduction of Sítá by an aboriginal or demon prince, who carried her off to Ceylon; her eventual recovery by Ráma; and the advance of the Aryans into Southern India, form the central story of the Rámáyana. It differs therefore from the central legend of the Mahábhárata, as commemorating a period when the main arena of Aryan enterprise had extended itself far

---

[1] The beautiful story of Sávitrí, the wife faithful to the end, is told in the Mahábhárata by the sage Márkandeya in answer to Yudishthira's question, whether any woman so true and noble as Draupadí had ever been known. Sávitrí, on the loss of her husband, dogged the steps of Yama, King of Death, until she wrung from him, one by one, many blessings for her family, and finally the reluctant restoration of her husband to life.

beyond their ancient settlements around Delhi; and as a pro- later than
duct of the Bráhman tendency to substitute abstract personifica- Mahá-
tions for human actors and mundane events. The nucleus of bhárata
Legend.
the Mahábhárata is a legend of ancient life; the nucleus of the
Rámáyana is an allegory. Its most modern form, the Adhyátma
Rámáyana, still further spiritualizes the story, and elevates Ráma
into a saviour and deliverer, a god rather than a hero.[1]

Its reputed author, Válmíki, is a conspicuous figure in Válmíki.
the epic, as well as its composer. He takes part in the
action of the poem, receives the hero Ráma in his hermitage,
and afterwards gives shelter to the unjustly banished Sítá and
her twin sons, nourishing the aspirations of the youths by
tales of their father's prowess. These stories make up the
main part of the Rámáyana, and refer to a period which has
been loosely assigned to about 1000 B.C. But the poem
could not have been put together in its present shape many
centuries, if any, before our era. Parts of it may be
earlier than the Mahábhárata, but the compilation as a whole
apparently belongs to a later date. The Rámáyana consists of
seven books (*Kándas*) and 24,000 *slokas*, or about 48,000 lines.

As the Mahábhárata celebrates the lunar race of Delhi, so Outline of
the Rámáyana forms the epic chronicle of the solar race of the Rámá-
Ajodhya or Oudh. The two poems thus preserve the legends yana.
of two renowned Aryan kingdoms at the two opposite, or
eastern and western, borders of the Middle Land (*Madhya-
desha*). The opening books of the Rámáyana recount the The local
wondrous birth and boyhood of Ráma, eldest son of Dasa- legend.
ratha, King of Ajodhya; his marriage with Sítá, as victor at her
swayam-vara, or tournament, by bending the mighty bow of
Siva in the public contest of chiefs for the princess; and his
appointment as heir-apparent to his father's kingdom. A
zanána intrigue ends in the youngest wife of Dasaratha
obtaining this appointment for her own son, Bharata, and in
the exile of Ráma, with his bride Sítá, for fourteen years to
the forest. The banished pair wander south to Prayág (Allahábád), already a place of sanctity; and thence across the river to
the hermitage of Válmíki, among the Bánda jungles, where a
hill is still pointed out as the scene of their abode. Meanwhile
Ráma's father dies, and the loyal youngest brother, Bharata,
although the lawful successor, refuses to enter on the inherit-

---

[1] The allegorical character of the Rámáyana has allowed scope for
various speculations as to its origin. Such speculations have been well
dealt with by Mr. Káshináth Trimbak Telang in his Essay, *Was the
Rámáyana copied from Homer?* (Bombay, 1873.)

ance, but goes in quest of Ráma to bring him back as rightful heir. A contest of fraternal affection takes place. Bharata at length returns to rule the family kingdom in the name of Ráma, until the latter shall come to claim it at the end of the fourteen years of banishment appointed by their late father.

The abduction of Sítá.

So far, the Rámáyana merely narrates the local chronicles of the court of Ajodhya. In the third book the main story begins. Rávana, the demon or aboriginal king of the far south, smitten by the fame of Sítá's beauty, seizes her at the hermitage while her husband is away in the jungle, and flies off with her in a magical chariot through the air to Lanka or Ceylon. The next three books (4th, 5th, and 6th) recount the expedition of the bereaved Ráma for her recovery. He makes alliances with the aboriginal tribes of Southern India, under the names of monkeys and bears, and raises a great army. The Monkey general, Hanumán, jumps across the straits between India and Ceylon, discovers the princess in captivity, and leaps back with the news to Ráma. The Monkey troops then build a causeway across the narrow sea,—the Adam's Bridge of modern geography,—by which Ráma marches across and, after slaying

Her rescue.

the monster Rávana, delivers Sítá. The rescued wife proves her unbroken chastity, during her stay in the palace of Rávana, by the ancient ordeal of fire. Agni, the god of that element, himself conducted her out of the burning pile to her husband ; and, the fourteen years of banishment being over, Ráma and Sítá return in triumph to Ajodhya. There they reigned gloriously ; and Ráma celebrated the great horse sacrifice (*aswa-medha*) as a token of his imperial sway over India. But a famine having smitten the land, doubts arose in Ráma's heart as to his wife's purity while in her captor's power at Ceylon. He banishes the faithful Sítá, who wanders forth again to Válmíki's hermitage, where she gives birth to Ráma's two sons. After sixteen years of exile, she is reconciled to her repentant husband, and Ráma and Sítá and their children are at last reunited.[1]

Later Sanskrit epics.

The Mahábhárata and the Rámáyana, however overladen with fable, form the chronicles of the kings of the Middle Land of the Ganges, their family feuds, and their national enterprises. In the later Sanskrit epics, the legendary element is more and more overpowered by the mythological. Among them the Raghu-vansa and the Kumára-sambhava, both

Raghu-vansa.

assigned to Kálidása, take the first rank. The Raghu-vansa

---

[1] Respectful mention should here be made of Growse's translation of the Hindi version of the *Rámáyana* by Tulsí Dás. (4to. Allahábád, 1883.)

celebrates the solar line of Raghu, King of Ajodhya; more particularly the ancestry and the life of his descendant Ráma. The Kumára-sambhava recounts the birth of the War-god.[1] It is still more didactic and allegorical, abounding in sentiment and in feats of prosody. But it contains passages of exquisite beauty of style and elevation of thought. From the astrological data which these two poems furnish, Jacobi infers that they cannot have been composed before 350 A.D.

Kumára-sambhava.

The name of Kálidása has come down, not only as the composer of these two later epics, but as the father of the Sanskrit drama. According to Hindu tradition, he was one of the 'Nine Gems' or distinguished men at the court of Vikramáditya. This prince is popularly identified with the King of Ujjain who gave his name to the *Samvat* era, commencing in the year 57 B.C. But, as Holtzmann points out, it may be almost as dangerous to infer from this latter circumstance that Vikramáditya lived in 57 B.C., as to place Julius Cæsar in the first year of the so-called Julian Calendar, namely, 4713 B.C. Several Vikramádityas figure in Indian history. Indeed, the name is merely a title, 'A very Sun in Prowess,' which has been borne by victorious monarchs of many of the Indian dynasties. The date of Vikramáditya has been variously assigned from 57 B.C. to 1050 A.D.; and the works of the poets and philosophers who formed the 'Nine Gems' of his court, appear from internal evidence to have been composed at intervals during that long period. The Vikramáditya, under whom Kálidása and the 'Nine Gems' are said to have flourished, ruled over Málwá probably from 500 to 550 A.D.

Kálidása.

King Vikramáditya.

550 A.D. ?

In India, as in Greece and Rome, scenic representations seem to have taken their rise in the rude pantomime of a very early time, possibly as far back as the Vedic ritual; and the Sanskrit word for the drama, *nátaka*, is derived from *nata*, a dancer. But the Sanskrit dramas of the classical age which have come down to us, probably belong to the period between the 1st century B.C. and the 8th century A.D. They make mention of Greek slaves, are acquainted with Buddhism in its full development, and disclose a wide divergence between Sanskrit and the dialects used by the lower classes. The Mahá-

Age of the Sanskrit drama.

---

[1] Translated into spirited English verse by Mr. Ralph T. H. Griffith, M.A., who is also the author of a charming collection of 'Idylls from the Sanskrit,' based on the Mahábhárata, Rámáyana, Raghu-vansa, and Kálidása's Seasons.

bhárata and Rámáyana appear in the Sanskrit drama as part of the popular literature,—in fact, as occupying very much the same position which they still hold.   No dramas are known to exist among the works which the Hindus who emigrated to Java, about 500 A.D., carried with them to their new homes.   Nor have any dramas been yet found among the Tibetan translations of the Sanskrit classics.

Sakuntalá.   The most famous drama of Kálidása is Sakuntalá, or the 'Lost Ring.'   Like the ancient epics, it divides its action between the court of the king and the hermitage in the forest. Prince Dushyanta, an ancestor of the noble Lunar race, weds by an irregular marriage a beautiful maiden, Sakuntalá, at her father's hermitage in the jungle.   Before returning to his capital, he gives his bride a ring as a pledge of his love ; but smitten by a curse from a holy man, she loses the ring, and cannot be recognised by her husband till it is found.   Sakuntalá bears a son in her loneliness, and sets out to claim recognition for herself and child at her husband's court.   But she is as one unknown to the prince, till, after many sorrows and trials, the ring comes to light.   She is then happily reunited with her husband, and her son grows up to be the noble Bharata, the chief founder of the Lunar dynasty whose achievements form the theme of the Mahábhárata.   Sakuntalá, like Sítá, is the type of the chaste and faithful Hindu wife ; and her love and sorrow, after forming the favourite romance of the Indian people for perhaps eighteen hundred years, have furnished a theme for the great European poet of our age.   'Wouldst thou,' says Goethe,

> ' Wouldst thou the young year's blossoms, and the fruits of its decline,
>   And all by which the soul is charmed, enraptured, feasted, fed,—
>   Wouldst thou the earth and heaven itself in one sole name combine ?
>   I name thee, O Sakuntalá ! and all at once is said.'

Other dramas ;   Sakuntalá has had the good fortune to be translated by Sir William Jones (1789), and to be sung by Goethe.   But other of the Hindu dramas and domestic poems are of almost equal interest and beauty.   As examples of the classical period, may be taken the Mrichchakatí, or 'Toy Cart,' a drama in ten Sanskrit,   acts, on the old theme of the innocent cleared and the guilty punished ; and the poem of Nala and Damayantí, or the 'Royal Gambler and the Faithful Wife.'   Such plays and poems frequently take an episode of the Mahábhárata or Rámáyana for their subject ; and in this way the main incidents in the two great epics have been gradually dramatized or reduced to the still more popular form of household song.   The modern drama was one of the first branches of Hindu secular literature and which accepted the spoken dialects; and the native theatre modern. forms the best, indeed the only, school in which an Englishman can acquaint himself with the in-door life of the people.

In our own day there has been a great dramatic revival Recent in India : new plays in the vernacular tongues issue rapidly dramatic from the press ; and societies of patriotic young natives form revival. themselves into dramatic companies, especially in Calcutta and Bombay. Many of the pieces are vernacular renderings of stories from the Sanskrit epics and classical dramas. Several have a political significance, and deal with the phases of development upon which India has entered under the influence of British rule. One Bengáli play, the Nil-darpan,[1] or the 'Indigo Factory,' became the subject of a celebrated trial in Calcutta ; while others—such as *Ekei ki bale Sabhyatá ?* 'Is this what you call civilisation?'—suggests many serious thoughts to a candid English mind. In 1877, 102 dramas were published in India in the native tongues ; and in 1882, 245.

Closely allied to the drama is the prose romance. In 1823, The Dr. H. H. Wilson intimated that Hindu literature contained Hindu collections of domestic narrative to an extent surpassing those novel. of any other people. The vast growth of European fiction since that date renders this statement no longer accurate. But Wilson's translations from the Vrihat-kathá may still be read with interest,[2] and the Sanskrit Beast-stories now occupy an Beast-even more significant place in the history of Indo-European stories ; literature than they did then. Many fables of animals familiar to the western world, from the time of Æsop downwards, had their original home in India. The relation between the fox and the lion in the Greek versions has no reality in nature. It was based, however, upon the actual relation between the lion and his follower the jackal, in the Sanskrit stories.[3] Weber thinks that complete cycles of Indian fables may have existed in the time of Pánini (350 B.C.). It is known that the Sanskrit Panchatantra, or Book of Beast Tales, was translated into the ancient their Persian as early as the 6th century A.D., and from that render- spread ing all the subsequent versions in Asia Minor and Europe have wards. been derived. The most ancient animal fables of India are at

---

[1] Literally, 'The Mirror of Indigo.'

[2] *Oriental Quarterly Magazine*, Calcutta, March 1824, pp. 63–77. Also vol. iii. of Wilson's Collected Works, pp. 156–268. London, 1864.

[3] See, however, Weber's elaborate footnote, No. 221, for the other view, *Hist. Ind. Lit.*, p. 211. Max Müller's charming essay on the Migration of Fables (*Chips*, vol. iv. pp. 145–209, 1875) traces the actual stages of a well-known story from the East to the West.

the present day the nursery stories of England and America. The graceful Hindu imagination delighted also in fairy tales; and the Sanskrit compositions of this class are the original source of many of the fairy tales of Persia, Arabia, and Christendom. The works of fiction published in the native languages in India in 1877 numbered 196; and in 1882, 237.

Sanskrit lyric poetry.

In mediæval India, a large body of poetry, half-religious, half-amorous, grew up around the legend of the youthful Krishna (the eighth incarnation of Vishnu) and his loves with the shepherdesses, the playmates of his sweet pastoral life. Káli-dása, according to Hindu tradition, was the father of the erotic lyric, as well as a great dramatic and epic poet. In his Megha-dúta or 'Cloud Messenger,' an exile sends a message by a wind-borne cloud to his love, and the countries beneath its long aerial route are made to pass like a panorama before the reader's eye. The Gíta Govinda, or Divine Herdsman of Jayadeva, is a Sanskrit 'Song of Solomon' of the 12th century A.D. A festival once a year celebrates the birthplace of this mystical love-poet, in the Birbhúm District of Lower Bengal; and many less famous compositions of the same class now issue from the vernacular press throughout India. In 1877, no fewer than 697 works of poetry were published in the native languages in India; and in 1882, 834.

The Puránas, 8th to 16th century A.D.

The mediæval Bráhmans displayed a marvellous activity in theological as well as in lyric poetry. The Puránas, literally ' The Ancient Writings,' form a collection of religious and philo-sophical treatises in verse, of which the principal ones number eighteen. The whole Puránas are said to contain 1,600,000 lines. The really old ones have either been lost or been incorporated in new compilations; and the composition of the existing Puránas probably took place from the 8th to the 16th century A.D. As the epics sang the wars of the Aryan heroes,

Contents of the Puránas.

so the Puránas recount the deeds of the Bráhman gods. They deal with the creation of the universe; its successive dissolu-tions and reconstructions; the stories of the deities and their incarnations; the reigns of the divine Manus; and the chronicles of the Solar and Lunar lines of kings who ruled, the former in the east and the latter in the west of the Middle Land (Madhya-desha).

Their sects.

The Puránas belong to the period after the mass of the people had split up into their two existing divisions, as wor-shippers of Vishnu or of Siva, *post*, 700 A.D. They are devoted to the glorification of one or other of these two rival gods, and thus embody the sectarian theology of Bráhmanism.   While claiming to be founded on Vedic inspira- Their tion, they practically superseded the Veda, and have formed influence. during ten centuries the sacred literature on which Hinduism rests.[1]

An idea of the literary activity of the Indian mind at the Indian present day may be formed from the fact, that 4890 works were works published in India in 1877, of which 4346 were in the native in 1877 languages.   Only 436 were translations, the remaining 4454 being original works or new editions.   The number of Indian publications constantly increases.   In 1882, 6198 works were and 1882. published in India, 5543 being in the native languages. The translations numbered 720, and the original works, including new editions, 5478.   These figures only show the publications officially registered under the Act.   A large number of unregistered pamphlets or brochures must be added ; together with the daily and weekly issue of vernacular newspapers, exceeding 230 in number and circulating over 150,000 copies.

This chapter has attempted to trace the intellectual and Absence of religious development of the early Aryans in India, and their territorial constitution into castes and communities.   Regarding their history. territorial history, it has said almost nothing.   It has, indeed, indicated their primeval line of march from their Holy Land among the seven rivers of the Punjab, to their Land of the Sacred Singers between the upper courses of the Jumna and the Ganges ; and thence to their more extensive settlements in the Middle Land of Bengal (*Madhya-desha*) stretching to beyond the junction of these two great rivers.   It has also told very briefly the legend of their advance into Southern India, in the epic rendering of the Rámáyana.   But the foregoing pages have refrained from attempts to fix the dates or to fill in the

---

[1] The foregoing pages have very briefly reviewed the most important branches of Sanskrit literature ; the influence of that literature upon Hinduism will be dealt with in a subsequent chapter.   To fully appreciate the connection between ancient thought and present practice in India, the student may also refer to Professor Monier Williams' *Modern India and the Indians* (Trübner, 1879).   That work unites the keen observation of a traveller new to the country with the previous learning acquired during a lifetime devoted to Oriental studies.   Professor Monier Williams is thus enabled to correlate the existing phenomena of Indian life with the historical types which underlie them.

details of these movements. For the territorial extension of the Aryans in India is still a battle-ground of inductive history.

Its inductive data.

Even for a much later period of Indian civilisation, the data continue under keen dispute. This will be amply apparent in the following chapters.[1] These chapters will open with the great upheaval of Buddhism against Bráhmanism in the 6th century before Christ. They will summarize the struggles of the Asiatic races in India during a period of twenty-three hundred years. They will close with the great military revival of Hinduism under the Maráthá Bráhmans in the 18th century of our era. An attempt will then be made, from the evidence of the vernacular literature and languages, to present a view of Indian thought and culture, when the European nations came in force upon the scene.

The Bráhmans in Indian history.

Meanwhile, the history of India, so far as obscurely known to us before the advent of the Greeks, 327 B.C., is essentially a literary history, and the memorials of its civilisations are mainly literary or religious memorials. The more practical aspects of those long ages, which were their real aspects to the people, found no annalist. From the commencement of the post-Vedic period, the Bráhmans strove with increasing success to bring the Aryan life and civilisation of India more and more into accord with their own priestly ideas.

In order to understand the long domination of the Bráhmans, and the influence which they still wield, it is necessary also to keep in mind their position as the great literary caste. Their priestly supremacy has been repeatedly assailed, and was during a space of nearly a thousand years overpowered by Buddhism.

The six attacks on Bráhmanism, 6th century B.C. to 19th century A.D.

But throughout twenty-two centuries the Bráhmans have been the counsellors of Hindu princes and the teachers of the Hindu people. They still represent the early Aryan civilisation of India. Indeed, the essential history of India is a narrative of the attacks upon the continuity of their civilisation,—that is to say, of attacks upon the Bráhmanical system of the Middle Land, and of the modifications and compromises to which that system has had to submit.

---

[1] Namely, on Buddhism, the Greeks in India, the Scythic Inroads, the Rise of Hinduism, Early Muhammadan Rulers, the Mughal Empire, and the Maráthá Power. We still await the complete evidence of coins and inscriptions ; although valuable materials have been already obtained from these silent memorials of the past. Mr. K. T. Telang's *Introduction to the Mudrárákshasa,* with Appendix, shows what can be gathered from a minute and critical examination of the historical data incidentally contained in the Hindu drama.

Those attacks mark out six epochs. First, the religious up- 1. Buddh-
rising of the non-Aryan and the partially Bráhmanized Aryan ism.
tribes on the east of the Middle Land of Bengal; initiated by
the preaching of Buddha in the 6th century B.C., culminating in
the Buddhist kingdoms about the commencement of our era,
and melting into modern Hinduism about the 8th century A.D.
Second, warlike inroads of non-Bráhmanical Aryans and Scythic 2. Greeks,
races from the west; strongly exemplified by the Greek invasions and
in the 4th century B.C., and continuing under the Greco-Bactrian Scythians
empire and its Scythic rivals to probably the 5th century A.D.
Third, the influence of the so-called aborigines or non-Aryan 3. Non-
tribes of India and of the non-Aryan low-castes incorporated Aryan
into the Hindu community; an influence ever at work—indeed tribes.
by far the most powerful agent in dissolving Bráhmanism into
Hinduism, and specially active after the decline of Buddhism
about the 7th century A.D.

Fourth, the reaction against the low beliefs, priestly oppres- 4. Hindu
sion, and bloody rites which resulted from this compromise sects.
between Bráhmanism and aboriginal worship. The reaction
received an impetus from the preaching of Sankar Achárya,
who founded his great Sivaite sect in the 8th century A.D.
It obtained its full development under a line of ardent
Vishnuite reformers from the 12th to the 16th centuries A.D.
The fifth solvent of the ancient Bráhmanical civilisation of 5. Muham-
India was found in the Muhammadan invasions and the rule madans.
of Islám, 1000 to 1765 A.D. The sixth, in the English 6. English.
supremacy, and in the popular upheaval which it has produced
in the 18th and 19th centuries. Each of these six epochs will,
so far as space permits, receive separate treatment in the
following chapters.

CHAPTER V.

BUDDHISM IN INDIA (543 B.C. TO 1000 A.D.).

Buddhism. THE first great solvént of Bráhmanism was the teaching of Gautama Buddha. The life of this celebrated man has three sides,—its personal aspects, its legendary developments, and its religious consequences upon mankind. In his own person, Buddha appears as a prince and preacher of ancient India. In the legendary developments of his story, Buddha ranks as a divine teacher among his followers, as an incarnation of Gautama Vishnu among the Hindus, and as a saint of the Christian Buddha. church, with a day assigned to him in both the Greek and Roman calendars. As a religious founder, he left behind a system of belief which has gained more disciples than any other creed in the world; and which is now more or less accepted by 500 millions of people, or nearly one-half the human race. According to the Páli texts, Buddha was born 622 B.C., and died 543 B.C.[1] Modern calculations fix his death about 480 B.C.[2]

The story The story of Buddha's earthly career is a typical one. It is of Buddha, modelled based on the old Indian ideal of the noble life which we have on the epic seen depicted in the Sanskrit epics. Like the Pándavas in type. the Mahábhárata, and like Ráma in the Rámáyana, Buddha is the miraculously born son of a king, belonging to one of the two great Aryan lines, the Solar and the Lunar; in Buddha's case, as in Ráma's, to the Solar. His youth, like that of the epic heroes, is spent under Bráhman tutors, and like the epic heroes he obtains a beautiful bride after a display of unexpected prowess with the bow; or, as the northern Buddhists relate, at an actual *swayam-vara*, by a contest in arms for the princess. A period of voluntary exile follows an interval of married happiness, and Buddha retires like Ráma to a Bráhman's hermitage in the forest.

Buddha The sending back of the charioteer to the bereaved father's and Ráma. capital forms an episode in the story of both the young princes. As in the Rámáyana, so in the legend of Buddha, it is to the

[1] Childers' *Dictionary of the Páli Language, s.v.* Buddho, p. 96.
[2] Oldenberg's *Buddha, Sein Leben* etc. (Hoey's excellent translation, p. 197). *Vide post,* p. 153.

jungles on the south of the Ganges, lying between the Aryan
settlements and the aboriginal races, that the royal exile
repairs.   After a time of seclusion, the Pándavas, Ráma,
and Buddha alike emerge to achieve great conquests; the two The
former by force of arms, the last by the weapons of the Spirit. Indian
legend.
Up to this point the outline of the three stories has followed
the same type; but henceforth it diverges.   The Sanskrit epics
depict the ideal Aryan man as prince, hermit, and hero.   In
the legend of Buddha, that ideal has developed into prince,
hermit, and saint.

Gautama, afterwards named Buddha, 'The Enlightened,' Parentage
and Siddhártha, 'He who has fulfilled his end,' was the only of Gautama
son of Suddhodana, King of Kapilavastu.   This prince, the Buddha.
chief of the Sákya clan, ruled over an outlying Aryan settlement on the north-eastern border of the Middle Land, about 622 B.C.
a hundred miles to the north of Benares, and within sight
of the snow-topped Himálayas.   A Gautama Rájput of the
noble Solar line, he wished to see his son grow up on the
warlike model of his race.   But the young prince shunned the His lonely
sports of his playmates, and retired to solitary day-dreams in youth, *æt.*
1-19.
nooks of the palace garden.   The king tried to win his son to
a practical career by marrying him to a beautiful and talented
girl; and the youthful Gautama unexpectedly proved his
manliness by a victory over the flower of the young chiefs at
a tournament.   For a while he forgot his solemn speculations
on the unseen, in the sweet realities of early married life.

But in his drives through the city he deeply reflected His mar-
on the types of old age, disease, and death which met ried life,
æt. 19-29.
his eye; and he was powerfully impressed by the calm of
a holy man, who seemed to have raised his soul above the
changes and sorrows of this world.   After ten years, his wife
bore to him an only son; and Gautama, fearing lest this new
tie should bind him too closely to the things of earth, retired
about the age of thirty to a cave among the forest-clad spurs
of the Vindhyas.   The story of how he turned away from the His Great
door of his wife's lamp-lit chamber, denying himself even a Renunciation, *æt.*
parting caress of his new-born babe lest he should wake the 29-30.
sleeping mother, and galloped off into the darkness, is one of
the many tender episodes in his life.   After a gloomy night ride,
he sent back his one companion, the faithful charioteer, with
his horse and jewels to his father.   Having cut off his long
Rájput locks, and exchanged his princely raiment for the rags
of a poor passer-by, he went on alone a homeless beggar.
This abandonment of earthly pomp and power, and of loved

wife and new-born son, is the Great Renunciation which forms a favourite theme of the Buddhist scriptures in Sanskrit, Páli, Tibetan, and Chinese. It has furnished, during twenty centuries, the type of self-sacrifice which all Indian reformers must follow if they are to win the trust of the people.

Buddha's forest life, *æt.* 30–36 or 29–34.*   For a time Buddha studied under two Bráhman recluses, near RAJAGRIHA, in Patná District, learning from them that the path to divine knowledge and tranquillity of soul lies through the subjection of the flesh. He then buried himself deeper in the south-eastern jungles, which at that time covered Gayá District, and during six years wasted himself by austerities in company with five disciples. The temple of BUDDH-GAYA marks the site of his long penance. But instead of earning peace of mind by fasting and self-torture, he reached a crisis of religious despair, during which the Buddhist scriptures affirm that the enemy of mankind, Mára, wrestled with him in bodily shape. Torn with doubts as to whether, after all his penance, he was not destined to perdition, the haggard ascetic, in a final paroxysm, fell senseless to the earth.

588 B.C.

His spiritual crisis.   When he recovered, the mental struggle had passed. He felt that the path to salvation lay not in self-torture in a mountain cave, but in preaching a higher life to his fellow-men. His five disciples, shocked by his giving up penance, forsook him; and Buddha was left in solitude to face the question whether he alone was right and all the devout minds of his age were wrong. The Buddhist scriptures depict him as

His temptation.   sitting serene under a fig-tree, while the great Enemy and his crew whirled round him with flaming weapons. 'When the conflict began between the Saviour of the World and the Prince of Evil,' says one of their sacred texts,[1] the earth shook; the sea uprose from her bed, the rivers turned back to the mountains, the hill-tops fell crashing to the plains, the sun was darkened, and a host of headless spirits rode upon the tempest. From his temptation in the wilderness, the ascetic emerged

His 'Enlightenment.'   with his doubts for ever laid at rest, seeing his way clear, and henceforth to be known as Buddha, literally 'The Enlightened.'[2]

This was Buddha's second birth; and the *pipal* fig or Bo (Bodhi), literally the Tree of the Enlightenment, under whose spreading branches its pangs were endured, has become

---

[1] The Madhurattha-Vilásiní, *Journal of the Bengal Asiatic Society*, vol. vii. p. 812.   Rhys Davids' *Buddhism*, p. 36.

[2] According to the Ceylonese texts, Buddha 'obtained Buddhahood' in 588 B.C. This would make him 34, not 36 years of age. Childers' *Páli Dictionary, s.v.* Buddho.

the sacred tree of 500 millions of mankind. It is the
Ficus religiosa of Western science. The idea of a second
birth was familiar to the twice-born Aryan castes of ancient *His story*
India, and was represented by their race-ceremony of in- *follows the*
vesting the boy at the close of childhood with the sacred *types.*
thread. In this, as in its other features, the story of Buddha
adheres to ancient Aryan types, but gives to them a new
spiritual significance. Having passed through the three prescribed stages of the Aryan saintly life,—as learner, house-
holder, and forest recluse,—he now entered on its fourth stage
as a religious mendicant. But he developed from the old
Bráhmanical model of the wandering ascetic, intent only on
saving his own soul, the nobler type of the preacher, striving
to bring deliverance to the souls of others.

Two months after his temptation in the wilderness, Buddha *Public*
commenced his public teaching in the Deer-Forest, on the *teaching of*
outskirts of the great city of Benares. Unlike the Bráhmans, *et.* 36-80.
he addressed himself, not to one or two disciples of the sacred
caste, but to the mass of the people. His first converts were
laymen, and among the earliest were women. After three
months of ministry, he had gathered around him sixty disciples,
whom he sent forth to the neighbouring countries with these *He sends*
words : 'Go ye now and preach the most excellent Law.' The *forth the*
essence of his teaching was the deliverance of man from the *Sixty.*
sins and sorrows of life by self-renunciation and inward self-
control. While the sixty disciples went on their missionary
tour among the populace, Buddha converted certain celebrated
hermits and fire-worshippers by an exposition of the philosophical side of his doctrine. With this new band he
journeyed on to Rájágriha, where the local king and his
subjects joined the faith, but where also he first experienced
the fickleness of the multitude. Two-thirds of each year he
spent as a wandering preacher. The remaining four months of
the rainy season he abode at some fixed place, often near
Rájágriha, teaching the people who flocked around his little
dwelling in the bamboo grove. His five old disciples, who *He con-*
had forsaken him in the time of his sore temptation in the *verts the*
wilderness, penitently rejoined their master. Princes, mer- *people,*
chants, artificers, Bráhmans and hermits, husbandmen and
serfs, noble ladies and repentant courtesans, were yearly added
to those who believed.

Buddha preached throughout a large part of Behar, *in the*
Oudh, and the adjacent Districts in the North - Western *Gangetic*
Provinces. In after ages monasteries marked his halting- *valley*

places; and the principal scenes of his life, such as
AJODHYA, BUDDH-GAYA, SRAVASTI, the modern SAHET MAHET,
RAJAGRIHA, etc., became the great places of pilgrimage for
the Buddhist world. His visit to his aged father at Kapilavastu, whence he had gone forth as a brilliant young prince,
and to which he returned as a wandering preacher, in dingy
yellow robes, with shaven head and the begging bowl in his
hand, is a touching episode which appeals to the heart of
Buddha
converts
his own
family.
universal mankind. The old king heard him with reverence.
The son, whom Buddha had left as a new-born babe, was
converted to the faith; and his beloved wife, from the
threshold of whose chamber he had ridden away into the
darkness, became one of the first of Buddhist nuns.

The Great Renunciation took place in his twenty-ninth year.
After silent self-preparation, his public ministry commenced
in his thirty-sixth, and during forty-four years he preached to
He pro-
phesies his
death.
the people. In prophesying his death, he said to his
followers: 'Be earnest, be thoughtful, be holy. Keep stedfast
watch over your own hearts. He who holds fast to the law
and discipline, and faints not, he shall cross the ocean of life
and make an end of sorrow.' He spent his last night in
preaching, and in comforting a weeping disciple; his latest
Buddha's
last words.
543 B.C.
words, according to one account, were, 'Work out your salvation with diligence.' He died calmly, at the age of eighty,[1]
under the shadow of a fig-tree, at Kusinagara, the modern
KASIA, in Gorakhpur District.

Different
versions
of the
Legend.
Such is the story of Gautama Buddha's life derived from
Indian sources, a story which has the value of gospel truth to
31 millions[2] of devout believers. But the two branches even
of Indian or Southern Buddhism have each their own version,
and the Buddha of the Burmese differs in important respects
from the Buddha of the Ceylonese.[3] Still wider is the diver-

---

[1] According to some accounts; according to others, at about seventy.
But the chronology of Buddha's life is legendary.

[2] The following estimate is given by Mr. Rhys Davids of the number
of the Southern Buddhists, substituting for his Indian figures the results
ascertained by the Census of 1881 :—

In Ceylon, ...	1,520,575
,, India and British Burma, . . .	nearly 4,000,000
,, Burma, ...	3,000,000
,, Siam, ...	10,000,000
,, Anam, ...	12,000,000
,, Jains, ...	485,020
Total, . .	31,005,595

[3] The original Páli text of the *Commentary of the Játakhas* is assigned

gence which the Northern or Tibetan Buddhists give to the legend of the life and to the teaching of their Master. The southern texts dwell upon the early career of Buddha up to the time of his Enlightenment in his 34th or 36th year. The incidents of that period have a peculiar pathos, and appeal to the most sacred experiences of humanity in all ages. They form the favourite episodes of European works on Buddhism. But such works are apt to pay perhaps too little attention to the fact that the first thirty-four years of Buddha's life were only a self-preparation for a social and religious propaganda prolonged to an extreme old age.

The forty-six years of intense personal labour, during which Later years of Buddha traversed wide regions, converted nations, withstood Buddha. kings, eluded assassins, and sifted out false disciples, receive more attention in the northern legends. These legends have lately been compiled from the Tibetan texts into a work which furnishes a new and most interesting view of Buddha's life.[1] The best authority on the Southern Buddhism of Burma states that the history of the Master 'offers an almost complete blank as to what regards his doings and preachings during a period of nearly twenty-three years.'[2]

The texts of the Northern Buddhists fill up this blank. Northern Southern Buddhism modelled its biographies of the Master Texts.

to Ceylonese scribes, *circ.* 450 A.D. The first part of it was published by Fausböll in 1875 (Copenhagen) ; and Mr. Rhys Davids' translation, with valuable introduction and notes, appeared under the title of *Buddhist Birth Stories* in 1880 (Trübner, London). Mr. Childers' *Dictionary of the Páli Language* is a storehouse of original materials from Ceylonese sources, and has been used for verifying all statements in the present chapter. A compendious view of Southern Buddhism, ancient and modern, will be found in Spence Hardy's *Manual of Buddhism,* translated from Singalese MS. The Burmese branch of Southern Buddhism is well represented by Bishop Bigandet's *Life or Legend of Gaudama* (third edition, 2 vols., Trübner, 1880), and by Mr. Alabaster's *The Wheel of the Law,* a translation or paraphrase of the Siamese *Pathama Sambodhiyan.* Mr. Rhys Davids' *Buddhism,* and his *Hibbert Lectures,* give an excellent review of the faith. The French works, the original authorities in Europe, have (in some respects) been superseded by Oldenberg's *Buddha, Sein Leben* etc.

[1] *The Life of the Buddha, and the Early History of his Order, derived from Tibetan Works in the Bkah-hgyur and Bstan-hgyur,* translated by W. Woodville Rockhill, Second Secretary to the United States Legation in China (Trübner & Co., London 1884). Mr. Beal's *Si-yu-ki, or Buddhist Records of the Western World,* translated from the Chinese of Hiuen Tsiang, throws curious side-lights upon the traditions which the Chinese pilgrim brought with him or heard in India regarding the local incidents of Buddha's life.

[2] From the fifty-sixth to the seventy-ninth year of his life. Bishop Bigandet's *Life or Legend of Gaudama,* vol. i. p. 260, and footnote.

The Indian epic type;

upon the Indian epic type. Such biographies, as already stated, reproduce the three stages in the life of an Aryan hero, depicted by the Mahábhárata and Rámáyana; except that the three ideal stages have developed from those of prince, hermit, and warrior, to those of prince, hermit, and saint. In the northern

The Tibetan type.

conditions of China and Tibet, Buddha appears by no means as an Aryan hero. He is rather the representative of a race with birth-customs and death-rites of its own—of a race dwelling amid the epic Aryan kingdoms of India, but with traces of a separate identity in the past. He is a Sakya (perhaps a Scythic) prince, whose clan had settled to the south of the Himálayas, and preserved relics of a non-Aryan type.

The philosophical type of the Southern Buddha.

The artificial character which the southern legends give to the life of Buddha, arose from their tendency to assimilate him with epic Indian types. It was intensified by the equally Indian tendency to convert actual facts into philosophical abstractions. Gautama or Sakya-Muni became only a link in a long series of just men made perfect. According to the Ceylonese texts, a Buddha is a human being who has obtained perfect self-control and infinite knowledge. Having attained Enlightenment himself, he spends the rest of his life in preaching the truth to others. At his death he is reabsorbed into the Divine Essence, and his religion flourishes for a certain period until it dies out, and a new Buddha appears to preach anew the lost truth. The attainment of Buddhahood is the final result of virtue and self-sacrifice during many previous lives. Innumerable Buddhas have been born in this world; 24 of whom are separately named. Gautama was only the latest, and his doctrine is destined to give place to the Metteya Buddha, or Buddha of Kindness, who is next to come.[1]

The northern concrete type.

The Buddha of the northern legends is a reformer of a more concrete type. The Tibetan texts give prominence to the political aspects of his Reformation. Incidentally, indeed, they amplify several of the touching episodes familiar to Southern Buddhism. The 'great Fear' which impelled the young prince forth from his palace into the darkness to seek a higher life; the dirt and stones thrown at the wanderer by the village girls; the parables of the Mango-tree, the Devout Slave, and many others; the rich young man who left all for the faith and was *not* exceeding sorry; and Buddha's own retirement from Benares to avoid the gifts and honours which were being thrust upon him,—receive fresh illustration from the Tibetan texts.[2]

---

[1] Mr. Childers' *Páli Dictionary*, p. 96. Sanskrit, *Maitraya*.

[2] The materials for the following paragraphs are derived mainly from Mr. Rockhill's work (1884), already cited.

But it is from the political and historical aspects that the Political Tibetan life of Buddha possesses its special value. We learn life of that Buddhism was in its origin only one of many conflicting Buddha. sects; indeed, that alike to its royal patrons and opponents it appeared at first in the light of a new order rather than in the light of a new faith.[1] The early struggles of Buddhism were neither with the old Aryan gods, nor with the Bráhmans as a caste; but with rival orders of philosophers or ascetics, and with schismatics among its own followers. The gods of the Veda, Brahma, Indra, and the Shining Ones, appear in friendly relations with Buddha, and attend upon him in more than one crisis of his life. The Bráhmans were no longer a caste altogether devoted to a spiritual life. The Tibetan texts disclose them as following partly religious, partly secular avocations, and as among ' the great nobles' of an Indian kingdom. The Bráhman attitude to the new faith was by no means one of confederate hostility. The main body of Bráhmans continued non-Buddhistic, and taught their doctrines at royal courts. But many conspicuous converts were drawn from among them, and the Tibetan texts almost uniformly speak of Bráhmans with respect.

The opponents of the Tibetan Buddha were rival sects Buddha's whom he found in possession of the field, and the false real brethren who arose among his own disciples. The older opponents. hostile sects were confuted, sometimes by fair discussion, but more often by superior magical feats. Indeed, transformations and miraculous appearances seem for a time to have furnished the most potent arguments of the new faith. But eventually Buddha forbade resort to such testimonies, and magic became to the orthodox Buddhist an unholy art. In his later years, Buddha more than once insists that his doctrine is essentially one to be understanded of the people; that he was keeping back His no secret for an initiated few; and that he was the preacher magical of a strictly popular religion without any esoteric side. arts.

It was from among his own disciples that his bitterest enemies came. The Sakya race of Kapilavastu had adopted his teaching as a nation, without much pretence of individual conversion. Buddha's modest beginnings, first with the five followers, then with the sixty, then with the thousand, now Wholesale took a national development. In the fervour of the new Sakya movement, the Sakyas proclaimed that one man out of every conversion family must enter the Buddhist mendicant order; and it was from this ordinance, to which Buddha was compelled to give a reluctant assent, that the troubles of his later life arose.

[1] Rockhill, *op. cit.* Also Rhys Davids' *Hibbert Lectures*, p. 156.

Schism of
Devadatta.

The discontent among the forced disciples found a leader in Buddha's own cousin, Devadatta, who aspired by superior asceticism to the headship. For the schism which he created, Devadatta won the support of the Heir-apparent of Magadha. A struggle, partly religious partly political, ensued. Devadatta was for a time triumphant. He abetted the murder of the Magadha king, the father of his ally; forced the aged Buddha into retirement; and plundered and oppressed the people. The miraculous deliverances of 'the Blessed One' from the catapult, and from the wild elephant let loose against him in a narrow street, mark, however, the turning-point in the fortunes of the schism. Devadatta was confuted by magical arts, and his royal patron was converted to the true faith. The traitor disciple having thus failed to usurp the spiritual leadership of the Sakyas, attempted to seduce the wife whom Buddha had left in solitude. The apostate hoped with her aid to stand forth as the king or temporal leader of the Sakya race. His contemptuous rejection by the loyal Sakya princess, his acts of

His fall
into hell.

despairing cruelty, and his fall into hell with a lie in his mouth, fitly close the career of the first great schismatic.

Buddha,
the Sakya
prince.

Throughout the Tibetan texts, Buddha figures as a typical Sakya; first as a young Kshattriya or prince of the royal line, and then as a saintly personage who turns back an army sent against his nation by the force of his piety alone. Such spiritual weapons, however, proved a feeble defence in early India. Eventually, the Sakya capital was attacked by over-whelming numbers. For a time the enemy were repulsed without the Buddhists incurring the sin of taking life. But their firm adherence to their Master's commandment, 'Thou shalt not kill,' in the end decided the fate of the Sakya city. Some escaped into exile and founded settlements in distant parts as far as the other side of the Punjab frontier. The fall of the city ended in the slaughter of 77,000 Sakyas, and in the dispersion of the remnants of the race. The story of the five hundred Sakya youths and five hundred Sakya maidens

Disasters
of his race.

who were carried into captivity is a pathetic one. The five hundred youths were massacred in cold blood; and the faithful Sakya maidens, having refused to enter the harem of their conqueror, were exposed to the populace with their hands and feet chopped off. How Buddha came to them in their misery, dressed their wounds, and comforted them with the hope of a better life, 'so that they died in the faith,' is affectingly told.

The foregoing narrative touches only on one or two aspects of the Tibetan texts. It suffices to show the characteristic

divergences between the northern and the southern legend. Other
In the northern, there is a gradually developed contrast be- aspects
tween two main figures, the traitor Devadatta and his brother Tibetan
Ananda, the Beloved Disciple. The last year of Buddha's Legend.
ministry is dwelt on by both. But its full significance and its
most tender episodes are treated with special unction in the
northern version of the Book of the Great Decease. The Fo-wei-
kian-king,[1] or 'Dying Instruction of Buddha,' translated into
Chinese between 397 and 415 A.D. from a still earlier Sanskrit
text, gives to the last scene a peculiar beauty. 'It was now in the Chinese
middle of the night,' it says, 'perfectly quiet and still; for the sake text of
of his disciples, he delivered a summary of the law.' After laying dying dis-
down the rules of a good life, he revealed the inner doctrines of course.
his faith. From these a few sentences may be taken. 'The heart
is lord of the senses : govern, therefore, your heart ; watch well
the heart.' 'Think of the fire that shall consume the world,
and early seek deliverance from it.' 'Lament not my going
away, nor feel regret. For if I remained in the world, then
what would become of the church? It must perish without
fulfilling its end. From henceforth all my disciples, practising
their various duties, shall prove that my true Body, the Body The
of the Law (*Dharmakaya*), is everlasting and imperishable. doctrines
of Buddha.
The world is fast bound in fetters; I now give it deliverance,
as a physician who brings heavenly medicine. Keep your
mind on my teaching; all other things change, this changes
not. No more shall I speak to you. I desire to depart. I
desire the eternal rest (*Nirvána*). This is my last exhortation.'

The secret of Buddha's success was that he brought spiritual
deliverance to the people. He preached that salvation was
equally open to all men, and that it must be earned, not by
propitiating imaginary deities, but by our own conduct. His
doctrines thus cut away the religious basis of caste, impaired the
efficiency of the sacrificial ritual, and assailed the supremacy of
the Bráhmans as the mediators between God and man. Buddha
taught that sin, sorrow, and deliverance, the state of a man in this
life, in all previous and in all future lives, are the inevitable results
of his own acts (*Karma*). He thus applied the inexorable law of Law of
cause and effect to the soul. What a man sows, he must reap. *Karma.*

As no evil remains without punishment, and no good deed
without reward, it follows that neither priest nor God can prevent

---

[1] Translated in Appendix to the Catalogue of the Manuscripts presented
by the Japanese Government to the Secretary of State for India, and now
in the India Office.—Concluding letter of Mr. Beal to Dr. Rost, dated
1st September 1874, sec. 5.

each act bearing its own consequences.   Misery or happiness in this life is the unavoidable result of our conduct in a past life ; and our actions here will determine our happiness or misery in the life to come.   When any creature dies, he is born again in some higher or lower state of existence, according to his meri or demerit.   His merit, or demerit, that is his character, consists of the sum total of his actions in all previous lives.

By this great law of *Karma*, Buddha explained the inequalities and apparent injustice of man's estate in this world as the consequence of acts in the past ; while Christianity compensates those inequalities by rewards in the future.   A system in which our whole well-being, past, present, and to come, depends on ourselves, theoretically leaves little room for the interference, or even existence, of a personal God.[1]   But the atheism of Buddha was a philosophical tenet, which so far from weakening the sanctions of right and wrong, gave them new strength from the doctrine of *Karma*, or the Metempsychosis of Character.

The liberation of the soul.

Nirvána.

To free ourselves from the thraldom of desire and from the fetters of selfishness, was to attain to the state of the perfect disciple, *Arahat* in this life, and to the everlasting rest after death, *Nirvána.*   Some Buddhists explain *Nirvána* as absolute annihilation, when the soul is blown out like the flame of a lamp.   Others hold that it is merely the extinction of the sins, sorrows, and selfishness of individual life.   The fact is, that the doctrine underwent processes of change and development, like all theological dogmas.   'But the earliest idea of *Nirvána,*' says one of the greatest authorities on Chinese Buddhism, 'seems to have included in it no more than the enjoyment of a state of rest consequent on the extinction of all causes of sorrow.'[2]   The great practical aim of Buddha's teaching was to subdue the lusts of the flesh and the cravings of self ; and *Nirvána* has been taken to mean the extinction of the sinful grasping condition of heart which, by the inevitable law of *Karma*, would involve the penalty of renewed individual existence.   As the Buddhist strove to reach a state of quietism or holy meditation in this world, namely, the

---

[1] 'Buddhism,' says Mr. Beal, *Catena of Buddhist Scriptures*, p. 153, ' declares itself ignorant of any mode of personal existence compatible with the idea of spiritual perfection, and so far, it is ignorant of God.'

[2] Beal, *Catena of Buddhist Scriptures from the Chinese*, p. 157, ed. 1871 ; and the *Buddhist Tripitaka*, App., Letter to Dr. Rost, sec. 6.   Max Müller deals with the word from the etymological and Sanskrit side in his *Chips from a German Workshop*, vol. i. pp. 279, 290, ed. 1867.   But see, specially, Childers' *Páli Dictionary*, *s.v.* Nilbánam, pp. 265-274.

state of the perfect disciple or *Arahat ;* so he looked forward
to an eternal calm in a world to come, *Nirvána.*

Buddha taught that this end could only be attained by the Moral
practice of virtue. He laid down eight precepts of morality, code.
with two more for the religious orders, making ten commandments (*dasa-síla*) in all. He arranged the besetting faults of
mankind into ten sins, and set forth the special duties appli- The Ten
cable to each condition of life ; to parents and children, to Command-
pupils and teachers, to husbands and wives, to masters and ments.
servants, to laymen and the religious orders. In place of the
Bráhman rites and sacrifices, Buddha prescribed a code of
practical morality as the means of salvation. The four
essential features of that code were—reverence to spiritual
teachers and parents, control over self, kindness to other men,
and reverence for the life of all sentient creatures.

He urged on his disciples that they must not only follow Missionary
the true path themselves, but that they should preach it to all aspects of
mankind. Buddhism has from the first been a missionary Buddhism.
religion. One of the earliest acts of Buddha's public ministry
was to send forth the Sixty ; and he carefully formulated the
four chief means of conversion. These were companionship
with the good, listening to the Law, reflection upon the truths
heard, and the practice of virtue. He also instituted a religious Order, one of whose special duties it was to go forth
and preach to the nations. While, therefore, the Bráhmans
kept their ritual for the twice-born Aryan castes, Buddhism
addressed itself not only to those castes and to the lower
mass of the people, but to all the non-Aryan races throughout India, and eventually to almost the whole Asiatic world.
Two features of the Buddhist Order were its fortnightly
meetings and public confession, or 'Disburdenment' of sins.

On the death of Buddha, five hundred of his disciples met The First
in a vast cave near Rájágriha to gather together his sayings. Council,
This was the First Council. They chanted the lessons of 543 B.C. (?)
their master in three great divisions—the words of Buddha to
his disciples ;[1] his code of discipline ;[2] and his system of
doctrine.[3] These became the Three Collections[4] of Buddha's
teaching ; and the word for a Buddhist Council[5] means
literally 'a singing together.' A century afterwards, a Second Second
Council, of seven hundred, was held at Vaisali, to settle disputes Buddhist
between the more and the less strict followers of Buddhism. 443 B.C. (?)
It condemned a system of ten 'Indulgences' which had grown

---

[1] *Sútras.* [2] *Vinaya.* [3] *Abhidharma.*
[4] *Pitakas,* lit. 'baskets ;' afterwards the five *Nikáyas.* [5] *Sangíti* in Páli.

up ; but it led to the separation of the Buddhists into two hostile parties, who afterwards split into eighteen sects.

Third Buddhist Council, 244 B.C. (?)
During the next two hundred years Buddhism spread over Northern India, perhaps receiving a new impulse from the Greek kingdoms in the Punjab. About 257 B.C., Asoka, the King of Magadha or Behar, became a zealous convert to the faith.[1] Asoka was grandson of the Chandra Gupta whom we shall meet as an adventurer in Alexander's camp, and afterwards as an ally of Seleukos. Asoka is said to have supported 64,000 Buddhist priests ; he founded many religious houses, and his kingdom is called the Land of the Monasteries (Vihára or Behar) to this day.

The work of Asoka.
Asoka did for Buddhism what Constantine afterwards effected for Christianity ; he organized it on the basis of a State religion. This he accomplished by five means—by a Council to settle the faith, by edicts promulgating its principles, by a State Department to watch over its purity, by missionaries to spread its doctrines, and by an authoritative revision or canon of the Buddhist scriptures. In 244 B.C., Asoka convened at Patná the Third Buddhist Council, of one thousand elders. Evil men, taking on them the yellow robe of the Order, had given forth their own opinions as the teaching of Buddha. Such heresies were now corrected ; and the Buddhism of Southern Asia practically dates from Asoka's Council.

(1) His Great Council.

---

[1] Much learning has been expended upon the age of Asoka, and various dates have been assigned to him. But, indeed, all Buddhist dates are open questions, according to the system of chronology adopted. The middle of the 3rd century B.C. may be taken as the era of Asoka. The following table from General Cunningham's *Corpus Inscriptionum Indicarum*, p. vii. (1877), exhibits the results of the latest researches on this subject :—

B.C. 264	ASOKA, Struggle with brothers, 4 years.
260	Comes to the throne.
257	Conversion to Buddhism.
256	Treaty with Antiochus.
255	Mahindo ordained.
251	Earliest date of rock edicts.
249	Second date of rock edicts.
248	Arsakes rebels in Parthia.
246	Diodotus rebels in Bactria.
244	Third Buddhist Council under Mogaliputra.
243	Mahindo goes to Ceylon.
242	Barábar cave inscriptions.
234	Pillar edicts issued.
231	Queen Asandhimitta dies.
228	Second Queen married.
226	Her attempt to destroy the Bodhi tree.
225	Asoka becomes an ascetic.
224	Issues Rúpnáth and Sasseram edicts.
223	Dies.
215	DASARATHA'S cave inscriptions, Nágárjuni.

In a number of edicts, before and after the synod, he published throughout India the cardinal principles of the faith. Such edicts are still found graven deep upon pillars, caves, and rocks, from the Yusafzai valley beyond Pesháwar on the north-western frontier, through the heart of Hindustán and the Central Provinces, to Káthiáwár in the west, and Orissa in the east coast of India. Tradition states that Asoka set up 84,000 memorial columns or topes. The Chinese pilgrims came upon them in the inner Himálayas. Forty-two inscriptions still surviving show how widely these royal sermons were spread over India itself.[1]

(2) His edicts.

In the year of the Council, Asoka founded a State Department to watch over the purity, and to direct the spread, of the faith. A Minister of Justice and Religion (Dharma Mahámátra) directed its operations; and, as one of its first duties was to proselytize, this Minister was charged with the welfare of the aborigines among whom his missionaries were sent. Asoka did not think it enough to convert the inferior races, without looking after their material interests. Wells were to be dug, and trees planted, along the roads; a system of medical aid was

(3) His Department of Public Worship.

---

[1] Major-General Cunningham, Director-General of the Archæological Survey of India, enumerates 14 rock inscriptions, 17 cave inscriptions, and 11 inscribed pillars. The rock inscriptions are at—(1) Sháhbázgarhi in the Yusafzai country, 40 miles east-north-east of Pesháwar; (2) Khálsi on the west bank of the Jumna; (3) Girnár in Káthiáwár, 40 miles north of Somnáth; (4 to 7) Dhauli in Cuttack, midway between Cuttack and Purí, and Jaugada in Ganjám District, 18 miles north-north-west of Barhampur,—two inscriptions at each, virtually identical; (8) Sasseram, at the north-east end of the Káimur range, 70 miles south-east of Benares; (9) Rúpnáth, a famous place of pilgrimage, 35 miles north of Jabalpur; (10 and 11) Bairát, 41 miles north of Jaipur; (12) the Khandgiri Hill, near Dhauli in Cuttack; (13) Deotek, 50 miles south-east of Nágpur; (14) Mánsera, north-west of Ráwal Pindi, inscribed in the Bactrian character. The cave inscriptions, 17 in number, are found at—(1, 2, 3) Barábar, and (4, 5, 6) Nágárjuni Hills, both places 15 miles north of Gayá; (7 to 15) Khandgiri Hill in Cuttack, and (16 and 17) Rámgarh in Sirguja. The eleven inscribed pillars are—(1) the Delhi-Siwálik, at Delhi; (2) the Delhi-Meerut, at Delhi; (3) the Allahábád at Jaipur; (4) the Lauriya-Araráj, at Lauriya, 77 miles north of Patná; (5) the Lauriya-Navandgarh, at another Lauriya, 15 miles north-north-west of Bettia; (6 and 7) two additional edicts on the Delhi-Siwálik, not found on any other pillar; (8 and 9) two short additional edicts on the Allahábád pillar, peculiar to itself; (10) a short mutilated record on a fragment of a pillar at Sánchi, near Bhílsa; (11) at Rámpura in the Tarái, north-east of the second Lauriya, near Bettia. The last-named pillar and the rock inscription at Mánsera (No. 14) are recent discoveries since the first edition of this work was published. The Mánsera rock inscription is interesting as being the second in the Bactrian character, and for its recording twelve Edicts complete.

K

established throughout his kingdom and the conquered Provinces, as far as Ceylon, for man and beast.[1] Officers were appointed to watch over domestic life and public morality,[2] and to promote instruction among the women as well as the youth.

(4) Missionary efforts.   Asoka recognised proselytism by peaceful means as a State duty.   The Rock Inscriptions record how he sent forth missionaries 'to the utmost limits of the barbarian countries,' to 'intermingle among all unbelievers,' for the spread of religion. They shall mix equally with soldiers, Bráhmans, and beggars, with the dreaded and the despised, both within the kingdom 'and in foreign countries, teaching better things.'[3] Conversion is to be effected by persuasion, not by the sword.   Buddhism was at once the most intensely missionary religion in the world, and the most tolerant.   This character of a proselytizing faith, which wins its victories by peaceful means, so strongly impressed upon it by Asoka, has remained a prominent feature of Buddhism to the present day.   Asoka, however, not only took measures to spread the religion, he also endeavoured to

(5) Reformed canon of Buddhist scriptures. secure its orthodoxy.   He collected the body of doctrine into an authoritative version, in the Mágadhí language or dialect of his central kingdom in Behar ; a version which for two thousand years has formed the canon (*pitakas*) of the Southern Buddhists.   In this way, the Mágadhí dialect became the Páli or sacred language of the Ceylonese.

Edicts of Asoka. Mr. Robert Cust thus summarizes Asoka's Fourteen Edicts :—

1. Prohibition of the slaughter of animals for food or sacrifice.
2. Provision of a system of medical aid for men and animals, and of plantations and wells on the roadside.
3. Order for a quinquennial humiliation and re-publication of the great moral precepts of the Buddhist faith.
4. Comparison of the former state of things, and the happy existing state under the king.
5. Appointment of missionaries to go into various countries, which are enumerated, to convert the people and foreigners.
6. Appointment of informers (or inspectors) and guardians of morality.
7. Expression of a desire that there may be uniformity of religion and equality of rank.
8. Contrast of the carnal pleasures of previous rulers with the pious enjoyments of the present king.
9. Inculcation of the true happiness to be found in virtue, through which alone the blessings of heaven can be propitiated.

---

[1] Rock Inscriptions, Edict ii., General Cunningham's *Corpus Inscriptionum*, p. 118.

[2] Rock Inscriptions, Edict vi. etc., *Corpus Inscriptionum*, p. 120. These Inspectors of Morals are supposed to correspond to the Sixth Caste of Megasthenes, the Ἐπίσκοποι of Arrian.

[3] Rock Inscriptions, Edict v. etc., *Corpus Inscriptionum*, p. 120.

10. Contrast of the vain and transitory glory of this world with the reward for which the king strives and looks beyond.

11. Inculcation of the doctrine that the imparting of *dharma* or teaching of virtue to others is the greatest of charitable gifts.

12. Address to all unbelievers.

13. (Imperfect) ; the meaning conjectural.

14. Summing up of the whole.

The fourth and last of the great Buddhist Councils was held under King Kanishka, according to one tradition four centuries after Buddha's death. The date of Kanishka is still uncertain ; but, from the evidence of coins and inscriptions, his reign has been fixed in the 1st century after Christ, or, say, 40 A.D.[1] Kanishka, the most famous of the Saka conquerors, ruled over North-Western India, and the adjoining countries. His authority had its nucleus in Kashmír, but it extended to both sides of the Himálayas, from Yarkand and Khokand to Agra and Sind. *{Fourth Council, Kanishka (40 A.D. ?)}*

Kanishka's Council of five hundred drew up three commentaries on the Buddhist faith. These commentaries supplied in part materials for the Tibetan or Northern Canon, completed at subsequent periods. The Northern Canon, or, as the Chinese proudly call it, the 'Greater Vehicle of the Law,' includes many later corruptions or developments of the Buddhism which was originally embodied by Asoka in the 'Lesser Vehicle,' or Canon of the Southern Buddhists (244 B.C.). The Buddhist Canon of China, a branch of the 'Greater Vehicle,' was gradually arranged between 67 and 1285 A.D. It includes 1440 distinct works, comprising 5586 books. The ultimate divergence between the Canons is great. They differ not only, as we have seen, in regard to the legend of Buddha's life, but also as to his teaching. With respect to doctrine, one example will suffice. According to the Northern or 'Greater Vehicle,' Buddhist monks who transgress wilfully after ordination may yet recover themselves ; while to such castaways the Southern or 'Lesser Vehicle' allowed no room for repentance.[2] *{'Greater Vehicle.' 'Lesser Vehicle.'}*

The original of the Northern Canon was written in the Sanskrit language, perhaps because the Kashmír and northern priests, who formed Kanishka's Council, belonged to isolated Himálayan settlements which had been little influenced by the *{Northern and Southern Canons.}*

---

[1] The latest efforts to fix the date of Kanishka are little more than records of conflicting authorities. See Dr. James Fergusson's paper in the *Journal of the Royal Asiatic Society*, Article ix., April 1880 ; and Mr. E. Thomas' comprehensive disquisition on the Sáh and Gupta coins, pp. 18-79 of the *Report of the Archæological Survey of Western India for* 1874-75, 4to, London, 1876.　　　　　[2] Beal, *Catena*, p. 253.

growth of the Indian vernacular dialects.   In one of these
dialects, the Mágadhí of Behar, the Southern Canon had been
compiled by Asoka and expanded by commentators.   Indeed,
the Buddhist compilations appear to have given the first literary
impulse to the Prákrits or spoken Aryan dialects in India ; as
represented by the Páli or Mágadhí of the Ceylonese Buddhist
scriptures, and the Maháráshtri of the ancient sacred books of
the Jains.   The northern priests, who compiled Kanishka's
Canon, preferred the 'perfected' Sanskrit, which had become
by that time the accepted literary vehicle of the learned
throughout India, to the Prákrit or 'natural' dialects of the
Gangetic valley.   Kanishka and his Kashmír Council (40
A.D. ?) became to the Northern or Tibeto-Chinese Buddhists,
what Asoka and his Patná Council (244 B.C.) had been to the
Buddhists of Ceylon and the South.

Buddhism
as a
national
religion ;
Buddhism was thus organized as a State religion by the
Councils of Asoka and Kanishka.   It started from Bráhmanical doctrines ; but from those doctrines, not as taught in
hermitages to clusters of Bráhman disciples, but as vitalized by
a preacher of rare power in the capital cities of India.   Buddha
did not abolish caste.   On the contrary, reverence to Bráhmans and to the spiritual guide ranked among the four great
sets of duties, with obedience to parents, control over self, and
acts of kindness to all men and animals.   He introduced,
however, a new classification of mankind, on the spiritual basis
of believers and unbelievers.

its religious
orders ;
The former took rank in the Buddhist community,—
at first, according to their age and merit ; in later times, as
laity[1] and clergy[2] (*i.e.* the religious orders).   Buddhism carried
transmigration to its utmost spiritual use, and proclaimed our
own actions to be the sole ruling influence on our past, present,
and future states.   It was thus led into the denial of any
external being or god who could interfere with the immutable
law of cause and effect as applied to the soul.   But, on the
other hand, it linked together mankind as parts of one
universal whole, and denounced the isolated self-seeking of
the human heart as 'the heresy of individuality.'[3]   Its mission
was to make men more moral, kinder to others, and happier
themselves ; not to propitiate imaginary deities.   It accordingly founded its teaching on man's duty to his neighbour,
instead of on his obligations to God ; and constructed its

---

[1] *Upasáka.*

[2] *Sramana, bhikshu* (monk or religious mendicant), *bhikshuní* (nun).

[3] *Sakdyaditthi.*

ritual on the basis of relic-worship or the commemoration of and
good men, instead of on sacrifice. Its sacred buildings were practical morality.
not temples to the gods, but monasteries (*vihâras*) for the
religious orders, with their bells and rosaries ; or memorial
shrines,[1] reared over a tooth or bone of the founder of the faith.

The missionary impulse given by Asoka quickly bore fruit. Spread of
In the year after his great Council at Patná (244 B.C.), his son Buddhism.
Mahindo[2] carried Asoka's version of the Buddhist scriptures
in the Mágadhí language to Ceylon. He took with him a In the
band of fellow-missionaries ; and soon afterwards, his sister, South,
the princess Sanghamittá, who had entered the Order, followed Ceylon, etc., 244
with a company of nuns. It was not, however, till six hundred B.C. to
years later (410–432 A.D.) that the Ceylonese Canon was 638 A.D.
written out in Páli, the sacred Mágadhí language of the
Southern Buddhists. About the same time, missionaries from
Ceylon finally established the faith in Burma (450 A.D.). The
Burmese themselves assert that two Buddhist preachers landed
in Pegu as early as 207 B.C. Indeed, some Burmese date the
arrival of Buddhist missionaries just after the Patná Council,
244 B.C., and point out the ruined city of Tha-tun, between the
Sitaung (Tsit-taung) and Salwín estuaries, as the scene of their
pious labours. Siam was converted to Buddhism in 638 A.D. ;
Java received its missionaries direct from India between the 5th
and the 7th centuries, and spread the faith to Bali and Sumatra.[3]
While Southern Buddhism was thus wafted across the In the
ocean, another stream of missionaries had found their way North,
China, etc.,
by Central Asia into China. Their first arrival in the Chinese 2nd century
empire is said to date from the 2nd century B.C., although it B.C. to
was not till 65 A.D. that Buddhism there became the estab- 552 A.D.
lished religion. The Greco-Bactrian kingdoms in the Punjab,
and beyond it, afforded a favourable soil for the faith. The
Scythian dynasties who succeeded the Greco-Bactrians accepted
Buddhism; and the earliest remains which recent discovery has

---

[1] *Stúpas, topes,* literally 'heaps or tumuli ;' *dagobas* or *dhátu-gopas,*
'relic-preservers ;' *chaityas.*   [2] Sanskrit, Mahendra.

[3] All these dates are uncertain. They are founded on the Singalese
chronology, but the orthodox in the respective countries place their national
conversion at remoter periods. Occasionally, however, the dates can be
tested from external sources. Thus we know from the Chinese traveller
Fa-Hian, that up to about 414 A.D. Java was still unconverted.   Fa-
Hian says, 'Heretics and Bráhmans were numerous there, and the law of
Buddha is in nowise entertained.' The Burmese chroniclers go back to a
time when the duration of human life was ninety millions of years ; and
when a single dynasty ruled for a period represented by a unit followed
by 140 cyphers. See *The Imperial Gazetteer of India,* Article SANDOWAY.

unearthed in Afghánistán are Buddhist.   Kanishka's Council, soon after the commencement of the Christian era, gave the great impetus to the faith beyond the Himálayas. Tibet, South Central Asia, and China, lay along the regular missionary routes of Northern Buddhism ; the Kirghiz are said to have carried the religion as far west as the Caspian; on the east, Buddhism was introduced into the Corea in 372 A.D., and thence into Japan in 552.

Buddhist influence on Christianity.

Buddhist doctrines are believed to have deeply affected religious thought in Alexandria and Palestine. The question is yet undecided as to how far the Buddhist ideal of the holy life, with its monks, nuns, relic-worship, bells, and rosaries, influenced Christian monachism ; and to what extent Buddhist philosophy aided the development of the Gnostic heresies, particularly those of Basilides and Manes, which rent the early church.   It is certain that the analogies are striking, and have been pointed out alike by Jesuit missionaries in Asia, and by oriental scholars in Europe.[1] The form of abjuration for those who renounced the Gnostic doctrines of Manes, expressly mentions Βόδδα and the Σκυθιανός (Buddha and the Scythian or Sákya)—seemingly, says Weber, a separation of Buddha the Sákya into two.   At this moment, the Chinese in San Francisco assist their devotions by pictures of the Buddhist Goddess of Mercy, imported on thin paper from Canton, which the Irish Roman Catholics identify as the Virgin Mary with the Infant in her arms, an aureole round her head, an adoring figure at her feet, and the Spirit hovering in the form of a bird.[2]

But it is right to point out that the early Nestorian Christians in China may have been the source of some of these resemblances. The liturgy of the Goddess of Mercy, Kwanyin, in which the analogies to the Eastern Christian office are most strongly marked, have been traced with certainty only as far back as 1412 A.D. in the Chinese Canon.[3] Professor Max

---

[1] For the latter aspect of the question, see Weber, founding on Lassen, Renan, and Beal, *Hist. Ind. Lit.*, p. 309, note 363, ed. 1878.

[2] See also *post*, p. 153. Polemical writers, Christian and Chinese, have with equal injustice accused Buddhism and Christianity of consciously plagiarizing each other's rites. Thus Kuang-Hsien, the distinguished member of the Astronomical Board, who brought about the Chinese persecution of the Christians from 1665 to 1671, writes of them : ' They pilfer this talk about heaven and hell from the refuse of Buddhism, and then turn round and revile Buddhism.'— *The Death-blow to the Corrupt Doctrines of T'len-chu (i.e.* Christianity), p. 46 (Shanghai, 1870). See also the remarks of Jao-chow—' The man most distressed in heart '—in the same collection.

[3] For an excellent account from the Chinese texts of the worship and liturgy of Kwan-yin, ' the Saviour,' or in her female form as the Goddess of Mercy, see Beal's *Catena of Buddhist Scriptures*, 383–397 (Trübner, 1871).

Müller endeavoured to show that Buddha himself is the original of Saint Josaphat, who has a day assigned to him by both the Greek and Roman churches.[1]

Professor Müller's Essay [2] has led to an examination of the whole evidence bearing on this subject.[3] The results may be thus summarized. The Roman Martyrology at the end of the saints for the 27th November, states: 'Apud Indos Persis finitimos sanctorum Barlaam et Josaphat (commemoratio), quorum actus mirandos Joannes Damascenus conscripsit.' *Among the Indians who border on Persia, Saints Barlaam and Josaphat, whose wonderful works have been written of by St. John of Damascus.* The story of these two saints is that of a young Indian prince, Josaphat, who is converted by a hermit, Barlaam. Josaphat undergoes the same awakening as Buddha from the pleasures of this world. His royal father had taken similar precautions to prevent the youth from becoming acquainted with the sorrows of life. But Josaphat, like Buddha, is struck by successive spectacles of disease, old age, and death; and abandons his princely state for that of a Christian devotee. He converts to the faith his father, his subjects, and even the magician employed to seduce him. For this magician, Theudas, the Buddhist schismatic Devadatta is supposed to have supplied the orginal; while the name of Josaphat is itself identified by philologers with that of Boddhisattwa, the complete appellation of Buddha.[4]

This curious transfer of the religious teacher of Asia to the Christian Martyrology has an equally curious history. Saint John of Damascus wrote in the 8th century in Greek, and an Arabic translation of his work, belonging to the 11th century, still survives. The story of Josaphat was popular in the Greek Church, and was embodied by Simeon the Metaphrast in the lives of the saints, *circ.* 1150 A.D. The Greek form of the name is 'Ιωάσαφ.[5] By the 12th century, the

Marginal notes: Buddha as a Christian Saint. Legend of Saints Barlaam and Josaphat. Early stages of the story.

---

[1] *Chips from a German Workshop,* vol. iv. pp. 177–189, ed. 1875.

[2] *Contemporary Review,* July 1870.

[3] For a list of the authorities, and an investigation of them from the Roman Catholic side, by Emmanuel Cosquin, see *Revue des Questions Historiques,* lvi. pp. 579-600; Paris, October 1880.

[4] The earlier form of Josaphat was Ioasaph in Greek and Youasaf or Youdasf in Arabic, an evident derivation from the Sanskrit Boddhisattwa, through the Persian form Boudasp (Weber). The name of the magician Theudas is in like manner an accurate philological reproduction of Devadatta or Thevdat.

[5] See the valuable note in Colonel Yule's *Marco Polo,* vol. ii. pp. 302-309 (2nd ed. 1875).]

Life of Barlaam and Josaphat had already reached Western
Europe in a Latin form.   During the first half of the 13th
century, Vincent de Beauvais inserted it in his *Speculum
Historiale ;* and in the latter half of that century it found a
place in the Golden Legend of Jacques de Voragine.   Mean-
while, it had also been popularized by the troubadour, Guy de
Cambrai.   From this double source, the Golden Legend of the
Church and the French poem of the people, the story of
Barlaam and Josaphat spread throughout Europe.   German,
Provençal, Italian, Polish, Spanish, English, and Norse versions
carried it from the southern extremity of the Continent to
Sweden and Iceland.

In 1583, the legend was entered in the Roman Martyrology
for the 27th day of November, as we have already seen, upon
the alleged testimony of St. John of Damascus.   A church in
Palermo still (1874) bears the dedication, *Divo Iosaphat.*[1]
The Roman Martyrology of Gregory XIII., revised under the
auspices of Urban VIII., has a universal acceptance throughout
Catholic Christendom ; although from the statements of Pope
Benedict XIV., and others, it would appear that it is to be
used for edification, rather than as a work resting on infallible
authority.[2]   However this may be, the text of the two legends,
and the names of their prominent actors, place beyond doubt
the identity of the Eastern and the Western story.

A Japanese   It is difficult to enter a Japanese Buddhist temple without
temple;   being struck by analogies to the Christian ritual on the one
its analo-
gies to   hand, and to Hinduism on the other.   The chantings of the
Hinduism   priests, their bowing as they pass the altar, their vestments,
and Chris-
tianity.   rosaries, bells, incense, and the responses of the worshippers,
remind one of the Christian ritual.   'The temple at Rokugo,'
writes a recent traveller to a remote town in Japan, 'was very
beautiful, and, except that its ornaments were superior in
solidity and good taste, differed little from a Romish church.
The low altar, on which were lilies and lighted candles, was
draped in blue and silver; and on the high altar, draped in
crimson and cloth of gold, there was nothing but a closed
shrine, an incense-burner, and a vase of lotuses.'[3]   In a
Buddhist temple at Ningpo, the Chinese goddess of mercy,

---

[1] Yule, *op. cit.* p. 308.

[2] This aspect of the question is discussed at considerable length by
Emmanuel Cosquin, pp. 583-594. He gives the two legends of Buddha
and of Barlaam-Josaphat in parallel columns, pp. 590-594 of the *Revue des
Questions Historiques,* vol. lvi., already cited.

[3] Miss Bird's *Unbeaten Tracks in Japan,* vol. i. p. 295 (ed. 1880).

Kwan-yin, whose resemblance to the Virgin Mary and Child Serpent ornamentation. has already been mentioned (p. 150), is seen standing on a serpent, bruising his head with her heel.

The Hindus, while denouncing Buddha as a heretic, have Buddha as an *avatár* of Vishnu. been constrained to admit him to a place in their mythology. They regard him as the ninth, and hitherto last, incarnation of Vishnu,—the Lying Spirit let loose to deceive men until the tenth or final descent of Vishnu, on the white horse, with a flaming sword like a comet in his hand, for the destruction of the wicked and the renovation of the world.

While on the one hand a vast growth of legends has arisen Buddha's personality denied. around Buddha, tending to bring out every episode of his life into strong relief, efforts have been made on the other hand to explain away his personal identity. No date can be assigned with certainty for his existence on this earth. The Northern Buddhists have fourteen different accounts, ranging from 2422 His date to 546 B.C.[1] The Southern Buddhists agree in starting from the 1st of June 543 B.C. as the day of Buddha's death. This latter date, 543 B.C., is usually accepted by European writers; but Indian chronology, as worked back from inscriptions and coins,[2] gives the date *circ.* 480. Some scholars, indeed, have argued that Buddhism is merely a religious development of the Bráhmanical Sánkhya philosophy of Kapila (*ante*, p. 99); that Buddha's birth is placed at a purely allegorical site, Kapila-vastu, 'the abode of Kapila'; that his mother is called Máyá-deví, in reference to the Máyá doctrine of Kapila's system; and that his own two names are symbolical ones, Siddartha, 'he who has fulfilled his end,' and Buddha, 'the enlightened.'

Buddhism and Bráhmanism are unquestionably united Links with Bráhmanism. by intermediate links. Certain of the sacred texts of the Bráhmans, particularly the Vrihad Aranyaka and the Atharva Upanishad of the Yoga system, teach doctrines which are essentially Buddhistic. According to Wilson and others, Buddha had possibly no personal existence;[3] Buddhism

---

[1] Csoma de Körös, on the authority of Tibetan MSS., *Tibetan Grammar*, p. 199. A debt long overdue has at length been paid to one of the most single-minded of oriental scholars by the publication of Dr. Theodore Duka's *Life and Works of Alexander Csoma de Körös*. (Trübner, 1885.)

[2] General Cunningham works back the date of Buddha's death to 478 B.C., and takes this as his starting-point in the *Corpus Inscriptionum Indicarum*, p. vii. The subject is admirably discussed by Mr. Rhys Davids in the *International Numismata Orientalia* (Ceylon fasciculus), pp. 38–56. He arrives at 412 B.C. as the most probable date. Dr. Oldenberg fixes it at about 480 B.C.

[3] Professor H. H. Wilson went so far as to say, 'It seems not impossible

Buddhism
merely the
Sánkhya
system?

Buddhism was merely the Sánkhya philosophy widened into a national religion; and the religious life of the Buddhistic orders was the old Bráhmanical type popularized.[1] The theory is at any rate so far true, that Buddhism was not a sudden invention of any single mind, but a development on a broader basis of a philosophy and religion which preceded it. Such speculations, however, leave out of sight the two great traditional features of Buddhism—namely, the preacher's appeal to the people, and the undying influence of his beautiful life. Senart's still more sceptical theory of Buddha as a Solar Myth, has completely broken down under the critical examination of Oldenberg.

Buddhism
did not
oust Bráh-
manism.

Buddhism never ousted Bráhmanism from any large part of India. The two systems co-existed as popular religions from the death of Buddha during thirteen hundred years (543 B.C. to about 800 A.D.), and modern Hinduism is the joint product of both. The legends of Buddha, especially those of the Northern Canon,[2] bear witness to the active influence of Bráhmanism during the whole period of Buddha's life. After his death, certain kings and certain eras were intensely Buddhistic; but the continuous existence of Bráhmanism is abundantly proved from the time of Alexander (327 B.C.) downwards. The historians who chronicled Alexander's march, and the Greek ambassador Megasthenes, who succeeded them (300 B.C.) in their literary labours, bear witness to the predominance of Bráhmanism in the period immediately preceding Asoka. Inscriptions, local legends, Sanskrit literature, and the drama, disclose the survival of Bráhman influence during the next six centuries (244 B.C. to 400 A.D.). From 400 A.D. we have the evidence of the Chinese pilgrims, who toiled through Central Asia into India to visit the birthplace of their faith.[3]

 ' Never did more devoted pilgrims,' writes the greatest living

that Sákya Muni is an unreal being, and that all that is related of him is as much a fiction as is that of his preceding migrations and the miracles that attended his birth, his life, and his departure.' The arguments are dealt with by Weber, *Hist. Ind. Lit.*, pp. 284–290, ed. 1878.

[1] Dr. Oldenberg's *Buddha, Sein Leben*, contains valuable evidence on this subject (Hoey's transl. pp. 46, 48 to 59, etc.). See also *The Sánkhya Aphorisms of Kapila*, Sanskrit and English, with illustrative texts from the Commentaries by Dr. Ballantyne, formerly Principal of the Benares College, 3rd ed. (Trübner, 1885.)

[2] See the *Life of the Buddha and the Early History of his Order*, derived from the Tibetan texts, by Mr. Woodville Rockhill of the U. S. Legation in China ; also Oldenberg's *Buddha*.

[3] The *Si-yu-ki, or Buddhist Records of the Western World*, translated from the Chinese, by Samuel Beal (Trübner, 2 vols. 1884), has completed

student of their lives,[1] 'leave their native country to encounter the perils of travel in foreign and distant lands; never did disciples more ardently desire to gaze on the sacred vestiges of their religion ; never did men endure greater sufferings by desert, mountain, and sea, than these simple-minded, earnest Buddhist priests.' Fa-Hian entered India from Afghánistán, and journeyed down the whole Gangetic valley to the Bay of Bengal in 399–413 A.D. He found Bráhman priests equally honoured with Buddhist monks, and temples to the Indian gods side by side with the religious houses of the Buddhist faith. Buddhism and Bráhmanism, 400 A.D. to 645 A.D. Fa-Hian, 399 A.D.

Hiuen Tsiang, a still greater pilgrim, also travelled to India from China by the Central Asia route, and has left a fuller record of the state of the two religions in the 7th century. His wanderings extended from 629 to 645 A.D. Everywhere throughout India he found the two systems eagerly competing for the suffrages of the people. By this time, indeed, Bráhmanism was beginning to reassert itself at the expense of the Buddhist religion. The monuments of the great Buddhist monarchs, Asoka and Kanishka, confronted him from the moment he neared the Punjab frontier ; but so also did the temples of Siva and his 'dread' queen Bhímá. Throughout North-Western India he found Buddhist convents and monks surrounded by 'swarms of heretics,' *i.e.* Bráhmanical sects. Hiuen Tsiang, 629 A.D.

The political power was also divided, though Buddhist sovereigns still predominated. A Buddhist monarch ruled over ten kingdoms in Afghánistán. At Peshawar, the great monastery built by Kanishka was deserted, but the populace remained faithful. In Kashmír, the king and people were devout Buddhists, under the teaching of 500 monasteries and

and perfected the work begun by Julien and Rémusat. Mr. Beal's new volumes throw a flood of light on the social, religious, and political condition of India from the 5th to 7th centuries A.D. The older authorities are Foe Koue Ki, *ou Relation des Royaumes Bouddhiques ; Voyages dans la Tartarie, l'Afghanistan et l'Inde à la fin du* iv. *siècle, par Chi-Fa-Hian,* translated by A. Rémusat, reviewed by Klaproth and Landresse, 1836. Mr. Beal's *Travels of the Buddhist Pilgrim Fa-Hian,* translated with Notes and Prolegomena, 1869 ; Julien's *Voyages des Pèlerins Bouddhistes,* t. i. ; *Histoire de la Vie de Hiouen-Thsang et de ses Voyages dans l'Inde,* translated from the Chinese, 1853, t. ii. and iii. ; *Mémoires sur les Contrées Occidentales, par Hiouen-Thsang,* translated from the Chinese, 1857–59. C. J. Neumánn's *Pilgerfahrten Buddhistischer Priester von China nach Indien, aus dem Chinesischen übersetzt,* 1883, of which only one volume is published ; General Cunningham's *Ancient Geography of India,* and his *Reports of the Archæological Survey of India* (various dates).

[1] *Si-yu-ki,* Mr. Beal's Introduction, pp. ix., x.

5000 monks. In the country identified with Jaipur, on the other hand, the inhabitants were devoted to heresy and war.

Buddhism in India, 629–645 A.D. Buddhist influence in Northern India seems, during the 7th century A.D., to have centred in the fertile plain between the Jumna and the Ganges, and in Behar. At Kanauj (Kanyákubja), on the Ganges, Hiuen Tsiang found a powerful Buddhist monarch, Síláditya, whose influence reached from the Punjab to North-Eastern Bengal, and from the Himálayas to the Narbadá river. Here flourished 100 Buddhist convents and 10,000 monks. But the king's eldest brother had been lately slain by a sovereign of Eastern India, a hater of Buddhism; and 200 temples to the Bráhman gods reared their heads under the protection of the devout Síláditya himself.

Síláditya appears as an Asoka of the 7th century A.D., and he practised with primitive vigour the two great Buddhist virtues of spreading the faith and charity. The former he Council of Síláditya, 634 A.D. attempted by means of a general Council in 634 A.D. Twenty-one tributary sovereigns attended, together with the most learned Buddhist monks and Bráhmans of their kingdoms. But the object of the convocation was no longer the undisputed assertion of the Buddhist religion. It dealt with the two phases of the religious life of India at that time. First, a discussion between the Buddhists and Bráhman philosophers of the Sánkhya and Vaiseshika schools; second, a dispute between the Buddhist sects who followed respectively the Northern and the Southern Canons, known as 'the Greater and the Lesser Vehicle of the Law.' The rites of the populace were of as composite a character as the doctrines of their teachers. On the first day of the Council, a statue of Buddha was installed with great pomp; on the second, an image of the Sun-god; on the third, an idol of Siva.

Síláditya's charity. Síláditya held a solemn distribution of his royal treasures every five years. Hiuen Tsiang describes how on the plain near Allahábád, where the Ganges and the Jumna unite their waters, the kings of the Empire, and a multitude of people, were feasted for seventy-five days. Síláditya brought forth the stores of his palace, and gave them away to Bráhmans and Buddhists, to monks and heretics, without distinction. At the end of the festival, he stripped off his jewels and royal raiment, handed them to the bystanders, and, like Buddha of old, put on the rags of a beggar. By this ceremony, the monarch commemorated the Great Renunciation of the founder of the Buddhist faith. At the same time, he discharged the highest duty inculcated alike by the Buddhist and Bráhmanical religions,

namely almsgiving. The vast monastery of Nalanda [1] formed Monastery of Nal-anda.
a seat of learning which recalls the universities of Mediæval
Europe.   Ten thousand monks and novices of the eighteen
Buddhist schools here studied theology, philosophy, law,
science, especially medicine, and practised their devotions.
They lived in lettered ease, supported from the royal funds.
But even this stronghold of Buddhism furnishes a proof that
Buddhism was only one of two hostile creeds in India.
During the brief period with regard to which the Chinese
records afford information, it was three times destroyed by the
enemies of the faith.[2]

Hiuen Tsiang travelled from the Punjab to the mouth of the Mingling of Buddh-ism and Bráhman-ism, 629–645 A.D.
Ganges, and made journeys into Southern India.   But every-
where he found the two religions mingled.   Buddh-Gayá, which
holds so high a sanctity in the legends of Buddha, had already
become a great Bráhman centre.   On the east of Bengal,
Assam had not been converted to Buddhism.   In the south-
west, Orissa was a stronghold of the Buddhist faith.   But in
the seaport of Tamlúk, at the mouth of the Húglí, the temples
to the Bráhman gods were five times more numerous than
the monasteries of the faithful.   On the Madras coast,
Buddhism flourished ; and indeed, throughout Southern India,
the faith seems still to have been. in the ascendant, although
struggling against Bráhman heretics and their gods.

During the 8th and 9th centuries A.D., Bráhmanism be- Victory of Bráhman-ism, 700–900 A.D.
came the ruling religion.   There are legends of persecutions,
instigated by Bráhman reformers, such as Kumaríla Bhatta
and Sankara Achárya.   But the downfall of Buddhism seems
to have resulted from natural decay, and from new movements
of religious thought, rather than from any general suppression
by the sword.   Its extinction is contemporaneous with the rise
of Hinduism, and belongs to a subsequent chapter.

In the 11th century, it was chiefly outlying States, like
Kashmír and Orissa, that remained faithful.   When the Muhammadans come permanently upon the scene, Buddhism as a
popular faith has almost disappeared from the interior Provinces
of India.   Magadha, the cradle of the religion, still continued
Buddhist under the Pál Rájás down to the Musalmán conquest
of Bakhtiyár Khilji in 1199 A.D.[3]

---

[1] Identified with the modern Baragáon, near Gayá. The Great Monastery can be traced by a mass of brick ruins, 1600 feet long by 400 feet deep. General Cunningham's *Ancient Geography of India*, pp. 468–470, ed. 1871.

[2] Beal's *Catena of Buddhist Scriptures from the Chinese*, p. 371, ed. 1871.

[3] MS. materials supplied to the author by General Cunningham, to

Buddhism an exiled religion, 1000 A.D.   During nearly a thousand years, Buddhism has been a banished religion from its native home.   But it has won greater triumphs in its exile than it could have ever achieved in the land of its birth.   It has created a literature and a religion for nearly half the human race, and has affected the beliefs of the other half.   Five hundred millions of men, or forty per cent. of the inhabitants of the world, still acknowledge, with more or less fidelity, the holy teaching of Buddha.   Afghánistán, Nepál, Eastern Túrkistán, Tibet, Mongolia, Manchuria, China, Japan, the Eastern Archipelago, Siam, Burma, Ceylon, and India, at one time marked the magnificent circumference

Its foreign conquests.   of its conquests.   Its shrines and monasteries stretched in a continuous line from what are now the confines of the Russian Empire to the equatorial islands of the Pacific.   During twenty-four centuries, Buddhism has encountered and outlived a series of powerful rivals.   At this day it forms, with Christianity and Islám, one of the three great religions of the world ; and the most numerously followed of the three.

Buddhist survivals in India.   In India its influence has survived its separate existence. The Buddhist period not only left a distinct sect, the Jains ; but it supplied the spiritual basis on which Bráhmanism finally developed from the creed of a caste into the religion of the people.   A later chapter will show how important and how permanent have been Buddhistic influences on Hinduism. The Buddhists in British India in 1881 numbered nearly $3\frac{1}{2}$ millions, of whom $3\frac{1}{4}$ millions were in British Burma ; and 166,892 on the Indian continent, almost entirely in North-Eastern Bengal and Assam.   Together with the Jain sect, the Buddhist subjects of the Crown in British India amount to close on four millions (1881).[1]   The revival of Buddhism is always a possibility in India.   This year (1885) an excellent Buddhist journal has been started in Bengalí, at Chittagong.

The Jains.   The Jains number about half a million in British India. Like the Buddhists, they deny the authority of the Veda, except

whose Archæological Reports and kind assistance this volume is deeply indebted.

[1] The Buddhists proper were returned in 1881 for British India at 3,418,476 ; of whom 3,251,584 were in British Burma ; 155,809 in the Lieutenant-Governorship of Bengal ; and 6563 in Assam.   The Jains proper were returned at 448,897 in British India by the Census of 1881. But except in a few spots, chiefly among the spurs of the Himálayas and in Assam and South-Eastern Bengal, the Indian Buddhists may be generally reckoned as Jains.

in so far as it agrees with their own doctrines. They disregard sacrifice; practise a strict morality; believe that their past and future states depend upon their own actions rather than on any external deity; and scrupulously reverence the vital principle in man and beast. They differ from the Buddhists chiefly in their ritual and objects of worship. The veneration of good men departed is common to both, but the Jains have expanded and methodized such adoration on lines of their own.

The Buddhists admit that many Buddhas have appeared in successive lives upon earth, and attained *Nirvána* or beatific extinction; but they confine their reverence to a comparatively small number. The Jains divide time into successive eras, and assign twenty-four *Jinas*, or just men made perfect, to each.[1] They name twenty-four in the past age, twenty-four in the present, and twenty-four in the era to come; and place colossal statues of white or black marble to this great company of saints in their temples. They adore above all the two latest, or twenty-third and twenty-fourth *Jinas* of the present era—namely, Pársvanáth[2] and Mahávíra. *Jain doctrines.*

The Jains choose wooded mountains and the most lovely retreats of nature for their places of pilgrimage, and cover them with exquisitely-carved shrines in white marble or stucco. Párasnáth Hill in Bengal, the temple city of Pálitána in Káthiáwár, and Mount Abú, which rises with its gems of architecture like a jewelled island from the Rájputána plains, form well-known scenes of their worship. The Jains are a wealthy community, usually engaged in banking or wholesale commerce, devoid indeed of the old missionary spirit of Buddhism, but closely knit together among themselves. Their charity is boundless; and they form the chief supporters of the beast hospitals, which the old Buddhistic tenderness for animals has left in many of the cities of India. *Jain temple cities.*

Jainism is, in its external aspects, Buddhism equipped with a mythology—a mythology, however, not of gods, but of saints. But in its essentials, Jainism forms a survival of beliefs anterior to Asoka and Kanishka. According to the old view, the Jains are a remnant of the Indian Buddhists who saved themselves from extinction by compromises with Hinduism, and so managed to erect themselves into a recognised caste. *Relation of Jainism to Buddhism.*

[1] Under such titles as Jagata-prabhu, 'lord of the world;' Kshínakarmá, 'freed from ceremonial acts;' Sarvajna, 'all-knowing;' Adhíswara, 'supreme lord;' Tírthankara, 'he who has crossed over the world;' and Jina, 'he who has conquered the human passions.'

[2] Popularly rendered Párasnáth.

Jains
earlier
than
Buddhists?

According to the later and truer view, they represent in an unbroken succession the Nigantha sect of the Asoka edicts. The Jains themselves claim as their founder, Mahávíra, the teacher or contemporary of Buddha ; and the Niganthas appear as a sect independent of, indeed opposed to, the Buddhists in the Rock Inscriptions of Asoka and in the Southern Canon (*pitakas*).

Mahávíra, who bore also the spiritual name of Vardhamána, 'The Increaser,' is the 24th Jina or 'Conqueror of the Passions,' adored in the present age of Jain chronology. Like Buddha, he was of princely birth, and lived and laboured in the same country and at the same time as Buddha. According to the southern Buddhistic dates, Buddha 'attained rest' 543 B.C., and Mahávíra in 526 B.C. According to the Jain texts, Mahávíra was the predecessor and teacher of Buddha.

Antiquity
of the
Jains.

A theory has accordingly been advanced that the Buddhism of Asoka (244 B.C.) was in reality a later product than the Nigantha or Jain doctrines.[1] The Jains are divided into theSwetámbaras, 'The White Robed,' and the Digambaras, 'The Naked.' The Tibetan texts make it clear that sects closely analogous to the Jains existed in the time of Buddha, and that they were antecedent and rival orders to that which Buddha established.[2] Even the Southern Buddhist Canon preserves recollections of a struggle between a naked sect like the Jain Digambaras, and the decently robed Buddhists.[3] This Digambara or Nigantha sect (Nirgrantha, 'those who have cast aside every tie') was very distinctly recognised by Asoka's edicts ; and both the Swetámbara and Digambara orders of the modern Jains find mention in the early copper-plate inscriptions of Mysore, *circ.* 5th or 6th century A.D. The Jains in our own day feel strongly on this subject, and the head of the community at Ahmadábád has placed many arguments before the writer of the present work to prove that their faith was anterior to Buddhism.

Until quite recently, however, European scholars did not admit the pretensions of the Jains to pre-Buddhistic antiquity.

[1] This subject was discussed in Mr. Edward Thomas' *Jainism, or the Early Faith of Asoka ;* in Mr. Rhys Davids' article in *The Academy* of 13th September 1879 ; in his *Hibbert Lectures,* p. 27 ; and in the *Numismata Orientalia* (Ceylon fasciculus), pp. 55, 60.

[2] Mr. Woodville Rockhill's *Life of the Buddha,* from the Bkah-Hgyur and Bstan-Hgyur in *variis locis.* 1884.

[3] See for example the curious story of the devout Buddhist bride from the Burmese sacred books, in Bishop Bigandet's *Life of Gaudama,* pp. 257-259, vol. i. ed. 1882.

H. H. Wilson questioned their importance at any period earlier than twelve centuries ago.[1] Weber regarded 'the Jains as merely one of the oldest sects of Buddhism;' and Lassen believed that they had branched off from the Buddhists.[2] M. Barth, after a careful discussion of the evidence, still thought that we must regard the Jains 'as a sect which took its rise in Buddhism.'[3] On the other hand, Oldenberg, who brings the latest light from the Páli texts to bear on the question, accepts the identity of the Jain sect with the Niganthas 'into whose midst the younger brotherhood of Buddha entered.'[4]

The learned Jacobi has now investigated this question from the Jain texts themselves.[5] Oldenberg had proved, out of the Buddhist scriptures, that Buddhism was a true product of Bráhman doctrine and discipline. Jacobi shows that both 'Buddhism and Jainism must be regarded as religions developed out of Bráhmanism not by a sudden reformation, but prepared by a religious movement going on for a long time.'[6] And he brings forward evidence for believing that Jainism was the earlier outgrowth; that it was probably founded by Pársvanáth, now revered as the 23rd Jina; and merely reformed by Mahávira, the contemporary of Buddha.[7] The outfit of the Jain monk, his alms-bowl, rope, and water vessel, was practically the equipment of the previous Bráhman ascetic.[8] In doctrine, the Jains accepted the Bráhman pantheistic philosophy of the *Atmán*, or Universal Soul. They believed that not only animals and plants, but the elements themselves, earth, fire, water, and wind, were endowed with souls. Buddha made a further divergence. He combated the Bráhman doctrine of the Universal Soul; and the Jain dogma, of the elements and

Jacobi's investigation of the question.

Jainism older than Buddhism.

---

[1] *Essays and Lectures on the Religion of the Hindus*, by H. H. Wilson. Dr. Reinhold Rost's edition, p. 329, vol. i. (1862).

[2] Weber's *Indische Studien*, xvi. 210, and Lassen's *Indische Alterthumskunde*, iv. 763 *et seq.*

[3] Barth's *Religions of India*, ed. 1882, p. 151; also Barth's *Revue de l'Histoire des Religions*, iii. 90.

[4] *Buddha, his Life, his Doctrine, his Order*, by Prof. Hermann Oldenberg. Hoey's translation (1882), p. 67. See also his pp. 66 and (footnote) 77, and 175.

[5] Jaina Sútras, Part I., the Acháránga Sútra, and the Kalpa Sútra, by Hermann Jacobi, forming vol. xxii. of Max Müller's *Sacred Books of the East*. Clarendon Press, 1884.

[6] Jacobi, *op. cit.* Introduction, xxxii.   [7] *Op. cit.* xxxiv.

[8] For slight differences, see Jacobi, xxviii.

L

minerals being endowed with souls, finds no place in Buddhist philosophy.[1]

Date of the Jain Scriptures. Jacobi believes that the Jain texts were composed or collected at the end of the 4th century B.C.; that the origin of the extant Jain literature cannot be placed earlier than about 300 B.C.; and that their sacred books were reduced to writing in the 5th century A.D.[2] He thinks that the two existing divisions of the Jains, the Swetambaras and the Digambaras, separated from each other about two or three hundred years after the death of the Founder; but 'that the development of the Jain church has not been at any time violently interrupted.'

Jains an independent sect. That, 'in fact, we can follow this development from its true beginning through its various stages, and that Jainism is as much independent from other sects, especially from Buddhism, as can be expected from any sect.'[3]

Modern Jainism. In its superficial aspects, modern Jainism may be described as a religion allied in doctrine to ancient Indian Buddhism, but humanized by saint-worship, and narrowed from a national religion to the exclusive requirements of a sect.

Survivals of Buddhism in India. The noblest survivals of Buddhism in India are to be found, however, not among any peculiar body, but in the religion of the people; in that principle of the brotherhood of man, with the re-assertion of which each new revival of Hinduism starts; in the asylum which the great Vaishnav sect affords to women who have fallen victims to caste rules, to the widow and the outcast; in that gentleness and charity to all men, which take the place of a poor-law in India, and give a high significance to the half-satirical epithet of the 'mild' Hindu.

[1] *Op. cit.* xxxiii.   [2] Jacobi, *op. cit.* xxxv. and xliii.   [3] *Op. cit.* xlvi.

CHAPTER VI.

THE GREEKS IN INDIA (327 TO 161 B.C.).

RELIGION AND PHILOSOPHY have been the great contributions of India to the world. We now come to deal with India, not as a centre of influence upon other nations, but as acted on by them.

THE EXTERNAL HISTORY OF INDIA commences with the Greek invasion in 327 B.C. Some indirect trade between India and the Mediterranean seems to have existed from very ancient times. Homer was acquainted with tin,[1] and other articles of Indian merchandise, by their Sanskrit names; and a list has been made of Indian products mentioned in the Bible.[2] The ship captains of Solomon and Hiram not only brought Indian apes, peacocks, and sandal-wood to Palestine ; they also brought their Sanskrit names.[3] This was about 1000 B.C. The Assyrian monuments show that the rhinoceros and elephant were among the tribute offered to Shalmaneser II. (859–823 B.C.).[4] But the first Greek historian who speaks clearly of India is Hekataios of Miletos (549–486 B.C.) ; the knowledge of Herodotos (450 B.C.) ended at the Indus ; and Ktesias, the physician (401 B.C.), brought back from his residence in Persia only a few facts about the products of India, its dyes and fabrics, monkeys and parrots. India to the east of the Indus was first made known to Europe by the historians and men of science who accompanied Alexander the Great in 327 B.C. Their narratives, although now lost, furnished materials to Strabo, Pliny, and Arrian. Soon afterwards, Megasthenes, as Greek

External sources of the history of India.

Early Greek writers, 549-401 B.C.

Megasthenes, 306-298 B.C.

---

[1] Greek, Kassiteros ; Sanskrit, Kastíra ; hence, the Kassiterides, the Tin or Scilly Islands. Elephas, ivory, through the Arabian *eleph* (from Arabic *el*, the, and Sanskrit *ibha*, domestic elephant), is also cited.

[2] Sir G. Birdwood's *Handbook to the British Indian Section of the Paris Exhibition of* 1878, pp. 22–35. For economic intercourse with ancient India, see Del Mar's *History of Money in Ancient Countries*, chaps. iv. and v. (1885).

[3] Hebrew, Kophim, tukijim, almugim = Sanskrit, *kapi, sikhí, valgukam.*

[4] Professor Max Duncker's *Ancient History of India*, p. 13 (ed. 1881).

ambassador resident at a court in the centre of Bengal (306–298 B.C.), had opportunities for the closest observation. The knowledge of the Greeks concerning India practically dates from his researches, 300 B.C.[1]

Alexander's expedition, 327–325 B.C. Alexander the Great entered India early in 327 B.C.; crossed the Indus above Attock, and advanced, without a struggle, over the intervening territory of the Taxiles[2] to the Jehlam (Jhelum) (Hydaspes). He found the Punjab divided into petty kingdoms jealous of each other, and many of them inclined to join an invader rather than to oppose him. One of these local monarchs, Porus, disputed the passage of the Jehlam with a force which, substituting chariots for guns, about equalled the army of Ranjít Singh, the ruler of the Punjab in the present century.[3] Plutarch gives a vivid description of the battle from Alexander's own letters. Having drawn up his troops at a bend of the Jehlam, about 14 miles west of the modern field of Chilianwála,[4] the Greek general crossed under cover of a tempestuous night. The chariots hurried out by Porus stuck in the muddy margin of the river. In the engagement which followed, the elephants of the Indian prince refused to face the

---

[1] The fragments of the Indika of Megasthenes, collected by Dr. Schwanbeck, with the first part of the Indika of Arrian; the Periplus Maris Erythræi, with Arrian's account of the voyage of Nearkhos; the Indika of Ktesias; and Ptolemy's chapters relating to India, have been edited in four volumes with prolegomena by Mr. J. W. M'Crindle, M.A. (Trübner, 1877, 1879, 1882, and 1885). They originally appeared in the *Indian Antiquary,* to which this volume and the whole *Imperial Gazetteer of India* are much indebted. General Cunningham's *Ancient Geography of India,* with its maps, and his *Reports of the Archæological Survey,* Vincent's *Commerce and Navigation of the Ancients* (2 vols. 4to, 1807), and the series of maps, on an unfortunately small scale, in General-Lieutenant von Spruner's *Historisch-Geographischen Atlas* (Gotha), have also been freely availed of.

[2] The Takkas, a Turanian race, the earliest inhabitants of RAWAL PINDI DISTRICT. They gave their name to the town of Takshásila or Taxila, which Alexander found 'a rich and populous city, the largest between the Indus and Hydaspes,' identified with the ruins of DERI SHAHAN. Taki or Asarúr, on the road between Lahore and Pindi Bhatiyán, was the capital of the Punjab in 633 A.D. When names are printed in capitals, the object is to refer the reader to the fuller information given in the *Imperial Gazetteer of India.*

[3] Namely, '30,000 efficient infantry; 4000 horse; 300 chariots; 200 elephants' [Professor Cowell]. The Greeks probably exaggerated the numbers of the enemy. Alexander's army numbered 'about 50,000, including 5000 Indian auxiliaries under Mophis of Taxila.'—General Cunningham, *Anc. Geog. of India,* p. 172. See his lucid account of the battle, with an excellent map, pp. 159–177, ed. 1871.

[4] And about 30 miles south-west of Jehlam town.

Greeks, and, wheeling round, trampled his own army under foot. His son fell early in the onset; Porus himself fled wounded; but on tendering his submission, he was confirmed in his kingdom, and became the conqueror's trusted friend. Alexander built two memorial cities on the scene of his victory, —Bucephala on the west bank, near the modern JALALPUR, named after his beloved charger, Bucephalus, slain in the battle; and Nikaia, the present MONG, on the east side of the river.

Alexander advanced south-east through the kingdom of the younger Porus to Amritsar, and after a sharp bend backward to the west, to fight the Kathaei at Sangala, he reached the Beas (Hyphasis). Here, at a spot not far from the modern battle-field of Sobráon, he halted his victorious standards.[1] He had resolved to march to the Ganges; but his troops were worn out by the heats of the Punjab summer, and their spirits broken by the hurricanes of the south-west monsoon. The native tribes had already risen in his rear, and the Conqueror of the World was forced to turn back, before he had crossed even the frontier Province of India. The Sutlej, the eastern Districts of the Punjab, and the mighty Jumna, still lay between him and the Ganges. A single defeat might have been fatal to his army; if the battle on the Jehlam had gone against him, not a Greek would probably have reached the Afghán side of the passes. Yielding at length to the clamour of his men, he led them back to the Jehlam. He there embarked 8000 of his troops in boats previously prepared, and floated them down the river; the remainder marched in two divisions along the banks.

Alexander in the Punjab, 327-326 B.C.

The country was hostile, and the Greeks held only the land on which they encamped. At Múltán, then as now the capital of the Southern Punjab, Alexander had to fight a pitched battle with the Malli, and was severely wounded in taking the city. His enraged troops put every soul within it to the sword. Farther down, near the confluence of the five rivers of the Punjab, he made a long halt, built a town,—Alexandria, the modern Uchh,—and received the submission of the neighbouring States. A Greek garrison and Satrap, whom he here left behind, laid the foundation of a more lasting influence. Having constructed a new fleet, suitable for the greater rivers on which he was now to embark, he proceeded southwards through Sind, and followed the course of the Indus until he reached

Alexander in Sind, 325 B.C.

[1] The change in the course of the Sutlej has altered its old position relative to the Beas at this point. The best small map of Alexander's route is No. v. in General Cunningham's *Anc. Geog. of India*, p. 104, ed. 1871.

the ocean. In the apex of the delta he founded or refounded a city—Patala—which survives to this day as Haidárábád, the native capital of Sind.[1] At the mouth of the Indus, Alexander beheld for the first time the majestic phenomenon of the tides. One part of his army he shipped off under the command of Nearkhos to coast along the Persian Gulf; the other he himself led through Southern Baluchistán and Persia to Susa, where, after terrible losses from want of water and famine on the march, he arrived in 325 B.C.[2]

Leaves India, August 325 B.C.

During his two years' campaign in the Punjab and Sind, Alexander captured no province, but he made alliances, founded cities, and planted Greek garrisons. He had transferred much territory from the tribes whom he had half-subdued, to the chiefs and confederations who were devoted to his cause. Every petty court had its Greek faction ; and the detachments which he left behind at various positions from the Afghán frontier to the Beas, and from near the base of the Himálayas to the Sind delta, were visible pledges of his return. At Taxila (DERI-SHAHAN) and Nikaia (MONG) in the Northern Punjab ; at Alexandria (UCHH) in the Southern Punjab ; at Patala (HAIDARABAD) in Sind ; and at other points along his route, he established military settlements of Greeks or their allies. A body of his troops remained in Bactria. In the partition of the Empire after Alexander's death in 323 B.C., Bactria and India eventually fell to Seleukos Nikator, the founder of the Syrian monarchy.

Results of Greek expedition, 327-325 B.C.

Seleukos, 323-312 B.C.

Meanwhile, a new power had arisen in India. Among the Indian adventurers who thronged Alexander's camp in the Punjab, each with his plot for winning a kingdom or crushing a rival, Chandra Gupta, an exile from the Gangetic valley, seems to have played a somewhat ignominious part. He tried to tempt the wearied Greeks on the banks of the Beas with

Chandra Gupta, 326 B.C. ;

---

[1] For its interesting appearances in ancient history, see General Cunningham's *Anc. Geog. of India*, pp. 279-287, under Patala or Nirankot. It appears variously as Pattala, Pattalene, Pitasila, etc. It was formerly identified with Tatta (Thatha), near to where the western arm of the Indus bifurcates. See also M'Crindle's *Commerce and Navigation of the Erythræan Sea*, p. 156 (Trübner, 1879). An excellent map of Alexander's campaign in Sind is given at p. 248 of Cunningham's *Anc. Geog. of India*.

[2] The stages down the Indus and along the Persian coast, with the geographical features and incidents of Nearkhos' *Voyage*, are given in the second part of the Indika of Arrian, chapter xviii. to the end. The river stages and details are of value to the student of the modern delta of the Indus.—M'Crindle's *Commerce and Navigation of the Erythræan Sea*, pp. 153-224 (1879).

schemes of conquest in the rich south-eastern Provinces; but having personally offended Alexander, he had to fly the camp (326 B.C.). In the confused years which followed, he managed, with the aid of plundering hordes, to found a kingdom on the ruins of the Nanda dynasty in Magadha, or Behar (316 *316 B.C.;* B.C.).[1] He seized their capital, Pataliputra, the modern Patná; established himself firmly in the Gangetic valley, and compelled the Punjab principalities, Greek and native alike, to acknowledge his suzerainty.[2] While, therefore, Seleukos Nikator was winning his way to the Syrian monarchy during the eleven years which followed Alexander's death, Chandra Gupta was building up an empire in Northern India. Seleukos reigned in Syria from 312 to 280 B.C.; Chandra Gupta in the *312 B.C.* Gangetic valley from 316 to 292 B.C. In 312 B.C., the power of both had been consolidated, and the two new sovereignties were soon brought face to face.

About that year, Seleukos, having recovered Babylon, pro- *Seleukos* ceeded to re-establish his authority in Bactria and the Punjab. *in India,* In the Punjab, he found Greek influence decayed.   Alex- *312–306 B.C.* ander had left a mixed force of Greeks and Indians at Taxila. But no sooner had he departed from India, than the Indians rose and slew the Greek governor.   The Macedonians next massacred the Indians.   A new governor, sent by Alexander, murdered the friendly Punjab prince, Porus; and was himself driven out of India, by the advance of Chandra Gupta from the Gangetic valley.   Seleukos, after a war with Chandra Gupta, determined to ally himself with the new power in India rather than to oppose it.   In return for 500 elephants, he ceded the Greek settlements in the Punjab and the Kábul valley; gave his daughter to Chandra Gupta in marriage; and stationed an ambassador, Megasthenes, at the Gangetic court (306–298 B.C.). *306–298* Chandra Gupta became familiar to the Greeks as Sandrokottos, *B.C.* King of the Prasii and Gangaridae; his capital, Pataliputra,[3] or Patná, was rendered into Palimbothra.   On the other hand, the Greeks and kings of Grecian dynasties appear in the rock-inscriptions under Indian forms.[4]

[1] *Corpus Inscriptionum Indicarum*, i. 7.   Jacobi's *Jaina Sútras*, xliii.
[2] For the dynasty of Chandra Gupta, see *Numismata Orientalia* (Ceylon fasciculus), pp. 41–50.
[3] The modern Patná, or Pattana, means simply 'the city.'   For its identification with Pataliputra by means of Mr. Ravenshaw's final discoveries, see General Cunningham's *Anc. Geog. of India*, p. 452 *et seq.*
[4] The Greeks as Yonas (Yavanas), from the 'Ιάονις or Ionians.   In the Inscriptions of Asoka, five Greek princes appear: Antiochus (of Syria); Ptolemy (Philadelphos of Egypt); Antigonos (Gonatos of Macedon);

The India of Megasthenes, 300 B.C.   Megasthenes has left a lifelike picture of the Indian people. Notwithstanding some striking errors, the observations which he jotted down at Patná, three hundred years before Christ, give as accurate an account of the social organization in the Gangetic valley as any which existed when the Bengal Asiatic Society commenced its labours at the end of the last century (1784). Up to the time of Megasthenes, the Greek idea of India was a very vague one. Their historians spoke of two classes of Indians,—certain mountainous tribes who dwelt in Northern Afghánistán under the Caucasus or Hindu Kush, and a maritime race living on the coast of Baluchistán. Of the India of modern geography lying beyond the Indus, they practically knew nothing. It was this India to the east of the Indus which Megasthenes opened up to the western world.

His seven classes of the people.   He describes the classification of the people, dividing them, however, into seven castes instead of four,[1]—namely, philosophers, husbandmen, shepherds, artisans, soldiers, inspectors, and the counsellors of the king. The philosophers were the Bráhmans, and the prescribed stages of their life are indicated. Megasthenes draws a distinction between the Bráhmans (Βραχμᾶνες) and the Sarmanai (Σαρμάναι), from which some scholars infer that the Buddhist Sramanas or monks were a recognised order 300 B.C., or fifty years before the Council of Asoka. But the Sarmanai might also include Bráhmans in the first and third stages of their life as students and forest recluses.[2] The inspectors,[3] or sixth class of Megasthenes, have been identified with the Buddhist supervisors of morals, afterwards referred to in the sixth edict of Asoka. Arrian's name for them, ἐπίσκοποι, is the Greek word which has become our modern Bishop or *overseer* of souls.

'Errors' of Megasthenes.   It must be borne in mind that Indian society, as seen by Megasthenes, was not the artificial structure described in Manu, with its rigid lines and four sharply demarcated castes. It was the actual society of the court, the camp, and the capital, at a time when Buddhist ideals were conflicting with Bráhmanical types. Some of the so-called errors of Megas-

Magas (of Kyrene); Alexander (II. of Epirus).—Weber, *Hist. Ind. Lit.*, pp. 179, 252. But see also Wilson, *Journ. Roy. As. Soc.*, vol. xii. (1850), and Cunningham's *Corpus Inscrip. Indic.*, pp. 125, 126.

[1] *Ancient India as described by Megasthenes and Arrian, being fragments of the Indika*, by J. W. M'Crindle, M.A., p. 40, ed. 1877.

[2] Brahmachárins and Vánaprasthas (ὑλόβιοι). Weber very properly declines to identify the Σαρμάναι exclusively with the Buddhist Sramanas. *Hist. Ind. Lit.*, p. 28, ed. 1878.

[3] The ἔφοροι (Deodorus, Strabo), ἐπίσκοποι (Arrian).

thenes have been imputed to him from a want of due appreciation of this fact. Others have been proved by modern inquiry
to be no errors at all. The knowledge of India derived by
the Greeks chiefly, although by no means exclusively, from
Megasthenes includes details which were scarcely known to
Europeans in the last century. The Aryan and Aboriginal
elements of the population, or the White and Dark Indians;
the two great harvests of the year in spring and autumn; the
salt-mines; the land-making silt brought down by the rivers
from the Himálayas; the great changes in the river-courses;
and even a fairly accurate measurement of the Indian
peninsula—were among the points known to the Greek writers.

From those sources, the present writer has derived pregnant The old
hints in regard to the physical configuration of India. The Indian
account which Megasthenes gives of the size of the Indus and rivers.
its lakes, points to the same conclusion as that reached by
the most recent observations, in regard to the Indian rivers
being originally lines of drainage through great watery regions.
In their upper courses they gradually scooped out their beds,
and thus produced a low-level channel into which the fens
and marshes eventually drained. In their lower courses they
conducted their great operations of land-making from the silt
which their currents had brought down from above. In regard
to the rivers, as in several other matters, the ' exaggerations '
of Megasthenes turn out to be nearer the truth than was
suspected until the Statistical Survey of 1871.

The Bráhmans deeply impressed Alexander by their learning Kalanos,
and austerities. One of them, Kalanos by name, was tempted, the Bráh-
notwithstanding the reproaches of his brethren, to enter the man.
service of the conqueror. But falling sick in Persia, Kalanos
determined to die like a Bráhman, although he had not consistently lived as one. Alexander, on hearing of the philosopher's
resolve to put an end to his life, vainly tried to dissuade him;
then loaded him with jewels, and directed that he should be
attended with all honours to the last scene. Distributing the
costly gifts of his master as he advanced, wearing a garland of 323 B.C.
flowers, and singing his native Indian hymns, the Bráhman
mounted a funeral pyre, and serenely perished in the flames.

The Greek ambassador observed with admiration the ab- Indian
sence of slavery in India, the chastity of the women, and the society,
courage of the men. In valour they excelled all other Asiatics; 300 B.C.
they required no locks to their doors; above all, no Indian was
ever known to tell a lie. Sober and industrious, good farmers,
and skilful artisans, they scarcely ever had recourse to a law-

suit, and lived peaceably under their native chiefs. The kingly government is portrayed almost as described in Manu, with its
Petty hereditary castes of councillors and soldiers. Megasthenes
kingdoms. mentions that India was divided into 118 kingdoms; some of which, such as that of the Prasii under Chandra Gupta, exercised suzerain powers. The village system is well described, each little rural unit seeming to the Greek an independent republic. Megasthenes remarked the exemption of the husbandmen (Vaisyas) from war and public services; and enumerates the dyes, fibres, fabrics, and products (animal, vegetable, and mineral) of India. Husbandry depended on the periodical rains; and forecasts of the weather, with a view to 'make adequate provision against a coming deficiency,' formed a special duty of the Bráhmans. 'The philosopher who errs in his predictions observes silence for the rest of his life.'

Indo- Before the year 300 B.C., two powerful monarchies had thus
Greek begun to act upon the Bráhmanism of Northern India, from
treaty, the east and from the west. On the east, in the Gangetic
256 B.C. valley, Chandra Gupta (316–292 B.C.) firmly consolidated the dynasty which during the next century produced Asoka (264–223 B.C.), established Buddhism throughout India, and spread its doctrines from Afghánistán to China, and from Central Asia to Ceylon. On the west, the heritage of Seleukos (312–280 B.C.) diffused Greek influences, and sent forth Greco-Bactrian expeditions to the Punjab. Antiochos Theos (grandson of Seleukos Nikator) and Asoka (grandson of Chandra Gupta), who ruled these probably conterminous monarchies, made a treaty with each other, 256 B.C. In the next century, Eukratides, King of Bactria, conquered as far as Alexander's royal city of Patala, the modern Haidarábád in the Sind Delta; and sent expeditions into Cutch and Gujarát, 181–161
Greeks in B.C. Menander advanced farthest into North-Western India,
India, and his coins are found from Kábul, near which he pro-
181–161 bably had his capital, as far as Muttra on the Jumna. The
B.C. Buddhist successors of Chandra Gupta profoundly modified the religion of Northern India from the east; the empire of Seleukos, with its Bactrian and later offshoots, deeply influenced the science and art of Hindustán from the west.

Greek in- We have already seen how much Bráhman astronomy owed
fluence on to the Greeks, and how the builders' art in India received its
Indian art. first impulse from the architectural exigencies of Buddhism. The same double influence, of the Greeks on the west and of the Buddhists on the east of the Bráhmanical Middle Land of

Bengal, can be traced in many details. What the Buddhists were to the architecture of Northern India, that the Greeks were to its sculpture. Greek faces and profiles constantly occur in ancient Buddhist statuary. They enrich almost all the larger museums in India, and examples may be seen at South Kensington. The purest specimens have been found in the Punjab, where the Greeks settled in greatest force. In the Lahore collection there was, among other beautiful pieces, an exquisite little figure of an old blind man feeling his way with a staff. Its subdued pathos, its fidelity to nature, and its living movement dramatically held for the moment in sculptured suspense, are Greek, and nothing but Greek. It is human misfortune, that has culminated in wandering poverty, age, and blindness —the very curse which Sophocles makes the spurned Teiresias throw back upon the doomed king—

> ' Blind, having seen ;
> Poor, having rolled in wealth ; he with a staff
> Feeling his way to a strange land shall go.

As we proceed eastward from the Punjab, the Greek type begins to fade. Purity of outline gives place to lusciousness of form. In the female figures, the artists trust more and more to swelling breasts and towering chignons, and load the neck with constantly-accumulating jewels. Nevertheless, the Grecian type of countenance long survived in Indian art. It is perfectly unlike the coarse, conventional ideal of beauty in modern Hindu sculptures, and may perhaps be traced as late as the delicate profiles on the so-called Sun Temple at KANARAK, built in the 12th century A.D. on the Orissa shore. *Greek and Hindu types of sculpture.*

Not only did the Greek impulse become fainter and fainter in Indian sculpture with the lapse of time, but that impulse was itself gradually derived from less pure and less vigorous sources. The Greek ideal of beauty may possibly have been brought direct to India by the officers and artists of Alexander the Great. But it was from Græco-Bactria, not from Greece itself, that the practical masters of Greek sculpture came to the Punjab. Indeed, it seems probable that the most prolific stream of such artistic inspirations reached India from the Roman Empire, and in Imperial times, rather than through even the indirect Grecian channels represented by the Bactrian kingdom. *Greek types die out.*

It must suffice here to indicate the ethnical and dynastic influences thus brought to bear upon India, without attempting to assign dates to the individual monarchs. The chronology of the twelve centuries intervening between the *Foreign influences on India.*

Græco - Bactrian period and the Muhammadan conquest still depends on a mass of conflicting evidence derived from inscriptions, legendary literature, unwritten traditions, and coins.[1] Four systems of computation exist, based upon the Vikramáditya, Saka, Seleucidan, and Parthian eras.

In the midst of the confusion, we see dim masses moving southwards from Central Asia into India. The Græco-Bactrian kings are traced by coins as far as Muttra on the Jumna. Their armies occupied for a time the Punjab, as far south as Gujarát and Sind. Sanskrit texts are said to indicate their advance through the Middle Land of the Bráhmans (*Madhya - desha*) to Sáketa (or AJODHYA), the capital of Oudh, and to Patná in Behar.[2] Megasthenes was

Greeks in Bengal. only the first of a series of Greek ambassadors to Bengal.[3] A Grecian princess became the queen of Chandra Gupta at Patná (*circ.* 306 B.C.). Græco-Bactrian girls, or Yavanís, were welcome gifts, and figure in the Sanskrit drama as the personal attendants of Indian kings. They were probably fair-complexioned slaves from the northern regions. It is right to add, however, that the word Yavan has a much wider application than merely to the Greeks or even to the Bactrians.

Greek survivals in India. The credentials of the Indian embassy to Augustus in 22–20 B.C. were written on skins; a circumstance which perhaps indicates the extent to which Greek usage had overcome Bráhmanical prejudices. During the century preceding the Christian era, Scythian or Tartar hordes began to supplant the Græco-Bactrian influence in the Punjab.

The 'Yavanas;' The term Yavana, or Yona, formerly applied to any non-Bráhmanical race, and especially to the Greeks, was now extended to the Sakæ or Scythians. It probably includes many various tribes of invaders from the west. Patient effort will be

Ancient and modern. required before the successive changes in the meaning of Yavana, both before and after the Greek period, are worked

---

[1] Report of the *Archæological Survey of Western India for* 1874–75, p. 49 (Mr. E. Thomas' monograph).

[2] Goldstucker assigned the Yavana siege of Saketa (AJODHYA), mentioned in the Mahábháshya, to Menander ; while the accounts of the Gárgí Sanhitá in the Yuga Purána speak of a Yavana expedition as far as Patná. But, as Weber points out (*Hist. Ind. Lit.*, p. 251, footnote 276), the question arises as to whether these Yavanas were Græco-Bactrians or Indo-Scythians. See, however, *Report of Archæological Survey of Western India for* 1874–75, p. 49, and footnote.

[3] Weber, *Hist. Ind. Lit.*, p. 251 (ed. 1878), enumerates four.

out. The word travelled far, and has survived with a strange vitality in out of the way nooks of India. The Orissa chroniclers called the sea-invaders from the Bay of Bengal, Yavanas, and in later times the term was applied to the Musalmáns.[1] At the present day, a vernacular form of the word is said to have supplied the local name for the Arab settlers on the Coromandel coast.[2]

[1] Hunter's *Orissa*, vol. i. pp. 25, 85, and 209 to 232 (ed. 1872).

[2] Bishop Caldwell gives Yavanas (Yonas) as the equivalent of the Sonagas or Muhammadans of the western coast : *Comparative Grammar of the Dravidian Languages*, 2nd edition, p. 2 (Trübner, 1875).

CHAPTER VII.

SCYTHIC INROADS INTO INDIA (126? B.C. TO 544 A.D.).

Migrations from Central Asia; THE foregoing chapters have dealt with two streams of population which, starting from Central Asia, poured through the north-western passes of the Himálayas, and spread themselves out upon the plains of Bengal. Those two great series of migrations are represented by the early Vedic tribes, and by the Græco-Bactrian armies. The first of them gave the race-type to Aryan, Indian civilisation; the second impressed an influence on Indian science and art, more important and more permanent than the mere numerical strength of the invaders would seem to justify. But the permanent settlement of the early Vedic tribes, and the shorter vehement impact of the Græco-Bactrian invaders, alike represent movements of the Aryan section of the human race. Another great family of mankind, the Turanian, and Tur-anian. had also its home in Central Asia. The earliest migrations of the Turanians belong to a period absolutely pre-historic; nor has inductive history yet applied its scrutiny to Turanian antiquity with anything like the success which it has achieved in regard to the beginnings of the Aryan peoples.

Scythic movements towards India. Yet there is evidence to show that waves of Turanian origin overtopped the Himálayas or pierced through their openings into India from very remote times. The immigrants doubtless represented many different tribes, but in the dim twilight of Indian history they are mingled together in confused masses known as the Scythians. There are indications that a branch of the Scythian hordes, who overran Asia about 625 B.C., made its way to Patala on the Indus, the site selected by Alexander in 325 B.C. as his place of arms in that delta, and long the capital of Sind under the name of Haidarábád. One portion of these Patala Scythians seems to have moved westwards by the Persian Gulf to Assyria; another section is supposed to have found its way north-east into the Gangetic valley, and to have branched off into the Sakyas of Kapilavastu, among whom Buddha was born.[1]   During the two hundred years before the Christian era, the Scythic movements come a little more clearly into sight, and in the first century after Christ those movements culminate in a great Indian sovereignty.   About 126 B.C., the Tartar tribe of Su are said to have conquered the Greek dynasty in Bactria, and the Græco-Bactrian settlements in the Punjab were overthrown by the Tue-Chi.[2] *Tue-Chi settlements 126 B.C. (?)*

Two centuries later, we touch solid ground in the dynasty whose chief representative, Kanishka, held the Fourth Bud-dhist Council, *circ.* 40 A.D., and became the royal founder of Northern Buddhism.   But long anterior to the alleged Tue-Chi settlements in the Punjab, tribes of Scythic origin had found their way into India, and had left traces of non-Aryan origin upon Indian civilisation.   The sovereignty of Kanishka in the first century A.D. was not an isolated effort, but the ripened fruit of a series of ethnical movements. *Kanishka, 40 A.D. (?)*

Certain scholars believe that even before the time of Buddha, there are relics of Scythic origin in the religion of India.   It has been suggested that the *Aswamedha,* or Great Horse Sacrifice, in some of its developments at any rate, was based upon Scythic ideas.   'It was in effect,' writes Mr. Edward Thomas, 'a martial challenge, which consisted in letting the victim who was to crown the imperial triumph at the year's end, go free to wander at will over the face of the earth; its sponsor being bound to follow its hoofs, and to conquer or conciliate' the chiefs through whose territories it passed.   Such a prototype seems to him to shadow forth the life of the Central Asian communities of the horseman class, 'among whom a captured steed had so frequently to be traced from camp to camp, and surrendered or fought for at last.'[3]   The curious connection between the Horse Sacrifice and the Man Sacrifice of the pre-Buddhistic religion of India has often been noticed.   That connection has been explained from the Indian point of view, by the substitution theory of a horse for a human victim.   But among the early shepherd tribes of Tibet, the two sacrifices coexisted as inseparable parts of The Great *Pre-Bud-dhistic Scythic influences.*   *The Horse Sacrifice.*

---

[1] *Catena of the Buddhist Scriptures from the Chinese,* by S. Beal, pp. 126–130. See also Herodotus, i. 103 to 106 ; Csoma de Körös, *Journal As. Soc. Beng.* 1833 ; and II. II. Wilson, *Ariana Antiqua,* p. 212, quoted by Weber, *Hist. Ind. Lit.* p. 285, ed. 1878.

[2] De Guignes, supported by Professor Cowell on the evidence of coins. Appendix to Elphinstone's *History of India,* p. 269, ed. 1866.

[3] *Report of Archæological Survey of Western India,* pp. 37, 38 (1876). But see, in opposition to Mr. Thomas' view, M. Senart in the French *Journ. Asiatique,* 1875, p. 126.

Oath. Each year the Tibetans took The Little Oath to their chiefs, and sacrificed sheep, dogs, and monkeys. But every third year they solemnized The Great Oath with offerings of men and horses, oxen and asses.[1]

Buddha, a Scythian(?)
Whatever significance may attach to this rite, it is certain that with the advent of Buddhism, Scythic influences made themselves felt in India. Indeed, it has been attempted to establish a Scythic origin for Buddha himself. One of his earliest appearances in the literature of the Christian Church is as Buddha the Scythian. It is argued that by no mere accident did the Fathers trace the Manichæan doctrine to Scythianus, whose disciple, Terebinthus, took the name of Buddha.[2] As already stated, the form of abjuration of the Manichæan heresy mentions Βόδδα and Σκυθιανός (Buddha and the Scythian or Sakya), seemingly, says Weber, a separation of Buddha Sakya-muni into two.[3] The Indian Buddhists of the Southern school would dwell lightly on, or pass over altogether, a non-Aryan origin for the founder of their faith. We have seen how the legend of Buddha in their hands assimilated itself to the old epic type of the Aryan hero. But a Scythic origin would be congenial to the Northern school of Buddhism : to the school which was consolidated by the Scythic monarch Kanishka, and which supplied a religion during more than ten centuries to Scythic tribes of Central Asia.

Meaning of Sakya.
We find, therefore, without surprise, that the sacred books of Tibet constantly speak of Buddha as the Sakya. In them, Buddha is the heir-apparent to the throne of the Sakyas ; his doctrine is accepted by the Sakya race; and a too strict adherence to its tenets of mercy ends in the destruction of the Sakya capital, followed by the slaughter of the Sakya people.[4] If we could be sure that Sakya really signified Scythian, this evidence would be conclusive. But the exact meaning of Sakya, although generally taken to be the Indian representative of Scythian, as the Persian Sakæ was the equivalent of Scythæ, has yet to be determined. At one time it seemed as if the

---

[1] Early History of Tibet, in Mr. Woodville Rockhill's *Life of the Buddha*, from the Tibetan Classics, p. 204 (Trübner, 1884).

[2] 'I believe the legend of Sakya was perverted into the history of Scythianus,' Beal's *Catena of the Buddhist Scriptures from the Chinese*, p. 129 (Trübner, 1871).

[3] Weber's *History of Indian Literature*, p. 309, footnote 363 (Trübner, 1878). But Buddhism probably reached the Early Church through the Scythians ; so that Buddha might be called Skuthianos, as the Scythian religious founder, without implying that he was a born Scythian. *Vide post*, chap. ix.   [4] *Vide ante*, p. 140.

Tibetan records might settle the point. These hopes have, however, been disappointed, as the earliest Tibetan records prove to be a reflex of foreign influences rather than a depository of indigenous traditions.

Tibet, Khoten, and other countries to the north of the Himálayas, on adopting Buddhism, more or less unconsciously re-cast their national traditions into Buddhist moulds.[1] These countries formed the meeting-place of two distinct streams of civilisation,—the material civilisation of China, and the religious civilisation of India. Some of the early Tibetan legends seem to be clumsy copies of the stories of the first Chinese sovereigns recorded in the Bamboo Books.[2] The Tibetan classics further obscure the historical facts, by a tendency to trace the royal lines of Central Asia to the family or early converts of Buddha; as certain mediæval families of Europe claimed descent from the Wise Men of the East; and noble *gentes* of Rome found their ancestors among the heroes of the Trojan war. Thus the first Tibetan monarch derived his line from Prasenadjit, King of Kosala, the life-long friend of Buddha; and the dynasty of Khoten claimed, as its founder, a son of King Dharmasoka.

Artificial nature of Tibetan traditions.

The truth is, that while Tibet obtained much of its material civilisation from China, its medicine, its mathematics, its weights and measures, its chronology, its clothing, its mulberries, tea, and ardent spirits; it received its religion and letters from India, together with its philosophy, and its ideal of the spiritual life. The mission of the seven Tibetan nobles to India to find an alphabet for the yet unwritten language of Tibet, is an historical event of the 7th century A.D. The Indian monastery of Nalanda was reproduced with fidelity in the great Hsamyas, or religious house at Lhasa. The struggle between Chinese and Indian influences disclosed itself alike in the public disputations of the Tibetan sects, and in the inner intrigues of the palace. One of the greatest of the Tibetan monarchs married two wives,—an Indian princess who brought Buddhist images from Nepal, and a Chinese princess who brought silk-brocades and whisky from China.[3] We must therefore receive with caution the evidence as to the original signification of the word Sakya, derived from the records of a nation which was so largely indebted for its ideas and its traditions to later foreign sources.

Sources of Tibetan ideas and traditions.

[1] Early Histories of Tibet and Khoten, in Mr. Rockhill's *Life of the Buddha*, p. 232, etc.

[2] *Idem*, p. 203.   [3] *Idem*, pp. 213-215.

Evidence of Tibetan traditions as to the Sakyas.

That evidence should, however, be stated. The Tibetan sacred books preserve an account of the Sakya creation; of the non-sexual procession of the ancient Sakya kings; and of the settlement of the Sakyas at Kapila, the birthplace of Buddha. Their chief seat was the kingdom of Kosala, near the southern base of the Himálayas. Tibetan traditions place the early Indian homes of the Sakyas on the banks of the Bhágírathí, as distinctly as the Vedic hymns place the homes of the primitive Aryans on the tributaries of the Indus. They claim, indeed, for Buddha a Kshattriyan descent from the noble Ishkvaku or Solar line. But it is clear that the race customs of the Indo-Sakyas differed in some respects from those of the Indo-Aryans.

Sakya race customs.

At birth, the Sakya infant was made to bow at the feet of a tribal image, Taksha Sakya-vardana, which, on the presentation of Buddha, itself bowed down to the divine child.[1] In regard to marriage, the old Sakya law is said to have allowed a man only one wife.[2] The dead were disposed of by burial, although cremation was not unknown. In the *topes* or funeral mounds of Buddhism is apparently seen a reproduction of the royal Scythian tombs of which Herodotus speaks.[3] Perhaps more remarkable is the resemblance of the great co-decease of Buddha's companions to the Scythian holocausts of the followers, servants and horses of a dead monarch.[4] On the death of Buddha, according to the Tibetan texts, a co-decease of 18,000 of his disciples took place. On the death of the faithful Maudgalyayana, the co-decease of disciples amounted to 70,000; while on that of Sariputra, the co-decease of Buddhist ascetics was as high as 80,000.[5] The composite idea of a co-decease of followers, together with a funeral mound over the relics of an illustrious personage, was in accordance with obsequies of the Scythian type.

Scythic Buddhism in India, 40-634 A.D.

Whatever may be the value of such analogies, the influence of the Scythian dynasties in Northern India is a historical fact. The Northern or Tibetan form of Buddhism, represented by the Scythian monarch Kanishka and the Fourth Council[6] in 40 A.D., soon made its way down to the plains of Hindustán, and during the next six centuries competed with the earlier Buddhism of Asoka. The Chinese pilgrim in 629-645

---

[1] Mr. Rockhill's *Life of the Buddha*, p. 17. [2] *Idem*, p. 15.

[3] Herodotus, iv. 71, 127.

[4] The slaughter of the king's concubine, cup-bearer, and followers is also mentioned in Herodotus, iv. 71 and 72.

[5] Mr. Rockhill's *Life of the Buddha*, p. 141, footnote 3, and p. 148.

[6] *Numismata Orientalia* (Ceylon fasc.), p. 54.

A.D. found both the Northern or Scythic and the Southern forms of Buddhism in full vigour in India. He spent fourteen months at China-pati, the town where Kanishka had kept his Chinese hostages in the Punjab ; and he records the debates between the Northern and Southern sects of Buddhists in various places. The town of China-pati, ten miles west of the Beas river,[1] bore witness to later ages of the political connection of Northern India with the Trans-Himálayan races of Central and Eastern Asia. The Scythic influence in India was a dynastic as well as a religious one. The evidence of coins and the names of Indian tribes or reigning families, such as the Sákas, Huns, and Nágas, point to Scythian settlements as far south as the Central Provinces.[2] *Scythic settlements in India.*

Some scholars believe that the Scythians poured down upon India in such masses as to supplant the previous population. The Jats or Játs,[3] who now number 4½ millions and form one-fifth of the inhabitants of the Punjab, are identified with the Getae ; and their great sub-division the Dhe with the Dahae, whom Strabo places on the shores of the Caspian. This view has received the support of eminent investigators, from Professor H. H. Wilson to General Cunningham, the late Director-General of the Archæological Survey of India.[4] The existing division between the Játs and the Dhe has, indeed, been traced back to the contiguity of the Massa-getae or Great Getae,[5] and the Dahae, who dwelt side by side in Central Asia, and who may have advanced together during the Scythian movements towards India on the decline of the Græco-Bactrian Empire. Without pressing such identifications too closely in the service of particular theories, the weight of authority is in favour of a Scythian origin for the Játs, the most numerous and valuable section of the agricultural population of the Punjab.[6] A similar descent has been assigned to certain of the Rájput *Scythian elements in the population.* *(1) The Játs.*

---

[1] General Cunningham's *Anc. Geog. of India*, p. 200.

[2] Muir's *Sanskrit Texts*, chap. v. vol. i. (1868) ; Sir C. Grant's *Gazetteer of the Central Provinces*, lxx., etc. (Nagpur, 1870) ; Reports of the *Archæological Survey of India and of Western India* ; Professor H. H. Wilson (and Dr. F. Hall), *Vishnu Purána*, ii. 134.

[3] The word occurs as Játs and Jats ; but the identity of the two forms has been established by reference to the *Aín-í-Akbarí.* Some are now Hindus, others Muhammadans.

[4] See among other places, part iv. of his *Archæological Reports*, p. 19.

[5] *Massa* means ' great ' in Pehlevi.

[6] It should be mentioned, however, that Dr. Trumpp believed them to be of Aryan origin (*Zeitsch. d. Deutsch. Morg. Gesellsch.*, xv. p. 690). See Mr J. Beames' admirable edition of Sir Henry Elliott's *Glossary of the Races of the North-Western Provinces*, vol. i. pp. 130-137, ed. 1869.

tribes. Colonel Tod, still the standard historian of Rájásthán, strongly insisted on this point.

(2) The Rájputs.

The relationship between the Játs and the Rájputs, although obscure, is acknowledged ; and although the *jus connubii* no longer exists between them, an inscription seems to show that they intermarried in the 5th century A.D.[1] Professor Cowell, indeed, regards the arguments for the Scythic descent of the Rájputs as inconclusive.[2] But authorities of weight have deduced, alike from local investigation [3] and from Sanskrit literature,[4] a Scythic origin for the Játs and for certain of the Rájput tribes. The question has lately been discussed, with the fulness of local knowledge, by Mr. Denzil Ibbetson, the chief Census officer for the Punjab in 1881. His conclusions are—First, that the terms Rájput and Ját indicate a difference in occupation and not in origin. Second, that even if they represent distinct waves of migration, separated by an interval of time, ' they belong to one and the same ethnic stock.' Third, 'that whether Játs and Rájputs were or were not originally distinct,' ' the two now form a common stock ; the distinction between Ját and Rájput being social rather than ethnic.' [5] We shall see that earlier migrations of Central Asian hordes also supplied certain of the Nágá, or so-called aboriginal, races of India.

Indian struggle against the Scythians.

The Scythic settlements were not effected without a struggle. As Chandra Gupta had advanced from the Gangetic valley, and rolled back the tide of Græco-Bactrian conquest, 312–306 B.C.,

[1] Inscription discovered in Kotah State ; No. 1 of Inscription Appendix to Colonel Tod's *Annals and Antiquities of Rájásthán*, vol. i. p. 701, note 3 (Madras Reprint, 1873). Although Tod is still the standard historian of Rájputána, and will ever retain an honoured place as an original investigator, his ethnical theories must be received with caution.

[2] Appendix to Elphinstone's *Hist. Ind.*, pp. 250 *et seq.*, ed. 1866.

[3] Tod's *Rájásthán*, pp. 52, 483, 500, etc., vol. i. (Madras Reprint, 1873).

[4] Dr. Fitz-Edward Hall's edition of Professor H. H. Wilson's *Vishnu Purána*, vol. ii. p. 134. The Húnas, according to Wilson, were ' the white Huns who were established in the Punjab, and along the Indus, as we know from Arrian, Strabo, and Ptolemy, confirmed by recent discoveries of their coins and by inscriptions.' ' I am not prepared,' says Dr. Fitz-Edward Hall, ' to deny that the ancient Hindus when they spoke of the Húnas included the Huns. In the Middle Ages, however, it is certain that a race called Húna was understood by the learned of India to form a division of the Kshattriyas.' Professor Dowson's *Dict. Hind. Mythology*, etc., p. 122.

[5] See the ethnographical volume of the Punjab Census for 1881, paras. 421, 422 *et seq.*, by Mr. Denzil Jelf Ibbetson, of the Bengal Civil Service, p. 220 (Government Press, Calcutta, 1883).

so the native princes who stemmed the torrent of Scythian invasion are the Indian heroes of the first century before and after Christ. Vikramáditya, King of Ujjain, appears to have won his paramount place in Indian story by driving out the invaders. An era, the *Samvat,* beginning in 57 B.C., was *Samvat* founded in honour of his achievements. Its date [1] seems era, 57 at variance with his legendary victories over the Scythian B.C. Kanishka in the 1st century after Christ.[2] But the very title of its founder suffices to commemorate his struggle against the northern hordes, as Vikramáditya Sakári, or Vikramáditya, the Enemy of the Scythians.

The name of Vikramáditya, 'A very Sun in Prowess,' was borne, as we have seen, by several Indian monarchs. In later ages their separate identity was merged in the ancient renown of the Slayer of the Scythians, who thus combined the fame of many Vikramádityas. There was a tendency to assign to his period the most eminent Indian works in science and poetry,—works which we know must belong to a date long after the first century of our era. His reign forms the Augustan era of Sanskrit literature; and tradition fondly ascribed the highest products of the Indian intellect during many later centuries to the poets and philosophers, or Nine Gems, of this Vikramáditya's Court. As Chandra Gupta, who freed India from the Greeks, is celebrated in the drama Mudrá-rákshasa; so Vikramáditya, the vanquisher of the Scythians, forms the central royal personage of the Hindu stage.

Vikramáditya's achievements, however, furnished no final de- *Sáka* or liverance, but merely form an episode in the long struggle between Scythian the Indian dynasties and new races from the north. Another era, 78 A.D. popular era, the *Sáka*, literally the Scythian, takes its commencement in 78 A.D.,[3] and is supposed to commemorate the defeat of the Scythians by a king of Southern India, Saliv,́hańá.[4] During the seven centuries which followed, three powerful monarchies, the Senas, Guptas, and Valabhís, established themselves

---

[1] *Samvatsara,* the 'Year.' The uncertainty which surrounds even this long-accepted finger-post in Indian chronology may be seen from Dr. J. Fergusson's paper 'On the Sáka and Samvat and Gupta eras' (*Journal Roy. As. Soc.*, New Series, vol. xii.), especially p. 172.

[2] The Hushka, Jushka, and Kanishka family of the *Rájá Tarangini*, or Chronicles of Kashmír, are proved by inscriptions to belong to the 4th century of the Seleucidan era, or the 1st century A.D.

[3] Monday, 14th March 78 A.D., Julian style.

[4] General Cunningham; see also Mr. Edw. Thomas' letter, dated 16th September 1874, to *The Academy,* which brings this date within the period of the Kanishka family (2 B.C. to 87 A.D.).

Sena (Sah) dynasty, 60 B.C. to 235 A.D.

in Northern and Western India. The Senas and Singhas, or Sátraps of Suráshtra, are traced by coins and inscriptions from 60 or 70 B.C. to after 235 A.D.[1] After the Senas come the Guptas of KANAUJ,[2] in the North-Western Provinces, the Middle Land of ancient Bráhmanism. The Guptas introduced an era of

Gupta dynasty, 319–470 A.D.

their own, commencing in 319 A.D.; and ruled in person or by viceroys over Northern India during 150 years, as far to the south-west as Káthiáwár. The Gupta dynasty was over-thrown by foreign invaders, apparently a new influx of Huns or Tartars from the north-west (450–470 A.D.).

Valabhí dynasty, 480–722 A.D.

The Valabhís succeeded the Guptas, and ruled over Cutch, north-western Bombay,[3] and Málwá, from 480 to after 722 A.D.[4] The Chinese pilgrim, Hiuen Tsiang, gives a full account of the court and people of Valabhí (630–640 A.D.). Buddhism was the State religion, but heretics, i.e. Bráhmans, abounded; and the Buddhists themselves were divided between the northern school of the Scythian dynasties, and the southern or Indian school of Asoka. The Valabhís seem to have been overthrown by the early Arab invaders of Sind in the 8th century.

Long struggle against Scythic invaders, 57 B.C. to 544 A.D.

The relations of these three Indian dynasties, the Senas, Guptas, and Valabhís, to the successive hordes of Scythians, who poured down on Northern India, are obscure. There is abundant evidence of a long-continued struggle, but the efforts to affix dates to its chief episodes have not yet produced results which can be accepted as final. Two Vikramá-ditya Sakáris, or vanquishers of the Scythians, are required for the purposes of chronology; and the great battle of Korúr near Múltán, in which the Scythian hosts perished, has been shifted backwards and forwards from 78 to 544 A.D.[5]

The truth seems to be that, during the first six centuries of the Christian era, the fortunes of the Scythian or Tartar races rose and fell from time to time in Northern India. They more than once sustained great defeats; and they more than once overthrew the native dynasties. Their presence is popularly

---

[1] By Mr. Newton. See Mr. E. Thomas on the Coins of the Sáh Kings, *Archæol. Rep. Western India*, p. 44 (1876); and Dr. J. Fergusson, *Journal Roy. As. Soc.*, 1880.

[2] Now a town of only 16,646 inhabitants in Farukhábád District, but with ruins extending over a semicircle of 4 miles in diameter.

[3] Lát-desha, including the collectorates of SURAT, BROACH, KAIRA, and parts of BARODA territory.

[4] The genealogy is worked out in detail by Mr. E. Thomas, *ut supra*, pp. 80–82.

[5] 78 A.D. was the popularly received date, commemorated by the *Sáka* era; 'between 524 and 544 A.D.' is suggested by Dr. Fergusson (p. 284 of *Journal Roy. As. Soc.*, vol. xii.) in 1880.

attested during the century before Christ by Vikramáditya (57 B.C. ?); during the 1st century after Christ, it is represented by the Kanishka family (2 B.C. to 87 A.D.); it was noted by Cosmas Indicopleustes, about 535 A.D.

A recent writer on the subject[1] believes that it was the white Huns who overthrew the Guptas between 465 and 470 A.D. He places the great battles of Korúr and Maushari, which 'freed India from the Sákas and Húnas,' between 524 and 544 A.D. But these dates still lie in the domain of inductive, indeed almost of conjectural, history. Cosmas Indicopleustes, who traded in the Red Sea about 535 A.D., speaks of the Huns as a powerful nation in Northern India in his days.[2]

While Greek and Scythic influences had thus been at work in Northern India during nine centuries (327 B.C. to 544 A.D.), another (so-called indigenous) element was profoundly affecting the future of the Indian people. A previous chapter has traced the fortunes, and sketched the present condition, of the pre-Aryan 'aborigines.' The Bráhmanical Aryans never accomplished a complete subjugation of these earlier races. The tribes and castes of non-Aryan origin numbered in 1872 about 18 millions in British territory; while the castes who claim a pure Aryan descent are under 16 millions.[3] The pre-Aryans have influenced the popular dialects of every Province, and in Southern India they still give their speech to 28 millions of people. *The pre-Aryan element in ancient India.*

The Vedic settlements along the five rivers of the Punjab were merely colonies or confederacies of Aryan tribes, who had pushed in among a non-Aryan population. When an Aryan family advanced to a new territory, it had often, as in the case of the Pándava brethren, to clear the forest and drive out the aboriginal people. This double process constantly repeated itself; and as late as 1657, when the Hindu Rájá founded the present city of BAREILLY, his first work was to cut down the jungle and expel the old Katheriyas. The ancient Bráhmanical kingdoms of the Middle Land (*Madhya-desha*), in the North-Western Provinces and Oudh, were surrounded by non-Aryan tribes. All the legendary advances beyond the northern centre of Aryan civilisation, narrated in the epic poets, were made into *Their lasting influence.*

---

[1] Dr. J. Fergusson, *Journal Roy. As. Soc.*, pp. 282-284, etc. (1880).

[2] *Topographia Christiana*, lib. xi. p. 338; *apud* Fergusson, *ut supra*.

[3] This latter number included both Bráhmans (10,574,444) and Kshattriyas and Rájputs (5,240,495). But, as we have just seen, some of the Rájput tribes are believed to be of Scythic origin, while others have been incorporated from confessedly non-Aryan tribes (*vide ante*, p. 91). Such non-Aryan Rájputs more than outnumber any survivals of the Vaisyas of pure Aryan descent.

the territory of non-Aryan races. When we begin to catch historical glimpses of India, we find the countries even around the northern Aryan centre ruled by non-Aryan princes. The Nandas, whom Chandra Gupta succeeded in Behar, appear as a Súdra or non-Aryan dynasty; and according to one account, Chandra Gupta and his grandson Asoka came of the same stock.[1]

Pre-Aryan kingdoms in Northern India.

The Buddhist religion did much to incorporate the pre-Aryan tribes into the Indian polity. During the long struggle of the Indo-Aryans against Græco-Bactrian and Scythian inroads (627 B.C. to 544 A.D.), the Indian aboriginal races must have had an increasing importance, whether as enemies or allies. At the end of that struggle, we discover them ruling in some of the fairest tracts of Northern India. In almost every District throughout Oudh and the North-Western Provinces, ruined towns and forts are ascribed to aboriginal races who ruled at different periods, according to the local legends, between the 5th and 11th centuries A.D. When the Muhammadan conquest supplies a firmer historical footing, after 1000 A.D., non-Aryan tribes were still in possession of several of these Districts, and had only been lately ousted from others.

The Takshaks of Ráwal Pindi District.

The Statistical Survey of India has brought together many survivals of these obscure races. It is impossible to follow that survey through each locality; the following paragraphs indicate, with the utmost brevity, a few of the results. Starting from the West, Alexander the Great found RAWAL PINDI District in the hands of the Takkas or Takshaks, from whom its Greek name of Taxila was derived. This people has been traced to a Scythian migration about the 6th century B.C.[2] Their settlements in the 4th century B.C. seem to have extended from the Paropamisan range[3] in Afghánistán to deep into Northern India. Their Punjab capital, Takshásila, or Taxila, was the largest city which Alexander met with between the Indus and the Jehlam (327 B.C.).[4] Salihávana, from whom the Sáka

The Takshaks.

Sixth Century B.C.;

327 B.C.

---

[1] The *Mudrá-rákshasa* represents Chandra Gupta as related to the last of the Nandas; the Commentator of the *Vishnu Puráia* says he was the son of a Nanda by a low-caste woman. Prof. Dowson's *Dict. Hindu Mythology*, etc., p. 68 (Trübner, 1879).

[2] Such dates have no pretension to be anything more than intelligent conjectures based on very inadequate evidence. With regard to the Takshaks, see Colonel Tod and the authorities which he quotes, *Rájásthán*, vol. i. p. 53 *passim*, pp. 93 *et seq.* (Madras Reprint, 1873).

[3] Where Alexander found them as the Parae-takae — *pahari* or Hill Takae(?).

[4] Arrian. The Bráhman mythologists, of course, produce an Aryan pedigree for so important a person as King Taksha, and make him the son of Bharata and nephew of Ráma-chandra.

or Scythian era took its commencement (78 A.D.), is held by The
some authorities to have been of Takshak descent.[1] In the Takshaks;
7th century A.D., Taki,[2] perhaps derived from the same race, 78 A.D.
was the capital of the Punjab. The Scythic Takshaks, indeed, 633 A.D.
are supposed to have been the source of the great Serpent Race, 1881 A.D.
the Takshakas or Nágás, who figure so prominently in Sanskrit
literature and art, and whose name is still borne by the Nágá
tribes of our own day. The Takkas remaining to the present
time are found only in the Districts of Delhi and Karnal.
They number 14,305, of whom about three - fourths have
adopted the faith of Islám.

The words Nágá and Takshaka in Sanskrit both mean The
a 'snake,' or tailed monster. As the Takshakas have been Nágás.
questionably connected with the Scythian Takkas, so the Nágás
have been derived, by conjecture in the absence of evidence,
from the Tartar patriarch Nagas, the second son of Elkhán.[3]
Both the terms, Nágás and Takshakas, seem to have been
loosely applied by the Sanskrit writers to a variety of non-Aryan
peoples in India, whose religion was of an anti-Aryan type.
We learn, for example, how the five Pándava brethren of
the Mahábhárata burned out the snake-king Takshaka from
his primeval Khándava forest. The Takshaks and Nágás
were the tree and serpent worshippers, whose rites and
objects of adoration have impressed themselves deeply on the
architecture and sculptures of India. They included, in a
confused manner, several different races of Scythic origin.

The chief authority on Tree and Serpent Worship in India Indo-
has deliberately selected the term 'Scythian' for the anti-Aryan Scythic
elements, which entered so largely into the Indian religions Nágás;
both in ancient and in modern times.[4] The Chinese records
give a full account of the Nágá geography of ancient India.
The Nágá kingdoms were both numerous and powerful, and
Buddhism derived many of its royal converts from them. The

---

[1] Tod, *Rájásthán*, vol. i. p. 95 (ed. 1873).

[2] Taki, or Asarur, 45 miles west of Lahore. General Cunningham, *Anc.
Geog. of India*, p. 191, and Map VI. (ed. 1871). This Taki lies, however,
considerably to the south-east of the Takshásila of Alexander's expedition.

[3] Tod, *Rájásthán*, vol. i. p. 53 (ed. 1873); a very doubtful authority.

[4] Dr. J. Fergusson's *Tree and Serpent Worship*, pp. 71, 72 (India
Museum, 4to, 1868). For the results of more recent local research, see
Mr. Rivett-Carnac's papers in the *Journal of the As. Soc., Bengal*, 'The
Snake Symbol in India,' 'Ancient Sculpturings on Rocks,' 'Stone Carv-
ings at Máinpuri,' etc.; the Honourable Ráo Sáhib Vishvanáks Náráyan
Mandlik's 'Serpent-Worship in Western India,' and other essays in the
Bombay As. Soc. Journal; also, *Reports of Archæological Survey*, Western
India.

Chinese chroniclers, indeed, classify the Nágá princes of India into two great divisions, as Buddhists and non - Buddhists. The serpent-worship, which formed so typical a characteristic of the Indo-Scythic races, led the Chinese to confound those tribes with the objects of their adorations; and the fierce Indo-Scythic Nágás would almost seem to be the originals of the Dragon races of Chinese Buddhism and Chinese art. The compromises to which Buddhism submitted, with a view to winning the support of the Nágá peoples, will be referred to in the following chapter, on the Rise of Hinduism.

become the Dragon-races of China.

As the Greek invaders found Ráwal Pindi District in possession of a Scythic race of Takkas in 327 B.C., so the Musalmán conqueror found it inhabited by a fierce non-Aryan race of Ghakkars thirteen hundred years later. The Ghakkars for a time imperilled the safety of Mahmúd of Ghazní in 1008. Farishta describes them as savages, addicted to polyandry and infanticide. The tide of Muhammadan conquest rolled on, but the Ghakkars remained in possession of their sub-Himálayan tract.[1] In 1205 they ravaged the Punjab to the gates of Lahore; in 1206 they stabbed the Muhammadan Sultán in his tent; and in spite of conversion to Islám by the sword, it was not till 1525 that they made their submission to the Emperor Bábar in return for a grant of territory. During the next two centuries they rendered great services to the Mughal dynasty against the Afghán usurpers, and rose to high influence in the Punjab. Driven from the plains by the Sikhs in 1765 A.D., the Ghakkar chiefs maintained their independence in the Murree (Marri) Hills till 1830, when they were crushed after a bloody struggle. In 1849, Ráwal Pindi passed, with the rest of the Sikh territories, under British rule. But the Ghakkars revolted four years afterwards, and threatened Murree, the summer capital of the Punjab, as lately as 1857. The Ghakkars are now found in the Punjab Districts of Ráwal Pindi, Jehlam, and Hazára. Their total number was returned at 25,789 in 1881. They are described by their British officers as 'a fine spirited race, gentlemen in ancestry and bearing, and clinging under all reverses to the traditions of noble blood.'[2]

The Ghakkars of Ráwal Pindi, 1008–1857 A.D.

The population of Ráwal Pindi District has been selected to illustrate the long-continued presence and vitality of the pre-Aryan element in India. Other parts of the country must be

Pre-Aryans of Bareilly District.

---

[1] For a summary of their later history, see article on RAWAL PINDI DISTRICT, *The Imperial Gazetteer of India.*

[2] *The Imperial Gazetteer of India*, article RAWAL PINDI DISTRICT.

more briefly dealt with. Proceeding inwards into the North-Western Provinces, we everywhere find traces of an early Buddhist civilisation in contact with, or overturned by, rude non-Aryan tribes. In Bareilly District, for example, the wild Ahírs from the north, the Bhíls from the south, and the Bhars from the east, seem to have expelled highly-developed Aryan communities at some period before 1000 A.D. Still farther to the east, all remains of pre-historic masonry in Oudh and the North-Western Provinces are assigned to the ancient Buddhists or to a non-Aryan race of Bhars.

The Bhars appear to have possessed the north Gangetic plains in the centuries coeval with the fall of Buddhism. *The Bhars in Oudh.* Their kingdoms extended over most of Oudh. Lofty mounds covered with ancient groves mark the sites of their forgotten cities; and they are the mysterious 'fort-builders' to whom the peasantry ascribe any ruin of unusual size. In the central valley of the Ganges, their power is said to have been crushed by the Sharki dynasty of Jaunpur in the end *In Jaun-* of the 14th century. In the Districts north of the Gan- *pur.* getic plain, the Bhars figure still more prominently in local traditions, and an attempt has been made to trace their continuous history. In GORAKHPUR DISTRICT, the aboriginal *In Gorakh-* Tharus and Bhars seem to have overwhelmed the early *pur.* outposts of Aryan civilisation several centuries before Christ. Their appearance on the scene is connected with the rise of Buddhism. They became vassals of the Buddhist kingdom of Behar on the south-east; and on the fall of that power, about 550 A.D., they regained their independence. The Chinese pilgrim in the 7th century comments in this region on the large number of monasteries and towers—the latter probably a monument of the struggle with the aboriginal Bhars, who were here finally crushed between the 7th and the 10th centuries A.D. In 1881, the total Bhar population of Oudh and the North-Western Provinces numbered 349,113.

As we advance still farther eastwards into Bengal, we find that the non-Aryan races have within historical time supplied a large part of the Hindu population. In the north, the Koch *The Koch* established their dominion upon the ruins of the Aryan *of Northern* kingdom of Kámrúp, which the Afghán King of Bengal had *Bengal.* overthrown in 1489. The Koch gave their name to the Native State of KUCH BEHAR; and their descendants, together *In Kuch* with those of other non-Aryan tribes, form the mass of the *Behar.* people in the neighbouring British Districts, such as RANGPUR. *In Rang-* In 1881, they numbered 1¼ million in Northern Bengal and *pur.*

Behar. One part of them got rid of their low origin by becoming Musalmáns, and thus obtained the social equality which Islám grants to all mankind. The rest have merged more or less imperfectly into the Hindu population; and about three-quarters of a million of them claim, in virtue of their position as an old dominant race, to belong to the Kshattriya caste. They call themselves Rájbansís, a term exactly corresponding to the Rájputs of Western India. The Hinduized Rájás of

Kuch Behar Rájás.

Kuch Behar obtained for their ancestors a divine origin from their Bráhman genealogists, in order to efface their aboriginal descent; and among the nobility all mention of the Koch tribe was avoided. The present Mahárájá married the daughter of the celebrated theistic apostle, Keshab Chandra Sen, the leader of the Brahmo Samáj. He is an honorary major in the British army, and takes a prominent part in Calcutta and Simla society.

Ahams of Assam.

Proceeding still eastwards, the adjacent valley of Assam was, until the last century, the seat of another non-Aryan ruling race. The Ahams entered Assam from the south-east about 1350 (?) A.D.; had firmly established their power in 1663; gradually yielded to Hinduism; and were overpowered by fresh Buddhist invasions from Burma between 1750 and 1825, when the valley was annexed to British India. The Ahams have been completely crushed as a dominant race; and their old national priests, to the number of 253,860, have been forced to become tillers of the soil for a living. But the people of Assam are still so essentially made up of aboriginal races and their Hinduized descendants, that not 130,000 persons of even alleged pure Aryan descent can be found in a population exceeding 4¾ millions.[1]

Pre-Aryan element south of the Ganges.

The foregoing summary has been confined to races north of the Ganges. Passing to the southern Gangetic plain, we find that almost every tract has traditions of a pre-Aryan tribe, either as a once-dominant race or as lying at the root of the local population. The great Division of Bundelkhand con-

Aborigines in Central India ;

tains several crushed peoples of this class, and takes its name from the Bundelas, a tribe of at least semi-aboriginal descent.

---

[1] The Bráhmans in Assam number only 119,075 (being fewer than the Kalitás or old priests of the Ahams, 253,860), out of a total population in Assam of 4,881,426; while the Koch alone number about 230,382, and even the crushed Ahams 179,314. For further particulars regarding these races, see *The Imperial Gazetteer of India*, article ASSAM.

As we rise from the Gangetic plains into the highlands of the Central Provinces, we reach the abiding home of the non-Aryan tribes. One such race after another—Gaulís, Nágás, Gonds, Ahírs, Bhíls—ruled from the Sátpura plateau.[1] Some of their chiefs and leading families now claim to be Kshattriyas; and a section of one of the lowest races, the Chauháns, borrowed their name from the noble ' Chauhán' Rájputs.

In the Lower Provinces of Bengal, we find the delta in Lower peopled by masses of pre-Aryan origin. One section of them Bengal; has merged into low-class Hindus; another section has sought a more equal social organization by accepting the creed of Muhammad. But such changes of faith do not alter their ethnical type; and the Musalmán of the delta differs as widely in race from the Afghán, as the low-caste Hindu of the delta differs from the Bráhman. Throughout Southern India, the in non-Aryan elements form almost the entire population, and Southern have supplied the great Dravidian family of languages, which India. are spoken by 28 millions of people. Two of our oldest and most faithful allies in the Madras Presidency, the enlightened dynasty of Travancore, and the ancient princes of Pudukotta, are survivals of the time when non-Aryan sovereigns ruled over Southern India.

The Scythic inroads, and the ancient Nágá and so-called Scythic aboriginal tribes, have, however, not merely left behind and Nágá remnants of races in individual Districts. They have affected on the character of the whole population, and profoundly Hinduism. influenced the religious beliefs and domestic institutions of India. In the Veda we see highly developed communities of the Aryan stock, worshipping bright and friendly gods, honouring woman, and assigning to her an important position in the family life. Husband and wife were the *Dampati*, or joint rulers of the Indo-Aryan household. Traditions of the freedom of woman among the ancient Aryan settlers survive in the *swayamvara* or Maiden's Own Choice of a Husband, in the epic poems.

The curtain of Vedic and Post-Vedic literature falls upon On the the scene before the 5th century B.C. When the curtain rises religion on the domestic and religious life of mediæval India, in the domestic life of

[1] See CENTRAL PROVINCES, *The Imperial Gazetteer of India.* The Gaulís modern are locally believed to have been earlier fort-builders than the Gonds (see India. for example, article SAONER); and some of the Gond chiefs trace their descent through 54 generations to a well-recorded ancestor assigned to 91 A.D. (see *The Imperial Gazetteer of India,* article SARANGHAR).

Puránas about the 10th century A.D., a vast change has taken place. The people are no longer sharply divided into civilised Aryans and rude non-Aryans, but into castes of a great mixed population. Their religion is no longer a worship of bright and friendly gods, but a composite product of Aryan spiritual conceptions and non-Aryan superstitions. The position of woman has also altered for the worse. Husband and wife are no longer 'joint rulers' of the household. The Maiden's Own Choice has fallen into disuse, or survived only as a Court pageant; the custom of child-marriage has grown up. The widow has been condemned to a life of privation, or has been taught the merit of extinguishing her existence on her husband's funeral pile.

The following chapter will exhibit this amorphous growth, popularly known as Hinduism. Orthodox Hindus are unfortunately in the habit of claiming the authority of the Veda for their mediæval institutions, for the evil as well as for the good. As a matter of fact, these institutions are the joint product of non-Aryan darkness and of Aryan light. The Scythic, and Nágá, and so-called aboriginal races, with their indifference to human suffering, their polyandric households, and their worship of fear and blood, have left their mark deep in the Hindu law-codes, in the terrorizing of the Hindu religion, and in the degradation of woman. English scholarship has shown that the worst feature of Hinduism, widow-burning, had no authority in the Veda. When it is equally well understood that the darker features of Hinduism, as a whole, rest not upon the Vedic scriptures, but are the result of a human compromise with non-Aryan barbarism, the task of the Indian reformer will be half accomplished. It is with a true popular instinct that the great religious movements of India in our day reject the authority of mediæval Hinduism, and appeal back to the Veda.

The appeal to the Veda.

CHAPTER VIII.

RISE OF HINDUISM (750 TO 1520 A.D.).

FROM these diverse races, pre-Aryan, Aryan, and Scythic, the population of India has been made up. The task of organizing them fell to the Bráhmans. That ancient caste, which had never quitted the scene even during the height of the Buddhistic supremacy, stepped forward to the front of the stage upon the decay of the Buddhist faith. The Chinese pilgrim, about 640 A.D., had found Bráhmanism and Buddhism co-existing throughout India. The conflict of creeds brought forth a great line of Bráhman apostles, from the 8th to the 16th century A.D., with occasional successors down to our own day. The disintegration of Buddhism, as we have seen, occupied many hundred years, perhaps from 300 to 1000 A.D.[1]

The Hindus take the 8th century as the turning-point in the struggle. About 750 A.D., arose a holy Bráhman of Bengal, Kumárila Bhatta by name, preaching the old Vedic doctrine of a personal Creator and God. Before this realistic theology, the impersonal abstractions of the Buddhists succumbed; and according to a later legend, the reformer wielded the sword of the flesh not less trenchantly than the weapons of the spirit. A Sanskrit writer, Madhava-Achárya, of the 14th century A.D., relates how Sudhanwan, a prince in Southern India, 'commanded his servants to put to death the old men and the children of the Buddhists, from the bridge of Ráma [the ridge of reefs which connects India with Ceylon] to the Snowy Mountain: let him who slays not, be slain.'[2]

Side-notes: RISE OF HINDUISM. Kumárila, 750 (?) A.D. Persecution (?) of Buddhism.

---

[1] From the language of the Saddharma Pundarika, translated into Chinese before the end of the 3rd century A.D., H. H. Wilson infers that even at that early date 'the career of the Buddhists had not been one of uninterrupted success, although the opposition had not been such as to arrest their progress' (*Essays*, vol. ii. p. 366, ed. 1862). The existence of Buddhism in India is abundantly attested to 1000 A.D.

[2] Quoted by H. H. Wilson, *ut supra.* See also Lassen's *Indische Alterthumskunde*, vol. iv. p. 708; Colebrooke's *Essays*, p. 190.

True value
of the
legend.

It is needless to say that no sovereign existed at that time in India whose power to persecute extended from the Himálayas to Cape Comorin. So far as the legend has any truth, it refers to one of many local religious reprisals which took place at the Indian courts during the struggle between the Buddhists and the Bráhmans. Such reprisals recurred in later days, on a smaller scale, between the rival Hindu sects. The legend of Kumárila is significant, however, as placing on a religious basis the series of many-sided evolutions which resulted in Hinduism. These evolutions were the result of ethnical processes, more subtle than the scheming of any caste of men. The Bráhmans gave a direction to Hinduism, but it was the natural development of the Indian races which produced it.

Twofold
basis of
Hinduism;
caste and
religion.

Hinduism is a social organization and a religious confederacy. As a social organization, it rests upon caste, with its roots deep down in the ethnical elements of the Indian people. As a religious confederacy, it represents the coalition of the old Vedic faith of the Bráhmans with Buddhism on the one hand, and with the ruder rites of the pre-Aryan and Indo-Scythic races on the other.

Caste basis
of Hinduism.

The ethnical basis of caste is disclosed in the fourfold division of the people into the 'twice-born' Aryan castes, including the Bráhmans, Kshattriyas (Rájputs), and Vaisyas; and the

The race-
origin of
caste.

'once-born' non-Aryan Súdras. The Census proves that this classification remains the fundamental one to the present day. The three 'twice-born' castes still wear the sacred thread, and claim a joint, although an unequal, inheritance in the holy books of the Veda. The 'once-born' castes are still denied the sacred thread, and their initiation into the old religious literature of the Indo-Aryans has only been effected by the secular teaching of our Anglo-Indian schools. But while caste has thus its foundations deep in the distinctions of race, its superstructure is regulated by another system of division, based on the occupations of the people. The early classification of the people may be expressed either ethnically as 'twice-born' Aryans, and 'once-born' non-Aryans; or socially, as priests,

Modified
by 'occu-
pation'
and 'lo-
cality.'

warriors, husbandmen, and serfs. On these two principles of classification, according to race and to employment, still further modified by geographical position, has been built up the ethnical and social organization of Indian caste.

Com-
plexity
of caste.

From the resulting cross-divisions arises an excessive complexity, which renders any brief exposition of caste superficial. As a rule, it may be said that the Aryan or 'twice-born' castes adhere most closely to the ethnical principle of division; the 'once-born' or distinctly non-Aryan to the same principle, but profoundly modified by the concurrent principle of employment; while the mixed progeny of the two are classified solely according to their occupation. But even among the Bráhmans, whose pride of race and continuity of tradition should render them the firmest ethnical unit among the Indian castes, classification by employment and by geographical situation plays a very important part; and the Bráhmans, so far from being a compact unit, are made up of several hundred castes, who cannot intermarry, nor eat food cooked by each other. They follow every employment, from the calm *pandits* of Behar in their stainless white robes, and the haughty priests of Benares, to the potato-growing Bráhmans of Orissa, 'half-naked peasants, struggling along under their baskets of yams, with a filthy little Bráhmanical thread over their shoulder.'[1]

Even the Bráhmans not an ethnical unit.

In many parts of India, Bráhmans may be found earning their livelihood as porters, shepherds, cultivators, potters, and fishermen, side by side with others who would rather starve and see their wives and little ones die of hunger, than demean themselves to manual labour, or allow food prepared by a man of inferior caste to pass their lips. Classification by locality introduces another set of distinctions among the Bráhmans. In Lower Bengal jails, a convict Bráhman from Behar or the North-Western Provinces used to be highly valued, as the only person who could prepare food for all classes of Bráhman prisoners. In 1864, the author saw a Bráhman felon try to starve himself to death, and submit to a flogging rather than eat his food, on account of scruples as to whether the birthplace of the North-Western Bráhman, who had cooked it, was equal in sanctity to his own native district. The Bráhmans are popularly divided into ten great septs, according to their locality; five on the north, and five on the south of the Vindhya range.[2] But the minor distinctions are innumerable. Thus, the first of the five northern Bráhman septs, the

The Bráhman caste analyzed.

---

[1] See Hunter's *Orissa*, vol. i. pp. 238 *et seq.* (ed. 1872), where 25 pages are devoted to the diversities of the Bráhmans in occupation and race. Also *Hindu Tribes and Castes*, by the Rev. M. A. Sherring, Introd. xxi. vol. ii. (4to, Calcutta, 1879).

[2] Thus tabulated according to a Sanskrit mnemonic *Sloka*:—
   I. The five Gauras north of the Vindhyá range—
      (1) The *Sáraswatas*, so called from the country watered by the river Saraswatí.
      (2) The *Kányakubjas*, so called from the Kányakubja or Kanauj country.

N

Sáraswatas in the Punjab, consist of 469 classes.[1]　Sherring enumerated 1886 separate Bráhmanical tribes.[2]　Dr. Wilson, of Bombay, carried his learned work on Caste to the length of two volumes, aggregating 678 pages, before his death ; but he had not completed his analysis of even a single caste—the Bráhmans.

The lower castes still more complex.　It will be readily understood, therefore, how numerous are the sub-divisions, and how complex is the constitution, of the lower castes.　The Rájputs now number 590 separately-named tribes in different parts of India.[3]　But a process of synthesis as well as of analysis has been going on among the Indian peoples.　In many outlying Provinces, we see non-Aryan chiefs and warlike tribes turn into Aryan Rájputs before our eyes.[4]　Well-known legends have been handed down of large bodies of aliens being incorporated from time to time even into the Bráhman caste.[5]　But besides these 'manufactured Bráhmans,' and the ethnical syncretisms which they represent, there has been a steady process of amalgamation among the Hindus by mixed marriage.[6]　The Súdras, says Mr. Sherring, 'display a great intermingling of races.　Every caste exhibits this confusion.　They form a living and practical testimony to the fact that in former times the upper and lower classes of native society, by which I

The building up of castes.

> (3) The *Gauras* proper, so called from Gaur, or the country of the Lower Ganges.
> (4) The *Utkalas*, of the Province of Utkala or Odra (Orissa).
> (5) The *Maithilas*, of the Province of Mithila (Tirhut).
>
> II. The five Dravidas south of the Vindhyá range—
> (1) The *Maháráshtras*, of the country of the Maráthí language.
> (2) The *Andhras* or *Tailangas*, of the country of the Telugu language.
> (3) The *Dravidas* proper, of the country of the Dravidian or Tamil language.
> (4) The *Karnátas*, of the Karnátika, or the country of the Canarese language.
> (5) The *Gurjaras*, of Gurjaráshtra, or the country of the Gujarátí language.

[1] Compiled by Pandit Rádhá Krishna, quoted by Dr. J. Wilson, *Indian Caste*, part ii. pp. 126–133.

[2] *Hindu Tribes and Castes*, pp. xxii.–xlvi. vol. ii. (4to, Calcutta, 1879).

[3] See Sherring, *Hindu Tribes and Castes*, vol. ii. pp. lv.–lxv.

[4] See Sherring, *Hindu Tribes and Castes*, vol. ii. p. lxvii.

[5] Hunter's *Orissa*, vol. i. p. 247 (in Oudh), p. 248 (in Bhágalpur), p. 254 (in Malabar), etc.

[6] See two interesting articles from opposite points of view, on the synthetic aspects of caste, by the Rev. Mr. Sherring, of Benares, and by Jogendra Chandra Ghose, in the *Calcutta Review*, Oct. 1880.

mean the Hindu and non-Hindu population of India, formed alliances with one another on a prodigious scale, and that the offspring of these alliances were in many instances gathered together into separate castes and denominated Súdras.'[1]

The Hindu custom now forbids marriage between (1) per- The slow sons of the same *gotra* or kindred, and (2) persons of different develop-ment of castes. But this precise double rule has been arrived at only Hindu after many intermediate experiments in endogamous and exo- marriage gamous tribal life. The transitions are typified by the polyandry law. of Draupadí in the Mahábhárata, and by many caste customs relating to marriage, inheritance, and the family tie, which survive to this day. Such survivals constitute an important branch of law, in fact, the domestic 'common law' of India,[2] and furnish one of the chief difficulties in the way of Anglo-Indian codification. Thus, to take a single point, the rules Survivals regarding marriage exhibit every phase from the compulsory of the process. polyandry of the old Nairs, the permissive polyandry of the Punjab Játs, and the condonement of adultery with a husband's brother or kinsman among the Kárakat Vellálars of Madura ; to the law of Levirate among the Ahírs and Nuniyás, the legal re-marriage of widows among the low-caste Hindus, and the stringent provisions against such re-marriages among the higher castes. At this day, the Nairs exhibit several of the stages in the advance from polyandric to monogamous institutions. The conflict between polyandry and the more civilised marriage system of the Hindus is going on before our eyes in Malabar. Among the Koils, although polyandry is forgotten, the right of disposing of a girl in marriage still belongs, in certain cases, to the *maternal* uncle,—a relic of the polyandric system of succession through females. This tribe also preserves the form of marriage by 'capture.'

The *Bráhmanas* indicate that the blood of the Hindus Ancient was, even in the early post-Vedic period, greatly intermingled.[3] mingling of castes. The ancient marriage code recognised as lawful, unions of men of higher caste with females from any of the lower ones, and their offspring[4] had a quite different social status from

---

[1] *Calcutta Review*, cxlii. p. 225.

[2] Among many treatises on this subject, Arthur Steele's *Law and Custom of Hindu Castes* (1868) deals with Western India ; Nelson's *View of Hindu Law* (1877), and Burnell's *Dayavibhága*, etc., may be quoted for the Madras Presidency ; Beames' admirable edition of Sir Henry Elliot's *Tribes of the North - Western Provinces*, and Sherring's *Hindu Tribes* (besides more strictly legal treatises), for Bengal.

[3] The *Taittiríya Bráhmana* of the Krishna Yajur Veda (quoted by Dr. J. Wilson, *Caste*, i. pp. 127-132) enumerates 159 castes.   [4] *Anuloma*.

the progeny [1] of illicit concubinage. The laws of Manu disclose how widely such connections had influenced the structure of Indian society 2000 years ago ; and the Census proves that the mixed castes still form the great body of the Hindu population. In dealing with Indian caste, we must therefore allow, not only for the ethnical and geographical elements into which it is resolvable, but also for the synthetic processes by which it has been built up.

The 'occupation' basis of caste.

The same remark applies to the other principle of classification on which caste rests, namely, according to the employments of the people. On the one hand, there has been a tendency to erect every separate employment in each separate Province into a distinct caste. On the other hand, there has

Changes of 'occupation' by castes.

been a practice (which European observers are apt to overlook) of the lower castes changing their occupation, and in some cases deliberately raising themselves in the social scale. Thus the Vaisya caste, literally the *vis* or general body of the Aryan settlers, were in ancient times the tillers of the soil. They have abandoned this laborious occupation to the Súdra and mixed castes, and are now the merchants and bankers of India. 'Fair in complexion,' writes the most accurate of recent students of caste,[2] 'with rather delicate features, and a certain refinement depicted on their countenances, sharp of eye, intelligent of face, and polite of

The Vaisyas.

bearing,' the Vaisyas 'must have radically changed since the days when their forefathers delved, sowed, and reaped.' Indeed, so great is the change, that a heated controversy is going on in Hindu society as to whether the Bengali *baniyás*, or merchant-bankers, are really of Vaisya descent or of a higher origin.

Such a rise in the social scale is usually the unconscious work of time, but there are also legends of distinct acts of self-assertion by individual castes. In Southern India, the gold-

Goldsmiths of Madras.

smiths strenuously resisted the rule of the Bráhmans, and for ages claimed to be the true spiritual guides, styling themselves *ácháryas*, 'religious teachers,' and wearing the sacred thread. Their pretensions are supposed to have given rise to the great division of castes in Madras, into the 'Right-hand,' or the cultivating and trading castes who supported the Bráhmans ;

[1] *Pratiloma.* For an arrangement of 134 Indian castes, according to their origin, or 'procession' from (1) regular full marriage by members of the same caste, (2) *anuloma*, (3) *pratiloma*, (4) *Vrátya-Santati*, (5) adultery, (6) incest, (7) degeneration ; Wilson, *Indian Caste*, ii. pp. 39-70.

[2] The Rev. M. A. Sherring (deceased, alas, since the above was written, after a life of noble devotion and self-sacrifice to the Indian people), *Calcutta Review*, October 1880, p. 220.

and the 'Left-hand,' chiefly craftsmen who sided with the artisan opposition to Bráhman supremacy.[1]

In Bengal, a similar opposition came from the literary class. The Dattas, a sept of the Káyasth or writer - caste, re- _{The Dattas of Bengal.} nounced the position assigned to them in the classification of Hindu society. They claimed to rank next to the Bráhmans, and thus above all the other castes. They failed; but a native author[2] states that one of their body, within the memory of men still living, maintained his title, and wore the sacred thread of the pure 'twice-born.' The Statistical Survey of India has disclosed many self-assertions of this sort, although of a more gradual character and on a smaller scale. Thus, in Eastern Bengal, where land is plentiful, the Sháhas, a section of the Surís or degraded spirit-sellers, have, _{The Sháhas.} in our own time, advanced themselves first into a respectable cultivating caste, and then into prosperous traders. Some of the Telís or oil-pressers in Dacca District, and certain of the _{Telís, Támbulís, etc.} Támbulís or *pán*-growers in Rangpur, have in like manner risen above their hereditary callings, and become bankers and grain merchants. These examples do not include the general opening of professions, effected by English education—the great solvent of caste.

There is therefore a plasticity as well as a rigidity in caste. _{Plasticity and rigidity in caste.} Its plasticity has enabled caste to adapt itself to widely separated stages of social progress, and to incorporate the various ethnical elements which make up the Indian people. Its rigidity has given strength and permanence to the corporate body thus formed. Hinduism is internally loosely coherent, but it has great powers of resistance to external pressure. Each caste is to some extent a trade- _{Caste, as a system of trade-guilds.} guild, a mutual assurance society, and a religious sect. As a trade-union, it insists on the proper training of the youth of its craft, regulates the wages of its members, deals with trade-delinquents, and promotes good fellowship by social gatherings. The famous fabrics of mediæval India, and the chief local industries in our own day, were developed under the supervision of caste or trade guilds of this sort. Such guilds may still be found in many parts of India, but not always with the same complete development.[3]

[1] This subject is involved in much obscurity. The above sentences embody the explanation given in Nelson's *View of the Hindu Law, as administered by the High Court of Madras*, p. 140 (Madras, 1877).

[2] Jogendra Chandra Ghose, *Calcutta Review*, cxlii. p. 279 (October 1880).

[3] The *Statistical Accounts* or *Gazetteers* of the Bombay Districts devote a special section to such trade-guilds in every District.

In AHMADABAD DISTRICT[1] each trade forms a separate guild. All heads of artisan households are ranged under their *Its regulation of wages.* proper guild. The objects of the guild are to regulate competition among the members, and to uphold the interest of the body in disputes with other craftsmen. To moderate competition, the guild appoints certain days as trade holidays, when any member who works is punished by a fine. A special case occurred in 1873 among the Ahmadábád bricklayers. Men of this class sometimes added 3d. to their daily wages by working extra time in the early morning. But several families were thereby thrown out of employment. Accordingly the guild met, and decided that as there was not employment for all, no man should be allowed to work extra time.

Working of the trade-guild. The decisions of the guild are enforced by fines. If the offender refuses to pay, and the members of the guild all belong to one caste, the offender is put out of caste. If the guild contains men of different castes, the guild uses its influence with other guilds to prevent the recusant member from getting work. The guild also acts in its corporate capacity against other crafts. For example, in 1872, the Ahmadábád cloth - dealers resolved among themselves to reduce the rates paid to the sizers or *tágiás.* The sizers' guild refused to prepare cloth at the lower rates, and *An Indian 'strike.'* remained six weeks on strike. At length a compromise was arrived at, and both guilds signed a stamped agreement.

Besides its punitive fines, the guild draws an income from fees levied on persons beginning to practise its craft. This custom prevails at Ahmadábád in the cloth and other industries. But no fee is paid by potters, carpenters, and inferior artisans. *Guild funds.* An exception is made, too, in the case of a son succeeding to his father, when nothing need be paid. In other cases, the amount varies, in proportion to the importance of the trade, from £5 to £50. The revenue from these fees and from punitive fines is expended in feasts to the members of the guild, in the support of poor craftsmen or their orphans, and in *Guild charities.* charity. A favourite device for raising money in Surat is for the members of a trade to agree to keep a certain date as a holiday, and to shut up all their shops except one. The right to keep open this one shop is let by auction, and the amount bid is credited to the guild-fund.

Trade-interests v. caste : Within the guild, the interests of the common trade often supersede the race element of the theoretically common caste. Thus, in Surat, each class of craftsmen, although including men

[1] See the article, *The Imperial Gazetteer of India.*

of different castes and races, combine to form a guild, with a council, a head-man, and a common purse for charity and entertainments. In Ahmadábád, Broach, and many industrial in trade centres, the trade organization into guilds co-exists with, or dominates, the race-structure of caste. A twofold organization also appears in the village community. Caste regulates the in the vil-theoretical position of every family within it; but the low-castes often claim the headship in the village government.

In Bárásat Sub-district in Bengal, of 5818 enumerated Village Heads, only 15 were Bráhmans or Rájputs, 4 were Káyasths, while 3524 belonged to the Súdra or inferior castes, down to the detested cow-skinners and corpse-bearers; the residue being Muhammadans, with 13 native Christians. In Southern India, the Village Head is sometimes of so low a caste that he cannot sit under the same roof with his colleagues in the village government. He therefore hands up his staff, which is set in the place of honour, while he himself squats on the ground outside. The trade-guild in the cities, and the village community throughout the country, act, together with caste, as mutual assurance societies, and under normal conditions allow none of their members to starve. Caste, and the trading or agricultural guilds concurrent with it, take the place of a poor-law in India.

It is obvious that such an organization must have some weapons for defending itself against lazy or unworthy members. The responsibility which the caste discharges with regard to feeding its poor, would otherwise be liable to abuses. As a matter of fact, the caste or guild exercises a surveillance over each of its members, from the close of childhood until death. If a man behaves well, he will rise to an honoured place in his caste; and the desire for such local distinctions exercises an important influence in the life of a Hindu. But the caste has its punishments as well as its rewards. Those punishments consist of fine and excommunication. The fine usually takes the form of a compulsory feast to the male members of the caste. This is the ordinary means of purification, or of making amends for breaches of the caste code.

Excommunication inflicts three penalties: First, an interdict against eating with the fellow-members of the caste. Second, an interdict against marriage within the caste. This practically amounts to debarring the delinquent and his family from respectable marriages of any sort. Third, cutting off the delinquent from the general community, by forbidding him the use of the village barber and washerman, and of the

[marginal notes:] in trade centres; in the village community. Low-caste Village Heads. Caste and 'mutual insurance.' No 'poor-law' in India. Caste rewards. Caste punishments. Excommunication.

priestly adviser. Except in very serious cases, excommunication is withdrawn upon the submission of the offender, and his payment of a fine. Anglo-Indian law does not enforce caste-decrees. But caste punishments exercise an efficacious restraint upon unworthy members of the community, precisely as caste rewards supply a powerful motive of action to good ones. A member who cannot be controlled by this mixed discipline of punishment and reward is eventually expelled; and, as a rule, an 'out-caste' is really a bad man. Imprisonment in jail carries with it that penalty; but may be condoned after release, by heavy expiations.

Recapitulation of caste.

Such is a brief survey of the nature and operation of caste. But the cross-divisions on which the institution rests; its conflicting principles of classification according to race, employment, and locality; the influence of Islám in Northern India; of the 'right-handed' and 'left-handed' branches in the South;[1] and the modifications everywhere effected by social or sectarian movements, render a short account of caste full of difficulties.

The religious basis of Hinduism.

Hinduism is, however, not only a social organization resting upon caste; it is also a religious federation based upon worship. As the various race elements of the Indian people have been welded into caste, so the simple old beliefs of the Veda, the mild doctrines of Buddha, and the fierce rites of the non-Aryan tribes have been thrown into the melting-pot, and poured out thence as a mixture of alloy and dross to be worked up into the Hindu gods. In the religious as in the social structure, the Bráhmans supplied the directing brain-power.

Its stages of evolution.

But both processes resulted from laws of human evolution, deeper than the workings of any individual will; and in both, the product has been, not an artificial manufacture, but a natural development. Hinduism merely forms one link in the golden chain of Indian religions. We have seen that the career of Buddha was but a combination of the ascetic and the heroic Aryan life as recorded in the Indian epics. Indeed, the discipline of the Buddhists organized so faithfully the prescribed stages of a Bráhman's existence, that it is difficult to decide whether the *Sarmanai* of Megasthenes were Buddhist clergy or Bráhman recluses. If accurate scholarship cannot accept Buddhism as simply the Sánkhya philosophy turned into a national religion, it admits that Buddhism is a natural development from Bráhmanism. An early set of

[1] See Crole's *Statistical Account of Chingleput District*, pp. 33, 34 (1879).

intermediate links is found in the *darsanas*, or philosophical systems, between the Vedic period and the establishment of Buddhism as a national religion under Asoka (1400? to 250 B.C.). A later set is preserved in the compromises effected during the final struggle between Buddhism and Bráhmanism, ending in the re-assertion of the latter in its new form as the religion of the Hindus (700 to 1000 A.D.).

Buddhism not only breathed into the new birth its noble spirit of charity, but bequeathed to Hinduism many of its institutions unimpaired, together with its scheme of religious life, and the material fabric of its worship. At this day, the *mahájan* or bankers' guild, in Surat, devotes part of the fees that it levies on bills of exchange to animal hospitals ; true survivals of Asoka's second edict, which provided a system of medical aid for beasts, 250 years before Christ. The cenobitic life, and the division of the people into laity and clergy, have passed almost unchanged from Buddhism into the present Hindu sects, such as the Vaishnavs or Vishnuites. *Buddhist influences on Hinduism. Beast hospitals.*

The Hindu monasteries in our own day vie with the Buddhist convents in the reign of Síláditya ; and Purí is, in many respects, a modern unlettered Nalanda. The religious houses of the Orissa delta, with their revenue of £50,000 a year,[1] are but Hindu developments of the Buddhist cells and rock-monasteries, whose remains still honeycomb the adjacent hills. *Monasteries.*

If we examine the religious life of the Vishnuite communities, we find their rules are Buddhistic, with Bráhmanical reasons attached. Thus the moral code of the Kabír-panthís consists of five rules :[2] First, life, whether of man or beast, must not be violated ; because it is the gift of God. Second, humanity is the cardinal virtue ; and the shedding of blood, whether of man or beast, a heinous crime. Third, truth is the great principle of conduct ; because all the ills of life and ignorance of God are due to original falsehood (*máyá*). Fourth, retirement from the world is desirable ; because the desires of the world are hostile to tranquillity of soul, and to the undisturbed meditation on God. Fifth, obedience to the spiritual guide is incumbent on all. This last rule is common to every sect of the Hindus. But the Kabír-panthís direct the pupil to examine well his teacher's life and doctrine before *The religious life.*

---

[1] Report by the Committee of native gentlemen appointed to inquire into the Orissa *maths*, dated 25th March 1869, par. 15.

[2] H. H. Wilson's *Religion of the Hindus*, vol. i. p. 94 (ed. 1862).

he resigns himself to his control. If we did not know that
Buddhism was itself an outgrowth from primitive Bráhmanism,
we might hold this code to be simple Buddhism, with the
addition of a personal God. But knowing, as we do, that
Bráhmanism and Buddhism were themselves closely connected, and that they combined to form Hinduism; it is
impossible to discriminate how far Hinduism was made up by
direct transmission from Buddhism or from Bráhmanism.

Buddhist influences on later religions.   The influence of Buddhism on the Christianity of the western
world has been referred to at p. 152. Whatever uncertainties
may still obscure that question, the effect of Buddhism upon
the present faiths of Eastern Asia admits of no doubt. The
best elements in the teaching of Buddha have survived in
modern Hinduism; and Buddhism carried with it essential
doctrines of Bráhmanism to China and Japan, together with
Serpent ornamen- tation :   certain characteristics of Indian religious art. The snake
ornamentation, which figures so universally in the religion
of India, is said to have been carried by Buddhism alike to
In Hinduism;   the east and the west. Thus, the canopy or baldachino over
Buddha's head delights in twisted pillars and wavy pat-
In Buddhism;   terns. These wave-like ornaments are conventionalized into
cloud curves in most of the Chinese and Japanese canopies;
but some of them still exhibit the original figures thus
symbolized as undulating serpents or Nágás. A serpent
baldachino of this sort may be seen in a monastery at Ningpo.[1]
It takes the place of the cobra-headed canopy, which in India
shelters the head of Siva, or of Vishnu as he slept upon the
In Chris- tian art.   waters at the creation of the world. The twisted columns
which support the baldachino at St. Peter's in Rome, and the
fluted ornamentation so common over Protestant pulpits, are
said to have a serpentine origin, and an eastern source. The
association of Buddha with two other figures, in the Japanese
temples, perhaps represents a recollection of the Bráhman
triad. The Bráhmanical idea of trinity, in its Buddhist
development as Buddha, Dharma (the Law), and Sangha (the
Congregation), deeply penetrates the faith. The Sacred Tooth
of Buddha at Ceylon is a reproduction of the phallic *linga* of
India.

Coalition of Buddh- ism with earlier religions :   Buddhism readily coalesced with the pre-existing religions
of primitive races. Thus, among the hill tribes of Eastern
Bengal, we see the Khyaungthas, or 'Children of the River,'

[1] The authority for this statement is an unpublished drawing by Miss
Gordon Cumming.

passing into Buddhists without giving up their aboriginal rites. In India ;
They still offer rice and fruits and flowers to the spirits of hill
and stream ;[1] and the Buddhist priests, although condemning
the custom as unorthodox, do not very violently oppose it. In In Japan.
Japan, a Buddhist saint visited the hill-slope of Hotoke Iwa in
767 A.D. ; declared the local Shinto deity to be only a manifestation of Buddha ; and so converted the old idolatrous high-
place into a Buddhist shrine. Buddhism has thus served as Shrines
a link between the ancient faiths of India and the modern common to
worship of the eastern world. It has given sanctity to the centres faiths.
of common pilgrimage, to which the great faiths of Asia resort.
Thus, the Siva-worshippers ascend the top of Adam's Peak in Adam's
Ceylon, to adore the footprint of their phallic god, the *Siva-* Peak.
pada ; the Buddhists repair to the spot to revere the same
symbol as the footmark of Buddha ; and the Muhammadans
venerate it as a relic of Adam, the Semitic father of
mankind.

Many common shrines of a similar character exist in India. Sakhi
The famous place of pilgrimage at Sakhi Sarwar crowns the Sarwar.
high bank of a hill stream at the foot of the Suláimán range,
in the midst of desert scenery, well adapted to penitents who
would mortify the flesh. To this remote spot, the Muhammadans come in honour of a Musalmán saint ; the Sikhs to
venerate a memorial of their theistic founder, Nának ; and the
Hindus to perform their own ablutions and rites. The mount
near Madras, associated in Catholic legend with the martyrdom
of St. Thomas, was originally a common hill-shrine for Muhammadans, Christians, and Hindus. Such hill-shrines for joint
worship are usually either rock-fortresses, like Kalinjar in the
North-Western Provinces and Chunar overhanging the Ganges,
or river-islands, like the beautiful islet on the Indus just below
the new railway bridge at Sakkar. The object of common
adoration is frequently a footmark in stone. This the Hindus
venerate as the footprint of Vishnu or Siva (*Vishnupad* or
Sivapad); while the Musalmáns revere it as the footprint
of Muhammad (*Kadam-rasul*). The mingled architecture of
some of these pilgrim-sites attests the various races and creeds
that combined to give them sanctity. Buddhism, which in
some respects was at first a revolt against Bráhman supremacy,
has done much to maintain the continuity between the ancient
and the modern religions of India.

Hinduism, however, derived its elements not merely from

[1] See Hunter's *Statistical Account of Bengal*, vol. vi. p. 40, etc.

Non-
Aryan
elements in
Hinduism.

Nágá rites.

Serpent-
worship in
Hinduism.

Phallic
emblems
in Hindu-
ism.

the two ancient Aryan faiths, the Bráhmanical and the Buddhist. In its popular aspects, it drew much of its strength,
and many of its rites, from the Nágá and other non-Aryan
peoples of India. Buddhists and Bráhmans alike endeavoured, during their long struggle, to enlist the masses on
their side. The Nágá kingdoms were divided, as we have
seen, by the Chinese geographers into those which had
accepted Buddhism, and those which had not. A chief feature
in Nágá-worship was the reverence for dragons or tailed
monsters. This reverence found its way into mediæval
Buddhism, and became an important element in Buddhist
mythology. The historian of Tree and Serpent worship goes
so far as to say that ' Buddhism was little more than a revival
of the coarser superstitions of the aboriginal races, purified and
refined by the application of Aryan morality.' [1]

The great monastery of Nalanda owed its foundation to the
supposed influence of a tailed monster, or Nágá, in a neighbouring tank. Many Hindu temples still support colonies of
sacred crocodiles ; and the scholar who has approached the
subject from the Chinese point of view, comes to the conclusion that ' no superstition was more deeply embedded in
the [ancient] Hindu mind than reverence for Nágás or dragons.
Buddhism from the first had to contend as much against the
under current of Nágá reverence in the popular mind, as
against the supercilious opposition of the philosophic Bráhman in the upper current. At last, as it would seem, driven
to an extremity by the gathering cloud of persecution, the
Buddhists sought escape by closing with the popular creed,
and endeavouring to enlist the people against the priests ;
but with no further success than such a respite as might be
included within some one hundred years.' [2]

This conception of the process is coloured by modern
ideas, but there can be no doubt that Hinduism incorporated
many aboriginal rites. It had to provide for the non-Aryan
as well as for the Aryan elements of the population, and it
combined the Bráhmanism and Buddhism of the Aryans with
the fetish-worship and religion of terror which swayed the non-
Aryan races. Some of its superstitions seem to have been
brought by Turanian or Scythian migrations from Central
Asia. Serpent-worship is closely allied to, if indeed it does

[1] Fergusson's *Tree and Serpent Worship*, pp. 62, with footnote, *et seq.*
(4to, 1868). This view must be taken subject to limitations.
[2] *Catena of Buddhist Scriptures from the Chinese*, pp. 415, 416. By
Samuel Beal (Trübner, 1871).

not take its origin in, that reverence for the symbols of human reproduction which formed one of the most widely-spread religions of pre-historic man. Phallic or generative emblems are on earth what the sun is in the heavens. The sun, as the type of celestial creative energy, was a primitive object of Aryan adoration. Later Bráhmanism, and its successor Hinduism, seem to have adopted not only the serpent, but the *linga* and *yoni*, or the terrestrial organs of male and female creative energy, from the non-Aryan races. The early Aryan ritual of the Vedas was addressed to the elements, particularly to Fire. The Hindu *linga* and *yoni*.

The worship of the phallic emblem or *linga* finds only a doubtful sanction, if any at all, in those ancient scriptures;[1] but the Puránas disclose it in full vigour (1000 A.D.); and the Muhammadans found it in every part of India. It is not only the chief religion to the south of the Vindhyas, but it is universally recognised by the Hindus. Such symbolism fitted well into the character of the third person of their triad—Siva, the Reproducer, as well as the All-Destroyer. To the Bráhmans it supplied a popular basis for their abstruse doctrines regarding the male and female energy in nature. Phallic worship harmonized also with their tendency to supply each god with a correlative goddess, and furnished an easily-understood symbolism for the *Sákta* sects, or worshippers of the divine creative power,[2] so numerous among the Hindus. For the semi-aboriginal tribes and half-Hinduized low-castes, this conception of Siva as the All-Destroyer and Reproducer, organized on a philosophical basis their old religion of propitiation by blood.[3] The 'creative energy.'

The fetish and tree worship of the non-Aryan races also entered largely into Hinduism. The first Englishman[4] who tried to study the natives as they actually are, and not as the Bráhmans described them, was struck by the universal prevalence of a worship quite distinct from that of the Hindu deities. A Bengal village has usually its local god, which it adores Fetish-worship in Hinduism, The *sála-grám*.

---

[1] H. H. Wilson's *Religion of the Hindus*, vol. i. p. 220 (ed. 1862).

[2] *Sakti.*

[3] The relation of these rites of the semi-Hinduized low-castes to the religion of the non-Aryan races is treated at considerable length, from personal observation, in Hunter's *Annals of Rural Bengal*, pp. 127-136 and 194, 5th edition.

[4] Dr. Francis Buchanan, who afterwards took the name of Hamilton. His survey of the North-Eastern Districts of Bengal, 1807-13, forms a noble

either in the form of a rude unhewn stone, or a stump, or a tree marked with red-lead. Sometimes a lump of clay placed under a tree does for a deity; and the attendant priest, when there is one, generally belongs to the half-Hinduized low-castes. The rude stone represents the non-Aryan fetish; and the tree seems to owe its sanctity to the non-Aryan belief that it forms the abode of the ghosts, or gods, of the village. We have seen how, in some Santáli hamlets, the worshippers dance round every tree; so that they may not, by any evil chance, miss the one in which the village spirits happen to dwell.

Vishnuite symbols. As the non-Aryan phallic emblems were utilized by Hinduism in the worship of Siva, the All-Destroyer and Reproducer, so the household fetish *sálagrám* has supplied a symbol for the rival Hindu deity Vishnu, the Preserver. The *sálagrám* (often an ammonite or curved stone) and the *tulasí* plant are the insignia of Vishnuism, as universally as the *linga* is of Sivaism. In both cases the Bráhmans enriched the popular fetish-worship with deep metaphysical doctrines, and with admirable moral codes. The Sivaite devotee carries round his neck, or hidden about his person, a miniature phallic emblem, *linga;* the *sálagrám* and *tulasí* are the objects of reverence among all the Vishnuite sects.[1]

The great Vishnuite festival of Bengal, the *rath-játra,* when Jagannáth, the 'Lord of the World,' is dragged in his car to his garden-house, is of Buddhist origin. But it has many a humbler counterpart in the forest excursions which the Bengal villagers make in their holiday clothes to some sacred tree in the neighbouring grove or jungle. These **Jungle rites.** jungle rites find special favour with the low-castes, and disclose curious survivals of the non-Hinduized element in the worshippers. Blood sacrifices and the eating of flesh have long been banished from the popular Vishnuite sects. But on such forest festivals, the fierce aboriginal instincts even in the mixed castes, who accept in ordinary life the restraints of Hinduism, break loose. Cowherds have been seen to

series of MS. folios in the India Office, much in need of a competent editor. Montgomery Martin made three printed volumes out of them by the process of drawing his pencil through the parts which did not interest him, or which he could not understand. These he published under the title of the *History, Antiquities, Topography, and Statistics of Eastern India* (3 vols., 1838).

[1] See, *inter alia,* pp. 15, 39, 50, 54, 116, 117, 140, 149, 179, 181, 246, vol. i. of H. H. Wilson's *Religion of the Hindus* (ed. 1862).

feed on swine-flesh, which at all other times they regard with abhorrence.

The ceremonies, where they can pretend to a conscious meaning, have a propitiatory or necromantic tinge. Thus, in Bírbhúm District the mixed and low castes of the chief town repair once a year to the jungle, and make offerings to a ghost who dwells in a *bel*-tree. Buchanan - Hamilton describes such sacrifices as 'made partly from fear, and partly to gratify the appetite for flesh.'[1] In examining the western ethnical frontier of Lower Bengal, the rites of the non-Aryan hillmen are found to merge into the Hinduism of the plains.[2] The evidence shows that the Hindus derived from non-Aryan sources their phallic emblem, the *linga*, their household fetish, the *sálagrám*, their village gods, *grám-devatas*, with the ghosts and demons that haunt so many trees, and the bloody rites of their national deity, Siva. Among the Hindus, these superstitions are often isolated and unconnected with each other ; among the Santáls and other non-Aryan races, they form riveted links in a ritual of fear and propitiation.

Non-Aryan rites merging into Hinduism.

The development of Hinduism out of pre-existing religious types, although a natural evolution, bears the impress of human guidance. Until the 12th century A.D., the Bráhmans supplied the directing energy in opposition to the Buddhists, and founded their reforms on a re-assertion of the personality of God. But by that period, Buddhism had ceased to struggle for a separate existence in India ; and the mass of the people began to strike out religious sects upon popular rather than on Bráhmanical lines. The work of the early Bráhman reformers was accordingly carried on after the 12th century, in part by low-caste apostles, who popularized the old Bráh-manical conception of a personal God, by infusing into it the Buddhist doctrine of the spiritual equality of man. Many of the Hindu sects form brotherhoods, on the Buddhist model, within which the classification by caste gives place to one based on the various degrees of perfection attained in the religious life.

Bráhman founders of Hinduism.

Low-caste apostles.

Most of the Hindu reformations since the 12th century thus preserve what was best in each of the two ancient faiths of India—namely, the personal God of the Bráhmans, and the spiritual equality of the Buddhists. Among the Hindus, every preacher who would really appeal to the

The Hindu apostolic type.

---

[1] *History, etc. of Eastern India*, from the Buchanan MSS., vol. i. p. 194.
[2] Hunter's *Annals of Rural Bengal*, p. 194, 5th edition.

popular heart must fulfil two conditions, and conform to a certain type. He must cut himself off from the world by a solemn act, like the Great Renunciation of Buddha; and he must come forth from his solemn communing with a simple message. The message need not be original. On the contrary, it must consist of a re-assertion, in some form, of the personality of God and the equality of men in His sight.

The Hindu Acta Sanctorum.

Hinduism boasts a line of religious founders stretching in almost unbroken succession from about 700 A.D. to the present day. The lives of the mediæval saints and their wondrous works are recorded in the Bhakta-Málá, literally, 'The Garland of the Faithful,' compiled by Nábhájí about three centuries ago.[1] This difficult Hindí work was popularized by later versions and commentaries,[2] and a vast structure of miracle and fable has been reared upon it. It is the Golden Legend and Acta Sanctorum of Hinduism. The same wonders are not recorded of each of its apostles, but divine interpositions abound in the life of all. The greater ones rank as divine

Miracles of the religious founders.

incarnations prophesied of old. Some were born of virgins; others overcame lions; raised the dead; their hands and feet when cut off sprouted afresh; prisons were opened to them; the sea received them and returned them to the land unhurt, while the earth opened and swallowed up their slanderers. Their lives were marvellous, and the deaths of some a solemn mystery.

Kabír's death.

Thus on Kabír's decease, both the Hindus and Musalmáns claimed the body, the former to burn it, the latter to bury it, according to their respective rites. While they wrangled over the corpse, Kabír suddenly stood in the midst, and, commanding them to look under the shroud, vanished. This they did. But under the winding-sheet they found only a heap of beautiful flowers, one-half of which they gave to be burned by the Hindus in their holy city, while the other half was buried in pomp by the Musalmáns. His name lives in the memory of the people; and to this day pilgrims from Upper India beg a spoonful of rice-water from the Kabír Monastery at Purí, at the extreme southern point of Bengal.

[1] H. H. Wilson, writing in the *Asiatic Researches* (Calcutta, 1828), says about ' 250 years ago.'—See *Journal of the Bombay Branch of the Asiatic Society*, vol. iii. p. 4.

[2] The best known are those of Náráyan Dás, about the time of Sháh Jahán (1627–58); the *tíká* of Krishna Dás (1713); and a later version 'in the more ordinary dialect of Hindustán.'—Wilson's *Religions of the Hindus*, vol. i. pp. 9, 10 (ed. 1862).

The first in the line of apostles was Kumárila, a *bhatta* or Bráhman of Behar. The legend relates that he journeyed into Southern India, in the 8th century A.D., commanding princes and people to worship one God. He stirred up a persecution against the Buddhists or Jains in the State of Rudrapur,—a local persecution which later tradition magnified into a general extermination of the Buddhists from the Himálayas to Cape Comorin.[1] In Hindu theology he figures as a teacher of the later Mímánsá philosophy, which ascribes the universe to a divine act of creation, and assumes an all-powerful God as the cause of the existence, continuance, and dissolution of the world. The doctrine of this personal deity, ' the ·one existent and universal soul,' ' without a second ' (*adwaita*), embodies the philosophical argument against the Buddhists. Kumárila bequeathed his task to his famous disciple Sankara Achárya, in whose presence he is said to have solemnly committed his body to the flames.

With the advent of Sankara Achárya we touch firmer historical ground. Born in Malabar, he wandered over India as an itinerant preacher as far north as Kashmír, and died at Kedarnáth in the Himálayas, aged 32. One of his disciples has narrated his life's work under the title of ' The Victory of Sankara,'[2] a record of his doctrines and controversial triumphs. Sankara moulded the later Mímánsá or Vedantic philosophy into its final form, and popularized it as a national religion. It is scarcely too much to say that, since his short life in the 8th or 9th century, every new Hindu sect has had to start with a personal God. He addressed himself to the high-caste philosophers on the one hand, and to the low-caste multitude on the other. He left behind, as the twofold result of his life's work, a compact Bráhman sect and a popular religion.

The Bráhman sect are the Smártas, still powerful in Southern India. Sankara taught that there was one sole and supreme God, *Bráhma Para Bráhma*, distinct alike from any member of the old Bráhman triad, or of the modern Hindu pantheon ; the

---

[1] The local persecution is recorded by Ananda Giri, a disciple of Sankara about the 8th or 9th century A.D., and the author of the *Sankara-Vijaya*. The magnified version appears in the *Sarva Darsana Sangraha* of Mádhava Achárya, in the 14th century. See, however, the Mackenzie MSS. in the India Office Library.

[2] The *Sankara-Vijaya* of Ananda Giri, published in the *Bibliotheca Indica*, and critically examined by Káshináth Trimbak Telang in vol. v. of the *Indian Antiquary*. But, indeed, Sankara is the first great figure in almost every Hindu hagiology, or book of saints, from the *Sarva Darsana Sangraha* of Mádhava Achárya downwards.

Ruler of the universe and its inscrutable First Cause, to be worshipped, not by sacrifices, but by meditation, and in spirit and in truth. The Smárta Bráhmans follow this philosophic side of his teaching; and of the religious houses which he founded some remain to this day, controlled from the parent monastery perched among the western ranges of Mysore.[1] But Sankara realized that such a faith is for the few. To those who could not rise to so high a conception of the godhead, he allowed the practice of any rites prescribed by the Veda, or by later orthodox teachers, to whatsoever form of the godhead they might be addressed. Tradition fondly narrates that the founders of almost all the historical sects of Hinduism—Sivaites, Vishnuites, Sauras, Sáktas, Gánapatyas, Bhairavas—were his disciples.[2] But Siva-worship claims Sankara as its apostle in a special sense. Siva-worship represents the popular side of his teaching, and the piety of his followers has elevated Sankara into an incarnation of Siva himself.[3]

His religion for the people.

Growth of Siva-worship;

Nothing, however, is altogether new in Hinduism, and it is needless to say that Siva had won his way high up into the pantheon long before the preaching of Sankara, in the 9th century A.D. Siva is the Rudra of the Vedas, as developed by Bráhman philosophy, and adapted by Sankara and others to popular worship. Rudra, the Storm-God of the Vedic hymns, had grown during this process into Siva, the Destroyer and Reproducer, as the third person of the Bráhman triad. The Chinese pilgrims supply evidence of his worship before the 7th century A.D., while his dread wife had a temple at the southernmost point of India at the time of the Periplus (2nd century A.D.), and gave her name to Cape Comorin.[4] Siva ranks high in the Mahábhárata, in various passages of uncertain date; but does not reach his full development till the Puránas, probably after the 10th century A.D. His worship in Bengal is said to have been formulated by Paramata Kálanála at Benares;[5] but Sankara's teaching gave an impulse to it

---

[1] See SRINGIRI (*The Imperial Gazetteer of India*) for a brief account of the chief-priest of the Smárta sect, which has its head-quarters in this monastery. Also the *Statistical Account of Mysore and Coorg*, by Lewis Rice, vol. ii. p. 413, etc. (Bangalore Government Press, 1876.)

[2] Wilson's *Religion of the Hindus*, vol. i. p. 28 (1862).

[3] This rank is claimed for Sankara by Mádhava Achárya in the 14th century A.D.; indeed, Siva's descent as Sankara is said to have been foretold in the *Skanda Purána*. Sankara is one of the names of Siva.

[4] From Kumári or Kanyá-kumári, the Virgin Goddess, a name of Durgá, wife of Siva.

[5] As Visweswara, or Lord of the Universe, under which name Siva is still the chief object of worship at Benares.

throughout all India, especially in the south ; and later tradition
makes Paramata himself a disciple of Sankara.

In the hands of Sankara's followers and apostolic suc- Its philo-
cessors, Siva-worship became one of the two chief religions sophical
of India. As at once the Destroyer and Reproducer, Siva aspects;
represented profound philosophical doctrines, and was early
recognised as being in a special sense the god of the Bráhmans.[1]
To them he was the symbol of death as merely a change of life.
On the other hand, his terrible aspects, preserved in his long list Its terrible
of names from the Roarer (Rudra)[2] of the Veda, to the Dread forms.
One (Bhíma) of the modern Hindu Pantheon, well adapted
him to the religion of fear and propitiation prevalent among
the ruder non-Aryan races. Siva, in his twofold character,
thus became the deity alike of the highest and of the lowest
castes. He is the Mahá-deva, or Great God of modern
Hinduism ; and his wife is Deví, pre-eminently THE Goddess.
His universal symbol is the *linga*, the emblem of reproduction ; his sacred beast, the bull, connected with the same
idea ; a trident tops his temples.

His images partake of his double nature. The Bráhmanical Twofold
conception is represented by his attitude as a fair-skinned man, aspects of
seated in profound thought, the symbol of the fertilizing Ganges Siva,
above his head, and the bull (emblem alike of procreation and
of Aryan plough-tillage) near at hand. The wilder non-Aryan
aspects of his character are signified by his necklace of skulls,
his collar of twining serpents, his tiger-skin, and his club with
a human head at the end. His five faces and four arms have
also their significance from this double aspect of his character,
Aryan and non-Aryan. His wife, in like manner, appears in her and of
Aryan form as Umá, ' Light,' the type of high-born loveliness ; Durgá, his
in her composite character as Durgá, a golden-coloured woman, queen.
beautiful but menacing, riding on a tiger ; and in her terrible
non-Aryan aspects, as Kálí, a black fury, of a hideous countenance, dripping with blood, crowned with snakes, and hung
round with skulls.

As an Aryan deity, Siva is Pasu-pati, the Lord of Animals Their two-
and the Protector of Cows ; Sambhu, the Auspicious ; Mrityun- fold sets of
jaya, the Vanquisher of Death ; Viswanátha, Monarch of All. names.
In his non-Aryan attributes, he is Aghora, the Horrible ; Virú-
páksha, of Mis-shapen Eyes ; Ugra, the Fierce ; Kapála-málin,

---

[1] A Sanskrit text declares Siva to be the *ádideva*, or special god of the
Bráhmans ; Vishnu, of the Kshattriyas ; Brahma, of the Vaisyas ; and
Ganesa, of the Súdras.

[2] From the root *rud*, weep.

Garlanded with Skulls. So also Deví, his female form, as an Aryan goddess is Umá, the lovely daughter of the mountain king, Himavat;[1] Aryá, the Revered; Gaurí, the Brilliant or Gold-coloured; Jagad-gaurí, the World's Fair One; Bhaváni, the Source of Existence; and Jagan-mátá, the Mother of the Universe. Her non-Aryan attributes appear in her names of Kálí or Syámá, the Black One; Chandí, the Fierce; Bhairaví, the Terrible; Rakta-dantí, the Bloody-Toothed.

Twofold aspects of Siva-worship. The ritual of Siva-worship preserves, in an even more striking way, the traces of its double origin. The higher minds still adore the Godhead by silent contemplation, as prescribed by Sankara, without the aid of external rites. The ordinary Bráhman hangs a wreath of blossoms around the phallic *linga*, or places before it offerings of flowers and rice. But the low-castes pour out the lives of countless victims at the feet of the terrible Kálí, and until lately, in time of pestilence and famine, tried in their despair to appease the relentless goddess by human blood. During the dearth of 1866, in a temple to Kálí within 100 miles of Calcutta, a boy was found with his *Human offerings, 1866.* neck cut, the eyes staring open, and the stiff clotted tongue thrust out between the teeth. In another temple at Húglí (a railway station only 25 miles from Calcutta), the head was left before the idol, decked with flowers.[2] Such cases are true survivals of the regular system of human sacrifices which we have seen among the non-Aryan tribes.[3] They have nothing to do with the old mystic *purusha-medha* or man-offering, whether real or symbolical, of the ancient Aryan faith;[4] but they form an essential part of the non-Aryan religion of terror, which demands that the greater the need, the greater shall be the propitiation.

Garlands of skulls. Such sacrifices are now forbidden, alike by Hindu custom and English law. H. H. Wilson found evidence that they were regularly offered by the Kápálika sect of Sivaite Hindus eight centuries ago; and representatives of those

---

[1] Monarch of the Himálayas.

[2] The Calcutta *Englishman* of 19th May 1866; *Annals of Rural Bengal,* p. 128, 5th edition.

[3] As among the Kandhs, *ante,* chap. iii.

[4] See Dr. Haug's *Origin of Bráhmanism,* p. 5 (Poona, 1863). The Purusha-sukta of the *Rig Veda,* x. 90, verses 7–15; and the Purusha-medha of the *Satapatha Bráhmana,* i. 2, 3, 6, and xiii. 6, i. 1; and of the *Aitareya Bráhmana,* ii. 8, with other passages quoted throughout Dr. Muir's *Sanskrit Texts,* seem to have an allegorical and mystical significance, rather than to refer to a real sacrifice. See also Wilson's Essay on Human Sacrifices, *Journal Roy. As. Soc.,* vol. viii. p. 96 (1852).

hideous votaries of Siva, 'smeared with ashes from the funeral pile, and their necks hung round with human skulls,' survive to this day.[1] Colonel Keatinge mentions that he has seen old sacrificial troughs near Jáintiapur, now used only for goats, which exactly fitted the size of a man. The new troughs are reduced to the dimensions of the animals at present offered; and the greater length of the ancient ones is explained by a legend of human sacrifices. The Statistical Survey of India has brought to light many traditions of such offerings. The hill tribes between Sylhet and Assam hunt a monkey at sowing-time, and crucify it on the margin of the village lands, apparently as a substitute for the Spring man-sacrifice.[2] A human life was sometimes devoted to the preservation of an artificial lake, or of a river embankment; a watchman of aboriginal descent being sacrificed,[3] or a virgin princess walled up in the breach.[4]

Animals substituted for human offerings.

Another Sivaite festival was the Charak-Pujá, or Hook-Swinging Festival, during which men were suspended from a pole by a hook thrust through the muscles of the back, and then swung in the air, in honour of Kálí. In 1863, the orders of Government for abolishing this festival were carried out in a border District, Bírbhúm, lying between the Hindu plains and the non-Aryan highlands. The low-castes, in reality semi-aborigines, and only half-Hinduized, assembled round the poles and foretold famine from the loss of their old propitiatory rites. As they thought the Spring ceremonies absolutely essential before commencing tillage, the British officer suggested they might swing a man by a rope round his waist instead of with a hook through his back. This compromise was accepted by some, but the better-informed cultivators gloomily assured the officer that the ceremonies would have no good effect on the crops without the spilling of blood.[5]

The Charak-Pujá.

The thirteen chief sects of Siva-worshippers faithfully represent the composite character of their god. Sankara left behind him a succession of teachers, many of whom rose to the rank of religious founders. The *Smárta* Bráhmans still maintain their life of calm monastic piety. The *Dandís*,

The thirteen Sivaite sects.

---

[1] H. H. Wilson's *Religion of the Hindus*, vol. i. p. 264.

[2] As among the Kandhs, *ante*, chap. iii.

[3] See SAKRAYPATNA, *The Imperial Gazetteer of India*.

[4] See ANANTASAGARAM, *The Imperial Gazetteer of India*.

[5] It is right to say that very little blood was lost, and the wounds caused were slight; indeed, slighter than those sometimes left behind by the skewers which were fixed through the cheek or tongue of the swinger during the performance.

or ascetics, divide their time between begging and meditation. Some of them adore, without rites, Siva as the third person of the Aryan triad. Others practise an apparently non-Aryan ceremony of initiation by drawing blood from the inner part of the novice's knee, as an offering to the god in his more terrible form, Bhairava. The *Dandís* follow the non-Aryan custom of burying their dead, or commit the body to some sacred stream.[1] The *Yogís* include every class of devotee, from the speechless mystic who, by long suppressions of the breath, loses the consciousness of existence in an unearthly union with Siva, to the impostor who sits upon air, and the juggler who travels with a performing goat. The thirteen Sivaite sects descend, through various gradations of self-mortification and abstraction, to the *Aghorís,* whose abnegation extends to eating carrion, or even human corpses, and gashing their own bodies with knives.

Gradations of Siva-worship.

Within the last few years a small Aghorí community took up their abode in a deserted building on the top of a mount near Ujjain. To inspire terror and respect, they descended to the burning *ghát,* snatched the charred bodies from the funeral pile, and retreated with them to their hill. The horror-stricken mourners complained to the local officer of the Mahárájá Sindhia, but did not dare to defend their dead against the squalid ministers of Siva. In the end, the Mahárájá's officer, by ensuring a regular supply of food for the devotees, put a stop to their depredations.

Sivaite corpse-eaters.

The lowest Sivaite sects follow non-Aryan rather than Aryan types, alike as regards their use of animal food and their bloody worship. These non-Aryan types are, however, spiritualized into a mystic symbolism by the Sivaite *Sáktas,* or worshippers of the creative energy in nature (*Sakti*). The 'right-hand' adorers[2] follow the Aryan ritual, with the addition of an offering of blood.[3] Their *Tantras* or religious works take the form of a dialogue between Siva and his lovely Aryan bride,[4] in which the god teaches her the true forms of prayer and ceremonial. But the 'left-hand' worship[5] is an organized five-fold ritual, of incantation, lust, gluttony, drunkenness, and blood. The non-Aryan origin of these secret rites is attested

Non-Aryan types, spiritualized by the Sákta or Tantrik sect.

---

[1] Cf. the Santáls and the Dámodar river, *ante,* chap. iii.

[2] Dakshinas or Bháktas.   [3] The *bali.*

[4] Usually in the form of Umá or Párvatí.

[5] Vámís or Vámácharís, whose worship comprises the five-fold Makára, ' which taketh away all sin,' namely—*mánsa* (flesh), *matsya* (fish, the symbol of ovarian fertility), *madya* (intoxicating spirits), *maithuna* (sexual intercourse), *mudrá* (mystical gesticulations).

by the use of meats and drinks forbidden to all respectable Hindus; perhaps also by the community of women, possibly an unconscious survival of the non-Aryan forms of polyandry and primitive marriage by capture.[1] The Kánchuliyas, one of the Secret lowest of the Sivaite sects, not only enforce a community of orgies. women, but take measures to prevent the exercise of individual selection, and thus leave the matter entirely to divine chance. Even their orgies, however, are spiritualized into a mystic symbolism; and the Dread Goddess surely punishes the votary who enters on them merely to gratify his lusts.

Siva-worship thus became a link between the highest and Siva and the lowest castes of Hindus. Vishnu, the second person compared. of the Aryan triad, supplied a religion for the intermediate classes. Siva, as a philosophical conception of the Bráhmans, afforded small scope for legend; and the atrocities told of him and his wife in their terrible forms, as adapted to the non-Aryan masses, were little capable of refined literary treatment. But Vishnu, the Preserver, furnished a congenial theme for sacred romance. His religion appealed, not to the fears, but to the hopes of mankind. Siva-worship combined the Bráhmanical doctrine of a personal God with non-Aryan bloody rites; Vishnu-worship, in its final form as a popular religion, represents the coalition of the same Bráhmanical doctrine of a personal God, with the Buddhist principle of the spiritual equality of man.

Vishnu had always been a very human god, from the time Vishnu when he makes his appearance in the Veda as a solar myth, always a the 'Unconquerable Preserver' striding across the universe in god. three steps.[2] His later incarnations made him the familiar friend of man. Of these 'descents'[3] on earth, ten or twenty- Vishnu as two in number, Vishnu-worship, with the unerring instinct of a hero.

[1] Cf. also the festival of the *Rukminí-haran-ekádasí* at Puri. See Hunter's *Orissa*, vol. i. p. 131.

[2] Probably at first connected with the rising, zenith, and setting of the sun in his daily course.

[3] *Avatáras.* The ten chief ones are: (1) the Fish incarnation; (2) the Tortoise, (3) the Boar, (4) the Man-Lion, (5) the Dwarf, (6) Parasu-ráma or Ráma with the Axe, (7) Ráma or Ráma-chandra, (8) Krishna, (9) Buddha, and (10) Kalkí, the White Horse, yet to come. The first four are mythological beasts, perhaps representing the progress of animal life through the eras of fishes, reptiles, and mammals, developing into half-formed man. From another aspect, the Fish represents the *yoni*, or ovarian fertility; the Tortoise, the *linga*; the Boar, the terrestrial fertilizer; and the Man-Lion, the celestial. These four appeared in the Satya Yuga, an

a popular religion, chose the two most beautiful and most human for adoration. As Ráma and Krishna, Vishnu attracted to himself innumerable loving legends. Ráma, his seventh incarnation, was the hero of the Sanskrit epic, the Rámáyana. In his eighth incarnation, as Krishna, Vishnu becomes the high-souled prince of the other epic, the Mahábhárata; he afterwards grew into the central figure of Indian pastoral poetry; was spiritualized into the supreme god of the Vishnuite Puránas; and now flourishes as the most popular deity of the Hindus.

His later develop-ments.

The worship of Vishnu, in one phase or another, is the religion of the bulk of the middle classes; with its roots deep down in beautiful forms of non‑Aryan nature-worship, and its top sending forth branches among the most refined Bráhmans and literary sets. It is a religion in all things graceful. Its gods are heroes or bright friendly beings, who walk and converse with men. Its legends breathe an almost Hellenic beauty. The pastoral simplicities and exquisite ritual of Vishnu belong to a later age than Siva‑worship, with its pandering to the grosser superstitions of the masses. Whatever may be the philosophical priority of the two creeds, Vishnuism made its popular conquests at a later period than Sivaite rites.

The Vishnu Purána, circ. 1045 *A.D.*

In the 11th century, the Vishnuite doctrines were gathered into a religious treatise. The *Vishnu Purána* dates from about 1045 A.D.,[1] and probably represents, as indeed its name implies, 'ancient' traditions which had co-existed with Sivaism and Buddhism for centuries. It derived its doctrines from the Vedas, not, however, in a direct channel, but filtered through the two great epic poems, the Rámáyana and the Mahábhárata. The *Vishnu Purána* forms one of the eighteen Puránas or Sanskrit theological works, in which the Bráhman moulders of Vishnuism and Sivaism embodied their rival systems.

The eighteen Puranas.

These works especially extol the second and third members of the Hindu triad, now claiming the pre-eminence for Vishnu

astronomical period anterior to the present world. The fifth or dwarf incarnation represents early man in the Treta Yuga, or second astronomical period, also long anterior to the present mundane one. The next three incarnations represent the Heroic Age; the ninth or Buddha, the Religious Age. The tenth stands for the end of all things, according to the Hindu apocalypse, when Vishnu shall appear on a white horse, a drawn sword, blazing like a comet, in his hand, for the destruction of the wicked and the renovation of the world. The *Bhágavata Purána* gives twenty-two incarnations of Vishnu.

[1] Preface to the *Vishnu Purána.* H. H. Wilson, p. cxii. (ed. 1864).

as the sole deity, and now for Siva; but in their higher flights
rising to a recognition that both are but forms for representing
the one eternal God. Their interminable dialogues are said
to run to 1,600,000 lines.[1] But they exhibit only the
Bráhmanical aspect of what were destined to become the two
national faiths of India, and they are devoid of any genuine
sympathy for the people.

The *Vishnu Purána* starts with an intolerance equal to Bráhmani-
that of the ancient code of Manu. It still declares the cal Vish-
priests to have sprung from the mouth, and the low-castes 1045 A.D.
from the feet, of God.[2] Its stately theogony disdains to touch
the legends of the people. It declares, indeed, that there is
One God ; but He is the God of the Bráhmans, to whom He
gives the earth as an inheritance, and in His eyes the ruder
Indian races are as naught. This is the general tenor of its
doctrines, although more enlightened, perhaps because later,
passages occur. In the *Vishnu Purána*, Buddha is still an
arch-heretic, who teaches the masses to despise the Veda, but
whose disciples are eventually crushed by the bright Aryan
gods. It is true that in the concluding book, when treating
of the last Iron Age, to which this world has now come, some
nobler idea of God's dealing with man gleams forth. In that
time of universal dissolution and darkness, the sage consoles
us with the assurance that devotion to Vishnu will suffice for
salvation to all persons and to all castes.[3]

Vishnuism had to preach a different doctrine before it could Popular
become, as it has for ages been, a religion of the people. Vishnu-
The first of the line of Vishnuite reformers was Rámánuja, a
Bráhman of Southern India. In the middle of the 12th cen- Rámánuja
tury, he led a movement against the Sivaites, proclaiming the *circ.* 1150
unity of God, under the title of Vishnu, the Cause and the A.D.
Creator of all things. Prosecuted by the Chola king, who
tried to enforce Sivaite conformity throughout his dominions,
Rámánuja fled to the Jain sovereign of Mysore. This prince
he converted to the Vishnuite faith by expelling an evil spirit
from his daughter. Seven hundred monasteries, of which
four still remain, are said to have marked the spread of his
doctrine before his death. Rámánuja accepted converts from
every class, but it was reserved for his successors to formally
enunciate the brotherhood of man.

At the end of the 13th century A.D., according to some

[1] Preface to the *Vishnu Purána*, p. xxiv. H. H. Wilson (ed. 1864).
[2] *Vishnu Purána*, lib. i. cap. vi. p. 89. H. H. Wilson (ed. 1864).
[3] *Vishnu Purána*, lib. vi. cap. ii. H. H. Wilson, p. cxxxviii.

authorities, or at the end of the 14th, according to others, the great reformation, which made Vishnu-worship a national religion of India, took place. Rámánand stands fifth in the apostolic succession from Rámánuja, and spread his doctrine through Northern India. He had his head-quarters in a monastery at Benares, but wandered from place to place preaching the One God under the name of Vishnu, and choosing twelve disciples, not from the priests or nobles, but among the despised castes. One of them was a leather-dresser, another a barber, and the most distinguished of all was the reputed son of a weaver. The list shows that every caste found free entrance into the new creed.

*Rámá-
nand,
1300–1400
A. D.*

*His low-
caste
disciples.*

The life of a disciple was no life of ease. He was called upon to forsake the world in a strictly literal sense, and to go about preaching or teaching, and living on alms. His old age found an asylum in some monastery of the brother-hood. Rámánuja had addressed himself chiefly to the pure Aryan castes, and wrote in the language of the Bráhmans. Rámánand appealed to the people, and the literature of his sect is in the dialects familiar to the masses. The Hindí vernacular owes its development into a written language, partly to the folk-songs of the peasantry and the war-ballads of the Rájput court-bards, but chiefly to the literary requirements of the new popular faith. Vishnuism has deeply impressed itself on the modern dialects of Northern India.[1]

*Kabír,
1380–1420
A. D.*

Kabír, one of the twelve disciples of Rámánand, carried his doctrines throughout Bengal. As his master had laboured to gather together all castes of the Hindus into one common faith, so Kabír, seeing that the Hindus were no longer the whole inhabitants of India, tried, about the beginning of the 15th century, to build up a religion that should embrace Hindu and Muhammadan alike. He rejected caste, denounced image-worship, and condemned the hypocrisy and arrogance of the Bráhmans. According to Kabír, the chief end of man is to obtain purity of life, and a perfect faith in God. The writings of his sect acknowledge that the god of the Hindu is also the god of the Musalmán. His universal name is The

*His doc-
trines.*

---

[1] The three best known sets of such religious treatises are—(1) the voluminous works ascribed to Kabír (*circ.* 1400 A.D.) and his followers, preserved at the head-quarters of his sect, the *Kabír Chaurá* at Benares ; (2) the *Granth*, or scriptures of various Bhágats or Vishnuite religious founders, especially of Dadú in Rájputána, and of the Sikh Gurús, beginning with Nának (1469) ; and (3) the *Bhaktamálá*, or Roll of the Bhaktas or apostles, the Golden Legend of Vishnuism already referred to.

Inner, whether He be invoked as the Alí of the Muhammadans, or as the Ráma of the Hindus. 'To Alí and to Ráma we owe our life,' say the scriptures of his sect,[1] 'and should show like tenderness to all who live. What avails it to wash your mouth, to count your beads, to bathe in holy streams, to bow in temples, if, whilst you mutter your prayers or journey on pilgrimage, deceitfulness is in your heart? The Hindu fasts every eleventh day; the Musalmán on the Ramazán. Who formed the remaining months and days, that you should venerate but one? If the Creator dwell in tabernacles, whose dwelling is the universe? The city of the Hindu god is to the east [Benares], the city of the Musalmán god is to the west [Mecca]; but explore your own heart, for there is the god, both of the Musalmáns and of the Hindus. Behold but One in all things. He to whom the world belongs, He is the father of the worshippers alike of Alí and of Ráma. He is my guide, He is my priest.'[2] Kabír was pre-eminently the Vishnuite apostle to Bengal; but his followers are also numerous in the Central Provinces, Gujarát, and the Deccan.

Kabír's teaching marks another great stride in the Vishnuite reformation. His master, Rámánand, had asserted an abstract equality of castes, because he identified the deity with the worshipper. He had regarded the devotee as but a manifestation of the divinity, and no lowness of birth could degrade the godhead. As Vishnu had taken the form of several of the inferior animals, such as the Boar and the Fish incarnations, so might he be born as a man of any caste. Kabír accepted this doctrine, but he warmed it by an intense humanity. All the chances and changes of life, the varied lot of man, his differences in religion, his desires, hopes, fears, loves, are but the work of *Máyá*, or illusion. To recognise the one Divine Spirit under these manifold illusions, is to obtain emancipation and the Rest of the Soul. That Rest is to be reached, not by burnt-offerings or sacrifices, but, according to Kabír, by faith (*bhaktí*), by meditation on the Supreme, by keeping His holy names, Harí, Rám, Govínd, for ever on the lips and in the heart.

The labours of Kabír may be placed between 1380 and 1420 A.D. In 1486, Chaitanya was born, who spread the Vishnuite doctrines, under the worship of Jagannáth, throughout the deltas of Bengal and Orissa. Signs and wonders

Marginal notes: Coalition of Vishnuism with Islám, 1420 A.D. — The One God of both. — Brotherhood of man. — The Rest of the Soul. — Faith. — Chaitanya, 1486-1527 A.D.

---

[1] The *Víjak* of Bhagodás, one of Kabír's disciples. The rival claims of the Hindus and Musalmáns to Kabír's body have already been mentioned.

[2] *Sabda*, lvi. Abridged from H. H. Wilson's *Works*, i. 81 (ed. 1864).

Chaitanya's life. attended Chaitanya through life, and during four centuries he has been worshipped as an incarnation of Vishnu. Extricating ourselves from the halo of legend which surrounds and obscures the apostle, we know little of his private life except that he was the son of a Bráhman settled at Nadiyá near Calcutta; that in his youth he married the daughter of a celebrated saint; that at the age of twenty-four he forsook the world, and, renouncing the state of a householder, repaired to Orissa, where he devoted the rest of his days to the propagation of the faith. He disappeared miraculously in 1527 A.D.

Chaitanya's teaching. With regard to Chaitanya's doctrine we have ample evidence. No race or caste was beyond the pale of salvation. The Musalmáns and Hindus shared his labours, and profited by his preaching. He held that all men are alike capable of faith, and that all castes by faith become equally pure. Implicit belief and incessant devotion were his watchwords. Contemplation rather than ritual was his pathway to salvation. Obedience to the religious guide is the great characteristic of his sect; but he warned his disciples to respect their teachers as second fathers, and not as gods. The great end of his system, as of all Indian forms of worship, is the

'Liberation' of the soul. liberation of the soul. He held that such liberation does not mean the mere annihilation of separate existence. It consists in nothing more than an entire freedom from the stains and the frailties of the body. The liberated soul dwells for ever, either in a blessed region of perfect beauty and sinlessness, or it soars into the heaven of Vishnu himself, high above the myths and mirages of this world, where God appears no more in his mortal incarnations, or in any other form, but is known in his supreme essence.[1]

The Chaitanya sect. The followers of Chaitanya belong to every caste, but they acknowledge the rule of the descendants of the original disciples (*gosáins*). These *gosáins* now number 23,062 in Bengal alone. The sect is open alike to the married and the unmarried. It has its celibates and wandering mendicants,

Its religious houses. but its religious teachers are generally married men. They live with their wives and children in clusters of houses around a temple to Krishna; and in this way the adoration of

---

[1] Besides the notices of Chaitanya in H. H. Wilson's works, the reader is referred to a very careful essay by Babu Jogendra Chandra Ghosh, entitled *Chaitanya's Ethics* (Calcutta, 1884). Mr. Ghosh bases his works upon the original writings of Chaitanya and his followers. The present author is indebted to him for a correction of one year in the date of Chaitanya's birth, calculated from the *Chaitanya Charitámrita.*

Chaitanya has become a sort of family worship throughout Orissa. The landed gentry worship him with a daily ritual in household chapels dedicated to his name. After his death, a sect arose among his followers, who asserted the spiritual independence of women.[1] In their monastic enclosures, male and female cenobites live in celibacy; the women shaving their heads, with the exception of a single lock of hair. The two sexes chant the praises of Vishnu and Chaitanya together, in hymn and solemn dance. One important doctrine of the Vishnuite sects is their recognition of the value of women as instructors of the outside female community. For long, their female devotees were the only teachers admitted into the *zanánas* of good families in Bengal. Fifty years ago, they had effected a change for the better in the state of female education, and the value of such instruction was assigned as the cause of the sect having spread in Calcutta.[2] Since that time, Vishnuite female ascetics of various sorts have entered the same field. In some instances the bad crept in along with the good, and an effort made in 1863 to utilize them in the mechanism of Public Instruction failed.[3]

The place it assigns to women.

The analogy of woman's position in the Vishnuite sects to that assigned to her by ancient Buddhism is striking. But the analogy becomes more complete when the comparison is made with the extra-mural life of the modern Buddhist nun on the Punjab frontier. Thus, in LAHUL (Lahaul) some of the nuns have not, as in Tibet, cloisters of their own. They are attached to monasteries, in which they reside only a few months of the year; and which they may permanently quit, either in order to marry or for other sufficient reasons. In 1868, there were seventy-one such Buddhist nuns in Lahul, able to read and write, and very closely resembling in their life and discipline the better orders of Vishnuite female devotees in Bengal. One of them was sufficiently skilled in astronomy to calculate eclipses.[4]

Modern Buddhist nuns.

The death of Chaitanya marked the beginning of a spiritual decline in Vishnu-worship. About 1520, Vallabha-Swámí preached in Northern India that the liberation of the soul did not depend upon the mortification of the body; and that

Vallabha-Swámí, *circ.* 1520 A.D.

[1] The Spashtha Dayakas.

[2] Wilson's *Religion of Hindus*, vol. i. p. 171 (ed. 1862).

[3] The official details of this interesting and once promising experiment at Dacca will be found in Appendix A. to the Report of the Director of Public Instruction, Bengal, for 1863-64, pp. 83-90; for 1864-65, pp. 155-158; and in each subsequent Annual Report to 1869.

[4] Sherring's *Hindu Tribes*, vol. ii. p. 9 (4to, Calcutta).

God was to be sought, not in nakedness and hunger and solitude, but amid the enjoyments of this life. An opulent sect had, from an early period, attached itself to the worship of Krishna and his bride Rádhá ; a mystic significance being, of course, assigned to their pastoral loves. Still more popular among women is the modern adoration of Krishna as the Bála Gopála, or the Infant Cowherd,—a faith perhaps uncon-

Child-worship.

sciously stimulated by the Catholic worship of the Divine Child. The sect, however, deny any connection of their Infant god with the babe Jesus, and maintain that their worship is a legitimate and natural development of Vishnuite conceptions. Another influence of Christianity on Hinduism may possibly be traced in the growing importance assigned by the Krishna sects to *bhakti*, or faith, as an all-sufficient instrument of salvation.

Krishna-worship.

Vallabhi-Swámí was the apostle of Vishnuism as a religion of pleasure. When he had finished his life's work, he descended into the Ganges ; a brilliant flame arose from the spot ; and, in the presence of a host of witnesses, his glorified form ascended to heaven. The special object of his homage was Vishnu in his pastoral incarnation, in which he took the form of the divine youth Krishna, and led an arcadian life in the forest. Shady bowers, lovely women, exquisite viands, and everything that appeals to the sensuousness of a tropical race, are mingled in his worship. His daily ritual consists of eight services, in which Krishna's image, as a beautiful boy, is delicately bathed, anointed with essences, splendidly attired, and sumptuously fed. The followers of the first Vishnuite reformers dwelt together in secluded monasteries, or went about scantily clothed, living upon alms. But the Vallabhi-Swámí sect performs its devotions arrayed in costly apparel, anointed with oil, and perfumed with camphor or sandal. It seeks its converts, not among weavers, or leather-dressers, or barbers, but among wealthy bankers and merchants, who look upon life as a thing to be enjoyed, and upon pilgrimage as a holiday excursion, or an opportunity for trade.

A religion of pleasure.

In a religion of this sort, abuses are inevitable. It was a revolt against a system which taught that the soul could approach its Maker only by the mortification of the body. It declared that God was present in the cities and marts of men, not less than in the cave of the ascetic. Faith and love were its instruments of salvation, and voluptuous contemplation its approved spiritual state. It delighted to clothe the deity in a beautiful human form, and mystical amorous poems make a

large part of its canonical literature. One of its most valued
theological treatises is entitled The Ocean of Love, *Prem* Love
Ságar; and although its nobler professors always recognised Poems.
its spiritual character, to baser minds it has become simply a
religion of pleasure. The loves of Rádhá and Krishna, that
woodland pastoral redolent of a wild-flower aroma as ethereal
as the legend of Psyche and Cupid, are sometimes materialized
into a sanction for licentious rites.

A few of the Vishnuite sects have been particularized in order Numerous
to show the wide area of religious thought which they cover, Vishnuite
and the composite conceptions of which their beliefs are sects.
made up. But any attempt at a complete catalogue of them The
is beyond the scope of this work. H. H. Wilson divided twenty
them into twenty principal sects, and the branches or lesser Vishnuite
brotherhoods number not less than a hundred. Their series sects.
of religious founders continued until the present century, when
they began to merge into the more purely theistic movements
of our day. Indeed, the higher Vishnuite teachers have always Theistic
been theistic. The Statistical Survey of India has disclosed move-
many such reformations, from the Kartábhajás[1] of the Districts ments.
around Calcutta, to the Satnámis[2] of the Central Provinces.

Some of these sects are poor local brotherhoods, with a
single religious house; others have developed into widespread and wealthy bodies; while one theistic church has
grown into a great nation, the Sikhs, the last military power The Sikhs.
which we had to subdue in India.[3] Nának Sháh, the spiritual Nának
founder of the Sikhs, was nearly contemporary with Kabír, and Sháh,
taught doctrines in the Punjab but little differing from those of 1469.
the Bengal apostle.[4] The Vishnuite sects now include almost
the whole population of Lower Bengal, excepting the very
highest and the very lowest castes. In many of their communities, caste is not acknowledged. Such sects form brother- Brotherhoods which recognise only spiritual distinctions or degrees; hoods.
and a new social organization is thus provided for the
unfortunate, the widow, or the out-caste. In lately Hinduized
Provinces like Assam, Vishnu-worship has become practically
the religion of the people.

The Car Festival of Jagannáth is perhaps the most typical Jagannáth.

---

[1] See Hunter's *Statistical Account of Bengal,* vol. i. pp. 73–75 (TWENTY-
FOUR PARGANAS); vol. ii. pp. 53–55 (NADIYA).

[2] See *The Imperial Gazetteer of India,* article CENTRAL PROVINCES.

[3] See *The Imperial Gazetteer of India,* articles AMRITSAR and PUNJAB.
For the theological aspects of the Sikhs, see Wilson's *Religion of the
Hindus,* vol. i. pp. 267–275 (ed. 1862).

[4] H. H. Wilson's *Religion of the Hindus,* vol. i. p. 269.

ceremony of the Vishnuite faith. Jagannáth, literally 'The Lord of the World,' represents, with unmistakeable clearness, that coalition of Bráhman and Buddhist doctrines which forms the basis of Vishnu - worship. In his temple are three rude images, unconsciously representing the Bráhmanical triad.

His Bráh-manical and Buddhist origin. His Car Festival is probably a once-conscious reproduction of the Tooth Festival of the Buddhists, although its original significance has dropped out of sight. The Chinese pilgrim Fa-Hian gives an account of the yearly procession of Buddha's Sacred Tooth from its chapel to a shrine some way off,[1] and of its return after a stay there. This was in the 5th century A.D.; but the account applies so exactly to the Car Festival at the present day, that Fergusson pronounces the latter to be 'merely a copy.'[2]

A similar festival is still celebrated with great rejoicing in Japan. As in the Indian procession of Jagannáth, the Japanese use three cars;[3] and Buddha sits in his temple, together with two other figures, like the Jagannáth triad of Orissa.[3] It is needless to add, that while Jagannáth is historically of Buddhist or composite origin, he is to his true believers the one supreme ' Lord of the World.'

Car Festi-val of Jagannath. The calumnies in which some English writers have indulged with regard to Jagannáth, are exposed in Hunter's work on Orissa. That work carefully examined the whole evidence on the subject, from 1580, when Abul Fazl wrote, through a long series of travellers, down to the police reports of 1870.[4] It English calumnies. came to the conclusion which H. H. Wilson had arrived at from quite different sources,[5] that self-immolation was entirely opposed to the worship of Jagannáth, and that the deaths at the Car Festival were almost always accidental. In a closely-packed, eager throng of a hundred thousand men and women at Purí, numbers of them unaccustomed to exposure or hard labour, and all of them tugging and straining to the utmost at the car, under a blazing sun, deaths must occasionally occur.

There 'were also isolated instances of pilgrims throwing themselves under the wheels in a frenzy of religious excite-Self-im-molation not prac-tised. ment. At one time, several unhappy people were killed or injured every year, but they were almost invariably cases

[1] From the chapel at Anurádhapura to Mehentele.

[2] *History of Architecture*, vol. ii. p. 590 (ed. 1867).

[3] See, among many interesting notices by recent travellers, Miss Bird's *Unbeaten Tracks in Japan*, vol. i. pp. 111, 115, etc. (ed. 1880).

[4] Hunter's *Orissa*, vol. i., particularly pp. 306-308; also pp. 132-136.

[5] Namely, the descriptions of the Car Festival or *Rath-Játra* in the work of Krishna Dás.

of accidental trampling. At an early period, indeed, the priests at Purí, probably by permitting a midnight sacrifice once a year within their precincts to the wife[1] of Siva, had fallen under suspicion of bloody rites.[2] But such rites arose from the ambition of the priests to make Purí the sacred city of all worships and all sects. The yearly midnight offerings to the Dread Goddess within Jagannáth's sacred precincts represent the efforts made from time to time towards a coalition of the Sivaite and Vishnuite worship, like the *chakra* or sacred disc of Vishnu which surmounts the pre-historic temple to Kálí at Tamluk.[3]

Such compromises had nothing to do with the worship of the true Jagannáth. A drop of blood even accidentally spilt in his presence pollutes the officiating priests, the people, and the consecrated food. The few suicides that occurred at the Car Festival were for the most part those of diseased and miserable objects, who took this means to put themselves out of pain.[4] The official returns now place the facts beyond doubt. Nothing could be more opposed to Vishnu-worship than self-immolation. Any death within the temple of Jagannáth renders the place unclean. The ritual suddenly stops, and the polluted offerings are hurried away from the sight of the offended god. *His bloodless worship.*

According to Chaitanya, the Orissa apostle of Jagannáth, the destruction of the least of God's creatures is a sin against the Creator. Self-slaughter he would have regarded with abhorrence. The copious literature of his sect frequently describes the Car Festival, but makes no mention of self-sacrifice, and contains not a single passage which could be twisted into a sanction for it.[5] Abul Fazl, the minister of Akbar, who conducted the survey of India for the Mughal Emperor, is silent about self-immolation to Jagannáth, although, from the context, it is almost certain that had he heard of the practice he would have mentioned it. In 1870, the present author compiled an index to all accounts by travellers and others of self-immolation at the Car Festival, from the 14th century downwards.[6] It proved that such *Evidence about Jagannáth; against self-slaughter.*

[1] Bimalá, the 'Stainless One.'
[2] See statement fròm the *Haft-iklim* (1485–1527 A.D.) in Hunter's *Orissa*, vol. i. p. 306.
[3] See *The Imperial Gazetteer*, article TAMLUK.
[4] See authorities quoted in Hunter's *Orissa*, vol. i. p. 134 ; Stirling's account, *Asiatic Researches*, vol. xv. p. 324 ; *Calcutta Review*, vol. x. p. 235 ; *Report of Statistical Commissioner to the Government of Bengal*, 1868, part ii. p. 8 ; Purí Police Reports ; Lieut. Laurie's *Orissa*, 1850.
[5] H. H. Wilson's *Religion of the Hindus*, vol. i. p. 155 (ed. 1862).
[6] Hunter's *Orissa*, vol. i. pp. 305–308.

suicides did at rare intervals occur, although they were opposed
to the spirit of the worship.

Libels on   An Indian procession means a vast multitude of excitable
Jagannáth. beings ready for any extravagance. Among Indian processions, that of Jagannáth to his country-house stands first;
and the frenzied affrays of the Muharram might as fairly
be assigned to the deliberate policy of the British Government, as the occasional suicides at the Car Festival may be
charged against the god. The travellers who tell the most
sensational stories are the ones whose narratives prove that
they went entirely by hearsay, or who could not themselves have seen the Car Festival at Purí. The number of
deaths, whether voluntary or accidental, as registered by the
dispassionate candour of English officials, has always been
insignificant, indeed far fewer than those incident to the party
processions of the Musalmáns; and under improved police
His gentle arrangements, they have practically ceased. So far from en-
doctrines. couraging religious suicides, the gentle doctrines of Jagannáth
tended to check the once common custom of widow-burning.
Even before the Government put a stop to *satí* in 1829, our
officials observed its comparative infrequency at Purí. Widow-
burning was discountenanced by the Vishnuite reformers, and
is stigmatized by a celebrated disciple as 'the fruitless union
of beauty with a corpse.'

The religi-   The worship of Siva and Vishnu operates as a religious
ous *nexus*
of Hindu- bond among the Hindus, in the same way as caste supplies
ism. the basis of their social organization. Theoretically, the
Hindu religion starts from the Veda, and acknowledges its
divine authority. But, practically, we have seen that Hinduism takes its origin from many sources. Vishnu-worship and
Sivaite rites represent the two most popular combinations of
The these various elements. The highly-cultivated Bráhman is a
'chosen
god,' *ishta-* pure theist; the less cultivated worships the divinity under
devatá. some chosen form, *ishta-devatá.* The conventional Bráhman,
especially in the south, takes as his 'chosen deity,' Siva in his
deep philosophical significance, with the phallic *linga* as his
emblem. The middle classes and the mercantile community
adore some incarnation of Vishnu. The low-castes propitiate
Siva the Destroyer, or rather one of his female manifestations,
such as the dread Kálí.

Practical   But every Hindu of education allows that his special object
faith of the of homage is merely his *ishta-devatá,* or own chosen form
Hindus
under which to adore the Deity, PARAM-ESWARA. He admits

that there is ample scope for adoring God under other Its toler-
ance.
manifestations, or in other shapes. Unless a new sect takes
the initiative, by rejecting caste or questioning the authority of the Veda, the Hindu is slow to dispute the orthodoxy
of the movement. Even the founder of the Brahmá Samáj,
or modern theistic church of Bengal, lived and died a Hindu.[1]
The Indian vernacular press cordially acknowledges the merits
of distinguished Christian teachers, like Dr. Duff of Calcutta,
or Dr. Wilson of Bombay. At first, indeed, our missionaries,
in their outburst of proselytizing zeal, spoke disrespectfully
of Hinduism, and stirred up some natural resentment. But
as they more fully realized the problems involved in conversion, they moderated their tone, and now live on friendly
terms with the Bráhmans and religious natives.

An orthodox Hindu paper, which had been filling its Hindu
fairness to
Chris-
tianity.
columns with a vigorous polemic entitled ' Christianity
Destroyed,' no sooner heard of the death of the late Mr.
Sherring, than it published a eulogium on that devoted missionary. It dwelt on ' his learning, affability, solidity, piety,
benevolence, and business capacity.' The editor, while a
stout defender of his hereditary faith, regretted that ' so little
of Mr. Sherring's teaching had fallen to his lot.'[2] The Hindus
are among the most tolerant religionists in the world.

Of the three members of the Hindu Triad, the first person, Modern
fate of the
Hindu
Triad.
Bráhma, has now but a few scattered handfuls of followers ;
the second person, Vishnu, supplies a worship for the middle
classes ; around the third person, Siva, in his twofold aspects,
has grown up that mixture of philosophical symbolism with
propitiatory rites professed by the highest and by the lowest
castes. But the educated Hindu willingly recognises that,
beyond and above his chosen Deity of the Triad, or his
favourite incarnation, or his village fetish, or his household
sálagrám, dwells the PARAM-ESWARA, the One First Cause, The One
God,
PARAM-
ESWARA.
whom the eye has not seen, and whom the mind cannot
conceive, but who may be worshipped in any one of the forms
in which he manifests his power to men.

[1] The best short account of this deeply interesting movement, and of
its first leader Rammohan Roy, will be found under the title of *Indian
Theistic Reformers*, by Professor Monier Williams, in the *Journal of the
Royal Asiatic Society*, Jan. 1881, vol. xiii. See also his *Modern India*
(Trübner, 1879) ; and Miss Collet's *Brahmo Year Book* (Williams &
Norgate, annually).

[2] The *Kaví-bachan Sudha*, quoted in the *Chronicle of the London Missionary Society* for November 1880, p. 792.

Recapitu-
lation.

Three
Western
influences;

(1) Chris-
tianity,

(2) Islám,

3) British
Rule.

The foregoing chapters indicate how, out of the early Aryan and non-Aryan races of India, as modified by Greek and Scythic invasions, the Hindu population and the Hindu religion were built up. We shall next consider three series of influences which, within historic times, have been brought to bear, by nations from the West, upon the composite people thus formed. The first set of these influences is represented by the early Christian Church of India, a Church which had its origin in a period long anterior to the mediæval Hinduism of the 9th century, and which is numerously represented by the Syrian Christians of Malabar in our own day. The second foreign influence brought to bear upon India from the West consisted of the Muhammadan invasions, which eventually created the Mughal Empire. The third influence is represented by the European settlements, which culminated in the British Rule.

CHAPTER IX.

CHRISTIANITY IN INDIA (*circa* 100 TO 1881 A.D.).

CHRISTIANITY now forms the faith of over two millions of Christian- the Indian population. Coeval with Buddhism during the ity coeval with last nine centuries of its Indian history, the teaching of Buddhism Christ has, after the lapse of another nine hundred years, for 900 years. more than twelve times more followers than the teaching of Buddha upon the Indian continent. Adding Burma, where the doctrines of Gautama still remain the creed of the people, there are over two millions of Christians to under three and a half millions of Buddhists; or to four millions of Buddhists and Jains. Christianity, while a very old religion in India, is also one of the most active at the present day. The Census of 1881 disclosed that the Christians in British and Feudatory India had increased by more than one-fifth since 1872; and this increase, while partly the result of more perfect enumeration, represents to a large extent a real growth.

The origin of Christianity in India is obscure. Early Origin tradition, accepted popularly by Catholics, and more doubtfully of Chris- tianity in by Protestants, connects it with St. Thomas the Apostle, India. who is said to have preached in Southern India, on the Malabar and Coromandel coasts; to have founded several The churches; and finally, to have been martyred at the Little orthodox tradition. Mount, near Madras, in 68 A.D. The Catholic tradition narrates further, that a persecution arose not long after, in which all the priests perished; that many years later, the Patriarch of Babylon, while still in communion with Rome, heard of the desolate state of the Indian Church, and sent forth bishops who revived its faith; that about 486 A.D., Nestorianism spread from Babylon into Malabar.

To orthodoxy this tradition has a twofold value. It assigns Value of the an apostolic origin to the Christianity of India; and it explains tradition. away the fact that Indian Christianity, when it emerges into history, formed a branch of the unorthodox Nestorian Church. Modern criticism has questioned the evidence for the evangel- istic labours of the Doubting Apostle in Southern India. It has brought to light the careers of two later missionaries, both bearing the name of Thomas, to whom, at widely separated dates, the honour of converting Southern India is assigned. Gibbon dismisses the question of their respective claims in a convenient triplet :—'The Indian missionary St. Thomas, an Apostle, a Manichæan, or an Armenian merchant.'[1]

Syrian Christians of India. This method of treatment scarcely satisfies the present century; and the Statistical Survey of India has thrown fresh light on the Syrian Christians of the Southern Peninsula. At this day they number 304,410,[2] or more than double the number of Native Protestants in India in 1861. Indeed, until within the past ten years, the remnants of the ancient Syrian Church had still a larger native following in India than all the Protestant sects put together.[3] It would be unsuitable to dismiss so ancient and so numerous a body without some attempt to trace their history. That history forms the longest continuous narrative of any religious sect in India except the Jains.

Their numbers and antiquity. The Syrian Church of Malabar had its origin in the period when Buddhism was still triumphant; it witnessed the birth of the Hinduism which superseded the doctrine and national polity of Buddha; it saw the arrival of the Muhammadans who ousted the Hindu dynasties; it suffered cruelly from the Roman inquisitors of the Portuguese; but it has survived its persecutors, and has formed a subject of interest to Anglican inquirers during the past eighty years.[4]

The three Legends of St. Thomas. The three legends of St. Thomas, the missionary of Southern India, may be summarized as follows. According to the Chaldæan Breviary and certain Fathers of the Catholic Church,

---

[1] *Decline and Fall of the Roman Empire* (quarto edition, 1788), vol. iv. p. 599, footnote 122.

[2] *Census of India*, 1881, vol. ii. pp. 20, 21. The Census officers return the whole as 'Syrians,' without discriminating between Jacobites and Syrian Catholics. A statement kindly supplied to the author by the Vicar-Apostolic of Verapoli returns the Syrian Catholics within his jurisdiction at over 200,000, and the Jacobites at about 100,000. The latter are chiefly under the jurisdiction of the Roman vicars-apostolic of Verapoli and Quilon, but are still distinguished as 'Catholics of the Syrian rite.'

[3] See *Protestant Missions in India, Burma, and Ceylon*, Statistical Tables, 1881, drawn up under the authority of the Calcutta Missionary Conference. This valuable compilation returns 138,731 Native Protestant Christians in 1861, and 224,258 in 1871, in India, exclusive of Burma.

[4] From the time of Claudius Buchanan and Bishop Heber downwards. See *Asiatic Researches*, vol. vii., 'Account of St. Thomé Christians on the coast of Malabar,' by Mr. Wrede; Buchanan's *Christian Researches in Asia*, 4th ed. (1811), pp. 106, 145; Heber's *Journal*, vol. ii.; Bishop Middleton's *Life of Le Bas*, chapters ix.-xii. (1831); Hough's *Hist. of Christianity in India*, 5 vols. (1839-60).

St. Thomas the Apostle converted many countries of Asia, and 52 to 68 found a martyr's death in India. The meagre tradition of the A.D. (?) early Church was expanded by the Catholic writers of the sixteenth and seventeenth centuries. The abstract by Vincenzo Maria makes the Apostle commence his work in Mesopotamia, First and includes Bactria, Central Asia, China, 'the States of the Legend: St.Thomas Great Mogul,' Siam, Germany, Brazil, and Ethiopia, in the the circle of his missionary labours. The apostolic traveller then Apostle (68 A.D.). sailed east again to India, converting the island of Socotra on the way, and after preaching in Malabar, ended his labours on the Coromandel coast.[1] The final development of the tradition fills in the details of his death. It would appear that on the 21st December 68 A.D., at Mailapur, a suburb of Madras, the Bráhmans stirred up a tumult against the Apostle, who, after being stoned by the crowd, was finally thrust through with a spear upon the spot now known as St. Thomas' Mount.

The second legend assigns the conversion of India to Second Thomas the Manichæan, or disciple of Manes, towards the Legend: Thomas end of the third century. Another legend ascribes the honour the Mani- to an Armenian merchant, Thomas Cana, in the eighth century. chæan (277 A.D.). The story relates that Mar Thomas, the Armenian, settled in Malabar for purposes of trade, married two Indian ladies, and Third grew into power with the native princes. He found that such Legend: Thomas Christians as existed before his time had been driven by the Ar- persecution from the coast into the hill-country. Mar Thomas menian secured for them the privilege of worshipping according to (780 A.D.?) their faith, led them back to the fertile coast of Malabar, and became their archbishop. On his death, his memory received the gradual and spontaneous honours of canonization by the Christian communities for whom he had laboured, and his name became identified with that of the Apostle.

Whatever may be the claims of the Armenian Thomas as the The three re-builder of the Church in Southern India, he was certainly Legends examined; not its founder. Apart from the evidence of Patristic literature, there is abundant local proof that Christianity flourished in Southern India long before the eighth century. In the sixth the third; century, while Buddhism was still at the height of its power, Kalyán, on the Bombay coast, was the seat of a Christian bishop from Persia.[2]

---

[1] *The Book of Ser Marco Polo the Venetian.* Colonel Yule's second edition, vol. ii. p. 343, note 4 (1875).

[2] *Gazetteer of the Bombay Presidency*, vol. xiii. part i., Thána District, pp. 66, 200, etc. It is not necessary to dispute whether the seat of this bishopric was the modern Kalyán or Quilon (Coilam), as the coast from Bombay southwards to Quilon bore indefinitely the name of Caliana.

the second legend ;

The claims of Thomas the Manichæan have the European support of the Church historians, La Croze,[1] Tillemont, and others. The local testimony of a cross dug up near Madras in 1547, bearing an inscription in the Pehlvi tongue, has also been urged in his favour. The inscription is probably of the seventh or eighth century A.D., and, although somewhat variously deciphered, bears witness to the sufferings of Christ.[2]

and the first.

For the claims of St. Thomas the Apostle, a longer and more ancient series of authorities are cited. The apocryphal history of St. Thomas, by Abdias, dating perhaps from the end of the first century, narrates that a certain Indian king, Gondaphorus, sent a merchant called Abban to Jesus, to seek a skilful architect to build him a palace. The story continues that the Lord sold Thomas to him as a slave expert in that art.[3] The Apostle converted King Gondaphorus, and then journeyed on to another country of India, under King Meodeus, where he

---

[1] *Histoire du Christianisme des Indes*, 2 vols. 12mo (The Hague, 1758).

[2] Professor Haug reads it thus : ' Whoever believes in the Messiah, and in God above, and also in the Holy Ghost, is in the grace of Him who bore the pain of the cross.' Dr. Burnell deciphers it more diffidently :—
' In punishment [?] by the cross [was] the suffering of this [one]: [He] who is the true Christ and God above, and Guide for ever pure.' Yule's *Marco Polo*, 2nd ed., p. 345, vol. ii.; also p. 339, where the cross is figured.

[3] This legend forms the theme of the *Hymnus in Festo Sancti Thomae Apostoli, ad Vesperum*, in the Mozarabic Breviary, edited by Cardinal Lorenzana in 1775. Its twenty-one verses are given as an appendix in Dr. Kennet's Madras monograph. Three stanzas will here suffice :—

> ' Nuncius venit de Indis
>   Quaerere artificem :
> Architectum construere
>   Regium palatium :
> In foro deambulabat
>   Cunctorum venalium.
>
> Habeo servum fidelem,
>   Locutus est Dominus,
> Ut exquiris talem, aptum
>   Esse hunc artificem :
> Abbanes videns, et gaudens,
>   Suscepit Apostolum.'

The hymn assigns the death of the Apostle to the priest of a sun temple which had been overthrown by St. Thomas :—

> ' Tunc sacerdos idolorum
>   Furibundus astitit,
> Gladio transverberavit
>   Sanctum Christi martyrem.
> Glorioso passionis
>   Laureatum sanguine.'

was slain by lances.[1] The existence of a King Gondaphorus has been established by coins, which would place him in the last century B.C., or within the first half of the first century of our era.[2] But, apart from difficulties of chronology, it is clear that the Gondaphorus of the coins was an Indo-Scythic monarch, reigning in regions which had no connection with Malabar. His coins are still found in numbers in Afghánistán and the Punjab, especially from Pesháwar to Ludhiána. He was essentially a Punjab potentate.

The mention of St. Thomas the Apostle in connection with India by the Fathers, and in the Offices of the Church, does not bring him nearer to Malabar, or to the supposed site of his martyrdom at Madras. For the term 'India,' at the period to which these authorities belong, referred to the countries beyond Persia, including Afghánistán and the basins of the Upper Oxus, Indus, and Ganges, rather than to the southern half of the peninsula. In the early accounts of the labours of St. Thomas, the vague term India is almost always associated with Persia, Media, or Bactria.[3] Nor does the appellation of St. Thomas as the Apostle of India in the Commemorations of the Church, help to identify him with the St. Thomas who preached on the Malabar and Coromandel coasts. For not only does the indeterminate character of the word still adhere to their use of 'India,' but the area assigned to the Apostle's labours is so wide as to deprive them of value for the purpose of local identification. Thus, the Chaldæan Breviary of the Malabar Church itself states that 'by St. Thomas were the

Wide meaning of 'India,'

in the Fathers,

---

[1] Colonel Yule's *Marco Polo*, second edition, vol. ii. p. 243. Dr. Kennet, in an interesting monograph entitled *St. Thomas, the Apostle of India,* p. 19 (Madras, 1882), says :—'The history of Abdias was published for the first time by Wolfgang Lazius, under the title of *Abdiæ Babyloniæ, Episcopi et Apostolorum Discipuli, de Historia certaminis Apostolici, libri decem ; Julio Africano Interprete.* Basiliæ, 1532.'

[2] For the various dates, see Colonel Yule's *Marco Polo*, second edition, vol. ii. p. 343. Colonel Yule's *Cathay* deals with the Chinese and Central Asian aspects of the legend of St. Thomas (2 vols. 1866).

[3] Thus the *Paschal Chronicle* of Bishop Dorotheus (born A.D. 254) says : 'The Apostle Thomas, after having preached the gospel to the Parthians, Medes, Persians, Germanians [an agricultural people of Persia mentioned by Herodotus, i. 125], Bactrians, and Magi, suffered martyrdom at Calamina, a town of India.' Hippolytus, Bishop of Portus (*circa* 220 A.D.), assigns to St. Thomas, Parthia, Media, Persia, Hercania, the Bactri, the Mardi, and, while ascribing the conversion of India to St. Bartholomew, mentions Calamina, a city of India, as the place of St. Thomas' martyrdom. The Metropolitan Johannes, who attended the Council of Nicæa in 325, subscribed as Bishop of 'India Maxima and Persia.' Dr. Kennet's monograph (Madras, 1882); Hough, i. pp. 30 to 116.

and
Church
Offices.

Chinese and the Ethiopians converted to the Truth,' while one of its anthems proclaims: 'The Hindus, the Chinese, the Persians, and all the people of the Isles of the Sea, they who dwell in Syria and Armenia, in Javan and Roumania, call Thomas to remembrance, and adore Thy Name, O Thou our Redeemer!'

First
glimpse at
Indian
Christians,
circa 190
A.D.

Candid inquiry must therefore decline to accept the connection of St. Thomas with the 'India' of the early Church as proof of the Apostle's identity with Thomas, the missionary to Malabar. Nevertheless, there is evidence to indicate that Christianity had reached Malabar before the end of the second century A.D., and nearly a hundred years previous to the supposed labours of Thomas the Manichæan (*circa* 277 A.D.). In

The
Roman
fleet from
Egypt.

the 2nd century a Roman merchant fleet of one hundred sail steered regularly from Myos Hormus on the Red Sea, to Arabia, Ceylon, and Malabar. It found an ancient Jewish colony, the remnants of which still remain to this day as the Beni-Israels,[1] upon the Bombay coast. Whether these Jews emigrated to India at the time of the Dispersion, or at a later period, their settlements probably date from before the second century of our era.

Jew
settlements
in ancient
Malabar.

The Red Sea fleet from Myos Hormus, which traded with this Jewish settlement in India, must in all likelihood have brought with it Jewish merchants and others acquainted with the new religion of Christ which, starting from Palestine, had penetrated throughout the Roman world. Part of the fleet, moreover, touched at Aden and the Persian Gulf, themselves early seats of Christianity. Indeed, after the direct sea-course to Malabar by the trade winds was known, the main navigation to India for some time hugged the Asiatic coast. Christian merchants from that coast, both of Jewish and other race, would in the natural course of trade have reached Malabar within the second century A.D.[2] The Buddhist polity then supreme in Southern India was favourable to the reception of a faith whose moral characteristics were humanity and self-sacrifice. Earlier Jewish settlers had already familiarized the native mind with the existence of an ancient and imposing

---

[1] For their present numbers and condition, see the *Bombay Gazetteer*, by Mr. J. M. Campbell, LL.D., of the Bombay Civil Service, vol. xi. pp. 85 and 421 ; vol. xiii. p. 273.

[2] The Roman trade with the southern coast of India probably dates from, or before, the Apostolic period. Of 522 silver *denarii* found near Coimbatore in 1842, no fewer than 135 were coins of Augustus, and 378 of Tiberius. Another find near Calicut about 1850 contained an *aureus* of Augustus, with several hundred coins, none later than the Emperor Nero.

religion in Palestine. When that religion was presented in its new and more attractive form of Christianity, no miraculous intervention was probably required to commend it to the tolerant Buddhist princes of Southern India.

About 190 A.D., rumours, apparently brought back by the Malabar Red Sea fleet, of a Christian community on the Malabar coast, fired the zeal of Pantænus of Alexandria. Pantænus, in his earlier years a Stoic philosopher, was then head of the celebrated school which formed one of the glories of his city. He started for India; and although it has been questioned whether he reached India Proper, the evidence seems in favour of his having done so. He 'found his own arrival anticipated by some who were acquainted with the Gospel of Matthew; to whom Bartholomew, one of the apostles, had preached; and had left them the same Gospel in the Hebrew, which also was preserved until this time.'[1] His mission may be placed at the end of the 2nd century. Early in the 3rd century, St. Hippolytus, Bishop of Portus (*circ.* 220 A.D.), also assigns the conversion of India to the Apostle Bartholomew. To Thomas he ascribes Persia and the countries of Central Asia, although he mentions Calamina, a city of India, as the place where Thomas suffered death. *{Malabar Christians, circ. 190 A.D. Pantænus. Hippolytus, circ. 220 A.D.}*

Indeed, the evidence of the early Christian writers, so far as it goes, tends to connect St. Thomas with the India of the ancient world,—that is to say, with Persia and Afghánistán,— and St. Bartholomew with the Christian settlements on the Malabar coast. Cosmos Indicopleustes writes of a Christian Church in Ceylon, and on the Callian or Malabar seaboard (*circ.* 547 A.D.). But he makes no mention of its foundation by St. Thomas, which, as an Alexandrian monk, he would have been almost sure to do had he heard any local tradition of the circumstance. He states that the Malabar Bishop was consecrated in Persia; from which we may infer that the Christians of Southern India had already been brought within the Nestorian fold. There is but slight evidence for fixing upon the Malabar coast as the seat of the orthodox Bishop Frumentius, sent forth by Athanasius to India and the East, *circ.* 355 A.D. *{Cosmos Indicopleustes, circ. 547 A.D.}*

The truth is, that the Christians of Southern India belonged from their first clear emergence into history to the Syrian rite. If, as seems probable, Christianity was first brought to Malabar by the merchant fleet from the Persian Gulf, or the *{Nestorian Church in Asia.}*

---

[1] Dr. Kennet, quoting Eusebius, in his monograph on *St. Thomas, the Apostle of India,* p. 9 (Madras, 1882).

Asiatic coast of the Arabian Sea, the Malabar Christians would follow the Asiatic forms of faith. When, therefore, in the 5th century, Nestorianism, driven forth from Europe and Africa, conquered the allegiance of Asia, the Church of Southern India would naturally accept the Nestorian doctrine.

It should be remembered that during the thousand years when Christianity flourished in Asia, from the 5th to the 15th century, it was the Christianity of Nestorius. The Jacobite sect dwelt in the midst of the Nestorians; and for nearly a thousand years, the Christianity of these types, together with Buddhism, formed the two intelligent religions of Central Asia. How far Buddhism and Christianity mutually influenced each other's doctrine and ritual still remains a complex problem. But Christianity in western Central Asia appears to have offered a longer resistance than Buddhism to the advancing avalanche of Islám; and in the countries to the west of Tibet it survived its Buddhist rival. 'Under the reign of the Caliphs,' says Gibbon, 'the Nestorian Church was diffused from China to Jerusalem and Cyprus; and their numbers, with those of the Jacobites, were computed to surpass the Greek and Latin communions.'[1]

Side by side with Buddhism for 1000 years.

The marvellous history of the Christian Tartar potentate, Prester John, king, warrior, and priest, is a mediæval legend based on the ascendancy of Christianity in some of the Central Asian States.[2] The travellers in Tartary and China, from the 12th to the 15th century, bear witness to the extensive survival, and once flourishing condition, of the Nestorian Church, and justify Pierre Bergeron's description of it as 'épandue par toute l'Asie.'[3] The term Catholicos, which the Nestorians applied to their Patriarch, and the Jacobites to their Metropolitan, survives in the languages of Central India. The mediæval travellers preserve it in various forms;[4] and the British Embassy to Yarkand, in 1873, still

Its wide diffusion.

[1] *Decline and Fall of the Roman Empire*, p. 598, vol. iv. (quarto ed. 1788). Gibbon quotes his authorities for this statement in a footnote. The whole subject of early Christianity in Central Asia and China has been discussed with exhaustive learning in Colonel Yule's *Cathay, and the Way Thither.* Hakluyt Society, 2 vols. 1866.

[2] 'Voyage de Rubruquis en Tartarie,' chap. xix., in the quarto volume of *Voyages en Asie*, published at the Hague in 1735. Guillaume de Rubruquis was an ambassador of Louis IX., sent to Tartary and China in 1253 A.D. Colonel Yule also gives the story of Prester John in *Marco Polo*, vol. i. pp. 229-233 (ed. 1875).

[3] 'Traité des Tartares,' par Pierre Bergeron, chap. iii. in the Hague quarto of *Voyages en Asie*, above quoted (1735).

[4] *Játhalík, Jatolic, Jatelic;* originally *Gáthalík.*

came upon a story of 'a poor and aged *Játlik*, or Christian priest.'[1]

Whether the Christians on the coast of Malabar were a direct offshoot of the Nestorian Church of Asia, or the result of an earlier seedling dropped by St. Thomas or St. Bartholomew on their apostolic travels, it is certain that from their first appearance in local history, the Malabar Christians obeyed bishops from Persia of the Nestorian rite.[2] By the 7th century, the Persian Church had adopted the name of Thomas Christians, and this title would in time be extended to all its branches, including that of Malabar. The early legend of the Manichæan Thomas in the 3rd century, and the later labours of the Armenian Thomas, the rebuilder of the Malabar Church, in the 8th, had endeared that name to the Christians of Southern India. In their isolation and ignorance, they confounded the three names, and concentrated their legends of the three Thomases in the person of the Apostle.[3] Before the 14th century, they had completed the process by believing that St. Thomas was Christ. *'Thomas Christians' of Persia; and of India.*

The fitness of things soon required that the life and death of the Apostle should be localized by the Southern Indian Church. Patristic literature clearly declares that St. Thomas had suffered martyrdom at Calamina, probably in some country east of Persia, or in Northern India itself. The tradition of the Church is equally distinct, that in 394 A.D. the remains of the Apostle were transferred to Edessa in Mesopotamia.[4] The attempt to localize the death of St. Thomas on the southwestern coast of India started, therefore, under disadvantages. A suitable site was, however, found at the Mount near Madras, one of the many hill shrines of ancient India which have formed a joint resort of religious persons of diverse faiths,— Buddhist, Muhammadan, and Hindu (*ante*, p. 203). *Legend of St. Thomas localized; in spite of difficulties, at Madras.*

Marco Polo, the first European traveller who has left an account of the place, gives the legend in its undeveloped form *13th century form of the legend.*

[1] Dr. Bellew's 'History of Káshgar,' in the *Official Report of Sir Douglas Forsyth's Mission*, p. 127. (Quarto, Foreign Office Press, Calcutta, 1875.)

[2] Mr. Campbell's *Bombay Gazetteer*, Thána District, chap. iii. (Bombay, 1882.)

[3] The Jacobites, or followers of Jacobus Baradaeus, prefer in the same way to deduce their name and pedigree from the Apostle James. Gibbon, iv. 603, footnote (ed. 1788).

[4] For the authorities, see Dr. Kennet's Madras monograph, *St. Thomas, the Apostle of India* (1882); and Colonel Yule's critical note, *Marco Polo*, vol. ii. p. 342 (2nd edition, 1875).

in the 13th century. The Apostle had, it seems, been accidentally killed outside his hermitage by a fowler, who, ' not
seeing the saint, let fly an arrow at one of the peacocks. And
this arrow struck the holy man in the right side, so that he
died of the wound, sweetly addressing himself to his Creator.'[1]
Miracles were wrought at the place, and conflicting creeds
claimed the hermit as their own. ' Both Christians and
Saracens, however, greatly frequent the pilgrimage,' says Marco
Polo truthfully, although evidently a little puzzled.[2] ' For the
Saracens also do hold the Saint in great reverence, and say
that he·was one of their own Saracens, and a great prophet.'
Not only the Muhammadans and Christians, but also the
Hindus seem to have felt the religious attractions of the spot.
About thirty years after Marco Polo, the Church itself was,
according to Odoric, filled with idols.[3] Two centuries later,
Joseph of Cranganore, the Malabar Christian, still testifies to
the joint worship of the Christian and the heathen at St.
Thomas' Mount. The Syrian bishops sent to India in 1504
heard ' that the Church had *begun* to be occupied by some
Christian people. But Barbosa, a few years later, found it half
in ruins, and in charge of a Muhammadan *fakir*, who kept a
lamp burning.'[4]

Brighter days, however, now dawned for the Madras legend.
Portuguese zeal, in its first fervours of Indian evangelization,
felt keenly the want of a sustaining local hagiology. Saint
Catherine had, indeed, visibly delivered Goa into their hands ;
and a parish church, afterwards the cathedral, was dedicated
to her in 1512. Ten years later, the viceroy Duarte Menezes
became ambitious of enriching his capital with the bones of an
apostle. A mission from Goa despatched to the Coromandel
coast in 1522, proved itself ignorant of, or superior to, the
well-established legend of the translation of the Saint's remains
to Edessa in 394 A.D., and found his sacred relics at the
ancient hill shrine near Madras, side by side with those of a
king whom he had converted to the faith. They were brought
with pomp to Goa, the Portuguese capital of India, and there
they lie in the Church of St. Thomas to this day.[5]

The finding of the Pehlvi cross, mentioned on a previous
page, at St. Thomas' Mount in 1547, gave a fresh colouring to

Side notes: Mixed worship at the shrine. — The legend as developed — by the Portuguese. — Relics at Goa. — Final form of the legend.

---

[1] Colonel Yule's *Marco Polo* (2nd edition, 1875), vol. ii. p. 340.
[2] *Idem*, ii. pp. 337–338.   [3] *Idem*, ii. p. 344.   [4] *Ibid*.
[5] *Ibid*. Colonel Yule's *Cathay* (2 vols. 1866) should also be referred to
by students of the legend of St. Thomas, and his alleged labours in Asia
and India.

the legend. So far as its inscription goes, it points to a Persian, and probably to a Manichæan origin. But at the period when it was dug up, no one in Madras could decipher its Pehlvi characters. A Bráhman impostor, knowing that there was a local demand for martyrs, accordingly came forward with a fictitious interpretation. The simple story of Thomas' accidental death from a stray arrow, had before this grown into a cruel martyrdom by stoning and a lance-thrust, with each spot in the tragedy fixed at the Greater and Lesser Mount near Madras. The Bráhman pretended to supply a confirmation of the legend from the inscription on the cross—a confirmation which continued to be accepted until Dr. Burnell and Professor Haug published their decipherments in our own day. 'In the 16th and 17th century,' says Colonel Yule, 'Roman Catholic ecclesiastical story-tellers seem to have striven in rivalry who should most recklessly expand the travels of the Apostle.'

The lying interpretation of the Bráhman, and the visible relics in the church at Goa, seem to have influenced the popular imagination more powerfully than the clear tradition of the early Church regarding the translation of the Apostle's relics to Edessa. Our own King Alfred has been pressed into the service of St. Thomas of Madras. 'This year,' 883 A.D., says the Anglo-Saxon Chronicle, 'Sighelm and Athelstane carried to Rome the alms which the king had vowed to send thither, and also to India to St. Thomas and to St. Bartholomew.'[1] Gibbon suspects 'that the English ambassadors collected their cargo and legend in Egypt.'[2] There is certainly no evidence to show that they ever visited the Coromandel coast, and much to indicate that the 'India' of Alfred was the India of the early Church, and far north-west of the Madras exploits of the Apostle. The legend of St. Thomas' Mount has in our own century been illustrated by the eloquence and learning of bishops and divines of the Anglo-Indian Church. 'But,' concludes Colonel Yule, 'I see that the authorities now ruling the Catholics at Madras are strong in disparagement of the special sanctity of the localities, and of the whole story connecting St. Thomas with Mailapur,' the alleged scene of his martyrdom.[3]

(margin: King Alfred's Embassy, but to which shrine)

---

[1] Hough, i. p. 104 (1839); Dr. Kennet's Madras monograph, *St. Thomas, the Apostle of India*, pp. 6, 7 (1882).

[2] *Decline and Fall of the Roman Empire*, vol. iv. p. 599, footnote 123 (ed. 1788); Hough, vol. i. pp. 105-107.

[3] Colonel Yule's *Marco Polo*, ii. p. 344 (ed. 1875).

As a matter of history, the life of the Nestorian Church in India has been a troubled one. A letter from the Patriarch Jesajabus to Simeon, Metropolitan of Persia, shows that before 660 A.D., the Christians along the Indian coast were destitute of a regular ministry.[1] In the 8th century, the Armenian friar Thomas found the Malabar Christians driven back into the recesses of the mountains. In the 14th century, Friar Jordanus declared them to be Christians only in name, without baptism. They even confounded St. Thomas with Christ.[2] A mixed worship, Christian, Muhammadan, and Hindu, went on at the old high place or joint hill shrine near Madras. In some centuries, the Church in Southern India developed, like the Sikhs in the Punjab, into a military sovereignty. In others, it dwindled away; its remnants lingering in the mountains and woods, or adopting heathen rites. The family names of a forest tribe[3] in Kánara, now Hindus, bear witness to a time when they were Christians; and there were probably many similar reversions to paganism.

The downfall of the Nestorian Church in India was due, however, neither to such reversions to paganism nor to any persecutions of native princes; but to the pressure of the Portuguese Inquisition, and the proselytizing energy of Rome. Before the arrival of Vasco da Gama in 1498, the St. Thomas
Christians had established their position as a powerful military caste in Malabar. The Portuguese found them firmly organized under their spiritual leaders, bishops, archdeacons, and priests, who acted as their representatives in dealing with the Indian princes. For long they had Christian kings, and at a later period chiefs, of their own.[4] In virtue of an ancient charter ascribed to Cherumal Perumal, Suzerain of Southern India in the ninth century A.D., the Malabar Christians enjoyed all the rights of nobility.[5] They even claimed precedence of the Nairs, who formed the heathen aristocracy. The St. Thomas Christians

---

[1] *Assemani Bibliotheca*, quoted by Bishop Caldwell, *Comparative Grammar of the Dravidian Languages*, p. 27, footnote (ed. 1875). Jesajabus died 660 A.D.

[2] Jordanus, quoted in Mr. J. M. Campbell's *Bombay Gazetteer*, vol. xiii. part i. p. 200 (ed. 1882).

[3] The Maráthí Sidis. For an interesting account of them, see Mr. J. M. Campbell's *Bombay Gazetteer*, Kánara District, vol. xv. part i. p. 397 (ed. 1883).

[4] *Histoire du Christianisme des Indes*, par M. V. La Croze, vol. i. p. 72, ii. p. 133, etc. (2 vols. 12mo, The Hague, 1758).

[5] *Idem*, i. p. 67. For details, see *The Syrian Church of Malabar*, by Edavalikel Philipos, p. 23, and footnote (Oxford, 1869). Local legend vainly places Cherumal Perumal and his grant as far back as 345 A.D.

and the Nairs were, in fact, the most important military castes
on the south-west coast.[1] They supplied the bodyguard of the Powerful
local kings ; and the Christian caste was the first to learn the and respected.
use of gunpowder and fire-arms. They thus became the
matchlockmen of the Indian troops of Southern India, usually
placed in the van, or around the person of the prince.

The Portuguese, by a happy chance, landed on the very Portu-
Province of India in which Christianity was most firmly estab- guese
efforts at
lished, and in which Christians had for long formed a recog- their con-
nised and respected caste. The proselytizing energy of the new- version to
Rome.
comers could not, however, rest satisfied with their good fortune.
That energy was vigorously directed both against the natives
and the ancient Christian communities. Indeed, the Nestorian
heresy of the St. Thomas Christians seemed to the fervour of the
friars to be a direct call from heaven for interference by the
orthodox Church. The Portuguese established the Inquisition,
as we shall presently see, at Goa in 1560. After various Portuguese attempts, strongly resisted by the St. Thomas Christians,
the latter were incorporated into the Catholic Church, by the
labours of Alexis de Menezes, Archbishop of Goa, in 1599.
The Synod held by him at Udayampura (or Diamper), near
Cochin, in that year denounced Nestorius and his heresies, and
put an end to the existence of the Indian Nestorian Church.

No document could be more exhaustively complete than Synod of
Diamper,
the Acts and Decrees of the Synod of Diamper, in its pro- 1599.
visions for bringing the Malabar Christians within the Roman
fold.[2] The sacred books of the St. Thomas congregations, their
missals, their consecrated oil and church ornaments, were
publicly burned ; and their religious nationality as a separate
caste was abolished. But when the firm hand of Archbishop
Menezes was withdrawn, his parchment conversions began to
lose their force. Notwithstanding the watchfulness of the
Goa Inquisition over the new converts, the Decrees of the
Synod of Diamper fell into neglect,[3] and the Malabar Christians
chafed under a line of Jesuit prelates from 1601 to 1653.

In 1653 they renounced their allegiance to their Jesuit

---

[1] For the military aspects of the Christian caste of St. Thomas, see
La Croze (*op. cit.*), ii. pp. 128, 129, 130, 140, 155, etc. The *History of
the Church of Malabar and Synod of Diamper*, by the learned Michael
Geddes, Chancellor of the Cathedral Church of Sarum (London, 1694), an
earlier and independent work, bears out this view.

[2] The Acts and Decrees of the Synod of Diamper (*i.e.* Udayampura)
occupy 346 pages of the Chancellor of Sarum's *History of the Church of
Malabar*, pp. 97–443 (ed. 1694).

[3] La Croze, ii. p. 193.

Reversions bishop. A Carmelite mission was despatched from Rome in
and Con-
versions, 1656 to restore order. The vigorous measures of its head,
1653-1663. Joseph of St. Mary, brought back a section of the old Christian
communities; and Joseph, having reported his success at
Rome, returned to India as their bishop in 1661. He found
the Protestant Dutch pressing the Portuguese hard on the
Malabar coast, 1661–1663. But the old military caste of
Malabar Christians rendered no assistance to their Catholic
superiors, and remained tranquil spectators of the struggle,
till the capture of Cochin by the Dutch brought about the
ruin of the Portuguese power in 1663.

Malabar   The Malabar Christians, thus delivered from the temporal
Christians
freed by   power of the Portuguese, re-asserted their spiritual independ-
the Dutch, ence. The Portuguese had compelled the native princes to
1663;   persecute the old Christian communities; and by confiscations,
imprisonments, and various forms of pressure, to drive the
Indian Nestorians into reconciliation with Rome.[1] Such a
persecution of a long recognised caste, especially of a valued
military caste, was as foreign to the tolerant spirit of Hinduism,
as it was repugnant to the policy of the Indian princes, and it
has left a deep impression on the traditions of the south-western
coast. The native Jacobite historian of the Church of Malabar
rises to the righteous wrath of an old Scottish covenanter in
recounting the bribing of the poorer chiefs by the Portuguese,
and the killings, persecutions, and separations of the married
clergy from their wives. The new Dutch masters of the southern
coast, after a short antagonism to the Carmelite prelate and
the native bishop whom he left behind, lapsed into indifference.
They allowed the Roman missionaries free scope, but put an
end to the exercise of the temporal power in support of the
Catholic bishop.[2]

The chief spiritual weapon of conversion, a weapon
dexterously used by the Portuguese Viceroys, had been the
interruption of the supply of Nestorian bishops from Persia.
receive a   This they effected by watching the ports along the west
Jacobite
bishop,   coast of India, and preventing the entrance of any Nestorian
1665.   prelate. The Syrian Church in India had therefore to struggle
on under its archdeacon, with grave doubts disturbing the
mind of its clergy and laity as to whether the archidiaconal
consecration was sufficient for the ordination of its priests.
The overthrow of the Portuguese on the seaboard put an end
to this long episcopal blockade. In 1665, the Patriarch of

[1] La Croze, vol. ii. pp. 169, 176, 183, 189, 192, 198, 203, etc.
[2] La Croze, vol. ii. pp. 204, 205.

Antioch sent a bishop, Mar Gregory, to the orphaned Syrian Church of India. But the new bishop belonged to the Jacobite instead of the Nestorian branch of the Asiatic Church. Indian Nestorianism may therefore be said to have received its death-blow from the Synod of Diamper in 1599.

Since the arrival of Mar Gregory in 1665, the old Syrian Church of India has remained divided into two sects. The *Pazheia kúttakár*, or Old Church, owed its foundation to Archbishop Menezes and the Synod of Diamper in 1599, and its reconciliation, after revolt, to the Carmelite bishop, Joseph of St. Mary, in 1656. It retains in its services the Syrian language and in part the Syrian ritual. But it acknowledges the supremacy of the Pope, and his vicars-apostolic. Its members are now known as Catholics of the Syrian Rite, to distinguish them from the converts made direct from heathenism to the Latin Church by the Roman missionaries. The other section of the Syrian Christians of Malabar is called the *Putten kúttakár*, or New Church. It adheres to the Jacobite tenets introduced by its first Jacobite bishop, Mar Gregory, in 1665. *(Marginal notes: Malabar Christians since 1665; (1) Syrian Catholics, 200,000; (2) Jacobites, 100,000?)*

The present Jacobites of Malabar condemn equally the errors of Arius, Nestorius, and the bishops of Rome.[1] They hold that the Bread and Wine in the Eucharist become the Real Body and Blood of Christ, and give communion in both kinds mixed together. They pray for the dead, practise confession, make the sign of the cross, and observe fasts. But they reject the use of images; honour the Mother of Jesus and the Saints only as holy persons and friends of God; allow the consecration of a married layman or deacon to the office of priest; and deny the existence of purgatory. In their Creed they follow the Council of Nicæa (325 A.D.). They believe in the Trinity; assert the One Nature and the One Person of Christ, and declare the procession of the Holy Ghost to be from the Father, instead of from the Father and the Son.[2] *(Marginal note: Tenets of the Malabar Jacobites.)*

The Syrian Catholics and Syrian Jacobites of Malabar maintain their differences with a high degree of religious vitality at the present day. Their congregations keep themselves distinct from the Catholics of the Latin Rite converted direct from heathenism, and from the Protestant sects. No Nestorian Church is now known to exist in Malabar.[3] The Syrian *(Marginal note: Nestorianism extinct in Malabar.)*

[1] *The Syrian Christians of Malabar*, being a Catechism of their doctrine and ritual, by Edavalikel Philipos, Chorepiscopus and Cathanar (*i.e.* priest) of the Great Church of Cottayam in Travancore, pp. 3, 4, 8 (Parker, 1869).

[2] The above summary is condensed from the Catechism of Edavalike Philipos, *op. cit.* pp. 9-13, 17, 19.   [3] *Idem*, p. 29.

Christians were returned in 1871 at about one-third of a million ; but the Census officers omitted to distinguish between Catholic Syrian and Jacobites. The Catholic Archbishop and Vicar-Apostolic of Verapoli, to whose kind assistance this chapter is indebted in many ways, estimates the Syrian Catholics at 200,000, and the Jacobites at 100,000. The totals for all Southern India cannot, however, be ascertained until the next Census of 1891.

Portu-guese mis-sionaries, 1500 A.D., Roman friars had visited India since the 13th century. The first regularly equipped Catholic mission, composed of Fran-ciscan brethren, arrived from Portugal in 1500. Their attacks on the native religions seemed part of the Portuguese policy of aggression on the Native States. The pious Portuguese monks were popularly identified with the brutal Portuguese soldiery, whose cruelties have left so deep a stain on early European enterprise in India. The military attempts of the Portuguese, and their ill-treatment of the native princes and the native population, provoked unmerited hatred against the disinterested, if sometimes ill-judged, zeal of the Portuguese missionaries.

identified with Portu-guese aggres-sions.

Native re-prisals or 'persecu-tions.' Native reprisals, which certain writers have dignified by the name of persecutions, occasionally took place in return for Portuguese atrocities. But the punishments suffered by the friars were usually inflicted for disobedience to the native civil power, or for public attacks on native objects of veneration ; such attacks as are provided for by the clauses in the Anglo-Indian Penal Code, which deal with words or signs calculated to wound the religious feelings of others. Attacks of this kind lead to tumults among an excitable population, and to serious breaches of the peace, often attended with bloodshed. The native princes, alarmed at the combined Portuguese assault on their territory and their religion, could not be expected to decide in such cases with the cold neutrality of an Anglo-Indian magistrate. Father Pedro de Covilham was killed in 1500.

Slow progress. For some time, indeed, missionary work was almost con-fined to the Portuguese settlements, although King Emmanuel (1498–1521) and his son John III. (1521–57) had much at heart the conversion of the Indians. The first bishop in India was Duarte Nunez, a Dominican (1514–17) ; and John de Albuquerque, a Franciscan, was the first bishop of Goa (1539–53). With St. Francis Xavier, who arrived in 1542, began the labours of the Society of Jesus in the East, and the progress of Christianity became more rapid.

Xavier and the Jesuits, 1542.

St. Francis' name is associated with the Malabar coast, and with the maritime tracts of Madura and Southern Madras.

He completed the conversion of the Paravars in Tinnevelli St. Francis District.[1] His relics repose in a silver shrine at Goa.[2] Xavier. Punnaikáyal, in Tinnevelli, was the scene, in 1549, of the death of Father Antonio Criminale, the protomartyr of the Society of Jesus ; and in the following year, several other lives were lost in preaching the gospel. Goa became an Archbishopric in 1577. In 1596 to 1599, the Archbishop of Goa, Alexis de Menezes, an Augustinian, succeeded in recon- Alexis de ciling the Indian Nestorians to Rome ; and at the Synod of Menezes. Diamper (Udayampura, near Cochin) in 1599, the affairs of the Indian Christians were settled. The use of the Syrian rite was Syrian rite retained after it had been purged of its Nestorianism. The reformed, later history of the Syrian Christians in Malabar has already tained, been traced. 1599.

The Jesuit mission to the Madras coast dates from 1606, The and is associated with the names of Robert de Nobili (its Madras founder, who died 1656), John de Britto (killed in Madura Jesuits. 1693), Beschi the great scholar (who died about 1746), and other illustrious Jesuits, chiefly Portuguese.[3] They laboured in Madura, Trichinopoli, Tanjore, Tinnevelli, Salem, etc. The mission of the Karnátic, also a Jesuit mission, was French in its origin, and due in some measure to Louis XIV. in 1700. Its centre was at Pondicherri.

The early Jesuit missions are particularly interesting. Their Good priests and monks became perfect Indians in all secular work done matters, dress, food, etc., and had equal success among all Jesuits. castes, high and low. In the south of the peninsula they brought, as we have seen, the old Christian settlements of the Syrian rite into temporary communion with Rome, and con- verted large sections of the native population throughout extensive districts. The Society of Jesus had also numerous although less important missions in the north of India. During the 17th and 18th centuries, religious troubles and difficulties arose in Western India through the action of the missionaries in regard to caste observances. Schisms troubled the Church. The Portuguese king claimed, as against the Pope, to appoint the Archbishop of Goa ; and the Dutch adventurers for a time persecuted the Catholics along the coast.

But in the 16th century it seemed as if Christianity was destined to be established by Jesuit preachers throughout

---

[1] See article TINNEVELLI DISTRICT, *The Imperial Gazetteer of India.*

[2] See article GOA, *The Imperial Gazetteer of India.*

[3] See articles MADURA and TINNEVELLI, *idem.*

a large part of India. The literary activity of missionaries belonging to the Order was also very great. Their early efforts in the cause of education, and in printing books in the various languages, are remarkable. De Nobili and Beschi have been named. Fathers Arnauld and Calmette should not be forgotten.

Letters of the Jesuits, 16th and 17th centuries.

But apart from works of scholarship, the early Indian Jesuits have left literary memorials of much interest and value. Their letters, addressed to the General of the Order in Europe, afford a vivid glimpse into the state of India during the 16th and 17th centuries. One volume,[1] which deals with the period ending in 1570, furnishes by way of preface a topographical guide to the Jesuit stations in the East. Separate sections are devoted to Goa, Cochin, Bassein, Thána, and other places in Western India, including the island of Socotra, in which the Jesuit brethren still found remnants of the Christians of St. Thomas.

Jesuit stations in India.

Basis of Portuguese rule.

The letters, as a whole, disclose at once the vitality and the weakness of the Portuguese position in the East. The Lusitanian conquest of India had a deeper fascination, and appeared at the time to have a higher moral significance for Christendom than afterwards attached to our more hesitating and matter-of-fact operations. Their progress formed a brilliant triumph of military ardour and religious zeal. They resolved not only to conquer India, but also to convert her. Only by slow degrees were they compelled in secret to realize that they had entered on a task, the magnitude of which they had not gauged, and the execution of which proved to be altogether beyond their strength. All that chivalry and enthusiastic piety could effect, they accomplished. But they failed to fulfil either their own hopes, or the expectations which they had raised in the minds of their countrymen at home. Their viceroys had to show to Europe results which they were not able to produce; and so they were fain to accept the shadow for the substance, and in their official despatches to represent appearances as realities. In their military narratives, every petty Rájá or village chief who sent them a few pumpkins or mangoes, becomes a tributary Rex, conquered by their arms or constrained to submission by the terror of their name. In their ecclesiastical epistles, the whole country is a land

Conquest and conversion.

---

[1] *Rerum a Societate Jesu in Oriente Gestarum Volumen*, Coloniæ, Anno 1574. It purports to have been translated into Latin from the Spanish. The author has to thank Mr. Ernest Satow, of H. B. M.'s Japanese Legation, for a loan of this curious volume.

flowing with milk and honey, and teeming with a population eager for sacramental rites.

The swift downfall of the Portuguese power, based upon conquest and conversion, will be exhibited in a later chapter. But the Portuguese are the only European nation who have created, or left behind them, a Christian State polity in India. To this day, their East India settlements are territorially arranged in parishes; and the traveller finds himself surrounded by churches and other ecclesiastical features of a Christian country, among the rice-fields and jungles of Goa and Damán. This parochial organization of Portuguese India was the direct result of the political system imposed on the viceroys from Europe. But, indirectly, it represents the method adopted by the Society of Jesus in its efforts at conversion. The Jesuits worked to a large extent by means of industrial settlements. Many of their stations consisted of regular agricultural communities, with lands and a local jurisdiction of their own. Indeed, both in the town and country, conversion went hand in hand with attempts at improved husbandry, or with a training in some mechanical art.

Parochial organization of Portuguese India.

This combination of Christianity with organized labour may best be understood from a description of two individual settlements:[1] Thána, a military agricultural station; and Cochin, a collegiate city and naval port. Thána, says a Jesuit letter-writer in the middle of the 16th century, is a fortified town where the Brethren have a number of converts. Once on a time a wrinkled and deformed old man came to them from distant parts, greatly desiring to be made a Christian. He was accordingly placed before a picture of the Blessed Virgin, and, having sought to kiss the Child, was forthwith baptized. He died in peace and joy next morning. Many boys and girls were likewise bought from the barbarians for a few pence a-piece. These swelled the family of Christ, and were trained up in doctrine and handicrafts. During the day they plied their trades as shoemakers, tailors, weavers, and iron-workers; on their return at evening to the College, they sang the catechism and litanies in alternate choirs. Others of them were employed in agriculture, and went forth to collect fruits or to work with the Christian cultivators in the fields.

Thána, a Jesuit station, 1550 A.D.

Christian craftsmen,

There was also a Christian village, the Hamlet of the

---

[1] The following details were chiefly condensed from the *Rerum a Societate Jesu in Oriente Gestarum Volumen,* already referred to. This book is no longer in the author's possession, and as no copy is procurable in India, the pages cannot be cited nor the exact words verified.

Trinity, 3000 paces off, upon temple lands bought up and consecrated by the Order. The Society had, moreover, certain

and culti-
vators.

farms, yielding 300 pieces of gold a year. This money supported the widows and orphans, the sick, and catechumens while engaged in their studies. The poorer converts were encouraged in agriculture by a system of advances. Everything seemed to prosper in the hands of the Jesuit Brethren, and their very goats had kids by couplets and triplets every year. The husbandmen 'are all excellent cultivators and good men,' well skilled in the Mysteries, and constant in the practice of their faith, assembling daily together *ad signum angelicæ salutationis.* ' Even in the woods, boys and men are heard chanting the Ten Commandments in a loud voice from the tops of the palm-trees.'

Jesuit rural
organiza-
tion.

The management of the mission stations seems to have been admirable. Four or five Brothers of the Order regulated alike the secular and the spiritual affairs of each community. One of them was a surgeon, who cured ulcers, sores, and dangerous maladies. The Christian village of the Trinity had, moreover, certain gardens which the inhabitants held in common, well irrigated and rich in *vines*, figs, and medicinal fruits. The catechism was publicly rehearsed once on ordinary days, twice on holidays. They held frequent musical services; the youths chanting the psalms, robed in white. The Thána choristers, indeed, enjoyed such a reputation that they were invited to sing at the larger gatherings at Bassein; and were much employed at funerals, at which they chanted the ' Misericordia ' to the admiration alike of Christians and heathens. Besides their civil and secular duties in the town of Thána, and at the Christian village and farms, the Brethren of the Order visited a circle of outposts within a distance of thirty thousand paces; ' to the great gain of their countrymen, whom they strengthen in their faith; and of the natives (*barbari*), whom they reclaim from their errors and superstitions to the religion of Christ.'

Cochin, a
collegiate
city.

The station of Thána discloses the regulated industry, spiritual and secular, which characterized the Jesuit settlements in India. Cochin may be taken to illustrate the educational labours of the Order and its general scheme of operations. The College of the Society, writes brother Hieronymus in 1570,[1] has two grammar schools, attended by 260 pupils, who have made excellent progress both in their studies and in the practice of the Christian sacraments. They are all skilled in

---

[1] Letter to the General of the Order, dated Cochin, February 1570.

the tenets of the faith; many of them have learned the catechism, arranged in questions and answers, and are now teaching it to the heathen. The rites of confession and communion are in constant use, and resorted to on saints' days by 300 or 400 persons. An equal concourse takes place when Indulgences are promulgated; and on a late occasion, when the jubilee granted by the Pope in 1568 was celebrated, 'such was the importunity of those seeking confession, that our priests could not find a breathing space for rest from morning to night.' At the College Church alone a thousand persons received the Eucharist, chiefly new communicants. A wholesale restitution of fraudulent gains took place, with a general reconciliation of enemies, and a great quickening of the faith in all. 'So vast was the concourse at this single church, without mentioning the other churches in the city, that we had from time to time to push out the throngs from the edifice into the courtyard, not without tears and lamentation on their part.'

The College of the Order likewise ministered to the Portuguese fleet stationed off Cochin; and the writer relates, with perhaps pardonable exaggeration, the strict discipline which the Brethren maintained among both officers and men. During the winter they had also collected a fund, and with it redeemed five Portuguese who, the year before, had fallen into captivity among 'the Moors.' These men, on coming to offer up public thanksgiving in church, edified the worthy fathers by relating how the Christians still remaining in captivity continued firm in the Catholic faith, although sorely tormented *incommodis et cruciatibus*. They told how one youth, in particular, 'who had attended our school, on being tied to a tree and threatened by the Moors with bows and arrows, had bravely answered that he would give up his life rather than his faith.' Upon which the Moors seem to have laid aside their lethal weapons, and let the lad off with a few kicks and cuffs. Another boy had at first apostatized; but his fellow-captives, foremost among them a nobleman of high station, threw themselves at his feet, and begged him to stand firm. The boy burst into tears, and declared that he had been led astray by terror, but that he would now rather die than abandon his religion. He proved himself as good as his word, rushed in front of his persecutors, and openly proclaimed himself to be still a Christian. 'The Moors,' as usual, seem to have taken the affair with much good nature; and, after another little comedy of tying him to a tree and threatening to shoot him and cut his throat, let their young apostate go.

Jesuit College at Cochin.

Jesuit itineraries.

'I come now,' continues Father Hieronymus, 'to the harvest of this year.' He goes on to describe the work of itinerating, from which we gather that the King of Cochin was friendly rather than otherwise to the members of the Order and their converts, protecting them by letters patent, and even giving rise to hopes of his own conversion. No fewer than 220 natives were baptized in one day; and the Father adduces, as a proof of their sincerity, the fact that they did not expect any material advantage from their conversion. 'For neither do they look for a present of new clothes at their baptism, nor for anything else from us, excepting spiritual food. They think themselves greatly honoured by the name of Christians, and labour to bring others to the truth.' Among the converts the Nairs figure a good deal; and an acolyte of this race, notwithstanding that he was harassed by the 'older Christians,' brought in other Nairs, by twos and threes, for baptism. The worthy Father uses 'Nair' as the name of 'a certain military class,' and so touches on the actual position held by this tribe three hundred years ago.

Conversions.

Conversion was not, however, always without its troubles. The story of a young Moor, whose mother was a cruel woman, and buried him in the ground up to his mouth for turning a Christian, is told with honest pride. His unkind parent likewise placed a huge stone round his head, designing that he should die a slow and painful death. But the boy managed to peep through a cleft in the stone, and spied some travellers passing that way, whereupon, although he had formerly known nothing of Latin, he managed to shout out the two words, '*exopto Christum.*' On hearing this, the travellers dug up the lad and took him before the Governor, who, in an obliging manner, gave over the boy to the College to be baptized, and sent the mother to prison. The neophytes seem to have been spirited lads; and the Father narrates how about two thousand of them took part in the military games held when the fleet was lying off Cochin, and distinguished themselves so greatly with various sorts of darts and weapons, that 'they came next to the Portuguese soldiers.'

Efforts at royal conversions.

The College took advantage of the illness of the king during the course of the year to try to convert him; but his majesty, although civil and friendly, declined their well-meaning efforts. They were more successful with two 'petty Rájás' (*reguli*) in the neighbourhood, who, 'being desirous of the Portuguese friendship,' professed an interest in spiritual matters on behalf of themselves and people. Three hundred, apparently of their subjects, promised to get themselves baptized as soon as a church should be built. 'But,' concludes the candid chronicler, 'as this particular people have a grievously bad reputation as liars, it is much to be prayed for that they will keep their word.' From another instance of a royal conversion, it appears that the introduction of Christianity, with 'letters of privilege' to converts, was a favourite method among the weaker Rájás for securing a Portuguese alliance.

The story of the Catholic missions thus graphically told by the *Rerum Gestarum Volumen* of the 16th century, is continued for the 17th and 18th by the letters from the Jesuit Fathers in Malabar. These letters have been edited by Le Père Bertrand in four volumes, which throw an important light, not only upon the progress of Christianity in India, but also upon the social and political state of the native kingdoms in which that progress was made.[1] The keynote to the policy of the Society of Jesus, in its work of Indian evangelization, is given in the following words :—'The Christian religion cannot be regarded as naturalized in a country, until it is in a position to propagate its own priesthood.'[2] *The Malabar Mission, 17th and 18th centuries.*

This was the secret of the wide and permanent success of the Catholic missions ; it was also the source of their chief troubles. For in founding Christianity on an indigenous basis, the Fathers had to accept the necessity of recognising indigenous customs and native prejudices in regard to caste. The disputes which arose divided the Jesuit missionaries for many years, and had to be referred, not only to the General of the Order, but to the Pope himself. The *Question des Rites Malabares* occupies many pages in Père Bertrand's volumes.[3] In the end, a special class of native priests was assigned to the low castes, while an upper class ministered to the Indians of higher degree. The distinction was rigidly maintained in the churches. Père Bertrand gives the plan of a *Question of caste.*

---

[1] *Mémoires Historiques sur les Missions des ordres religieux* (1 vol. 2nd ed., Paris, 1862) : *La Mission du Maduré d'après des documents inédits* (3 vols., Paris, 1848, 1850, 1854). The first edition of the *Mémoires Historiques* (Paris, 1847) formed apparently an introduction to the three volumes of Letters which constitute Père Bertrand's *La Mission du Maduré*. The author takes this opportunity of acknowledging his obligations to the authorities of St. Xavier's College, Calcutta, for the loan of Père Bertrand's works, and for much kind assistance in his inquiries.

[2] Condensed from Père Bertrand, *Missions*, vol. i. p. 1.

[3] For example, *Mémoires Historiques*, vol. i. pp. 353 *et seq.* Indeed, this volume is largely devoted to the polemics of the question. Also *La Mission du Maduré*, vol. ii. pp. 140 *et seq.* ; vol. iv. pp. 404 to 496 ; and in many other places of Père Bertrand's work.

Malabar church as laid before the sovereign Pontiff in 1725, which shows a systematic demarcation between the high and low castes even during divine service. Whatever may have been lost of the primitive Christian equality by this system, it had the merit of being adpated to native habits of thought, and it was perhaps unavoidable in an Indian church which endeavoured to base itself upon an indigenous priesthood.[1] The adoption of native terms by the Jesuit Fathers, such as *guru*, teacher; *sanyásí*, hermit, etc., also led to embittered discussions.

Letters from Malabar, 17th and 18th centuries.

The letters disclose, however, other and more agreeable aspects of the early missions to India. A few of them complain of the dangers and discomforts of missionary life in a tropical climate and among a suspicious people.[2] But, as a rule, they are full of keen observation and triumphant faith. Some of them are regularly divided into two parts; the first being devoted to the secular history of the period, or 'Evènements politiques;' the second to the current affairs and progress of the mission. Others are of a topographical and statistical character. Many of them record signs and wonders vouch-safed on behalf of their labours. A pagan woman, for example, who had been possessed of a devil from birth, is delivered from her tormentor by baptism, and enters into a state of joy and peace. Another native lady, who had determined to burn herself on her husband's funeral pile, and had resisted the counter entreaties of her family and the Village Head, miraculously renounced her intention when sprinkled with ashes consecrated by the priest. Throughout, the letters breathe a desire for martyrdom, and a spiritual exultation in sufferings endured for the cause.

Political events.

Miracles.

One very touching epistle is written by de Britto from his prison the day before his execution. 'I await death,' he writes to the Father Superior, 'and I await it with impatience. It has always been the object of my prayers. It forms to-day the most precious reward of my labours and my sufferings.'[3] Another letter relates the punishment of Father de Saa, several of whose teeth were knocked out by blows, so that he almost died under the pain (A.D. 1700). His tormentor was, however, miraculously punished and converted to the faith.[4] The more

Martyr-doms.

---

[1] The plan of the church is given at p. 434 of Père Bertrand's *Mission du Maduré*, vol. iv. ed. 1854. The merits of the question are so fully discussed in that volume that it is unnecessary to reopen the question here.

[2] For example, *Lettre du Père Balthazar*, dated Tanjore, 1653, *op. cit.* vol. iii. pp. 1 *et seq.*

[3] *La Mission du Maduré*, vol. iii. p. 447. Letter dated 3rd February 1693.   [4] Vol. iv. pp. 63-68.

striking events take place in Malabar and Cochin. But in other parts of India, also, there were triumphs and sufferings. 'Even here,' writes Père Petit from Pondicherri, 'we are not altogether without some hope of martyrdom, the crown of apostleship.'[1] It is natural that such writers should regard as martyrs, their brethren who fell victims to popular tumults stirred up by their own preaching. Penalties for sectarian affrays, or for insults to the native religions, such as would now be punished by the Indian Penal Code, figure as 'persecutions.' The Salvationists have of late suffered several 'persecutions' of this sort from Anglo-Indian magistrates.

Nor are the literary labours of the Fathers without a fitting record. Bishop Caldwell lately expressed his regret that the biography of Father Beschi, the Tamil scholar and poet, should yet be unwritten.[2] But the defect is supplied, not only in an elaborate notice of Beschi's life and works, but also by Beschi's own letters to the General of the Order.[3] Several epistles of de Nobili are of scarcely less interest in the annals of Indian Christianity. Literary labours of the Jesuits.

The arguments of the Catholic missionaries were enforced by the weapons of the secular power. In 1560, the Portuguese established the Inquisition at Goa, under the Dominican Order. At first the establishment was of a modest and tentative character; the functionaries numbering only five, and the whole salaries amounting in 1565 to £71 a year.[4] But by degrees it extended its operations, until in 1800 the functionaries numbered 47. The Goa Inquisition has formed the subject of much exaggerated rumour, and the narrative of one of its prisoners startled and shocked Europe during the seventeenth century.[5] Dr. Claudius Buchanan recalled public attention to the subject by his vividly coloured letters at the beginning of the nineteenth century.[6] The calmer narrative of Da Fonseca, derived from the archives of Goa, proves that the reality was sufficiently terrible. No continuous statistics exist of the The Portuguese Inquisition, 1560-1812.

---

[1] Vol. iv. p. 158.

[2] *A Political and General History of the District of Tinnevelli*, by Bishop Caldwell (Madras Government Press, 1881), p. 239.

[3] Père Bertrand, vol. iv. pp. 342-375.

[4] *O Chronista de Tissuary*, vol. iv. p. 51. Quoted in Fonseca's *Goa*, p. 217 (Bombay, 1878).

[5] *Relation de l'Inquisition de Goa*, by the Physician Dellon, who was confined in one of its cells in 1674. Pyrard, Fryer, and other travellers have also left notices of the Goa Inquisition.

[6] See his Letters and Journal dated 1808, pp. 150-176 of *Christian Researches in Asia*, 4th ed. (1811).

punishments inflicted.   But the records repeatedly speak of the necessity for additional cells, and in 1674 they numbered two hundred. Seventy-one *autos da fé*, or general jail deliveries, are mentioned between 1600 and 1773. The total number of persons condemned on these occasions is unknown. But at a few of the *autos* it is said that ' 4046 persons were sentenced to various kinds of punishment, of whom 3034 were males and 1012 females.'[1]   These punishments included 105 men and 16 women condemned to the flames, of whom 57 were burned alive and 64 in effigy.

Number of autos da fé.

It is not necessary to inquire how far such examples of religious punishment in Portuguese territory were responsible for the persecution of the Catholic missionaries in Cochin and Malabar.   Nor, in passing judgment on the Hindu princes, should we forget the perpetual military aggressions and occasional cold-blooded massacres by the Portuguese on the southern and western coasts.   Christian missions in Northern India had scarcely anything to fear from the native powers. Indeed, under Akbar, and almost throughout the entire period of the Mughal Emperors until the accession of Aurungzeb, Christianity seems to have been regarded with an enlightened interest, and certainly without disfavour, by the Delhi court. More than one of the Mughal queens and princes are said to have been Christians; and the faith was represented both by Imperial grants and in the Imperial seraglio.   Many of the great Hindu Feudatories also displayed a courteous indifference to the Christian missionaries, and a liberal recognition of their scientific and secular attainments.

Christians set example of religious persecution

The Inquisition at Goa was temporarily suspended in 1774, but re-established in 1779.   It was abolished in 1812, and the ancient palace in which it had been held was pulled down in 1820.   The *débris* were finally removed in 1859 on the occasion of the exposition of the body of St. Francis Xavier.[2]

Inquisition abolished 1812.

In 1759, Portugal broke up the Society of Jesus, seized its property, and imprisoned its members.   France did the same in 1764; and to prevent greater evils, Clement XIV. in 1773 was forced to suppress the Society altogether.   The French Revolution followed.   These events deprived the Indian

The Jesuits suppressed, 1759-73.

[1] Da Fonseca's *Goa*, p. 220.   The original authorities quoted are *O Chronista de Tissuary, Historia dos Principaes actos e Procedimêntos da Inquisição em Portugal*, Lisboa, 1845, p. 38 ; and F. N. Xavier in the *Gabinête Litterario*, vol. iii. pp. 89 and 280 ; *Narração da Inquisição de Goa*, pp. 143 *et seq.* (*Nova Goa*, 1866).

[2] A popular account of its history will be found in Mr. E. Rehatsek's ' Holy Inquisition at Goa,' *Calcutta Review*, No. 145, April 1881.

Jesuit missions alike of priests and of funds, and for a long time they languished, served in the south only by a few priests from Goa and Pondicherri. That dismal period, however, presents some illustrious names; among them two well-known writers, the Abbé Dubois of Mysore, and the Carmelite Fra Paolino de San Bartholomeo (in India 1774–90). In the absence of priests to sustain the courage of the Christians, every occasional or local persecution told. Tipú, about 1784, forcibly circumcised 30,000 Catholics of Kánara, and deported them to the country above the Gháts. Many native Christians lived and died without ever seeing a priest; they baptized their own children, taught them the prayers, and kept up daily worship in their churches.

Better days, however, dawned. In 1814, the Society of Jesus was re-established; under Gregory XVI., its missions began a new life, and have since made great progress. Their prosperity is, however, hampered by the action taken in Europe against the religious orders. The claims of Portugal to appoint the Archbishop of Goa, and through him to regulate clerical patronage, as opposed to the right of the Pope, have occasioned schisms in the past, and still give rise to discord.

The Jesuits re-established, 1814.

The Roman Catholics throughout all India, British, Feudatory, and Foreign, number altogether 1,356,037 souls, as returned in the table to be presently given from the *Madras Catholic Directory* for 1885. The Census Report of 1881, adding the latest figures for Portuguese and French India, gives a total of 1,248,801.

Number of Roman Catholics in India.

The Roman Catholic missions are maintained by many of the European nations, and are nearly equally divided between the secular and regular clergy. Almost every mission contains a mixture of races among its priests; even Holland, Scotland, and Germany being ably represented. Although all are directed by Europeans, seven-eighths of the priests are natives. It is also worthy of remark that, in the list of bishops during the last 300 years, the names of several natives are found, some of them Bráhmans. The Roman Catholic missions are presided over by sixteen bishops (vicars and prefects apostolic), the delegates of the Pope, who governs the missions himself, without the intervention of the Camera. Side by side with these papal vicars-apostolic, who are also bishops, the Archbishop of Goa (appointed by the King of Portugal) has an independent jurisdiction over a certain number of Catholics outside his diocese, who are scattered over India, but chiefly in the south. The prefect-apostolic of Pondicherri

Organization of the Roman Catholic missions.

Archbishop of Goa.

presides over the Catholics in several British Districts and throughout the southern French possessions. In Pondicherri he has technically jurisdiction only over 'those who wear hats.'

His separate jurisdiction.

The independent jurisdiction of the Archbishop of Goa, and the dissensions to which it gave rise, have been referred to.

Jus patronatus 1600.

It had its origin in the *Jus patronatus* granted by Pope Clement VIII. to King Philip. By the Pontifical Bull, the Portuguese king was charged with the support of the Catholic churches in India, and in return was invested with the patronage of their clergy. On the ruin of the Portuguese power in India by the Dutch, it was held that the sovereign was no longer in a position to fulfil his part of the agreement. The Indian clergy became a growing charge upon Rome.

Curtailed, 1673.

In 1673, therefore, Clement X. abrogated the jurisdiction of the Portuguese Archbishop of Goa beyond the limits of the Portuguese settlements. In 1674, two Briefs declared that the Portuguese bishops had no authority over the vicars and missionaries-apostolic sent from Rome to India. These orders only produced a long ecclesiastical dispute. Accordingly, in 1837, Gregory XVI. published his Bull, *Multa præclare*, dividing the whole of India into vicariates-apostolic, and forbade the Goanese prelates to interfere in their management.

Concordat of 1857.

The Portuguese Archbishop of Goa disregarded this decree, and the *Indo-Lusitanum schisma* continued until 1861. In 1857, a concordat was agreed to by the Pope and the King of Portugal, by which such churches as were then under the apostolic vicars should remain under the same, while those which then acknowledged the Goanese jurisdiction should

Settlement of 1861.

continue under the Archbishop of Goa. In 1861, joint commissioners were sent out from Rome and Portugal to put this arrangement into execution. In the end, the Pope granted for some time, '*ad tempus*,' to the Archbishop of Goa an extraordinary jurisdiction over certain churches, served by Goanese priests, but beyond the Portuguese dominions. Such churches are still to be found in Malabar, Madura, Ceylon, Madras, Bombay, and apparently in the lower delta of Bengal. It is intended that this independent jurisdiction of the Portuguese Archbishop of Goa shall in time lapse to the vicars-apostolic appointed from Rome. But meanwhile it continues to this day, and still gives rise to occasional disputes.[1]

---

[1] The foregoing two paragraphs on the extraordinary jurisdiction of the Archbishop of Goa are condensed from MS. materials supplied to the author by the papal Vicar-Apostolic of Verapoli.

As the ecclesiastical and civil divisions of India do not Distribu-
correspond, it is difficult to compare missionary with official tion of Roman
statistics. The Catholics in French territory numbered, Catholics.
according to the *Madras Catholic Directory* for 1885, 33,226,
and in Portuguese territory in 1881, 252,477. This leaves
1,070,334 Catholics for British India and the Native States,
according to the *Madras Directory* for 1885, or 963,058
according to the Census Report of 1881. Catholics are most
numerous in the Native States of Travancore and Cochin
(comprised in the vicariates of Verapoli and Quilon). The
archdiocese of Goa, with 660 priests, nearly all natives, for a
very small territory containing over 250,000 Catholics, is a
witness to the sternly proselytizing system of the Portuguese.

Verapoli, the smallest in area of the Roman vicariates, The
contains the largest number of priests and Catholics. These Verapoli vicariate
are chiefly the descendants of the Nestorians converted to (Travan-
Rome in the 16th century, and were divided by the Census core).
of 1881 into two classes—of the Syrian rite, 141,386, and of
the Latin rite, 80,600. They were directed by 14 European
Carmelite priests, and by 375 native priests, 39 of the Latin
rite, and 336 of the Syrian rite.

The Census of 1881 returned the Syrian Christians alto- Syrian and
gether apart from the Roman Catholics, but did not distin- Roman Catholic
guish between Jacobites and Catholics of the Syrian rite. Out Christians.
of a total of 304,410 Syrians in all India, 301,442 are returned
by the Census Report as within the Native States of Travancore and Cochin (the vicariates of Verapoli and Quilon). The
Census Report returned the total number of Roman Catholics
in Travancore and Cochin at 274,734; while the returns officially
accepted by the heads of the Catholic Church give the number
in the *Madras Catholic Directory* at 378,096. From private
inquiries since made, it appears that the discrepancy arises
from the fact that the number of Catholics was underrated at
the time of the Census. About 100,000 Roman Catholics of
the Syrian rite, belonging to the jurisdiction of the vicars-
apostolic of Verapoli and Quilon, seem to have been included
among the Syrian Jacobites.

The Pondicherri and Madura vicariates represent parts of
the famous Jesuit missions of Madura and of the Karnátic.
In Bombay city, and along the fertile maritime strip or Konkan
between the Western Gháts and the sea, the Roman Catholics
form an important section of the native population.

The following table shows the Roman Catholic population
for all India, as returned by the authorities of the Church.

R

ROMAN CATHOLIC POPULATION OF BRITISH INDIA AND NATIVE STATES.

(According to the ' Madras Catholic Directory' for 1885.)

	Number.
Vicariate-Apostolic of Madras, ...	56,548
,, ,, Haidarábád (Nizám's Dominions), .	9,100
,, ,, Vizagapatam, ...	13,287
,, ,, Mysore, ...	27,429
,, ,, Coimbatore, ...	24,027
,, ,, Madura, ...	176,169
,, ,, Quilon (South Travancore), . .	97,496
,, ,, Verapoli (North Travancore and Cochin),	280,600
,, ,, Mangalore, ...	76,000
,, ,, Pondicherri (within British Territory),	174 441
,, ,, Bombay, ...	51,025
,, ,, Agra, ...	8,400
,, ,, Patná, ...	10,000
,, ,, Punjab, ...	5,900
,, ,, Western Bengal, ...	18,000
Prefecture-Apostolic of Central Bengal, ...	1,678
Vicariate-Apostolic of Eastern Bengal, ...	16,000
,, ,, Southern Burma, ...	17,580
,, ,, Eastern Burma, ...	6,654
Total in British India and Native States, . .	1,070,334

ROMAN CATHOLIC POPULATION OF PORTUGUESE SETTLEMENTS IN INDIA.

(According to the Census of February 17*th,* 1881.)

Goa, ...	250,645
Damán, ...	1,497
Diu, ...	335
Total in Portuguese Settlements in India, . .	252,477

ROMAN CATHOLIC POPULATION OF FRENCH SETTLEMENTS IN INDIA.

(According to the ' Madras Catholic Directory' for 1885.)

Pondicherri, ...	18,889
Karikal, ...	12,787
Chandarnagar, ...	300
Yanaon, ...	450
Mahé, ...	800
Total in French Settlements in India, . . .	33,226
Grand Total in British, Native, and Foreign India, . .	1,356,037

The Roman Catholics in India steadily increase; and as in former times, the increase is chiefly in the south, especially in the missions of Pondicherri and Madura. The number of Catholics in British and French India and the Native States, but exclusive of the Portuguese Possessions, rose from 732,887 in 1851, to 934,400 in 1871, and to 1,103,560 in 1881. The Pondicherri mission lately performed over 50,000 adult baptisms in three years. In the Madura vicariate, the increase is principally in Tinnevelli and Rámnád. The converts are chiefly agriculturists, but are by no means confined to the low castes.

The principal Catholic colleges in India are those of the Society of Jesus, at Calcutta, Bombay, and Negapatam. Another Jesuit college has lately been opened at Mangalore in South Kánara, a District in which there are over 3000 Catholic Bráhmans. England, being a Protestant country, supplies few priests, and hence Catholic missions have much difficulty in maintaining colleges where English is the vehicle of higher education. The statistics of the Catholic schools are incomplete, owing to want of information about certain parts of the Goa jurisdiction. But the number of Catholic schools actually returned in 1880, including Goa, was 1514, with 51,610 pupils. In British India and the Native States, the children in Catholic schools increased from 28,249 in 1871, to 44,699 in 1881.

The Roman Catholics work in India with slender pecuniary resources. They derive their main support from two great Catholic organizations, the Association for the Propagation of the Faith, and the Society of the Holy Childhood. The former contributes £24,464 yearly to Indian missions, and the latter £12,300, making a total of £36,764. This is exclusive of the expenditure within the Archbishopric of Goa; but it represents the European contributions to the whole Vicariates under the Pope. In 1880 they maintained a staff of 16 bishops and 1118 priests, teaching 1236 schools, with 40,907 pupils, and giving religious instruction to 1,002,379 native Christians. The Roman Catholic priests deny themselves the comforts considered necessaries for Europeans in India. In many Districts they live the frugal and abstemious life of the natives, and their influence reaches deep into the social life of the communities among whom they dwell.

The first Protestant missionaries in India were Lutherans, Ziegenbalg and Plutschau, who in 1705 began work under the patronage of the King of Denmark at the Danish settlement of Tranquebar. Ziegenbalg and many of the early Lutheran missionaries were men of great ability; and, besides their translations of the Scriptures, some of their writings still hold a high place in missionary literature. Ziegenbalg began the translation of the Bible into Tamil, and his successor Schultze completed it in 1725. This was the first Protestant translation of the Scriptures in India. Schultze also translated the whole Bible into Hindustání. Ziegenbalg died in 1719, leaving 355 converts. In spite of the patronage of the Kings of Denmark and England, and the liberal assistance of friends in Europe, the Lutheran mission made at first but slow progress, and was much hindered and opposed by the local Danish authorities. Gradually it extended itself into Madras, Cuddalore, and Tanjore; schools were set up, and conversion and education went hand in hand.

Transla-
tion of the
Bible,
1725.

In 1750, arrived the pious Schwartz, whose name is bound up with the history of Tanjore and adjacent Districts until his death in 1798. He was the founder of the famous Tinnevelli missions.[1] Next to the Lutherans come the Baptists of Serampur, with the honoured names of Carey, Marshman, and Ward. In the 18th century, the English East India Company did not discourage the labours of Protestant missionaries. It had allowed Kiernander, originally sent out by the Danes, to establish himself at Calcutta in 1758. But subsequently, it put every obstacle in the way of missionaries, and deported them back to England on their landing. Carey arrived in 1793. In 1799, to avoid the opposition of the English East India Company, he established himself with four other missionaries at Serampur (15 miles from Calcutta), at that time, like Tranquebar, a Danish possession. Then began that wonderful literary activity which has rendered illustrious the group of 'Serampur missionaries.' In ten years, the Bible was translated, and printed, in whole or part, in 31 languages; and by 1816, the missionaries had about 700 converts. The London Missionary Society (established 1795) entered the field in 1798, and its missions have gradually grown into importance.

Schwartz
in Tan-
jore,
1750-98.
Serampur
mission-
aries.

Kier-
nander in
Calcutta,
1758.

Carey,
1793.

31 transla-
tions of the
Bible.

The opposition of the East India Company continued till 1813, when it was removed by the new Charter. The same document provided for the establishment of the bishopric of Calcutta, and three archdeaconries, one for each Presidency. Up to this period the Established Church of England had attempted no direct missionary work, although some of the East India Company's chaplains had been men of zeal, like the

Official
opposi-
tion with-
drawn,
1813.

---

[1] See article TINNEVELLI, *The Imperial Gazetteer of India.*

ardent Henry Martyn (1806–11). The first Bishop of Calcutta Bishopric (Middleton) arrived in 1814. From this time the Church of of Calcutta, cutta, England has constantly kept up a missionary connection with 1814. India, chiefly by means of its two great societies—the Church Missionary Society, which sent out its first representative in 1814; and the Society for the Propagation of the Gospel, which did so in 1826. Their most successful stations are in Southern India, where they have gathered in the seed sown by the Lutheran missions. The second Bishop of Calcutta was the well-known Heber (1823–26). In 1835, under a new Charter of the East Indian India Company, the see of Madras was established, and in Sees. 1837, that of Bombay. In 1877, owing to the extension of mission work in Tinnevelli, two missionaries were appointed bishops, as assistants to the Bishop of Madras; the dioceses of Lahore and Rangoon also were separated from Calcutta, and bishops appointed. The missionary bishopric of Travancore and Cochin was established in 1879. It has no connection with Government, nor have the assistant bishops in Madras.

The first missionary of the Church of Scotland was Dr. Presby- Alexander Duff (1830–63), to whom the use of English as terian missions, the vehicle of higher education in India is largely due. Mis- 1830–63. sionaries of numerous other Protestant societies (European Other and American) have since entered India, and established missions. numbers of churches and schools. They have furnished memorable names to the roll of Indian educators, such as Judson (Baptist) in Burma, 1813–50, and John Wilson (Presbyterian) of Bombay, 1843–75.

The progress of the several Protestant missions in India Statistics may be thus stated:— In 1830 there were 9 societies at of Protestant work, and about 27,000 native Protestants in all India, missions. Ceylon, and Burma. By 1870 there were no less than 35 societies at work; and in 1871 there were 318,363 converts (including Ceylon, etc., as above). In 1852 there were 459 Protestant missionaries, and in 1872 there were 606. Between 1856 and 1878, the converts made by the Baptist Progress, Societies of England and America, in India, Ceylon, and 1856 to 1878. Burma, increased from about 30,000 to between 80,000 and 90,000. Those of the Basle missions of Germany multiplied from 1060 to upwards of 6000; those of the Wesleyan Methodist missions of England and America, from 7500 to 12,000; those of the American Board, from 3302 to

Protestant progress, 1856-1878. about 12,000 ; those of the Presbyterian missions of Scotland, England, Ireland, and America, connected with 10 societies, from 821 to 10,000 ; those of the missions of the London Missionary Society, from 20,077 to 48,000 ; and those of the Church Missionary Society and of the Society for the Propagation of the Gospel, from 61,442 to upwards of 164,000.[1]

Great increase of native Protestants, 1851-1881. The increased activity of the Protestant missionary bodies in India, during the past third of a century, may be seen from the table [2] on the following page. Between 1851 and 1881, the number of mission stations has increased nearly threefold ; while the number of Native Protestant Christians has multiplied by more than fivefold, the number of communicants by nearly tenfold, and the number of churches or congregations by sixteenfold. This is partly due to the extended employment of native agency in the work. The native ordained pastors have been increased from 21 in 1851 to 575 in 1881, and the native lay preachers from 493 to 2856. The Protestant Church in India has greatly gained in strength by making a freer use of, and reposing a more generous confidence in, its native agents. Its responsible representatives report the increase of Native Christians in India, Burma, and Ceylon,[3] from 1851 to 1861, at 53 per cent.; from 1861 to 1871, at 61 per cent.; and from 1871 to 1881, at 86 per cent.

Extended use of native agency.

School work of Protestant missions, The activity of the Protestant missions has not, however, been confined to the propagation of their faith. Their services to education, and especially in the instruction of the people in the vernacular languages, will hereafter be referred to. But the vast extension of these services during late years is less generally recognised. The number of pupils in Protestant mission schools and colleges has risen from 64,043 in 1851 to 196,360 in 1881, or more than threefold. The standard of instruction has risen at an equal pace, and the mission institutions successfully compete with the Government colleges at the examinations of the Calcutta, Madras, and Bombay Universities. Female education has always formed a subject

Its rapid development, 1851-81.

Female education.

[1] The Rev. M. A. Sherring, in the *Chronicle of the London Missionary Society*, August 1879.

[2] Compiled from *The Statistical Tables for* 1881, issued under instructions of the Calcutta Missionary Conference (Thacker, Spink, & Co., Calcutta, 1882). It should be remembered that the statistical organization was more perfect in 1881 than in 1851. To Mr. W. Rees Philipps this chapter is indebted for many materials and figures regarding Indian Christian missions in their earlier years.

[3] The table given on next page deals only with India and Burma, and excludes Ceylon. *Op. cit.* pp. x. and xiii.

of peculiar care among the missionary bodies. The number of girls' day schools belonging to Protestant missions in India alone has risen from 285 in 1851 to 1120 in 1881. This is exclusive of girls' boarding schools and *zanána* work. The total number of female pupils, under Protestant mission teaching in India alone, exclusive of Burma, has multiplied from 11,193 in 1851 to 57,893 in 1881.

The great success of the missionaries of late years in their school work, as in their preaching, is due to the extended use of native agency. Complete statistics are available on this point only for 1871 and 1881. The number of 'Foreign'[1] and Eurasian male teachers belonging to Protestant missions in India and Burma, has decreased from 146 in 1871 to 101 in 1881; while the native Christian teachers have been doubled, from 1978 in 1851 to 3675 in 1881. In 1881, there were also 2468 non-Christian native teachers employed; making a total of 6143 native teachers in missionary employ in 1881, against 101 'Foreign' and Eurasian teachers. The native female teachers, Christian and non-Christian, have increased from 863 in India and Burma in 1871, to 1996 in 1881. The following table may now be left to speak for itself :— *Extended use of native agency.*

SUMMARY OF PROTESTANT MISSIONS IN INDIA
AND BURMA.

	Number in 1851.	Number in 1861.	Number in 1871.	Number in 1881.
Stations, ...	222	337	448	601
Foreign *a* and Eurasian or-				
dained agents, . .	339	501	517	622
Native ordained agents, .	21	143	302	575
Foreign and Eurasian lay				
preachers, . . .	...	...	...	77
Native lay preachers, .	493	1,677	2,344	2,856
Churches or congregations,	267	643	2,631	4,180
Native Christians, . .	91,092	198,097	286,987	492,882
Communicants, . .	14,661	43,415	73,330	138,254
Male pupils in schools, .	52,850*b*	64,828	100,750	138,477
Female pupils in schools, .	11,193*b*	17,035	27,627	57,893
Total male and female				
pupils, ...	64,043*b*	81,863	128,377	196,360*c*

a Including British, European, American, and all others, not natives of India.

b The pupils for 1851 were in India only; no returns being available for Burma for that year.

c The return of total pupils is exclusive of 65,728 boys and girls attending Sunday schools. The returns for 1851 and 1861 are as a whole less complete than those for 1871 and 1881.

---

[1] Including British, European, American, and all non-Indian teachers.

General
Statistics
of Chris-
tian popu-
lation in
India.

The foregoing pages have briefly traced the history of Christianity in India, and disclose the recent progress made by its main branches, Catholic and Protestant, among the natives. It remains to exhibit the Christian population as a whole, including both Europeans and Indians. In comparing the results, it must be borne in mind that the figures have been derived from various sources, and that the areas of enumeration in some cases overlap each other. Thus, the jurisdictions of the Catholic vicars-apostolic supply a basis for calculation which differs from the territorial areas adopted

European
and
Native.

by the Census of British India. Every effort has been made to allow for such causes of error, and to render the following tables a true presentment of the Christian population of India, British, Feudatory, and Foreign. It will be observed that the total number of Christians has increased during the nine years from 1872 to 1881 by 365,251. In British India alone the increase has been 270,807, or 30·2 per cent. The total number of Christians was 2,148,228 in 1881, as against 1,782,977 in 1872.

TOTAL CHRISTIAN POPULATION IN INDIA IN 1872 AND IN 1881.

	1872.	1881.	Increase.	Percentage of Increase.	
In British India, .	897,682	1,168,489	270,807	30·2	Figures for 1872 less complete than for 1881.
In Native States, .	620,295	694,036	73,741	11·9	
In Portuguese India,	235,000	252,477	17,477	7·4	
In French India, .	30,000	33,226	3,226	10·7	
Total, .	1,782,977	2,148,228	365,251	20·4	

Denomi-
national
Statistics,
1881.

The Census of 1881 returned the Christian population in British and Native India, according to sect. This return is useful as affording a test of the figures given in the foregoing pages from the Roman Catholic and Protestant missions. It will be observed that the two sets of figures practically agree, allowing for differences in the areas of the enumeration. In the total for all India these sources of discrepancy disappear; but it must be remembered that that total includes both Europeans and natives.

CHRISTIAN POPULATION OF INDIA ACCORDING TO SECT

(As returned by the Census of 1881).

	Church of England.	Church of Scotland.	Lutherans.	Other Protestant Sects.	Roman Catholics.	Syrians.	Greeks and Armenians.	Others and Unspecified.	Total.
BRITISH DISTRICTS.									
Madras,	182,218	1,637	4,667	20,161	473,352	2,885	314	25,993[1]	711,037
Bombay,	1,109	5,762	80	2,286	109,456	4	56	19,574	138,317
Bengal,	32,690	3,939	23,593	18,962	20,725	67	1,383	20,741	128,100
Punjab,	20,838	1,619	4	1,063	8,021	10	34	1,831	33,420
North-Western Provinces and Oudh,	27,924	3,443	483	3,232	9,384	2	85	3,096	47,649
Central Provinces,	4,523	715	17	222	5,833	...	14	625	11,949
Assam,	1,676	290	221	3,320	351	...	5	1,227	7,090
Berâr,	...	71	5	41	620	...	...	595	1,335
Ajmere,	934	659	...	51	468	...	15	98	2,225
Coorg,	392	35	152	65	2,508	...	...	...	3,152
British Burma,	9,980	655	346	56,112	16,281	...	226	615	84,215
Total in British India,	282,284	18,825	29,568	105,418	652,999	2,968	2,132	74,295	1,168,489
NATIVE STATES.									
Bombay,	45	95	1	22	6,059	...	...	615	6,837
Central Provinces,	7	...	...	...	...	...	...	17	24
Punjab,	157	90	...	...	12	...	...	23	279
Baroda,	3°1	20	1	44	405	...	...	...	771
Central India,	1,588	3 3	6	195	1,882	...	2	3,089	7,065
Cochin,	1,409	...	...	...	120,919[2]	14,033	...	...	136,361
Haidarâbâd,	4,909	450	1	184	6,436	...	1	1,733	13,614
Mysore,	5,586	242	...	2,012	20,010	...	7	892	29,249
Râjputâna,	109	9	...	11	...	...	...	1,144	1,294
Travancore,	57,313	...	...	...	153,815	287,409	...	...	498,542
Total in Native States,	71,429	1,209	9	2,468	310,059	301,442	10	7,410	694,036
Grand Total in British India and Native States,	353,713	20,034	29,577	107,886	963,058	304,410	2,142	81,705	1,862,525
Portuguese India, general return, practically all Catholics,									257,477
French India, Do.									33,226
Grand Total for all India and Burma									2,148,228

NOTE.—No details are available of the different sects of Christians in Portuguese and French India. But for all practical purposes the number of Roman Catholics may be taken as the total Christian population. Adding, therefore, to the above figures, 252,477 Catholics in Portuguese Settlements (1881), and 33,226 Catholics in French Settlements (1885), a grand total of 2,148,228 Christians is obtained for all India, British, Feudatory, and Foreign.

[1] Including the Madras Native States of Pudukotai, Banganapalli, and Sandur.

[2] A considerable discrepancy occurs between the number of Roman Catholics in Travancore and Cochin States as returned by the Census of 1881, and that returned by the Roman Catholic authorities, as shown on a previous page. This difference, it has been explained, apparently arises from the fact that the Roman Catholics were under-estimated in the Census returns by the exclusion of about 100,000 Syrian Christians who acknowledge the jurisdiction of the Vicars-Apostolic of Verapoli and Quilon, and by their inclusion among the Jacobites who are unconnected with the Roman Catholic Church.

The Government of India maintains an ecclesiastical establishment for its European soldiers and officials. It devotes on an average £660,000 a year to their medical requirements, and £160,000 to their spiritual wants.[1] The two following tables show the ecclesiastical staff, and the number of soldiers and Government servants who attend their ministrations. In making up the second table, it has not been found practicable to bring the statistics of attendance beyond the date of the last Parliamentary return of 1880. During the year 1879, to which the attendance columns in the second table refer, a large European force was absent in the field, and the church attendance of European troops was decreased by about 13,000 officers and men.

INDIAN ECCLESIASTICAL STAFF, 1884.

	BISHOPS.		ARCH-DEACONS.		CHAPLAINS.			REGISTRARS.	
	No.	Pay.	No.	Pay.	No.	Pay (sen.).	Pay (jun.).	No.	Pay.
Church of England—		£		£		£	£		£
Calcutta, .	1	4598	1	1280	}			1a	480
Lahore, . .	1	960	1	960	} 92	960	600	...	...
Rangoon, . .	1	960	1	960	}			1	60
Madras, . .	1	2560	1	1280	39	960	600	1	256
Bombay, . .	1	2560	1	1280	26	960	600	1	180
Church of Scotland—									
Bengal, . .	...	...	1b	1351	4	960	600	...	...
Madras, . .	...	...	1b	1140	3	960	600	...	...
Bombay, . .	...	...	1b	1140	3	990	600	...	...
Roman Catholic Priests—									
Bengal, . .	2	600c	...	...	42	360d	240	...	...
Madras, . .	1	600c	...	...	15	360d	240	...	...
Bombay, . .	1	600c	...	...	18	360d	240	...	...
Total, . .	9	...	8	...	242	...	...	4	...

a The registrar of the Calcutta Diocese is also registrar of the Lahore Diocese.
b These are the senior Presbyterian Chaplains in the three Presidencies.
c This is an allowance for furnishing ecclesiastical returns for transmission to England, paid to certain Roman Catholic Bishops in official communication with the British Government. The number of Catholic Bishops is sixteen for all India.
d There is also an intermediate class on £300 per annum. In addition to their rates of pay, Roman Catholic priests receive horse allowance at £36 per annum.

In the following table, it should be borne in mind that the salaries and number of chaplains refer to 1884, while the attendance is that of 1879, when a large force was in the field. The attendance in ordinary years is estimated

[1] The average cost of the ecclesiastical establishment during the ten years ending 1883 was £160,657.

at over 50,000. This would raise the total Church attendance of British troops and Government servants (exclusive of women and children) to about 55,000.

INDIAN ECCLESIASTICAL MINISTRATIONS.

	Salaries and Allowances (1884).	No. of Bishops, Archdeacons, Chaplains or Ministers (1884).	Number of European Troops and Officers ordinarily attending Church (1879).	Number of other Government Servants (excluding Wives and Children) ordinarily attending Church (1879).	Total of Government Servants attending Church (1879).
Church of England, . .	£124,175	167	23,842	3191	27,033
Church of Scotland, . .	10,445	13	2,782	479	3,261
Church of Rome, . . .	31,251	79	10,586	621	11,207
Total, ...	£165,871	259	37,210	4291	41,501

CHAPTER X.

EARLY MUHAMMADAN RULERS (711 TO 1526 A.D.).

WHILE Buddhism was giving place to Hinduism throughout India, and Christianity under Nestorian bishops was spreading along the coast of Malabar, a new faith had arisen in Arabia. Muhammad, born in 570 A.D., created a conquering religion, and died in 632. Within a hundred years after his death, his followers had invaded the countries of Asia as far as the Hindu Kush. Here their progress was stayed, and Islám had to consolidate itself, during three more centuries, before it grew strong enough to grasp the rich prize of India. But, almost from the first, the Arabs had fixed eager eyes upon that wealthy country. Fifteen years after the death of the prophet, Usmán sent a sea-expedition to Thána and Broach on the Bombay coast (647 ? A.D.). Other raids towards Sind took place in 662 and 664, with no results.

Early Arab expeditions to Bombay coast, 636-711 A.D.

In 711, however, the youthful Kásim advanced into Sind, to claim damages for an Arab ship which had been seized at an Indian port. After a brilliant campaign, he settled himself in the Indus valley; but the advance of the Musalmáns depended on the personal daring of their leader, and was arrested by his death in 714 A.D. The despairing valour of the Hindus struck the invaders with wonder. One Rájput garrison preferred extermination to submission. They raised a huge funeral pile, upon which the women and children first threw themselves. The men then bathed, took a solemn farewell of each other, and, throwing open the gates, rushed upon the besiegers and perished to a man. In 750, the Rájputs are said to have expelled the Muhammadan governor, but it was not till 828 A.D. that the Hindus regained Sind.

Muhammadan settlement in Sind, 711-828 ?

Their expulsion, 828 A.D.

The armies of Islám had carried the crescent from the Hindu Kush westwards, through Asia, Africa, and Southern Europe, to distant Spain and Gaul, before they obtained a foothold in the Punjab. This long delay was due, not only to the daring of individual tribes, such as the Sind Rájputs just

India on the eve of the Muhammadan conquest, 1000 A.D.

mentioned, but to the military organization of the Hindu kingdoms. To the north of the Vindhyas, three separate groups of princes governed the great river-valleys. The Rájputs ruled in the north-west, throughout the Indus plains, and along the upper waters of the Jumna. The ancient Middle Land of Sanskrit times (Madhya-desha) was divided among powerful kingdoms, with their suzerain at Kanauj. The lower Gangetic valley, from Behar downwards, was still in part governed by Pál or Buddhist dynasties, whose names are found from Benares to jungle-buried hamlets deep in the Bengal delta.[1] The Vindhya ranges stretched their wall of forest and mountain between the northern and southern halves of India. Their eastern and central regions were peopled by fierce hill tribes. At their western extremity, towards the Bombay coast, lay the Hindu kingdom of Málwá, with its brilliant literary traditions of Vikramáditya, and a vast feudal array of fighting men. India to the south of the Vindhyas was occupied by a number of warlike princes, chiefly of non-Aryan descent, but loosely grouped under three great over-lords, represented by the Chera, Chola, and Pándya dynasties.[2]

Hindu kingdoms —(1) of the north;

(2) of the south.

Each of these groups of kingdoms, alike in the north and in the south, had a certain power of coherence to oppose to a foreign invader; while the large number of the groups and units rendered conquest a very tedious process. For even when the over-lord or central authority was vanquished, the separate groups and units had to be defeated in detail, and each State supplied a nucleus for subsequent revolt. We have seen how the brilliant attempt in 711, to found a lasting Muhammadan dynasty in Sind, failed. Three centuries later, the utmost efforts of two great Musalmán invaders from the north-west only succeeded in annexing a small portion of the frontier Punjab Province, between 977 and 1176 A.D. The Hindu power in Southern India was not completely broken till the battle of Tálikot in 1565; and within a hundred years, in 1650, the great Hindu revival had commenced which, under the form of the Maráthá confederacy, was destined to break up the Mughal

Hindu power of resistance.

Slow progress of Muhammadans in India.

---

[1] For example, at Sábhár, on the northern bank of the Burígangá, once the capital of the Bhuiya or Buddhist Pál Rájá Harischandra. In 1839, the only trace that remained of his traditional residence was a brick mound, covered with jungle. See Hunter's *Statistical Account of Bengal*, vol. v. pp. 72, 73, 118. In Lower Bengal, the Buddhist Páls had given place to the Bráhmanized Sens of Nadiyá before the Muhammadans reached that Province for the first time in 1199.

[2] See *The Imperial Gazetteer of India*, articles CHERA, CHOLA, and PANDYA.

Their
success
short-
lived.

Empire in India. That Empire, even in the north of India, had only been consolidated by Akbar's policy of incorporating Hindu chiefs and statesmen into his government (1556–1605). Up to Akbar's time, and even during the earlier years of his reign, a series of Rájput wars had challenged the Muhammadan supremacy. In less than two centuries after his death, the successor of Akbar was a puppet in the hands of the Hindu Maráthás at Delhi.

Muham-
madan
conquests
only par-
tial,

The popular notion that India fell an easy prey to the Musalmáns is opposed to the historical facts. Muhammadan rule in India consists of a series of invasions and partial conquests, during eleven centuries, from Usmán's raid, *circ.* 647, to Ahmad Sháh's tempest of invasion in 1761 A.D. They represent in Indian history the overflow of the nomad tribes of Central Asia, towards the south-east; as the Huns, Túrks, and various Tartar tribes disclose in early European annals the westward movements from the same great breeding-ground of nations. At no time was Islám triumphant throughout the whole of India. Hindu dynasties always ruled over large areas. At the height of the Muhammadan power, the Hindu princes paid tribute, and sent agents to the Imperial Court. But

and tem-
porary.

even this modified supremacy of Delhi lasted for little over a century (1578–1707). Before the end of that brief period, the Hindus had begun the work of reconquest. The native chivalry of Rájputána was closing in upon Delhi from the south; the religious confederation of the Sikhs was growing

Hindus
reconquer
India from
the Musal-
máns,
1707–61.

into a military power on the north-west. The Maráthás had combined the fighting powers of the low-castes with the statesmanship of the Bráhmans, and were subjecting the Muhammadan kingdoms throughout all India to tribute. So far as can now be estimated, the advance of the English power at the beginning of the present century alone saved the Mughal Empire from passing to the Hindus.

This chapter will necessarily confine its survey to the essential stages in the spread of the Musalmán conquest, and will pass lightly over the intermediate princes or minor dynasties who flit across the scene.[1] The annexed summary presents a view of the whole :—

---

[1] The Hon. Mountstuart Elphinstone's *History of India* is still the standard popular work on the Muhammadan period. Professor Cowell's edition (Murray, 1866) incorporated some of the new materials accumulated since Mr. Elphinstone wrote. But much of the original work is a reproduction of *Firishta*, and requires to be re-written from Sir Henry Elliot's *Persian Historians* and the results of the Archæological and

SUMMARY OF MUHAMMADAN CONQUERORS AND DYNASTIES
OF INDIA (1001–1857).

I. HOUSE OF GHAZNI (Túrkí).
1001–1186. Mahmúd of Ghazní
to Sultán Khusrú. Pp. 272-75.

II. HOUSE OF GHOR (Afghán?).
1186–1206. Muhammad Ghori
(Shahab-ud-dín). Pp. 275-78.

III. SLAVE KINGS (chiefly Túrkí).
1206–1290. Kutab-ud-dín to Balban and Kaikubád. Pp. 278-80.

IV. HOUSE OF KHILJI (Túrkí?).
1290–1320. Jalál-ud-dín to Násír-
ud-dín Khusrú. Pp. 280-83.

V. HOUSE OF TUGHLAK (Punjab
Túrks), 1320–1414. Pp. 283-86.
1320. Ghiyás - ud - dín Tughlak.
P. 283.
1324. Muhammad Tughlak. Pp.
283-85.
1351. Firuz Tughlak. P. 285.
1414. End of the dynasty. P. 286.
[Irruption of the Mughals under
Timúr (Tamerlane) in 1398–
99, leaving behind him a fifteen
years' anarchy under the last
of the line of Tughlak, until
the accession of the Sayyids
in 1414. P. 285.]

VI. THE SAYYIDS.
1414–1450. Curtailed power of
Delhi. P. 286 *passim*.

VII. THE LODIS (Afgháns).
1450–1526. Feeble reigns; independent States. P. 286.

VIII. HOUSE OF TIMUR (Mughal),
1526–1857.
1526–1530. Bábar. P. 290.
1530–1556. Humáyún. Pp. 290-91.

[Sher Sháh, the Afghán governor of Bengal, drives Humáyún out of India in 1540,
and his Afghán dynasty rules
till 1555. P. 291.]
1556–1605. Akbar the Great.
Pp. 291-300.
1605–1627. Jahángír. Pp. 300-302.
1628–1658. Sháh Jahán, deposed.
Pp. 302-305.
1658–1707. Aurangzeb or Alamgír I. Pp. 306-312.
1707–1712. Bahádur Sháh, or
Sháh Alam I. P. 312.
1712. Jahandar Sháh. P. 312.
1713–1718. Farrukhsiyyar. P. 312.
1719–1748. Muhammad Sháh
(after two boy Emperors). Pp.
312-313.
[Irruption of Nádir Sháh the
Persian, 1738–1739. Pp.
313-15.]
1748–1754. Death of Muhammad
Sháh; and accession of Ahmad
Sháh, deposed 1754. P. 313.
1754–1759. Alamgír II. P. 313.
[Six invasions of India by
Ahmad Sháh Duráni, the
Afghán, 1748–1761. Pp.
313-15.]
1759–1806. Sháh Alam II., titular
Emperor. P. 313.
1806–1834. Akbar II., titular Emperor. P. 313.
1834–1857. Muhammad Bahádur
Sháh, titular Emperor; the
seventeenth and last Mughal
Emperor; died a State prisoner
at Rangoon in 1862. P. 313.

Statistical Surveys. The present chapter has chiefly used, besides
Elphinstone, the following works for the Muhammadan period :—(1) Sir
Henry Elliot's *History of India as told by its own Historians, i.e.* the
Arab and Persian travellers and writers, edited by Professor Dowson,
8 vols. 1867–77 (Trübner); (2) Mr. Edward Thomas' *Chronicles of
the Pathán Kings of Delhi,* especially for reigns from 1193 to 1554, for
which period he gives the initial dates of the Hijra years (Trübner, 1871);
(3) Mr. Edward Thomas' *Revenue Resources of the Mughal Empire,* with
his manuscript marginal notes; (4) Lieut.-Colonel Brigg's Translation of
Muhammad Kásim Firishta's *History of the Rise of the Muhammadan*

First
Túrkí
invasions.

The first collision between Hinduism and Islám on the Punjáb frontier was the act of the Hindus. In 977, Jaipál, the Hindu chief of Lahore, annoyed by Afghán raids, led his troops up the passes against the Muhammadan kingdom of Ghazní, in Afghánistán. Subuktigín, the Ghaznivide prince, after severe fighting, took advantage of a hurricane to cut off the Hindu retreat through the pass. He allowed them, how-

Subukti-
gín, 977
A.D.

ever, to return to India on the surrender of fifty elephants, and the promise of one million *dirhams* (about £25,000).[1] Tradition relates how Jaipál, having regained his capital, was counselled by the Bráhman, standing at his right hand, not to disgrace himself by paying ransom to a barbarian; while his nobles and warrior chiefs, standing at his left, implored him to keep faith. In the end, Subuktigín swept down the passes to enforce his ransom, defeated Jaipál, and left an Afghán officer with 10,000 horse to garrison Peshádwar. Subuktigín was soon afterwards called away to fight in Central Asia, and his Indian raid left behind it only this outpost.[2] But henceforth, the Afgháns held both ends of the passes.

Mahmúd
of Ghazní,
1001–1030.

In 997, Subuktigín died, and was succeeded by his son, Mahmúd of Ghazní, aged sixteen. This valiant monarch reigned for thirty-three years,[3] and extended the limits of his father's little Afghán kingdom from Persia on the west, to deep into the Punjab on the east. Having spent four years in consolidating his power to the west of the Khaibar Pass, he led

His seven-
teen inva-
sions,
1001–1026.

forth in 1001 A.D. the first of his seventeen[4] invasions of India.

Power in India; (5) Reports of the Archæological Survey of Western India, and materials supplied by the Statistical Survey of the various Provinces of India; (6) Professor Blochmann's *Aín-i-Akbari* (Calcutta, 1873), together with Gladwin's older translation (2 vols. 1800). When the dates or figures in this chapter differ from Elphinstone's, they are derived from the original Persian authorities, as adopted by Sir Henry Elliot and Mr. Thomas.

[1] The *Táríkh Yamíní*, written *circ.* 1020, by Al 'Utbí, a secretary of Sultán Mahmúd, is the contemporary authority for this invasion. It is translated in Sir Henry Elliot's *Persian Historians*, vol. ii. pp. 18–24. The materials for the invasions of Subuktigín are *Firishta*, i. pp. 11–25 (ed. 1829); and Sir Henry Elliot's *Persian Historians*, vols. ii. iii. iv. and vi.

[2] His chronicler, Al 'Utbí, never once mentions Delhi or Lahore.

[3] The *Tabakát-i-Násirí* (Sir Henry Elliot's *Persian Historians*, vol. ii. p. 270) speaks of the '36th year of his reign.' But the dates 997 to 1030 seem authoritative. The original materials for the invasions of Mahmúd are *Firishta*, i. pp. 37–82; and Sir Henry Elliot's *Persian Historians*, vols. i. ii. iii. and iv.

[4] This number, and subsequent details, are taken from the authorities translated in Sir Henry Elliot's *Persian Historians*, vols. ii. iii. iv.; and critically examined in the Appendix to his second volume, pp. 434–478 (1869).

Of these, thirteen were directed to the subjugation of the
Punjab; one was an unsuccessful incursion into Kashmír; the
remaining three were short but furious raids against more
distant cities—Kanauj, Gwalior, and Somnáth.

Jaipál, the Hindu frontier chief of Lahore, was again
defeated. According to Hindu custom, a twice-conquered
prince was deemed unworthy to reign; and Jaipál, mount-
ing a funeral pile, solemnly made over his kingdom to his Patriotic
son, and burned himself in his regal robes. Another local devotion
of the
chief, rather than yield himself to the victor, fell upon his Hindus,
own sword. In the sixth expedition (1008 A.D.), the Hindu 1008 A.D
ladies melted their ornaments, while the poorer women spun
cotton, to support their husbands in the war. In one great
battle, the fate of the invaders hung in the balance. Mahmúd,
alarmed by a coalition of the Indian kings as far as Oudh
and Málwá, entrenched himself near Pesháwar. A sortie
which he made was driven back, and the wild Ghakkar
tribe [1] burst into the camp and slaughtered nearly 4000
Musalmáns.

But each expedition ended by further strengthening the Mahmúd's
Muhammadan foothold in India. Mahmúd carried away progress in
India,
enormous booty from the Hindu temples, such as Thaneswar 1001–1024.
and Nagarkot, and his sixteenth and most famous expedition
was directed against the temple of Somnáth in Gujarát (1024
A.D.). After bloody repulses, he stormed the town; and the
Hindu garrison, leaving 5000 dead, put out in boats to sea.
The famous idol of Somnáth was merely one of the twelve
lingas or phallic emblems erected in various parts of India.
But Mahmúd having taken the name of the 'Idol-Smasher,' Expedition
the modern Persian historians gradually converted the plunder to Somnáth, 1024.
of Somnáth into a legend of his pious zeal. Forgetting the
contemporary accounts of the idol as a rude stump of stone,
Firishta tells how Mahmúd, on entering the temple, was offered

---

[1] Firishta says, '30,000 Ghakkars with their heads and feet bare.'
Colonel Brigg's *Firishta*, vol. i. p. 47 (ed. 1829). Elphinstone gives the
number of Mahmúd's expeditions somewhat differently from the number
and order adopted in the above text from the Persian authorities, translated
by Sir Henry Elliot. Thus Elphinstone gives the expedition of 1008 A.D.
as the fourth (p. 328), while Sir Henry Elliot gives it as the sixth
(*Persian Historians*, vol. i. p. 444). In the same way, Elphinstone gives the
Somnáth expedition as the twelfth (p. 334, ed. 1866), while Sir Henry
Elliot gives it as the sixteenth (vol. ii. p. 468). These instances must
suffice to indicate the differences between Elphinstone and the later
materials derived from Sir Henry Elliot and Mr. Edward Thomas. In
subsequent pages, the more accurate materials will be used without pausing
to point out such differences.

Fiction of the jewel-bellied god.

an enormous ransom by the priests if he would spare the image.[1] But Mahmúd cried out that he would rather be remembered as the breaker than the seller of idols, and clove the god open with his mace. Forthwith a vast treasure of jewels poured forth from its vitals, which explained the liberal offers of the priests, and rewarded the disinterested piety of the monarch. The growth of this myth can be clearly traced,[2] but it is still repeated by uncritical historians. The *linga* or solid stone fetish of Somnáth, had no stomach, and could contain no jewels.

The sandal-wood gates.

Mahmúd carried off the temple gates, with fragments of the phallic emblem, to Ghazní,[3] and on the way nearly perished with his army in the Indus desert. But the famous 'Sandal-wood gates of Somnáth,' brought back as a trophy from Ghazní by our troops in 1842, and paraded through Northern India, were as clumsy a forgery as the story of the jewel-bellied idol itself. Mahmúd died at Ghazní in 1030 A.D.

Results of Mahmúd's invasions, 1030 A.D.

As the result of seventeen invasions of India, and twenty-five years' fighting, Mahmud had reduced the western districts of the Punjab to the control of Ghazní, and left the remembrance of his raids as far as Kanauj on the east, and Gujarát in the south. He never set up as a resident sovereign in India. His expeditions beyond the Punjab were the adventures of a religious knight-errant, with the plunder of a temple-city, or the demolition of an idol, as their object, rather than serious efforts at conquest. But as his father had left Peshá-war as an outpost garrison, so Mahmúd left the Punjab as an outlying Province of Ghazní.

The Punjab conquered.

Mahmúd's justice and thrift.

The Muhammadan chroniclers tell many stories, not only of Mahmúd's valour and piety, but also of his thrift. One day a poor woman complained that her son had been killed by robbers in a distant desert of Irak. Mahmúd said he was very sorry, but that it was difficult to prevent such accidents so far from the capital. The old woman rebuked him with these words,

---

[1] Colonel Brigg's *Firishta*, vol. i. pp. 72, 73 (ed. 1829).

[2] Sir H. Elliot's *History of India from the Persian Historians*, vol. ii. p. 270, from the *Tabakát-i-Násirí*; also Appendix, vol. ii. p. 476; vol. iv. pp. 182, 183, from the *Habibu-s-Siyar* of Khondamir. But see, even in 1832, II. H. Wilson in the *Asiatic Researches*, vol. xvii. pp. 194 *et seq.* A foundation for Firishta's invention is, however, to be found in the contemporary account of Al Biruni (970–1029 A.D.), who says that the top of the *linga* was garnished with gems of gold.

[3] Of the four fragments, he deposited one in the Jamá Masjid at Ghazní, another at the entrance of his palace, and the third he sent to Mecca, and the fourth to Medina. *Tabakát-i-Násirí.*

'Keep therefore no more territory than you can rightly govern.'
The Sultán forthwith rewarded her, and sent troops to guard
all caravans passing that way.   Mahmúd was an enlightened
patron of poets, and his liberality drew the great Ferdousi to Ferdousi.
his court.   The Sultán listened with delight to his *Sháh-námah*,
or Book of Kings, and promised him a *dirham*, meaning a
golden one, for each verse on its completion.   After thirty
years of labour, the poet claimed his reward.   But the Sultán
finding that the poem had run to 60,000 verses, offered him
60,000 silver *dirhams*, instead of *dirhams* of gold.   Ferdousi
retired in disgust from the court, and wrote a bitter satire
which records to this day the base birth of the monarch.
Mahmúd forgave the satire, but remembered the great epic,
and, repenting of his meanness, sent 100,000 golden *dirhams*
to the poet.   The bounty came too late.   For as the royal
messengers bearing the bags of gold entered one gate of
Ferdousi's city, the poet's corpse was being borne out by
another.

During a century and a half, the Punjab remained under House of
Mahmúd's successors, as a Province of Ghâzní.   But in 1152, Ghor,
the Afgháns of Ghor[1] overthrew the Ghaznívide dynasty; and 1152–1186.
Khusrú, the last of Mahmúd's line, fled to Lahore, the capital
of his outlying Indian territory.   In 1186, this also was Obtains
wrested from him;[2] and the Ghorian prince Shahâb-ud-dín, the
better known as Muhammad of Ghor, began the conquest of Punjab,
India on his own account.   But each of the Hindu princi- 1186.
palities fought hard, and some of them still survive seven
centuries after the torrent of Afghán invasion swept over their
heads.

On his first expedition towards Delhi, in 1191, Muhammad Muham-
of Ghor was utterly defeated by the Hindus at Thaneswar, mad of
badly wounded, and barely escaped with his life.   His scattered invasions,
hosts were chased for 40 miles.   But he gathered together 1191–1206.
the wreck at Lahore, and, aided by new hordes from Central His first
Asia, again marched into Hindustán in 1193.   Family quarrels 1191.
among the Rájputs prevented a united effort against him.

[1] Ghor, one of the oldest seats of the Afghán race, is now a ruined
town of Western Afghánistán, 120 miles south-east of Herát.   The feud
between Ghor and Ghazní was of long standing and great bitterness.
Mahmúd of Ghazní had subdued Ghor in 1010 A.D.; but about 1051
the Ghorian chief captured Ghazní, and dragged its chief inhabitants to
Ghor, where he cut their throats, and used their blood for making mortar
for the fortifications.   After various reprisals, Ghor finally triumphed over
Ghazní in 1152.

[2] *Tabakát-i-Násirí.*   Sir H. Elliot's *Persian Historians*, vol. ii. p. 281.

Dissensions among the Hindu princes.

The cities of Delhi and Kanauj stand forth as the centres of rival Hindu monarchies, each of which claimed the first place in Northern India. A Chauhán prince, ruling over Delhi and Ajmere, bore the proud name of Prithwí Rájá or Suzerain. The Ráhtor king of Kanauj, whose capital can still be traced across eight square miles of broken bricks and rubbish,[1] celebrated a feast, in the spirit of the ancient Horse-sacrifice,[2] to proclaim himself the Over-lord.

Court pageant at Kanauj, 12th century A.D.

At such a feast, all menial offices had to be filled by royal vassals; and the Delhi monarch was summoned as a gate-keeper, along with the other princes of Hindustán. During the ceremony, the daughter of the King of Kanauj was nominally to make her *swayamvara*, or 'own choice' of a husband, a pageant survival of the reality in the Sanskrit epics. The Delhi Rájá loved the maiden, but he could not brook to stand at another man's gate. As he did not arrive, the Kanauj

A *swayamvara*, or maiden's choice.

king set up a mocking image of him at the door. When the princess entered the hall to make her choice, she looked calmly round the circle of kings, then stepping proudly past them to the door, threw her bridal garland over the neck of the ill-shapen image. Forthwith, says the story, the Delhi monarch rushed in, sprang with the princess on his horse, and galloped off towards his northern capital. The outraged father led out his army against the runaways, and, having called in the Afgháns to attack Delhi on the other side, brought about the ruin of both the Hindu kingdoms.

Distribution of Rájputs, *circ.* 1184.

The tale serves to record the dissensions among the Rájput princes, which prevented a united resistance to Muhammad of Ghor. He found Delhi occupied by the Tomára clan, Ajmere by the Chauháns, and Kanauj by the Ráhtors. These Rájput States formed the natural breakwaters against invaders from the north-west. But their feuds are said to have left the King of Delhi and Ajmere, then united under one Chauhán Over-lord, only 64 out of his 108 warrior chiefs. In 1193, the Afgháns again swept down on the Punjab. Prithwí Rájá of Delhi and Ajmere[3] was defeated and slain. His heroic princess burned herself on his funeral pile. Muhammad of Ghor, having occupied Delhi, pressed on to Ajmere; and in

---

[1] See article KANAUJ, *The Imperial Gazetteer of India.*

[2] *Aswa-medha,* described in a previous chapter.

[3] Descended from the eponymous Rájá Aja of Ajmere, *circ.* 145 A.D.; and on the mother's side, from Anang Pál Tuar, Rájá of Delhi, who adopted him; thus uniting Delhi to Ajmere. See article AJMERE-MERWARA, in *The Imperial Gazetteer of India.*

1194, overthrew the rival Hindu monarch of Kanauj, whose body was identified on the field of battle by his false teeth. The brave Ráhtor Rájputs of Kanauj, with other of the Rájput Rájput clans in Northern India, quitted their homes in large migrations bodies rather than submit to the stranger. They migrated putána. into Ráj- to the regions bordering on the eastern desert of the Indus, and there founded the military kingdoms which bear their race-name, Rájputána, to this day.

History takes her narrative of these events from the matter-of-fact statements of the Persian annalists.[1] But the Hindu court-bard of Prithwí Rájá left behind a patriotic version of the fall of his race. His ballad-chronicle, known as the *Prithwíráj Rásau* of Chánd, is one of the earliest poems in Hindí. It depicts the Musalmán invaders as beaten in all the battles except the last fatal one. Their leader is taken prisoner by the Hindus, and released for a heavy ransom. But the quarrels of the chiefs ruined the Hindu cause.

Setting aside these patriotic songs, Benares and Gwalior mark the south-western limits of Muhammad of Ghor's own advance. But his general, Bakhtiyár Khiljí, conquered Behar in 1199,[2] Muham-and Lower Bengal down to the delta in 1203. On the conquest of approach of the Musalmáns, the Bráhmans advised Lakshman Bengal, Sen, the King of Bengal, to remove his residence from Nadiyá 1203. to some more distant city. But the prince, an old man of eighty, could not make up his mind until the Afghán general had seized his capital, and burst into the palace one day while his majesty was at dinner. The monarch slipped out by a back door without having time to put on his shoes, and fled to Purí in Orissa, where he spent his remaining days in the service of Jagannáth.[3]

Meanwhile the Sultán, Muhammad Ghorí, divided his time between campaigns in Afghánistán and Indian invasions; and he had little time to consolidate his Indian conquests. Even in the Punjab, the tribes were defeated rather than sub-dued. In 1203, the Ghakkars issued from their mountains,

[1] *Firishta* (i. 161-187), the *Tabakát-i-Násirí* of Minháju-s-Siráj, and others; translated in Sir Henry Elliot's *Persian Historians*, vols. ii. v. and vi.

[2] *History of Bengal from the first Muhammadan Invasion to* 1757, by Major Charles Stewart, p. 25 (Calcutta, 1847). The nearly contemporary authority is the *Tabakát-i-Násirí* (1227-41); Sir H. Elliot's *Persian Historians*, vol. ii. pp. 307-309.

[3] Stewart, p. 27. The *Tabakát-i-Násirí* merely says 'he went towards Sanknát' (*sic*) (Jagannáth?); Sir H. Elliot's *Persian Historians*, vol. ii. p. 309.

took Lahore,[1] and devastated the whole Province.[2] In 1206,
a party of the same clan swam the Indus, on the bank of
which the Afghán camp was pitched, and stabbed the Sultán
to death while asleep in his tent.[3]

Muhammad of Ghor's work in India, 1191–1206.   Muhammad of Ghor was no religious knight-errant like
Mahmúd of Ghazní, but a practical conqueror. The objects
of his distant expeditions were not temples, but Provinces.
Subuktigín had left Peshawar as an outpost of Ghazni (977
A.D.); and Mahmúd had reduced the western Punjab to an
outlying Province of the same kingdom (1030 A.D.). That
was the net result of the Túrkí invasions of India. But
Muhammad of Ghor left the whole north of India, from the
delta of the Indus to the delta of the Ganges, under Muhammadan generals, who on his death set up for themselves.

Northern India subdued.   His Indian Viceroy, Kutab-ud-dín, proclaimed himself sovereign of India at Delhi, and founded a line which
lasted from 1206 to 1290. Kutab claimed the control over
Kutab-ud-dín, 1206-10; all the Muhammadan leaders and soldiers of fortune in
India from Sind to Lower Bengal. His name is preserved
at his capital by the Kutab Mosque, with its graceful
colonnade of richly-sculptured Hindu pillars, and by the
Kutab *Minár*,[4] which raises its tapering shaft, encrusted with
chapters from the Kurán, high above the ruins of old Delhi.
first 'Slave King.' Kutab-ud-dín had started life as a Túrkí slave, and several of
his successors rose by valour or intrigue from the same low
condition to the throne. His dynasty is accordingly known
as that of the Slave Kings. Under them India became for
the first time the seat of resident Muhammadan sovereigns.
Kutab-ud-dín died in 1210.[5]

The Slave Dynasty, 1206-90.   The Slave Dynasty found itself face to face with the three
perils which have beset the Muhammadan rule in India from
the outset, and beneath which that rule eventually succumbed.
First, rebellions by its own servants, Musalmán generals,
or viceroys of Provinces; second, revolts of the Hindus;

---

[1] *Firishta*, vol. i. pp. 182–184.

[2] As far south as the country near Múltán, *Táju-l-Ma-ásir;* Sir H.
Elliot's *Persian Historians*, vol. ii. pp. 233–235 ; *Tárikh-i-Alfí*, v. 163.
The Muhammadan historians naturally minimize this episode.

[3] Sir H. Elliot's *Persian Historians*, vol. ii. pp. 235, 297, 393. Brigg's
Firishta, vol. i. pp. 185, 186.

[4] *The Imperial Gazetteer of Indian*, article DELHI CITY.

[5] The original materials for Kutab-ud-dín Aibak's reign are to be found
in *Firishta*, vol. i. pp. 189-202 (ed. 1829) ; and the *Persian Historians*,
translated by Sir Henry Elliot, vols. ii. iii. iv. and v.

third, fresh invasions, chiefly by Mughals, from Central Asia.

Altamsh, the third and greatest Sultán of the Slave line Its difficul-(1211–36 A.D.), had to reduce the Muhammadan Governors of ties. Lower Bengal and Sind, both of whom had set up as independent rulers; and he narrowly escaped destruction by a Mughal invasion. The Mughals under Changíz Khán swept through the Indian passes in pursuit of an Afghán prince; but their progress was stayed by the Indus, and Delhi remained untouched. Before the death of Altamsh (1236 A.D.), the Hindus Altamsh, had ceased for a time to struggle openly; and the Muhammadan 1211–36. Viceroys of Delhi ruled all India on the north of the Vindhya range, including the Punjab, the North-Western Provinces, Oudh, Behar, Lower Bengal, Ajmere, Gwalior, Málwá, and Sind. The Khálif of Baghdád acknowledged India as a separate Muhammadan kingdom during the reign of Altamsh, and struck coins in recognition of the new Empire of Delhi (1229 A.D.).[1] Altamsh died in 1236.

His daughter Raziyá was the only lady who ever occupied The the Muhammadan throne of Delhi (1236–39 A.D.). Learned Empress Raziyá, in the Kurán, industrious in public business, firm and energetic 1236–39. in every crisis, she bears in history the masculine name of the *Sultán* Raziyá. But the favour which she showed to the master of the horse, an Abyssinian slave, offended her Afghán generals; and after a troubled reign of three and a half years, she was deposed and put to death.[2]

Mughal irruptions and Hindu revolts soon began to under- Mughal mine the Slave dynasty. The Mughals are said to have burst irruptions 1244-88. through Tibet into North-Eastern Bengal in 1245;[3] and during the next forty-four years, repeatedly swept down the Afghán passes into the Punjab (1244–88). The wild Indian tribes, such as the Ghakkars[4] and the hillmen of Mewát, ravaged the Muhammadan lowlands almost up to the capital.

[1] *Chronicles of the Pathán Kings of Delhi*, by Edward Thomas, p. 46 (Milne, 1871). Original materials for Shams-ud-dín Altamsh : *Firishta*, vol. i. pp. 205-212 (1829) ; Sir Henry Elliot's *Persian Historians*, vols. ii. iii. iv.

[2] Thomas' *Chronicles of the Pathán Kings*, pp. 104-108 ; *Firishta*, vol. i. pp. 217-222 ; Sir Henry Elliot's *Persian Historians*, vols. ii. and iii.

[3] This invasion of Bengal is discredited by the latest and most critical historian, Mr. Edward Thomas, in his *Pathán Kings of Delhi*, p. 121, note (ed. 1871). On the other side, see *Firishta*, vol. i. p. 231, but cf. Col. Brigg's footnote ; and the *Tabakát-i-Násirí* in Sir H. Elliot's *Persian Historians*, vol. ii. pp. 264, 344 ; ' In March 1245, the infidels of Changíz Khán came to the gates of Lakhnautí ' (Gaur).

[4] For an account of the Ghakkars, *vide ante*, p. 186, chap. vii

Rájput
revolts.

Rájput revolts foreshadowed that inextinguishable vitality of the Hindu military races, which was to harass, from first to last, the Mughal Empire, and to outlive it. Under the Slave kings, even the north of India was only half subdued to the Muhammadan sway. The Hindus rose again and again in Málwá, Rájputána, Bundelkhand, along the Ganges, and in the Jumna valley, marching to the river bank opposite Delhi itself.[1]

Balban,
1265-87.

The last monarch but one of the Slave line, Balban (1265-87 A.D.), had not only to fight the Mughals, the wild non-Aryan tribes, and the Rájput clans; he was also compelled to massacre his own viceroys. Having in his youth entered into a compact for mutual support and advancement with forty of his Túrkí fellow-slaves in the palace, he had, when he came to the throne, to break the powerful confederacy thus formed. Some of his provincial governors he publicly scourged; others were beaten to death in his presence; and a general, who failed to reduce the rebel Muhammadan

His
cruelties
to the
Hindus.

Viceroy of Bengal, was hanged. Balban himself moved down to the delta, and crushed the Bengal revolt with a merciless skill. His severity against Hindu rebels knew no bounds. He nearly exterminated the Jadún Rájputs of Mewát, to the south of Delhi, putting 100,000 persons to the sword. He then cut down the forests which formed their retreats, and opened up the country to tillage. The miseries caused by the Mughal hordes in Central Asia, drove a crowd of princes and

His fifteen
royal pen-
sioners.

poets to seek shelter at the Indian court. Balban boasted that no fewer than fifteen once independent sovereigns had fed on his bounty, and he called the streets of Delhi by the names of their late kingdoms, such as Bághdad, Kharizm, and Ghor. He died in 1287 A.D.[2] His successor was poisoned, and the Slave dynasty ended in 1290.[3]

House of
Khiljí,
1290-1320.

In that year Jalál-ud-dín, a ruler of Khiljí, succeeded to the Delhi throne, and founded a line which lasted for thirty years (1290-1320 A.D.). The Khiljí dynasty extended the Muhammadan power into Southern India. Alá-ud-dín, the nephew and successor of the founder, when Governor of Karra,[4] near Allahábád, pierced through the Vindhyá ranges

---

[1] Thomas' *Pathán Kings*, 131.

[2] Materials for the reign of Balban (Ghiyás-ud-dín Balban) : Sir Henry Elliot's *Persian Historians*, vol. iii. pp. 38, 97, 546, 593 (1871) ; *Firishta*, vol. i. pp. 247-272 (1829).

[3] Mr. E. Thomas' *Pathán Kings*, pp. 138-142.

[4] Forty miles north-west of Allahábád, once the capital of an important fief, now a ruined town. See *The Imperial Gazetteer of India*, article KARRA.

with his cavalry, and plundered the Buddhist temple city of Bhílsa, 300 miles off. After trying his powers against the rebellious Hindu princes of Bundelkhand and Málwá, he conceived the idea of a grand raid into the Deccan. With a band of 8000 horse, he rode into the heart of Southern India. On the way he gave himself out as flying from his uncle's court, to seek service with the Hindu King of Rájáma-hendri. The generous Rájput princes abstained from attacking a refugee in his flight, and Alá-ud-dín surprised the great city of Deogiri, the modern Daulatábád, at that time the capital of the Hindu kingdom of Maháráshtra. Having suddenly galloped into its streets, he announced himself as only the advance guard of the whole imperial army, levied an immense booty, and carried it back 700 miles to the seat of his Governorship on the banks of the Ganges. He then lured the Sultán Jalál-ud-dín, his uncle, to Karra, in order to divide the spoil; and murdered the old man in the act of clasping his hand (1295 A.D.).[1]

Alá-ud-dín scattered his spoils in gifts or charity, and pro-claimed himself Sultán (1295-1315 A.D.).[2] The twenty years of his reign founded the Muhammadan sway in Southern India. He reconquered Gujarát from the Hindus in 1297; captured Rintimbur,[3] after a difficult siege, from the Jaipur Rájputs in 1300; took the fort of Chittor, and partially sub-jected the Sesodia Rájputs (1303); and having thus reduced the Hindus on the north of the Vindhyas, prepared for the conquest of the Deccan. But before starting on this great expedition, he had to meet five Mughal inroads from the north. In 1295 he defeated a Mughal invasion under the walls of his capital, Delhi; in 1304-5 he encountered four others, sending all prisoners to Delhi, where the chiefs were trampled by elephants, and the common soldiery slaughtered in cold blood. He crushed with equal severity several rebellions which took place among his own family during the same period; first putting out the eyes of his insurgent nephews, and then beheading them (1299-1300).

Having thus arranged his affairs in Northern India, he under-took the conquest of the South. In 1303 he had sent his eunuch slave, Malik Káfur, with an army through Bengal, to attack Warangal, the capital of the Hindu kingdom of Teling-

Marginal notes:
Alá-ud-dín's Southern raids, 1294.

Reign of Alá-ud-dín, 1295-1315.

Alá-ud-dín's re-conquest of N. India, 1295-1303.

His con-quest of Southern India, 1303-15.

---

[1] Thomas' *Pathán Kings*, p. 144.
[2] Materials for the reign of Alá-ud-dín Khiljí : Sir Henry Elliot's *Persian Historians*, vol. iii. (1871) ; *Fírishta*, vol. i. pp. 321-382 (1829).
[3] See article RINTIMBUR, *The Imperial Gazetteer of India*.

ána. In 1306, Káfur marched victoriously through Málwá and Khándesh into the Maráthá country, where he captured Deogiri, and persuaded the Hindu king Rám Deo to return with him to do homage at Delhi. While the Sultán Alá-ud-dín was conquering the Rájputs in Márwár, his slave general, Káfur, made expeditions through the Karnátic and Maháráshtra, as far south as Adam's Bridge, at the extremity of India, where he built a mosque.

His general, Malik Káfur.

The Muhammadan Sultán of India was no longer merely an Afghán king of Delhi. Three great waves of invasion from Central Asia had created a large Muhammadan population in Northern India. First came the Túrkís, represented by the house of Ghazní; then the Afgháns (commonly so called), represented by the house of Ghor; finally the Mughals, having failed in their repeated attempts to conquer the Punjab, took service in great numbers with the Sultáns of Delhi. Under the Slave Kings the Mughal mercenaries had become so powerful as to require to be massacred (1286). About 1292, three thousand Mughals, having been converted from their old Tartar rites to Muhammadanism, received a suburb of Delhi, still called Mughalpur, for their residence. Other immigrations of Mughal mercenaries followed. After various plots, Alá-ud-dín slaughtered 15,000 of the settlers, and sold their families as slaves (1311 A.D.).

Extent of the Muhammadan power in India, 1306.

Muhammadan population in India, 1286-1311.

The unlimited supply of soldiers which Alá-ud-dín could thus draw upon from the Túrkí, Afghán, and Mughal races in Northern India and the countries beyond, enabled him to send armies farther south than any of his predecessors. But in his later years, the Hindus revolted in Gujarát; the Rájputs reconquered Chittor; and many of the Muhammadan garrisons were driven out of the Deccan. On the capture of Chittor in 1303, the garrison had preferred death to submission. The peasantry still chant an early Hindí ballad, telling how the queen and thirteen thousand women threw themselves on a funeral pile, while the men rushed upon the swords of the besiegers. A remnant cut their way to the Aravalli Hills; and the Rájput independence, although in abeyance during Alá-ud-dín's reign, was never crushed. Having imprisoned his sons, and given himself up to paroxysms of rage and intemperance, Alá-ud-dín died in 1315, helped to the grave, it is said, by poison given by his favourite general, Káfur.

Mughal mercenaries, 1286-1311.

Hindu revolts.

A renegade Hindu Emperor, 1316-20;

During the four remaining years of the house of Khiljí, the actual power passed to Khusrú Khán, a low-caste renegade

Hindu, who imitated the military successes and vices of his Khusrú. patron, Malik Káfur, and then personally superintended his murder.[1] Khusrú now became all in all to the debauched Emperor Mubárik; slew him, and seized the throne. While outwardly professing Islám, Khusrú desecrated the Kurán by using it as a seat, and degraded the pulpits of the mosques into pedestals for Hindu idols. In 1320 he was slain, and the Khiljí dynasty disappeared.[2]

The leader of the rebellion was Ghiyás-ud-dín Tughlak, who had started life as a Túrkí slave, and risen to the frontier Governorship of the Punjab. He founded the Tughlak House of dynasty, which lingered on for ninety-four years (1320–1414), Tughlak, 1320-1414. although submerged for a time by the invasion of Timúr (Tamerlane) in 1398. Ghiyás-ud-dín Tughlak (1320–24 A.D.) removed the capital from Delhi to a spot about four miles farther east, and called it Tughlakábád.

His son and successor, Muhammad Tughlak (1324–51), Muham- was an accomplished scholar, a skilful captain, and a severely mad abstinent man.[3] But his ferocity of temper, perhaps inherited 1324-51. from the tribes of the steppes, rendered him merciless as a judge and careless of human suffering. The least opposition drove him into outbursts of insane fury. He wasted the treasures accumu- Muham- lated by Alá-ud-dín in buying off the Mughal hordes, who again mad and again swept down on the Punjab. On the other hand, in mad ex- fits of ambition, he raised an army for the invasion of Persia, peditions, and sent out an expedition of 100,000 men against China. 1324-51. The first force broke up for want of pay, and plundered his own dominions; the second perished almost to a man in the Himá- layan passes. He planned great conquests into Southern India, and dragged the whole inhabitants of Delhi, 800 miles His off, to Deogiri, to which he gave the name of Daulatábád. cruelties. Twice he allowed the miserable suppliants to return to Delhi; twice he compelled them on pain of death to quit it. One of these forced migrations took place amid the horrors of a famine; the citizens perished by thousands, and in the end the king had to give up the attempt. Having drained his treasury, he issued a forced currency of copper coins, by His forced which he tried to make the king's brass equal to other men's currency.

---

[1] Thomas' *Pathán Kings*, pp. 178, 179.   [2] *Idem*, pp. 184, 185.

[3] Materials for his reign : Sir Henry Elliot's *Persian Historians*, vols. i. iii. v. vi. vii. ; *Firishta*, vol. i. pp. 408-443 (ed. 1829) ; Elphinstone's narrative of this reign is an admirable specimen of his spirited style of work, pp. 403-410 (ed. 1866).

silver.[1] During the same century, the Mughal conqueror of
China, Kublai Khán, had expanded the use of paper notes,
early devised by the Chinese; and Kai Khátú had introduced
a bad imitation of it into Persia.   Tughlak's forced currency
quickly brought its own ruin.   Foreign merchants refused the
worthless brass tokens, trade came to a stand, and the king
had to take payment of his taxes in his own depreciated
coinage.

Revolt of the Provinces, 1338-51.
Meanwhile the Provinces began to throw off the Delhi yoke.
Muhammad Tughlak had succeeded in 1324 to the greatest
Empire which had, up to that time, acknowledged a Muhammadan Sultán in India.   But his bigoted zeal for Islám forbade
him to trust either Hindu princes or Hindu officers; and he
thus found himself compelled to fill every high post with
foreign Muhammadan adventurers, who had no interest in
the stability of his rule.   The annals of the period present a
long series of outbreaks, one part of the Empire renouncing
its allegiance as soon as another had been brought back to
He flays his nephew.
subjection.   His own nephew rebelled in Málwá, and being
caught, was flayed alive (1338).   The Punjab governor revolted
(1339), was crushed, and put to death.   The Musalmán Viceroys of Lower Bengal and of the Coromandel coast set up
for themselves (about 1340), and could not be subdued.
The Hindu kingdoms of Karnáta and Telingána recovered
their independence (1344), and expelled the Musalmán
His reign one long revolt.
garrisons.   The Muhammadan governors in the Deccan also
revolted, while the troops in Gujarát rose in mutiny.   Muhammad Tughlak rushed with an army to the south to take
vengeance on the traitors, but hardly had he put down their
rising than he was called away by insurrections in Gujarát,
Málwá, and Sind.   He died in 1351, while chasing rebels in
the lower valley of the Indus.

Muhammad Tughlak's revenue exactions, 1325-51.
Muhammad Tughlak was the first Musalmán ruler of India
who can be said to have had a revenue system.   He increased
the land-tax between the Ganges and the Jumna; in some
Districts ten-fold, in others twenty-fold.   The husbandmen fled
before his tax-gatherers, leaving their villages to lapse into
jungle, and formed themselves into robber clans.   He cruelly
punished all who trespassed on his game preserves; and he
invented a kind of man-hunt without precedent in the annals
His 'man-hunt.'
of human wickedness.   He surrounded a large tract with his
army, 'and then gave orders that the circle should close

[1] Thomas' *Pathán Kings*, p. 243.   See his valuable monograph entitled
'Muhammad Bin Tughlak's Forced Currency,' *op. cit.* pp. 239-261.

towards the centre, and that all within it (mostly inoffensive peasants) should be slaughtered like wild beasts. This sort of hunt was more than once repeated; and on a subsequent occasion, there was a general massacre of the inhabitants of the great city of Kanauj. These horrors led in due time to famine; and the miseries of the country exceeded all powers of description.'[1]

His son, Fíruz Tughlak (1351–88), ruled mercifully, but had to recognise the independence of the Muhammadan kingdoms of Bengal and the Deccan, and suffered much from bodily infirmities and court intrigues.[2] He undertook many public works, such as dams across rivers for irrigation, tanks, caravan-saráis, mosques, colleges, hospitals, and bridges. But his greatest achievement was the old Jumna Canal. This work drew its waters from the Jumna, near a point where it leaves the mountains, and connected that river with the Ghaggar and the Sutlej by irrigation channels.[3] Part of it has been reconstructed by the British Government, and spreads a margin of fertility on either side to this day. But the dynasty of Tughlak soon sunk amid Muhammadan mutinies and Hindu revolts; and under Mahmúd, its last real king, Northern India fell an easy prey to the great Mughal invasion of 1398. Fíruz Sháh Tughlak, 1351–88.
His canals.
Mahmúd Tughlak.

In that year, Timúr (Tamerlane) swept through the Afghán passes at the head of the united hordes of Tartary. He defeated the Tughlak King, Mahmúd, under the walls of Delhi, and entered the capital. During five days, a massacre raged; 'some streets were rendered impassable by heaps of dead,'[4] while Timúr calmly looked on and held a feast in honour of his victory. On the last day of 1398 he resumed his march, with a 'sincere and humble tribute of grateful praise' to God, in Fíruz's marble mosque on the banks of the Jumna. He crossed the Ganges, and proceeded as far as Hardwár, after another great massacre at Meerut. Then, skirting the foot of the Himálayas, he retired through their north-western passes into Central Asia (1399). Timúr's (Tamer-lane's) invasion, 1398.

Timúr left no traces of his power in India, save ruined cities. On his departure, Mahmúd Tughlak crept back from Ruin of the Tugh-laks, 1399.

[1] Elphinstone's *History of India,* pp. 405, 406 (ed. 1866).

[2] Materials for his reign: Sir Henry Elliot's *Persian Historians,* vols. i. iii. iv. vi. viii. ; *Firishta,* vol. i. pp. 444–465 (ed. 1829).

[3] Thomas' *Pathán Kings,* p. 294. See article JUMNA CANAL, WESTERN, *The Imperial Gazetteer of India.*

[4] *Firishta,* vol. i. p. 493. His whole account of Timúr's invasion is very vivid, vol. i. pp. 485 497 (ed. 1829).

his retreat in Gujarát, and nominally ruled till 1412. The Tughlak line ended in 1414.

The Sayyids, 1414-50. It was succeeded by the Sayyid dynasty, who ruled from 1414 till 1450. The Afghán house of Lodi followed, from 1450 to 1526. But some of these Sultáns reigned over only a few miles round Delhi; and during the whole period, the Hindu princes and the local Muhammadan kings were practically independent throughout the greater part of India. The house of Lodi was crushed beneath the Mughal invasion of Bábar in 1526.

The Lodis, 1450-1526.

Hindu kingdoms of the Deccan. Bábar founded the Mughal Empire of India, whose last representative died a British State prisoner at Rangoon in 1862. Before entering on the story of that great Empire, we must survey for a moment the kingdoms, Hindu and Muhammadan, on the south of the Vindhya range. The three ancient kingdoms, Chera, Chola, and Pándya occupied, as we have seen,[1] the Dravidian country peopled by Tamil-speaking races. Pándya, the largest of them, had its capital at Madura, and traces its foundation to the 4th century B.C. The Chola kingdom had its head-quarters successively at Combaconum and Tanjore. Talkad, in Mysore, now buried by the sands of the Káveri, was the capital of the Chera kingdom. The 116th king of the Pándya dynasty was overthrown by the Muhammadan general Malik Káfur, *circ.* 1304. But the Musalmáns failed to establish their power in the extreme south, and a series of Hindu dynasties ruled from Madura over the old Pándya kingdom until the 18th century. No European kingdom can boast a continuous succession such as that of Madura, traced back by the piety of genealogists to the 4th century B.C. The Chera kingdom enumerates fifty kings, and the Chola sixty-six, besides minor dynasties.

Chera, Chola, and Pándya.

Kingdom of Vijaya-nagar, 1118-1565. But authentic history in Southern India begins with the Hindu kingdom of Vijayanagar or Narsinha, which flourished from 1118 to 1565 A.D. The capital can still be traced within the Madras District of Bellary, on the right bank of the Tungabhadra river,—vast ruins of temples, fortifications, tanks, and bridges, now inhabited by hyænas and snakes. For at least three centuries, Vijayanagar dominated the southern part of the Indian peninsula. Its Rájás waged war and made peace on equal terms with the Muhammadan Sultáns of the Deccan.

Those Sultáns derived their origin from the conquest of

[1] At the beginning of this chapter; and articles CHERA, CHOLA, PANDYA, in *The Imperial Gazetteer of India.*

Alá-ud-dín (*post* 1303 A.D.). After a period of confused fighting, Muham-
the Bahmaní kingdom of the Deccan emerged as the represen- madan States
tative of Muhammadan rule in Southern India. Its founder, in the
Zafar Khán, an Afghán general during the reign of Muhammad Deccan,
Tughlak (1325-51), defeated the Delhi troops, and set up as 1303.
Musalmán sovereign of the Deccan. Having in early youth
been the slave of a Bráhman who had treated him kindly and
foretold his future greatness, he took the title of Bahmaní,[1]
and transmitted it to his successors.

The rise of the Bahmaní dynasty is usually assigned to The
the year 1347, and it lasted for 178 years, until 1525.[2] Its Bahmaní dynasty,
successive capitals were Gulbargah, Warangal, and Bídar, all in 1347-1525.
the Haidarábád territory ; and it loosely corresponded with the
Nizám's Dominions of the present day. At the height of
their power, the Bahmaní kings claimed sovereignty over half
the Deccan, from the Tungabhadra river in the south to Orissa
in the north, and from Masulipatam on the east to Goa on the
west. Their direct government was, however, much more
confined. In their early struggle against the Delhi throne, they
derived support from the Hindu southern kingdoms of Vijayanagar and Warangal. But during the greater part of its career,
the Bahmaní dynasty represented the cause of Islám against
Hinduism on the south of the Vindhyas. Its alliances and
its wars alike led to a mingling of the Musalmán and Hindu
populations.

For example, the King of Málwá invaded the Bahmaní Composite
dominions with a mixed force of 12,000 Afgháns and Rájputs. armies, 1347-1525.
The Hindu Rájá of Vijayanagar recruited his armies from
Afghán mercenaries, whom he paid by assignments of land,
and for whom he built a mosque. The Muhammadan Bahmaní
troops, on the other hand, were often led by converted Hindus.
The Bahmaní army was itself made up of two hostile Mingling
sects of Musalmáns. One sect consisted of Shiás, chiefly of Hindus and Musal-
Persians, Túrks or Tartars from Central Asia ; the other, of máns.
native-born Musalmáns of Southern India, together with Abyssinian mercenaries, both of whom professed the Sunni faith.
The rivalry between these Musalmán sects frequently imperilled
the Bahmaní throne. The dynasty reached its highest power Fall of
under the Bahmaní Alá-ud-dín II. about 1437, and was broken Bahmaní dynasty,
up by its discordant elements between 1489 and 1525. 1489-1525.

---

[1] His royal name in full was Sultán (or Sháh) Alá-ud-dín Gángo Bahmaní.

[2] These extreme dates are taken from Thomas' *Pathán Kings,* pp.
340, 341. Materials for the Bahmaní dynasty : Sir Henry Elliot's *Persian
Historians,* vols. iv. vii. viii. ; *Firishta,* vol. ii. pp. 283-558 (ed. 1829).

Five Mu-
hammadan
States
of the
Deccan,
1489-1688.
Out of its fragments, five independent Muhammadan king-doms in the Deccan were formed. These were—(1) The Adil Sháhí dynasty, with its capital at Bijápur, founded in 1489 by a son of Amurath II., Sultán of the Ottomans ; annexed by the Mughal Emperor Aurangzeb in 1686--88. (2) The Kutab Sháhí dynasty, with its capital at Golconda, founded in 1512 by a Túrkomán adventurer ; also annexed by Aurangzeb in 1687–88. (3) The Nizám Sháhí dynasty, with its capital at Ahmadnagar, founded in 1490 by a Bráhman renegade from the Vijayanagar Court ; subverted by the Mughal Emperor Sháh Jahán in 1636. (4) The Imad Sháhí dynasty of Berar, with its capital at Ellichpur, founded in 1484 also by a Hindu from Vijayanagar ; annexed to the Ahmadnagar kingdom (No. 3) in 1572. (5) The Baríd Sháhí dynasty, with its capital at Bídar, founded 1492–1498 by a Túrkí or Georgian slave. The Barid Sháhí territories were small and undefined ; independent till after 1609. Bídar fort was finally taken by Aurangzeb in 1657.

Fall of
Hindu
kingdom
of Vijaya-
nagar.
Space precludes any attempt to trace the history of these local Muhammadan dynasties of Southern India. They preserved their independence until the firm establishment of the Mughal Empire in the north, under Akbar's successors. For a time they had to struggle against the great Hindu kingdom of Vijayanagar. In 1565 they combined against that power, and, aided by a rebellion within Vijayanagar itself, they overthrew it at Tálikot in 1565.

Battle of
Tálikot,
1565.

The battle of Tálikot marks the final downfall of Vijaya-nagar as a centralized Hindu kingdom. But its local Hindu chiefs or Náyaks seized upon their respective fiefs, and the Muhammadan kings of the south were only able to annex a part of its dominions. From the Náyaks are descended the well-known Palegárs of the Madras Presidency, and the present Mahárájá of Mysore. One of the blood-royal of Vijayanagar fled to Chandragiri, and founded a line which exercised a prerogative of its former sovereignty by granting the site of Madras to the English in 1639. Another scion, claiming the same high descent, lingers to the present day near the ruins of Vijayanagar, and is known as the Rájá of Anagundi, a feudatory of the Nizám of Haidarábád. The independence of the local Hindu chiefs in Southern India, throughout the Muhammadan period, is illustrated by the Manjarábád family, which maintained its authority from 1397 to 1799.[1]

Independ-
ent Náyaks
and Pále-
gárs of
Southern
India.

Lower Bengal threw off the authority of Delhi in 1340. Its

[1] See article MANJARABAD, *The Imperial Gazetteer of India.*

Muhammadan governor, Fakír-ud-dín, set up as sovereign, with Indepen-
his capital at Gaur, and stamped coin in his own name. A dence of
succession of twenty independent kings ruled Bengal until 1538, 1340-1576;
when it was temporarily annexed to the Mughal Empire by
Humáyún.   It was finally incorporated with that Empire by
Akbar in 1576.   The great province of Gujarát in Western India Of Guja
had in like manner grown into an independent Muhammadan rát, 1391--
kingdom, which lasted for two centuries, from 1391 till con- 1573;
quered by Akbar in 1573.   Málwá, which had also set up as
an independent State under its Muhammadan governors, was
annexed by the King of Gujarát in 1531.   Even Jaunpur, Of Jaun-
including the territory of Benares, in the very centre of the pur, 1394-
Gangetic valley, maintained its independence as a separate 1478.
Musalmán State for nearly a hundred years from 1394 to 1478,
under the disturbed rule of the Sayyids and of the first Lodí at
Delhi.

CHAPTER XI.

THE MUGHAL EMPIRE (1526 TO 1761 A.D.).

State of India in 1526.

WHEN, therefore, BABAR invaded India in 1526, he found it divided among a number of local Muhammadan kings and Hindu princes. An Afghán Sultán of the house of Lodí, with his capital at Agra, ruled over what little was left of the historical kingdom of Delhi. Bábar, literally the Lion, born in 1482, was the sixth in descent from Timúr the Tartar. At the early age of twelve, he succeeded his father in the petty kingdom of Ferghána on the Jaxartes (1494); and after romantic adventures, conquered Samarkand, the capital of Tamerlane's line in 1497. Overpowered by rebellion, and driven out of the Valley of the Oxus, he seized the kingdom of Kábul in 1504. During twenty-two years he grew in strength on the Afghán side of the Indian passes, till in 1526 he burst through them into the Punjab, and defeated the Delhi sovereign Ibráhím Lodí at Pánípat. This was the first of the three great battles which decided the fate of India on that same plain, viz. in 1526, 1556, and 1761. Having entered Delhi, he received the allegiance of the Muhammadans, but was speedily attacked by the Rájputs of Chittor. In 1527, Bábar defeated them at Fatehpur Síkri near Agra, after a battle memorable for its perils and for Bábar's vow, in his extremity, never again to touch wine. He rapidly extended his power as far as Múltán and Behar. He died at Agra in 1530, leaving an Empire which stretched from the river Amu in Central Asia to the borders of the Gangetic delta in Lower Bengal.

Early life of Bábar, 1482-1526.

Invades India, 1526.

Battles of Pánípat.

Conquers Northern India, 1526-30.

Humáyún, Emperor, 1530-56.

His son, HUMAYUN, succeeded him in India, but had to make over Kábul and the Western Punjab to his rival brother Kámrán.[1] Humáyún was thus left to govern a new conquest,

A.D. [1] REIGN OF HUMAYUN :—

1530. Accession to the throne. Capture of Lahore and occupation of the Punjab by his rival brother Kámrán. Final defeat of the Lodís under Mahmúd Lodí, and acquisition of Jaunpur by Humáyún.
1532. Humáyún's campaigns in Málwá and Gujarát.

[Footnote continued on next page.

and at the same time was deprived of the base from which his
father had drawn his supplies. The Mughal hordes who had
accompanied Bábar were more hateful to the long-settled
Indian Afgháns than the Hindus themselves. After ten years
of fighting, Humáyún was driven out of India by the Bengali Humáyún
Afgháns under Sher Sháh, the Governor of Bengal. While fly- expelled
ing through the desert of Sind, as an exile to Persia, his famous Sháh.
son Akbar was born to him in the petty fort of Umarkot (1542).
Sher Sháh set up as Emperor, but was killed while storming Afghán
the rock-fortress at Kálinjar (1545). His son succeeded to dynasty of
his power. But under his grandson, the third of the Afghán 1540-56.
house, the Provinces revolted, including Málwá, the Punjab,
and Bengal. Humáyún returned to India, and with Akbar, then
only in his thirteenth year, defeated the Indo-Afghán army
after a desperate battle at Pánípat (1556). India now passed
finally from the Afgháns to the Mughals. Sher Sháh's line dis- Humáyún
appears; and Humáyún, having recovered his Kábul dominions, regains
reigned again for a few months at Delhi, but died in 1556. his throne.

AKBAR THE GREAT, the real founder of the Mughal Empire Akbar the
as it existed for two centuries, succeeded his father at the age of Great,
fourteen.[1] Born in 1542, his reign lasted for almost fifty years, 1556-1605.
from 1556 to 1605, and was therefore contemporary with that
of our own Queen Elizabeth (1558–1603). His father, Humáyún, left but a small kingdom in India, scarcely extending
beyond the districts around Agra and Delhi. At the time of
Humáyún's death, Akbar was absent in the Punjab under the
guardianship of Bairám Khán, fighting the revolted Afgháns.
Bairám, a Túrkomán by birth, had been the support of the
exiled Humáyún, and held the real command of the army
which restored him to his throne at Pánípat in 1556. He now

1539. Humáyún defeated by Sher Sháh, the Afghán ruler of Bengal, at
   Chapar Ghát, near Baxár, the Mughal army being utterly routed.
   Retreats to Agra.
1540. Humáyún finally defeated by Sher Sháh near Kanauj, and escapes
   to Persia as an exile. Sher Sháh ascends the Delhi throne.
1556. Humáyún's return to India, and defeat of the Afgháns at Pánípat by
   his young son Akbar. Remounts the throne, but dies in a few
   months, and is succeeded by Akbar.
For dates see Thomas' *Pathán Kings*, pp. 379, 380. Materials for Humáyún's reign: Sir Henry Elliot's *Persian Historians*, vols. iv. v. vi.; *Firishta*,
vol. ii. pp. 154–180 (1829); Elphinstone, pp. 441–472 (1866).

[1] Materials for reign of Akbar: the *Aín-i-Akbarí*, of Abul Fazl (old
translation by Francis Gladwin, 2 vols., 1800; best edition by Professor
Blochmann (Calcutta, 1873), left unfinished at his death); Sir Henry
Elliot's *Persian Historians*, vols. i. v. and vi.; *Firishta*, vol. ii. pp. 1812–82;
Elphinstone, 495–547 (1866).

Bairám
Regent,
1556–60.

Akbar
reigns for
himself,
1560.

became the Regent for the youthful Akbar, under the honoured title of Khán Bába, equivalent to 'the King's Father.' Brave and skilful as a general, but harsh and overbearing, he raised many enemies; and Akbar, having endured four years of thraldom, took advantage of a hunting-party to throw off his minister's yoke (1560). The fallen Regent, after a struggle between his loyalty and his resentment, revolted, was defeated, but pardoned. Akbar granted him a liberal pension; and Bairám was in the act of starting on a pilgrimage to Mecca, when he fell beneath the knife of an Afghán assassin, whose father he had slain in battle.

Akbar's
work in
India.

The chief events in the reign of Akbar are summarized below.[1] India was seething with discordant elements. The earlier invasions by Túrks, Afgháns, and Mughals had left a powerful Muhammadan population in India under their own chiefs. Akbar reduced these Musalmán States to Provinces of the Delhi Empire. Many of the Hindu kings and Rájput nations had also regained their independence; Akbar brought them into political dependence to his authority. This double task he effected partly by force of arms, but in part also by

[1] REIGN of AKBAR, 1556–1605 :—

1542. Born at Umarkot in Sind.
1555–56. Regains the Delhi throne for his father by the great victory over the Afgháns at Pánípat (Bairám Khán in actual command). Succeeds his father after a few months in 1556, under regency of Bairám Khán.
1560. Akbar assumes the direct management of the kingdom. Revolt of Bairám, who is defeated and pardoned.
1566. Invasion of the Punjab by Akbar's rival brother Hákim, who is defeated.
1561–68. Akbar subjugates the Rájput kingdoms to the Mughal Empire.
1572–73. Akbar's campaign in Gujarát, and its re-annexation to the Empire.
1576. Akbar's re-conquest of Bengal; its final annexation to the Mughal Empire.
1581–93. Insurrection in Gujarát. The Province finally subjugated in 1593 to the Mughal Empire.
1586. Akbar's conquest of Kashmír; its final revolt quelled in 1592.
1592. Akbar's conquest and annexation of Sind to the Mughal Empire.
1594. His subjugation of Kandahár, and consolidation of the Mughal Empire over all India north of the Vindhyas as far as Kábul and Kandahár.
1595. Unsuccessful expedition of Akbar's army to the Deccan against Ahmadnagar under his son Prince Murád.
1599. Second expedition against Ahmadnagar by Akbar in person. Captures the town, but fails to establish Mughal rule.
1601. Annexation of Khándesh, and return of Akbar to Northern India.
1605. Akbar's death at Agra.
N.B. — Such phrases as 'Akbar's conquest' or 'Akbar's campaign' mean the conquest or campaign by Akbar's armies, and do not necessarily imply his personal presence.

alliances. He enlisted the Rájput princes by marriage and Concilia-
by a sympathetic policy in the support of his throne. He tion of
Hindus.
then employed them in high posts, and played off his Hindu
generals and Hindu ministers against the Mughal party in
Upper India, and against the Afghán faction in Bengal.

On his accession in 1556, he found the Indian Empire
confined to the Punjab, and the districts around Agra and
Delhi. He quickly extended it at the expense of his nearest Akbar
neighbours, namely, the Rájputs. Jaipur was reduced to a extends
the
fief of the Empire; and Akbar cemented his conquest by Empire.
marrying the daughter of its Hindu prince. Jodhpur was in
like manner overcome; and Akbar married his heir, Salím,
who afterwards reigned under the title of Jahángír, to the
grand-daughter of the Rájá. The Rájputs of Chittor were
overpowered after a long struggle, but disdained to mingle their Reduction
high-caste Kshattriyan blood even with that of an Emperor. of Rájputs,
1561-68.
They found shelter among the mountains and in the deserts
of the Indus, whence they afterwards emerged to recover
most of their old dominions, and to found their capital of
Udaipur, which they retain to this day. They still boast that
alone, among the great Rájput clans, they never gave a
daughter in marriage to a Mughal Emperor.

Akbar pursued his policy of conciliation towards all the Hindu
States. He also took care to provide a career for the lesser Employ-
Hindu nobility. He appointed his Hindu brother-in-law, the ment of
Hindus.
son of the Jaipur Rájá, to be Governor of the Punjab. Rájá
Mán Singh, also a Hindu relative, did good war-service for Akbar Mán
from Kábul to Orissa. He ruled as Akbar's Governor of Singh.
Bengal from 1589 to 1604; and again for a short time under
Jahángír in 1605-06. Akbar's great finance minister, Rájá Todar
Todar Mall, was likewise a Hindu, and carried out the first Mall.
land settlement and survey of India. Out of 415 *mansabdárs*,
or commanders of horse, 51 were Hindus. Akbar abolished
the *jaziah*, or tax on non-Musalmáns, and placed all his subjects upon a political equality. He had the Sanskrit sacred
books and epic poems translated into Persian, and showed a
keen interest in the literature and religion of his Hindu subjects. He respected their laws, but he put down their in- Reform of
human rites. He forbade trial by ordeal, animal sacrifices, Hindu
customs.
and child-marriages before the age of puberty. He legalized
the re-marriage of Hindu widows, but he failed to abolish
widow-burning on the husband's funeral pile, although he took
steps to ensure that the act should be a voluntary one.

Akbar thus incorporated his Hindu subjects into the

Indian
Muham-
madan
States
reduced by
Akbar.

effective machinery of his Empire. With their aid he reduced the independent Muhammadan kings of Northern India. He subjugated the Musalmán potentates from the Punjab to Behar. After a struggle, he wrested Bengal from its Afghán princes of the house of Sher Sháh, who had ruled it from 1539 to 1576. From the latter date, Bengal remained during two centuries a Province of the Mughal Empire, under governors appointed from Delhi (1576–1765). In 1765 it passed by an imperial grant to the British. Orissa, on the Bengal seaboard, submitted to Akbar's armies under his Hindu general, Todar Mall, in 1574.

On the opposite coast of India, Gujarát was reconquered from its Muhammadan king in 1572–73, although not finally subjugated until 1593. Málwá had been reduced in 1570–72. Kashmír was conquered in 1586, and its last revolt quelled in 1592. Sind was also annexed in 1591–92; and by the recovery of Kandahár in 1594, Akbar had extended the Mughal Empire from the heart of Afghánistán across all India north of the Vindhyas to Orissa and Sind. The magnificent circumference of Mughal conquest in Northern India and Afghánistán was thus complete.

Capital
changed
from Delhi
to Agra.

Akbar also removed the seat of the Mughal government from Delhi to Agra, and founded Fatehpur Síkrí to be the future capital of the Empire. From this latter project he was, however, dissuaded, by the superior position of Agra on the great water-way of the Jumna. In 1566 he built the Agra fort, whose red sandstone battlements majestically overhang the river to this day.

Akbar's
efforts in
Southern
India.

His efforts to establish the Mughal Empire in Southern India were less successful. Those efforts began in 1586, but during the first twelve years were frustrated by the valour and states-manship of Chánd Bíbí, the queen-regent of Ahmadnagar. This celebrated lady skilfully united the Abyssinian and the Persian factions [1] in the Deccan, and strengthened herself by an alliance with Bijápur and other Muhammadan States of the south. In 1599, Akbar led his armies in person against the princess; but, notwithstanding her assassination by her mutinous troops, Ahmadnagar was not reduced till the reign of Sháh Jahán, in 1637. Akbar subjugated Khándesh; and with this somewhat precarious annexation, his conquests in the Deccan ceased. He returned to Northern India, perhaps feeling that the conquest of the south was beyond the strength of his young Empire. His last years were rendered miserable by the intrigues of his family, and by the misconduct of his

Only
annexed
Khándesh.

---

[1] Professing the hostile Sunní and Shiah creeds.

beloved son, Prince Salím, afterwards Jahángír. In 1605 he died, and was buried in the noble mausoleum at Sikandra, whose mingled architecture of Buddhist design and Arabesque tracery bear witness to the composite faith of the founder of the Mughal Empire. In 1873, the British Viceroy, Lord Northbrook, presented a cloth of honour to cover the plain marble slab beneath which Akbar lies. His death.

Akbar's conciliation of the Hindus, and his interest in their literature and religion, made him many enemies among the pious Musalmáns. His favourite wife was a Rájput princess; another of his wives is said to have been a Christian; and he ordered his son Prince Murád, when a child, to take lessons in Christianity. On Fridays (the Sabbath of Islám) he loved to collect professors of many religions around him. He listened impartially to the arguments of the Bráhman and the Musalmán, the Pársí, the ancient fire-worshipper, the Jew, the Jesuit, and the sceptic philosopher. The history of his life, the *Akbar-námah*, records such a conference, in which the Christian priest Redíf disputed with a body of Muhammadan *mullás* before an assembly of the doctors of all religions, and is given the best of the argument. Starting from the broad ground of general toleration, Akbar was gradually led on by the stimulant of cosmopolitan discussion to question the truth of his inherited beliefs. Akbar's religious principles.

The counsels of his friend Abul Fazl,[1] coinciding with that sense of superhuman omnipotence which is bred of despotic power, led him at last to promulgate a new State religion,—' the Divine Faith,' based upon natural theology, and comprising the best practices of all known creeds. Of this eclectic creed Akbar himself was the prophet, or rather the head of the Church. Every morning he worshipped in public the sun, as the representative of the divine soul which animates the universe, while he was himself worshipped by the ignorant multitude. It is doubtful how far he encouraged this popular adoration, but he certainly allowed his disciples to prostrate themselves before him in private. The stricter Muhammadans accused him, therefore, of accepting a homage permitted only to God.[2] His new faith. Divine honours to Akbar.

---

[1] Abul Fazl is accused, by the unanimous voice of the Muhammadan historians, of leading away Akbar's religious sympathies from Islám. See the valuable biography of *Shaikh Abul Fazl-i-'Allámí*, prefixed to Blochmann's *Aín-i-Akbarí*, p. xxix., etc.

[2] Akbar's perversion from Islám has formed the subject of much learned censure by Mullá 'Abdul Kádir Badáúní and other Musalmán writers. The question is exhaustively dealt with by Blochmann in a ' Note ' of 46 pages : *Aín-i-Akbarí*, pp. 167–213. See also Sir Henry Elliot's *Persian Historians*, vol. v. pp. 477 *et seq.*

Akbar's organization of the Empire.

Akbar not only subdued all India to the north of the Vindhya Mountains, he also organized it into an Empire. He partitioned it into Provinces, over each of which he placed a Governor, or Viceroy, with full civil and military control. This control was divided into three departments—the military,

Army reforms.

the judicial, including the police, and the revenue. With a view to preventing mutinies of the troops, or assertions of independence by their leaders, he reorganized the army on a new basis. He substituted, as far as possible, money payments to the soldiers, for the old system of grants of land (*jágírs*) to the generals. Where this change could not be carried out, he brought the holders of the old military fiefs under the control of the central authority at Delhi. He further checked the independence of his provincial generals by a sort of feudal organization, in which the Hindu tributary princes took their place side by side with the Mughal nobles.

Akbar's system of justice,

The judicial administration was presided over by a lord justice (*Mir-i-adl*) at the capital, aided by *Kázís* or law-officers in the principal towns. The police in the cities were under a superintendent or *kotwál*, who was also a magistrate. In country districts where police existed at all, they were left to the management of the landholders or revenue officers. But throughout rural India, no regular police force can be said to have existed for the protection of person and property until

and police.

after the establishment of British rule. The Hindu village had its hereditary watchman, who in many parts of the country was taken from the predatory castes, and as often leagued with the robbers as opposed them. The landholders and revenue-officers had each their own set of myrmidons who plundered the peasantry in their names.

Akbar's revenue system.

Akbar's revenue system was based on the ancient Hindu customs, and survives to this day. He first executed a survey to measure the land. His officers then found out the produce of each acre of land, and settled the Government share, amounting to one-third of the gross produce. Finally, they fixed the rates at which this share of the crop might be commuted into a money payment. These processes, known as the land settlement, were at first repeated every year. But to save the peasant from the extortions and vexations incident to an annual inquiry, Akbar's land settlement was afterwards made for ten years. His officers strictly enforced the payment of a third of the whole produce, and Akbar's land revenue from Northern India exceeded what the British take at the present day.

From his fifteen Provinces, including Kábul beyond the Afghán frontier, and Khándesh in Southern India, Akbar demanded 14 millions sterling per annum; or excluding Kábul, Khándesh, and Sind, $12\frac{1}{3}$ millions. The British land-tax from a much larger area of Northern India was only $11\frac{3}{4}$ millions in 1883.[1] Allowing for the difference in area and in the purchasing power of silver, Akbar's tax was about three times the amount which the British take. Two later returns show the land revenue of Akbar at $16\frac{1}{2}$ and $17\frac{1}{2}$ millions sterling. The Provinces had also to support a local militia (*búmí* = *bhúmí*) in contradistinction to the regular royal army, at a cost of at least 10 millions sterling. Excluding both Kábul and Khándesh, Akbar's demand from the soil of Northern India exceeded 22 millions sterling per annum, under the two items of land revenue and militia cess. There were also a number of miscellaneous taxes. Akbar's total revenue is estimated at 42 millions.[2]

Akbar's land revenue.

His total revenue.

[1] Namely, Bengal, £3,816,796; Assam, £385,504; North-Western Provinces and Oudh, £5,700,816; and Punjab, £1,889,807: total, £11,792,923. — *Administration Reports* (1882-83).

[2] PROVINCES OF THE DELHI EMPIRE UNDER AKBAR, CIRC. 1580.

	Land-tax in Rupees.
1. Allahábád, ...	5,310,677
2. Agra, ...	13,656,257
3. Oudh, ...	5,043,954
4. Ajmere, ...	7,153,449
5. Gujarát, ...	10,924,122
6. Behar, ...	5,547,985
7. Bengal, ...	14,961,482
8. Delhi, ...	15,040,388
9. Lahore, ...	13,986,460
10. Múltán, ...	9,600,764
11. Málwá, ...	6,017,376
12. Berar, ...	17,376,117
13. Khándesh, ...	7,563,237
14. Ahmadnagar (only nominally a Province, yielded no revenue), . . .	...
15. Tatta (Sind), ...	1,656,284
Total, .	133,838,552
16. Kábul (omitting payments in kind), .	8,071,024
Grand Total, .	141,909,576

The land revenue was returned at $16\frac{1}{2}$ millions sterling in 1594, and £17,450,000 at Akbar's death in 1605. The aggregate taxation of Akbar was 32 millions sterling; with 10 millions for militia cess (*búmí*); total, 42 millions sterling. See Thomas' *Revenue Resources of the Mughal Empire*, pp. 5-21 and p. 54 (Trübner, 1871). These and the following conversions

The large totals of Mughal taxation.   Since the first edition of this work was written, the author has carefully reconsidered the evidence for the large revenue totals under the Mughal Emperors. The principal authority on the subject is Mr. Edward Thomas, F.R.S., who has summed up the results of a lifetime devoted to Indian numismatics, in his *Revenue Resources of the Mughal Empire from* A.D. 1593 *to* A.D. 1707.[1] No one can study that work without acknowledging the laborious and accurate research which Mr. Thomas has devoted to the points involved. His results were accepted

Are they to be relied on?   without reserve in the first edition of *The Imperial Gazetteer of India*. Since the publication of this work, however, the author has received several communications from Mr. H. G. Keene, questioning the soundness of Mr. Thomas' conclusions. Those conclusions point to a comparatively heavier taxation under the Mughal Emperors than under British rule; and have been made the basis of contrasts flattering to the British administration. The author felt it, therefore, incumbent on him to submit Mr. Keene's views to the scrutiny of the two most eminent numismatists now living, namely General Cunningham and Mr. Edward Thomas himself.

General Cunningham's view.   Mr. Thomas, after examining the counter-statements, adheres to his former conclusions. General Cunningham is inclined to think that the great totals of revenue recorded by Muhammadan writers, could not have been actually enforced from India at the different periods to which they refer. He thinks that individual items may be reduced by a technical scrutiny.[2] But that scrutiny only affects certain of the entries. He rests his general conclusion on wider grounds, and believes that the revenues recorded by the Muhammadan writers represent rather the official demand than the amounts actually realized. The following pages will reproduce Mr. Edward Thomas' conclusions, as revised by himself for the first edition of this work. But they are reproduced subject to the considerations stated in the present paragraph.

are made at the nominal rate of 10 rupees to the pound sterling. But the actual rate was then about 8 or 9 rupees to the £. The real revenues of the Mughal Emperors represented, therefore, a considerably larger sum in sterling than the amounts stated in the text and footnotes. The purchasing power of silver, expressed in the staple food-grains of India, was two or three times greater than now.

[1] This monograph was written as a supplement to Mr. Thomas' *Chronicles of the Pathán Kings of Delhi.* (Trübner & Co., 1871.)

[2] See General Cunningham's Letter, dated 5th July 1883, printed in the paper 'On some Copper Coins of Akbar,' in the *Journal of the Asiatic Society of Bengal*, vol. liv. Part I., 1885.

It may be here convenient to exhibit the revenues of the Mughal Empire in India, as compiled by Mr. Edward Thomas, from Muhammadan authorities and European travellers, during the century from its practical foundation by Akbar to its final expansion under Aurangzeb in 1697, and thence to its fall in 1761:—

Mughal revenues, 1697-1761 A.D.

REVENUES OF THE MUGHAL EMPERORS AT THIRTEEN VARIOUS PERIODS FROM 1593 TO 1761,[1] FROM A SMALLER POPULATION THAN THAT OF BRITISH INDIA.

	Mughal Emperors.	Authority.	Land Revenue.	Revenue from all Sources.
1	Akbar, A.D. 1593,	Nizám-ud-dín Ahmad: not for all India, / Allowance for Provincial Troops (búmí),	...	£32,000,000 / 10,000,000
				nett £42,000,000
2	,, 1594,	Abul Fazl MSS.: not for all India,	*nett* £16,574,388	
3	,, 1605,	Official Documents: not for all India,	*nett* 16,582,440	
4	Jahángír, 1609-11,	Indian Authorities quoted by De Läet,	*nett* 17,450,000	
5	,, 1628,	Captain Hawkins,	*nett* 17,500,000	*nett* 50,000,000
6	Sháh Jahán, 1648-49,	Abdul Hamíd Láhorí,	*nett* 22,000,000	...
7	,, 1655,	,,	*gross* 26,743,970	...
8	Aurangzeb, 1655,	Official Documents,	*nett* 24,059,114	...
9	,, 1670?	Later Official Documents,	*gross* 35,641,431	...
10	,, 1695,	Gemelli Careri,	*nett* 34,505,890	...
11	,, 1697,	Manucci (Catrou),	*nett* 38,719,400	*nett* 80,000,000
12	,, 1707,	Ramusio,	*nett* 30,179,692	*nett* 77,438,800
13	Sháh Alam, 1761,	Official Statement presented to Ahmad Sháh Abdáli on his entering Delhi,	*nett* 34,506,640	...

[1] The above Table is reproduced from Mr. Edward Thomas' *Revenue Resources of the Mughal Empire*, published in 1871. Mr. Thomas has kindly revised it, from materials collected since that date. The words *nett* and *gross* are inserted by his direction.

Rája Todar Mall.

Abul Fazl.

Akbar's Hindu minister, Rájá Todar Mall, conducted the revenue settlement, and his name is still a household word among the husbandmen of Bengal. Abul Fazl, the man of letters and Finance Minister of Akbar, compiled a Statistical Survey of the Empire, together with many vivid pictures of his master's court and daily life, in the *Aín-i-Akbarí*—a work of perennial interest, and one which has proved of great value in carrying out the Statistical Survey of India at the present day.[1] Abul Fazl was killed in 1602, at the instigation of Prince Salím, the heir to the throne.

Jahángír, Emperor, 1605-27.

SALIM, the favourite son of Akbar, succeeded his father in 1605, and ruled until 1627 under the title of JAHANGIR, or Conqueror of the World. The chief events of his reign are summarized below.[2] His reign of twenty-two years was spent in reducing the rebellions of his sons, in exalting the influence

---

[1] The old translation is by Gladwin (1800); the best is by the late Mr. Blochmann, Principal of the Calcutta *Madrasah*, or Muhammadan college, whose early death was one of the greatest losses which Persian scholarship has sustained in this century.

[2] REIGN OF JAHANGIR, 1605-27 :—

1605. Accession of Jahángír.
1606. Flight, rebellion, and imprisonment of his eldest son, Khusrú.
1610. Malik Ambar recovers Ahmadnagar from the Mughals, and re-asserts independence of the Deccan dynasty, with its new capital at Aurang-ábád.
1611. Jahángír's marriage with Núr Jahán.
1612. Jahángír again defeated by Malik Ambar in an attempt to recover Ahmadnagar.
1613-14. Defeat of the Udaipur Rájá by Jahángír's son Sháh Jahán. Unsuccessful revolt in Kábul against Jahángír.
1615. Embassy of Sir T. Roe to the Court of Jahángír.
1616-17. Temporary re-conquest of Ahmadnagar by Jahángír's son Sháh Jahán.
1621. Renewed disturbances in the Deccan; ending in treaty with Sháh Jahán. Capture of Kandahár from Jáhangír's troops by the Persians.
1623-25. Rebellion against Jahángír by his son Sháh Jahán, who, after defeating the Governor of Bengal at Rájmahál, seized that Province and Behar, but was himself overthrown by Mahábat Khán, his father's general, and sought refuge in the Deccan, where he unites with his old opponent Malik Ambar.
1626. The successful general Mahábat Khán seizes the person of Jahángír. Intrigues of the Empress Núr Jahán.
1627. Jahángír recovers his liberty, and sends Mahábat Khán against Sháh Jahán in the Deccan. Mahábat joins the rebel prince against the Emperor Jahángír.
1627. Death of Jahángír.
Materials for Jahángír's reign : Sir Henry Elliot's *Persian Historians*, vols. v. vi. and vii. ; Elphinstone, pp. 550-603.

of his wife, and in drunken self-indulgence. In spite of long
wars in the Deccan, he added little to his father's territories.
India south of the Vindhyas still continued apart from the
northern Empire of Delhi.   Malik Ambar, the Abyssinian
minister of Ahmadnagar, maintained, in spite of reverses, the
independence of that kingdom.   At the end of Jahángír's _{Rebellion} ‹Rebellion›
reign, his rebel son, Prince Sháh Jahán, was a refugee in the _{of his son.} ‹of his son.›
Deccan, in alliance with Malik Ambar against the Mughal
troops.   The Rájputs also began to re-assert their independence.   In 1614, Prince Sháh Jahán on behalf of the Emperor
defeated the Udaipur Rájá.   But the conquest was only
partial and for a time.   Meanwhile, the Rájputs formed an ‹Revolt›
important contingent of the imperial armies, and 5000 of ‹of the›
their cavalry aided Shán Jahán to put down a revolt in Kábul. ‹Rájputs.›
The Afghán Province of Kandahár was wrested from Jahángír
by the Persians in 1621.   The land-tax of the Mughal Empire
remained at $17\frac{1}{2}$ millions under Jahángír, but his total revenues
were estimated at 50 millions sterling.[1]

The principal figure in Jahángír's reign is his Empress, Núr ‹The Em-›
Jahán,[2] the Light of the World.   Born in great poverty, but ‹press Núr Jahán.›
of a noble Persian family, her beauty won the love of Jahángír
while they were both in their first youth, during the reign of
Akbar.   The old Emperor tried to put her out of his son's
way, by marrying her to a brave soldier, who obtained high
employment in Bengal.   Jahángír on his accession to the
throne commanded her divorce.   Her husband refused, and
was killed.   His wife, being brought into the imperial palace,
lived for some time in chaste seclusion as his widow, but in
the end emerged as Núr Jahán, the Light of the World.   She
surrounded herself with her relatives, and at first influenced
Jahángír for his good.   But the jealousy of the imperial
princes and of the Mughal generals against her party led to
intrigue and rebellion.   In 1626, her successful general,
Mahábat Khán, found himself compelled, in self-defence, to
turn against her.   He seized the Emperor, whom he kept,
together with Núr Jahán, in captivity for six months.   Jahángír
died in the following year, 1627, in the midst of a rebellion
against him by his son Sháh Jahán and his greatest general,
Mahabát Khán.

Jahángír's personal character is vividly portrayed by Sir ‹Jahángír's›
Thomas Roe, the first British Ambassador to India (1615). ‹personal character.›

---

[1] Mr. Edward Thomas' *Revenue Resources of the Mughal Empire*,
pp. 21-26 and p. 54.

[2] Otherwise known as Núr Mahal, the Light of the Palace.

Agra continued to be the central seat of the government, but the imperial army on the march formed in itself a splendid capital. Jahángír thought that Akbar had too openly severed himself from the Muhammadan faith. The new Emperor conformed more strictly to outward observances, but lacked the

His drunken feasts.

inward religious feeling of his father. While he forbade the use of wine to his subjects, he spent his own nights in drunken revelry. He talked religion over his cups until he reached a certain stage of intoxication, when he ' fell to weeping, and to various passions, which kept them to midnight.' In public he maintained a strict appearance of virtue, and never allowed any person whose breath smelled of wine to enter his presence. A courtier who had shared his midnight revels, and indiscreetly referred to them next morning, was gravely examined as to who were the companions of his debauch, and one of them was bastinadoed so that he died.

Jahángír's justice.

During the day-time, when sober, Jahangír tried to work wisely for his Empire. A chain hung down from the citadel to the ground, and communicated with a cluster of golden bells in his own chamber, so that every suitor might apprise the Emperor of his demand for justice without the intervention of the courtiers. Many European adventurers repaired to his court, and Jahángír patronized alike their arts and their religion. In his earlier years he had accepted the eclectic faith of his father. It is said that on his accession he had even permitted the divine honours paid to Akbar to be continued to himself. His first wife was a Hindu princess ;

His religion.

figures of Christ and the Virgin Mary adorned his rosary ; and two of his nephews embraced Christianity with his full approval.[1]

Shah Jahán, Emperor, 1628-58.

SHAH JAHAN hurried north from the Deccan in 1627, and proclaimed himself Emperor at Agra in January 1628.[2] He

[1] Elphinstone's *Hist.*, p. 560 (ed. 1866), on the authority of Roe, Hawkins, Terry, Coryat.

[2] Materials for Sháh Jahán's reign : Sir Henry Elliot's *Persian Historians*, vols. vi. vii. and viii. ; Elphinstone, pp. 574-603.

REIGN OF SHAH JAHAN, 1628-58 :—

1627. Imprisonment of Núr Jahán on the death of Jahángír, by Asaf Khán on behalf of Sháh Jahán.

1628. Sháh Jahán returns from the Deccan and ascends the throne (January). He murders his brother and kinsmen.

1628-30. Afghán uprisings against Sháh Jahán in Northern India and in the Deccan.

[*Footnote continued on next page.*

put down for ever the court faction of the Empress Núr Jahán, by confining her to private life upon a liberal allowance ; and by murdering his brother Shahriyár, with all members of the house of Akbar who might prove rivals to the throne. He was, however, just to his people, blameless in his private habits, a good financier, and as economical as a magnificent court, splendid public works, and distant military expeditions could permit.

Under Sháh Jahán, the Mughal Empire was finally shorn of Sháh its Afghán Province of Kandahár; but it extended its con- Jahán quests in the Deccan, and raised the magnificent buildings in Kandahár, Northern India which now form its most splendid memorials. finally in After a temporary occupation of Balkh, and the actual re-con- 1653. quest of Kandahár by the Delhi troops in 1637, Shah Jahán lost much of his Afghán territories, and the Province of Kandahár was severed from the Mughal Empire by the Persians in 1653. On the other hand, in the Deccan, the kingdom of Ahmadnagar (to which Ellichpur had been united in 1572) was at last annexed to the Mughal Empire in 1636. Bídar fort was taken in 1657, while the remaining two of the Conquests five Muhammadan kingdoms of Southern India,[1] namely Deccan. Bijápur and Golconda, were forced to pay tribute, although not finally reduced until the succeeding reign of Aurangzeb. But the Maráthás now appear on the scene, and commenced,

1629-35. Sháh Jahán's wars in the Deccan with Ahmadnagar and Bijápur ; unsuccessful siege of Bijápur.

1634. Sháhjí Bhonsla, grandfather of Sivají, the founder of the Maráthá power, attempts to restore the independent King of Ahmadnagar, but fails, and in 1636 makes peace with the Emperor Sháh Jahán.

1636. Bijápur and Golconda agree to pay tribute to Sháh Jahán. Final submission of Ahmadnagar to the Mughal Empire.

1637. Re-conquest of Kandahár by Sháh Jahán from the Persians.

1645. Invasion and temporary conquest of Bálkh by Sháh Jahán. Bálkh was abandoned two years later.

1647-53. Kandahár again taken by the Persians, and three unsuccessful attempts made by the Emperor's sons Aurangzeb and Dárá to recapture it. Kandahár finally lost to the Mughal Empire, 1653.

1655-56. Renewal of the war in the Deccan under Prince Aurangzeb. His attack on Haidarábád, and temporary submission of the Golconda king to the Mughal Empire.

1656. Renewed campaign of Sháh Jahán's armies against Bijápur.

1657-58. Dispute as to the succession between the Emperor's sons. Aurangzeb defeats Dárá ; imprisons Murád, his other brother ; deposes his father by confining him in his palace, and openly assumes the government. Sháh Jahán dies, practically a State prisoner in the fort of Agra, in 1666.

[1] *Vide ante*, end of chap. x.

unsuccessfully at Ahmadnagar in 1637, that series of persistent Hindu attacks which were destined in the next century to break down the Mughal Empire.

Aurangzeb and his brothers carried on the wars in Southern India and in Afghánistán for their father, Sháh Jahán. Save for one or two expeditions, the Emperor lived a magnificent life in the north of India. At Agra he raised the exquisite mausoleum of the Táj Mahál, a dream in marble, designed by Titans and finished by jewellers.[1] His Pearl Mosque, the *Motí Masjid*, within the Agra fort is perhaps the purest and loveliest house of prayer in the world. Not content with enriching his grandfather Akbar's capital, Agra, with these and other architectural glories, he planned the re-transfer of the seat of Government to Delhi, and adorned that city with buildings of unrivalled magnificence. Its Great Mosque, or *Jamá Masjid*, was commenced in the fourth year of his reign and completed in the tenth. The palace at Delhi, now the fort, covered a vast parallelogram, 1600 feet by 3200, with exquisite and sumptuous buildings in marble and fine stone. A deeply-recessed portal leads into a vaulted hall, rising two storeys like the nave of a gigantic Gothic cathedral, 375 feet in length; 'the noblest entrance,' says the historian of architecture, 'to any existing palace.'[2] The *Diwán-i-Khás*, or Court of Private Audience, overlooks the river, a masterpiece of delicate inlaid work and poetic design. Sháh Jahán spent many years of his reign at Delhi, and prepared the city for its destiny as the most magnificent capital in the world under his successor Aurangzeb. But exquisite as are its public buildings, the manly vigour of Akbar's red-stone fort at Agra, with its bold sculptures and square Hindu construction, has given place to a certain effeminate beauty in the marble structures of Sháh Jahán.[3]

Marginal notes: Sháh Jahán's buildings. Táj Mahál. Delhi Mosque. Sháh Jahán's palace at Delhi.

[1] Sháh Jahán's architectural works are admirably described in Dr. James Fergusson's *Hist. Architecture*, vol. iii. pp. 589-602 (ed. 1876). See also article AGRA CITY, *The Imperial Gazetteer of India*.

[2] Fergusson's *Hist. Architecture*, vol. iii. p. 592. See also article DELHI CITY, *The Imperial Gazetteer of India*.

[3] PROVINCES OF THE DELHI EMPIRE UNDER SHAH JAHAN, 1648-49 :—

In India—					Land-tax in Rupees.
1. Delhi,	.	.	.	.	25,000,000
2. Agra,	.	.	.	.	22,500,000
3. Lahore, .	.	.	.	.	22,500,000
4. Ajmere, .	.	.	.	.	15,000,000
					————————
Carry forward,		.	.	.	85,000,000

Akbar's dynasty lay under the curse of rebellious sons. As Jahángír had risen against his most loving father, Akbar ; and as Sháh Jahán had mutinied against Jahángír ; so Sháh Jahán in his turn suffered from the intrigues and rebellions of his family. In 1658, Sháh Jahán, old and worn out, fell ill ; and in the following year his son Aurangzeb, after a treacherous conflict with his brethren, deposed his father, and proclaimed himself Emperor in his stead. The unhappy Sháh Jahán was kept in confinement for seven years, and died a State prisoner in the fort of Agra in 1666.

Rebellion of Prince Aurang-zeb, 1657.

Sháh Jahán deposed, 1658.

Under Sháh Jahán, the Mughal Empire attained its highest union of strength with magnificence. His son Aurangzeb added to its extent, but at the same time sowed the seeds of its decay. Akbar's land revenue of 17½ millions had been raised, chiefly by new conquests, to 22 millions sterling under Sháh Jahán. But this sum included Kashmír, and five Provinces in Afghánistán, some of which were lost during Sháh Jahán's reign. The land revenue of the Mughal Empire within India, under Sháh Jahán, was 20¾ millions. The magnificence of Sháh Jahán's court was the wonder of European travellers. His Peacock Throne, with its tail blazing in the shifting natural colours of rubies, sapphires, and emeralds, was valued by the jeweller Tavernier at 6½ millions sterling.

Sháh Jahán's revenues.

Brought forward,	.	Rs. 85,000,000
5. Daulatábád,	. . . .	13,750,000
6. Berar, .	. . .	13,750,000
7. Ahmadábád,	. . .	13,250,000
8. Bengal, .	. . .	12,500,000
9. Allahábád,	. . .	10,000,000
10. Behar, .	. . .	10,000,000
11. Málwá, .	. . .	10,000,000
12. Khándesh,	. . .	10,000,000
13. Oudh, .	. . .	7,500,000
14. Telingána,	. . .	7,500,000
15. Múltán, .	. . .	7,000,000
16. Orissa, .	. . .	5,000,000
17. Tatta (Sind),	. . .	2,000,000
18. Baglánah,	. . .	500,000
Land Revenue of India,	.	207,750,000
19. Kashmír,	. . .	3,750,000
20. Kábul, .	. . .	4,000,000
21. Balkh, .	. . .	2,000,000
22. Kandahár,	. . .	1,500,000
23. Badakhshan,	. . .	1,000,000

Total Rs. 220,000,000

— Mr. Edward Thomas *Revenue Resources of the Mughal Empire*, p. 28.

Aurang-
zeb's
usurpa-
tion, 1658.

AURANGZEB proclaimed himself Emperor in 1658, in the room of his imprisoned father, with the title of Alamgír, the Conqueror of the Universe, and reigned until 1707. Under Aurangzeb, the Mughal Empire reached its widest limits.[1] But his long rule of forty-nine years merely presents on a more magnificent stage the old unhappy type of a Mughal reign. In its personal character, it commenced with his rebellion against his father; consolidated itself by the murder of his brethren; and darkened to a close amid the mutinies, intrigues, and gloomy jealousies of his own sons. Its public aspects consisted of a magnificent court in Northern India; conquests of the independent Muhammadan kings in the south; and wars against the Hindu powers, which, alike in Rájputána and the Deccan, were gathering strength for the overthrow of the Mughal Empire.

His reign,
1658-1707.

The chief events of the reign of Aurangzeb are summarized below.[2] The year after his accession, he defeated and put to death his eldest brother, the noble but impetuous Dárá

---

[1] Materials for Aurangzeb's reign : Sir Henry Elliot's *Persian Historians*, vols. vii. and viii. ; Elphinstone, pp. 598-673.

[2] REIGN OF AURANGZEB, 1658-1707 :—

1658. Deposition of Sháh Jahán, and usurpation of Aurangzeb.

1659. Aurangzeb defeats his brothers Shujá and Dárá. Dárá, his flight being betrayed by a chief with whom he sought refuge, is put to death by order of Aurangzeb.

1660. Continued struggle of Aurangzeb with his brother Shujá, who ultimately fled to Arakan, and there perished miserably.

1661. Aurangzeb executes his youngest brother, Murád, in prison.

1662. Unsuccessful invasion of Assam by Aurangzeb's general Mir Jumlá. Disturbances in the Deccan. War between Bijápur and the Maráthás under Sivají. After various changes of fortune, Sivají, the founder of the Maráthá power, retains a considerable territory.

1662-1665. Sivají in rebellion against the Mughal Empire. In 1664 he assumed the title of Rájá, and asserted his independence ; but in 1665, on a large army being sent against him, he made submission, and proceeded to Delhi, where he was placed under restraint, but soon afterwards escaped.

1666. Death of the deposed Emperor, Sháh Jahán. War in the Deccan, and defeat of the Mughals by the King of Bijápur.

1667. Sivají makes peace on favourable terms with Aurangzeb, and obtains an extension of territory. Sivají levies tribute from Bijápur and Golconda.

1670. Sivají ravages Khándesh and the Deccan, and there levies for the first time *chauth*, or a contribution of one-fourth of the revenue.

1672. Defeat of the Mughals by the Maráthá Sivají.

1677. Aurangzeb revives the *jaziah* or poll-tax on non-Muhammadans.

[*Footnote continued on next page.*

(1659). After another twelve months' struggle, he drove out of India his second brother, the self-indulgent Shujá, who perished miserably among the insolent savages of Arakan (1660–61).[1] His remaining brother, the brave young Murád, was executed in prison the following year (1661). Aurangzeb, having thus killed off his brethren, set up as an orthodox sovereign of the strictest sect of Islám; while his invalid father, Sháh Jahán, lingered on in prison, mourning over his murdered sons, until 1666, when he died.

He murders his brothers.

Aurangzeb continued, as Emperor, that persistent policy of the subjugation of Southern India which he had so brilliantly commenced as the lieutenant of his father, Sháh Jahán. Of the five Muhammadan kingdoms of the Deccan, three, namely Bídar, and Ahmadnagar-with-Elichpur, had fallen to Aurangzeb's arms before his accession to the Delhi throne.[2] The two others, Bijápur and Golconda, struggled longer, but Aurangzeb was determined at any cost to annex them to the Mughal Empire. During the first half of his reign, or exactly twenty-five years, he waged war in the south by means of his generals (1658–83). A new Hindu power had arisen in the Deccan, the Maráthás.[3] The task before Aurangzeb's armies was not only the old one of subduing the Muhammadan kingdoms of Bijápur and Golconda,

Subjugation of Southern India.

Rise of the Maráthá power.

1679. Aurangzeb at war with the Rájputs. Rebellion of Prince Akbar, Aurangzeb's youngest son, who joins the Rájputs, but whose army deserts him. Prince Akbar is forced to fly to the Maráthás.

1681. Aurangzeb has to continue the war with the Rájputs.

[1672–1680. Maráthá progress in the Deccan. Sivají crowns himself an independent sovereign at Ráigarh in 1674. His wars with Bijápur and the Mughals. Sivají dies in 1680, and is succeeded by his son, Sambhají.]

1683. Aurangzeb invades the Deccan in person, at the head of his Grand Army.

1686-88. Aurangzeb conquers Bijápur and Golconda, and annexes them to the Empire (1688).

1689. Aurangzeb captures Sambhají, and barbarously puts him to death.

1692. Guerilla war with the Maráthás under independent leaders.

1698. Aurangzeb captures Jinjí from the Maráthás.

1699–1701. The Maráthá war. Capture of Sátára and Maráthá forts by the Mughals under Aurangzeb. Apparent ruin of Maráthás.

1702-05. Successes of the Maráthás.

1706. Aurangzeb retreats to Ahmadnagar, and

1707. Miserably dies there (February).

[1] See article AKYAB, *The Imperial Gazetteer of India.*

[2] The five kingdoms have been described in chapter x.

[3] For the rise and history of the Maráthás, see next chapter, xii.

but also of crushing the quick growth of the Maráthá confederacy.

During a quarter of a century his efforts failed. Bijápur and
Golconda were not conquered. In 1670, the Marátha leader,
Sivají, levied *chauth*, or one-fourth of the revenues, as tribute
from the Mughal Provinces in Southern India; and in 1674,

Sivají crowns himself. enthroned himself an independent sovereign at Ráigarh. In
1680–81, Aurangzeb's rebel son, Prince Akbar, gave the
prestige of his presence to the Marátha army. Aurangzeb
felt that he must either give up his magnificent life in the
north for a soldier's lot in the Deccan, or he must relinquish
his most cherished scheme of conquering Southern India.
He accordingly prepared an expedition on an unrivalled scale

Aurang- zeb's southern campaign, 1683-1707. of numbers and splendour, to be led by himself. In 1683 he
arrived at the head of his Grand Army in the Deccan, and
spent the next half of his reign, or twenty-four years, in the
field. Golconda and Bijápur fell after another long struggle,
and were finally annexed to the Mughal Empire in 1688.

His 20 years' Marátha war, 1688-1707. But the conquests of these two last of the five Muhammadan kingdoms of the Deccan only left the arena bare for
the Maráthás. Indeed, the attacks of the Maráthás on the
two Muhammadan States had prepared the way for the annexation of those States by Aurangzeb. The Emperor waged
war during the remaining twenty years of his life (1688–1707)
against the rising Hindu power of the Maráthás. Their first
great leader, Sivají, had proclaimed himself king in 1674, and
died in 1680. Aurangzeb captured his son and successor
Sambhají in 1689, and cruelly put him to death; seized the
Marátha capital, with many of their forts, and seemed in the
first year of the new century to have almost stamped out their
existence (1701). But after a guerilla warfare, the Maráthás

His 'Grand Army' worn out, 1705. again sprang up into a vast fighting nation. In 1705 they recovered their forts; while Aurangzeb had exhausted his health,
his treasures, and his troops, in the long and fruitless struggle.
His soldiery murmured for arrears; and the Emperor, now old
and peevish, told the malcontents that if they did not like his
service they might quit it, while he disbanded some of his
cavalry to ease his finances.

Aurangzeb hemmed in. Meanwhile the Maráthás were pressing hungrily on the
imperial camp. The Grand Army of Aurangzeb had grown
during a quarter of a century into an unwieldy capital. Its
movements were slow, and incapable of concealment. If
Aurangzeb sent out a rapid small expedition against the Maráthás who plundered and insulted the outskirts of his camp,

they cut it to pieces. If he moved out against them in force, they vanished. His own soldiery feasted with the enemy, who prayed with mock ejaculations for the health of the Emperor as their best friend. In 1706, the Grand Army was so disorganized that Aurangzeb opened negotiations with the Maráthás. He even thought of submitting the Mughal Provinces to their tribute or *chauth.* But their insolent exultation broke off the treaty, and the despairing Aurangzeb, in 1706, sought shelter in Ahmadnagar, where he died the next year. Dark suspicion of his sons' loyalty, and just fears lest they should subject him to the fate which he had inflicted on his own father, left him alone in his last days. On the approach of death, he gave utterance in broken sentences to his worldly counsels and adieus, mingled with terror and remorse, and closing in an agony of desperate resignation : 'Come what may, I have launched my vessel on the waves. Farewell! Farewell! Farewell!'[1]

His despair, 1706.

Aurangzeb's death, 1707.

The conquest of Southern India was the one inflexible purpose of Aurangzeb's life, and has therefore been dealt with here in a continuous narrative. In the north of India, great events had also transpired. Mír Jumlá led the imperial troops as far as Assam, the extreme eastern Province of India (1662). But amid the pestilential swamps of the rainy season, the army melted away, its supplies were cut off, and its march was harassed by swarms of natives who knew the country and defied the climate. Mír Jumlá succeeded in extricating the main body of his troops, but died of exhaustion and a broken heart before he reached Dacca.

Mír Jumlá's expedition to Assam, 1662.

In the west of India, Aurangzeb was not more fortunate. During his time the Sikhs were growing into a power, but it was not till the succeeding reigns that they commenced the series of operations which in the end wrested the Punjab from the Mughal Empire. Aurangzeb's bigotry arrayed against him the Hindu princes and peoples of Northern India. He revived the *jaziah* or insulting poll-tax on non-Musalmáns (1677), drove the Hindus out of the administration, and oppressed the widow and children of his father's faithful Hindu general Jaswant Singh. A local sect of Hindus was forced into rebellion in 1676 ; and in 1677, the Rájput States combined against him. The Emperor waged a protracted war

Aurangzeb's bigoted policy. Oppresses the Hindus. The Rájputs revolt,

---

[1] Aurangzeb's *Letters* form a popular Persian book in India to this day. His counsels to his sons are edifying and most pathetic ; and the whole work is written in a deeply religious tone, which could scarcely have been assumed.

against them; at one time devastating Rájputána, at another time saving himself and his army from extermination only by a stroke of genius and rare presence of mind. In 1679, his son, Prince Akbar, rebelled and joined the Rájputs with his division of the Mughal army. From that year, the permanent alienation of the Rájputs from the Mughal Empire dates; and the Hindu chivalry, which had been a source of strength to Akbar the Great, became an element of ruin to Aurangzeb and his successors. The Emperor sacked and slaughtered throughout the Rájput States of Jaipur, Jodhpur, and Udaipur. The Rájputs retaliated by ravaging the Muhammadan Provinces of Málwá, defacing the mosques, insulting the ministers of Islám, and burning the Kurán. In 1681, the Emperor patched up a peace in order to allow him to lead the Grand Army into the Deccan, from which he was destined never to return.

and can-
not be
subdued.

Aurang-
zeb's
revenues.

All Northern India except Assam, and the greater part of Southern India, paid revenue to Aurangzeb. His Indian Provinces covered nearly as large an area as the British Empire at the present day, although their dependence on the central Government was less direct. From these Provinces his net land-revenue demand is returned at 30 to 38 millions sterling; a sum which represented at least three times the purchasing power of the land revenue of British India at the present day. But it is doubtful whether the enormous demand of 38 millions was fully realized during any series of years, even at the height of Aurangzeb's power before he left Delhi for his long southern wars. It was estimated at only 30 millions in the last year of his reign, after his absence of a quarter of a century in the Deccan. Fiscal oppressions led to evasions and revolts, while some or other of the Provinces were always in open war against the Emperor.

The land
revenue,
30 to 38
millions.

Maximum
Mughal
land-tax.

The following statements exhibit the Mughal Empire in its final development, just before it began to break up. The standard return of Aurangzeb's land revenue was *net* £34,505,890; and this remained the nominal demand in the accounts of the central exchequer during the next half-century, notwithstanding that the Empire had fallen to pieces. When the Afghán invader, Ahmad Sháh Duráni, entered Delhi in 1761, the treasury officers presented him with a statement showing the land revenue of the Empire at £34,506,640. The highest land revenue of Aurangzeb, after his annexations in Southern India, and before his final reverses, was 38½ millions sterling;

of which close on 38 millions were from Indian Provinces.[1] Highest
The total revenue of Aurangzeb was estimated in 1695 at 80 total revenue, 80
millions, and in 1697 at $77\frac{1}{2}$ millions sterling.[2] The gross millions,
taxation levied from British India, deducting the opium excise, 1695.
which is paid by the Chinese consumer, averaged $35\frac{1}{2}$ millions
sterling during the ten years ending 1879; and $40\frac{3}{4}$ millions
from 1879 to 1883. The table on a previous page, showing the
growth of the revenues of the Mughal Empire from Akbar to
Aurangzeb, may be contrasted with the taxation of British
India, as given in chapter xv.

[1] PROVINCES OF THE DELHI EMPIRE UNDER AURANGZEB.

LAND REVENUE OF AURANGZEB IN 1697 (according to Manucci).		LAND REVENUE OF AURANGZEB in 1707 (according to Ramusio).	
	Rupees.		Rupees.
1. Delhi, . .	12,550,000	1. Delhi, . .	30,548,753
2. Agra, . .	22,203,550	2. Agra, . .	28,669,003
3. Lahore, .	23,305,000	3. Ajmere, .	16,308,634
4. Ajmere, .	21,900,002	4. Allahábád, .	11,413,581
5. Gujarát, .	23,395,000	5. Punjab, .	20,653,302
6. Málwá, .	9,906,250	6. Oudh, . .	8,058,195
7. Behar, .	12,150,000	7. Múltán, .	5,361,073
8. Múltán, .	5,025,000	8. Gujarát, .	15,196,228
9. Tatta (Sind), .	6,002,000	9. Behar, .	10,179,025
10. Bakar, .	2,400,000	10. Sind, . .	2,295,420
11. Orissa, .	5,707,500	11. Daulatábád, .	25,873,627
12. Allahábád, .	7,738,000	12. Málwá, .	10,097,541
13. Deccan, .	16,204,750	13. Berar, . .	15,350,625
14. Berar, .	15,807,500	14. Khándesh, .	11,215,750
15. Khándesh, .	11,105,000	15. Bídar, . .	9,324,359
16. Baglána, .	6,885,000	16. Bengal, .	13,115,906
17. Nande (Nandair),	7,200,000	17. Orissa, .	3,570,500
18. Bengal, .	40,000,000	18. Haidarábád, .	27,834,000
19. Ujjain, .	20,000,000	19. Bijápur, .	26,957,625
20. Rájmahál, .	10,050,000		
21. Bijápur, .	50,000,000	Total, .	292,023,147
22. Golconda, .	50,000,000	20. Kashmír, .	5,747,734
		21. Kábul, .	4,025,983
Total, .	379,534,552		
23. Kashmír, .	3,505,000	Grand Total, .	301,796,864
24. Kábul, .	3,207,250	or £30,179,686	
Grand Total, .	386,246,802		
or £38,624,680			

The above lists are taken from Mr. Edward Thomas' *Revenue Resources
of the Mughal Empire*, pp. 46 and 50. The whole subject is admirably
discussed in his chapter entitled 'Aurangzeb's Revenues,' pp. 33 *et seq.*
The four returns of the land revenue for his reign are, *nett*, 24 millions
in 1655; $34\frac{1}{2}$ millions in later official documents; $38\frac{3}{4}$ millions in 1697;
30 millions in 1707.

[2] Mr. Edward Thomas' *Revenue Resources of the Mughal Empire*, p. 54,
etc. (1871).

Character
of Aurang-
zeb.

Aurangzeb tried to live the life of a model Muhammadan Emperor. Magnificent in his public appearances, simple in his private habits, diligent in business, exact in his religious observances, an elegant letter - writer, and ever ready with choice passages alike from the poets and the Kurán, his life would have been a blameless one, if he had had no father to depose, no brethren to murder, and no Hindu subjects to oppress. But his bigotry made an enemy of every one who did not share his own faith; and the slaughter of his kindred compelled him to entrust his government to strangers. The Hindus never forgave him; and the Sikhs, the Rájputs, and the Maráthás, immediately after his reign, began to close in upon the Empire. His Muhammadan generals and viceroys, as a rule, served him well during his vigorous life. But at his death they usurped his children's inheritance. The succeeding Emperors were puppets in the hands of the too powerful soldiers or statesmen who raised them to the throne, controlled them while on it, and killed them when it suited their purposes to do so. The subsequent history of the Empire is a mere record of ruin. The chief events in its decline and fall are summarized below.[1]

Decline
of the
Mughal
Empire.

[1] THE DECLINE AND FALL OF THE MUGHAL EMPIRE,

From death of Aurangzeb to that of Muhammad Bahádur Sháh, 1707-1862.

1707. Succession contest between Muázzim and Alam, two sons of Aurangzeb; victory of the former, and his accession under the title of Bahádur Sháh; controlled by the General Zul-fíkar Khán. Revolt of Prince Kambaksh; his defeat and death.

1710. Expedition against the Sikhs.

1712. Death of Bahádur Sháh, and accession of his eldest son, Jahándar Sháh, after a struggle for the succession; an incapable monarch, who only ruled through his *wazír*, Zul-fíkar Khán. Revolt of his nephew, Farukhsiyyar; defeat of the Imperial army, and execution of the Emperor and his prime minister.

1713. Accession of Farukhsiyyar, under the auspices and control of Husáin Alí, Governor of Behar, and Abdullá, Governor of Allahábád.

1716. Invasion by the Sikhs; their defeat, and cruel persecution.

1719. Deposition and murder of Farukhsiyyar by the Sayyid chiefs Husain Alí and Abdullá. They nominate in succession three boy Emperors, the first two of whom died within a few months after their accession. The third, Muhammad Sháh, commenced his reign in September 1719.

1720. Murder of Husain Alí, and overthrow of the Sayyid 'king-makers.'

1720-48. The Governor of the Deccan, or Nizám-ul-Mulkh, establishes his independence, and severs the Haidarábád Provinces from the Mughal Empire.

1732-43. The Governor of Oudh, who was also *Wazír* of the Empire, becomes practically independent of Delhi.

[*Footnote continued on next page.*

For a time, Mughal Emperors still ruled India from Delhi. But of the six immediate successors of Aurangzeb, two were under the control of an unscrupulous general, Zul-fikár Khán,[1] while the four others were the creatures of a couple of Sayyid adventurers who well earned their title of the 'king-makers.' From the year 1720, the breaking up of the Empire took a more open form. The Nizám-ul-Mulkh, or Governor of the

The six 'Puppet' kings.

1735-51. General decline of the Empire; revolts within, and invasion of Nádír Sháh from Persia (1739). The Maráthás obtain Málwá (1743), followed by the cession of Southern Orissa and tribute from Bengal (1751). First invasion of India by Ahmad Sháh Duráni, who had obtained the throne of Kandahár (1747); his defeat in Sirhind (1748).

1748. Death of Muhammad Sháh.

1748-50. Accession of Ahmad Sháh, his son; disturbances by the Rohillá Afgháns in Oudh, and defeat of the Imperial troops.

1751. The Rohillá insurrection crushed with the aid of the Maráthás.

1751-52. Second invasion of India by Ahmad Sháh Duráni, and cession of the Punjab to him.

1754. Deposition of the Emperor, and accession of Alamgír II.

1756. Third invasion of India by Ahmad Sháh Duráni, and sack of Delhi.

1759-61. Fourth invasion of India by Ahmad Sháh Duráni, and murder of the Emperor Alamgír II. by his *wazír*, Ghází-ud-dín. The Marátha conquests in Northern India. The Maráthás complete their organization for the conquest of Hindustán; capture of Delhi.

1761-1805. The third battle of Pánípat, between the Afgháns under Ahmad Sháh and the Maráthás; defeat of the latter. From this time the Mughal Empire ceased to exist, except in name. The victory of Baxar, gained by Major Munro, breaks the Mughal power in Bengal. The Diwáni, or administration, of Bengal, Behar, and Orissa is granted by the Emperor to the British in 1765. The nominal Emperor on the death of Alamgír II. was Sháh Alam II., an exile, who resided till 1771 in Allahábád, a pensioner of the British. In 1771 he threw in his fortunes with the Maráthás, who restored him to a fragment of his hereditary dominions. The Emperor was blinded and imprisoned by rebels. He was afterwards rescued by the Maráthás, but was virtually a prisoner in their hands till 1803, when the Marátha power was overthrown by Lord Lake. Sháh Alam died in 1806, and was succeeded by his son,

1806-1837. Akbar II., who succeeded only to the nominal dignity, and lived till 1837; when he was followed by

1837-62. Muhammad Bahádur Sháh, the seventeenth Mughal Emperor, and last of the race of Timúr. For his complicity in the Mutiny of 1857 he was deposed and banished for life to Rangoon, where he died, a British State prisoner, in 1862. Two of his sons and grandson were shot by Hodson in 1857, to prevent a rescue, and for their participation in the murder of English women and children at Delhi.

[1] Sir Henry Elliot's *Persian Historians*, vol. vii. pp. 348-558 (Trübner, 1877).

Indepen-
dence
of the
Deccan,
1720-48;
of Oudh,
1732-43.

Deccan,[1] established his independence, and severed the largest part of Southern India from the Delhi rule (1720-48). The Governor of Oudh,[2] originally a Persian merchant, who had risen to the post of Wazír or Prime Minister of the Empire, established his own dynasty in the Provinces which had been committed to his care (1732-43).

Hindu
risings.

Oppres-
sion of
the Sikhs,
1710-16.

The Hindu subjects of the Empire were at the same time establishing their independence. The Sikh sect in the Punjab, driven by oppression into revolt, had been mercilessly crushed in 1710-16. The indelible memory of the cruelties then inflicted by the Mughal troops nerved the Sikh nation with that hatred to Delhi which served the British cause so well in 1857. In 1716, the Sikh leader, Banda, was carried about by the insulting Mughals in an iron cage, tricked out in the mockery of imperial robes, with scarlet turban and cloth of gold. His son's heart was torn out before his eyes, and thrown in his face. He himself was then pulled to pieces with red-hot pincers, and the Sikhs were exterminated like mad dogs (1716).

Rájput
indepen-
dence.
1715.
The
Marátha
chauth,
1751.

The Hindu princes of Rájputána were more fortunate. Ajít Singh of Jodhpur asserted his independence, and Rájputána practically severed its connection with the Mughal Empire in 1715. The Maráthás having enforced their claim to black-mail (*chauth*) throughout Southern India, burst through the Vindhyas upon the north, obtained the cession of Málwá (1743) and Orissa (1751), with an Imperial grant for tribute from Bengal (1751). But the great Hindu military revival represented by the Marátha power demands a separate section for itself, and will be narrated in the next chapter.

Invasions
from the
north-
west,
1739-61.
Nádir
Sháh,
1739.

While the Muhammadan governors and Hindu subjects of the Empire were thus asserting their independence, two new sets of external enemies appeared. The first of these consisted of invasions from the north-west. In 1739, Nádir Sháh, the Persian, swept down with his destroying host, and, after a massacre in the streets of Delhi and a fifty-eight days' sack, went off with a booty estimated at 32 millions sterling.[3] Six times the Afgháns burst through the passes under Ahmad Sháh Duráni, plundering, slaughtering, and then scornfully retiring to their homes with the plunder of the Empire. In 1738, Kábul, the last Afghán Province of the Mughals, had been severed from Delhi; and in 1752, Ahmad Sháh the Afghán obtained the

---

[1] Chin Khilich Khán or Azaf Sháh, a Túrkomán Sunní.

[2] Saádat Alí Khán, a Persian Shiah.

[3] Mill's *History of British India*, vol. ii. p. 456 (Wilson's edition, 1840).

cession of the Punjab. The cruelties inflicted upon Delhi and Northern India during these six invasions form an appalling tale of bloodshed and wanton cruelty. The miserable capital opened her gates, and was fain to receive the Afgháns as guests. Yet on one occasion it suffered for six weeks every enormity which a barbarian army can inflict upon a prostrate foe. Meanwhile the Afghán cavalry were scouring the country, slaying, burning, and mutilating in the meanest hamlet as in the greatest town. They took especial delight in sacking the holy places of the Hindus, and murdering the defenceless votaries at the shrines. Ahmad Sháh, 1748-61. Afghán invasions, 1747-61.

A horde of 25,000 Afghán horsemen swooped down upon the sacred city of Muttra during a festival, while it was thronged with peaceful Hindu pilgrims engaged in their devotions. 'They burned the houses,' says the Tyrolese Jesuit Tieffenthaler, who was in India at that time, 'together with their inmates, slaughtering others with the sword and the lance ; hauling off into captivity maidens and youths, men and women. In the temples they slaughtered cows,' the sacred animal of the Hindus, 'and smeared the images and pavement with the blood.' The border-land between Afghánistán and India lay silent and waste ; indeed, districts far within the frontier, which had once been densely inhabited, and which are now again thickly peopled, were swept bare of inhabitants. Misery of the Provinces, 1747-61. Afghán atrocities.

Another set of invaders came from the sea. In the wars between the French and English in Southern India, the last vestiges of the Delhi authority in the Madras Presidency disappeared (1748-61). The victory of Baxar, gained by Major Munro in 1764, broke the Mughal power in Northern India, and drove the Emperor himself to seek shelter in our camp. Bengal, Behar, and Orissa were handed over to the English by an imperial grant in 1765. We technically obtained these fertile Provinces as the nominee of the Emperor ; but the third battle of Pánípat had four years previously reduced the throne of Delhi to a shadow. The third battle of Pánípat was fought in 1761, between the Afghán invader Ahmad Sháh and the Maráthá powers, on the memorable plain on which Bábar in 1526, and in Akbar in 1556, had twice won the sovereignty of India. Invaders from the sea. Fall of the Empire. Battle of Pánípat, 1761.

That sovereignty was now, after little more than two centuries of Mughal rule, lost for ever by their degenerate descendants. The Afgháns defeated the Maráthás at Pánípat in 1761 ; and during the anarchy which followed, the British patiently built up a new power out of the wreck of the Mughal Empire.

Mughal pensioners and imperial puppets reigned still at Delhi over a numerous seraglio under such lofty titles as Akbar II. or Alamgír (Aurangzeb) II.   But their power was confined to the palace, while Maráthás, Sikhs, and Englishmen struggled for

Last of the Mughals, 1862.

the sovereignty of India.   The last nominal Emperor emerged for a moment as a rebel during the Mutiny of 1857, and died a State prisoner in Rangoon in 1862.

CHAPTER XII.

THE MARATHA POWER (1634 TO 1818 A.D.).

THE British won India, not from the Mughals, but from the British
Hindus. Before we appeared as conquerors, the Mughal India won,
Empire had broken up. Our conclusive wars were neither with the
the Delhi King, nor with his revolted governors, but with the Mughals,
two Hindu confederacies, the Maráthás and the Sikhs. Our the
last Maráthá war dates as late as 1818, and the Sikh Confedera- Hindus.
tion was not finally overcome until 1849.

About the year 1634, a Maráthá soldier of fortune, SHAHJI Rise of the
BHONSLA by name, began to play a conspicuous part in Maráthás.
Southern India.[1] He fought on the side of the two independent Sháhjí
Muhammadan States, Ahmadnagar and Bijápur, against the 1634.
Mughals ; and left a band of followers, together with a military
fief, to his son Sivají, born in 1627.[2] Sivají formed a national Sivají.
party out of the Hindu tribes of Southern India, as opposed
alike to the imperial armies from the north, and to the
independent Muhammadan kingdoms of the Deccan. There
were thus, from 1650 onwards, three powers in the Deccan :

[1] The original authorities for the Maráthá history are—(1) James Grant
Duff's *History of the Maráthás*, 3 vols. (Bombay reprint, 1863) ; (2) Edward
Scott Waring's *History of the Maráthás* (quarto, 1810) ; (3) Major William
Thorne's *Memoir of the War in India conducted by General Lord Lake*
(quarto, 1818) ; (4) Sidney J. Owen's *Selections from the Despatches of the
Marquis of Wellesley* (1877) ; (5) his *Selections from the Indian Despatches
of the Duke of Wellington* (1880) ; and (6) Henry T. Prinsep's *Narrative
of Political and Military Transactions of British India under the Marquis
of Hastings* (quarto, 1820). The very brief notice of the Maráthás which
the scope of the present work allows, precludes an exhaustive use of these
storehouses. But it should be mentioned that the later history of the
Maráthás (since 1819) has yet to be written. The leading incidents of that
history are described in separate articles in *The Imperial Gazetteer of India*.
To save space, this chapter confines itself, as far as practicable, to referring
in footnotes to those articles. Ample materials will be found in the
Gazetteers of the Bombay Districts and Central Provinces.

[2] Grant Duff's *History of the Maráthás*, vol. i. p. 90 (ed. 1863).

Three parties in the Deccan, 1650. first, the ever-invading troops of the Delhi Empire; second, the forces of the two remaining independent Muhammadan States of Southern India, namely, Ahmadnagar and Bijápur; third, the military organization of the local Hindu tribes, which ultimately grew into the Maráthá confederacy.

Strength of the Hindu or third party. During the eighty years' war of Sháh Jahán and Aurangzeb, with a view to the conquest of Southern India (1627–1707), the third or Hindu party fought from time to time on either side, and obtained a constantly-increasing importance. The Mughal armies from the north, and the independent Muhammadan kingdoms of the south, gradually exterminated each other. Being foreigners, they had to recruit their exhausted forces chiefly from outside. The Hindu confederacy drew its inexhaustible native levies from the wide tract known as Maháráshtra, stretching from the Berars in Central India to

Courted by the other two. near the south of the Bombay Presidency. The Maráthás were therefore courted alike by the Imperial generals and by the independent Muhammadan sovereigns of the Deccan. With true Hindu statecraft, their leader, Sivají, from time to time aided the independent Musalmán kingdoms of the Deccan against the Mughal avalanche from the north. Those kingdoms, with the help of the Maráthás, long proved a match for the imperial troops. But no sooner were the Delhi armies driven back, than the Maráthás proceeded to despoil the independent Musalmán kingdoms. On the other hand, the Delhi generals, when allied with the Maráthás, could completely overpower the independent Muhammadan States.

Sivají, born 1627, died 1680. SIVAJI saw the strength of his position, and, by a course of treachery, assassination, and hard fighting, won for the Maráthás the practical supremacy in Southern India.[1] As a basis for his operations, he perched himself safe in a number of impregnable hill forts in the Bombay Presidency. His troops consisted of Hindu spearmen, mounted on hardy ponies. They were the peasant proprietors of Southern India, and could be dispersed or called together on a moment's notice, at the proper seasons of the agricultural year. Sivají had therefore the command of an unlimited body of troops, without the expense of a standing army. With these he swooped down upon his enemies, exacted tribute, or forced

His hill forts.

His army of horsemen.

His tactics. them to come to terms. He then paid off his soldiery by a part of the plunder; and while they returned to the sowing or

[1] The career of Sivají is traced in Grant Duff's *History of the Maráthás*, vol. i. pp. 90–220. The Bombay reprint of Grant Duff's *History*, in three volumes, 1863, is invariably referred to in this chapter.

reaping of their fields, he retreated with the lion's share to his hill forts. In 1659 he lured the Bijápur general into an ambush, stabbed him at a friendly conference, and exterminated his army. In 1662–64, Sivají raided as far as the extreme north of the Bombay Presidency, and sacked the Imperial city of Surat. In 1664 he assumed the title of king (Rájá), with the royal prerogative of coining money in his own name.[1]

Coins money.

The year 1665 found Sivají helping the Mughal armies against the independent Musalmán State of Bijápur. In 1666 he was induced to visit Delhi. Being coldly received by the Emperor Aurangzeb, and placed under restraint, he escaped to the south, and raised the standard of revolt.[2] In 1674, Sivají enthroned himself with great pomp at Ráigarh, weighing himself in a balance against gold, and distributing the precious counterpoise among his Bráhmans.[3] After sending forth his hosts as far as the Karnátik in 1676, he died in 1680.

Visits Delhi, 1666.

Enthrones himself, 1674.

Died, 1680.

The Emperor Aurangzeb would have done wisely to have left the independent Musalmán Kings of the Deccan alone, until he had crushed the rising Maráthá power. Indeed, a great statesman would have buried the old quarrel between the Muhammadans of the north and south, and united the whole forces of Islám against the Hindu confederacy which was rapidly organizing itself in the Deccan. But the fixed resolve of Aurangzeb's life was to annex to Delhi the Muhammadan kingdoms of Southern India. By the time he had carried out this scheme, he had wasted his armies, and left the Mughal Empire ready to break into pieces at the first touch of the Maráthás.

Aurang-zeb's mis-taken policy, 1688-1707.

SAMBHAJI succeeded his father, Sivají, in 1680, and reigned till 1689.[4] His life was entirely spent in wars with the Portuguese and Mughals. In 1689, Aurangzeb captured him. The Emperor burnt out his eyes with a red-hot iron, cut out the tongue which had blasphemed the Prophet, and struck off his head.

Sambhají, 1680-89.

His son, SAHU, then six years of age, was also captured and kept a prisoner till the death of Aurangzeb. In 1707 he was restored, on acknowledging allegiance to Delhi. But his long captivity among the Mughals left him only half a Maráthá.[5]

Sahu, 1707.

---

[1] Grant Duff's *History of the Maráthás,* vol. i. p. 146.

[2] *Idem,* vol. i. chap. v. *ad finem.*   [3] *Idem,* vol. i. pp. 191–193.

[4] For the career of Sambhají, see Grant Duff's *History of the Maráthás,* vol. i. pp. 220–261.

[5] The career of Sahu is traced in Grant Duff's *History of the Maráthás,* vol. i. pp. 297–306.

He wasted his life in his seraglio, and resigned the rule of his territories to his Bráhman minister Báljí Vishwanáth, with the title of Peshwá.[1] This office became hereditary, and the power of the Peshwá superseded that of the Maráthá kings. The family of Sivají only retained the little principalities of Sátára and Kolhápur. Sátára lapsed, for want of a direct heir, to the British in 1848. Kolhápur has survived through their clemency, and was ruled, under their control, by the last adopted representative of Sivají's line[2] until 1883. On his death, in December 1883, another Maráthá youth of high family was placed by the British Government, in virtue of the adoption *sanad*, on the State cushion of Kolhápur.

Rise of the Peshwás.

Sátára and Kolhápur ; the last of Sivají's line.

Meanwhile the PESHWAS were building up at Poona the great Marátha confederacy. In 1718, Baljí, the first Peshwá, marched an army to Delhi in support of the Sayyid 'king-makers.'[3] In 1720[4] he extorted an Imperial grant of the *chauth* or 'one-fourth' of the revenues of the Deccan. The Maráthás were also confirmed in the sovereignty of the countries round Poona and Sátára. The second Peshwá, Bájí Ráo (1721-40), converted the tribute of the Deccan granted to his father into a practical sovereignty. In fifteen years he wrested the Province of Málwá from the Empire (1736), together with the country on the north-west of the Vindhyas, from the Narbada to the Chambal.[5] In 1739[6] he captured Bassein from the Portuguese.

Progress of the Peshwás, 1718.

Second Peshwá conquers the Deccan, 1721-40.

The third Peshwá, Báljí Bájí Ráo, succeeded in 1740, and carried the Marátha terror into the heart of the Mughal Empire.[7] The Deccan became merely a starting-point for a vast series of their expeditions to the north and the east. Within the Deccan itself he augmented his sovereignty, at the expense of the Nizám, after two wars. The great centres of the Marátha power were now fixed at Poona in Bombay and Nágpur in the Berars. In 1741-42, a general of the Berar branch of the Maráthás known as the Bhonslas, swept down upon Bengal; but, after plundering to the suburbs of the Muhammadan capital Murshidábád, he was driven back through Orissa by the Viceroy Alí Vardí Khán. The 'Marátha Ditch,' or

Third Peshwá, 1740-61.

Conquests in the Deccan.

Expeditions beyond it :

To Bengal, 1742-51 ;

[1] For Baljí's career, see Grant Duff's *Hist. of the Maráthás*, vol. i. pp. 307-339.

[2] See articles KOLHAPUR and SATARA, *Imperial Gazetteer of India.*

[3] *Vide ante*, p. 313.

[4] Grant Duff's *History of the Maráthás*, vol. i. pp. 324, 325.

[5] Grant Duff's *History of the Maráthás*, vol. i. pp. 393-395.

[6] For Bájí Ráo's career, see *op. cit.* vol. i. pp. 344-410.

[7] His career is sketched in *op. cit.* vol. ii. pp. 1-115.

semicircular moat around part of Calcutta, records to this day
the panic which then spread throughout Bengal.   Next year,
1743, the head of the Berar Maráthás, Raghují Bhonsla, himself
invaded Bengal in force.   From this date, in spite of quarrels
between the Poona and Berar Maráthás over the spoil, the
fertile Provinces of the Lower Ganges became a plundering
ground of the Bhonslas.   In 1751 they obtained a formal
grant from the Viceroy Alí Vardí of the *chauth* or 'quarter-
revenue' of Bengal, together with the cession of Orissa.
In Northern India, the Poona Maráthás raided as far as the To the
Punjab, and drew down upon them the wrath of Ahmad Sháh, Punjab,
the Afghán, who had wrested that Province from Delhi.   At 1760.
the third battle of Pánípat, the Maráthás were overthrown, by Pánípat,
the combined Muhammadan forces of the Afgháns and of 1761.
the Provinces still nominally remaining to the Mughal Empire
(1761).

The fourth Peshwá, Madhu Ráo, succeeded to the Maráthá Fourth
sovereignty in this moment of ruin.[1]   The Hindu confederacy Peshwá,
seemed doomed to destruction, alike by internal treachery and 1761-72.
by the superior force of the Afghán arms.   As early as 1742,
the Poona and Berar branches had taken the field against each
other, in their quarrels over the plunder of Bengal.   Before
1761, two other branches, under Holkar and Sindhia, had set
up for themselves in the old Mughal Province of Málwá and
the neighbouring tracts, now divided between the States of
Indore and Gwalior.   At Pánípat, Holkar, the head of the
Indore branch, deserted the Hindu line of battle when he saw
the tide turn, and his treachery rendered the Maráthá rout
complete.   The fourth Peshwá was little more than the
nominal centre of the five great Maráthá branches, with their The five
respective head-quarters at Poona, the seat of the Peshwás; Maráthá
at Nágpur, the capital of the Bhonslas, in Berar; at Gwalior, branches.
the residence of Sindhia; at Indore, the capital of Holkar;
and at Baroda, the seat of the rising power of the Gáekwárs.
Madhu Ráo, the fourth Peshwá, just managed to hold his own
against the Muhammadan princes of Haidarábád and Mysore,
and against the Bhonsla branch of the Maráthás in Berar.
His younger brother, Náráyan Ráo, succeeded him as fifth Fifth
Peshwá in 1772, but was quickly assassinated.[2] Peshwá,
1772.

From this time the Peshwá's power at Poona begins to Decline
recede, as that of his nominal masters, the lineal descendants of the
Peshwás,

For his career, see Grant Duff's *Hist. of the Maráthás*, vol. ii. pp. 1772-1818.
115-172.

[2] Grant Duff's *History of the Maráthás*, vol. ii. pp. 174-178.

X

of Sivají, had faded out of sight at Sátára and Kolhápur. The Peshwás came of a high Bráhman lineage, while the actual fighting force of the Maráthás consisted of low-caste Hindus. It thus happened that each Marátha general who rose to independent territorial sway, was inferior in caste, although possessed of more real power than the Peshwá, the titular head of the confederacy. Of the two great northern houses, Holkar was descended from a shepherd,[1] and Sindhia from a slipper-bearer.[2] These potentates lay quiet for a time

Progress of the northern Maráthás. after their crushing disaster at Pánipat. But within ten years of that fatal field, they had finally established themselves throughout Málwá, and invaded the Rájput, Ját, and Rohillá Provinces, from the Punjab on the west to Oudh on the east

Sindhia and Holkar, 1761-1803. (1761-71). In 1765, the titular Emperor, Sháh Alam, had sunk into a British pensioner after his defeat at Baxar. In 1771 he made overtures to the Maráthás. Holkar and Sindhia nominally restored him to his throne at Delhi, but held him a virtual prisoner till 1803-04, when they were overthrown by our second Marátha war.

The Bhonslas of Berar, 1751-1853. The third of the northern Marátha houses, namely, the Bhonslas of Berar and the Central Provinces, occupied themselves with raids to the east. Operating from their basis at Nágpur,[3] they had extorted, by 1751, the *chauth* or 'quarter-revenue' of Bengal, together with the sovereignty of Orissa. The accession of the British in Bengal (1756-65) put a stop to their raids in that Province. In 1803, a division of our army drove them out of Orissa. In 1817, their power was finally broken by our last Marátha war. Their head-quarter territories, now forming the Central Provinces,[4] were administered under the guidance of British Residents from 1817 to 1853. On the death of the last Raghují Bhonsla, without issue, in 1853, Nágpur lapsed to the British.

The Gáekwárs of Baroda. The fourth of the northern Marátha houses, namely, Baroda,[5] extended its power throughout Gujarát, on the north-western coast of Bombay, and the adjacent peninsula of Káthiáwár. The scattered but wealthy dominions known as the Territories of the Gáekwár were thus formed. Since our last Marátha war, in 1817, Baroda has been ruled by the Gáekwár, with the help of a British Resident and a

---

[1] See article INDORE, *The Imperial Gazetteer of India.*
[2] See article GWALIOR, *The Imperial Gazetteer of India.*
[3] See article NAGPUR, *The Imperial Gazetteer of India.*
[4] See article CENTRAL PROVINCES, *The Imperial Gazetteer of India.*
[5] See article BARODA, *The Imperial Gazetteer of India.*

subsidiary force. In 1874, the reigning Gáekwár, having Baroda in attempted to poison the Resident, was tried by a High Com- 1874. mission consisting of three European and three native members, found guilty, and deposed. But the British Government refrained from annexing the State, and raised a descendant of the founder of the family from poverty to the State cushion.

While these four northern houses of the Maráthás were pursuing their separate careers, the Peshwá's power was being broken to pieces by family intrigues. The sixth Peshwá, Sixth Madhu Ráo Náráyan, was born after his father's death, and Peshwá, during his short life of twenty-one years the power remained 1774-95. in the hands of his minister, Náná Farnavis. Raghubá, the uncle of the late Peshwá, disputed the birth of the posthumous child, and claimed for himself the office of Peshwá. The infant's guardian, Náná Farnavis, having invoked the aid of the French, the British sided with Raghubá. These alliances brought on the first Maráthá war (1779–81), ending with the First Mar- treaty of Salbái (1782). That treaty ceded the islands of áthá war,
1779–81. Salsette and Elephanta with two others to the British, secured to Raghubá a handsome pension, and confirmed the child - Peshwá in his sovereignty. The latter, however, only reached manhood to commit suicide at the age of twenty-one.

His cousin, Bájí Ráo II., succeeded him in 1795 as the Seventh seventh and last Peshwá. The northern Maráthá house of and last
Peshwá, Holkar now took the lead among the Maráthás, and forced the 1795-1818. Peshwá into the arms of the English. By the treaty of Bassein in 1802, the Peshwá agreed to receive and pay for a British force to maintain him in his dominions. The northern Maráthá houses combined to break down this treaty. The second Maráthá war followed (1803–04). General Wellesley Second crushed the forces of the Sindhia and Nágpur houses on the Marátná
war, great fields of Assaye and Argaum in the south, while Lord 1803-04. Lake disposed of the Marátá armies at Laswári and Delhi in the north. In 1804, Holkar was completely defeated at Díg. These campaigns led to large cessions of territory to the British, the overthrow of the French influence in India, and the replacement of the titular Delhi Emperor under the protection of the English. In 1817–18, the Peshwá, Holkar, Last Mar- and the Bhonsla Maráthás at Nágpur took up arms, each on átná war,
1817-18. his own account, against the British, and were defeated in detail. That war finally broke the Maráthá power. The Peshwá, Bájí Ráo, surrendered to the British, and his territories

were annexed to our Bombay Presidency.[1]   The Peshwá
remained a British pensioner at Bithúr, near Cawnpore, on a
End of the magnificent allowance, till his death.   His adopted son grew
Peshwás, up into the infamous Náná Sáhib of the Mutiny of 1857, when
1849. the last relic of the Peshwás disappeared from the eyes of
men.

[1] For a summary of the events of this last Maráthá war, *vide post*, pp.
401, 402.   Also Grant Duff's *History of the Maráthás*, vol. iii. *passim*.

CHAPTER XIII.

THE INDIAN VERNACULARS AND THEIR LITERATURE.

THE foregoing chapters have summarized the successive settlements of Asiatic peoples in India. The remainder of this volume will deal with altogether different aspects of Indian history. For the three essential stages in that history are— first, the long struggle for India by the races of Asia; second, a shorter struggle for India by European nations; third, the consolidation of India under British rule. From the great contest of five thousand years, England emerged the victor. We have seen how the tidal waves of Asiatic populations— pre-Aryan, Aryan, Scythic, Afghán, and Mughal—swept across India from the north. The next chapter (xiv.) will exhibit the briefer, but not less eventful, efforts of the European maritime powers to enter India from the sea. The conquest of India by the British, and an account of the administration which they have established throughout its widely separated Provinces, will conclude this volume.

The three stages in Indian history: (1) Struggle for India by the Asiatic races; (2) by the European nations; (3) Consolidation of India under British rule.

The inroads under Alexander the Great and his successors had proved momentary episodes,—episodes, moreover, of an Asiatic rather than of a European type. The Greek and Græco-Bactrian hosts entered India from the north; they effected no settlements beyond the frontier Province; and the permanent element in their forces consisted of Asiatic rather than of European troops. The civilisation and organization of India, from a prehistoric period many thousand years before Christ down to the 15th century A.D., had been essentially the work of Asiatic races. Since the end of that century, when the Portuguese landed on the Malabar coast, the course of Indian history has been profoundly influenced by European nations.

Greek inroads temporary, and semi-Asiatic in type.

Before entering on this new period, therefore, it is desirable to obtain a clear idea of India, as moulded by the survival of the fittest among the Asiatic peoples who had struggled for the Indian supremacy during so many thousand years. The social constitution of the Indian races on the

Asiatic civilisation of India.

twofold basis of religion and caste, has been fully explained. Their later political organization under the Afgháns, Mughals, and Maráthás, has been more briefly summarized. It remains, however, to exhibit the geographical distribution of the Indian races, and the local landmarks, literatures, and languages, which the Europeans found on their arrival in India.

As found by the European Powers.

India in the 1st century A. D.

Before the beginning of the Christian era, Northern India was partitioned out among civilised communities in which the Aryan element prevailed, while the southern peninsula was covered with forests, and dotted with the settlements of non-Aryan peoples. The Northern Aryans had a highly developed literary language, Sanskrit. They spoke less artificial cognate dialects, called Prákrits, which (equally with the Sanskrit) had grown out of the primitive Indo-Germanic tongue. The non-Aryans of Southern India at that period knew nothing of the philosophy or sciences which flourished in the north. They had not even a grammatical settlement of the principles of their own language; and they used vernaculars so uncouth as to earn for them, from the civilised Aryans, the name of Mlechchhas, meaning the people of imperfect utterance or broken speech.[1]

India in the 16th century A. D.

When the European nations arrived in India during the 16th and 17th centuries, all this had changed. The stately Sanskrit of the Northern Aryans had sunk into a dead language, still used as a literary vehicle by the learned, but already pressed hard by a popular literature in the speech of the people. The Prákrits, or ancient-spoken dialects, had given place to the modern vernaculars of Northern India. In Southern India a still greater change had taken place. The obscure non-Aryan races had there developed a political organization and a copious literature, written in vernaculars of their own,—vernaculars which, while richly endowed for literary uses, remained non-Aryan in all essentials of structure and type.

The Dravidians.

Leaving aside, for the moment, the changes among the Aryans in the north, let us briefly examine this survival of prehistoric non-Aryan life in the southern peninsula. The non-Aryan races of the south were spoken of by Sanskrit authors under the general name of Dravidas, and their

---

[1] For the ideas connoted by this word, and its later application to the Huns and Musalmáns, see the Honourable K. T. Telang's *Essay on the Mudrárákhasa,* pp. 4–7, 12, etc., and footnotes. Bombay.

languages under the vague term *Paisáchí.* The latter term covered, however, a wider linguistic area, from the speech of the Bhotas of Tibet to that of the Pándyas or Tamil-speaking tribes of Southern India.

Modern philology, rejecting any generic term, proves that the scattered non-Aryan languages of India belong to separate stocks. Some of the isolated tribes, who still survive in their hill and forest retreats around Bengal, entered from the north-east, and brought with them dialects akin to the Chinese. The great body of Dravidian speech in the south seems, however, to have had its origin, equally with the Aryan languages, to the north-west of the Himálayas. It would appear that long before the Aryan invasions, a people speaking a very primitive Central Asian language, had entered by the Sind passes. These were the Dravidas or Dravidians of later times. Other non-Aryan races from the north pushed them onwards to the present Dravidian country in the south of the peninsula. But the Dravidians had left more than one colony on their line of march. The Brahuís of the Sind frontier, the Gonds and Kus of the Central Provinces, the Uráons of Chutiá Nágpur, with a tribal offshoot in the Rájmahál hills overlooking the Gangetic valley,[1] remain to this day as landmarks along the Dravidian route through India.

The Dravidian language contains words apparently belonging to a phase of human speech, anterior to the separation of the Indo-Germanic from the Scythian stocks.[2] It presents affinities to the present Ugrian of Siberia, and to the present Finnish of Northern Europe; while its analogies to the ancient Behistun tablets of Media have been worked out by the great Dravidian scholar of our times.[3] Those tablets recorded the life of Darius Hystaspes in the old Persian, together with a rendering in the speech of the Scythians of the Medo-Persian Empire. They date from the 5th century B.C., and they indicate a common starting-place of the Turanian family of languages whose fragments have been scattered to the shores of

The Dravidian route.

The Dravidian language.

Its place in philology.

[1] *Introduction to the Malto Language,* p. iv. (Agra, 1884), by the Rev. Ernest Droese; to whom the author is indebted for valuable local details which he hopes to incorporate hereafter in a larger work.
[2] *Comparative Grammar of the Dravidian Languages,* by Bishop Caldwell, p. 46, ed. 1875. Unfortunately, the paging of that edition repeats itself, running as far as p. 154 in the introduction, and commencing again (in a slightly different type) at p. 1 of the Grammar itself. Except when otherwise mentioned, the pages cited in this book refer to the first or introductory series of Bishop Caldwell's numerals.
[3] *Idem,* pp. 68-72, and 106.

the Baltic, the Steppes of Northern Siberia, and the Malabar coast. This family belongs to the primæval agglutinative phase of human speech, as opposed to the inflectional stage which the later Aryan migrations into India represent. The Dravidians found refuge, after their long wanderings, in the sea-girt extremity of the Indian peninsula. In its isolation this Turanian speech has there preserved its primitive type, and forms one of the most ancient relics of the prehistoric world.

The Dravidians in Sanskrit literature.

The extrusion of the Dravidians from Northern India had taken place before the arrival of the Aryan-speaking races. The Dravidians are to be distinguished from the later non-Aryan immigrants, whom the Vedic tribes found in possession of the valleys of the Indus and Ganges. These later non-Aryans were in their turn subjugated or pushed out by the Aryan newcomers; and they accordingly appear in the Vedic hymns as the 'enemies' (Dasyus) and 'serfs' (Súdras) of the Indo-Aryan settlers. The Dravidian non-Aryans of the south, on the other hand, appear from the first in the Sanskrit as friendly forest folk, the monkey armies who helped the Aryan hero Ráma on his march through Southern India against the demon king of Ceylon.

The Tamil language still preserves evidence of a Dravidian civilisation before the southern advance of the Aryans which the Rámáyana represents. 'They had "kings,"' writes Bishop Caldwell,[1] 'who dwelt in "strong houses," and ruled over small "districts of country." They had "minstrels" who recited "songs" at "festivals," and they seem to have had alphabetical "characters" written with a stylus on palmyra leaves. A bundle of those leaves was called a "book." They acknowledged the existence of God, whom they styled Kô or King. They erected to his honour a "temple," which they called Kô-il, God's house. Marriage existed among them. They were acquainted with the ordinary metals, with the exception of tin, lead, and zinc; with all the planets ordinarily known to the ancients, excepting Mercury and Saturn. They had numerals up to a hundred, some of them up to a thousand. They had "medicines;" "hamlets" and "towns," but no cities; "canoes," "boats" and even "ships" (small decked coasting vessels).

Pre-Aryan Dravidian civilisation.

Dravidian arts.

'They were well versed in "agriculture," and delighted in "war." They were armed with "bows" and "arrows," with "spears" and "swords." All the ordinary or necessary arts of life, including "spinning," "weaving," and "dyeing," existed

[1] *Comparative Grammar of the Dravidian Languages*, condensed from pp. 117, 118.

among them. They excelled in "pottery," as their places of sepulture show. They were ignorant, not only of every branch of "philosophy," but even of "grammar." Their undeveloped intellectual condition is especially apparent in words relating to the operations of the mind. To express "the will" they would have been obliged to describe it as "that which in the inner part says, I am going to do so and so."'

While the Dravidians appear in Sanskrit literature as friends or allies, the Aryans were not their conquerors, but their 'instructors' or 'fathers.' The first Bráhman settlers in the south came as hermits or sages, who diffused around them a halo of higher civilisation. The earliest of such Bráhman colonies among the Dravidians, led by the holy Agastya, has long faded into the realms of mythology. 'The Vindhya Mountains,' it is said, 'prostrated themselves before Agastya,' still fondly remembered as the Tamir-muni, pre-eminently the Sage to the Tamil race. He introduced philosophy at the court of the first Pándyan king, wrote many treatises for his royal disciple, and now lives for ever in the heavens as Canopus, the brightest star in the Southern Indian hemisphere. He is worshipped as Agasteswara, the Lord Agastya, near Cape Comorin. But the orthodox still believe him to be alive, although invisible to sinful mortals, hidden away in the conical mountain called Agastya's Hill, from which the sacred river of Tinnevelli springs. *Legend of Agastya.*

This legend serves to indicate the influence of Sanskrit civilisation and learning among the Dravidian race. That influence was essentially a friendly one. The Bráhmans became the 'fathers' of the less advanced race; and although they classified the non-Aryan multitude as Súdras, yet this term did not connote in Southern India the ideas of debasement and servitude which it affixed to the non-Aryan races in the north. The Buddhist missionaries were probably the first Aryan instructors of the Dravidian kings and peoples, and their labours must have begun before the commencement of the Christian era. *Bráhmanic influence on the Dravidians.*

Bishop Caldwell takes the Aryan emigration under Vijaya, from Magadha in Bengal to Ceylon, *circa* B.C. 550, as the starting-point of Aryan civilisation in Southern India. Dr. Burnell, however, believes that Aryan civilisation had not penetrated deeply among the Dravidians until the advent of Kumárila, the Bráhman reformer from Behar in the 8th century A.D.[1] *Commencement of that influence.*

[1] Dr. Burnell's article in the *Indian Antiquary* for October 1872.

Bráhman hermits had doubtless taught the Dravidian peoples, and Bráhman sages had adorned Dravidian courts long before this latter date. But it was from the great religious revival of the 8th century, that the continuous and widespread influence of Bráhman civilisation in Southern India took its rise.

Dravidian speech developed
The Bráhman apostles of the Sivaite and Vishnuite faith, from the 8th to the 12th century A.D.,[1] composed their religious treatises in Sanskrit. The intellectual awakening, produced by their teaching, also gave the first impulse to the use of the vernacular languages of India for literary purposes. The Dravidians gratefully acknowledge that they owe the settlement of the grammatical principles of their speech to Sanskrit sages, among whom the legendary Agastya holds the highest rank.

into vernacular literatures.
But the development of that speech into a vernacular literature was chiefly the work of the Dravidians themselves. Indeed, the first outburst of their vernacular literature sprang from the resistance of their previous Buddhistic faith to the Bráhmanical religious revival.

The Dravidian dialects.
Before the arrival of the European nations in the 16th and 17th centuries, four Dravidian dialects had developed literatures. The Tamil, the Telugu, the Kánarese, and the Malayálam are now literary languages of established reputation. But space compels us to concentrate our attention on the oldest and most influential of the vernacular literatures of Southern India,—the Tamil.

The Tamil.
This language, in its structure and its vocabulary, forms the best representative of cultivated Dravidian speech. It has not feared to incorporate such philosophical, religious, and abstract terms as it required from the Sanskrit. But its borrowings in this respect are the mere luxuries or delicacies of the language, and they have left unaffected its robust native fabric. 'Tamil,' writes Bishop Caldwell, 'can readily dispense with the greater part or the whole of its Sanskrit, and by dispensing with it, rises to a purer and more refined style.'[2] He maintains that the Ten Commandments can be translated into classical Tamil with the addition of a single Sanskrit word. That word is 'image.'

First cultivation of Tamil.
According to native tradition, Tamil was first cultivated by the sage Agastya. Many works, besides a grammar and treatises on philosophy and science, are ascribed to him. His name served indeed as a centre around which Tamil compositions of widely separated periods, including some of recent date, gather. The oldest Tamil grammar now extant,

[1] *Vide ante*, pp. 209 and 217. [2] *Comparative Grammar*, pp. 50, 51.

the Tol-Káppiyam, is assigned to one of his disciples. But the rise of a continuous Tamil literature belongs to a later period. The Sivaite and Vishnuite revival of the Bráhman apostles in Southern India, from the 8th century onwards, stirred up a counter movement on the part of the Jains. Jain cycle of Tamil literature. Before that period, the Buddhism of the Dravidian kingdoms had modelled itself on the Jain type. We shall see hereafter that early Buddhism in Northern India adopted the Prákrit or vernacular speech for its religious treatises. On the same analogy, Buddhism in Southern India, as the religion of the people, defended itself against the Bráhmanical revival of the 8th century by works in the popular dialects. The Dravidian Buddhists or Jains created a cycle of Tamil literature, anti-Bráhmanical in tone, stretching from the 9th to the 13th century. 9th to 13th century A.D.

Its first great composition, the Kural of Tiruvalluvar, not later than the 10th century A.D., is said to have been the work of a poet sprung from the Pariah or lowest caste. It enforces the old Sankya philosophy in 1330 distichs or poetical aphorisms, dealing with the three chief desires of the human heart; wealth, pleasure, and virtue. To the sister of its author, a Pariah poetess, are ascribed many compositions of the highest moral excellence, and of undying popularity in Southern India. The Jain period of Tamil literature includes works on ethics and language; among them the Divákaram, literally the 'Day-making' Dictionary. The period culminated in the Chintámaní, a romantic epic of 15,000 lines by an unknown Jain author. Indeed, it is worthy of remark that several of the best Indian authors, whether Sanskrit or vernacular, have left no indication of their names. As it was the chief desire of an Indian sage to merge his individual existence in the Universal Existence; so it appears to have been the wish of many Indian men of letters of the highest type to lose their literary individuality in the school or cycle of literature to which they belonged. Its great Pariah poet, 900 A.D. (?) The Jain epic.

Contemporaneous with the Jain cycle of Tamil literature, the great adaptation of the Rámáyana was composed by Kambar for the Dravidian races. This work is a Tamil paraphrase or imitation, rather than a translation of the ancient Sanskrit epic. A stanza prefixed to the work states that it was finished in the year corresponding to 886 A.D. But this stanza may itself be a later addition; and Bishop Caldwell, after a careful examination of the whole evidence, places the work after 1100. The Tamil Rámáyana.

Tamil Sivaite hymnologies. Between that period and the 16th century, two encyclopædic collections of Tamil hymns in praise of Siva were gradually formed. They breathe a deeply religious spirit, and the earlier collection (*post* 1200 A.D.) still holds its place in the affections of the Tamil-speaking people. The later collection was the work of a Sivaite devotee and his disciples, who devoted themselves to uprooting Jainism (*circ.* 1500 A.D.). During the same centuries, the Vishnuite apostles were equally

Tamil Vishnuite hymnology. prolific in Tamil religious song. Their Great Book of the Four Thousand Psalms constitutes a huge hymnology dating from the 12th century onwards. After a period of literary inactivity, the Tamil genius again blossomed forth in the 16th and 17th centuries with a poet-king as the leader of the literary revival.

The Sittar Tamil poets. In the 17th century arose an anti-Bráhmanical Tamil literature known as the Sittar school. The Sittars or sages were a Tamil sect who, while retaining Siva as the name of the One God, rejected everything in Siva-worship inconsistent with

Their pure theism. pure theism. They were quietists in religion, and alchemists in science. They professed to base their creed upon the true original teaching of the Rishís, and indeed assumed to themselves the names of these ancient inspired teachers of mankind. They thus obtained for their poems, although written in a modern colloquial style, the sanction of a venerable antiquity. Some scholars believe that they detect Christian influences in works of the Sittar school. But it must be remembered that the doctrines and even the phraseology of ancient Indian theism and of Indian Buddhism approach closely to the subsequent teaching and, in some instances, to the very language of Christ.[1]

---

[1] The following specimens of the Sittar school of Tamil poetry are taken from Bishop Caldwell's *Comparative Grammar*, p. 148. The first is a version of a poem of Siva-vákya, given by Mr. R. C. Caldwell, the Bishop's son, in the *Indian Antiquary* for 1872. He unconsciously approximates the verses to Christian ideas, for example, by the title, 'The Shepherd of the Worlds,' which Bishop Caldwell states may have meant to the poet only 'King of the Gods.'

THE SHEPHERD OF THE WORLDS.

How many various flowers
Did I, in bygone hours,
Cull for the gods, and in their honour strew ;
In vain how many a prayer
I breathed into the air,
And made, with many forms, obeisance due.

The Tamil writers of the 18th and 19th centuries are Modern classified as modern. The honours of this period are divided Tamil between a pious Sivaite and the Italian Jesuit, Beschi. This writers. missionary of genius and learning not only wrote Tamil prose Beschi. of the highest excellence, but he composed a great religious epic in classical Tamil, which has won for him a conspicuous rank among Dravidian poets. His work, the Tembávani, gives a Tamil adaptation of the narrative and even of the geography of the Bible, suited to the Hindu taste of the 18th century.

Since the introduction of printing, the Tamil press has Recent been prolific. A catalogue of Tamil printed books, issued in Statistics. Madras up to 1865, enumerated 1409 works. In the single year 1882, no fewer than 558 works were printed in the vernaculars in Madras, the great proportion of them being in Tamil.

While the non-Aryans of Southern India had thus evolved

> Beating my breast, aloud
> How oft I called the crowd
> To drag the village car ; how oft I stray'd,
> In manhood's prime, to lave
> Sunwards the flowing wave,
> And, circling Saiva fanes, my homage paid.

> But they, the truly wise,
> Who know and realize
> Where dwells the Shepherd of the Worlds, will ne'er
> To any visible shrine,
> As if it were divine,
> Deign to raise hands of worship or of prayer.

The Unity of God and of Truth.

God is one, and the Veda is one ;
The disinterested, true Guru is one, and his initiatory rite one ;
When this is obtained his heaven is one ;
There is but one birth of men upon the earth,
And only one way for all men to walk in :
But as for those who hold four Vedas and six shastras,
And different customs for different people,
And believe in a plurality of gods,
Down they will go to the fire of hell !

God is Love.

The ignorant think that God and love are different.
None knows that God and love are the same.
Did all men know that God and love are the same,
They would dwell together in peace, considering love as God.

Aryan languages of Northern India ; Sanskrit. a copious literature and cultivated spoken dialects out of their isolated fragments of prehistoric speech, a more stately linguistic development was going on in the Aryan north. The achievements of Sanskrit as a literary vehicle in the various departments of poetry, philosophy, and science, have been described in chapter iv. at such length as the scope of this work permits. But Sanskrit was only the most famous of several Aryan dialects in the north. One of its eminent modern teachers defines it as 'that dialect which, regulated and established by the labours of the native grammarians, has led for the last 2000 years or more an artificial life, like that of the Latin during most of the same period in Europe.'[1] The Aryan vernaculars of modern India are the descendants not of Sanskrit, but of the spoken languages of the Aryan immigrants into the north. The Bráhmanical theory is that these ancient spoken dialects, or Prákrits, were corruptions of the purer Sanskrit. European philology has disproved this view, and the question has arisen whether Sanskrit was ever a spoken language at all.

Was Sanskrit ever a vernacular ?

Dr. John Muir's affirmative answer. This question has a deep significance in the history of the Indian vernaculars, and it is necessary to present, with the utmost brevity, the views of the leading authorities on the subject. Dr. John Muir, that *clarum et venerabile nomen* in Anglo-Indian scholarship, devotes many pages to 'reasons for supposing that the Sanskrit was originally a spoken language.'[2] He traces the Sanskrit of the philosophical period to the earlier forms in the Vedic hymns, and concludes 'that the old spoken language of India and the Sanskrit of the Vedas were at one time identical.'[3]

Professor Benfey's view ;

affirmative. Professor Benfey gives the results of his long study of the question in even greater detail. He believes that Sanskrit-speaking migrations from beyond the Himálayas continued to follow one another into India down to perhaps the 9th century B.C. That Sanskrit became the prevailing Indian vernacular dialect throughout Hindustán, and as far as the southern borders of the Maráthá country. That it began to die out as a spoken language from the 9th century B.C., and had become extinct as a vernacular in the 6th century B.C. ; its place being taken by derivative dialects or Prákrits. But that it still lingered in the schools of the Bráhmans ; and that, about the 3rd century

---

[1] Professor Whitney's *Sanskrit Grammar*, p. ix. Leipzig, 1879.
[2] Muir's *Sanskrit Texts*, vol. ii. pp. 144–160, ed. 1874.
[3] *Idem,* p. 160, and Dr. Muir's long footnote, No. 181.

B.C., it was brought back into public life as a sacred language with a view to refuting the Buddhistic teachers who wrote in the vernacular or Prákrit dialects. Professor Benfey also holds that about the 5th century A.D. Sanskrit had diffused itself over the whole of India as a literary language. We know that a subsequent revival of Sanskrit for the Puránic or orthodox treatises of the Bráhmans, as opposed to the new doctrines of the reformers who used the vernacular, actually took place about the 10th century A.D.

Lassen inclines to the same general view. He thinks that, in the time of Asoka, the main body of Aryans of Northern India spoke local dialects; while Sanskrit still remained the speech of Bráhmans, and of dignitaries of State. *Lassen's view.*

Sanskrit scholars of not less eminence have come to the conclusion that Sanskrit was not at any time a vernacular tongue. Professor Weber assigns it to the learned alone. He thinks that the Prákrits, or Aryan vernaculars of Northern India, were derived directly from the more ancient Vedic dialects; while Sanskrit was 'the sum of the Vedic dialects constructed by the labour and zeal of grammarians, and polished by the skill of learned men.' Professor Aufrecht agrees 'in believing that Sanskrit proper (*i.e.* the language of the epic poems, the law books, nay, even that of the Bráhmanas) was never actually spoken, except in schools or by the learned.' *Sanskrit never a spoken language. Weber's view. Aufrecht's view.*

The question has been finally decided, however, not by Sanskrit scholars in Europe, but by students of the modern Aryan vernaculars in India. During the past fourteen years, a bright light has been brought to bear upon the language and literature of ancient India, by an examination of the actual speech of the people at the present day. *Evidence from present Indian speech.*

Two learned Indian civilians, Mr. Salmon Growse and Mr. John Beames, led the way from not always concurrent points of view. In 1872, Mr. Beames' *Comparative Grammar of the Modern Aryan Languages of India* [1] opened up a new field of human knowledge, and began to effect for the Aryan dialects of the North, what Bishop Caldwell's great work accomplished for non-Aryan speech in Southern India. Dr. Ernest Trumpp's *Grammar of the Sindhí Language* followed, and would probably have modified some of Mr. Beames' views. Another learned German officer of the Indian Government, Professor Rudolf *The new study of the vernaculars, 1872-1885.*

[1] Three volumes, Trübner & Co. The first volume was published in 1872 ; the last in 1879.

Hœrnle, further specialized the research by his *Comparative Grammar of the Gaudian Languages* (1880), with particular reference to the Hindí. The same scholar and Mr. George Grierson, of the Civil Service, have, during the present year (1885), jointly brought out the first part of a *Comparative Dictionary of the Bihárí Language*, which will enable every European inquirer to study the structure and framework of a modern Aryan vernacular for himself. These and other cognate works have accumulated a mass of new evidence, which settles the relationship of the present Aryan vernaculars to the languages of ancient India.

Results disclosed by the vernaculars.
They prove that those vernaculars do not descend directly from Sanskrit. They indicate the existence of an Aryan speech older than Sanskrit, older, perhaps, than the Vedic hymns; from which the Sanskrit, the Prákrits or ancient spoken dialects of India, and the modern vernaculars were alike derived. Passing beyond the Vedic period, they show that ancient Aryan speech diverged into two channels. The one channel poured its stream into the ocean of Sanskrit, a language 'at once archaic and artificial,' elaborated by the Bráhmanical schools.[1] The other channel branched out into the Prákrits or ancient spoken vernaculars. The artificial Sanskrit (*Samskrita, i.e.* the perfected language) attained its complete development in the grammar of Pánini (*circ.* 350 B.C.).[2] The Prákrits (*i.e.* naturally evolved dialects) found their earliest extant exposition in the grammar of Vararuchi, about the 1st century B.C.[3] But the 4000 algebraic aphorisms of Pánini mark the climax of the labours of probably a long antecedent series of Sanskrit elaborators, while Vararuchi stands at the head of a long series of subsequent Prákrit grammarians.

Divergence of Sanskrit and Prákrit.

Pánini and Vararuchi.

The Prákrits spread south.
The spread of the Aryans from Northern India is best marked by the southern advance of their languages. The three great routes of Prákrit speech to the southward were—down the Indus valley on the west; along the Ganges valley to the east; and through certain historical passes of the

[1] Hœrnle and Grierson's *Comparative Dictionary of the Bihárí Language*, pp. 33 and 34. Secretariat Press, Calcutta, 1885. It should be remembered that Indian grammarians, when speaking of the Vedic language technically, do not call it Sanskrit, but *Chhandas.* They restrict the technical application of Sanskrit to the scholastic language of the Bráhmans, elaborated on the lines of the earlier Vedic.

[2] *Vide ante*, pp. 100 *et seq.*

[3] Hœrnle's *Comparative Grammar of the Gaudian Languages*, p. xviii. *et seq.*, ed. 1880.

Vindhyas in the centre. Between 500 B.C. and 500 A.D., the Their western or Apabhramsa dialects of Prákrit had spread across three lines of march. the Indus basin, and down the Bombay coast. During the same period dialects of Eastern or Magadhí Prákrit had occupied the valleys of the Jumna and the Ganges. Aryan tribes, speaking the Maháráshtrí and Sauraseni Prákrits, had poured through the Vindhyan passes, one of their great lines of march being that followed by the Jabalpur Railway at the present day. The Maháráshtrí dialect reached as far south as Goa on the western coast. The peninsula, to the south and east of the Maháráshtrí linguistic frontier, was inhabited by the Dravidian or Paisáchí-speaking races.

By degrees the main Prákrits, or spoken Aryan dialects, Classifica-differentiated themselves into local vernaculars, each occupying tion of Prákrits. a more contracted area. A series of maps has been compiled showing the stages of this process between 500 B.C. and 1800 A.D.[1] Various classifications have been framed, both of the modern vernaculars and of the ancient Prákrits. Vararuchi, Vara-the earliest Prákrit grammarian extant, enumerates four classes ruchi's four classes. in the 1st century B.C.,—Maháráshtrí, now Maráthí;[2] Saura-sení, now the Braj of the North-Western Provinces; Magadhí, now Bihárí; and Paisáchí, loosely applied to outlying non-Aryan dialects from Nepál to Cape Comorin.

Apart from the last-named Paisáchí, the literary Prákrits The two really divide themselves between two great linguistic areas. main Prákrits. Saurasení, with the so-called Maháráshtrí, occupied the upper part of the North-Western Provinces, and sent forth offshoots through the Vindhya passes as far south as Goa. Magadhí spread itself across the middle valley of the Ganges, with its brightest literary centre in Behar. These were the two parents of the most highly developed of the Aryan vernaculars of modern India. The Apabhramsa, or 'broken' dialects of the Indus region, may for the moment be left out of sight.

The Prákrits, or spoken Aryan dialects of ancient India, Prákrits received their first literary impulse from Buddhism. As the developed by Buddh-Bráhmans elaborated Sanskrit into the written vehicle for their ists,

---

[1] Prefixed to Hœrnle and Grierson's *Comparative Dictionary of the Bihárí Language.* See also the Language Map appended to Hœrnle's *Comparative Grammar of the Gaudian Languages.*

[2] Mr. Beames thinks that there is as much of the Magadhí and Saura-sení type in the modern Maráthí as there is of the Maháráshtrí Prákrit, *Comparative Grammar of the Modern Aryan Languages,* vol. i. p. 34, ed. 1872. He holds that Maráthí reproduces the name rather than the sub-stance of Maháráshtrí.

orthodox religion, so the teachers of the new faith appealed to the people by works in the popular tongues. The Buddhist missionaries to Ceylon, *circ.* 307 B.C., carried with them the spoken Prákrit of the Gangetic kingdom of Magadha. This dialect of Northern Indian became Páli, literally the series or *catena* of holy scripture in Ceylon. While the early Buddhists thus raised the Eastern or Magadhí Prákrit of Behar to a sacred language, the Jains made use of the Maháráshtrí Prákrit of Western India for their religious treatises. In this way, the two most characteristic of the spoken Aryan dialects of ancient India obtained a literary fixity, during the centuries shortly before and after the commencement of our era.

for their scriptures;

and by the Jains.

The Prákrits also remained the speech of the people, and underwent those processes of development, decay, and re-generation to which all spoken languages are subject. On the one hand, therefore, we have the literary Magadhí and Maháráshtrí Prákrits of the beginning of the Christian era, the former embalmed in the Buddhist scriptures of Ceylon, the latter in the Jain sacred books of Western India. On the other hand, we have the spoken representatives of these two ancient Prákrits in the modern vernaculars of Behar and of the Maráthá country.[1]

The Prákrits also remained spoken languages.

The evolution of the modern vernaculars from the ancient Prákrits is involved in deep obscurity. The curtain falls on the era of Prákrit speech within a few hundred years after the birth of Christ, and does not again draw up until the 10th century. When it rises, Prákrit dialects have receded from the stage, and their place has been taken by the modern vernaculars. During the dark interval, linguistic changes had taken place in the old Prákrits not less important than those which transformed Latin into Italian and Anglo-Saxon into English. Those changes are now being elucidated by the series of comparative grammars and dictionaries mentioned on pp. 335–36. It is only practicable here to state the most important of the results.

Evolution of modern vernaculars from Prákrits.

Obscure interval, 400-1000 A.D.

The old Prákrits were synthetical in structure. The

---

[1] This statement leaves untouched the question how far Maráthí is the direct representative of Maháráshtrí, or how far it is derived from the Saurasení Prákrit. As already mentioned, both the Saurasení and Maháráshtrí poured through the Vindhya passes into South-Western India, and combined to form the second of the two main Prákrits referred to in the classification on a previous page.

modern Aryan vernaculars of India are essentially analytical. The
During the eight centuries while the curtain hangs down synthetic
before the stage, the synthetic inflections of the Prákrits Prákrits
had worn out. The terminals of their nouns and verbs
had given place to post-positions, and to the disjointed
modern particles to indicate time, place, or relation. The
function performed in the European languages by prepositions
for the nouns are discharged, as a rule, by post-positions in
the modern Indian vernaculars. The process was spontaneous, become
and it represents the natural course of the human mind. analytical
'The flower of synthesis,' to use the words at once eloquent lars.
and accurate of Mr. Beames, 'budded and opened; and
when full-blown began, like all other flowers, to fade. Its
petals, that is its inflections, dropped off one by one; and in
due course the fruit of analytical structure sprung up beneath
it, and grew and ripened in its stead.'[1]

As regards their vocabularies, the Aryan vernaculars of Three
modern India are made up of three elements. One class of elements
their words is named Tatsama, 'the same as' the corresponding culars;
words in Sanskrit. A second class is termed Tadbhava, 'similar Sanskrit
in nature or origin' to the corresponding words in Sanskrit. *tatsamas.*
The third class is called Desaja, or 'country-born.' This Prákrit
classification is an ancient one of the Indian grammarians, and Non-
it is so far artificial that it refers the modern vernaculars to Aryan
Sanskrit standards; while we know that the modern vernaculars *desajas.*
were derived not from the Sanskrit, but from the Prákrits. It
suffices, however, for practical purposes.

The great body of modern Indian speech belongs to the Their
second or Tadbhava class of words, and may be taken loosely Prákrit
to represent its inheritance from the old spoken dialects or work;
Prákrits. But the vernaculars have enriched themselves for
literary purposes by many terms imported directly from the
Sanskrit; to represent religious, philosophical, or abstract ideas. and Sans-
These are the Tatsamas, 'the same as' in Sanskrit. The dif- krit enrich-
ferent vernaculars borrow such 'identical' words from Sanskrit ments.
in widely varying proportions. The strongest of the vernaculars,
such as Hindí and Maráthí, trust most to their own Tadbhava
or Prákrit element; while the more artificial of them, like
the Bengalí and Uriyá, are most largely indebted to direct
importations of Sanskrit words.

The third element in modern vernacular speech is the
Desaja, or 'country-born.' This represents the non-Aryan and

[1] Mr. Beames' *Comparative Grammar of the Modern Aryan Languages
of India,* vol. i. p. 45 (ed. 1872).

Non-Aryan element in the vernaculars ; other words not derived either from the Sanskrit or the Prákrits. At one time it was supposed, indeed, that the modern vernaculars of India were simply made up of the Sanskrit of the Aryan settlers, modified by, and amalgamated with, the speech of the ruder non-Aryan races whom they subdued. Modern philology renders this theory no longer tenable. It has proved that Sanskrit played a comparatively unimportant function in the formation of those vernaculars. It also tends to show that

less important than formerly supposed. the non-Aryan element is less influential than was supposed. Both in structure and in vocabulary the modern vernaculars of India are the descendants neither of the written Sanskrit, nor of the aboriginal tongues, but of the Prákrits or spoken dialects of the ancient Aryans.

Proportion of non-Aryan words ; In regard to grammatical structure, this position is now firmly established. But the proportion of aboriginal or non-Aryan words in the modern Indian vernaculars still remains undetermined. The non-Aryan scholars, with Brian Hodgson and Bishop Caldwell at their head, assign a considerable influence to the non-Aryan element in the modern vernaculars.[1]

in Sindhí, Dr. Ernest Trumpp believes that nearly three-fourths of the Sindhí words commencing with a cerebral are taken from some non-Aryan or Scythic language, which he would prefer to call Tátár. He thinks, indeed, that there is very strong proof to show that the cerebral letters themselves were borrowed, by the Prákrits and modern Indian vernaculars, from some idiom

in Gangetic vernaculars, anterior to the introduction of the Aryan languages into India. Bishop Caldwell states that the non-Aryan element, even in the Northern Indian languages, has been estimated at one-

in Maráthí. tenth of the whole, and in the Maráthí at one-fifth.[2]

The real proportion still unknown. Such generalizations are not accepted by the most eminent students of the Indo-Aryan vernaculars. Mr. Beames strongly expresses his view that the speech of the conquering Aryans completely overmastered that of the aboriginal tribes. The early grammarians were wont to regard as Desaja, or non-Aryan, all words for which they could not discover a Tatsama

---

[1] See Mr. Brian Houghton Hodgson's *Aborigines of India*, Calcutta, 1849 ; and pp. 1-152 of vol. ii. of his *Miscellaneous Essays* (Trübner, 1880). Also the Rev. Dr. Stevenson's paper in the *Journal of the Asiatic Society of Bombay*.

[2] Bishop Caldwell's *Comparative Grammar of the Dravidian Languages*, introd. p. 57 (ed. 1875). Lassen held that the aboriginal tribes not only introduced ' peculiar varieties into the Prákrit dialects,' but also ' occasioned very great corruptions of sound and form in the Indo-Aryan languages ' (*Indische Alterthumskunde*, ii. 1149). But the more recent investigations of Beames, Hœrnle, and Grierson render these *dicta* doubtful.

or Tadbhava origin. But the more delicate processes of modern philology have reduced the number of this class, and tend still further to diminish it. The truth is, that until a complete examination is made with the new lights, both of the vocabulary and of the structure of the Indian vernaculars, no final conclusion can be arrived at.

Dr. Hœrnle thus sums up the existing knowledge in regard to the group of Indian vernaculars on which he is the highest authority: ' That there are non-Aryan elements in the Bihari, I have no doubt. Considering that the Aryans immigrated into India, and absorbed large masses of the indigenous population into their ranks, it would be a wonder if no portion of the aboriginal languages had become incorporated into the Aryan speech. But what the several constituents of that aboriginal portion are, and what proportion they bear to the Aryan element in the vernacular language, it is impossible at present to form any scientific opinion. And what is more,— it is impossible to say whether the assumed aboriginal portion of the Aryan speech was Dravidian, or some other language, such as Kolarian or Tibeto-Burman.' [1]

Present position of the question.

---

[1] Letter from Dr. Rudolf Hœrnle to the author, dated 28th May 1885. Dr. Hœrnle continues—' Attempts have been made now and then (*e.g.* in *The Indian Antiquary*) to show that some particular selected words of the North Indian languages are really Dravidian. But these, even supposing they had been successful, would not enable any one to pronounce an opinion on the general question of the proportion of non-Aryan words in the Gaudian languages. As a matter of fact, some of these attempts, notably those referring to the genitive and dative post-positions (*ká, ke, kí,* etc.), have been conspicuous failures. It is now, I think, generally admitted that these post-positions are thoroughly Aryan. The truth is, that the way in which the question of the non-Aryan element in the vernaculars should be approached has been hitherto almost entirely misconceived. A little consideration must convince any one that whatever aboriginal elements there may be in the vernaculars, they must have been incorporated into them before the present vernacular times, that is, in the period when Sanskrit and Prákrit flourished. The question therefore properly stands thus—What are the aboriginal elements in Sanskrit and Prákrit? The vernaculars arose from Prákrit (and in a certain sense from Sanskrit) according to certain phonetic laws peculiar to the Aryan languages. Hence it is next to useless to try to refer Bihari (or any Aryan) vernacular words direct to the Dravidian. They must in the first place be referred back (by the well-known Aryan phonetic laws) to their earlier forms in Prákrit and Sanskrit. Only when this is done, the question can properly be asked whether they are Aryan or non-Aryan. And in order to decide this question, it will, among other points, have to be considered whether they possess correlates in the other Aryan languages (*e.g.* of Europe). But there is every probability that there is a considerable number of words in Sanskrit and Prákrit which are not Aryan, but only

Fourfold composition of the vernaculars :

(1) Prákrit element.

(2) Aboriginal element.

(3) Sanskrit borrowings.

(4) Persian terms.

At present, therefore, we cannot advance further than the four following conclusions :—First, that in grammatical structure and in their vocabularies, the modern analytical vernaculars of India represent the old synthetic Prákrits ; after a process of development, decay, and regeneration, which has been going on, as the result of definite linguistic laws, during the past fifteen hundred years. Second, that the modern vernaculars contain a non-Aryan element, derived from the so-called aborigines of India ; but that this element has very slightly affected their grammatical structure, and that the proportion which it holds in their vocabularies is yet undetermined. Third, that the modern vernaculars have enriched themselves, for literary and philosophical purposes, by direct and conscious borrowings from the Sanskrit. Fourth, that they have also imported many terms connected with the administration, the land revenue, judicial business, and official life, from the Persian court language of the Afghán and Mughal dynasties.

The seven Aryan vernaculars.

(1) Sindhí.

(2) Punjabí.

(3) Gujaráthí.

(4) Hindí.

(5) Maráthí.

The Aryan vernaculars of modern India may be distributed according to their geographical areas into seven main languages.

Towards the north-western frontier, Sindhí is spoken by the descendants of the shepherd tribes and the settlements who were left behind by the main stream of the prehistoric Aryan immigrants. The Sindhí language abounds in words of non-Aryan origin ; it contains very few Tatsamas, *i.e.* Sanskrit words in their original shape ; and it is almost destitute of an original literature. The Punjabí language is spoken in the valleys of the Indus and its tributaries. Like the Sindhí, it contains few Tatsamas, *i.e.* words borrowed directly from the Sanskrit.

Gujaráthí occupies the area immediately to the south of Punjabí ; while Hindí is conterminous with the Punjabí on the east. These two languages rank next to Punjabí in respect to the paucity of words borrowed directly from the Sanskrit. They are chiefly composed of Tadbhava, *i.e.* words representing the Prákrits or old spoken dialects. Maráthí is spoken in the Districts to the south and east of the Guja-

Aryanized. The question, however, has never been systematically or satisfactorily investigated. Some attempts have latterly been made in this direction by showing that not a few Sanskrit words are, in reality, Prákrit words Sanskritized. The next step will be to show that some Prákrit words are non-Aryan words Prákritized (*i.e.* Aryanized).'

ráthí frontier ; Bengalí succeeds to Hindí in the east of Bengal (6)Bengalí.
and the Gangetic delta ; while Uriyá occupies the Mahánadi (7) Uriyá.
delta and the coast of the Bay of Bengal from near the mouth
of the Húglí to the northern Districts of Madras. These
three last-named vernaculars, Maráthí, Bengalí, and Uriyá, are
most largely indebted to modern and artificial importations
direct from the Sanskrit.

With the exception of Sindhí, the modern vernaculars of Vernacular
India have each a literature of their own. Some of them, literature.
indeed, possess a very rich and copious literature. This subject
still awaits careful study. The lamented Garcin de Tassy has Garcin de
shown how interesting, and how rich in results, that study may Tassy.
be rendered. His history of Hindí literature,[1] and his yearly
review of works published in the Indian vernaculars, form a
unique monument to the memory of a scholar who worked
under the disadvantage of never having resided in India.
But the unexhausted literary stores of the Indian vernaculars
can only be appreciated by personal inquiry among the natives
themselves. The barest summary of the written and unwritten
works in the modern Indian vernaculars is altogether beyond
the scope of the present work. It can merely indicate the
wealth of unprinted, and in many cases unwritten, works
handed down from generation to generation, arranged in
geographical areas. The chapter will then conclude by
selecting for description a few authors from three of the most
advanced of the vernaculars — namely Hindí, Maráthí, and
Bengalí. It will not touch on the Persian or Musalmán
literature of the Delhi Empire.

As regards the isolated vernacular of Orissa, the present Vernacular
writer has elsewhere given an analytical catalogue of 107 Uriyá writers
authors, with a brief description of 47 Uriyá manuscripts of in Uriyá ;
undetermined authorship.[2] Several of the Uriyá poets and
theologians were prolific authors, and have left behind them
a number of distinct compositions. Thus, Dina Krishna Dás
(*circ.* 1550 A.D.) was so popular a writer as to earn for
himself the title of 'The Son of God Jagannáth.' His
separate works number fifteen, and embrace a wide range
of subjects, from ' the Waves of Sentiment,' an account of
the youthful sports of Krishna, to severe medical treatises.
Another Orissa poet of the 16th century composed 23 works,

[1] *Histoire de la Littérature Hindouie et Hindoustanie*, par M. Garcin
de Tassy, 3 vols. large octavo, 2nd ed., Paris, 1870-71.
[2] Hunter's *Orissa*, vol. ii. App. ix. ed. 1872.

on religious and metaphysical subjects, such as 'A Walk round the Sacred Enclosures of the Puri Temple,' and 'The Sea of the Nectar of Faith.' The greatest of the Uriyá poets, Upendra Bhanj, a Rájá of Gumsar, belongs to nearly the same period. He left behind him 42 collections of poems and treatises, some of them of great length.

Messrs. Hœrnle and Grierson have lately exhibited the local literature of Behar, and its sub-divisions, with admirable learning and distinctness.[1] It must suffice here to refer the student to their lists of works in Bihárí and the modern dialects of the Gaudian group.

in Bihárí.

An idea of the wealth of poetry current in Rájputána may be gathered from the following statement. The figures are taken from a manuscript note forwarded to the author by the Rev. John Traill, Presbyterian missionary at Jaipur. Besides the ordinary Hindí works, such as translations from the Sanskrit, the Rájputs have a vast store of religious poetry and traditional song, still living in the mouths of the people. The works of only a single sect can be specified in detail.

Rájputána literature.

Dadu, a religious reformer, born at Ahmadábád in 1544, left behind him a Báni, or body of sacred poetry, extending to twenty thousand lines. His life, by Jai Gopál, runs to three thousand lines. Fifty-two disciples spread his doctrine throughout Rájputána and Ajmere, each of them leaving a large collection of religious verse. The literary fertility of the sect may be inferred from the works of nine of the disciples. The poems and hymnology of Gharib Dás are said to amount to 32,000 lines; Jaisá is stated to have composed 124,000 lines; Prayág Dás, 48,000 lines; Rajab-jí, 72,000 lines; Bakhna-jí, 20,000 lines; Bábá Banwárí Dás, 12,000 lines; Shankar Dás, 4400 lines; Súndar Dás, 120,000 lines; and Mádhu Dás, 68,000 lines.

Dadu.

Sacred poetry of a single sect.

These figures are stated on the authority of Mr. Traill, and they are subject to the qualification that no European scholar has yet collected the writings of the sect. They are given as reported by the natives among whom the poems are still current. It is to be regretted that so little has yet been done to edit the stores of vernacular literature in the Feudatory States of India. A noble task lies before the more enlightened of the native princes; and in this task they would receive the willing assistance of English scholars now in India.

Dadu hymnologies.

[1] *Comparative Dictionary of the Bihárí Language,* pp. 38-42 (quarto; Calcutta, 1885).

A very brief notice of the most distinguished authors in Selected vernacular authors. Hindí, Maráthí, and Bengalí must conclude this chapter. For practical purposes, those three vernaculars represent the highest modern development of the modern Indian mind. This is, of course, exclusive of the Dravidian literature in the south of India, which has already been dealt with at the beginning of the chapter. The monastic literature of Burma is almost entirely a reproduction of the ancient Buddhist writings, and does not come within the scope of this work.

Hindí ranks, perhaps, highest among the Indian vernaculars Hindí authors: in strength and dignity. At the head of Hindí authors is Chand Bardái. Chand was a native of Lahore, but lived at Chand Bardái, 12th century A.D. the court of Prithwi Rájá, the last Hindu sovereign of Delhi, at the close of the twelfth century.[1] His poems are a collection of ballads in which he recites, in his old age, the gallant deeds of the royal master whom he had served, and whose sad fate he had survived. They disclose the ancient Prákrit in the very act of passing into the modern vernacular. In grammatical structure they still retain many relics of the synthetic or inflectional type ; although the analytical forms of the modern vernaculars are beginning to crowd out these remnants of the earlier phase of the Indian speech. Chand's ballads have been printed, but they also survive in the mouths of the people. They are still sung by wandering bards throughout North-Western India and Rájputána, to near the mouths of the Indus, and to the frontier of Baluchistán.

The vernacular literatures derived their chief impulse, how-Later Hindí authors. ever, not from court minstrelsy, but from religious movements. Each new sect seems to have been irresistibly prompted to embody its doctrines in verse. Kabír, the Indian Luther of 15th century A.D. the fifteenth century, may be said to have created the sacred literature of Hindí.[2] His Ramainís and Sabdas form an immense body of religious poetry and doctrine. In the following century, Súr Dás of Mathura, Nabhají and 16th century. Keshava Dás of Bijápur, wrote respectively the Súrságar, the Bhaktamálá, and the Rámchandrika. A brief notice of the Bhaktamálá has already been given at page 208. In the 17th century. seventeenth century, Bihárí Lál, of the ancient city of Amber near Jaipur, composed his famous Satsai ; and Bundel-khand produced its prince of poets, Lál Kavi, the author of the Chhatra Prakás. All these were natives of western

---

[1] For Prithwi Rájá, *vide ante*, chap. x. p. 276.

[2] For Kabír's work as a religious reformer, *vide ante*, pp. 208, 218.

Hindustán, except Kabír, who belonged to the Benares district.

18th century.

The last troubled years of the Mughal dynasty in the eighteenth century brought about a silence in Hindí literature. That silence was effectually broken by the introduction of the

19th century.

printing press in the nineteenth century. It has been succeeded by a great outburst of Hindí activity in prose and verse. Every decade now produces hundreds of Hindí publications, to some extent reproductions or translations of ancient authors, but also to a large extent original work.

Maráthí literature.

The Maráthás are scarcely more celebrated as a military than as a literary race. Their language is highly developed, and possesses structural complications attractive to the Indian

Nám Deva, 13th century A.D.

student. The first Maráthí poet of fame was Nám Deva, about the end of the thirteenth century. Like his contemporary, Dnyánoba the author of the celebrated Dnyáneshwarí,

Dnyánoba, 13th century A.D.

he was deeply impressed with the spiritual aspects of life. Indeed, almost all the Maráthí writers are religious poets. About the year 1571, Srídhar compiled his huge Maráthí adaptation or paraphrase of the Sanskrit Puránas.

Tukarám, 17th century A.D.

Maráthí poetry reached its highest flight in the Abhangas or spiritual poems of Tukarám or Tukoba (*circ.* 1609). This famous ascetic started life as a petty shopkeeper; but failing in retail trade, he devoted himself to religion and literature. The object of his adoration was Vithoba, a corruption of Bishtu or Vishnu. Tukarám was the popular poet in Western India of the reformed Vishnuite faith which Chaitanyá had taught in Bengal. He inveighed with peculiar unction and beauty against the riches of the world, which in his earlier years he had himself failed to secure.

Mayúr Pandit, 18th century A.D.

About 1720, Mayúr Pandit or Moropanth poured forth his copious song in strains which some regard as even more elevated than the poems of Tukarám.

Besides its accumulations of religious verse, Maráthí possesses a prose literature, among which the chief compositions are the Bakhars or Annals of the Kings. It is also rich in love songs, and farcical poetry of a broad style of wit.

Bengalí literature;

Bengalí is, in some respects, the most modern of the Indian vernaculars. As a spoken language, it begins on the north, where Hindí ends on the south; that is to say, in the Gangetic valley below Behar. From Rájmahal on the north to the Bay of Bengal, and from Assam on the east to Orissa on the

west, Bengalí forms the speech of about 50 millions of people its geo-
in the valleys and deltas of the Brahmaputra and the Ganges. graphical
area;
The language exhibits clearly marked dialectical modifications
in the north, the east, and the west, of this great area. But
for literary purposes, Bengalí may be regarded as a linguistic
entity. Indeed, literary Bengalí of the modern type is, to
some extent, an artificial creation. Much more than the and
Hindí, it has enriched itself by means of words directly im- linguistic
features.
ported from the Sanskrit. Such words not only supply the
philosophical, religious, and abstract terms of Bengalí literature, but they enter largely into the every-day language of
the people. This is to some extent due to the circumstance
that the Bengalís have very rapidly adopted western ideas.
With the introduction of such ideas arose the necessity for new
terms; and for these terms, Bengalí writers naturally turned
towards the Sanskrit.

The process has not been confined, however, to philosophic Sanskritiz-
works. Even in poetry, the best Bengalí writers of the present ing tendency of
day affect a more classical style than that of their predecessors Bengalí.
from the fourteenth to the eighteenth century. In 17 lines
of Bengalí verse taken from a contemporary periodical, the
Banga-darshana, there are only six or seven words which are
not Sanskrit importations. 'If we progress in this direction a
century longer,' writes a native author, 'the Bengalí language
will be distinguishable from the Sanskrit only by the case
terminations and mood and tense terminations.'[1] The framework of the colloquial language still continues to be derived
from the Prákrit, although Sanskrit terms are diffusing themselves even among the spoken language of the educated
classes.

Bengalí literature commences with the vernacular poets of Three
the fourteenth century. During its first two hundred years, periods of
Bengalí
Bengalí song was devoted to the praises of Krishna, and the literature;
loves of the young god. In the sixteenth century two great (1) 14th to
revolutions, religious and political, took place in Bengal. 16th century.
In the political world, the independent Afghán dynasty
of Bengal succumbed to the advancing Mughal power; and

---

[1] *The Literature of Bengal*, by Arcy Dae, p. 43, Calcutta, 1877. This
interesting volume is based on the more elaborate Bengalí work of Pandit
Rámgati Nyaratna. A complete treatment of the subject is still a desider-
atum, which it is hoped that Bengalí research will before long supply.
Mr. Dae, whose volume has been freely used in the following pages, would
confer a benefit both on his countrymen and on European students of the
Indian vernaculars, by undertaking the task.

Bengal was finally incorporated as a Province of the Delhi Empire.

(2) 16th to 18th century. In religion, a reformation of the Sivaite religion was effected under Bráhman impulses, and Krishna - worship receded from its literary pre-eminence. During the next two hundred and fifty years Bengalí poetry found its chief theme in the praises of Kálí or Chandí, the queen of Siva, who is alike the god of Destruction and of Reproduction. Early in the

(3) 19th century. nineteenth century, European influences began to impress themselves on Bengalí thought. Bengalí literature accordingly entered upon a third period, the period through which it is still passing, and which corresponds to the imported Western civilisation of India in the nineteenth century.

Bidyápati Thákur, 14th century. Putting aside Jayadeva of Bírbhúm, the Sanskrit singer in the twelfth century, Bengalí poetry commences with Bidyápati Thákur, a Bráhman of Tirhút. Bidyápati adorned the court of King Sivasinha of Tirhút in the fourteenth century ; and a deed of gift, still existing, proves that he had made his fame before 1400 A.D. Although popularly claimed as the Chaucer of Bengal, he wrote in what must now be regarded as a Bihárí rather than a Bengalí dialect ; and recited in learned verse the

Chandí Dás, 15th century. loves of Rádhá and Krishna. About the same period Chandí Dás, a Bírbhúm Bráhman, took up the sacred strain in the Bengalí tongue. Originally a devotee of the goddess Chandí, queen of Siva, he was miraculously converted to the worship of Krishna, whose praises he celebrated in a less learned, but more forcible colloquial style. To these two poets and their followers, Krishna was a lover rather than a deity ; and his mistress Rádhá, more of a pastoral beauty than a goddess. But their poetry constantly realizes that beneath the human amours of the divine pair, lies a deep spiritual significance.

Verses by Bidyápati. This didactic side of their poetry may be illustrated by three verses of Bidyápati to Krishna under his title of Mádhava, 'The Honeyed One.'

A HYMN TO KRISHNA.

'O ! Mádhava ! our final stay,
The Saviour of the world Thou art,
In mercy look upon the weak,
To Thee I turn with trustful heart.

Half of my life in sleep has past ;
In illness—boyhood—years have gone,
In pleasure's vortex long I roamed,
Alas ! forgetting Thee, the One.

> Unnumbered beings live and die,
>   They rise from Thee and sink in Thee,
>   (Thou uncreate and without end !)
>   Like ripples melting in the sea.'[1]

At the beginning of the sixteenth century, the great religious reformer Chaitanyá[2] gave a more serious turn to the poetry of Bengal. He preached the worship of Vishnu, and the doctrine of saving faith in that deity. Krishna was the pastoral incarnation of the god; but the Vishnuism taught by Chaitanyá spiritualized the human element in the amours which the earlier poets had somewhat warmly sung. Chaitanyá declared the spiritual equality of mankind, and combated the cruel distinctions of caste. His doctrine amounted to a protest against the Hinduism of his day, although it has been skilfully incorporated by the later Hinduism of our own. The opposition, excited by Chaitanyá's Vishnuite reformation, took the form of a revival of the worship of Siva and his queen. *Religious movements of the 16th century. The Vishnuite Revival.*

There were thus, in the sixteenth century, two great religious movements going on in Bengal; the one in favour of Vishnu, the second person of the Hindu triad; and the other in favour of Siva, the third person of that trinity. The more serious aspect which Chaitanyá gave to Vishnuism did not lend itself to popular song so easily as the human loves of Krishna, celebrated by the earlier Vishnuite poets. On the other hand, the counter revival of Sivaism accepted as its objects of adoration, some form or other of the Goddess of Destruction and Reproduction under her various names[3] of Umá, Párvatí, Durgá, Kálí, or Chandí. These names suggested alike the terrors and the mercies of the Queen of Siva, and appealed in a special manner to a people dwelling amid the stupendous catastrophes of nature in a deltaic Province like Bengal. *The Sivaite Revival. Bengalí Sivaite poetry.*

The result was an outburst of Bengalí song, which took as its theme the praises of Chandí, the wife of Siva. Kirtibás Ojhá, a Bráhman of Nadiyá District in the sixteenth century, marks the transition stage. Kirtibás drew his inspiration from the Sanskrit epics, and his great work is the Bengalí version of the *Rámáyana.* His translation is still recited by Ghattaks or bards at a thousand religious and festive gatherings every year throughout Bengal. Its modern versions have received much *Kirtibás Ojhá, 16th century. The transition poet.*

---

[1] Slightly altered from the rendering of Mr. Dae's *Literature of Bengal,* p. 60 (Bose & Co., Calcutta, 1877).

[2] *Vide ante,* pp. 219–21.

[3] For the different names of the wife of Siva, and the aspects of the goddess which these names connote, *vide ante,* pp. 211, 212.

re-touching from later poets of the classical or Sanskritizing school; but an old copy of 1693 proves that Kirtibás wrote in a strong colloquial style, with a ring and rhythm of peculiar beauty. The *Rámáyana* recites the achievements of the heroic incarnation of Vishnu, and Kirtibás Ojhá may therefore be claimed as a Vishnuite poet. But in reality his work marks the Sanskrit revival which gave the impulse to the Sivaite or Chandí poets of the next two and a half centuries.

His Bengalí *Rámáyana.*

These Sivaite poets kept possession of Bengalí literature during the 250 years which elapsed before the commencement of the third or present period. First among them was Makunda Rám Chakravarti, a Bráhman of Bardwán District, and a contemporary of Kirtibás Ojhá in the 16th century. He was driven from his home by the oppressions of Muhammadan officers, and his verses give a lifelike picture of the Muhammadan land settlement of Lower Bengal. All classes, he says, were crushed with an equal tyranny; fallow lands were entered as arable, and by a false measurement, three-fourths of a *bighá* were taxed as a full *bighá*. In the collection of the revenue, the oppressions were not less than in the assessment. The treasury officers deducted more than one rupee in seven for short weight and exchange. The husbandmen fled from their lands, and threw their cattle and goods into the markets, 'so that a rupee worth of things sold for ten annas.' Makunda Rám's family shared the common ruin; but the young poet, after a wandering life, found shelter as tutor in the family of Bánkurá Deb, a powerful landholder of Bírbhúm and Midnapur Districts. He was honoured with the title of Kabi Kankan, or the Jewel of Bards, and wrote two great poems besides minor songs.

Sivaite and Chandí poets, 16th to 18th century.

Makunda Rám.

His most popular work is the story of Kálketu, the hunter. Kálketu, a son of Indra, King of Heaven, is born upon earth as a poor hunter. In his celestial existence he had a devoted wife, and she, too, is born in this world, and becomes his faithful companion throughout their allotted earthly career. Their mortal births had been brought about by the goddess Chandí, queen of Siva, in order that she might have a city founded and dedicated to herself. The poor hunter and his wife, Fullorá, after years of hardship, are guided to a buried treasure by their kind patroness, Chandí. With this, the hunter builds a city, and dedicates it to the goddess. But misled by a wicked adviser, he goes to war with the King of Kalinga on the south, is defeated, and cast into prison. In due time Chandí rescues her foolish but faithful servant. At

The story of Kálketu, by Makunda Rám.

last the hunter and his true wife die and ascend to heaven. He lives again as the son of Indra, while Fullorá again becomes his celestial spouse.

The other poem of Makunda Rám narrates the adventures of a spice merchant, Dhanapati, and his son, Srímanta Sadá-gar. A celestial nymph, Khulloná, is sent down to live on earth as penance for a venial offence. She grows into a beautiful girl, and is wedded by the rich merchant, Dhanapati, who has, however, already a first wife. Before the marriage can be consummated, the king of the country sends off the merchant to Eastern Bengal to procure a golden cage for a favourite bird. The bride is left with his elder wife in the family home upon the banks of the Adjai, a river which separates Bírbhúm and Bardwán Districts in South-Western Bengal. A wicked handmaid excites the jealousy of the elder wife, and the girl-bride is condemned to menial offices, and sent forth as a goat-herd to the fields. The kind goddess Chandí, however, converts the elder lady to a better frame of mind; the girl-bride is received back; and on the return of her husband becomes his favourite wife. In due time she bears him a son, Srímanta Sadágar, the hero of the subsequent story.

The Srí-manta Sadágar of Makunda Rám.

The king next sends the merchant for spices to Ceylon, and his voyage down the great rivers of Bengal and across the sea is vividly described. From the towns mentioned on his route, it appears that in those days the water-way from Bardwán District and the neighbouring country, to the Bay of Bengal, lay by the Húglí as far down as Calcutta, and then struck south-eastward by what is now the dead river of the Adí-Gangá.[1] The poor merchant is imprisoned by the King of Ceylon, and there languishes until he is sought out by his brave son, Srímanta Sadágar, from whom the poem takes its name. Srímanta is also seized, and led out to execution by the cruel king. But the kind goddess Chandí delivers both father and son, and the beautiful Khulloná receives back with joy her lost treasures from the sea.

Voyage viâ the Húglí and Adí Gangá to Ceylon, 16th century.

In the 17th century, the second of the two great Sanskrit epics, the *Mahábhárata*, was translated by Kási Rám Dás. This poet also belonged to Bardwán District. His version still holds its place in the affections of the people, and is chanted by professional bards throughout all Bengal. The more tender episodes are rendered with feeling and grace;

Kási Rám Dás, 17th century.

The Bengalí Rámáy-ana.

---

[1] See article HUGLI RIVER in *The Imperial Gazetteer of India.*

but the fiery quarrels and heroic spirit of the Sanskrit original lose much in the Bengalí translation.

Bengalí poets of the 18th century. The 18th century produced two great Bengalí poets. In 1720, Rám Prasád Sen, of the Vaidya caste, was born in Nadiyá District. Sent at an early age as clerk to a Calcutta office, he scribbled verses when he should have been casting up accounts, and was reported for punishment by the chief clerk. The head of the business read the rhymes, dismissed the poet, but assigned to him a pension of Rs. 30 a month. With this he retired to his native village, and wrote poetry for the rest of his life. Rám Prasád was a devout Tantrik or worshipper of the wife of Siva, and his poems consist chiefly of appeals to the goddess under her various names of Kálí, Sakti, etc. His songs, however, are more often complaints of her cruelty than thanksgivings for her mercies.[1]

The Court of Nadiyá, 18th century. The little Hindu court of Nadiyá then formed the centre of learning and literature in Bengal, and the Rájá endowed Rám Prasád with 33 acres of rent-free land. The grateful poet in return dedicated to the prince his *Kabiranjan*, or version of the tale of *Bidyá Sundar*. The fame of this version has, however, been eclipsed by the rendering of the same story by a rival poet Bhárat Chandra. Two other well-known works, the *Kálí Kirtan* and the *Krishna Kirtan*, in honour respectively of Kálí and Krishna, with many minor poems, have also come down from the pen of Rám Prasád.

Bhárat Chandra Rái. The other great Bengal poet of the 18th century was Bhárat Chandra Rái, who died 1760. The son of a petty Rájá, he was driven from his home by the oppressions of the Rájá of Bardwán, and after many adventures and imprisonment, obtained the protection of the chief native officer of the French Settlement at Chandarnagar. The generosity of the Rájá of Nadiyá[2] afterwards raised him to comfort, and he devoted his life to three principal poems. His version of the *Bidyá Sundar* is a passionate love poem, and remains the accepted rendering of that tale to the present day. The goddess Kálí interposes at the end to save the life of the frail heroine. His other two principal poems, the *Annadá Mangal* and the *Mánsinha*, form continuations of the same work; and, like it, are devoted to the glorification of the queen of Siva under her various names.

With the printing press, and the Anglo-Indian School, arose

[1] Dae's *Literature of Bengal*, p. 147. (Calcutta, 1877.)
[2] Mr. Dae says, inadvertently, the Rájá of Bardwán.

a generation of Bengalís whose chief ambition is to live by the Recent
pen. The majority find their career in official, mercantile, or Bengalí literature,
professional employment. But a large residue become writers, 19th cenof books; and Bengal is at present passing through a grand tury.
literary climacteric. Nearly 1300 works per annum are published in the vernacular languages of Lower Bengal alone.
It is an invidious task to attempt to single out the most
distinguished authors of our own day. Amid such a climax of
literary activity, much inferior work is produced. But it is not
too much to say that in poetry, philosophy, science, the novel
and the drama, Bengalí literature has, in this century, produced
masterpieces without rivals in its previous history. In two
departments it has struck out entirely new lines. Bengalí
prose practically dates from Rám Mohan Rái; and Bengalí
journalism is essentially the creation of the third quarter of the
present century.[1]

As Bengalí poetry owed its rise in the 14th century, and its Bengalí
fresh impulse in the 16th, to outbursts of religious song; so prose, 19th century.
Bengalí prose is the offspring of the religious movement
headed by the Rájá Rám Mohan Rái in the 19th. This great
theistic reformer felt that his doctrines and arguments required
a more serious vehicle than verse. When he died in 1833, he
at once received the position of the father of Bengalí prose,—
a position which he still enjoys in the grateful memories of his
countrymen.[2] Of scarcely less importance, however, in the
creation of a good prose style, were two rival authors born in
1820. Akkhai Kumár Datta enforced the theistic doctrines
of the Brahma Samáj with indefatigable ability in his religious
journal, the *Tatwabodhiní Patriká.* Reprints of his articles
still rank as text-books of standard Bengalí prose. Iswar
Chandra Vidyaságar, also born in 1820, devoted himself to
social reform upon orthodox Hindu lines. The enforced
celibacy of widows, and the abuses of polygamy, have formed
the subject of his life-long attacks.

An older worker, Iswar Chandra Gupta, born 1809, took the
lead in the modern popular poetry of Bengal. His fame has

---

[1] From no list of 19th century Bengalí authors should the following
names be omitted :—Rám Mohan Rái, Akkhai Kumár Datta, Iswar
Chandra Vidyaságar, Iswar Chandra Gupta, Madhu Sudan Datta, Hem
Chandra Banarji, Bankim Chandra Chattarjí, Dino Bandhu Mitra, and
Nabin Chandra Sen.

[2] Rájá Rám Mohan Rái (Rammohun Roy) is also well known for his
English works, of which it is pleasant to record that a collected reprint is
now appearing under the editorship of Babu Gogendra Chandra Ghose,
M.A. (Calcutta, 1885).

Modern
Bengalí
poets,
19th cen-
tury.

been eclipsed, however, by Madhu Sudan Datta, born 1828, who now ranks higher in the estimation of his countrymen than any Bengalí poet of this or any previous age.   Madhu Sudan's epic, the *Meghnád Badh Kábya*, is reckoned by Bengalí critics as second only to the masterpieces of Válmiki, Kálidása, Homer, Dante, and Shakspeare.   This generous appreciation is characteristic of the catholic spirit of Hinduism.   For

Madhu
Sudan
Datta,
1828-1875.

Madhu Sudan Datta became a Christian, lectured as professor in a Christian college, went to England, and returned to Bengal only to die, after a too brief career, in 1875.   His epic relates the death of Meghnad or Indrajít, greatest of the sons of Ravana, and takes its materials from the well-known episode in the *Rámáyana.*   Among Bengalí poets still living, Hem Chandra Banarji occupies perhaps the highest place of honour.

The
Bengalí
Drama.

In the Bengalí drama, Dina Bandhu Mitra, born 1829, died 1873, led the way.   His first and greatest work, the *Níl Darpan* or Mirror of Indigo, startled the community by its picture of the abuses of indigo planting a quarter of a century ago.   It was translated into English by the well-known missionary and philanthropist, the Rev. James Long; and formed the ground of an action for libel, ending in the fine and imprisonment of the latter gentleman.   In prose fiction, Bunkim Chandra Chattarjí, born 1838, ranks first.   The Bengalí novel is essentially a creation of the last half century, and the *Durgesh Nandini* of this author has never been surpassed. But many new novelists, dramatists, and poets are now establishing their reputation in Bengal; and the force of the literary impulse given by the State School and the printing press seems still unabated.   It is much to be regretted that so little of that intellectual activity has flowed into the channels of biography and critical history.

The mean-
ing of this
chapter.

This chapter has dealt at some length with the vernacular literature of India, because a right understanding of that literature is necessary for the comprehension of the chapters which follow.   It concludes the part of the present book which treats of the struggle for India by the Asiatic races.   In the next chapter the European nations come upon the scene.   How they strove among themselves for the mastery will be briefly narrated.   The conquest of India by any one of them formed a problem whose magnitude not one of them appreciated. The Portuguese spent the military resources of their country, and the religious enthusiasm of their Church, in the vain attempt to establish an Indian dominion by the Inquisition and the Sword. This chapter has shown the strength and the extent of the indigenous civilisation which they thus ignorantly and unsuccessfully strove to overthrow.

Assaults on the indigenous civilisation of India.

The Indian races had themselves confronted the problems for which the Portuguese attempted to supply solutions from without. One religious movement after another had swept across India ; one philosophical school after another had presented its explanation of human existence and its hypothesis of a future life. A popular literature had sprung up in every Province. The Portuguese attempt to uproot these native growths, and to forcibly plant in their place an exotic civilisation and an exotic creed, was foredoomed to failure. From any such attempt the Dutch and the French wisely abstained. One secret of the success of the British power has been its non-interference with the customs and the religions of the people.

English non-interference.

CHAPTER XIV.

EARLY EUROPEAN SETTLEMENTS (1498 TO 18TH CENTURY A.D.).

The Portu-
guese in
India.
Vasco da
Gama,
1498.

THE Muhammadan invaders of India had entered from the north-west. Her Christian conquerors approached by sea from the south. From the time of Alexander to that of Vasco da Gama, Europe held little direct intercourse with the East. An occasional traveller brought back stories of powerful kingdoms and of untold wealth; but the passage by sea was scarcely dreamed of, and by land, wide deserts and warlike tribes lay between. Commerce, indeed, struggled overland and *viâ* the Red Sea; being carried on chiefly by the Italian cities on the Mediterranean, which traded to the ports of the Levant.[1] But to the Europeans of the 15th century, India was an unknown land, which powerfully attracted the imagination of spirits stimulated

[1] The following is a list of the most noteworthy early travellers to the East, from the 9th century to the establishment of the Portuguese as a conquering power in India in the 16th. The Arab geographers will be found in Sir Henry Elliot's first volumes of the Indian Historians. The standard European authority is *The Book of Ser Marco Polo the Venetian*, edited by Colonel Henry Yule, C.B., 2 vols., second edition, 1875. The author's best thanks are due to Colonel Yule for the assistance he has kindly afforded both here and in those articles of *The Imperial Gazetteer of India*, which came within the scope of Colonel Yule's researches. The authorities for the more ancient travellers and Indian geographers are, as already stated, M'Crindle's *Megasthenes and Arrian*, his *Ktesias*, and his *Navigation of the Erythræan Sea*, which originally appeared in the *Indian Antiquary*, and were republished by Messrs. Trübner. *The Commerce and Navigation of the Ancients in the Indian Ocean*, by Dr. William Vincent, Dean of Westminster (2 vols. quarto, 1807), may still be perused with interest, although Dr. Vincent's materials have been supplemented by fuller and more accurate knowledge.

883 A.D. King Alfred sends Sighelm of Sherburn to the shrine of Saint Thomas in 'India.' The site of the shrine is doubtful, see chap. ix.

851-916. Suláimán and Abu Zaid, whose travels furnished the *Relations* of Reinaud.

912-30. The geographer Mas'udi.

1159-73. Rabbi Benjamin of Tudela; visited Persian Gulf, reported on India.

1260-71. The brothers Nicolo and Maffeo Polo, father and uncle of Marco Polo; make their first trading venture through Central Asia.

by the renaissance, and ardent for discovery. The materials for this period have been collected by Sir George Birdwood in his admirable official *Report on the Old Records of the India Office* (1879), to which the following paragraphs are largely indebted. The history of the various European settlements will be found in greater detail, under their respective articles, in *The Imperial Gazetteer of India.*

In 1492, Christopher Columbus sailed westwards under the Portuguese Spanish flag to seek India beyond the Atlantic, bearing with voyages. him a letter to the great Khán of Tartary. He found America instead. An expedition under Vasco da Gama started from Lisbon five years later, in the opposite, or south-eastern, direction. It doubled the Cape of Good Hope, and cast anchor off the city of Calicut on the 20th May 1498, after a protracted voyage of nearly eleven months. An earlier Portuguese emissary, Covilham, had reached Calicut overland about 1487.

1271. They started on their second journey, accompanied by Marco Polo; and about 1275, arrived at the Court of Kublai Khán in Shangtu, whence Marco Polo was entrusted with several missions to Cochin China, Khanbulig (Pekin), and the Indian Seas.

1292. Friar John of Monte Corvino, afterwards Archbishop of Pekin; spent thirteen months in India on his way to China.

1304-78. Ibn Batuta, an Arab of Tangiers; after many years in the East, attached himself to the Court of Muhammad Tughlak at Delhi, 1334-42, whence he was despatched on an Embassy to China.

1316-30. Odorico di Pordenone, a Minorite friar; travelled in the East and through India by way of Persia, Bombay, and Surat (where he collected the bones of four missionaries martyred in 1321), to Malabar, the Coromandel coast, and thence to China and Tibet.

1328. Friar Jordanus of Severac, Bishop of Quilon.

1338-49. John de Marignolli, a Franciscan friar; on his return from a mission to China, visited Quilon in 1347, and made a pilgrimage to the shrine of St. Thomas in India in 1349.

1327-72. Sir John Mandeville; wrote his travels in India (supposed to be the first printed English book, London, 1499); but beyond the Levant his travels are invented or borrowed.

1419-40. Nicolo Conti, a noble Venetian; travelled throughout Southern India and along the Bombay coast.

1442-44. Abd-ur-Razzak; during an embassy to India, visited Calicut, Mangalore, and Vijayanagar, where he was entertained in state by the Hindu sovereign of that kingdom.

1468-74. Athanasius Nikitin, a Russian; travelled from the Volga, through Central Asia and Persia, to Gujarát, Cambay, and Chaul, whence he proceeded inland to Bídar and Golconda.

1494-99. Hieronimo di Santo Stefano, a Genoese; visited the port of Malabár and the Coromandel coast as a merchant adventurer, and after proceeding to Ceylon and Pegu, sailed for Cambay.

1503-08. Travels of Ludovico di Varthema. In the *Hakluyt Series.*

From the first, Da Gama encountered hostility from the Moors, or rather Arabs, who monopolized the sea-borne trade ; but he seems to have found favour with the Zamorin or Hindu Rájá of Malabar. An Afghán of the Lodí dynasty was then on the throne of Delhi, and another Afghán king was ruling over Bengal. Ahmadábád formed the seat of a Muhammadan dynasty in Gujarát. The five independent Muhammadan kingdoms of Ahmednagar, Bijápur, Elichpur, Golconda, and Bídar had partitioned out the Deccan. But the Hindu Rájá of Vijayanagar still ruled as paramount in the south, and was perhaps the most powerful monarch to be found at that time in India, not excepting the Lodí dynasty at Delhi.

State of India on arrival of Portuguese.

After staying nearly six months on the Malabar coast, Da Gama returned to Europe, bearing with him the following letter from the Zamorin to the King of Portugal :—' Vasco da Gama, a nobleman of your household, has visited my kingdom and has given me great pleasure. In my kingdom there is abundance of cinnamon, cloves, ginger, pepper, and precious stones. What I seek from thy country is gold, silver, coral, and scarlet.' The safe arrival of Da Gama at Lisbon was celebrated with national rejoicings as enthusiastic as those which had greeted the return of Columbus. If the West Indies belonged to Spain by priority of discovery, Portugal might claim the East Indies by the same right. The Portuguese mind became intoxicated by dreams of a mighty oriental empire.

Rájá of Calicut's letter, 1498.

The early Portuguese navigators were not traders or private adventurers, but admirals with a royal commission to conquer territory and to promote the spread of Christianity. A second expedition, consisting of thirteen ships and twelve hundred soldiers, under the command of Cabral, was despatched in 1500. 'The sum of his instructions was to begin with preaching, and if that failed, to proceed to the sharp determination of the sword.' On his outward voyage, Cabral was driven by stress of weather to the coast of Brazil. Ultimately he reached Calicut, and established factories both there and at Cochin, in spite of active hostilities from the natives.

Portuguese expedition, 1500.

In 1502, the King of Portugal obtained from Pope Alexander VI. a bull constituting him ' Lord of the Navigation, Conquests, and Trade of Ethiopia, Arabia, Persia, and India.' In that year Vasco da Gama sailed again to the East, with a fleet numbering twenty vessels. He formed an alliance with the Rájás of Cochin and Cananore against the Zamorin of Calicut, and bombarded the latter in his palace. In 1503, the great Alfonso d'Albuquerque sailed to the East in command of

Portuguese supremacy in eastern seas, 1500-1600.

one of three expeditions from Portugal. In 1505, a large fleet of twenty-two sail and fifteen thousand men was sent under Francisco de Almeida, the first Portuguese Governor and Viceroy of India.

In 1509, Albuquerque succeeded as Governor, and widely extended the area of Portuguese influence. Having failed in an attack upon Calicut, he in 1510 seized Goa, which has since remained the capital of Portuguese India. Then, sailing round Ceylon, he captured Malacca, the key to the navigation of the Indian archipelago, and opened a trade with Siam and the Spice Islands. Lastly, he sailed back westwards, and after penetrating into the Persian Gulf and the Red Sea, returned to Goa only to die in 1515. In 1524, Vasco da Gama came out to the East for the third time, and he too died at Cochin, in 1527. For exactly a century, from 1500 to 1600, the Portuguese enjoyed a monopoly of Oriental trade.[1] 'From Japan and the Spice Islands to the Red Sea and the Cape of Good Hope, they were the sole masters and dispensers of the treasures of the East; while their possessions along the Atlantic coast of Africa and in Brazil completed their maritime empire.'[2]

Albuquerque takes Goa, 1510.

But the Portuguese had neither the political strength nor the personal character necessary to maintain such an Empire. Their national temper had been formed in their contest with the Moors at home. They were not traders, but knights-errant and crusaders, who looked on every pagan as an enemy of Portugal and of Christ. Only those who have read the contemporary narratives of their conquests, can realize the superstition and the cruelty with which their history in the Indies is stained.

Cruelties of Portuguese in India.

Albuquerque alone endeavoured to conciliate the goodwill of the natives, and to live in friendship with the Hindu princes, who were naturally better pleased to have the Portuguese, as governed by him, for their neighbours and allies, than the Muhammadans whom he had expelled or subdued. The justice and magnanimity of his rule did as much to extend and confirm the power of the Portuguese in the East, as his courage and the success of his military achievements.

Albuquerque's policy of conciliation.

---

[1] For a full account of the Portuguese in India, and the curious phases of society which they developed, see article GOA, *The Imperial Gazetteer of India.* Also for local notices, see articles DAMAN, DIU, BASSEIN, CALICUT.

[2] This and the following paragraphs are condensed from Sir George Birdwood's official *Report on the Miscellaneous Old Records in the India Office,* dated 1st November 1878 (folio, 1879).

In such veneration was his memory held, that the Hindus of
Goa, and even the Muhammadans, were wont to repair to his
tomb, and there utter their complaints, as if in the presence of
his shade, and call upon God to deliver them from the tyranny
of his successors.

Later
Viceroys ;

their
bravery.

'The cruelties of Soarez, Sequeyra, Menezes, Da Gama,
and succeeding viceroys, drove the natives to desperation,
and encouraged the princes of Western India in 1567 to form
a league against the Portuguese, in which they were joined by
the King of Achín.' But the undisciplined Indian troops were
unable to stand against the veteran soldiers of Portugal; 200
of whom, at Malacca, routed 15,000 natives with artillery.
When, in 1578, Malacca was again besieged by the King of
Achín, the small Portuguese garrison destroyed 10,000 of his
men, and all his cannon and junks. Twice again, in 1615
and for the last time in 1628, Malacca was besieged, and on
each occasion the Achinese were repulsed with equal bravery.
But the increased military forces sent out to resist these
attacks proved an insupportable drain on the revenues and
population of Portugal.

Spanish
influences,
1580.

In 1580, the Portuguese crown was united with that of
Spain, under Philip II. This proved the ruin of the maritime
and commercial supremacy of Portugal in the East. The interests of Portugal in Asia were henceforth subordinated to the
European interests of Spain. In 1640, Portugal again became
a separate kingdom. But in the meanwhile the Dutch and
English had appeared in the Eastern Seas ; and before their
indomitable competition, the Portguese empire of the Indies
withered away as rapidly as it had sprung up. The period of
the highest development of Portuguese commerce was probably
from 1590 to 1610 on the eve of the subversion of their commercial power by the Dutch, and when their political administration in India was at its lowest depth of degradation. At
this period a single fleet of Portuguese merchantmen sailing
from Goa to Cambay or Surat would number as many as 150
or 250 *carracks*. Now, only one Portuguese ship sails from
Lisbon to Goa in the year.[1]

Downfall
of Portu-
guese in
India,
1639-1739.

The Dutch besieged Goa in 1603, and again in 1639. Both
attacks were unsuccessful on land ; but the Portuguese were
gradually driven off the sea. In 1683, the Maráthás plundered
to the gates of Goa. The further history of the Portuguese in
India is a miserable chronicle of pride, poverty, and sounding

[1] Reproduced, without verification, from Sir George Birdwood's Report,
p. 70.

titles. The native princes pressed upon them from the land. On the sea they gave way to more vigorous European nations.

The only remaining Portuguese possessions in India are Goa, Damán, and Diu, all on the west coast, with a total area of 2365 square miles, and a total population of 475,172 in 1881.[1] The general Census of 1871 also returned 426 Portuguese in British India, not including those of mixed descent. About 30,000 of the latter are found in Bombay ('Portuguese' half-castes), and 20,000 in Bengal, chiefly in the neighbourhood of Dacca and Chittagong. The latter are known as Firinghis; and, excepting that they retain the Roman Catholic faith and European surnames, they are scarcely to be distinguished either by colour, language, or habits of life from the natives among whom they live. *Portuguese Possessions in 1881.* *Mixed descendants.*

The Dutch were the first European nation who broke through the Portuguese monopoly. During the 16th century, Bruges, Antwerp, and Amsterdam became successively the great emporiums whence Indian produce, imported by the Portuguese, was distributed to Germany, and even to England. At first the Dutch, following in the track of the English, attempted to find their way to India by sailing round the northern coast of Europe and Asia. William Barents is honourably known as the leader of three of these arctic expeditions, in the last of which he perished. *The Dutch in India, 1602-1824.*

The first Dutchman to double the Cape of Good Hope was Cornelius Houtman, who reached Sumatra and Bantam in 1596. Forthwith private companies for trade with the East were formed in many parts of the United Provinces; but in 1602 they were all amalgamated by the States-General into 'The Dutch East India Company.' Within fifty years the Dutch had established factories on the continent of *Dutch India Companies.*

---

[1] This number, 475,172, is the 'actual' population of all the Portuguese Settlements in India, as shown in the General Statement No. 1 of the Census of Portuguese India, taken on the 17th February 1881. The same table shows the 'nominal' population at 481,467. Both these returns differ somewhat from the totals obtained from the detailed tables showing the males and females, age, and civil condition of the people. Thus, the total obtained for Goa is 444,449 from the detailed statements, while the General Statement No. 1 of the Portuguese Settlements shows an 'actual' population for Goa of 413,698 and a 'nominal' population of 420,868. Similar differences on a smaller scale may be detected in the general and detailed statements of the Settlement of Damán. In both cases, the separate articles in *The Imperial Gazetteer of India* follow the detailed tables of male and female, age, and civil condition; while in general statements of population for Portuguese India, the general totals issued under the authority of the Portuguese Government are accepted.

India, in Ceylon, in Sumatra, in the Persian Gulf, and in the Red Sea, besides having obtained exclusive possession of the Moluccas. In 1619 they laid the foundation of the city of Batavia in Java, as the seat of the supreme government of the Dutch possessions in the East Indies, which had previously been at Amboyna. At about the same time the Dutch discovered the coast of Australia; while in North America they founded the city of New Amsterdam or Manhattan, now New York.

Their progress, 1619.

During the 17th century the Dutch were the foremost maritime power in the world. Their memorable massacre of the English at Amboyna, in 1623, forced the British Company to retire from the Eastern Archipelago to the continent of India, and thus led to the foundation of our Indian Empire. The long naval wars and bloody battles between the English and the Dutch within the narrow seas were not terminated until William of Orange united the two countries in 1689. In the Eastern Archipelago the Dutch ruled without a rival, and expelled the Portuguese from almost all their territorial possessions. In 1635 they occupied Formosa; in 1640 they took Malacca, a blow from which the Portuguese never recovered; in 1647 they were trading at Sadras, on the Pálár river; in 1651 they founded a colony at the Cape of Good Hope, as a half-way station to the East; in 1652 they built their first Indian factory at Pálakollu, on the Madras coast; in 1658 they captured Jaffnapatam, the last stronghold of the Portuguese in Ceylon. Between 1661 and 1664 the Dutch wrested from the Portuguese all their earlier settlements on the pepper-bearing coast of Malabar; and in 1669 they expelled the Portuguese from St. Thomé and Macassar.

Dutch supremacy in eastern seas, 1600–1700.

Their brilliant progress, 1635–69.

The fall of the Dutch colonial empire resulted from its short-sighted commercial policy. It was deliberately based upon a monopoly of the trade in spices, and remained from first to last destitute of sound economical principles. Like the Phœnicians of old, the Dutch stopped short of no acts of cruelty towards their rivals in commerce; but, unlike the Phœnicians, they failed to introduce their civilisation among the natives with whom they came in contact. The knell of Dutch supremacy was sounded by Clive, when in 1759 he attacked the Dutch at Chinsurah both by land and water, and forced them to an ignominious capitulation. In the great French wars from 1793 to 1811, England wrested from Holland every one of her colonies; although Java was restored in 1816, and Sumatra exchanged for Malacca in 1824.

Their short-sighted policy.

Stripped of their Indian possessions, 1759-1811.

At present, the Dutch flag flies nowhere on the mainland of India. But quaint houses, Dutch tiles and carvings, at Chinsurah, Negapatam, Jaffnapatam, and at petty ports on the Coromandel and Malabar coast, with the formal canals in some of these old Settlements, remind the traveller of scenes in the Netherlands. The passage between Ceylon and the mainland still bears the name of the Dutch governor, Palk. In the Census of 1872, only 70 Dutchmen were enumerated throughout all British India, and 79 in 1881.[1] *Dutch relics in India.*

The earliest English attempts to reach India were made by the North-west passage. In 1496, Henry VII. granted letters patent to John Cabot and his three sons (one of whom was the famous Sebastian) to fit out two ships for the exploration of this route. They failed, but discovered the island of Newfoundland, and sailed along the coast of America from Labrador to Virginia. In 1553, the ill-fated Sir Hugh Willoughby attempted to force a passage along the north of Europe and Asia, the successful accomplishment of which has been reserved for a Swedish savant of our own day. Sir Hugh perished miserably; but his second in command, Chancellor, reached a harbour on the White Sea, now Archangel. Thence he penetrated by land to the court of the Grand Duke of Moscow, and laid the foundation of 'the Russia Company for carrying on the overland trade between India, Persia, Bokhara, and Moscow.' *Early English adventurers, 1496-1596. The North-west passage, 1553-1616.*

Many English attempts were made to find a North-west passage to the East Indies, from 1576 to 1616. They have left on our modern maps the imperishable names of Frobisher, Davis, Hudson, and Baffin. Meanwhile, in 1577, Sir Francis Drake had circumnavigated the globe, and on his way home had touched at Ternate, one of the Moluccas, the king of which island agreed to supply the English nation with all the cloves which it produced. *Later attempts.*

The first modern Englishman known to have visited the Indian Peninsula was Thomas Stephens, in 1579. William of Malmesbury states, indeed, that in 883 Sighelmus of Sherborne, sent by King Alfred to Rome with presents to the Pope, proceeded thence to 'India,' to the tomb of St. Thomas, and brought back jewels and spices. But, as already pointed out, it by no means follows that the 'India' of William of *Stephens, first Englishman in India, 1579.*

---

[1] For local notices of the Dutch in India, see articles SADRAS, PALA-KOLLU, CHINSURAH, NEGAPATAM, PALK'S PASSAGE, etc., in their respective volumes of *The Imperial Gazetteer of India.*

Malmesbury meant the Indian peninsula. Stephens (1579) was educated at New College, Oxford, and became rector of the Jesuit College in Salsette. His letters to his father are said to have roused great enthusiasm in England to trade directly with India.

Fitch, Newberry, Leedes, 1583.

In 1583, three English merchants, Ralph Fitch, James Newberry, and Leedes, went out to India overland as mercantile adventurers. The jealous Portuguese threw them into prison at Ormuz, and again at Goa. At length Newberry settled down as a shopkeeper at Goa; Leedes entered the service of the Great Mughal; and Fitch, after a lengthened peregrination in Ceylon, Bengal, Pegu, Siam, Malacca, and other parts of the East Indies, returned to England.[1]

The defeat of the 'Invincible Armada' in 1588, at which time the crowns of Spain and Portugal were in union, gave a fresh stimulus to maritime enterprise in England; and the successful voyage of Cornelius Houtman in 1596 showed the way round the Cape of Good Hope, into waters hitherto monopolized by the Portuguese.

English East India Companies.

The following paragraph on the early history of the English East India Companies is condensed, with little change, from Sir George Birdwood's official report.[2] In 1599, the Dutch, who had now firmly established their trade in the East, raised the price of pepper against us from 3s. per lb. to 6s. and 8s. The merchants of London held a meeting on the 22nd September at Founders' Hall, with the Lord Mayor in the chair, and agreed to form an association for the purposes of trading directly with India. Queen Elizabeth also sent Sir John Mildenhall by Constantinople to the Great Mughal to apply for privileges for an English Company. On the 31st December 1600,[3] the English East India Company was in-

First charter, 31st December 1600.

corporated by royal charter under the title of 'The Governor and Company of Merchants of London trading to the East Indies.' The original Company had only 125 shareholders, and a capital of £70,000, which was raised to £400,000 in 1612–13, when voyages were first undertaken on the joint-stock account.

Courten's Association, known as 'The Assada Merchants,' from a factory subsequently founded by it in Madagascar, was

---

[1] Condensed from *Report on Old Records in the India Office*, pp. 75-77.

[2] Condensed from *Report on Old Records in the India Office*, pp. 77 *et seq.*

[3] Auber gives the date as the 30th December, *Analysis of the Constitution of the East India Company*, by Peter Auber, Assistant-Secretary to the Honourable Court of Directors, p. ix. (London, 1826).

established in 1635, but, after a period of internecine rivalry, Later
was united with the London Company in 1650. In 1654-55, companies,
the 'Company of Merchant Adventurers' obtained a charter 1635,
from Cromwell to trade with India, but united with the 1655,
original Company two years later. A more formidable rival
subsequently appeared in the English Company, or 'General
Society trading to the East Indies,' which was incorporated
under powerful patronage in 1698, with a capital of 2 millions 1698,
sterling. According to Evelyn, in his *Diary* for March 5,
1698, 'the old East India Company lost their business against
the new Company by 10 votes in Parliament; so many of their
friends being absent, going to see a tiger baited by dogs.'
However, a compromise was effected through the arbitration
of Lord Godolphin [1] in 1708; by which the amalgamation of 1708.
the 'London' and the 'English' Companies was finally carried Amalga-
out in 1709, under the style of 'The United Company of mated
Company,
Merchants of England trading to the East Indies.' About 1709.
the same time, the Company advanced loans to the English
Government aggregating £3,200,000 at 5 per cent. interest, in
return for the exclusive privilege to trade to all places between
the Cape of Good Hope and the Straits of Magellan. [2]

The early voyages of the Company from 1600 to 1612 are English
distinguished as the 'separate voyages,' twelve in number. Voyages,
1600-12.
The subscribers individually bore the expenses of each voyage,
and reaped the whole profits. With the exception of the
fourth, all these separate voyages were highly prosperous, the
profits hardly ever falling below 100 per cent. After 1612,
the voyages were conducted on the joint-stock account.

The English were promptly opposed by the Portuguese. First
But James Lancaster, even in the first voyage (1601-2), English
voyages,
established commercial relations with the King of Achín and 1601-06.
at Priaman in the island of Sumatra; as well as with the
Malaccas, and at Bantam in Java, where he settled a 'House
of Trade' in 1603. In 1604 the Company undertook their
second voyage, commanded by Sir Henry Middleton, who
extended their trade to Banda and Amboyna. The success
of these voyages attracted a number of private merchants to
the business; and in 1606, James I. granted a licence to Sir
Edward Michelborne and others to trade 'to Cathay, China,
Japan, Corea, and Cambaya.' But Michelborne, on arriving

---

[1] Under the award of Lord Godolphin, by the Act of the 6th of Queen
Anne, in 1708, cap. 17. Auber's *Analysis*, p. xi.

[2] Mill, *Hist. Brit. Ind.*, vol. i. p. 151 (ed. 1840). Auber gives a detailed
statement of these loans, from 1708 to 1793; *Analysis*, p. xi. etc.

in the East, instead of exploring new sources of commerce like the East India Company, followed the pernicious example of the Portuguese, and plundered the native traders among the islands of the Indian Archipelago. He in this way secured a considerable booty, but brought disgrace on the British name, and seriously hindered the Company's business at Bantam.

Voyages, 1608-11.

In 1608, Captain D. Middleton, in command of the fifth voyage, was prevented by the Dutch from trading at Banda, but succeeded in obtaining a cargo at Pulo Way. In this year also, Captain Hawkins proceeded from Surat, as envoy from James I. and the East India Company, to the court of the Great Mughal. He was graciously received by the Emperor (Jahángír), and remained three years at Agra. In 1609, Captain Sharpay obtained the grant of free trade at Aden, and a cargo of pepper at Priaman in Sumatra. In 1609, also, the Company constructed the dockyard at Deptford, which was the beginning, observes Sir William Monson, 'of the increase of great ships in England.' In 1611, Sir Henry Middleton, in command of the sixth voyage, arrived before Cambay. He resolutely fought the Portuguese, who tried to beat him off, and obtained important concessions from the Native Powers. In 1610–11, also, Captain Hippon, commanding the seventh voyage, established agencies at Masulipatam, and in Siam, at Patania or Patany on the Malay Peninsula, and at Pettipollee. We obtained leave to trade at Surat in 1612.

Swally fight, 1615.

In 1615, the Company's fleet, under Captain Best, was attacked off Swally, the port of Surat, at the mouth of the river Tápti, by an overwhelming force of Portuguese.[1] But the assailants were utterly defeated in four engagements, to the astonishment of the natives, who had hitherto considered them invincible. The first-fruit of this decisive victory was the pre-eminence of our factory at Surat, with subordinate agencies at Gogra, Ahmadábád, and Cambay. Trade was also opened with the Persian Gulf. In 1614, an agency was established at Ajmere by Mr. Edwards of the Surat factory. The chief seat of the Company's government in Western India remained at Surat until 1684–87, when it was transferred to Bombay.[2]

---

[1] For this date and account of the engagement, see *Bombay Gazetteer*, SURAT and BROACH, vol. ii. pp. 77, 78 (Bombay Government Press, 1877).

[2] Orders issued, 1684 ; transfer commenced, 1686 ; actually carried out, 1687. *Bombay Gazetteer*, vol. ii. p. 98.

In 1615, Sir Thomas Roe was sent by James I. as am- Sir
bassador to the court of Jahángír, and succeeded in placing Roe, 1615.
Thomas
the Company's trade in the Mughal dominions on a more
favourable footing. In 1618, the English established a factory
at Mocha; but the Dutch compelled them to resign all pretensions to the Spice Islands. In that year also, the Company
failed in its attempt to open a trade with Dabhol, Baticola, and
Calicut, through a want of sincerity on the part of the Zamorin
or Calicut Rájá. In 1619 we were permitted to establish a
factory and build a fort at Jask, in the Persian Gulf.

In 1619, the 'Treaty of Defence' with the Dutch, to Treaty
prevent disputes between the English and Dutch companies, with
was ratified. When it was proclaimed in the East, the Dutch 1619.
Dutch,
and English fleets, dressed out in all their flags, and with
yards manned, saluted each other. But the treaty ended in
the smoke of that stately salutation, and the perpetual strife
between the Dutch and English Companies went on as bitterly
as ever. Up to this time, the English Company did not
possess any territory in sovereign right in the 'Indies,' excepting in the island of Lantore or Great Banda. The island was
governed by a commercial agent of the Company, who had
under him thirty Europeans as clerks and warehousemen.
This little band, with two hundred and fifty armed Malays,
constituted the only force by which it was protected. In the
islands of Banda and Pulo Roon and Rosengyn, the English
Company had factories, at each of which were ten agents.
At Macassar and Achín they possessed agencies; the
whole being subordinate to a head factory at Bantam in
Java.

In 1620, the Dutch, notwithstanding the Treaty of Defence, English
concluded the previous year, expelled the English from Pulo by Dutch,
attacked
Roon and Lantore; and in 1621 from Bantam in Java. The 1620.
fugitive factors tried to establish themselves, first at Pulicat, and
afterwards at Masulipatam on the Coromandel coast, but were
effectually opposed by the Dutch. In 1620, the Portuguese
also attacked the English fleet under Captain Shillinge, but
were defeated with great loss. From this time the estimation
in which the Portuguese were held by the natives declined,
while that of the English rose. In 1620, too, the English
Company established agencies at Agra and Patná. In 1622
they joined with the Persians, attacked and took Ormuz from
the Portuguese, and obtained from Sháh Abbas a grant in perpetuity of the customs of Gombroon. This was the first time
that the English took the offensive against the Portuguese.

Masuli-
patam fac-
tory, 1622.

The mas-
sacre of
Amboyna,
1623.

English
driven out
of Archi-
pelago,
1624.

English
retire to
India,
1625.

Their
early
factories,
1625–53.

Trade to
Bengal,
1634.

In the same year, 1622, our Company succeeded in re-establishing their factory at Masulipatam.

The massacre of Amboyna, which made so deep an impression on the English mind, marked the climax of the Dutch hatred to us in the eastern seas. After long and bitter recriminations, the Dutch seized our Captain Towerson at Amboyna, with 9 Englishmen, 9 Japanese, and 1 Portuguese sailor, on the 17th February 1623. They tortured the prisoners at their trial, and found them guilty of a conspiracy to surprise the garrison. The victims were executed in the heat of passion, and their torture and judicial murder led to an outburst of indignation in England. Ultimately, commissioners were appointed to adjust the claims of the two nations; and the Dutch had to pay a sum of £3615 as satisfaction to the heirs of those who had suffered. But from that time the Dutch remained masters of Lantore and the neighbouring islands. They monopolized the whole trade of the Indian Archipelago, until the great naval wars which commenced in 1793. In 1624, the English, unable to oppose the Dutch, withdrew nearly all their factories from the Archipelago, the Malay Peninsula, Siam, and Java. Some of the factors and agents retired to the island of Lagundy, in the Strait of Sunda, but were forced by its unhealthiness to abandon it.

Driven out of the Eastern Archipelago by the Dutch, and thus almost cut off from the lucrative spice trade, the English betook themselves in earnest to founding settlements on the Indian seaboard. In 1625–26, the English established a factory at Armagáon on the Coromandel coast, subordinate to Masulipatam.[1] But in 1628, Masulipatam was, in consequence of the oppressions of the native governors, for a time abandoned in favour of Armagáon, which now mounted 12 guns, and had 23 factors and agents. In 1629, our factory at Bantam in Java was re-established as an agency subordinate to Surat; and in 1630, Armagáon, reinforced by 20 soldiers, was also placed under the presidency of Surat. In 1632, the English factory was re-established at Masulipatam, under a grant, the 'Golden Firman,' from the King of Golconda. In 1634, by a *farmán* dated February 2, the Company obtained from the Great Mughal liberty to trade in Bengal. But their ships were to resort only to Pippli

---

[1] These brief chronological abstracts follow, with a few omissions, additions and corrections of dates, Sir George Birdwood's official *Report on the Old Records in the India Office* (folio), p. 83. For notices of the Indian towns mentioned, see the articles in *The Imperial Gazetteer of India.*

in Orissa, now left far inland by the sea.   The Portuguese were in the same year expelled for a time from Bengal.

In 1634-35, the English factory at Bantam in Java was again raised to an independent presidency, and an agency was established at Tatta, or 'Scindy.'   In 1637, Courten's Association (chartered 1635) settled agencies at Goa, Baticola, Kárwár, Achín, and Rájápur.   Its ships had the year before plundered some native vessels at Surat and Diu.   This act disgraced the Company with the Mughal authorities (who could not comprehend the distinction between the Company and the Association), and depressed the English trade with Surat, while that of the Dutch proportionately increased. Bantam Presidency, 1635.

In 1638, Armagáon was abandoned as unsuited for commerce ; and in 1639, Fort St. George or Madraspatnam (Chennapat-nam) [1] was founded by Francis Day, and the factors at Armagáon were removed to it.   It was made subordinate to Bantam in Java, until raised in 1653 to the rank of a Presidency.   In 1640, the Company established an agency at Bussorah, and a factory at Kárwár.   Trade having much extended, the Company's yard at Deptford was found too small for their ships, and they purchased some copyhold ground at Blackwall, which at that time was a waste marsh, without an inhabitant. Here they opened another dockyard, in which was built the *Royal George,* of 1200 tons, the largest ship up to that time constructed in England. Madras founded, 1639.

Our factory at Húglí in Bengal was established in 1640, and at Balasor in 1642.   In 1645, in consequence of professional services rendered by Mr. Gabriel Boughton, surgeon of the *Hopewell,* to the Emperor Sháh Jahán, additional privileges were granted to the Company ; and in 1646, the Governor of Bengal, who had also been medically attended by Boughton, made concessions which placed the factories at Balasor and Húglí on a more favourable footing.   In 1647, Courten's Association established its colony at Assada, in Madagascar. In 1652, Cromwell declared war against the Dutch on account of their accumulated injuries against the English Company. In 1653, the English factory at Lucknow was withdrawn. No record has been found of its establishment.   In 1658, the Company established a factory at Kásimbázár (spelt 'Castle Bazaar' in the records), and the English establishments in Húglí, 1640. Mada-gascar, 1647.

---

[1] Bishop Caldwell derives Madras from the Telugu *maduru,* the sur-rounding wall of a fort.   Its native name is obtained from Chennappa, the father-in-law of the Nayakkur or Chief of Chinglepat.   *Comparative Grammar of the Dravidian Languages,* p. 10 (ed. 1875).

Bengal were made subordinate to Fort St. George or Madras, instead of to Bantam.

Bombay ceded, 1661.

In 1661, Bombay was ceded to the British crown as part of the dower of Catharine of Braganza, but was not delivered up until 1665. King Charles II. transferred it to the East India Company, for an annual payment of £10, in 1668. The seat of the Western Presidency was removed to it from Surat in 1684–87. The Company's establishments in the East Indies then consisted in 1685 of the Presidency of Bantam in Java, with its dependencies of Jambí, Macassar, and minor agencies in the Indian Archipelago; Fort St. George and its dependent factories on the Coromandel coast and Bengal; Surat, with its affiliated dependency of Bombay; and factories at Broach, Ahmadábád, and other places in Western India; also at Gombroon (Bandar Abbas) and Bussorah in the Persian Gulf and Euphrates valley. In 1661, the factory at Biliapatam was founded. In 1663, the English factories established at Patná, Balasor, and Kásimbázár were ordered to be discontinued, and purchases to be made only at Húglí. In 1664, Surat was pillaged by the Maráthá Sivají, but Sir George Oxenden bravely defended the English factory; and the Mughal Emperor, in admiration of his conduct, granted the Company an exemption from customs for one year.

Our factories, 1685. Bantam. Madras. Bombay. Persian Gulf. Bengal.

Bengal separated from Madras, 1681.

In 1681, Bengal was separated from Madras, and Mr. Hodges appointed 'agent and governor' of the Company's affairs 'in the Bay of Bengal, and of the factories subordinate to it, at Kásimbázár, Patná, Balasor, Maldah, and Dacca. A corporal of approved fidelity, with 20 soldiers, to be a guard to the agent's person at the factory of Húglí, and to act against interlopers.' In 1684, Sir John Child was made 'Captain-General and Admiral of India;' and Sir John Wyborne, 'Vice-Admiral and Deputy Governor of Bombay.'

Bombay a Presidency, 1687.

In 1687, the seat of the Presidency was finally transferred from Surat to Bombay. In 1686, Kásimbázár, in common with the other English factories in Bengal, had been condemned to confiscation by the Nawáb Shaistá Khán. The Húglí factory was much oppressed, and the Company's business throughout India suffered from the wars of the Mughals and Maráthás.

'Governor-General.'

Sir John Child was appointed 'Governor-General,'[1] with full power in India to make war or peace; and was ordered to

[1] Sir George Birdwood's *Report on the Old Records of the India Office*, p. 85, quotes this title from the MSS. It is therefore, nominally, a century older than is usually supposed; but Hastings was the first real Governor-General, 1774.

proceed to inspect the Company's possessions in Madras and
Bengal, and arrange for their safety. On the 20th of Decem- Calcutta
ber 1686, the Company's Agent and Council were forced by founded,
1686.
the exactions of the Muhammadan Governor to quit their
factory at Húglí. They retired down the river to Sutanati
(Calcutta). Tegnapatam (Fort St. David) was founded in this
year (1686), and definitively established in 1691–92.

In 1687–88, the Company's servants, broken in spirit by the English
oppressions of the native Viceroy, determined to abandon their resolve
to quit
factories in Bengal. In 1688, Captain Heath of the *Resolution,* Bengal,
in command of the Company's forces, embarked all its servants 1687–88.
and goods, sailed down the Húglí, and anchored off Balasor
on the Orissa coast. They were, however, soon invited to
return by the Emperor, who granted them the site of the
present city of Calcutta for a fortified factory. In 1689, our
factories at Vizagapatam and Masulipatam on the Madras
coast were seized by the Muhammadans, and the factors
were massacred.

But in this same year, the Company determined to consoli- The Com-
date their position in India on the basis of territorial sovereignty, pany em-
barks on
to enable them to resist the oppression of the Mughals and territorial
Maráthás. With that view, they passed the resolution, which sway,
1689.
was destined to turn their clerks and factors throughout India
into conquerors and proconsuls : 'The increase of our revenue
is the subject of our care, as much as our trade ; 'tis that must
maintain our force when twenty accidents may interrupt our
trade ; 'tis that must make us a nation in India. Without that
we are but a great number of interlopers, united by His
Majesty's royal charter, fit only to trade where nobody of power
thinks it their interest to prevent us. And upon this account
it is that the wise Dutch, in all their general advices that
we have seen, write ten paragraphs concerning their government, their civil and military policy, warfare, and the increase
of their revenue, for one paragraph they write concerning
trade.' The subsequent history of the English East India
Company and its settlements will be narrated in the next
chapter.

The Portuguese at no time attempted to found a Company, Other
but kept their eastern trade as a royal enterprise and monopoly. 'East
India
The first incorporated Company was the English, established Com-
in 1600, which was quickly followed by the Dutch in 1602. panies.'
The Dutch conquests, however, were made in the name of the Dutch ;
State, and ranked as national colonies, not as semi-commercial

French ;   possessions. Next came the French, whose first East India Company was founded in 1604; the second, in 1611; the third, in 1615; the fourth (Richelieu's), in 1642; the fifth (Colbert's), in 1644. The sixth was formed by the union of the French East and West India, Senegal, and China Companies under the name of 'The Company of the Indies,' in 1719. The exclusive privileges of this Company were, by the French king's decree, suspended in 1769; and the Company was finally abolished by the National Assembly in 1796.

French possessions.   Dupleix, the governor of the French factories and possessions on the Madras coast, first conceived the idea of founding an Indian Empire upon the ruins of the Mughal dynasty; and for a time the French nation successfully contended with the English for the supremacy in the East. The French settlements in India are still five in number, with an area of 203 square miles, and a population of 273,611 souls. The brilliant history of our great national rivals is summarized under the article FRENCH POSSESSIONS in *The Imperial Gazetteer of India*, vol. iv. (2nd edition).

Danish ;   The first Danish East India Company was formed in 1612, and the second in 1670. The settlements of Tranquebar and Serampur were both founded in 1616, and acquired by the English by purchase from Denmark in 1845. Other Danish settlements on the mainland of India were Porto Novo ; with Eddova and Holcheri on the Malabar coast. The Company

Scotch ;   started by the Scotch in 1695 may be regarded as having been still-born. The 'Royal Company of the Philippine

Spanish ;   Islands,' incorporated by the King of Spain in 1733, had little to do with India proper.

German, or Ostend Company.   Of more importance was 'The Ostend Company,' incorporated by the Emperor of Austria in 1722 ;[1] its factors and agents being chiefly persons who had served in the Dutch and English Companies. This enterprise forms the subject of Carlyle's 'Third Shadow Hunt' of the Emperor Karl VI.[2] 'The Kaiser's Imperial Ostend East India Company, which convulsed the diplomatic mind for seven years to come, and

Described by Carlyle.   made Europe lurch from side to side in a terrific manner, proved a mere paper Company ; never sent ships, only produced Diplomacies, and "had the honour to be." ' Carlyle's

---

[1] The deed of institution is dated 17th December 1722.
[2] *History of Friedrich II. of Prussia, called Frederick the Great*, by Thomas Carlyle, vol. i. pp. 555-557 (3rd ed. 1859).

picturesque paragraphs do not disclose the facts. The Ostend Company formed the one great attempt of the German Empire, then with Austria at its head, to secure a share of the India trade. It not only sent ships, but it founded two settlements in India which threatened the commerce of the older European Companies. One of its settlements was at Coblom *Its Indian* or Covelong, between the English Madras and the Dutch *settlements.* Sadras, on the south-eastern coast. The other was at Bankipur, or 'Banky-bazaar,' on the Húglí River, between the English Calcutta and the Dutch Chinsura. Each of these German settlements was regarded with hatred by the English *Threaten-* and Dutch ; and with a more intense fear by the less successful *ing attitude* French, whose adjacent settlements at Pondicherri on the *Ostend* Madras coast, and at Chandarnagar on the Húglí, were also *Company.* threatened by the Ostend Company.

So far from the German association being 'a mere paper Company' never sending ships, as Carlyle supposes, its formation was the result of a series of successful experimental voyages. In 1717, Prince Eugene ordered two vessels to sail for India, under the protection of his own passports. The profits of *Its experi-* the expedition led to others in succeeding years, and each *mental voyages,* voyage proved so fortunate, that the Austrian Emperor found *1717–22.* it necessary to protect and consolidate the property of the adventurers by a charter in 1722. This deed granted to the Ostend Company more favourable terms than any of the other European Companies enjoyed. Its capital was one million *Their great* sterling, and so great were the profits during its first years *success.* that its shares brought in 15 per cent. The French, Dutch, and English Companies loudly complained of its factories, built at their very doors, both on the Húglí River and on the Madras coast. These complaints were warmly taken up by their respective Governments in Europe.

For the object which the Emperor Karl VI. had in view *Political* was political not less than commercial. Prince Eugene had *objects of* urged that an India Company might be made to form the *Company.* nucleus of a German fleet, with a first-class naval station at Ostend on the North Sea, and another at Fiume or Trieste on the Adriatic. Such a fleet would complete the greatness of Germany by sea as by land ; and would render her independent of the Maritime Powers, especially of England and Holland. The Empire would at length put its ports on the Baltic and the Adriatic to a proper use, and would thenceforth exert a commanding maritime influence in Europe.

The existing Maritime Powers objected to this ; and the

Ostend Company opposed by the Maritime Powers;

Ostend Company became the shuttlecock of European diplomacy for the next five years. The Dutch and English felt themselves particularly aggrieved. They pleaded the treaties of Westphalia and Utrecht. After long and loud altercations, the Emperor sacrificed the Ostend Company in 1727 to gain the acceptance of a project nearer his heart—the Prag-

and sacrificed to the Pragmatic Sanction, 1727.

matic Sanction for the devolution of his Imperial heritage. To save his honour, the sacrifice at first took the form of a suspension of the Company's charter for seven years. But the Company was doomed by the Maritime Powers. Its shareholders did not, however, despair. They made attempts to transfer their European centre of trade to Hamburg, Trieste, Tuscany, and even Sweden.

Ostend settlement destroyed, 1733;

Meanwhile the other European Companies in Bengal had taken the law into their own hands. They stirred up the Muhammadan Government against the new-comers. In 1733, the Muhammadan military governor of Húglí picked a quarrel, in the name of the Delhi Emperor, with the little German settlement at Bankipur, which lay about eight miles below Húglí town on the opposite side of the river. The Muhammadan troops besieged Bankipur; and the garrison, reduced to fourteen persons, after a despairing resistance against overwhelming numbers, abandoned the place, and set sail for Europe. The Ostend agent lost his right arm by a cannon ball during the attack; and the Ostend Company, together with the German interests which it represented, became thenceforward merely a name in Bengal. Its chief

and disappeared from the map.

settlement, Bankipur or ' Banky-bazaar,' has long disappeared from the maps; and the author could only trace its existence from a chart of the last century, aided by the records of that period, and by personal inquiry on the spot.[1] The Ostend Com-

Ostend Company bankrupt, 1784;

pany, however, still prolonged its existence in Europe. After a miserable struggle, it became bankrupt in 1784; and was finally extinguished by the arrangements made at the renewal

and extinguished, 1793.

of the English East India Company's charter in 1793.

Prussian Companies.

What the Emperor of Austria had failed to effect, Frederick the Great, King of Prussia, resolved to accomplish. Having got possession of East Friesland in 1744, he tried to convert

[1] There is an interesting series of MSS. labelled *The Ostenders* in the India Office. See also the Abbé Raynal's *History of the Settlements and Trade of the Europeans in the East and West Indies*, Book v. (pp. 176-182, vol. ii. of the 1776 edition); and the article BANKIPUR on the Húglí in *The Imperial Gazetteer of India.*

its capital, Embden, into a great northern port. Among other Asiatic Trading Company of Embden, 1750. Embden Bengal-ische Handels-gesellschaft, 1753. measures, he gave his royal patronage to the Asiatic Trading Company, started 1st September 1750, and founded the *Bengalische Handelsgesellschaft* on the 24th January 1753.[1] The first of these Companies had a capital of £170,625; but six ships sent successively to China only defrayed their own expenses, and yielded a profit of 10 per cent. in seven years. The Bengal Company of Embden proved still more unfortunate; its existence was summed up in two expeditions which did not pay, and a long and costly lawsuit.[2]

The failure of Frederick the Great's efforts to secure for Their failure. Prussia a share in the India trade, resulted to some extent from the jealousy of the rival European Companies in India. The Dutch, French, and English pilots refused to show the Dutch and English jealousy of the Embden Companies. way up the dangerous Húglí river to the Embden ships, ' or any other not belonging to powers already established in India.'[3] It is due to the European Companies to state that in thus refusing pilots to the new-comers, they were carrying out the orders of the Native Government of Bengal to which they were then strictly subject. 'If the Germans come here,' the The Nawáb's orders against the Prussians. Nawáb had written to the English merchants on a rumour of the first Embden expedition reaching India, 'it will be very bad for all the Europeans, but for you worst of all, and you will afterwards repent it; and I shall be obliged to stop all your trade and business. . . . Therefore take care that these German ships do not come.'[4] 'God forbid that they should come,' was the pious response of the President of the English Council; 'but should this be the case, I am in hopes they will be either sunk, broke, or destroyed.'

They came nevertheless, and some years later the English English agents privately trade with Prussian Company. Court of Directors complain that their Bengal servants are anxious to trade privately with the Embden Company. ' If any of the Prussian ships,' wrote the Court, 'want the usual assistance of water, provisions, or real necessaries, they are to be supplied according to the customs of nations in amity one with the other. But you are on no pretence whatsoever to

[1] These dates are taken from Carlyle's *Frederick the Great*, vol. iv. pp. 367, 368 (ed. 1864). Carlyle's account of the Embden Companies is unfortunately of slight historical value.

[2] The commercial details of these Companies are given by the Abbé Raynal, *op. cit.* ii. pp. 201, 202.

[3] Despatch from the Calcutta Council to the Court of Directors, dated 6th September 1754, para. 11.

[4] Letter from the Nawáb of Murshidábád : Bengal Consultations of 19th August 1751.

have any dealings with them, or give the least assistance in their mercantile affairs.'[1]   The truth is that the German Company had effected an entrance into Bengal, and found the French, English, and Dutch merchants quite willing to trade with it on their private account.   But the German invest-

Frederick sacrifices the Company.

ments were made without experience, and the Embden Company was before long sacrificed by the Prussian king to the exigencies of his European diplomacy.

Swedish Company, 1731.

The last nation of Europe to engage in maritime trade with India was Sweden.   When the Ostend Company was suspended, a number of its servants were thrown out of employment.   Mr. Henry Köning, of Stockholm, took advantage of their knowledge of the East, and obtained a charter for the 'Swedish Company,' dated 13th June 1731.   This Company was reorganized in 1806, but did little ; and after many troubles, disappeared from India.

Causes of failure : of the Portuguese ;

Such is a summary of the efforts by European nations to obtain a share in the India trade.   The Portuguese failed, because they attempted a task altogether beyond their strength ; the conquest and the conversion of India.   Their memorials are the epic of the Lusiad, the death-roll of the Inquisition, an indigent half-caste population, and three decayed patches

of the Dutch ;

of territory on the Bombay coast.   The Dutch failed on the Indian continent, because their trade was based on a monopoly which it was impossible to maintain, except by great and costly armaments.   Their monopoly, however, still flourishes

of the French.

in their isolated island dominion of Java.   The French failed, in spite of the brilliancy of their arms and the genius of their generals, from want of steady support at home.   Their ablest Indian servants fell victims to a corrupt Court and a careless people.   Their surviving settlements disclose that talent for careful administration which, but for French monarchs and their ministers and their mistresses, might have been displayed throughout a wide Indian Empire.

Causes of failure of the Germans.

The German Companies, whether Austrian or Prussian, were sacrificed to the diplomatic necessities of their royal patrons in Europe ; and to the dependence of the German States in the wars of the last century upon the Maritime Powers.   But the German people has never abandoned the struggle.   The share in the Indian trade which Prussian King

---

[1] Letter from the Court of Directors to the Calcutta Council, March 25, 1756, para. 71.

and Austrian Kaiser failed to grasp in the 18th century, has been gradually acquired by German merchants in our own day. An important part of the commerce of Calcutta and Bombay is now conducted by German firms; German mercantile agents are to be found in the rice districts, the jute districts, the cotton districts; and persons of German nationality have rapidly increased in the Indian Census returns. Revival of German trade in India.

England emerged the prize-winner from the long contest of the European nations for India. Her success was partly the good gift of fortune, but chiefly the result of four elements in the national character. There was—first, a marvellous patience and self-restraint in refusing to enter on territorial conquests or projects of Indian aggrandizement, until she had gathered strength enough to succeed. Second, an indomitable persistence in those projects once they were entered on; and a total incapacity, on the part of her servants in India, of being stopped by defeat. Third, an admirable mutual confidence of the Company's servants in each other in times of trouble. Fourth, and chief of all, the resolute support of the English nation at home. England has never doubted that she must retrieve, at whatever strain to herself, every disaster which may befall Englishmen in India; and she has never sacrificed the work of her Indian servants to the exigencies of her diplomacy in Europe. She was the only European power which unconsciously but absolutely carried out these two principles of policy. The result of that policy, pursued during two and a half centuries, is the British India of to-day. Causes of England's success in India. Fixed policy of England in India.

The extent to which the chief continental nations of Europe now resort to British India, may be inferred from the following figures. These figures are exclusive of Europeans in French and Portuguese territory, and in the Native States. Germans numbered 655 in 1872, and 1170 in 1881; French, 631 in 1872, and 1013 in 1881; Portuguese, 426 in 1872, and 147 in 1881; Italians, 282 in 1872, and 788 in 1881; Greeks, 127 in 1872, and 195 in 1881; Swedes, 73 in 1872, and 337 in 1881; Russians, 45 in 1872, and 204 in 1881; Dutch, 70 in 1872, and 79 in 1881; Norwegians, 58 in 1872, and 358 in 1881; Danes, 45 in 1872, and 126 in 1881; Spaniards, 32 in 1872, and 87 in 1881; Belgians, 20 in 1872, and 180 in 1881; Swiss, 19 in 1872, and 87 in 1881; Turks, 18 in 1872, and 355 in 1881; Austrians, 53 in 1872, and 296 in 1881. European traders in 1872 and 1881.

[378]

CHAPTER XV.

HISTORY OF BRITISH RULE (1757 TO 1885 A.D.).

Our first territorial possession. Madras, 1639. THE political history of the British in India begins in the 18th century with the French wars in the Karnátik. Fort St. George, the nucleus of Madras, founded by Francis Day in 1639, was our earliest possession. The French settlement of Pondicherri, about 100 miles lower down the Coromandel coast, was established in 1674; and for many years the English and French traded side by side without rivalry or territorial ambition. The English paid a rent of 1200 pagodas (£500) to the deputies of the Mughal Empire when Aurangzeb annexed the south, and on two occasions bought off a besieging army by a heavy bribe.

Southern India after 1707. After the death of Aurangzeb in 1707, the whole of Southern India became practically independent of Delhi. In the Deccan Proper, the Nizám-ul-Mulk founded a hereditary dynasty, with Haidarábád for its capital, which exercised a nominal authority over the entire south. The Karnátik, or the lowland tract between the central plateau and the eastern sea, was ruled by a deputy of the Nizám, known as the Nawáb **Local rulers.** of Arcot. Farther south, Trichinopoli was the capital of a Hindu Rájá; Tanjore formed another Hindu kingdom under a degenerate descendant of Sivají. Inland, Mysore was gradually growing into a third Hindu State; while everywhere local chieftains, called *pálegárs* or *naiks*, were in semi-independent possession of citadels or hill-forts. These represented the fief-holders of the ancient Hindu kingdom of Vijayanagar; and many of them had maintained a practical independence since its fall in 1565.

French and English in the Karnátik. Such was the condition of affairs in Southern India when war broke out between the English and the French in Europe in 1744. Dupleix was at that time Governor of Pondicherri, and Clive was a young writer at Madras. An English fleet first appeared on the Coromandel coast, but Dupleix, by a judicious present, induced the Nawáb of Arcot to interpose and prevent hostilities. In 1746, a French squadron arrived,

under the command of La Bourdonnais. Madras surrendered First
almost without a blow; and the only settlement left to the French
English was Fort St. David, a few miles south of Pondicherri, 1746-48.
where Clive and a few other fugitives sought shelter. The We lose
Nawáb, faithful to his impartial policy, marched with 10,000 Madras,
men to drive the French out of Madras, but was defeated. 1746.
In 1748, an English fleet arrived under Admiral Boscawen,
and attempted the siege of Pondicherri, while a land force
co-operated under Major Lawrence, whose name afterwards
became associated with that of Clive. The French repulsed
all attacks; but the treaty of Aix-la-Chapelle, in the same
year, restored Madras to the English.[1]

The first war with the French was merely an incident in the Second
greater contest in Europe. The second war had its origin in French
Indian politics, while England and France were at peace. 1750-61.
The easy success of the French arms had inspired Dupleix Dupleix.
with the ambition of founding a French empire in India,
under the shadow of the Muhammadan powers. Disputed successions at Haidarábád and at Arcot supplied his opportunity.
On both thrones Dupleix placed his nominees, and posed as
the arbiter of the entire south. The English of Madras,
under the instinct of self-preservation, had supported another
candidate to the throne of Arcot, in opposition to the nominee
of Dupleix. Our candidate was Muhammad Alí, afterwards known in history as Wálá-jáh. The war which ensued
between the French and English in Southern India has been
exhaustively described by Orme. The one incident that Clive's
stands out conspicuously is the capture and subsequent defence of
defence of Arcot by Clive in 1751. This heroic feat, even 1751.
more than the battle of Plassey, spread the fame of English
valour throughout India. Shortly afterwards, Clive returned
to England in ill-health, but the war continued fitfully for
many years. On the whole, English influence predominated in
the Karnátik or Madras coast, and their candidate, Muhammad
Alí, maintained his position at Arcot. But, inland, the French
were supreme in the Deccan, and they were able to seize the
maritime tract called 'the Northern Circars.'

The final struggle did not take place until 1760. In that Wande-
year Colonel (afterwards Sir Eyre) Coote won the decisive wash,
1760.

[1] The authorities for the French and English wars in Southern India
are—(1) Orme's *Indostan*, 2 vols., Madras reprint, 1861; (2) Mill's
History of British India (ed. 1840); and (3) for the French views of those
transactions, Colonel Malleson's admirable *History of the French in India*
(London, 1868), and *Final Struggles of the French in India* (London, 1878).

victory of Wandewash over the French General, Lally, and proceeded to invest Pondicherri, which was starved into capitulation in January 1761. A few months later the hill-fortress of Ginjee (Gingi) also surrendered.[1] In the words of Orme: 'That day terminated the long hostilities between the two rival European powers in Coromandel, and left not a single ensign of the French nation avowed by the authority of its Government in any part of India.'[2]

Gingi surrendered, 5th April 1761.

The English in Bengal, 1634-96.

Meanwhile, the narrative of British conquest shifts with Clive to Bengal. The first English settlement near the Gangetic estuary was Pippli in Orissa, at which the East India Company was permitted to trade in 1634, five years before the foundation of Madras. The river on which Pippli stood has since silted up, and the very site of the English settlement is now a matter of conjecture. In 1640, a factory was opened at Húglí; in 1642, at Balasor; and in 1681, Bengal was erected into a separate presidency, though still subordinate to Madras. The name of Calcutta is not heard of in the Company's records till 1686, when Job Charnock, the English chief, was forced to quit Húglí by the deputy of Aurangzeb, and settled lower down the river on the opposite bank. There he acquired a grant of the three petty villages of Sutanati, Gobindpur, and Kálíghát (Calcutta), and founded the original Fort William in 1696.

Native rulers of Bengal, 1707-56.

At the time of Aurangzeb's death, in 1707, the Nawáb or Governor of Bengal was Murshid Kulí Khán, known also in European history as Jafar Khán. By birth a Bráhman, and brought up as a slave in Persia, he united the administrative ability of a Hindu with the fanaticism of a renegade. Hitherto the capital of Bengal had been at Dacca, on the eastern frontier of the empire, whence the piratical attacks of the Portuguese and of the Arakanese or Maghs could be most easily checked. Murshid Kulí Khán transferred his residence to Murshidábád, in the immediate neighbourhood of Kásim-bázár, which was then the chief emporium of the Gangetic trade. The English, the French, and the Dutch had each factories at Kásimbázár, as well as at Dacca, Patná, and Maldah. But

---

[1] A full account of GINGI is given, *sub verbo,* in *The Imperial Gazetteer of India.* In like manner, the local history of each Presidency, Province, or town is treated in the separate article upon it, and can therefore only be very briefly summarized here. Thus, with regard to Calcutta, the reader is referred to article CALCUTTA in *The Imperial Gazetteer of India.*

[2] Orme's *History of Military Transactions in Indostan* (1803), Madras reprint, vol. ii. p. 733 (1861).

Calcutta was the head-quarters of the English, Chandarnagar European of the French, and Chinsurah of the Dutch. These three settle- headments were situated not far from one another upon reaches of quarters, the Húglí, where the river was navigable for sea-going ships. 1740. Calcutta is about 80 miles from the sea; Chandarnagar, 24 miles by river above Calcutta; and Chinsurah, 2 miles above Chandarnagar. Húglí town, to which reference has so often been made, is almost conterminous with Chinsurah, but lies one mile above it.

Murshid Kulí Khán ruled over Bengal prosperously for twenty-one years, and left his power to a son-in-law and a grandson. The hereditary succession was broken in 1740 by Alí Vardi Alí Vardi Khán, a usurper, but the last of the great Nawábs of Bengal. Khán, In his days the Maráthá horsemen began to ravage the 1740–56. country, and the inhabitants of Calcutta obtained permission in 1742 to erect an earthwork, known to the present day as the Maráthá ditch. Alí Vardi Khán died in 1756, and was succeeded by his grandson, Siráj-ud-Daulá (Surajah Dowlah), Siráj-ud-a youth of only eighteen years, whose ungovernable temper Daulá, led to a rupture with the English within two months after 1756. his accession.

In pursuit of one of his own family who had escaped from his vengeance, he marched upon Calcutta with a large army. Many of the English fled down the river in their ships. The remainder surrendered after a brave resistance, and were thrust for the night into the 'Black Hole' or military jail 'Black of Fort William, a room about 18 feet square, with only two Hole' of Calcutta, small windows barred with iron. It was our ordinary garrison 1756. prison in those times of cruel military discipline. But although the Nawáb does not seem to have been aware of the consequences, it meant death to a crowd of 146 English men and women in the stifling heats of June. When the door of the prison was opened next morning, only 23 persons out of 146 remained alive.[1]

The news of this disaster fortunately found Clive back again Clive and at Madras, where also was a squadron of the King's ships Watson. under Admiral Watson. Clive and Watson promptly sailed to

---

[1] The contemporary record of that terrible night is Holwell's Narrative. The original materials have been carefully examined, and much misrepresentation has been cleared away by Dr. H. E. Busteed, in the Calcutta *Englishman*, several dates, 1880. The site of the 'Black Hole' has been lately identified, at the entrance to the lane behind the General Post-Office; and the spot has been paved with fine stone (1884).

the mouth of the Ganges with all the troops they could get

Calcutta recovered, 1757. together. Calcutta was recovered with little fighting, and the Nawáb consented to a peace which restored to the Company all their privileges, and gave them ample compensation for their losses. It is possible that matters might have ended thus, if a fresh cause of hostilities had not suddenly arisen. War had just been declared between the English and French in Europe; and Clive, following the traditions of warfare in the Karnátik, captured the French settlement of Chandarnagar. The Nawáb Siráj-ud-Daulá, enraged by this breach of the peace within his dominions, took the side of the French. But Clive, acting upon the policy which he had learned from Dupleix, provided himself with a rival candidate (Mír Jafar) to the throne.

Battle of Plassey, 1757. Undaunted, he marched out to the grove of Plassey, about 70 miles north of Calcutta, at the head of 1000 Europeans and 2000 sepoys, with 8 pieces of artillery. The Bengal Viceroy's army numbered 35,000 foot and 15,000 horse, with 50 cannon.

How the victory was gained. Clive is said to have fought in spite of his Council of War. The truth is, he could scarcely avoid a battle. The Nawáb attacked with his whole artillery, at 6 A.M.; but Clive kept his men well under shelter, 'lodged in a large grove, surrounded with good mud banks.' At noon the enemy drew off into their entrenched camp for dinner. Clive only hoped to make a 'successful attack at night.' Meanwhile, the enemy being probably undressed over their cooking-pots, he sprang upon one of their advanced posts, which had given him trouble, and stormed 'an angle of their camp.' Several of the Nawáb's chief officers fell. The Nawáb himself, dismayed by the unexpected confusion, fled on a camel; his troops dispersed in a panic, and Clive found he had won a great victory. Mír Jafar's cavalry, which had hovered undecided during the battle, and had been repeatedly fired on by Clive, 'to make them keep their distance,' now joined our camp; and the road to Murshidábád lay open.[1]

The battle of Plassey was fought on June 23, 1757, an anniversary afterwards remembered when the Mutiny of 1857 was at its height. History has agreed to adopt this date as the beginning of the British Empire in the East. But the imme-

Its small results at first. diate results of the victory were comparatively small, and several years passed in hard fighting before even the Bengalis would admit the superiority of the British arms. For the

---

[1] These numbers and the account of the battle are taken by the author from Clive's MS. Despatch to the Secret Committee, dated 26th July 1757. The quotations are Clive's own words.

moment, however, all opposition was at an end.   Clive, again
following in the steps of Dupleix, placed Mír Jafar upon the Mír Jafar,
Vic_eregal throne at Murshidábád, being careful to obtain a 1757.
patent of investiture from the Mughal court.

Enormous sums were exacted from Mír Jafar as the price of Pecuniary
his elevation.   The Company claimed 10 million rupees as com- compensa-
pensation for its losses.   For the English, native, and Armenian English.
inhabitants of Calcutta were demanded, respectively, 5 million,
2 million, and 1 million rupees; for the naval squadron and the
army, $2\frac{1}{2}$ million rupees apiece.   The members of the Council
received the following amounts :—Mr. Drake, the Governor,
and Colonel Clive, as second member of the Select Committee, 280,000 rupees each.   Colonel Clive also received
200,000 rupees as Commander-in-Chief, and 1,600,000 rupees
' as a private donation;' Mr. Becker, Mr. Watts, and Major
Kilpatrick, 240,000 rupees each, besides 'private donations,'
amounting in the case of Mr. Watts to 800,000 rupees.   The
gratifications of a personal character, including the donation
to the troops and the fleet, aggregated £1,238,575;[1] while
the whole claim amounted to £2,697,750.   The English stil
cherished extravagant ideas of Indian wealth.   But no funds
existed to satisfy their inordinate demands, and they had to be
contented with one-half the stipulated sums.   Even of this
reduced amount, one-third had to be taken in jewels and
plate, there being neither coin nor bullion left.

At the same time, the Nawáb made a grant to the Com- Grant of
pany of the *zamíndárí* or landholder's rights over an extensive Twenty-
tract of country round Calcutta, now known as the District ganás,
of the Twenty-four Parganás.   The area of this tract was 882 1757.
square miles.   In 1757 the Company obtained only the
zamíndárí rights—*i.e.*, the rights to collect the cultivators'
rents, with the revenue jurisdiction over them.   The superior
lordship, or right to receive the land-tax, remained with the
Nawáb.   But in 1759 this also was granted by the Delhi
Emperor, the nominal Suzerain of the Nawáb, in favour of
Clive, who thus became the landlord of his own masters,
the Company.   Clive was enrolled among the highest nobility
of the Mughal Empire, with the rank of commander of 6000
foot and 5000 horse, and a large allotment of land near
Calcutta, in 1759.

This military fief, or Clive's *jágír*, as it was called, subse- Clive's
quently became a matter of inquiry in England.   Lord Clive's *jágír*, 1759.

[1] For a full statement of the personal donations, see Mill's *History of
British India,* vol. iii. pp. 367, 368 (Wilson's ed. 1840).

claims to the property as feudal Suzerain over the Company were contested in 1764. On the 23rd June 1765, when he returned to Bengal, a new deed was issued, confirming the unconditional *jágír* to Lord Clive for ten years, with reversion afterwards to the Company in perpetuity. This deed, having received the Emperor's sanction on the 12th August 1765, gave absolute validity to the original *jágír* grant in favour of Lord Clive. It transferred, in reversion, to the Company the Twenty-four Parganás as a perpetual property based upon a *jágír* grant. The sum of Rs. 222,958, the amount at which the land was assessed when first made over to the Company in 1757, was paid to Lord Clive from 1765 until his death in 1774, when the whole proprietary right reverted to the Company.[1]

Clive, first Governor of Bengal, 1758 ; In 1758, Clive was appointed by the Court of Directors the first Governor of all the Company's settlements in Bengal.[2]

[1] For a full account of the different grants, and the powers granted by them, see Hunter's *Statistical Account of Bengal*, vol. i. (TWENTY-FOUR PARGANAS), pp. 19, 20.

[2] GOVERNORS AND GOVERNORS-GENERAL OF INDIA UNDER THE EAST INDIA COMPANY, 1758-1858.

1758. Lord Clive, Governor.	1805. Sir George Barlow (*pro tem.*).
1760. Mr. Z. Holwell (*pro tem.*).	1807. Earl of Minto.
1760. Mr. Vansittart.	1813. Earl of Moira, Marquis of Hastings.
1765. Lord Clive (second time).	
1767. Harry Verelst.	1823. John Adam (*pro tem.*).
1769. John Cartier.	1823. Lord Amherst.
1772. Warren Hastings (first Governor-General, 1774).	1828. Mr. Butterworth Bayley (*pro tem.*).
1785. Sir John Macpherson (*pro tem.*).	1828. Lord William Cavendish Bentinck.
1786. Marquis of Cornwallis.	1835. Sir Chas. Metcalfe, afterwards Lord Metcalfe (*pro tem.*).
1793. Sir John Shore (Lord Teignmouth).	
1798. Sir Alured Clarke (*pro tem.*).	1836. Earl of Auckland.
1798. Lord Mornington (Marquis Wellesley).	1842. Earl of Ellenborough.
	1844. Viscount Hardinge.
1805. Marquis of Cornwallis (second time).	1848. Earl (afterwards Marquis) of Dalhousie.
	1856. Earl Canning.

VICEROYS OF INDIA UNDER THE CROWN, 1858-85.

1858. Earl Canning.	1869. Earl of Mayo.
1862. Earl of Elgin.	1872. Sir John Strachey (*pro tem.*).
1863. Sir R. Napier, afterwards Lord Napier of Magdala (*pro tem.*).	1872. Lord Napier of Merchistoun (*pro tem.*).
1863. Sir William Denison (*pro tem.*).	1872. Earl of Northbrook.
	1876. Earl of Lytton.
1864. Sir John Lawrence (Lord Lawrence).	1880. Marquis of Ripon.
	1884. Lord Dufferin.

Two powers threatened hostilities. On the west, the Sháhzáda or Imperial prince, known afterwards as the Emperor Sháh Alam, with a mixed army of Afgháns and Maráthás, and supported by the Nawáb Wazír of Oudh, was advancing his own claims to the Province of Bengal. In the south, the influence of the French under Lally and Bussy was over-shadowing the British at Madras.

The vigour of Clive exercised a decisive effect in both directions. Mír Jafar was anxious to buy off the Sháhzáda, who had already invested Patná. But Clive marched in person to the rescue, with an army of only 450 Europeans and 2500 sepoys, and the Mughal army dispersed without striking a blow. Clive also despatched a force southwards from Bengal under Colonel Forde, in 1759, which recaptured Masulipatam from the French, and permanently established British influence throughout the Northern Circars, and at the court of Haidarábád. He next attacked the Dutch, the only other European nation who might yet prove a rival to the English. He defeated them both by land and water; and their settlement at Chinsurah existed thenceforth only on sufferance. *scatters Oudh army; overcomes French in Madras; defeats Dutch.*

From 1760 to 1765, Clive was in England. He had left no system of government in Bengal, but merely the tradition that unlimited sums of money might be extracted from the natives by the terror of the English name. In 1761, it was found expedient and profitable to dethrone Mír Jafar, the English Nawáb of Murshidábád, and to substitute his son-in-law, Mír Kásim, in his place. On this occasion, besides private donations, the English received a grant of the three Districts of Bardwán, Midnapur, and Chittagong, estimated to yield a net revenue of half a million sterling. But Mír Kásim soon began to show a will of his own, and to cherish dreams of independence. He retired from Murshidábád to Monghyr a strong position on the Ganges, commanding the only means of communication with the north-west. There he proceeded to organize an army, drilled and equipped after European models, and to carry on intrigues with the Nawáb Wazír of Oudh. He resolved to try his strength with the English, and found a good pretext. *Misman-agement, 1760-64. Mír Kásim set up, 1761.*

The Company's servants claimed the privilege of carrying on their private trade throughout Bengal, free from inland dues and all imposts. The assertion of this claim caused affrays between the customs officers of the Nawáb and the native traders, who, whether truly or not, represented that *Mír Kásim breaks with the English.*

2 B

they were acting on behalf of the servants of the Company. The Nawáb alleged that his civil authority was everywhere set at nought. The majority of the Council at Calcutta would not listen to his complaints. The Governor, Mr. Vansittart, and Warren Hastings, then a junior member of Council, attempted to effect some compromise. But the controversy had become too hot. The Nawáb's officers fired upon an English boat, and forthwith all Bengal rose in arms. Two

Patná Massacre, 1763.

thousand of our sepoys were cut to pieces at Patná; about 200 Englishmen, who there and in various other parts of the Province fell into the hands of the Muhammadans, were massacred.[1]

But as soon as regular warfare commenced, Mír Kásim met with no more successes. His trained regiments were defeated in two pitched battles by Major Adams, at Gheriah and at Udhanálá (Oodeynullah); and he himself took refuge with the Nawáb Wazír of Oudh, who refused to deliver him up. This led to a prolongation of the war. Sháh Alam, who had succeeded his father as Delhi Emperor, and Shujá-ud-Daulá the Nawáb Wazír of Oudh, united their forces, and threatened

First sepoy mutiny, 1764.

Patná, which the English had recovered. A more formidable danger appeared in the English camp, in the form of the first sepoy mutiny. This was quelled by Major (afterwards Sir Hector) Munro, who ordered 24 of the ringleaders to be blown

Battle of Baxár, 1764.

from guns—an old Mughal punishment. In 1764, Major Munro won the decisive battle of Baxár, which laid Oudh at the feet of the conquerors, and brought the Mughal Emperor a suppliant to the English camp.

Clive's second governorship, 1765-67.

Meanwhile, the Council at Calcutta had twice found the opportunity they loved of selling the government of Bengal to a new Nawáb. But in 1765, Clive (now Baron Clive of Plassey in the peerage of Ireland) arrived at Calcutta, as Governor of Bengal for the second time. Two landmarks stand out in his policy. First, he sought the substance, although not the name, of territorial power, under the fiction of a grant from the Mughal Emperor. Second, he desired to purify the Company's service, by prohibiting illicit gains, and by guaranteeing a reasonable pay from honest sources. In neither respect were his plans carried out by his immediate successors. But the beginning of our Indian rule dates from

---

[1] The massacre of Patná is described in sufficient detail under article PATNA DISTRICT in *The Imperial Gazetteer of India*, and in Hunter's *Statistical Account of Bengal*, vol. xi. pp. 71 *et seq.*

this second governorship of Clive, as our military supremacy had dated from his victory at Plassey.

Clive landed, advanced rapidly up from Calcutta to Allah-ábád, and there settled in person the fate of nearly half of India. Oudh was given back to the Nawáb Wazír, on condition of his paying half a million sterling towards the expenses of the war. The Provinces of Allahábád and Kora,[1] forming the greater part of the Doáb, were handed over to Sháh Alam, the Delhi Emperor, who in his turn granted to the Company the *diwáni* or fiscal administration of Bengal, Behar, and Orissa, with the jurisdiction of the Northern Circars. A puppet Nawáb was still maintained at Murshidábád, with an annual allowance from us of £600,000. Half that amount, or about £300,000, we paid to the Emperor as tribute from Bengal.[2] Thus was constituted the dual system of Government, by which the English received the revenues of Bengal and undertook to maintain the army; while the criminal jurisdiction, or *nizámat*, was vested in the Nawáb. In Indian phraseology, the Company was *diwán*, and the Nawáb was *nizám*. The actual collection of the revenues still remained for some years in the hands of native officials.

Clive's other great task was the reorganization of the Company's service. All the officers, civil and military alike, were tainted with the common corruption. Their legal salaries were paltry and quite insufficient for a livelihood. But they had been permitted to augment them, sometimes a hundred-fold, by means of private trade and gifts from the native powers. Despite the united resistance of the civil servants, and an actual mutiny of two hundred military officers, Clive carried through his reforms. Private trade and the receipt of presents were prohibited for the future, while a substantial increase of pay was provided out of the monopoly of salt.

Lord Clive quitted India for the third and last time in 1767. Between that date and the governorship of Warren Hastings in 1772, little of importance occurred in Bengal beyond the terrible famine of 1770, which is officially reported to have swept away one-third of the inhabitants. The dual system of government, established in 1765 by Clive, had proved a

Marginal notes: Clive's partition of Gangetic valley, 1765. — Diwání grant of Bengal, 1765. — Clive's reorganization of the Company's service, 1766. — Dual system of administration 1767-72;

---

[1] The 'Corah' of the E. I. Company's records; the capital of an ancient Muhammadan governorship, now a decayed town in Fatehpur District. article KO RA in *The Imperial Gazetteer of India*.

[2] The exact sums were Sikka Rs. 5,386,131 to the Nawáb, and Sikka Rs. 2,600,000 to the Emperor.

failure. Warren Hastings, a tried servant of the Company, distinguished alike for intelligence, for probity, and for knowledge of oriental manners, was nominated Governor by the Court of Directors, with express instructions to carry out a predetermined series of reforms. In their own words, the Court had resolved to 'stand forth as *díwán*, and to take upon themselves, by the agency of their own servants, the entire care and administration of the revenues.' In the execution of this plan, Hastings removed the exchequer to Calcutta from Murshidábád, which had up to that time remained the revenue head-quarters of Bengal. He also appointed European officers, under the now familiar title of Collectors, to superintend the revenue collections and preside in the courts.

Dual system abolished, 1772.

Clive had laid the territorial foundations of the British Empire in Bengal. Hastings may be said to have created a British administration for that Empire. The wars forced on him by Native Powers in India, the clamours of his masters in England for money, and the virulence of Sir Philip Francis with a faction of his colleagues at the Council table in Calcutta, retarded the completion of his schemes. But the manuscript records disclose the patient statesmanship and indomitable industry which he brought to bear upon them. From 1765 to 1772, Clive's dual system of government, by corrupt native underlings and rapacious English chiefs, prevailed. Thirteen years were now spent by Warren Hastings in experimental efforts at rural administration by means of English officials (1772–85). The completion of the edifice was left to his successor. But Hastings was the administrative organizer, as Clive had been the territorial founder, of our Indian Empire.

Warren Hastings, 1772–85.

His administrative reforms.

Hastings' true fame as an Indian ruler rests on his administrative work. He reorganized the Indian service, reformed every branch of the revenue collections, created courts of justice and some semblance of a police. History remembers his name, however, not for his improvements in the internal administration, but for his bold foreign policy, and for the crimes into which it led him. From 1772 to 1774, he was Governor of Bengal; from the latter date to 1785, he was the first Governor-General, presiding over a Council nominated, like himself, under a statute of Parliament known as the Regulating Act (1773). In his domestic policy he was greatly hampered by the opposition of his colleague in council, Sir Philip Francis. But in his external relations with Oudh, with the Maráthás, and with Haidar Alí, he was generally able to compel assent to his views.

Hastings' policy with native powers.

Warren Hastings first Governor-General, 1774.

His relations with the native powers, like his domestic His two-fold aims. policy, formed a well-considered scheme. Hastings had to find money for the Court of Directors in England, whose thirst for the wealth of India was not less keen, although more decorous, than that of their servants in Bengal. He had also to protect the Company's territory from the Native Powers, which, if he had not destroyed them, would have annihilated him. An honest man under such circumstances might be led into questionable measures. Hastings in his personal dealings, and as regards his personal gains, seems to have been a high-minded English gentleman. But as an Anglo-Indian statesman, he shared the laxity which he saw practised by the native potentates with whom he had to deal. Parts of his policy were vehemently assailed in Parliament, and cannot be upheld by right-thinking men. It is the object of the present summary neither to attack nor to defend his measures, but to give a short account of them as a connected whole.

Warren Hastings had in the first place to make Bengal pay. Hastings makes Bengal pay. This he could not do under Clive's dual system of administration. When he abolished that double system, he cut down the Nawáb's allowance to one-half, and so saved about £160,000 a year. In defence of this act, it may be stated that the titular Nawáb, being then a minor, had ceased to render even any nominal service for his enormous pension. Clive had himself reduced the original £600,000 to £450,000 on the accession of a new Nawáb in 1766, and the grant was again cut down to £350,000 on a fresh succession in 1769.[1] The allowance had practically been of a fluctuating and personal character.[2] Its further reduction in the case of the new child-Nawáb had, moreover, been expressly ordered by the Court of Directors six months before Hastings took office.

Hastings' next financial stroke was the sale of Allahábád and Sells Allahábád and Kora, 1773. Kora Provinces to the Wazír of Oudh. These Provinces had been assigned by Clive, in his partition of the Gangetic valley, to the Emperor Sháh Alam, together with a tribute of about £300,000 (26 *lákhs* of rupees), in return for the grant of Bengal to the Company. But the Emperor had now been

---

[1] The detailed history of these transactions, and a sketch of each of the 14 Nawábs of Bengal from 1704 to 1884, will be found under District Murshidábád, vol. ix. pp. 172–195 of Hunter's *Statistical Account of Bengal.*

[2] See separate agreements with the successive Nawábs of 30th September 1765, 19th May 1766, and 21st March 1770, in each of which the grant is to the Nawáb, without mention of heirs or successors.—Aitchison's *Treaties and Engagements,* vol. i. pp. 56–59 (ed. 1876).

seized by the Maráthás.   Hastings held that His Majesty
was no longer independent, and that it would be a fatal policy
for the British to pay money to the Maráthás in Northern
India, when it was evident that they would soon have to fight
them in the south.   He therefore withheld the tribute of the
£300,000 from the puppet Emperor, or rather from his
Maráthá custodians.

Withholds the Emperor's tribute.

Clive, at the partition of the Gangetic valley in 1765, assigned
the Provinces of Allahábád and Kora to the Emperor.   The
Emperor, now in the hands of the Maráthás, had made them
over to his new masters.   Warren Hastings held that by so
doing His Majesty had forfeited his title to these Provinces.
Hastings accordingly resold them to the Wazír of Oudh.   By
this measure he freed the Company from a military charge of
nearly half a million sterling (40 *lákhs* of rupees), and obtained
a price of over half a million (50 *lákhs*) for the Company.

The Rohillá war, 1773-74.

The sale included the loan of the British troops to subdue
the Rohillá Afgháns, who held a large tract in those Provinces
ever since Ahmad Sháh's desolating invasion in 1761.   The
Rohillás were foreigners, and had cruelly lorded it over the
peasantry.[1]   They now resisted bravely, and were crushed with
the merciless severity of Asiatic warfare by the Wazír of Oudh,
aided by his British troops.   By these measures Warren Hastings
bettered the finances of Bengal to the extent of a million
sterling a year on both sides of the account; but he did so at
the cost of treaties and pensions granted by his predecessor
Clive.

Plunder of Chait Singh, 1780.

He further improved the financial position of the Company
by what is known as the plunder of Chait Singh and the
Begam of Oudh.   Chait Singh, the Rájá of Benares, had grown
rich under British protection.   He resisted the demand of
Warren Hastings to subsidize a military force, and an alleged
correspondence with the enemies of the British Government led
to his arrest.   He escaped, headed a rebellion, and was crushed.
His estates were forfeited, but transferred to his nephew subject to an increased tribute.[2]

Hastings fines the Oudh Begam, 1782.

The Begam, or Queen-Mother, of Oudh was charged with
abetting the Benares Rájá in his rebellion.   A heavy fine was
laid upon her, which she resisted to the utmost.   But after

---

[1] For the history of the Rohillá Afgháns, on whom much sentiment
has been needlessly lavished, see article BAREILLY DISTRICT, *The Imperial
Gazetteer of India,* and other Districts of Rohilkhand.

[2] See *The Imperial Gazetteer of India,* articles BENARES DISTRICT and
BENARES ESTATE.

cruel pressure on herself and the eunuchs of her household, over a million sterling was extorted for the English Company.

On his return to England, Warren Hastings was impeached, Charges in 1786, by the House of Commons for these and other alleged against acts of oppression. He was solemnly tried by the House of Hastings. Lords, and the proceedings dragged themselves out for seven years (1788–95). They form one of the most celebrated State trials in English history, and ended in a verdict of not guilty on all the charges. Meanwhile, the cost of the defence had ruined Warren Hastings, and left him dependent upon the charity of the Court of Directors—a charity which never failed.

The real excuse, such as it is, for some of Hastings' measures Hastings' is that he had to struggle for his very existence; that native poor perfidy gave him his opportunity; and that he used his oppor- excuse. tunity, on the whole, less mercilessly than a native Viceroy would have done. It is a poor excuse for the clearest English head, and the firmest administrative hand, that ever ruled India. In his dealings with Southern India, Warren Hastings had not to regard solely the financial results. He there appears as the great man that he really was; calm in council, cautious of enterprise, but swift in execution, and of indomitable courage in all that he undertook.

The Bombay Government was naturally emulous to follow the example of Madras and Bengal, and to establish its supre- macy at the Court of Poona by placing its own nominee upon the throne. This ambition found its scope in 1775 by the treaty of Surat, by which Raghunáth Ráo, one of the claimants to the throne of the Peshwá, agreed to cede Salsette and Bassein to the English, in consideration of being himself restored to Poona. The military operations that followed are First Mar- known as the first Maráthá war. Warren Hastings, who in his áthá war, capacity of Governor-General claimed some degree of control 1778–81. over the decisions of the Bombay Government, strongly dis- approved of the treaty of Surat. But when war actually broke out, he threw the whole force of the Bengal army into the scale. One of his favourite officers, General Goddard, marched across Goddard's the peninsula from sea to sea, and conquered the rich Province march, of Gujarát almost without a blow. Another, Captain Popham, 1778–79. snatched by storm the rock-fortress of Gwalior, which was regarded as the key of Hindustán.

These brilliant successes of the Bengal troops atoned for the contemporaneous disgrace of the convention of Wargaum in 1779, when the Maráthás overpowered and dictated terms to our Bombay force. The war in Bombay lasted till 1781.

Treaty of
Salbai,
1782.

It was closed by the treaty of Salbai (1782), which practically restored the *status quo*. Raghunáth Ráo, the English claimant to the Peshwáship, was set aside on a pension; Gujarát was restored to the Maráthás; and only Salsette, with Elephanta and two other small islands, was retained by the English.

Meanwhile, Warren Hastings had to deal with a more formidable enemy than the Maráthá confederacy. The reckless conduct of the Madras Government had roused the hostility

War with
Mysore,
1780–84.

both of Haidar Alí of Mysore and of the Nizám of the Deccan, the two strongest Musalmán powers in India. These princes began to draw the Maráthás into an alliance against the English. The diplomacy of Hastings won back the Nizám and the Maráthá Rájá of Nágpur; but the army of Haidar Alí fell like a thunderbolt upon the British possessions in the Karnátik. A strong detachment under Colonel Baillie was cut to pieces at Pollilore, and the Mysore cavalry ravaged the country up to the walls of Madras. For the second time the Bengal army, stimulated by the energy of Hastings, saved the honour of the English name. He despatched Sir Eyre Coote, the victor of Wandewash, to relieve Madras by sea, with all the men and money available, while Colonel Pearse marched south overland to overawe the Rájá of Berar and the Nizám. The war was hotly contested, for the aged Sir Eyre Coote had lost his energy, and the Mysore army was not only well disciplined and equipped, but skilfully handled by Haidar and

Death of
Haidar
Alí, 1782.

his son Tipú. Haidar died in 1782; and peace was finally concluded with Tipú in 1784, on the basis of a mutual restitution of all conquests.

Lord
Corn-
wallis,
1786–93.

Two years later, Warren Hastings was succeeded by Lord Cornwallis, the first English nobleman of rank who undertook the office of Governor-General of India. Between these two great names an interval of twenty months took place under Sir John Macpherson, a civil servant of the Company (Feb. 1785 to Sept. 1876). Lord Cornwallis twice held the high post of Governor-General. His first rule lasted from 1786 to 1793, and is celebrated for two events—the introduction of the Permanent Settlement into Bengal, and the second Mysore war. If the foundations of the system of civil administration were laid by Hastings, the superstructure was raised by Cornwallis. It was he who first entrusted criminal jurisdiction to Europeans, and established the Nizámat Sadr Adálat, or Supreme Court of Criminal Judicature, at Calcutta.

It was he, also, who separated the functions of the District Collector and Judge.

The system thus organized in Bengal was afterwards ex- His tended to Madras and Bombay, when those Presidencies also revenue reforms. acquired territorial sovereignty. But the achievement most familiarly associated with the name of Cornwallis is the Permanent Settlement of the land revenue of Bengal. During four years, 1786-90, he laboured, with the help of an able Bengal civilian, John Shore, to arrive at the facts of the case. Warren Hastings had introduced, unsuccessfully and only for a period, a five years' settlement of the land revenue. Lord Cornwallis, after three years of inquiry and of provisional measures, introduced a ten years' or 'decennial' settlement The De- (1789-91). Up to this time, the revenue had been collected cennial pretty much according to the old Mughal system. The ment, *zamíndárs*, or Government farmers, whose office always tended 1789-91. to become hereditary, were recognised as having a right to collect the revenue from the actual cultivators. But no principle of assessment existed, and the amount actually realized varied greatly from year to year. Hastings seems to have looked to experience, as acquired from a succession of quinquennial settlements, to furnish the standard rate of the future. Francis, on the other hand, Hastings' great rival, advocated the fixing of the State demand in perpetuity. The same view recommended itself to the authorities at home, Period of partly because it would place their finances on a more stable experi- basis, partly because it seemed to identify the *zamíndár* with the landlord of the English system of property. Accordingly, Cornwallis took out with him in 1786 instructions to introduce a Permanent Settlement.

The process of assessment began in 1789, and terminated in The Per- 1791. No attempt was made to measure the fields or calculate manent Settlement the out-turn, as had been done by Akbar, and as is now done of Bengal, whenever settlements are made in the British Provinces. The 1793. amount to be paid in the future was fixed by reference to what had been paid in the past. At first the settlement was called decennial, but in 1793 it was declared permanent for ever. The total assessment amounted to Sikka Rs. 26,800,989, or about 3 millions sterling for Bengal. Lord Cornwallis carried the scheme into execution ; but the praise or blame, so far as details are concerned, belongs to Sir John Shore, afterwards Lord Teignmouth, a civil servant, whose knowledge of the country was unsurpassed in his time. Shore would have proceeded more cautiously than Cornwallis' preconceived English idea of a proprietary body, and the Court of Directors' haste after fixity, permitted.[1]

Second Mysore war, 1790-92.

The second Mysore war of 1790–92 is noteworthy on two accounts. Lord Cornwallis, the Governor-General, led the British army in person, with a pomp and a magnificence of supply which recalled the campaigns of Aurangzeb. The two great southern powers, the Nizám of the Deccan and the Maráthá confederacy, co-operated as allies of the British. In the end, Tipú Sultán submitted when Lord Cornwallis had commenced to beleaguer his capital. He agreed to yield one-half of his dominions to be divided among the allies, and to pay 3 millions sterling towards the cost of the war. These conditions he fulfilled, but ever afterwards he burned to be revenged upon his English conquerors.

Sir John Shore, 1793-98.

The period of Sir John Shore's rule as Governor-General, from 1793 to 1798, was uneventful. In 1798, Lord Mornington, better known as the Marquis of Wellesley, arrived in India, already inspired with imperial projects which were destined to change the map of the country. Mornington was the friend and favourite of Pitt, from whom he is thought to have derived his far-reaching political vision, and his

Marquis of Wellesley, 1798-1805.

antipathy to the French name. From the first he laid down as his guiding principle, that the English must be the one paramount power in the peninsula, and that native princes could only retain the insignia of sovereignty by surrendering their political independence. The history of India since his time has been but the gradual development of this policy, which received its finishing touch when Queen Victoria was proclaimed Empress of India on the 1st of January 1877.[2]

French influence in India, 1798-1800.

To frustrate the possibility of a French invasion of India, led by Napoleon in person, was the governing idea of

[1] The Permanent Settlement will be referred to in greater detail, and its practical working exhibited, under the Administrative chapter.

[2] An admirable account of Lord Wellesley's policy will be found in the Despatch of the Governor-General in Council to the Secret Committee of the Court of Directors, dated Fort William, 12th April 1804. This Despatch extends to 791 paragraphs, and covers all the great Indian questions of that eventful period. It was printed by John Stockdale, Piccadilly, in 1805, as a quarto volume, entitled, *History of all the Events and Transactions which have taken place in India*, etc. It will continue to form the most authentic record of any Governor-Generalship of India, until the seal is taken off Lord Dalhousie's long closed diaries.

Wellesley's foreign policy. France at this time, and for many years later, filled the place afterwards occupied by Russia in the imagination of English statesmen. Nor was the danger so remote as might now be thought. French regiments guarded and overawed the Nizám of Haidarábád. The soldiers of Sindhia, the military head of the Maráthá confederacy, were disciplined and led by French adventurers. Tipú Sultán of Mysore carried on a secret correspondence with the French Directorate, allowed a tree of liberty to be planted in his dominions, and enrolled himself in a republican club as 'Citizen Tipú.' The islands of Mauritius and Bourbon afforded a convenient half-way rendezvous for French intrigue and for the assembling of a hostile expedition. Above all, Napoleon Buonaparte was then in Egypt, dreaming of the conquests of Alexander ; and no man knew in what direction he might turn his hitherto unconquered legions.

Wellesley conceived the scheme of crushing for ever the French hopes in Asia, by placing himself at the head of a great Indian confederacy. In Lower Bengal, the conquests of Clive and the policy of Warren Hastings had made the English paramount. Before Lord Wellesley's arrival, our power was consolidated from the seaboard to Benares, high up the Gangetic valley. Beyond our frontier there, the Nawáb Wazír of Oudh had agreed to pay a subsidy for the aid of British troops. This sum in 1797 amounted to £760,000 a year ; and the Nawáb, being always in arrears, entered into negotiations for a cession of territory in lieu of a cash payment. In 1801, the treaty of Lucknow made over to the British the *doáb*, or fertile tract between the Ganges and the Jumna, together with Rohilkhand. In Southern India, our possessions were chiefly confined in 1798, before Lord Wellesley, to the coast Districts of Madras and Bombay. *India before Lord Wellesley, 1798 ; in the north ; in the south.*

Wellesley resolved to make the British supreme as far as Delhi in Northern India, and to compel the great powers of the south to enter into subordinate relations to the Company's government. The intrigues of the native princes gave him his opportunity for carrying out his plan without breach of faith. The time had arrived when the English must either become supreme in India, or be driven out of it. The Mughal Empire was completely broken up ; and the sway had to pass either to the local Muhammadan governors of that Empire, or to the Hindu confederacy represented by the Maráthás, or to the British. Lord Wellesley determined that it should pass to the British. *Lord Wellesley's scheme.*

Lord Wellesley's work;,   His work in Northern India was at first easy. By the treaty of Lucknow in 1801, he made us territorial rulers as far as the heart of the present North-Western Provinces, and in the north;   established our political influence in Oudh. Beyond those limits, the northern branches of the Maráthás practically held sway, with the puppet Emperor in their hands. Lord Wellesley left them untouched for a few years, until the second Maráthá war (1802–04) gave him an opportunity for dealing effectively with their nation as a whole.

in the south.   In Southern India, Lord Wellesley quickly perceived that the Muhammadan Nizám at Haidarábád stood in need of his protection, and he converted him into a useful follower throughout the succeeding struggle. The other Muhammadan power of the south, Tipú Sultán of Mysore, could not be so easily handled. Lord Wellesley resolved to crush him, and had ample provocation for so doing. The third power of Southern India—namely, the Hindu Maráthá confederacy—was so loosely organized that Lord Wellesley seems at first to have hoped to live on terms with it. When several years of fitful alliance had convinced him that he had to choose between the supremacy of the Maráthás or of the British in Southern India, he did not hesitate in his decision.

Treaty with the Nizám, 1798.   Lord Wellesley first addressed himself to the weakest of the three southern powers, the Nizám at Haidarábád. Here he won a diplomatic success, which turned a possible rival into a subservient ally. The French battalions at Haidarábád were disbanded, and the Nizám bound himself by treaty [1] not to take any European into his service without the consent of the English Government,—a clause since inserted in every leading engagement entered into with Native Powers.

Wellesley next turned the whole weight of his resources against Tipú, whom Cornwallis had defeated, but had not subdued. Tipú's intrigues with the French were laid bare, and he was given an opportunity of adhering to the new subsidiary Third Mysore war, 1799.   system. On his refusal, war was declared, and Wellesley came down in viceregal state to Madras to organize the expedition in person, and to watch over the course of events. One English army marched into Mysore from Madras, accompanied by a contingent from the Nizám. Another advanced from the western coast. Tipú, after a feeble resistance in the field, retired into Seringapatam, and, when his capital was stormed, died fighting bravely in the breach, 1799. Since the battle of Plassey

[1] Dated 1st September 1798.—Aitchison's *Treaties and Engagements,* vol. v. pp. 173–176 (ed. 1876).

no event had so greatly impressed the native imagination as Fall of Seringapatam, 1799. the capture of Seringapatam, which won for General Harris a peerage, and for Wellesley an Irish Marquisate.

In dealing with the territories of Tipú, Wellesley acted with moderation. The central portion, forming the old State of Mysore, was restored to an infant representative of the Hindu Rájás, whom Haidar Alí had dethroned; the rest of Tipú's dominions was partitioned between the Nizám, the Maráthás, and the English. At about the same time, the Karnátik, or the part of South-eastern India ruled by the Nawáb of Arcot, and also the principality of Tanjore, were placed under direct British administration, thus constituting the Madras Presidency almost as it has existed to the present day. The sons of the slain Tipú were treated by Lord Wellesley with paternal tenderness. They received a magnificent allowance, with semi-royal establishment, first at Vellore, and afterwards in Calcutta. The last of them, Prince Ghulam Muhammad, was long well known as a public-spirited citizen of Calcutta, and an active Justice of the Peace. He died only a few years ago (about 1877).

The Maráthás had been the nominal allies of the English The Maráthás in 1800. in both their wars with Tipú. But they had not rendered active assistance, nor were they secured to the English side as the Nizám now was. The Marátha powers at this time were five in number. The recognised head of the confederacy was the Peshwá of Poona, who ruled the hill country of the Western Gháts, the cradle of the Marátha race. The fertile Province of Gujarát was annually harried by the horsemen of the Gáekwár of Baroda. In Central India, two military leaders, Sindhia of Gwalior and Holkar of Indore, alternately held the pre-eminence. Towards the east, the Bhonsla Rájá of Nágpur reigned from Berar to the coast of Orissa.

Wellesley laboured to bring these several Marátha powers Wellesley's dealings with the Maráthás. within the net of his subsidiary system. In 1802, the necessities of the Peshwá, who had been defeated by Holkar, and driven as a fugitive into British territory, induced him to sign the treaty of Bassein. By this he pledged himself to the British to hold communications with no Power, European or Native, except ourselves. He also granted to us Districts for the maintenance of a subsidiary force. This greatly extended the English territorial influence in the Bombay Presidency. But it led to the second Marátha war, as neither Sindhia nor the Rájá of Nágpur would tolerate the Peshwá's betrayal of Marátha independence.

Second
Marátha
war,
1802-04.

British
victories,
1802-03.

The campaigns which followed are perhaps the most glorious in the history of the British arms in India. The general plan, and the adequate provision of resources, were due to the Marquis of Wellesley, as also the indomitable spirit which refused to acknowledge defeat. The armies were led by Sir Arthur Wellesley (afterwards Duke of Wellington), and General (afterwards Lord) Lake. Wellesley operated in the Deccan, where, in a few short months, he won the decisive victories of Assaye and Argaum, and captured Ahmadnagar. Lake's campaign in Hindustán was no less brilliant, although it has received less notice from historians. He won pitched battles at Alígarh and Láswárí, and took the cities of Delhi and Agra. He scattered the French troops of Sindhia, and at the same time stood forward as the champion of the Mughal Emperor in his hereditary capital. Before the end of 1803, both Sindhia and the Bhonsla Rájá of Nágpur sued for peace.

Additions
to British
India,
1803.

Later dis-
asters,
1804-05.

Sindhia ceded all claims to the territory north of the Jumna, and left the blind old Emperor Sháh Alam once more under British protection. The Bhonsla forfeited Orissa to the English, who had already occupied it with a flying column in 1803 ; and Berar to the Nizám, who gained a fresh addition by every act of complaisance to the British Government. The freebooter Jaswant Ráo Holkar alone remained in the field, supporting his troops by raids through Málwá and Rájputána. The concluding years of Wellesley's rule were occupied with a series of operations against Holkar, which brought little credit on the British name. The disastrous retreat of Colonel Monson through Central India (1804) recalled memories of the convention of Wargáum, and of the destruction of Colonel Baillie's force by Haidar Alí. The repulse of Lake in person at the siege of Bhartpur (Bhurt-pore) is memorable as an instance of a British army in India having to turn back with its object unaccomplished (1805). Bhartpur was not finally taken till 1827.

India after
Lord
Wellesley,
1805 ;

in the
north ;

in the
south.

Lord Wellesley during his six years of office carried out almost every part of his territorial scheme. In Northern India, Lord Lake's campaigns, 1803-05, brought the North-Western Provinces (the ancient *Madhya-desha*) under British rule, together with the custody of the puppet Emperor. The new Districts were amalgamated with those previously acquired from the Nawáb Wazír of Oudh into the 'Ceded and Con-quered Provinces.' This partition of Northern India remained till the Sikh wars of 1845 and 1848–49 gave us the Punjab. In South-eastern India, we have seen that Lord Wellesley's conquests constituted the Madras Presidency almost as it exists at this date. In South-western India, the Peshwá was reduced to a vassal of the Company. But the territories now under the Governor of Bombay were not finally built up into their present form until the last Maráthá war in 1818.

The financial strain caused by these great operations of Lord Wellesley had meanwhile exhausted the patience of the Court of Directors at home. In 1805, Lord Cornwallis was sent out as Governor-General a second time, with instructions to bring about peace at any price, while Holkar was still unsubdued, and with Sindhia threatening a fresh war. But Cornwallis was now an old man, and broken down in health. Travelling up to the north-west during the rainy season, he sank and died at Gházípur, before he had been ten weeks in the country. *Marquis of Cornwallis again, 1805.*

His immediate successor was Sir George Barlow, a civil servant of the Company, who as a *locum tenens* had no alternative but to carry out the commands of his employers. Under these orders, he curtailed the area of British territory, and, in violation of engagements, abandoned the Rájput chiefs to the cruel mercies of Holkar and Sindhia. During his administration, also, occurred the mutiny of the Madras sepoys at Vellore (1806), which, although promptly suppressed, sent a shock of insecurity throughout the Empire. The feebly economical policy of this interregnum proved a most disastrous one. But, fortunately, the rule soon passed into firmer hands. *Sir George Barlow, 1805.*

Lord Minto, Governor-General from 1807 to 1813, consolidated the conquests which Wellesley had acquired. His only military exploits were the occupation of the island of the Mauritius, and the conquest of Java by an expedition which he accompanied in person. The condition of Central India continued to be disturbed, but Lord Minto succeeded in preventing any violent outbreaks without himself having recourse to the sword. The Company had ordered him to follow a policy of non-intervention, and he managed to obey his orders without injuring the prestige of the British name. Under his auspices, the Indian Government opened relations with a new set of foreign powers, by sending embassies to the Punjab, to Afghánistán, and to Persia. The ambassadors had been trained in the school of Wellesley, and formed, perhaps, the most illustrious trio of 'politicals' whom the Indian services have produced. Metcalfe went as envoy to the Sikh Court of Ranjít Singh at Lahore; Elphinstone met the Sháh of Afghán- *Earl of Minto, 1807-13.*

istán at Peshawar; and Malcolm was despatched to Persia. It cannot be said that these missions were fruitful of permanent results; but they introduced the English to a new set of diplomatic relations, and widened the sphere of their influence.

Lord Moira (Marquis of Hastings), 1814-23.
The successor of Lord Minto was the Earl of Moira, better known by his later title as the Marquis of Hastings. The Marquis of Hastings completed Lord Wellesley's conquests in Central India, and left the Bombay Presidency almost as it stands at present. His long rule of nine years, from 1814 to 1823, was marked by two wars of the first magnitude—namely, the campaigns against the Gúrkhas of Nepál, and the last Marathá struggle.

The Gúrkhas of Nepál.
The Gúrkhas, the present ruling race in Nepál, trace their descent from Hindu immigrants and claim a Rájput origin. The indigenous inhabitants, called Newars, belong to the Indo-Tibetan stock, and profess Buddhism. The sovereignty of the Gúrkhas dates only from 1767–68, when they overran the valley of Khatmandu, and gradually extended their power over the hills and valleys of Nepál. Organized upon a military and feudal basis, they soon became a terror to their neighbours, marching east into Sikkim, west into Kumáun, and south into the Gangetic plains. In the last quarter their victims were British subjects (natives of Bengal), and it became necessary to check their advance. Sir George Barlow and Lord Minto had remonstrated in vain, and nothing was left to Lord Moira but to take up arms.

Nepál war, 1814-15.
The first campaign of 1814 was unsuccessful. After overcoming the natural difficulties of a malarious climate and precipitous hills, our troops were on several occasions fairly worsted by the impetuous bravery of the little Gúrkhas, whose heavy knives or *kukris* dealt terrible execution. But in the cold weather of 1814, General Ochterlony, who advanced by way of the Sutlej, stormed one by one the hill forts which still stud the Himálayan States, now under the Punjab Government, and compelled the Nepál *darbár* to sue for peace. In the following year, 1815, the same general made his brilliant march from Patná into the lofty valley of Khatmandu, and finally dictated the terms which had before been rejected, within a few miles of the capital. By the treaty of Segauli, which defines the English relations with Nepál to the present day, the Gúrkhas withdrew on the south-east from Sikkim; and on the south-west, from their advanced posts in the outer

Second campaign.

Treaty of Segauli; cedes Himálayan tracts, 1815.

ranges of the Himálayas, which enabled us to obtain the
health-giving stations of Naini Tál, Massuri, and Simla.

Meanwhile, the condition of Central India was every year
becoming more unsatisfactory. The great Marátha chiefs had
learned to live as princes rather than as predatory leaders.
But their original habits of lawlessness were being followed by
a new set of freebooters, known as the Pindárís. As opposed to
the Maráthás, who were at least a Hindu nationality bound by
the traditions of a united government, the Pindárís were merely
plundering bands, closely corresponding to the free companies
of mediæval Europe. Of no common race, and of no common
religion, they welcomed to their ranks the outlaws and broken
men of all India—Afgháns, Maráthás, or Játs. They represented the débris of the Mughal Empire, which had not been
incorporated by any of the local Muhammadan or Hindu
powers that sprang up out of its ruins. For a time, indeed,
it seemed as if the inheritance of the Mughal might pass to
these armies of banditti. In Bengal, similar hordes had
formed themselves out of the disbanded Muhammadan troops
and the Hindu predatory castes. But they had been dispersed under the vigorous rule of Warren Hastings. In
Central India, the evil lasted longer, attained a greater scale,
and was only stamped out by a regular war.

The Pindárí head-quarters were in Málwá, but their depredations were not confined to Central India. In bands, sometimes of a few hundreds, sometimes of many thousands, they
rode out on their forays as far as the opposite coasts of Madras
and of Bombay. The most powerful of the Pindárí captains,
Amír Khán, had an organized army of many regiments, and
several batteries of cannon. Two other leaders, known as
Chítu and Karím, at one time paid a ransom to Sindhia of
£100,000. To suppress the Pindárí hordes, who were supported by the sympathy, more or less open, of all the Marátha
chiefs, Lord Hastings (1817) collected the strongest British
army which had yet been seen in India, numbering 120,000
men. One-half operated from the north, the other half
from the south. Sindhia was overawed, and remained quiet.
Amír Khán disbanded his army, on condition of being
guaranteed the possession of what is now the principality of
Tank. The remaining bodies of Pindárís were attacked in
their homes, surrounded, and cut to pieces. Karím threw
himself upon the mercy of the conquerors. Chítu fled to
the jungles, and was killed by a tiger.

In the same year (1817) and almost in the same month

The Pindárís, 1804-17.

Pindárí bands, 1815.

Pindárí leaders.

Pindárí war, 1817.

2 C

(November) as that in which the Pindárís were crushed, the three great Maráthá powers at Poona, Nágpur, and Indore rose separately against the English. The Peshwá, Bájí Ráo, had long been chafing under the terms imposed by the treaty of Bassein (1802). A new treaty of Poona, in June 1817, now freed the Gáekwár from his control, ceded further districts to the British for the pay of the subsidiary force, and submitted all future disputes to the decision of our Government.

New Maráthá treaty, 1817.

Elphinstone, then our Resident at his Court, foresaw a storm, and withdrew to Kírki, whither he had ordered up a European regiment. The next day the Residency was burnt down, and Kírki was attacked by the whole army of the Peshwá. The attack was bravely repulsed, and the Peshwá immediately fled from his capital, Poona. Almost the same plot was enacted at Nágpur, where the honour of the British name was saved by the sepoys, who defended the hill of Sítábaldi against enormous odds.

The Maráthá attack.

It had now become necessary to crush the Maráthás. Their forces under Holkar were defeated in the following month at the pitched battle of Mehidpur. All open resistance was now at an end. Nothing remained but to follow up the fugitives, and to impose conditions for a general pacification. In both these duties Sir John Malcolm played a prominent part. The dominions of the Peshwá were annexed to the Bombay Presidency, and the nucleus of the present Central Provinces was formed out of the territory rescued from the Pindárís. The Peshwá himself surrendered, and was permitted to reside at Bithúr, near Cawnpur, on a pension of £80,000 a year. His adopted son was the infamous Náná Sáhib of the Mutiny of 1857.

Last Maráthá war, 1817-18.

Bombay territories annexed, 1818.

To fill the Peshwá's place, as the traditional head of the Maráthá confederacy, the lineal descendant of Sivají was brought forth from obscurity and placed upon the throne of Sátára. An infant was recognised as the heir of Holkar, and a second infant was proclaimed Rájá of Nágpur under British guardianship. At the same time, the States of Rájputána accepted the position of feudatories to the paramount British power.

Sátára;

Rájputána.

The map of India, as thus drawn by Lord Hastings, remained substantially unchanged until the time of Lord Dalhousie. But the proudest boast of Lord Hastings and Sir John Malcolm was, not that they had advanced the *pomœrium*, but that they had conferred the blessings of peace and good government upon millions who had groaned under the extortions of the Maráthás and Pindárís.

Map of India, 1818-48.

The Marquis of Hastings was succeeded by Lord Amherst, Mr. Adam, after the interval of a few months, during which Mr. Adam, 1823. a civil servant, acted as Governor-General. The Maráthá war in the Peninsula of India was hardly completed when our armies had to face new enemies beyond the sea. Lord Lord Amherst's administration lasted for five years, from 1823 to Amherst, 1828. It is known in history by two prominent events, the first Burmese war and the capture of Bhartpur.

For some years past, our north-eastern frontier had been disturbed by Burmese raids. Burma, or the country Ancient which fringes the western shore of the Bay of Bengal, Burma. and runs up the valley of the Irawadi, has a people of Tibeto-Chinese origin, and a history of its own. Tradition asserts that its civilisation was introduced from the coast of Coromandel, by a people who are supposed to preserve a trace of their origin in their name of Talaing (*cf.* Telingána). However this may be, the Buddhist religion, professed by the Burmese at the present day, certainly came from India at a very early date. Waves of invasion from Siam on the south, and from the wild mountains of China in the north, have passed over the land. These conquests were marked by the wanton and wholesale barbarity which seems to characterize the Tibeto-Chinese race; but the civilisation of Buddhism survived every shock, and flourished around the ancient pagodas. European travellers in the 15th century visited Pegu and Tenasserim, which they Burma, describe as flourishing seats of maritime trade. During the 15th cent. Portuguese predominance in the East, Arakan in Northern A.D. Burma became an asylum for desperate European adventurers. With their help, the Arakanese conquered Chittagong on the Bengal seaboard, and (under the name of the Maghs) became the terror of the Gangetic delta. About 1750, a new Burmese dynasty arose, founded by Alaung-paya or Alompra, with its capital at Ava. Alompra's successors ruled Independent Burma until its annexation to British India in 1886.[1]

The dynasty of Alompra, after having subjugated all Burmese Burma, and overrun (1800) Assam, which was then an inde- encroach- pendent kingdom, began a series of encroachments upon the India. British Districts. As they rejected all peaceful proposals with scorn, Lord Amherst was at last compelled to declare war in 1824. Little military glory could be gained by beating First Bur- the Burmese, who were formidable chiefly from the pestilential mese war, 1824.

[1] For the history of Burma, see the articles BURMA, BRITISH, and BURMA, INDEPENDENT, in *The Imperial Gazetteer of India.*

character of their country.   One expedition with gunboats proceeded up the Brahmaputra into Assam.   Another marched by land through Chittagong into Arakan, as the Bengal sepoys refused to go by sea.   A third, and the strongest, sailed from Madras direct to the mouth of the Irawadi.   The war was protracted over two years.   After a loss to us of about 20,000 lives, chiefly from disease, and an expenditure of £14,000,000, the King of Ava signed, in 1826, the treaty of

Assam, etc., annexed, 1826.

Yandabu.   By this he abandoned all claim to Assam, and ceded the Provinces of Arakan and Tenasserim, already in the military occupation of the British.   He retained the whole valley of the Irawadi, down to the sea at Rangoon.

Bhartpur taken, 1827.

The capture of Bhartpur in Central India by Lord Combermere, in January 1827, wiped out the repulse which Lake had received before that city in January 1805.   A disputed succession led to the British intervention.   Artillery could make little impression upon the massive walls of mud.   But at last a breach was effected by mining, and the city was taken by storm, thus removing the popular notion throughout India that it was impregnable—a notion which had threatened to become a political danger.

Lord William Bentinck, 1828–35.

The next Governor-General was Lord William Bentinck, who had been Governor of Madras twenty years earlier, at the time of the mutiny of Vellore (1806).   His seven years' rule (from 1828 to 1835) is not signalized by any of those victories or extensions of territory by which chroniclers measure the growth of an Empire.   But it forms an epoch in administrative reform, and in the benign process by which a subject population is won over to venerate as well as to dread its alien rulers.   The modern history of the British in India, as benevolent administrators, ruling the country with an eye to the good of the natives, may be said to begin with Lord William Bentinck.   According to the inscription upon his statue at Calcutta, from the pen of Macaulay : ' He abolished cruel rites ; he effaced humiliating distinctions ; he gave liberty to the expression of public opinion ; his constant study was to elevate the intellectual and moral character of the nations committed to his charge.'

His financial reforms.

Lord William Bentinck's first care on arrival in India was to restore equilibrium to the finances, which were tottering under the burden imposed upon them by the Burmese war.   This he effected by three series of measures—first, by reductions in permanent expenditure, amounting to 1½ million

sterling a year ; second, by augmenting the revenue from lands
which had surreptitiously escaped assessment ; third, by duties
on the opium of Málwá. He also widened the gates by which
educated natives could enter the service of the Company.
Some of these reforms were distasteful to the covenanted
service and to the officers of the army. But Lord William
was staunchly supported by the Court of Directors and by the
Whig Ministry at home.

His two most memorable acts are the abolition of *sati*, or Abolition
widow-burning, and the suppression of the *thags*. At this of *sati*, 1829.
distance of time it is difficult to realize the degree to which
these two barbarous practices had corrupted the social system
of the Hindus. European research has clearly proved that
the text in the Vedas adduced to authorize the immolation
of widows, was a wilful mistranslation.[1] But the practice had
been enshrined in Hindu opinion by the authority of centuries, and had acquired the sanctity of a religious rite. The
Emperor Akbar prohibited it, but failed to put it down. The
early English rulers did not dare to violate the religious
traditions of the people. In the year 1817, no less than 700
widows are said to have been burned alive in the Bengal
Presidency alone. To this day, the holy spots of Hindu
pilgrimage are thickly dotted with little white pillars, each
commemorating a *sati*. In spite of strenuous opposition, both
from Europeans and natives, Lord William Bentinck carried a
regulation in Council on the 4th December 1829, by which
all who abetted *sati* were declared guilty of ' culpable homicide.'

The honour of suppressing *thagí* must be shared between Suppres-
Lord William Bentinck and Captain Sleeman. *Thags* were sion of *thagí*.
hereditary assassins, who made strangling their profession.
They travelled in bands, disguised as merchants or pilgrims,
and were sworn together by an oath based on the rites of the
bloody goddess Kálí. Between 1826 and 1835, as many as
1562 *thags* were apprehended in different parts of British India ;
and, by the evidence of approvers, these abominable brotherhoods were gradually stamped out.

Two other historical events are connected with the admini- Renewal
stration of Lord William Bentinck. In 1833, the Charter of of charter, 1833.
the East India Company was renewed for twenty years, bu
upon the condition that the Company should abandon its
trade and permit Europeans to settle in the country. At the
same time, a fourth or ' Law-member ' was added to the
Governor-General's Council, who might not be a servant of the

[1] *Vide ante*, chap. iv. p. 78.

Company; and a Commission was appointed to revise and codify the law. Macaulay was the first Law-member of Council, and the first President of the Law Commission.

Mysore protected, 1830.

In 1830–31, it was found necessary to take the State of Mysore under British administration. It continued so up to March 1881, when it was restored to native government. In 1834, the frantic misrule of the Rájá of Coorg brought on a sharp and short war. The Rájá Lingaráj was permitted to retire to Vellore, then to Benares, and finally to England, where he died. The brave and proud inhabitants of his mountainous little territory decided to place themselves under the sway of the Company. This was the only annexation effected by Lord William Bentinck, and it was done ' in consideration of the unanimous wish of the people.'

Coorg annexed, 1834.

Lord Metcalfe, 1835–36.

Sir Charles (afterwards Lord) Metcalfe succeeded Lord William as senior member of Council. His short term of office is memorable for the measure which his predecessor had initiated, but which he carried into execution, for giving entire liberty to the press. From this time the Indian Government lost the power of deporting journalists who made themselves formidable by their pens. Public opinion in India, as well as the express wish of the Court of Directors at home, pointed to Metcalfe as the fittest person to carry out the policy of Bentinck, not provisionally, but as Governor-General for a full term.

Lord Auckland, 1836–42.

Party exigencies, however, led to the appointment of Lord Auckland. From this date commences a new era of war and conquest, which may be said to have lasted for twenty years. All looked peaceful until Lord Auckland, prompted by his evil genius, attempted by force to place Sháh Shujá upon the throne of Kábul ; an attempt conducted with gross mismanagement, and ending in the annihilation of the British garrison placed in that city.

Afghán-istán under the Duránís, 1747–1826.

For the first time since the days of the Sultáns of Ghazní and Ghor, Afghánistán had obtained a national king in 1747 in Ahmad Sháh Duráni. This resolute soldier found his opportunity in the confusion which followed the death of the Persian conqueror, Nádir Sháh. Before his own decease in 1773, Ahmad Sháh had conquered a wide empire, from Herát to Pesháwar, and from Kashmír to Sind. His intervention on the field of Pánípat (1761) turned back the tide of Maráthá conquest, and replaced a Mughal Emperor on the throne of Delhi. But Ahmad Sháh never cared to settle down in India, and alternately kept state at his two Afghán capitals of Kábul and Kandahár. The Duráni kings were prolific in children, who fought to the death with one another on each succession. At last, in 1826, Dost Muhammad, head of the powerful Barakzai family, succeeded in establishing himself as ruler of Kábul, with the title of Amír, while two fugitive brothers of the Duráni line were living under British protection at Ludhiána, on the Punjab frontier.

The attention of the English Government had been directed to Afghán affairs ever since the time of Lord Wellesley, who feared that Zamán Sháh, the Afghán Amír, then holding his court at Lahore (1800), might follow in the path of Ahmad Sháh, and overrun Hindustán. The growth of the powerful Sikh kingdom of Ranjít Singh effectually dispelled these alarms. Subsequently, in 1809, while a French invasion of India was still a possibility to be guarded against, Mountstuart Elphinstone was sent by Lord Minto on a mission to Sháh Shujá to form a defensive alliance. Before the year expired, Sháh Shujá had been driven into exile, and a third brother, Mahmúd Sháh, was on the throne. In 1837, when the curtain rises upon the drama of English interference in Afghánistán, the usurper Dost Muhammad, Barakzai, was firmly established at Kábul. His great ambition was to recover Pesháwar from the Sikhs. When, therefore, Captain Alexander Burnes arrived on a mission from Lord Auckland, with the ostensible object of opening trade, the Dost was willing to promise everything if only he could get Pesháwar. *Our early dealings with Kábul, 1800-37.*

Dost Muhammad, 1837.

But Lord Auckland had another and more important object in view. At this time the Russians were advancing rapidly in Central Asia, and a Persian army, not without Russian support, was besieging Herát, then as now the bulwark of Afghánistán on the west. A Russian envoy was at Kábul at the same time as Burnes. The latter was unable to satisfy the demands of Dost Muhammad in the matter of Pesháwar, and returned to India unsuccessful. Lord Auckland forthwith resolved upon the hazardous plan of placing a more subservient ruler upon the throne of Kábul. *Russian influence, 1837.*

Sháh Shujá, one of the two exiles of Ludhiána, was selected for the purpose. At this time both the Punjab and Sind were independent kingdoms. Sind was the less powerful of the two, and accordingly a British army escorting Sháh Shujá made its way by that route into southern Afghánistán through the Bolan Pass. Kandahár surrendered ; Ghazní was taken by storm. Dost Muhammad fled across the Hindu Kush, and

Sháh
Shujá
installed,
1839.
Sháh Shujá was triumphantly led into the Bala Hissár at Kábul in August 1839. After one more brave struggle, Dost Muhammad surrendered, and was sent to Calcutta as a State prisoner.

But although we could enthrone Sháh Shujá, we could not win for him the hearts of the Afgháns. To that nation he seemed a degenerate exile thrust back upon them by foreign arms. During two years, Afghánistán remained in the military Kábul
occupied,
1839-41. occupation of the British. The catastrophe occurred in November 1841, when our Political Agent, Sir Alexander Burnes, was assassinated in the city of Kábul. The troops in the cantonments were under the command of General Elphinstone (not to be confounded with the able civilian and historian, the Hon. Mountstuart Elphinstone). Sir William Macnaghten was the political officer. Elphinstone, an old man, proved unequal to the responsibilities of the position. Macnaghten was treacherously murdered at an interview with the Afghán chief Akbar Khán, eldest son of Dost Muhammad.

After lingering amid disgraceful dissensions and with The
winter
retreat. fatal indecision in their cantonments for two months, the British army set off in the depth of winter, under a fallacious guarantee from the Afghán leaders, to find its way back to India through the passes. When they started, they numbered 4000 fighting men with 12,000 camp followers. A single sur- Our
garrison
annihil-
ated, 1842. vivor, Dr. Brydon, reached the friendly walls of Jalálábád, where Sale was gallantly holding out. The rest perished in the snowy defiles of Khurd-Kábul and Jagdalak, from the knives and matchlocks of the Afgháns, or from the effects of cold. A few prisoners, chiefly women, children, and officers, were considerately treated by the orders of Akbar Khán.

The first Afghán enterprise, begun in a spirit of aggression, and conducted amid disagreements and mismanagement, had The shock
in Eng-
land. ended in the disgrace of the British arms. The real loss, which amounted only to a single garrison, and cost fewer soldiers than many a victory, was magnified by the horrors of the winter march, and by the completeness of the annihilation.

Earl of
Ellen-
borough,
1842-44.
Within a month after the news reached Calcutta, Lord Auckland had been superseded by Lord Ellenborough, whose first impulse was to be satisfied with drawing off in safety the garrisons from Kandahár and Jalálábád. But bolder counsels The army
of retribu-
tion, 1842. were forced upon him. General Pollock, who was marching straight through the Punjab to relieve Sale, was allowed to penetrate to Kábul. General Nott, although ordered to withdraw from Afghánistán, resolved to take Kábul on the way!

Lord Ellenborough gave his commands in well-chosen words, which would leave his Generals responsible for any disaster.[1] General Nott took that responsibility, and instead of retreating south-east to the Indus, boldly marched north in nearly the opposite direction to Kábul. After hard fighting, the two British forces, under Pollock and Nott, met at their common destination at Kábul City in September 1842. The great *bázár* at Kábul was blown up with gunpowder, to fix a stigma upon the city ; the prisoners were recovered ; and the British troops marched back to India, leaving Dost Muhammad to take undisputed possession of his throne.

The drama closed with a bombastic proclamation from Lord Ellenborough, who had caused the gates from the tomb of Mahmúd of Ghazní to be carried back as a memorial of 'Somnáth revenged.' Lord Ellenborough, in his craze for historical melodrama, declared these doors to be the ones carried away from the spoliation of the Somnáth temple by Mahmúd of Ghazní, 1024 A.D.[2] The gates were a modern forgery ; and their theatrical procession through the Punjab formed a vainglorious sequel to Lord Ellenborough's diffidence, while the fate of our armies hung in the balance. The histrionic travesty which closed the first Kábul war was scarcely less distasteful to the serious English mind than the unrighteous interference which led to its commencement, or the follies and feeble division of counsels which produced its disasters.

Lord Ellenborough, who loved military pomp, had his taste gratified by two more wars. In 1843, the Muhammadan rulers of Sind, known as the *Mírs* or Amírs, whose chief fault was that they would not surrender their independence, were crushed by Sir Charles Napier. The victory of Miání, in which 3000 British troops defeated 20,000 Baluchís, is one of the brilliant feats of arms in Anglo-Indian history. But valid reasons can scarcely be found for the annexation of the country. In the same year, a disputed succession at Gwalior, fomented by feminine intrigue, resulted in an outbreak of the overgrown army which the Sindhia family kept up. Peace was restored by the battles of Mahárájpur and Punniah, at the former of which Lord Ellenborough was present in person.

In 1844, Lord Ellenborough was recalled by the Court of

The 'Gates of Somnath,' 1842.

Sind war, 1843.

Gwalior outbreak, 1843.

---

[1] *The Indian Administration of Lord Ellenborough, being his Correspondence.* Edited by Lord Colchester, 1874. See Lord Ellenborough's own Letters, pp. 29, 30, 39, etc.

[2] *Vide ante,* chap. x. p. 274.

Directors, who differed from him on points of administration, disliked his theatrical display, and distrusted his erratic genius.

Lord Hardinge, 1844-48.
He was succeeded by Sir Henry (afterwards Lord) Hardinge, who had served through the Peninsular war, and lost a hand at Ligny. It was felt on all sides that a trial of strength between the British and the remaining Hindu power in India, the great Sikh nation, drew near.

The Sikhs, 1469.
The Sikhs were not a nationality like the Maráthás, but a religious sect bound together by the additional tie of military discipline. They trace their origin to Nának Sháh, a pious Hindu reformer, born near Lahore in 1469, before the

Nának Sháh.
ascendancy of either Mughals or Portuguese in India. Nának, like other zealous preachers of his time, preached the abolition of caste, the unity of the Godhead, and the obligation of leading a pure life.[1] From Nának, ten *gurus* or apostles are traced down to Govind Singh in 1708, with whom the succession stopped. Cruelly persecuted by the ruling Muhammadans, almost exterminated under the miserable successors of Aurangzeb,[2] the Sikh martyrs clung to their faith with unflinching zeal. At last the downfall of the Mughal Empire transformed the Sikh sect into a territorial power. It was the only political organization remaining in the Punjab. The

Sikh confederacies.
Sikhs in the north, and the Maráthás in Southern and Central India, thus became the two great Hindu powers who partitioned the Mughal Empire. Even before the rise of Ranjít Singh, offshoots from the Sikh *misls* or confederacies, each led by its elected *sardár*, had carved out for themselves feudal principalities along the banks of the Sutlej, some of which endure to the present day.

Ranjít Singh, 1780-1839.
Ranjít Singh, the 'Lion of the Punjab' and founder of the Sikh kingdom, was born in 1780. In his twentieth year he obtained the appointment of Governor of Lahore from the Afghán Amír, and formed the project of erecting his personal rule upon the fanaticism of his Sikh countrymen. He organized their church militant, or 'the liberated,' into an army under European officers, which for steadiness and religious fervour has had no parallel since the

His kingdom.
'Ironsides' of Cromwell. From Lahore, as his capital, he extended his conquests south to Múltán, west to Pesháwar,

---

[1] *Vide ante*, pp. 207-8. The life of Nának and growth of his sect are summarized in articles AMRITSAR and PUNJAB, *The Imperial Gazetteer of India.* The religious aspects of the Sikhs are fully treated in Wilson's *Religion of the Hindus*, vol. i. pp. 267-275 (ed. 1862).

[2] *Vide ante*, p. 314.

and north to Kashmír. On the east side alone he was hemmed in by the Sutlej, up to which river the authority of the British Government had advanced in 1804. Until his death, in 1839, Ranjít Singh was ever loyal to the engagements which he had entered into with Metcalfe in 1809. But he left no son capable of wielding his sceptre. Lahore was torn by dissensions between rival generals, ministers, and queens. *Its dis-* The only strong power was the army of the Central Com- *sensions.* mittee of Generals or *khálsá*,[1] which, since our disaster in Afghánistán, burned to measure its strength with the British Sepoys. The French or European Generals, Avitabile and Court, were foolishly ousted by the Sikh commanders, and the supreme military command was vested in a series of *panchayats* or elective committees of five.

In 1845, the Sikh army, numbering 60,000 men with 150 *First* guns, crossed the Sutlej and invaded British territory. Sir *Sikh war,* Hugh Gough, the Commander-in-Chief, together with the *1845.* Governor-General, hurried up to the frontier. Within three weeks, four pitched battles were fought, at Múdkí, Firozshahr, Aliwál, and Sobráon. The British loss on each occasion was heavy; but by the last victory, the Sikhs were fairly driven back into the Sutlej, and Lahore surrendered to the British. The British, however, declined to annex the prostrate province; but appointed a Sikh protectorate. By the terms of peace which we then dictated, the infant son of Ranjít, Dhulíp *Dhulíp* Singh, was recognised as Rájá; the Jalandhar Doáb, or tract *Singh,* between the Sutlej and the Rávi, was annexed to British terri- *1845.* tory; the Sikh army was limited to a specified number; Major Henry Lawrence was appointed Resident, to assist the Sikh Council of Regency, at Lahore; and a British force was sent to garrison the Punjab on behalf of the child-Rájá. The Governor-General, Sir H. Hardinge, received a peerage, and returned to England in 1848.

Lord Dalhousie succeeded. The eight years' rule of this *Earl of* greatest of Indian proconsuls (1848–56) left more conspicuous *Dalhousie,* results than that of any Governor-General since Clive. A *1848–56.* high-minded statesman, of a most sensitive conscience, and earnestly desiring peace, Lord Dalhousie found himself forced against his will to fight two wars, and to embark on a policy of annexation. His campaigns in the Punjab and in Burma

---

[1] The Persian word *khálisah*, literally 'pure' or 'sincere,' means in Indian official language the royal exchequer, and hence more loosely the bureau of the central administration.

ended in large acquisitions of territory; while Nágpur, Oudh, and several minor States also came under British rule. But Dalhousie's deepest interest lay in the advancement of the moral and material condition of the country. His system of administration carried out in the conquered Punjab, by the two Lawrences and their assistants, is probably the most successful piece of difficult work ever accomplished by Englishmen. British Burma has prospered under our rule not less than the Punjab. In both cases, Lord Dalhousie himself laid the foundations of our administrative success, and deserves a large share of the credit.

His administrative reforms.

No branch of the administration escaped his reforming hand. He founded the Public Works Department, with a view to creating the network of roads, railways, and canals which now cover India. He opened the Ganges Canal, still the largest work of the kind in the country; and he turned the sod of the first Indian railway. He promoted steam communication with England *viâ* the Red Sea, and introduced cheap postage and the electric telegraph. It is Lord Dalhousie's misfortune that these benefits are too often forgotten in the recollections of the Mutiny, which followed his policy of annexation, after the firm hand which had remodelled British India was withdrawn. But history is compelled to record not only that no other Governor-General since the time of Lord Wellesley had ruled India with such splendid success from the military and political point of view, but also that no other Governor-General had done so much to improve the internal administration since the days of Warren Hastings.

His Public Works.

Lord Dalhousie had not been six months in India before the second Sikh war broke out. The attempt to govern the Punjab by a Sikh protectorate broke down. The Council of Regency was divided against itself, corrupt and weak. The Queen-Mother had chosen her paramour as prime minister. In 1848, the storm broke. Two British officers were treacherously assassinated at Múltán. Unfortunately, Henry Lawrence was at home on sick leave. The British army was not ready to act in the hot weather; and, despite the single-handed exertions of Lieutenant (afterwards Sir Herbert) Edwardes, this outbreak of fanaticism led to a general rising of the Sikh confederacies.

Second Sikh war, 1848-49.

The *khálsá* army again came together, and once more fought on even terms with the British. On the fatal field of Chiliánwála,[1] which our patriotism prefers to call a drawn battle, the British

Chilián-wála, 1849.

---

[1] See articles CHILIANWALA and GUJRAT, *The Imperial Gazetteer of India.*

lost 2400 officers and men, besides four guns and the colours of three regiments (13th January 1849). But before reinforcements could come out from England, bringing Sir Charles Napier as Commander-in-Chief, Lord Gough had restored his reputation by the crowning victory of Gujrát, which absolutely Gujrát destroyed the Sikh army. Múltán had previously fallen; and victory. the Afghán horse under Dost Muhammad, who had forgotten their hereditary antipathy to the Sikhs in their greater hatred of the British name, were chased back with ignominy to their native hills. The Punjab, annexed by proclamation on the 29th March 1849,[1] became a British Province—a virgin field for the administrative talents of Dalhousie and the two Lawrences. Mahárájá Dhulíp Singh received an allowance of £58,000 a year, on which he now lives as an English country gentleman in Norfolk.

The first step in the pacification of the Punjab[2] was a general The disarmament, which resulted in the delivery of no fewer than Punjab annexed, 120,000 weapons of various kinds. Then followed a settle- 1849. ment of the land-tax, village by village, at an assessment much Its pacifi- below that to which it had been raised by Sikh exactions; and cation. the introduction of a loose but equitable code of civil and criminal procedure. Roads and canals were laid out by Colonel Robert Napier (afterwards Lord Napier of Magdala). The security of British peace, and the personal influence of British officers, inaugurated a new era of prosperity, which was felt to the farthest corners of the Province. It thus happened that, when the Mutiny broke out in 1857, the Punjab remained not only quiet, but loyal.

The second Burmese war, in 1852, arose out of the ill- Second treatment of some European merchants at Rangoon, and the Burmese war, 1852. insults offered to the captain of a British frigate who had been sent to remonstrate.[3] The lower valley of the Irawadi, from Rangoon to Prome, was occupied in a few months; and as the King of Ava refused to treat, it was annexed by proclama- British tion on the 20th December 1852, under the name of Pegu, Burma annexed, to the Provinces of Arakan and Tenasserim acquired in 1826. 1852. Since annexation, the inhabitants of the town of Rangoon have multiplied nearly fifteen-fold. The trade of this

---

[1] In terms of the agreement with Mahárájá Dhulíp Singh, of same date. —Aitchison's *Treaties and Engagements*, vol. vi. p. 47 (ed. 1876).

[2] For the annexation and administrative history of the Punjab, see article PUNJAB in *The Imperial Gazetteer of India*.

[3] For further details, see article BURMA, *The Imperial Gazetteer of India*.

port, which four years after annexation (1857–58) only amounted to £2,131,055, had increased to £8,192,025 in 1877–78, and to £13,174,094 in 1883.[1]

Its prosperity under our rule. The towns and rural parts have alike prospered. Before its annexation in 1826, Amherst District was the scene of perpetual warfare between the Kings of Siam and Pegu, and was stripped of inhabitants. In February 1827, a Talaing chief with 10,000 followers settled in the neighbourhood of Maulmain; and after a few years, a further influx of 20,000 immigrants took place. In 1855, the population of Amherst District amounted to 83,146 souls; in 1860, to 130,953; in 1875, to 275,432; and in 1881, to 301,086. Or, to take the case of a seaport, —in 1826, when we occupied that part of the Province, Akyab was a poor fishing village. By 1830, it had developed into a little town with a trade valued at £7000. In 1879, the trade exceeded 2 millions sterling; so that the trade of Akyab had multiplied itself close on three hundred-fold in fifty years.

The Feudatory States. Lord Dalhousie's dealings with the Feudatory States of India revealed the whole nature of the man. That rulers only exist for the good of the ruled, was his supreme axiom of government, of which he gave a conspicuous example in his own daily life. That British administration was better for the people than native rule, followed from this axiom. He was thus led to regard native chiefs from somewhat the same point of view as the Scotch regarded the hereditary jurisdictions after 1745, namely, as mischievous anomalies, to be abolished by every fair means. Good faith must be kept with rulers on Dalhousie's doctrine of 'lapse.' the throne, and with their legitimate heirs. But no false sentiment should preserve dynasties which had forfeited our sympathies by generations of misrule, nor prolong those that had no natural successor. The 'doctrine of lapse' was the practical application of these principles, complicated by the Indian practice of adoption.

Hindu doctrine of adoption. According to Hindu private law, an adopted son entirely fills the place of a natural son, whether to perform the religious obsequies of his father or to inherit his property. In all respects he continues the *persona* of the deceased. But it was argued that, both as a matter of historical fact and as one of political expediency, the succession to a throne stood upon a

---

[1] See article RANGOON, *The Imperial Gazetteer of India.* For growth of trade in other Burmese ports, see also article AKYAB, *The Imperial Gazetteer of India.*

different footing. It was affirmed, not always with a complete knowledge of the facts, that the Mughal Emperors had asserted an interest in successions to the great fiefs, and demanded heavy payments for recognising them. It was therefore maintained that the paramount power could not acknowledge without limitations a right of adoption, which might be used as a fraud to hand over the happiness of millions to a base-born impostor. Here came in Lord Dalhousie's maxim of 'the good of the governed.' In his mind, benefits to be conferred through British administration weighed heavier than a superstitious and often fraudulent fiction of inheritance.

The first State to escheat to the British Government in accordance with these principles was Sátára, which had been reconstituted by Lord Hastings on the downfall of the Peshwá in 1818. The Rájá of Sátára, the last lineal representative of Sivají, died without a male heir in 1848, and his deathbed adoption was set aside (1849). In the same year, the independence of the Rájput State of Karauli was saved by the Court of Directors, who drew a fine distinction between a dependent principality and a protected ally. In 1853, Jhánsí suffered the same fate as Sátára. *Lapsed States. Sátára, 1849. Jhánsí.*

But the most conspicuous application of the doctrine of lapse was the case of Nágpur. The last of the Marátha Bhonslas, a dynasty older than the British Government itself, died without a son, natural or adopted, in 1853. His territories were annexed, and became the Central Provinces. That year also saw British administration extended to the Berars, or the Assigned Districts, which the Nizám of Haidarábád was induced to hand over to us, as a territorial guarantee for his arrears of subsidy, and for the pay of the Haidarábád contingent which he perpetually kept in arrear. The relics of three other dynasties also passed away in 1853, although without any attendant accretion to British territory. In the extreme south, the titular Nawáb of the Karnátik and the titular Rájá of Tanjore both died without heirs. Their rank and their pensions died with them, but compassionate allowances were continued to their families. In the north of India, Báji Ráo, the ex-Peshwá who had been dethroned in 1818, lived on till 1853 in the enjoyment of his annual pension of £80,000. His adopted son, Nána Sáhib, inherited his accumulated savings, but could obtain no further recognition. *Nágpur, 1853. Berars handed over, 1853.*

Lord Dalhousie annexed the Province of Oudh on different grounds. Ever since the Nawáb Wazír, Shujá-ud-Daulá, received back his forfeited territories from the hands of Lord *Annexation of Oudh, 1856.*

Clive in 1765, the existence of his dynasty had depended on the protection of British bayonets.[1] Guarded alike from foreign invasion and from domestic rebellion, the long line of Nawábs had sunk into private debauchees and public oppressors. Their one virtue was steady loyalty to the British Government. The fertile districts between the Ganges and the Gogra, which now support a denser population than any rural area of the same size on the globe, had been groaning for generations under an anarchy for which each British Governor-General felt himself in part responsible. Warning after warning had been given to the Nawábs (who had assumed the title of Sháh or King since 1819) that they must put their house in order.

What the benevolent Bentinck and the soldierly Hardinge had only threatened, was reserved for Lord Dalhousie, who united honesty of purpose with stern decision of character, to perform. He laid the whole case before the Court of Directors, who, after long and painful hesitation, resolved on annexation. Lord Dalhousie, then on the eve of retiring, felt that it would be unfair to leave the perilous task to his successor in the first moments of his rule. The tardy decision of the Court of Directors left him, however, only a few weeks to carry out the work. But he solemnly believed that work to be his duty to the people of Oudh. 'With this feeling on my mind,' he wrote in his private diary, 'and in humble reliance on the blessing of the Almighty (for millions of His creatures will draw freedom and happiness from the change), I approach the execution of this duty, gravely and not without solicitude, but calmly and altogether without doubt.'

Lord Dalhousie's view of the measure.

At the commencement of 1856, the last year of his rule, he issued orders to General (afterwards Sir James) Outram, then Resident at the Court of Lucknow, to assume the direct administration of Oudh, on the ground that 'the British Government would be guilty in the sight of God and man if it were any longer to aid in sustaining by its countenance an administration fraught with suffering to millions.' The proclamation was issued on the 13th February 1856. The king, Wájid Alí, bowed to irresistible force, although he refused to recognise the justice of his deposition. After a mission to England, consisting of his mother, brother, and son, by way of protest and appeal, he settled down in the pleasant suburb of Garden Reach near Calcutta. There he still lives (1885) in

Grounds of annexation.

---

[1] For the history of Oudh since 1765, and the misrule which compelled its annexation, see article OUDH, *The Imperial Gazetteer of India.*

'the enjoyment of a pension of £120,000 a year. Oudh was thus annexed without a blow. But this measure, on which Lord Dalhousie looked back with the proudest sense of rectitude, was perhaps the one act of his rule that most alarmed native public opinion.

The Marquis of Dalhousie resigned office in March 1856, being then only forty-four years of age ; but he carried home with him the seeds of a lingering illness, which resulted in his death in 1860. Excepting Cornwallis, he was the first, although by no means the last, of English statesmen who have fallen victims to their devotion to India's needs. Lord Dal-
housie's
death,
1860.

Lord Dalhousie completed the fabric of British rule in India. The Empire as mapped out by Lord Wellesley and Lord Hastings, during the first quarter of the century, had received the addition of Sind in 1843. The Marquis of Dalhousie finally filled in the wide spaces covered by Oudh, by the Central Provinces, and by smaller States within India ; together with the great outlying territories of the Punjab on the North-Western Frontier, and the richest part of British Burma beyond the sea. His work
in India.

The great Governor-General was succeeded by his friend Lord Canning, who, at the farewell banquet in England given to him by the Court of Directors, uttered these prophetic words, ' I wish for a peaceful term of office. But I cannot forget that in the sky of India, serene as it is, a small cloud may arise, no larger than a man's hand, but which, growing larger and larger, may at last threaten to burst and overwhelm us with ruin.' In the following year, the Sepoys of the Bengal army mutinied, and all the valley of the Ganges from Patná to Delhi rose in rebellion. Earl
Canning,
1856–62. The Sepoy
Mutiny,
1857.

The various motives assigned for the Mutiny appear inadequate to the European mind. The truth seems to be that native opinion throughout India was in a ferment, predisposing men to believe the wildest stories, and to rush into action in a paroxysm of terror. Panic acts on an oriental population like drink among a European mob. The annexation policy of Lord Dalhousie, although dictated by the most enlightened considerations, was distasteful to the native mind. The spread of education, the appearance of the steam-engine and the telegraph wire, seemed simultaneous disclosures of a deep plan to substitute an English for an Indian civilisation. Causes
of the
Mutiny.

The Bengal Sepoys thought that they could see farther than the rest of their countrymen. Most of them were Hindus of Temper
of the
Sepoys.

high caste ; many of them were recruited from Oudh. They regarded our reforms on Western lines as attacks on their own nationality, and they knew at first hand what annexation meant. They believed it was by their prowess that the Punjab had been conquered, and that all India was held. The numerous dethroned princes, or their heirs and widows, were the first to learn and to take advantage of this spirit of disaffection and panic. They had heard of the Crimean war, and were told that Russia was the perpetual enemy of England. Our munificent pensions had supplied the funds with which they could buy the aid of skilful intriguers. They had much to gain, and little to lose, by a revolution.

In this critical state of affairs, of which the Government had scant official knowledge, a rumour ran through the cantonments that the cartridges of the Bengal army had been greased with the fat of cows and pigs. This was affirmed to be part of a general plot by the British Government to destroy the religion alike of the Hindu and of the Muhammadan Sepoy. As a matter of fact, cow's tallow had been culpably and ignorantly used. Steps were taken to prevent the defiling cartridges from reaching the hands and mouths of the native army. But no assurances could quiet the minds of the Sepoys. Fires occurred nightly in the native lines ; officers were insulted by their men ; confidence was gone, and scarcely the form of discipline remained.

The 'greased' cartridges, 1857.

The events which followed form contemporary annals. Any narrative of them beyond the barest summary would involve the criticism of measures on which history has not yet pronounced her calm verdict, and would lead to personal praise or blame of still living men.[1] Each episode of the Mutiny is treated in *The Imperial Gazetteer of India*, under the town or District where it occurred. But it may not be out of place to mention here, that the outbreak of the storm found the native regiments denuded of many of their best officers. The administration of the great Empire, to which Dalhousie put the corner-stone, required a larger staff than the civil service could supply. The practice of selecting the ablest military men for civil posts, which had long existed, received a sudden and vast development. Oudh, the Punjab, the Central Provinces, British Burma, were administered to a large extent

The army drained of its talent.

---

[1] The Mutiny of 1857 has already a copious literature. Sir John Kaye's *History of the Sepoy War* (3 vols.), with its able and eloquent continuation by Colonel Malleson, C.S.I., as *The History of the Indian Mutiny* (3 vols.), forms the standard work.

by picked officers from the Company's regiments. Some skilful commanders remained; but the native army had nevertheless been drained of many of its brightest intellects and firmest wills at the very crisis of its fate.

On the afternoon of Sunday, 10th May 1857, the Sepoys at Meerut (Merath) broke into open mutiny.[1] They burst into the jail, and rushed in a wild torrent through the cantonments, cutting down a few Europeans whom they met. They then streamed off to the neighbouring city of Delhi, to stir up the native garrison and the criminal population of that great city, and to place themselves under the authority of the discrowned Mughal Emperor. Meerut was the largest military station in Northern India, with a strong European garrison of foot, horse, and guns, sufficient to overwhelm the mutineers before ever they reached Delhi. But as the Sepoys acted in irrational haste, so the British officers, in but too many cases, acted with equally irrational indecision. The news of the outbreak was telegraphed to Delhi, and nothing more was done that night. At the moment when one strong will might have saved India, no soldier in authority at Meerut seemed able to think or act. The next morning the Muhammadans of Delhi rose, and all that the Europeans there could do was to blow up the magazine. *Outbreak of the Mutiny, May 1857.* *At Meerut.* *At Delhi.*

A rallying centre and a traditional name were thus given to the revolt, which forthwith spread like wild-fire through the North-Western Provinces and Oudh down into Lower Bengal. The same narrative must suffice for all the outbreaks, although each episode has its own story of sadness and devotion. The Sepoys rose on their officers, usually without warning, sometimes after protestations of fidelity. The Europeans, or persons of Christian faith, were frequently massacred; occasionally, also, the women and children. The jail was broken open, the treasury plundered, and the mutineers marched off to some centre of revolt, to join in what had now become a national war. *Spread of the Mutiny, summer of 1857.*

In the Punjab the Sepoys were anticipated by measures of repression and disarmament, carried out by Sir John Lawrence and his lieutenants, among whom Edwardes and Nicholson stand conspicuous. The Sikh population never wavered. Crowds of willing recruits came down from the Afghán hills. And thus the Punjab, instead of being itself a source of danger, was able to furnish a portion of its own garrison for the siege of Delhi. In Lower Bengal many of the Sepoys mutinied, and then dispersed in different directions. The native armies of Madras and Bombay remained true to their *Loyalty of the Sikhs.*

[1] See article MEERUT, *The Imperial Gazetteer of India.*

colours. In Central India, the contingents of some of the great chiefs sooner or later joined the rebels, but the Muhammadan State of Haidarábád was kept loyal by the authority of its able minister, the late Sir Sálar Jang.

Cawnpur. The main interest of the Sepoy War gathers round the three cities of Cawnpur, Lucknow, and Delhi. Cawnpur contained one of the great native garrisons of India. At Bithúr, not far off, was the palace of Dundhu Panth, the heir of the last Peshwá (*ante*, pp. 324, 402), who had inherited his savings, but had failed to procure a continuance of his pension ; and whose **Nána** more familiar name of Nána Sáhib will ever be handed down **Sáhib.** to infamy. At first the Nána was profuse in his professions of loyalty ; but when the Sepoys at Cawnpur mutinied on the 6th June, he put himself at their head, and was proclaimed Peshwá of the Maráthás.

The Europeans at Cawnpur, numbering more women and **Our ill-** children than fighting men, shut themselves up in an ill-chosen **chosen** hasty entrenchment, where they heroically bore a siege for **position.** nineteen days under the sun of a tropical June. Every one had courage and endurance to suffer or to die ; but the directing mind was again absent. On the 27th June, trusting to a safe-conduct from the Nána as far as Allahábád, they surrendered, and, to the number of 450, embarked in boats **Massacre** on the Ganges. Forthwith a murderous fire was opened **of Cawn-** upon them from the river bank. Only a single boat escaped, **pur.** and but four men, who swam across to the protection of a friendly Rájá, ultimately survived to tell the tale. The rest of the men were massacred on the spot. The women and children, numbering 125, were reserved for the same fate on the 15th July, when the avenging army of Havelock was at hand.[1]

Lucknow. Sir Henry Lawrence, the Chief Commissioner of Oudh, had foreseen the storm. He fortified and provisioned the Residency at Lucknow, and thither he retired with all the European inhabitants and a weak British regiment on 2nd July. Two days later, he was mortally wounded by a shell. Whatever **Sir Henry** opinion may be formed of Sir Henry Lawrence's capacity as **Lawrence.** a soldier in his one unfortunate engagement, he clearly perceived the main strategic and political points in the struggle. Lawrence had deliberately chosen his position ; and the little garrison held out under unparalleled hardships and against enormous odds, until relieved by Havelock and Outram on 25th September. But the relieving force was itself invested by fresh swarms of rebels ; and it was not until November that

[1] See article CAWNPUR, *The Imperial Gazetteer of India.*

Sir Colin Campbell (afterwards Lord Clyde) cut his way into Lucknow, and effected the final deliverance of the garrison [1] (16th November 1857). Our troops then withdrew to more urgent work, and did not finally re-occupy Lucknow till March 1858.

The siege of Delhi began on 8th June, one month after the original outbreak at Meerut. Siege in the proper sense of the word it was not; for the British army, encamped on the historic 'ridge,' at no time exceeded 8000 men, while the rebels within the walls were more than 30,000 strong. In the middle of August, Nicholson arrived with a reinforcement from the Punjab; but his own inspiring presence was even more valuable than the reinforcement he brought. On 14th September the assault was delivered, and after six days' desperate fighting in the streets, Delhi was again won. Nicholson fell at the head of the storming party. Hodson, the intrepid leader of a corps of irregular horse, hunted down next day the old Mughal Emperor, Bahádur Sháh, and his sons. The Emperor was afterwards sent a State prisoner to Rangoon, where he lived till 1862. As the mob pressed in on the guard around the Emperor's sons, near Delhi, Hodson found it necessary to shoot down the princes (who had been captured unconditionally) with his own hand. [2]

Siege of Delhi, June to Sept. 1857.

Nicholson.

After the fall of Delhi and the final relief of Lucknow, the war loses its dramatic interest, although fighting went on in various parts of the country for eighteen months longer. The population of Oudh and Rohilkhand, stimulated by the presence of the Begam of Oudh, the Nawáb of Bareilly, and Nána Sáhib himself, had joined the mutinous Sepoys *en masse.* In this quarter of India alone, it was the revolt of a people rather than the mutiny of an army that had to be quelled. Sir Colin Campbell (afterwards Lord Clyde) conducted the campaign in Oudh, which lasted through two cold seasons. [3] Valuable assistance was lent by Sir Jang Bahádur of Nepál, at the head of his gallant Gúrkhas. Town after town was occupied, fort after fort was stormed, until the last gun had been re-captured, and the last fugitive had been chased across the frontier by January 1859.

Oudh reduced

by Lord Clyde.

In the meanwhile, Sir Hugh Rose (afterwards Lord Strathnairn), with another army from Bombay, was conducting an equally brilliant campaign in Central India. His most formid-

Sir Hugh Rose in Central India.

---

[1] See article LUCKNOW, *The Imperial Gazetteer of India.*
[2] See article DELHI CITY, *The Imperial Gazetteer of India.*
[3] See article BAREILLY, *The Imperial Gazetteer of India.*

able antagonists were the disinherited Ráni or Princess of Jhánsi, and Tantiá Topí, whose military talent had previously inspired Nána Sáhib with all the capacity for resistance which he ever displayed. The Princess died fighting bravely at the head of her troops in June 1858.[1] Tantiá Topí, after doubling backwards and forwards through Central India, was at last betrayed and run down in April 1859.

Renewals of the Company's Charter, 1813-15.   The Company's charter had been granted from time to time for periods of twenty years, and each renewal had formed an opportunity for a national inquest into the management of India. The Parliamentary Inquiry of 1813 abolished the Company's monopoly of Indian trade, and compelled it to direct its energies in India to the good government of the people. The Charter Act of 1833 did away with its remaining Chinese trade, and opened up administrative offices in India to the natives, irrespective of caste, creed, or race. The Act

Its privileges curtailed.   of 1853 abolished the patronage by which the Company filled up the superior or covenanted branch of its civil service. It laid down the principle that the administration of India was too national a concern to be left to the chances of benevolent nepotism ; and that England's representatives in India must be chosen openly, and without favour, from the youth of England.

Downfall of the Company, 1858.   The Mutiny sealed the fate of the East India Company, after a life of more than two and a half centuries. The original Company received its charter of incorporation from Elizabeth in 1600. Its political powers, and the constitution of the Indian Government, were derived from the Regulating

Its history epito- mized, 1773-1858.   Act of 1773, passed by the Ministry of Lord North. By that statute the Governor of Bengal was raised to the rank of Governor-General ; and, in conjunction with his Council of four other members, he was entrusted with the duty of superintending and controlling the Governments of Madras and Bombay, so far as regarded questions of peace and war : a Supreme Court of Judicature was appointed at Calcutta, to which the judges were appointed by the Crown : and a power of making rules, ordinances, and regulations was conferred upon the Governor-General and his Council. Next came the

Act of 1784.   India Bill of Pitt (1784), which founded the Board of Control, strengthened the supremacy of Bengal over the other Presidencies, and first authorized the historical phrase, ' Governor-General-in-Council.'

The new Charter Act which abolished the Company's

[1] See article JHANSI, *The Imperial Gazetteer of India.*

Chinese trade in 1833, introduced successive reforms into the constitution of the Indian Government. It added to the Act of Council a Law-member who need not be chosen from among 1833. the Company's servants, and was entitled to be present only at meetings for making Laws and Regulations. It accorded the authority of Acts of Parliament to the Laws and Regulations so made, subject to the disallowance of the Court of Directors. It appointed a Law Commission; and it gave the Governor-General-in-Council a control over the other Presidencies, in all points relating to the civil or military administration. The Charter of the Company was renewed for the last time in 1853, not for a definite period of years, but only Act of for so long as Parliament should see fit. On this occasion 1853. the number of Directors was reduced, and, as above stated, their patronage as regards appointments to the covenanted civil service was taken away, to make room for the principle of open competition.

The Act for the better government of India (1858), which India finally transferred the entire administration from the Company transferred to the Crown, was not passed without an eloquent protest from Crown, the Directors, nor without acrimonious party discussion in 1858. Parliament. It enacts that India shall be governed by, and in the name of, the Queen of England through one of her principal Secretaries of State, assisted by a Council of fifteen members. The Governor-General received the new title of 'The Viceroy. The European troops of the Company, numbering Viceroy.' about 24,000 officers and men, were amalgamated with the royal service, and the Indian navy was abolished. By the Indian Councils Act (1861), the Governor-General's Council, and also the Councils at Madras and Bombay, were augmented by the addition of non-official members, either natives or Europeans, for legislative purposes only. By another Act also passed in 1861, High Courts of Judicature were constituted out of the old Supreme Courts at the Presidency towns.

It fell to the lot of Lord Canning both to suppress the India Mutiny, and to introduce the peaceful revolution which followed. under the It suffices to say that he preserved his equanimity unruffled in 1858–62. the darkest hours of peril, and that the strict impartiality of his conduct incurred alternate praise and blame from partisans of both sides. The epithet then scornfully levelled at him of 'Clemency' Canning, is now remembered only to his honour. Queen's On 1st November 1858, at a grand *darbár* held at Alláhábád, Proclamation, 1st he published the Royal Proclamation, which announced that Nov. 1858.

the Queen had assumed the government of India. This document, which is, in the truest and noblest sense, the Magna Charta of the Indian people, proclaimed in eloquent words a policy of justice and religious toleration ; and granted an amnesty to all except those who had directly taken part in the murder of British subjects. Peace was proclaimed throughout India on the 8th July 1859. In the following cold weather, Lord Canning made a viceregal progress through the northern Provinces, to receive the homage of loyal princes and chiefs, and to guarantee to them the right of adoption.

Cost of the Mutiny.   The suppression of the Mutiny increased the debt of India by about 40 millions sterling, and the military changes which ensued augmented the annual expenditure by about 10 millions. To grapple with this deficit, a distinguished political economist and parliamentary financier, Mr. James Wilson, was sent out

Financial reforms.   from England as financial member of Council. He re-organized the customs system, imposed an income-tax and a licence duty, and created a State paper currency. He died in the midst of his splendid task ; but his name still lives as that

Legal reforms.   of the first and greatest finance minister of India. The Penal Code, originally drawn up by Macaulay in 1837, passed into law in 1860; together with Codes of Civil and Criminal Procedure in 1861.[1]

Lord Elgin, 1862-63.   Lord Canning left India in March 1862, and died before he had been a month in England. His successor, Lord Elgin, only lived till November 1863. He expired at the Himálayan station of Dharmsálá, and there he lies buried.

Lord Lawrence, 1864-69.   He was succeeded by Sir John (afterwards Lord) Lawrence, the saviour of the Punjab. The chief incidents of Lord Lawrence's rule were the Bhután war, followed by the annexation of the Bhután Dwárs in 1864, and the terrible Orissa famine of 1866.

In a later famine in Bundelkhand and Upper Hindustán in 1868-69, Lord Lawrence laid down the principle, for the first time in Indian history, that the officers of the Government would be held personally responsible for taking every possible

Events of his Vice-royalty.   means to avert death by starvation. An inquiry was conducted into the status of the peasantry of Oudh, and an Act was passed with a view to securing them in their customary rights. After a period of fratricidal war among the sons of Dost Muhammad, the Afghán territories were concentrated in the

[1] On the subject of Anglo-Indian Codification, *Vide ante*, chap. iv.

hands of Sher Alí, and the latter was acknowledged as Amír by Lord Lawrence. A commercial crisis took place in 1866, which seriously threatened the young tea industry in Bengal, and caused widespread ruin in Bombay. Sir John Lawrence retired in January 1869, after having passed through every grade of Indian service, from an assistant magistracy to the viceroyalty. On his return to England, he was raised to the peerage. He died in 1879, and lies in Westminster Abbey.

Lord Mayo succeeded Lord Lawrence in 1869, and urged on the material progress of India. The Ambálá *darbár,* at which Sher Alí was recognised as Amír of Afghánistán, although in one sense the completion of what Lord Lawrence had begun, owed its success to Lord Mayo. The visit of His Royal Highness the Duke of Edinburgh in 1869-70 gave great pleasure to the natives of India, and introduced a tone of personal loyalty into our relations with the feudatory princes. *Lord Mayo, 1869-72. Ambálá darbár, 1869.*

Lord Mayo reformed several of the great branches of the administration, created an Agricultural Department, and introduced the system of Provincial Finance. The impulse to local self-government given by the last measure has done much, and will do more, to develop and husband the revenues of India; to quicken the sense of responsibility among the English administrators; and to awaken political life among the people. Lord Mayo also laid the foundation for the reform of the Salt Duties. He thus enabled his successors to abolish the old pernicious customs-lines which walled off Province from Province, and strangled the trade between British India and the Feudatory States. He developed the material resources of the country by an immense extension of roads, railways, and canals, thus carrying out the beneficent system of Public Works which Lord Dalhousie had inaugurated. Lord Mayo's splendid vigour defied alike the climate and the vast tasks which he imposed on himself. He anxiously and laboriously studied with his own eyes the wants of the farthest Provinces of the Empire. But his life of noble usefulness was cut short by the hand of an assassin, in the convict settlement of the Andaman Islands, in 1872. *Lord Mayo's reforms. Provincial finance. Customs-lines abolished. Lord Mayo's death, 1872.*

His successor was Lord Northbrook, whose ability found pre-eminent scope in the department of finance.[1] During his *Lord Northbrook, 1872-76.*

[1] It would be unsuitable for an officer of the Government to attempt anything beyond the barest summary of events in India since the death of

viceroyalty, a famine which threatened Lower Bengal in 1874 was successfully obviated by a vast organization of State relief; the Maráthá Gáekwár of Baroda was dethroned in 1875 for misgovernment and disloyalty, but his dominions were continued to a child selected from the family; and the Prince of Wales made a tour through the country in the cold weather of 1875–76. The presence of His Royal Highness evoked a passionate burst of loyalty never before known in the annals of British India. The feudatory chiefs and ruling houses of India felt for the first time that they were incorporated into the Empire of an ancient and a splendid dynasty.

Prince of Wales' tour, 1875-1876.

Lord Lytton, 1876-80.
The 'Empress of India.'

Lord Lytton followed Lord Northbrook in 1876. On January 1, 1877, Queen Victoria was proclaimed Empress of India at a *darbár* of unparalleled magnificence, held in the old Delhi cantonment behind the historic 'ridge'—the 'ridge' from which in 1857 the British had reconquered the revolted Mughal capital. But while the princes and high officials of the country were flocking to this gorgeous scene, the shadow of famine was darkening over Southern India. Both the monsoons of 1876 had failed to bring their due supply of rain, and the season of 1877 was little better. This long-continued drought stretched from the Deccan to Cape Comorin, and subsequently invaded Northern India, causing a famine more widespread than any similar calamity since 1770. Despite vast importations of grain by sea and rail, despite the most strenuous exertions of the Government, which incurred a total expenditure on this account of 11 millions sterling, the loss of life from actual starvation and its attendant train of diseases was lamentable. The deaths from want of food, and from the diseases incident to a famine-stricken population, were estimated at $5\frac{1}{4}$ millions.

Famine of 1877-78.

Afghán affairs, 1878-81.

In the autumn of 1878, the affairs of Afghánistán again forced themselves into notice. Sher Alí, the Amír, who had been hospitably entertained by Lord Mayo, was found to be favouring Russian intrigues. A British embassy was refused admittance to the country, while a Russian mission was received with honour. This led to a declaration of war. British armies advanced by three routes — the Khaibar (Khyber), the Kuram, and the Bolán; and without much opposition occupied the inner entrances of the passes. Sher

Lord Mayo in 1872. The four Viceroys who have ruled during the past fourteen years, are, happily, still living; their policy forms the subject of keen contemporary criticism; and the administrators, soldiers, and diplomatists who gave effect to that policy still hold possession of the scene.

Alí fled to Afghán Turkistán, and there died. A treaty was entered into with his son, Yákub Khán, at Gandamak, by which the British frontier was advanced to the crests or farther sides of the passes, and a British officer was admitted to reside at Kábul. Within a few months the British Resident, Sir Louis Cavagnari, was treacherously attacked and massacred together with his escort, and a second war became necessary. Yákub Khán abdicated, and was deported to India.

At this crisis of affairs, a general election in England resulted in a defeat of the Conservative Ministry. Lord Lytton resigned simultaneously with the Home Government, and the Marquis of Ripon was nominated as his successor in April 1880. In that year, a British brigade received a defeat between Kandahár and the Helmand river from the Herát troops of Ayúb Khán; a defeat promptly and completely retrieved by the brilliant march of General Sir Frederick Roberts from Kábul to Kandahár, and by the total rout of Ayúb Khán's army on 1st September 1880. Abdurrahman Khán, the eldest male representative of the stock of Dost Muhammad, was recognised by us as Amír. The British forces retired from Kábul, leaving him, as our friend, in possession of the capital. The withdrawal of our troops from Kandahár was also effected. Soon afterwards Ayúb Khán advanced with an army from Herát, defeated the Amír Abdurrahman's troops, and captured Kandahár. His success was short-lived. The Amír Abdurrahman marched south with his forces from Kábul, completely routed Ayúb Khán, re-occupied Kandahár, and still reigns as undisputed Amír of Afghánistán (1886). In 1884, a Boundary Commission was appointed with the consent of the Amír to settle, in conjunction with Russian Commissioners, the north-western frontier of Afghánistán. *Marquis of Ripon, 1880-81.* *Afghán affairs, 1880-84.*

The Native State of Mysore, which had been administered by the British on behalf of the Hindu ruling family since 1831, was replaced under its hereditary dynasty on the 25th March 1881. *Mysore, 1881.*

During the remaining years of Lord Ripon's administration (1881-84) peace was maintained in India. The Viceroy took advantage of this lull to carry out certain important reforms in the internal government of the country. The years 1882-84 will be memorable for these great measures. By the repeal of the Vernacular Press Act, he set free the native journals from the last restraints on the free discussion of public questions. *Lord Ripon's internal administration, 1881-84.*

His scheme of local self-government developed the municipal institutions which had been growing up since India passed to the Crown. By a series of enactments, larger powers of local self-government were given to rural and urban boards, and the Local Government Acts. elective principle received a wider application. Where rural boards did not exist, he endeavoured to utilize the local materials available for their formation; and from this point of view he may be said to have extended the principle of local self-government from the towns to the country. Where rural boards already existed he increased their powers; and as far as possible sought to give them a representative basis.

Amendment of Criminal Procedure. An attempt to extend the jurisdiction of the rural criminal courts over European British subjects, independently of the race or nationality of the presiding judge, excited strong public feeling, and ended in a compromise. The principle was asserted in regard to native officers belonging to the Superior Civil Service who had attained to a certain standing, namely District Magistrates and Sessions Judges. At the same time the European community received a further extension of trial by jury, which enables European British subjects to claim a jury, if they see fit to do so, in nearly all cases before the District criminal tribunals.

Department of Agriculture, 1881–84. One of the earliest acts of Lord Ripon's viceroyalty was the re-establishment of the Department of Revenue and Agriculture in accordance with the recommendation of the Famine Commission. This department had been originally instituted by Lord Mayo; but some years after his death, its functions had been distributed between the Finance and Home Departments. It was now reconstituted substantially on its former basis, as a distinct secretariat of the Government of India. It at once took up the recommendations of the Famine Commission; both those bearing on famine relief, and those dealing with organic reforms in the administration of the land revenue. Agricultural improvements, exhibitions of Indian produce, whether in India or in Europe, and works elucidating the raw produce Revenue reforms. of the country, received its special attention. Its reforms in the administration of the land revenue were largely directed to prevent re-settlements in temporarily settled districts from bearing too heavily on the cultivators. Such re-settlements are in future, except in special cases, to avoid re-measurement and vexatious inquisitions, and are to leave to the landlord or husbandman the entire profits accruing from improvements carried out by himself.

Henceforth, an enhancement of the land revenue is to be

made mainly on the grounds (1) of a rise in prices, (2) of an increase in the cultivated area, and (3) of improvements which have been made at the expense of the Government. The Agricultural Department superintends a variety of important operations bearing on the development of the country and the welfare of the people ; including surveys, emigration, the meteorological bureau, the extension of veterinary science, and the statistics of internal trade.

Lord Ripon also appointed an Education Commission with a view to the spread of popular instruction on a broader basis. This Commission, after hearing evidence and collecting data throughout the Presidencies and Provinces of India, reported in 1883. The result of its labours was a Resolution of the Governor-General in Council, which, while encouraging all grades of education, provided specially for the advance of primary instruction at a more equal pace with higher education. The Recommendations of the Commission, and the Government Resolution based upon them, gave encouragement to the indigenous schools which in some Provinces had not previously received a sufficient recognition from the State Department of Public Instruction. *Education Commission, 1882–1883.*

The Commission's Recommendations strongly affirmed the principle of self-help in the extension of high schools and colleges, and laid particular stress on the duty of assisting primary education from Provincial and Municipal funds. They endeavoured to provide for certain sections of the people, particularly the Muhammadans, who for various causes had found themselves unable to avail themselves fully of the State system of public instruction, or in regard to whom that system had proved defective. The general effect of the Commission's labours, and of the Government Resolution based thereon, is to give a more liberal recognition to private effort of every kind, and to schools and colleges conducted on the system of grants-in-aid.

In 1882, Lord Ripon's Finance Minister, Sir Evelyn Baring, took off the import duties on cotton goods; and with them, almost the whole import customs, saving a few exceptions such as those on arms, liquors, etc., were abolished. *Abolition of customs duties, 1882.* In 1884, a Committee of the House of Commons took evidence on railway extension in India, and embodied their recommendations in a Parliamentary Report. The condition of the agricultural population in Bengal occupied the close attention of Lord Ripon throughout his whole viceroyalty. After keen discussions, prolonged during many years, he left a Tenancy *Bengal Tenancy Bill.*

Bill, regulating the relations of landlord and tenant in Bengal, almost ready to be passed by his successor.

Earl of Dufferin, 1884.
The Marquis of Ripon retired from the viceroyalty at the end of 1884, and was succeeded by the Earl of Dufferin. In the spring of 1885, Lord Dufferin passed the Bengal Tenancy Bill through its final stage in the Legislature; and held a Darbár at Rawál Píndi for the reception of the Amír of Afghánistán. The result of the meeting was to strengthen the British relations with that ruler.

Burmese affairs, 1885.
During the summer of the same year, 1885, the hostile attitude of the king of Independent Burma forced itself upon the attention of the British Government. After repeated but fruitless remonstrances, a British expedition was despatched from Bengal and Madras to Rangoon. It advanced up the Irawadi valley (November–December 1885), and occupied Mandalay, the capital of Independent Burma. King Thebau, who had inaugurated his reign by a family massacre, and had steadily refused to redress the wrongs of certain British subjects whom he had injured, remained defiant. He vainly sought aid against the English from foreign powers. In the end he surrendered, almost without a blow, was dethroned, and deported for safe custody to British India. The authority of the Viceroy of India was substituted for that of King Thebau throughout Upper Burma by Proclamation on the 1st January 1886. In February 1886, Lord Dufferin proceeded in person to Burma, to settle the administration of the new British Province. As all pacific proposals were rejected, a military force under General Prendergast moved up the Irawadi in a flotilla of steamers. The opposition encountered was insignificant. On November 28 the capital of Mandalay was occupied without fighting; King Thebau surrendered, and was sent as a prisoner to Rangoon.

CHAPTER XVI.

BRITISH ADMINISTRATION OF INDIA.

THE Act of 1858, which transferred India from the Company to the Crown, also laid down the scheme of its government. Under the Company, the Governor-General was an autocrat, responsible only to the distant Court of Directors. The Court of Directors had been answerable to the shareholders, or Court of Proprietors, on the one hand; and, through the Board of Control, to the Sovereign and to Parliament on the other. The Act of 1858 did away with these intermediary bodies between the Governor-General and the British Ministry. For the Court of Directors, the Court of Proprietors, and the Board of Control, it substituted a Secretary of State, aided by a Council appointed by the Crown. *Control of India in England. Under the Company. Under the Crown.*

The Secretary of State for India is a Cabinet Minister, who comes into and goes out of office with the other members of the Ministry. His Council was originally appointed for life. Its members are now appointed for ten years only;[1] but may be re-appointed for another five years for special reasons. The Secretary of State rules in all ordinary matters through the majority of his Council. But in affairs of urgency, and in questions which belong to the Secret Department, including political correspondence, he is not required to consult his Council. The Viceroy or Governor-General is appointed by the Crown, and resides in India. His ordinary term of office is five years. *The Secretary of State. His Council in England. Office of Viceroy.*

The supreme authority in India is vested by a series of Acts of Parliament[2] in the Viceroy or Governor-General-in-Council, subject to the control of the Secretary of State in England. Every executive order and every legislative statute runs in the name of the 'Governor-General-in-Council;[3] but in *Administration in India. 'Governor-General-in-Council.'*

[1] Under 32 and 33 Vict. c. 97.
[2] The chief of these Acts are 13 Geo. III. c. 63; 33 Geo. III. c. 52; 3 and 4 Will. IV. c. 85; 21 and 22 Vict. c. 106; and 24 and 25 Vict. c. 67.
[3] A style first authorized by 33 Geo. III. c. 52, sec. 39.

certain cases,[1] a power is reserved to the Viceroy to act independently. The Governor-General's Council is of a two-fold character.

Executive Council.

First, the ordinary or Executive Council,[2] usually composed of about six official members besides the Viceroy, which may be compared with the cabinet of a constitutional country. It meets regularly at short intervals, usually once a week, discusses and decides upon questions of foreign policy and domestic administration, and prepares measures for the Legislative Council. Its members divide among themselves the chief departments of State, such as those of Foreign Affairs, Finance, War, Public Works, etc. The Viceroy combines in his own person the duties of constitutional Sovereign with those of Prime Minister;[3] and has usually charge of the Foreign Department. As a rule, the Viceroy is himself the initiating Member of Council for Foreign and Feudatory Affairs.

Second,[4] the Legislative Council, which is made up of the same members as the preceding, with the addition of the Governor of the Province in which it may be held; certain officials selected by the Governor-General from Bengal, Madras, Bombay, or other Provinces; and nominated members, representative of the non-official Native and European communities. The official additional members thus appointed

Legislative Council.

to the Legislative Council must not exceed in number the non-officials, and the total of the additional members must not exceed twelve. The meetings of the Legislative Council are held when and as required, usually once a week. They are open to the public; and a further guarantee for publicity is ensured by the proviso that draft Bills must be published a

---

[1] 'Cases of high importance, and essentially affecting the public interest and welfare' (33 Geo. III. c. 52, sec. 47) ; 'when any measure is proposed whereby the safety, tranquillity, or interests of the British possessions in India may, in the judgment of the Governor-General, be essentially affected' (3 and 4 Will. IV. c. 85, sec. 49) ; 'cases of emergency' (24 and 25 Vict. c. 67, sec. 23).

[2] This is the lineal descendant of the original Council organized under the charters of the Company, first constituted by Parliamentary sanction in 1773 (13 Geo. III. c. 63, sec. 7).

[3] The mechanism and working of the Governor-General's Council, and of the Secretariats, and chief Departments of the Indian Administration, are described in Hunter's *Life of the Earl of Mayo*, vol. i. pp. 189-202 (2nd ed.)

[4] Originally identical with the Executive Council, upon which legislative powers were conferred by 13 Geo. III. c. 63, sec. 36. The distinction between the two Councils was first recognised in the appointment of 'the fourth member' (3 and 4 Will. IV. c. 85, sec. 40).

certain number of times in the *Gazette*. As a matter of practice, these draft Bills have usually been first subjected to the criticism of the several Provincial governments. Provincial Legislative Councils have also been appointed for the Presidencies of Madras and Bombay, and for the Lieutenant-Governorship of Bengal. The members of these local Legislative Councils are appointed, in the case of Madras and Bombay, by the Governors of those Provinces; and in Bengal, by the Lieutenant-Governor, subject to the approval of the Governor-General. The Acts of these Provincial Legislative Councils, which can deal only with provincial matters, are subject to sanction by the Governor-General.

The Presidencies of Madras and Bombay, and the Lieutenant-Governorships of Bengal and of the North-Western Provinces, have each a High Court,[1] supreme both in civil and criminal business, but with an ultimate appeal to the Judicial Committee of the Privy Council in England. Of the minor Provinces, the Punjab has a Chief Court, with three judges; the Central Provinces and Oudh have each a Judicial Commissioner, who sits alone. British Burma has a Judicial Commissioner and a Recorder. In this Province, the Judicial Commissioner has jurisdiction over the territory outside Rangoon (save that in cases of European British subjects the Recorder has the powers of a High Court). The Recorder has jurisdiction in the town of Rangoon, and in all criminal cases in any part of Burma where the accused are European British subjects. The Judicial Commissioner and the Recorder of Rangoon sit together as a 'Special Court' for certain purposes. Appeals from the Recorder of Rangoon in civil suits where the subject-matter ranges from Rs. 3000 to Rs. 10,000, lie to the High Court at Calcutta. The latter Court also decides references from the 'Special Court' of Rangoon when the members are equally divided in opinion. For Assam, the High Court at Calcutta is the highest judicial authority, except in the three Hill Districts, namely, the Gáro Hills, the Khási and Jaintia Hills, and the Nágá Hills. In these Districts, the Chief Commissioner of Assam is judge without appeal in civil and criminal matters. Special rules apply to the Dwárs bordering on Bhután.

High Courts of Justice

The law administered in the Indian Courts consists mainly of—(1) the enactments of the Indian Legislative Councils (Imperial and Provincial), as above described, and of the bodies

The law of British India.

[1] Constituted out of the Supreme Courts and the Sudder (Sadr) Courts in 1861 (24 and 25 Vict. c. 104).

which preceded them; (2) statutes of the British Parliament which apply to India; (3) the Hindu and Muhammadan laws of inheritance, and their domestic law, in causes affecting Hindus and Muhammadans; (4) the Customary Law affecting particular castes and races. Much has been done towards consolidating special sections of the Indian law;[1] and in the Indian Penal Code, together with the Codes of Civil and Criminal Procedure, we have memorable examples of such efforts.

But although the Governor-General-in-Council is theoretically supreme over every part of India alike,[2] his actual authority is not everywhere exercised in the same direct manner. For ordinary purposes of administration, British India is partitioned into Provinces, each with a government of its own; and certain of the Native States are attached to those Provinces with which they are most nearly connected geographically. These Provinces, again, enjoy various degrees of independence. The two Presidencies of Madras and Bombay, including Sind, retain many marks of their original equality with Bengal. They each have an army and a civil service of their own. They are each administered by a Governor appointed direct from England. They have each an Executive and a Legislative Council, whose functions are analogous to those of the Councils of the Governor-General, although subject to his control.[3] They thus possess a domestic legislature; and in administrative matters, also, the interference of the Governor-General-in-Council is sparingly exercised.

Of the other Provinces, Bengal, or rather Lower Bengal, occupies a peculiar position. Like the North-Western Provinces and the Punjab, it is administered by a single official with the style of Lieutenant-Governor, who is controlled by no Executive Council; but, unlike those two Provinces, Bengal has a Legislative Council, so far preserving a sign of its early pre-eminence. The other Northern Provinces, Assam, Oudh, and the Central Provinces, whether ruled by a Lieutenant-Governor or a Chief Commissioner, may be regarded from a historical point of view as fragments of the original Bengal Presidency,[4] which, as thus defined, would be co-extensive with all British India not included under Madras or Bombay. Garrisons on the Madras or Bombay establishment may be posted in out-

Marginal notes: Provincial Administration. Madras. Bombay. Bengal. Minor Provinces.

[1] *Ante*, chap. iv. p. 117.
[2] 3 and 4 Will. IV. c. 85, secs. 39 and 65.
[3] 24 and 25 Vict. c. 67, sec. 42.
[4] See article BENGAL PRESIDENCY, *The Imperial Gazetteer of India.*

lying tracts of the old Bengal territories, but civil officers of the
Madras and Bombay Services are excluded. The Lieutenant-
Governors and most of the Chief Commissioners are chosen
from the Covenanted Civil Service. In executive matters they
are the practical rulers, but, excepting the Lieutenant-Governor
of Bengal, they have no legislative authority.

To complete the total area of territory under British admini- Minor
stration, it is necessary to mention, besides Bengal, the North- admini-
Western Provinces, the Punjab, Oudh, and Assam, certain strations.
quasi-Provinces, under the immediate control of the Viceroy.
These are—BRITISH BURMA, part of which was annexed in
1826 and part in 1852; the CENTRAL PROVINCES, lapsed in
1853; ASSAM, annexed in 1826; AJMERE, transferred from
Rájputána; BERAR, or the Districts assigned by the Nizám of
Haidarábád, for the support of the Haidarábád Contingent;
and the little territory of COORG, in the extreme south.[1] The
State of Mysore was under British administration from 1831 to
1881, when it was restored to its native Rájá, on his attaining
his majority.

Another difference of administration, although now of less 'The
importance than in former times, derives its name from the Regula-
old Regulations, or laws and judicial rules of practice which tions.'
preceded the present system of Acts of the Legislature. From
these Regulations certain tracts of country have been from
time to time exempted—tracts which, owing to their backward
state of civilisation or other causes, seemed to require exceptional treatment. In non-Regulation territory, broadly speak- Non-
ing, a larger measure of discretion is allowed to the officials, Regulation
both in the collection of revenue and in the administration territory.
of civil justice; strict rules of procedure yield to the local
exigencies; and the judicial and executive departments are to
a great extent combined in the same hands.

A wider field is also permitted for the selection of the
administrative body, which is not entirely confined to the
Covenanted Civil Service, but includes military officers on the
staff and also uncovenanted civilians. The title of the highest
executive official in a District of a Regulation Province is that
of Collector-Magistrate. In a non-Regulation District, the 'Deputy
corresponding officer is styled the Deputy Commissioner; and Commis-
the supreme authority in a non-Regulation Province (with the sioners.'
exception of the Punjab) is called, not a Lieutenant-Governor,
but a Chief Commissioner. The Central Provinces, Assam,

---

[1] For the constitution of each of these Provinces, see their articles in
The Imperial Gazetteer of India.

and British Burma are examples of non-Regulation Provinces; but non-Regulation Districts are to be found also in Bengal and the North-Western Provinces. Their existence is always disclosed by the term 'Deputy Commissioner' as the title of the chief executive officer of the District.

The 'District' or territorial unit.

Alike in Regulation and in non-Regulation territory, the unit of administration is the District—a word of very definite meaning in official phraseology. The District officer, whether known as Collector-Magistrate or as Deputy Commissioner, is the responsible head of his jurisdiction. Upon his energy and personal character depends ultimately the efficiency of our Indian Government. His own special duties are so numerous and so various as to bewilder the outsider; and the work of his subordinates, European and native, largely depends upon the stimulus of his personal example. His position has been compared to that of the French *préfet;* but such a comparison is unjust in many ways to the Indian District officer. He is not a mere subordinate of a central bureau, who takes his colour from his chief, and represents the political parties or the permanent officialism of the capital. The Indian Collector is a strongly individualized worker in every department of rural well-being, with a large measure of local independence and of individual initiative.

The District Officer or 'Collector-Magistrate.'

Duties of the 'Collector-Magistrate.'

As the name of Collector-Magistrate implies, his main functions are two-fold. He is a fiscal officer, charged with the collection of the revenue from the land and other sources; he also is a revenue and criminal judge, both of first instance and in appeal. But his title by no means exhausts his multifarious duties. He does in his smaller local sphere all that the Home Secretary superintends in England, and a great deal more; for he is the representative of a paternal and not of a constitutional government. Police, jails, education, municipalities, roads, sanitation, dispensaries, the local taxation, and the imperial revenues of his District, are to him matters of daily concern. He is expected to make himself acquainted with every phase of the social life of the natives, and with each natural aspect of the country. He should be a lawyer, an accountant, a surveyor, and a ready writer of State papers. He ought also to possess no mean knowledge of agriculture, political economy, and engineering.

Number of Districts in British India.

The total number of Districts in British India is about 235. They vary greatly in size and number of inhabitants. The average area is 3840 square miles, ranging from 14,115 square miles in Sind (Karáchi), 12,045 square miles in Bengal (Lohárdagá), and 11,885 square miles in the Central Provinces (Ráipur) ; down to 937 square miles in the North-Western Provinces (Tarái), 957 square miles in Madras (Nílgiris), and 989 square miles in Oudh (Lucknow). The average population is 800,723 souls, similarly ranging from 3,051,916 in Bengal (Maimansingh), 2,617,120 in the North-Western Provinces Their (Gorakhpur), and 2,365,035 in Madras (Malabar) ; down to varying size. 91,034 in Madras (Nílgiris), 144,070 in the North-Western Provinces (Dehra), and to 231,341 in the Central Provinces (Nimar). Districts from their extreme smallness, or other circumstances which render them quite exceptional,—such as the little hill District of Simla, the backward and only partially inhabited tract of Northern Arakan, the Calcutta-Suburban District of Howrah,—are not included in the above. The Madras Districts are, on an average, the most extensive in area, and the most populous. In every other Province but Madras, the Districts are grouped into larger areas, known as Divisions, each under the charge of a Commissioner. But these Divisions are not properly units of administration, as the Districts are. They are aggregates of units, formed only for convenience of supervision, so that an intermediate authority may exercise the universal watchfulness which would be impossible for a distant Lieutenant-Governor.

The Districts are again partitioned out into lesser tracts, Sub-called Sub-divisions in Bengal, *táluks* in Madras and in Districts. Bombay, and *tahsíls* in Northern India generally. These Sub-Districts are the primary units of fiscal administration. The *thání*, or police circle, is the unit of police administration over the whole of British India.

The preceding sketch of Indian administration would be The Secre-incomplete without a reference to the Secretariat, or central tariat : bureau of each Province, which controls and gives unity to the whole. From the Secretariat are issued the orders that regulate or modify the details of administration ; into the Secretariat come the multifarious reports from the local officers, to be there digested for future reference. But although the Secretaries may enjoy the social life of the Presidency capitals, with higher salaries and better prospects of promotion, the efficiency of our rule rests ultimately upon the shoulders of the District officers, who bear the burden and heat of the day, of the with fewer opportunities of winning fame or reward. The Govern-ment of Secretariat of the Supreme Government of India consists of India ;

seven branches, each of which deals with a special department of the administration. The officers who preside over them are named respectively, the Foreign Secretary, the Home Secretary, the Secretary in the Department of Revenue and Agriculture, the Financial Secretary, the Military Secretary, the Public Works Secretary, and the Secretary in the Legislative Department. In the Presidencies, Lieutenant-Governorships, and Chief-Commissionerships, the Provincial Secretariat is formed on the same model, but the Secretaries are only from one to three or four in number.

of the local government.

Land-Tax.

THE LAND-TAX.—The land furnishes the chief source of Indian revenue, and the collection of the land-tax forms the main work of Indian administration. No technical term is more familiar to Anglo-Indians, and none more obscure to the English public, than that of 'land settlement.' Nor has any subject given rise to more voluminous controversy. It will here suffice to explain the general principles upon which the system is based, and to indicate the chief differences in their application to the several Provinces. That the State should appropriate to itself a share of the produce of the soil, is a maxim of finance which has been recognised throughout the East from time immemorial. The germs of rival systems in India can be traced in the survival of military and other service tenures, and in the poll-tax of Assam and Burma.

Land Settlement.

The early development of the Indian land system was due to two conditions,—a comparatively high state of agriculture, and an organized plan of administration,—both of which were supplied by the primitive Hindu village community. During the lapse of generations, despite domestic anarchy and foreign conquest, the Hindu village preserved its customs, written on the imperishable tablets of tradition. In the ancient Hindu village community, the land was held, not by private owners, but by occupiers under the village corporation : the revenue was due, not from individuals, but from the village community represented by its head-man. The harvest of the hamlet was dealt with as a common fund ; and before the general distribution, the head-man was bound to set aside the share of the king. No other system of taxation could be theoretically more just, or in practice less obnoxious, to a primitive people. This ancient land system may still be found in parts of India, both under British and native rule ; and it prevailed almost universally before the Muhammadan conquest.

Ancient land system of India.

The Musalmáns brought with them the avarice of conquerors,

and a stringent system of revenue collection. Under the Musalmán Mughal Empire, as organized by Akbar the Great, the share land-tax. of the State was fixed at one-third of the gross produce of the soil; and an army of tax-collectors intervened between the cultivator and the supreme government. The vocabulary of our own land system is borrowed from the Mughal administration. The *zamíndár* himself is a creation of the The Muhammadans, unknown to the early Hindu system. He *zamíndár.* was originally a mere tax-collector, or farmer of the land revenue, who agreed to pay a lump sum from the tract of country assigned to him. But the Hindu chief or local mag- His two- nate was often accepted by the Mughals as the *zamíndár*, or fold origin. revenue contractor, for the lands under his control. In this way, the Indian *zamíndárs* as a body are of mixed origin, and represent in some cases not merely an official status, but heredi- tary rights. If the Hindu village system may be praised for its justice, the Mughal farming system had at least the merit of efficiency. Sháh Jahán and Aurangzeb, as we have seen,[1] ex- tracted a larger land revenue than we obtain at the present day.

When the responsibility of governing the country was first The Com- undertaken by the East India Company, an attempt was made pany's to understand the social system upon which the payment of efforts. land revenue was based. Elaborate orders were issued to this end in 1769; but the Company's servants were too engrossed with conquest, with the 'annual investment,' and with their private trade, to find time for minute inquiries into the rights of the peasantry. The *zamíndár* was conspicuous and useful; The the village community and the cultivating *ráyat* did not force *zamíndár* themselves into notice. The *zamíndár* seemed a solvent landlord. person, capable of keeping a contract; and his official position as tax-collector was confused with the proprietary rights of an English landlord. In Bengal, the *zamíndár*, under the Per- manent Settlement of 1793, was raised to the status of proprietor, holding at a quit-rent payable to the State, fixed in perpetuity. In Madras, under the *ráyatwárí* system of holding direct from the State, and in most other parts of India, the actual cultivator has been raised to the same status, subject also to a quit-rent, fixed at intervals of thirty years. The aim of Growth of the British authorities has everywhere been to establish private private property in the soil, consistently with the punctual payment of rights. the revenue.

The annual Government demand, like the succession duty in

[1] This subject has been fully discussed in the chapter on the Mughal Empire. *Vide ante*, pp. 298, 299, 305, 311, etc.

Landed property in India.

England, is the first liability on the land. When that is satisfied, the registered landholder in Bengal has powers of sale or mortgage scarcely more restricted than those of an English tenant in fee-simple. At the same time, the possible hardships, as regards the cultivator, of this absolute right of property vested in the owner have been anticipated by the recognition of occupancy rights or fixity of peasant-tenures, under carefully ascertained conditions.

Individual proprietary rights.

Legal titles have everywhere taken the place of unwritten customs. Land, which was merely a source of livelihood to the cultivator and of revenue to the State, has become a valuable property to the owner. The fixing of the revenue demand has conferred upon the landholder a credit which he never before possessed, and created for him a source of future profit arising out of the unearned increment. This credit he may use improvidently; and he sometimes does so with disastrous results. But none the less has the land system of India been raised from a lower to a higher stage of civilisation; that is to say, from holdings in common to holdings in severalty, and from the corporate possession of the village community to individual proprietary rights.

Rates of land-tax.

With regard to the money rates of the assessment, the Famine Commissioners in 1880 reported the average rate throughout India at about 2s. per cultivated acre, ranging from 4d. to 4s. 6d., according to the quality of the land. In the North-Western Provinces the rates of assessment average Rs. 1. 11. 4. per cultivated acre. In the Punjab, with the same system of Land Settlement, but with an inferior soil, they average just under one rupee. These latter figures are taken from the Census Report of 1881. Taking the nominal conversion of the rupee at 2s., the average rate in the North-Western Provinces would be 3s. 5d., and in the Punjab a fraction under 2s., per acre. The rupee, however, is now (1885) worth, at the current rate of exchange, only 1s. 6d., and not 2s. The actual sterling land-tax would therefore be about 2s. 7d. in the North-Western Provinces, and 1s. 6d. in the Punjab, per acre.

Government share of the crop.

The actual share of the crop, represented by these rates, is a very difficult problem. The Mughal assessment was fixed at one-third of the produce. Under many native rulers, this rate was increased to one-half, and under some to three-fifths. For example, the author found that in Párikud the Rájá's officers used to take $\frac{48}{80}$ths of the crop on the threshing-floor, leaving only two-fifths to the cultivator.[1]

[1] See Hunter's *Orissa*, vol. i. p. 34 (ed. 1872).

The English revenue officers adhere to the old theory of a third of the produce, but they make so many deductions in favour of the peasant, as to reduce the Government share in practice to about one-seventeenth. This question will be discussed in some detail in dealing with the general comparison of English and Mughal taxation. It must here suffice to say that the Famine Commissioners, the only body who have had the whole evidence before them, estimate the land-tax throughout British India ' at from 3 per cent. to 7 per cent. of the gross out-turn.' The old native basis of division, although retained in name in some Provinces, has disappeared in practice. Instead of the ruling power taking from 33 to 60 per cent., the average land-tax of the British Government throughout India is, according to the Famine Commissioners, only 5½ per cent. of the produce of the fields.

The means by which the land revenue is assessed is known as Settlement, and the assessor is styled a Settlement Officer. In Lower Bengal, the assessment existing in 1793 was declared to be fixed in perpetuity; but throughout the greater part of India the process is ever going on. The details vary in the different Provinces ; but, broadly speaking, a Settlement may be described as the ascertainment of the agricultural capacity of the land. Prior to the Settlement is the work of Village Survey, which determines the area of every village, and, as a rule, of every field. Then comes the Settlement Officer, whose duty it is to estimate the character of the soil, the kind of crop, the opportunities for irrigation, the present means of communication, their probable development, and all other circumstances which tend to affect the value of the land and its produce. With these facts before him, he proceeds to assess the Government demand upon the land, according to certain general principles, which may vary in the several Provinces. The final result is a Settlement Report, which records, as in a Domesday Book, the whole agricultural statistics concerning the District.

LOWER BENGAL, and a few adjoining Districts of the North-Western Provinces and of Madras, enjoy a Permanent Settlement, *i.e.* the land revenue has been fixed in perpetuity. When the Company obtained the *díwání* or financial administration of Bengal in 1765, the theory of a Settlement, as described above, was unknown. The existing Muhammadan system was adopted in its entirety. Engagements, sometimes yearly, sometimes for a term of years, were entered into with the *zamíndárs*

[margin notes: The Land Settlement. / Village Survey. / Process of Settlement. / The Permanent Settlement of Bengal. / Our first attempts, 1768-89.]

to pay a lump sum for the area over which they exercised control. If the offer of the *zamíndár* was not deemed satisfactory, another contractor was substituted in his place. But no steps were taken, and perhaps no steps were then possible, to ascertain in detail the amount which the country could afford to pay. For more than twenty years this practice of temporary engagements continued, and received the sanction of Warren Hastings, the first Governor - General of India. Hastings' great rival, Francis, was among those who urged the superior advantages of a permanent assessment. At last, in 1789, a slightly more accurate investigation into the agricultural resources of Bengal was carried out; and the Settlement based upon the imperfect data yielded by this inquiry was declared perpetual by Lord Cornwallis in 1793.[1]

Permanent Settlement, 1793.

The *zamíndárs* were thus raised to the status of landlords, with rights of transfer and inheritance, subject only to the payment in perpetuity of a rent-charge. In default of due payment, their lands were to be sold to the highest bidder. The assessment of Lower Bengal was fixed at *sikká* Rs. 26,800,989, equivalent to Rs. 28,587,722, then about equal to three millions sterling. By the year 1871-72, the total land-tax realized from the same area had increased to over $3\frac{1}{2}$ millions sterling, chiefly owing to the inclusion of estates which had escaped the original assessment on various pretexts. In 1883-84, the land revenue of Bengal was returned at $3\frac{3}{4}$ millions sterling, apart from the road and local cesses based on the land-tax. If these are added, the total exceeds 4 millions sterling, popularly lumped together as ' land revenue.'

Proprietors created by law.

Fixed land-tax of Lower Bengal, 1793.

While the claim of Government against the *zamíndárs* was thus fixed for ever, the law intended that the rights of the *zamíndárs* over their own tenants should equitably be restricted. But no detailed record of tenant-right was inserted in the Settlement papers; and as a matter of fact, the cultivators lost rather than gained in security of tenure. The rights of the landlord, as against the State, were defined by the Regulations of 1793 ; and the rights of the tenants, as against the landlord, were formerly ' reserved' by those Regulations, but were not defined. The landlord could therefore go into Court with a precise legal status; the cultivator could only shelter himself under vague customary rights. As the pressure of population on the soil increased, and land in Bengal became

Rights of the cultivators.

---

[1] The personal aspects of this measure, and the parts played by the Court of Directors, the Governor-General (Lord Cornwallis), and his chief Indian adviser (John Shore), are briefly narrated, *ante*, p. 393.

a subject of competition among the cultivators, the tenant found himself unprovided with any legal provisions to enable him to resist rack-rents. He could only plead ancient but undefined custom : the landlord could urge a proprietary right, based on express sections of the law. The result was a gradual decadence of peasant-right during the sixty-five years following the Permanent Settlement of 1793.

The *zamíndár* was the revenue-paying unit recognised by the Permanent Settlement. But in a large number of cases the *zamíndár* has in effect parted with all his interest in the land, by means of the creation of perpetual leases or *patnis*. These leases are usually granted in consideration of a lump Inter-sum paid down and an annual rent. The *patnidár* may in mediate turn create an indefinite series of sub-tenures, such as *dar-* tenure-holders. *patnis*, *se-patnis*, etc., beneath his own tenure; and between himself and the actual cultivator.

It has been mentioned that the Permanent Settlement of 1793 was not preceded by any systematic survey. But in the course of the past thirty years, Lower Bengal has been subjected to a professional survey, which determined the boundaries of Imperfect every village, and issued maps on the scale of four inches to survey of the mile. This survey, however, has only a topographical Bengal. value. Few statistical inquiries were made, and no record obtained of rights in the soil. Even the village landmarks then set up have been suffered to fall into decay. It was not until 1869 that a Statistical Survey of Bengal was, after several Statistical costly failures dating as far back as 1769 and 1807, organized Survey. on an efficient basis. The work was conducted to a successful issue during the ten following years (1869 to 1879); and the results of the survey were published in twenty-two volumes, containing a systematic account of each of the sixty Districts of Bengal and Assam, with their 74 millions of people.

By two stringent Regulations in 1799 and 1812, the tenant Cultivators was placed at the mercy of a rack-renting landlord. If he oppressed, failed to pay his rent, however excessive, his property was 1799-1812. rendered liable to distraint, and his person to imprisonment. At the same time, the operation of the revenue sale law had introduced a new race of *zamíndárs*, who were bound to their tenants by no traditions of hereditary sympathy, but whose sole object was to make a profit out of their newly-purchased property. The rack-rented peasantry found little protection in our courts until 1859, when an Act was passed which con- Land Law siderably restricted the landlord's powers of enhancement in of 1859. certain specified cases.

Land reform of 1859.

The Land Law of 1859 divided the cultivators into four classes :—First, those who had held their holdings at the same rates since 1793. It ordained that the rents of such tenants should not be raised at all. Second, those who had held their land at the same rent for twenty years. It ordained that such tenants should be presumed by law to have held since 1793, unless the contrary was proved. Third, those who had held for twelve years. To such tenants it gave a right of occupancy, under which their rents could be raised only for certain specified reasons by a suit at law. Fourth, those who had held for less than twelve years. These were left by Act x. of 1859 to make what bargain they could with the landlords.

Subsequent rise in rent.

Rent Commission, 1879.

Further experience, since 1859, has shown that even these provisions are inadequate to avert the wholesale enhancement of rents in Bengal, and especially in Behar. In 1879, the Government issued a Commission to inquire into the questions involved. The Commissioners of 1879 desired to confirm all the rights given to the peasant by the Land Code of 1859, and proposed to augment them. They recommended that the first class of cultivators, who have held their land at the same rates since 1793, should never have their rent raised.

Its proposals, 1880.

That the second class, or those who have thus held for twenty years, should still be presumed to have held since 1793. That the third class of cultivators, who have held for twelve years, should have their privileges increased. The occupancy rights of this class would, by the recommendations of the Commission, be consolidated into a valuable peasant-tenure, transferable by sale, gift, or inheritance. The Commissioners also proposed that any increase in the value of the land or of the crop, not arising from the agency of either the landlord or the 'occupancy tenant,' shall henceforth be divided equally between them. This provision is a very important one in a country like Bengal, where new railways, new roads, and the increase of the people and of trade constantly tend to raise the price of the agricultural staples. What political economists call the 'unearned increment,' would, if this proposal were adopted, be halved between the proprietor and the cultivator with occupancy rights.

Three years' tenants.

But the great changes proposed by the Rent Commissioners of 1879 referred to the fourth or lowest class of husbandmen, who have held for less than twelve years, and whom the Land Code of 1859 admitted to no rights whatever. The Commissioners proposed to accord a quasi-occupancy right to all tenants who had held for three years. If the landlord demanded an increased rent from such tenant, and the tenant preferred to leave rather than submit to the enhancement, then the landlord would have to pay to him—first, a substantial compensation for disturbance, and second, a substantial compensation for improvements. Compensation for disturbance.

The proposals of the Commissioners were partially, but only partially, embodied in the Bengal Tenancy Act of 1885.

Finally, after a long and acrimonious discussion, a Rent Law for Bengal, substantially based upon the Report of the Commission of 1879, was passed in the present year (1885). Rent Law of 1885.

The Permanent Settlement was confined to the three Provinces of Bengal, Behar, and Orissa, according to their boundaries at that time. Orissa proper, which was conquered from the Maráthás in 1803, is subject to a temporary Settlement, of which the current term of thirty years will not expire until 1897. The assessment is identical with that fixed in 1838, which was based upon a careful field-measurement and upon an investigation into the rights of every landholder and undertenant. The Settlement, however, was made with the landholder, and not with the tenant; and in practice the rights of the cultivators are on the same footing as in Bengal. Orissa Settlements, 1803-38.

In Assam Proper, or the Brahmaputra valley, the settlement is simple and effective. The cultivated area is artificially divided into *mauzás* or blocks, over each of which is placed a native official or *mauzádár*. Every year the *mauzádár* ascertains the area actually under cultivation, and then assesses the fields, according to their character, at a prescribed rate. Assam Settlement, yearly.

The prevailing system throughout the Madras Presidency is the *ráyatwárí*, which takes the cultivator or peasant proprietor as its rent-paying unit, as the Bengal system takes the *zamíndár*. This system cannot be called indigenous to the country, any more than the *zamíndárí* is to Bengal. When the British declared themselves heir to the Nawáb of the Karnátik at the beginning of the present century, they had no adequate experience of revenue management. The authorities in England favoured the *zamíndárí* system already at work in Bengal,—a system which appeared best calculated to secure punctual payment. The Madras Government was accordingly instructed to enter into permanent engagements with *zamíndárs;* and where no *zamíndárs* could be found, to create substitutes out of enterprising contractors. The attempt resulted in utter failure, except in tracts where the *zamíndárs* happened to be the representatives of ancient lines or powerful chiefs. Several such chiefs exist in the extreme south and in the north of the *Ráyatwárí* Settlement in Madras. Its history. *Zamíndárí* system failed.

Presidency. Their estates have been guaranteed to them on payment of a *peshkash* or permanent tribute, and are saved by the custom of primogeniture from the usual fate of sub-division.

Sir Thomas Munro, 1820. Throughout the rest of Madras, the influence of Sir Thomas Munro led to the adoption of the *ráyatwárí* system, which will always be associated with his name.

Madras method of assessment : According to this system, an assessment is made with the cultivator for the land actually taken for cultivation. Neither *zamíndár* nor village community intervenes between the cultivator and the State. The early *ráyatwárí* settlements in Madras were based upon insufficient experience. They were preceded by no survey, and they had to adopt the crude estimates of native officials. Since 1858, a department of Revenue Survey has been organized, and the assessment carried out *de novo*.

first, measurement ; second, estimate of produce ; third, fixing the rates. Nothing can be more complete in theory than a Madras *ráyatwárí* settlement. First, the area of the entire District, whether cultivated or uncultivated, and of each field within the District, is accurately measured. The next step is to calculate the estimated produce of each field, having regard to every kind of both natural and artificial advantage. Lastly, an equitable rate is fixed upon every field. The elaborate nature of these inquiries and calculations may be inferred from the fact that as many as 35 different rates are sometimes struck for a single District, ranging from as low as 6d. to as high as

Thirty years' settlement. £1, 4s. per acre. The rates thus ascertained by the revenue survey are fixed for a term of thirty years.

But during that period the aggregate rent-roll of a District is liable to be affected by several considerations. New land may be taken up for cultivation, or old land may be abandoned ; and occasional remissions may be permitted under no fewer than eighteen specified heads. Such

Madras yearly *jamábandi.* matters are decided by the Collector at the *jamábandi*, or inquest held every year for ascertaining the amount of revenue to be paid by each *ráyat* for the current season. This annual inquiry has sometimes been mistaken for a yearly re-assessment of the *ráyat's* holding. It is not, however, a change in the rates for the land which he already holds, but an inquiry into and record of the changes in his holding, or of any new land he may wish to take up.

Permanent Settlement in Madras. Certain of the Madras Districts on the seaboard adjoining Bengal were granted on a Permanent Settlement to *zamíndárs*, hereditary native chiefs or revenue-farmers. The land thus permanently settled forms one-eighth of the area of

Madras. Throughout the other seven-eighths, the *ráyatwárí* settlement has raised the cultivator into a peasant proprietor. This person was formerly the actual tiller of the soil. But as population increased under British rule, the value of the land rose, and the peasant proprietor has in many cases been able to sub-let his holding to poorer cultivators, and to live, in whole or part, off the rent. The Government has during the same period decreased rather than increased its average land-tax per acre throughout the Madras Presidency. For as the people multiplied, they were forced back upon inferior soils, and the average Government demand per acre has been proportionately diminished. But the very same process of falling back on the inferior soils has, according to economical principles, created the possibility of levying a rent from the superior soils. This rent is enjoyed by the former cultivators, many of whom are thus growing into petty landholders, living upon the rent of fields which their fathers tilled with their own hands. *The cultivator grows into a proprietor.*

An idea of the increase of population in Madras, and of the extension of cultivation, may be obtained from the following figures : — In 1853, the general population was estimated at 22 millions ; in 1878, at 31½ millions, showing an increase of 43 per cent., or nearly one-half ; and in 1881 (after the great famine of 1876–78), at a little over 31 millions. The cultivated land, held by husbandmen direct from the State, had, between 1853 and 1878, increased from 12 to 20 millions of acres, or 66 per cent., exactly two-thirds. The area of tillage had, therefore, not only kept pace with the increase of population, but had extended at a ratio of 50 per cent. more rapidly. This resulted partly from the fact that the inferior lands, now reclaimed, could not support so large an average of people as the superior lands, which were already in cultivation at the commencement of the period. The Government recognised this, and has accordingly increased its rental only from 3 millions to 3⅘ millions sterling ; being only 26 per cent., or one-fourth, while the area of cultivation has increased by 66 per cent. The Government, in fact, has reduced its average rental over the total area of cultivation from 5s. an acre in 1853 to 3s. 10d. an acre in 1878, or over 23 per cent., say one-fourth. According to the ordinary theory of rent, rates should have risen enormously during that period ; and they have risen enormously wherever the land is held by private proprietors. *Extension of tillage in Madras, 1853–81.* *Exceeds the growth of the population.*

As regards the Madras Presidency, the facts may be recapitu-

Reduction of average land-tax. lated thus. During the 25 years ending 1878, the area of cultivation had increased by 66 per cent., or two-thirds ; the population by 43 per cent., or nearly one-half; and the Government rental by only 26 per cent., or one-fourth ; while the average rates of land-tax per cultivated acre had been actually reduced by about one-fourth, from 5s. an acre in 1853 to 3s. 10d. an acre in 1878, and to 3s. 8d. an acre in 1883. Instead of taking advantage of the increase of population to enhance the rental, the Madras Government has realized the fact that the increase in numbers means a harder struggle for life, and has reduced instead of enhancing, according to the economic laws of rent, the average rates throughout its domains.

Land system of Bombay. Bombay has also a land system of its own, which requires to be distinguished from the *ráyatwári* of Madras, although resembling it in principle. In the early days of our rule, no regular method existed throughout the Bombay Presidency ; and at the present time there are tracts where something of the old confusion survives. The modern

The 'survey tenure' of Bombay. 'survey tenure,' as it is called, dates from 1838, when it was first introduced into one of the *táluks* of Poona District : it has since been gradually extended over the greater part of the Presidency. As its name implies, the Settlement is preceded by survey. Each field is measured, and an assessment placed upon it according to the quality of the soil and the crop. This assessment holds good for a term of thirty years. The

Its rates. ordinary rates vary in different Districts from 4s. 6d. an acre in the rich black-soil lands of Gujarát, to 10d. an acre in the hills of the Konkan.

Its simplicity. The primary characteristic of the Bombay system is its simplicity. The Government fixes a minimum area as the revenue assessment unit, below which it refuses to recognise sub-divisions. This minimum area, technically called a ' field,' varies from 20 acres upwards, in different Bombay Districts. The 'field' is therefore the unit, and its actual occupier is the only person recognised by the revenue law. He knows exactly what he will have to pay, and the State knows what it will receive, during the currency of the term. The assessment is, in fact, a quit-rent liable to be modified at intervals of thirty years. The Bombay system is also characterized by its fairness to the tenant. He possesses ' a transferable and heritable property, continuable without question at the expiration of a settlement lease, on his consenting to the revised rate.' To borrow a metaphor from English law, his position has been raised from that of a villein to that of a copyholder.

In place of the bare permission to occupy the soil, he has received a right of property in it.

Its advantages to the provident.

Some of the Bombay peasants have proved unequal to the responsibilities of property which they had not won by their own exertions. In rich districts, the men who were recorded as the actual occupiers are able to let their land to poorer cultivators, and so live off the toil of others upon fields which they themselves had formerly to till. But these proprietary rights give the peasant a power of borrowing which he did not possess before. In certain parts, especially in the dry Districts of the high-lying Deccan, the husbandmen have got hopelessly into debt to the village bankers. The peasant was often improvident, the seasons were sometimes unfortunate, the money-lender was always severe.

Its disadvantages to the improvident.

Amid the tumults of native rule, the usurers lent comparatively small sums. If the peasant failed to pay, they could not evict him or sell his holding; because, among other reasons, there was more land than there were people to till it. The native Government, moreover, could not afford to lose a tenant. Accordingly the bankrupt peasant went on, year after year, paying as much interest as the money-lender could squeeze out of him; until the next Maráthá invasion or Muhammadan rebellion swept away the whole generation of usurers, and so cleared off the account. Under our rule there is no chance of such relief for insolvent debtors; and our rigid enforcement of contracts, together with the increase of the population, has armed the creditor with powers formerly unknown. For the peasant's holding under the British Government has become a valuable property, and he can be readily sold out, as there are always plenty of husbandmen anxious to buy in. The result is two-fold. In the first place, the village banker lends larger sums, for the security is increased; and in the second place, he can push the peasantry to extremities by eviction, a legal process which was economically impossible, and politically impermissible, under native rule.

Debts of the Deccan peasant.

In Bengal, the cry of the peasant is for protection against the landlord. In South-western India, it is for protection against the money-lender. After a careful inquiry, the Government determined to respond to that cry. It has practically said to the village bankers : 'A state of things has grown up under British rule which enables you to push the cultivators, by means of our Courts, to extremities unknown under the native dynasties, and repugnant to the customs of India. Henceforth, in considering the security on which you lend money,

Bombay Relief Acts, 1879 and 1881.

2 F

please to know that the peasant cannot be imprisoned or sold out of his farm to satisfy your claims; and we shall free him from the lifelong burden of those claims by a mild bankruptcy law.' Such is the gist of the Southern India Agriculturists' Relief Acts of 1879 and 1881.

Its provisions for the husbandman;

This Act of 1879 provides, in the first place, for small rural debtors of £5 and under. If the Court is satisfied that such a debtor is really unable to pay the whole sum, it may direct the payment of such portion as it considers that he can pay, and grant him a discharge for the balance. The Act gives powers to the Court to go behind the letter of the bond, to cut down interest, and to fix the total sum which may seem to the judge to be equitably due.

As a rural Insolvency Act.

To debtors for amounts exceeding £5, it gives the full protection of an Insolvency Act. No agriculturist shall henceforth be arrested or imprisoned in execution of a decree for money. In addition to the old provisions against the sale of the necessary implements of his trade, no agriculturist's immoveable property shall be attached or sold in execution of any decree, unless it has been specifically mortgaged for the debt to which such decree relates. But even when it has been specifically mortgaged, the Court may order the debtor's holding to be cultivated, for a period not exceeding seven years, on behalf of the creditor, after allowing a sufficient portion of it for the support of the debtor and his family. At the end of the seven years, the debtor is discharged.

Rural Insolvency Procedure.

If the debtor himself applies for relief under the Insolvency clauses, the procedure is as follows :—His moveable property, less the implements of his trade, are liable to sale for his debts. His immoveable property, or farm, is divided into two parts, one of which is set aside as 'required for the support of the insolvent and members of his family dependent on him,' while the remainder is to be managed on behalf of his creditors. But 'nothing in this section shall authorize the Court to take into possession any houses or other buildings belonging to, and occupied by, an agriculturist.' Village

'Conciliators.'

arbitrators or 'conciliators' are appointed by the same Act, and every creditor must first try to settle his claims before them. If the effort at arbitration fails, the 'conciliator' shall give the applicant a certificate to that effect. No such suit shall be entertained by any Civil Court, unless the plaintiff produces a certificate from the local 'conciliator' that arbitration has been attempted and failed. The Act of 1879 has been somewhat modified by the amending Act of 1881.

The North-Western Provinces and the Punjab have practically one land system. In those parts of India, the village community has preserved its integrity more completely than elsewhere. Government therefore recognises the village, and not the *zamíndár's* estate or the *ráyat's* field, as the unit of land administration. The village community takes various forms. Sometimes it holds all the village lands in joint-ownership; the share of each co-owner being represented by a fractional part of the gross rental. Sometimes part of the lands is held in common and part in severalty; while sometimes no common lands remain, although a joint responsibility for the Government revenue still subsists. *[Land system of N.W. Provinces and Punjab. Corporate holdings.]*

The Settlement in the North-Western Provinces and the Punjab is more comprehensive than in Madras or Bombay. In addition to measurement and agricultural appraisement, it includes the duty of drawing up an exhaustive record of all rights and sub-tenures existing in every village. The proprietors are alone responsible for the revenue; but while the State limits its claims against them, it defines the rights of all other parties interested in the soil. The term of settlement in the North-Western Provinces and in the Punjab is thirty years. The principle of assessment is that the Government revenue shall be equal to one-half of the rent, leaving the other half as the share of the landlord, who is liable for due payment, and has the trouble of collecting it from the cultivators. The average rate of assessment is 3s. 5d. per acre in the North-Western Provinces, and 2s. in the Punjab. This is at the nominal conversion of 10 rupees to the pound sterling. At the actual value of the rupee (1885), the rates would be 2s. 7d. in the North-Western Provinces, and 1s. 6d. in the Punjab, per acre. *[Land Settlement in North-Western Provinces and Punjab.]*

Oudh, the Indian Province most recently acquired, has a peculiar land system, arising out of its local history. The Oudh *tálukdárs* resemble English landlords more closely even than do the *zamíndárs* of Bengal. In origin, they were not revenue-farmers but territorial magnates, whose influence was derived from feudal authority, military command, or hereditary sway. Their present status dates from the pacification after the Mutiny of 1857. The great *tálukdárs* were then invited to become responsible each for a gross sum for the estates which they were found to hold prior to our annexation of Oudh. The exceptional position of the *tálukdárs* was recognised by conferring upon them, not only the privilege of succession by primogeniture, but also the power of bequest by will—a landright unknown alike to Hindu and Muhammadan law. Land *[Land system of Oudh. The táluk-dárs.]*

not comprised in *tálukdárí* estates was settled in the ordinary way with its proprietors or *zamíndárs* for a term of thirty years. The whole of Oudh has since been accurately surveyed.

Land system of Central Provinces. The Central Provinces contain many varieties of land tenure, from the feudatory chiefs, who pay a light tribute, to the village communities, who are assessed after survey. Population is sparse and agriculture backward, so that the incidence of land revenue is everywhere low. The survey was conducted generally on the Punjab system, adopting the 'estate' as the unit of assessment. But in the Central Provinces the British Government gave proprietary rights to the former revenue-farmers, or fiscal managers of villages, under native rule. It thus created a body of landholders between itself and the cultivators. Of the rental paid by the husbandmen, the Government ordinarily takes one-half as land-tax, and allows one-half to the proprietary body. The current settlement, for a term of thirty years, will expire in 1897.

Land revenue of British India. The gross land revenue realized from territory under British administration in India, amounted to £21,876,067 in 1882–83. During the ten years ending 1882–83, it averaged £21,283,764, which is raised to about 22¾ millions by the inclusion of certain local rates and cesses levied on land. This latter figure shows an average of a fraction less than 10d. per cultivated acre. The average annual cost of collecting the land revenue during the ten years ending 1882–83 was £2,945,151, or close on three millions sterling. The highest average rate of assessment estimated per head, is in Bombay, namely, 3s. 10¼d. per head of population; the lowest, 1s. 2½d. per head, in Bengal and Assam. The *net* land revenue realized from British India, deducting charges of collection, during the ten years ending March 1883, averaged 18⅓ millions sterling. In 1882–83, the land revenue of British India was 21¾ millions *gross*, and 18¾ millions *net*.[1]

Salt administration.

Sources of salt. THE SALT DUTY.—Salt ranks next to land revenue among the items of actual taxation in India; opium being excluded, as paid by the Chinese consumer. Broadly speaking, the salt consumed in India is derived from four sources—(1) importation by sea, chiefly from the mines of Cheshire; (2) solar evaporation in shallow tanks along the seaboard; (3) gatherings from the Salt Lakes in Rájputána; (4) quarrying in the Salt Hills of the Northern Punjab. Until recently, the tax

[1] Parliamentary Return.

levied upon salt varied very much in different parts of the
country; and a numerous preventive staff was stationed along
a continuous barrier hedge, which almost cut the peninsula
into two fiscal sections.

The reforms of Sir J. Strachey in 1878, by which the Equaliza-
higher rates were reduced while the lower rates were raised, tion of
and their subsequent equalization over the whole country, salt duty.
have effectually abolished this engine of oppression. Communication is now free; and it has been found that prices
are lowered by thus bringing the consumer nearer to his
market, even though the rate of taxation be increased. In the
Punjab and Rájputána, salt administration has become, as
in Lower Bengal, a simple matter of weighing quantities and
levying a uniform tax. In Bombay, also, the manufacture is Systems
now conducted with a minimum of expense at large central of manu-
depôts in Gujarát (Guzerát), under a thorough system of excise facture.
supervision. Along the eastern coast, however, from Orissa
to Cape Comorin, the process of evaporating sea-water is
carried on as a private industry, although under official supervision and on Government account.

The process of manufacture in Madras is exceedingly simple, Process
and at the same time free from temptations to smuggling. The of manu-
season lasts from about January to July, in which latter month facture.
the downpour of rain usually puts a stop to operations. A
site is selected in the neighbourhood of one of the backwaters or inlets which abound along the coast. Before
commencing, the proprietor of the salt-pan must each year
obtain the consent of the Collector of the District, and must
engage to supply a certain quantity of salt. The first step is
to form a series of pans or reservoirs of varying degrees of
shallowness by banking up the earth, with interconnecting
channels. Into the outer and deepest of these pans, the sea-
water is baled by means of a lever and bucket-lift, and there
allowed to stand for some days until it has by evaporation
acquired the consistency of brine. The brine is then passed
through the channels into the remainder of the series of
gradually shallowing pans. At last it becomes crystallized
salt, and is scraped off for conveyance to the wholesale depôt.
It is estimated that, in a favourable season, this process may be
repeated *de novo* from twelve to fifteen times, according as the
weather permits. But a single shower of rain will spoil the
whole operation at any stage.

Like the poppy cultivation in Bengal, the manufacture of
salt in Madras is a monopoly, which can be defended by the

Working
of the
monopoly
in Madras.

circumstances of the case. No one is compelled to manufacture, and rights of property in a salt-pan are strictly respected ; while the State endeavours, by means of a careful staff of supervisors, to obtain the maximum of profit with a minimum of interference. The system as at present carried on has been gradually developed from the experience of nearly a century. The manufacturers belong to the same class as the ordinary cultivators ; and, as a rule, their condition is somewhat more prosperous, for they possess a hereditary privilege carrying with it commercial profits. They do not work upon a system of advances, as is the case with so many other Indian industries ; but they are paid at a certain rate when they bring their salt to the Government depôt. This rate of payment, known as *kudiva-ram*, is at present fixed at an average of 1 *ánná* 5·8 *pies* (or about 2¼d.) per *maund* of 82⅔ lbs.; the other expenses of the

Cost of
salt in
Madras.

Salt Department for supervision, etc., raise the total cost to 3 *ánnás* 5·6 *pies* (or about 5¼d.) per *maund*. The price charged to the consumer by the Madras Government, up to

Duty of
salt.

March 1882, was Rs. 2. 8. (or about 5s.) per *maund*, the balance being net profit.

Equalization of
duty.

The equal rate of salt duty which now prevails throughout all continental India is Rs. 2 per *maund*, or 5s. 5d. a cwt. In British Burma, only 3 *ánnás* per *maund*, or 6d. a cwt., are charged for local consumption, and a transit duty of 1 per cent. *ad valorem* for salt sent across the frontier. In the salt tracts on the west of the Indus, excluding the Kalábágh mines, a special rate of 8 *ánnás* per local *maund* of 103 lbs. is charged. The total salt revenue of British India in 1882–83 was returned at £6,177,781, the average for ten years being £6,627,194.

Excise
administration.

EXCISE DUTIES in India are not a mere tax levied through the private manufacturer and retailer, but (like salt) a species of Government monopoly. The only excisable articles are intoxicants and drugs ; and the object of the State is to check consumption, not less than to raise revenue. The details vary in the different Provinces, but the general plan of administration is the same. The right to manufacture, and the right to retail, are both monopolies of Government, let out to private individuals upon strict conditions. Distillation of country spirits is permitted under two systems—either to the highest bidder under official supervision ; or only upon certain spots set apart

Central
distillery
system.

for the purpose. The latter is known as the *sadr* or central distillery system. The right of sale is also farmed out to the

highest bidder, subject to regulations fixing the quantity of Rice-beer.
liquor that may be sold at one time. The brewing of beer
from rice and other grains, a process universal among the hill
tribes and other aboriginal races, is practically untaxed and
unrestrained. The numerous European breweries at the hill
stations pay a tax at the rate of 6d. a gallon. A large business
in brewing is now done at Simla, Marri (Murree), Kasaulí,
Massuri, Nainí Tál, Solán, and in the Nílgiris. An attempt
is being made to establish breweries on the plains.

Excise duties are also levied upon the sale of a number of
intoxicating or stimulant drugs, of which the most important
are opium and *gánjá* or *bhang*. Opium is issued for local Opium.
consumption in India from the Government manufactories at
Patná and Benares, and sold through private retailers at a
monopoly price. This drug is chiefly consumed in Assam,
Burma, and the Punjab. *Gánjá* is an intoxicating preparation Gánjá.
made from the flowers and leaves of Indian hemp (*Cannabis
sativa*, var. *indica*). The cultivation of hemp for this purpose
is chiefly confined to a limited area in Rájsháhí District,
Bengal, and to the inner valleys of the Himálayas, whence the
drug is imported under the name of *charas*. Its use is a fre- Charas.
quent cause, not only of crime, but also of insanity. Government attempts to check consumption—first, by fixing the retail
duty at the highest rate that will not encourage smuggling;
and second, by continually raising that rate as experience
allows. Strictly speaking, *gánjá* consists of the flowering
and fruiting heads of the female plant; *bháng* or *siddhi*, of the
dried leaves and small stalks, with a few fruits; while *charas*
is the resin itself, collected in various ways as it naturally
exudes.

No duty is at present levied upon tobacco in any part Tobacco.
of British India. The plant is universally grown by the
cultivators for their own smoking, and, like everything else,
was subject to taxation under native rule; but the impossibility
of accurate excise supervision has caused the British Government to abandon this impost. The total excise revenue of
British India in 1882–83 was returned at £3,609,561, the
average for ten years being £2,774,073.

THE MUNICIPALITIES at present existing in India are a Municipal
creation of the Legislature; indeed, a recent branch of our admini-
system of administration. Their origin is to be traced, not to stration.
the native *panchádyat*, but to the necessity for relieving the
District officer from some of the details of his work. The

The old 'Council of Five;' *panchdyat* or elective Council of Five is one of the institutions most deeply rooted in the Hindu mind. By it the village community was ruled, the head-man being only its executive official, not the legislator or judge. By it caste disputes were settled; by it traders and merchants were organized into powerful guilds, to the rules of which even European outsiders have had to submit. By a development of the *panchdyat*, the Sikh army of the *khdlsd* was despotically governed, when the centralized system of Ranjít Singh fell to pieces at his death.

Municipalities succeed it. The village organization was impaired or broken up under Mughal rule. Municipal institutions have gradually developed in place of the old Hindu mechanism of rural government, which had thus worn out or disappeared. Police, roads, and sanitation are the three main objects for which a modern Indian municipality is constituted. In rural tracts, these departments are managed (in different Provinces) by the Collector, or by one of his subordinate staff, or by a Local Fund Board. Within municipal limits, they are delegated to a Committee, who, until lately, derived their practical authority from the Collector's sanction, implied or expressed. Except in the larger towns, the municipalities can scarcely be said as yet to exhibit the attributes of popular representation or of vigorous corporate life. But the Local Government Acts, passed during Lord Ripon's Viceroyalty (*ante*, p. 428), have given a new impulse to the rural and municipal boards. As education advances, they will doubtless be further developed.

Municipal statistics. 1877-83. In 1876-77, excluding the three Presidency capitals, there were altogether 894 muncipalities in British India, with 12,381,059 inhabitants, or just 7 per cent. of the total population. Out of an aggregate number of 7519 members of municipal committees, concerning whom information is available, 1794 were Europeans and 5725 natives; 1863 were *ex-officio*, 4512 were nominated by Government, and 1144 elected, the last class being almost confined to the North-Western and Central Provinces. The financial statistics of these municipalities are given in a later section of this chapter.

In 1882-83, the municipalities in British India, exclusive of the three Presidency cities, numbered 783, with 12,923,494 inhabitants. The passing of the Local Self-Government Acts (1882-84) has extended the elective principle, in a larger or smaller measure, all over India. The three great municipalities in the Presidency towns of Calcutta, Madras, and Bombay administered a population in 1877 of $1\frac{1}{2}$ million. Their governing bodies aggregated 176 members, of whom 122 were natives. Eighty of the members were elected by the ratepayers. In 1882–83, the municipalities of Calcutta, Bombay, and Madras governed a population of $1\frac{2}{3}$ million; the members of the three municipal bodies numbered 171, of whom 93 were elected.[1]

FINANCE. — It is difficult to present a view of Indian finance, which shall be at once concise and intelligible. The subject is full of controversies, and obscured by different

Imperial finance.

---

[1] *Note on Indian Statistics.*

It may here be convenient to explain the considerations which have led to the selection of the years for which statistics are given in this and the following chapters. The Indian returns are rendered with great promptitude by the Government of India, in India itself. But these returns deal with a dozen Provinces and Administrations, covering an area equal to Europe less Russia. A considerable interval necessarily elapses between the local issue of the returns by the Indian Government and their final compilation and revision for Parliamentary purposes. During this revision, the totals are frequently altered owing to inter-provincial adjustments and other operations of account. The final presentment to Parliament is, however, the only authoritative English source of Indian statistics. It has therefore been adopted, so far as possible, in the present work. The latest return, in its final shape, as presented to both Houses of Parliament by command of Her Majesty, which has reached the author before the sheets went to press in the summer of 1885, is the Blue Book entitled the *Statistical Abstract relating to British India from 1873-74 to 1882-83.* This admirable compilation of Mr. Charles Prinsep, Statistical Reporter in the India Office, has therefore been accepted as fixing the period to which information should be brought down in the present work—namely, the 31st March 1883.

But the present author has also been guided in his selection of dates by other considerations—(1) The only two Census enumerations of the Indian population as a whole were taken respectively in 1872 and in 1881. These years are, therefore, the two great landmarks in Indian statistics. (2) The first edition of the present work took the year 1877, or in some cases 1878, as the latest period for which the final presentment of Indian statistics was available when it was written. The author has felt that it may be convenient to enable the reader to compare the progress during the quinquennial interval (1878 to 1883). He has therefore, in most cases, given the two sets of figures for 1877-78 and 1882-83. (3) In some departments it has been found practicable to bring down the final figures to 1884, and even to March 1885. This has only been done when it seemed to the author that the later statistics were required to exhibit really salient facts. In conclusion, the author begs it will be believed that in each case careful consideration has been devoted to the selection of the years for which the statistics are given. The individual considerations in different departments are too numerous to specify. It should always be remembered that the final presentment to Parliament of Indian statistics and accounts, available to the author when the sheets went to the press, refers to the decade ending 1882-83.

presentments of the same sets of accounts. In the first place,
the aggregate revenue and expenditure are officially returned
according to a system which, although necessary for Indian
purposes, is apt to mislead the English critic. The Indian
Government is not a mere tax-collecting agency, charged
with the single duty of protecting person and property. Its

*Its ob-
scurities.*

system of administration is based upon the view that the
British power is a paternal despotism, which owns, in a
certain sense, the entire soil of the country, and whose duty
it is to perform the various functions of a wealthy and an

*The 'busi-
ness' of
the Indian
Govern-
ment.*

enlightened proprietor. It collects its own rents. It provides,
out of its own capital, facilities for irrigation, means of communication, public buildings, schools, and hospitals. It also
takes on itself the businesses of a railway owner, and of a
manufacturer on a grand scale, in the case of opium and salt.
These departments swell the totals on both sides of the
balance-sheet with large items, neither of the nature of taxation
nor of administrative expenditure.

*Changes
in system
of account.*

In the second place, the methods of keeping the Indian
public accounts have been subjected to frequent changes during
recent years, to such an extent as to vitiate all comparative
statements for long periods of time. The commercial traditions, inherited from the days of the Company, regulated the
Indian accounts until about the year 1860. From that date
efforts have been made to bring the methods of Indian accounting into conformity with the English system of public accounts.
It results that the same entries represent different facts at
different periods. Thus, under the Company, the items usually
represented the *net* sums ; they now represent the gross sums.
At one period, the gross receipts are shown, with a *per contra*
for the charges of collection or for refunds. At another time,
important classes of charges have been transferred from the
Imperial to the Provincial Budgets, to be brought back again
after an interval of a few years to the Imperial Budget, and again
transferred to Local Finance. Capital expenditure on public
works, at one period charged to current revenue, is at another
period excluded, as being 'extraordinary' or 'reproductive.'

*The result-
ing ob-
scurities.*

The entire net income of the railways, whether the property of
the State or of guaranteed companies, has now been entered as
Imperial revenue, and the interest to shareholders as Imperial
expenditure. The Indian accounts represent, therefore, not
only the Indian taxation and the cost of administration. They
represent the trade expenses and profits of the Government as
a great railway owner, canal maker, opium manufacturer, salt

monopolist, and pioneer of new industries. They also represent these profits and expenses under diverse systems of account at different periods.

The following pages will first endeavour to exhibit the actual taxation of British India, as compared with that of the Mughal Empire. They will then show the gross revenue and expenditure of British India, whether of the nature of taxation or otherwise, and analyze its principal items.

THE ACTUAL TAXATION paid by the people of British India during the ten years ending 1879, averaged 35⅓ millions. The subjoined tables show the *gross* items, exclusive of the opium duty which is paid by the Chinese consumer, tributes from foreign or feudatory States, forest receipts, and the Mint. The actual taxation arranges itself under seven branches, as given in Statement I. on the next page, from 1869 to 1879. *Gross taxation of British India.*

This table was compiled from a special Parliamentary Return, and shows the net taxes, after deducting drawbacks and items not of the nature of actual taxation. Statement II. shows the revenue from the same items during the four following years, 1880–83, but without deductions or drawbacks. The average of these four years is 40¾ millions, without deductions or drawbacks, against 35⅓ millions, after deductions and drawbacks, during the ten years ending 1879.

The *net* taxation of British India, that is to say, the sums realized, less the cost of collection, averaged 32 millions [1] during the ten years ending 1879. Returns of *net* taxation, however, depend much upon the method on which they are prepared. But the final accounts as presented to Parliament enable us to arrive accurately at the gross taxation paid by the Indian people, which, as above shown, was 35⅓ millions during the ten years ending 1879, or a rate of 3s. 8d. per head. *Net and gross taxation of British India.*

This rate contrasts alike with that now paid by the taxpayer in England, and with that formerly paid in India under the Mughal Empire. The 34 millions of people in Great Britain and Ireland pay 68 millions of Imperial taxation, [2] besides heavy local and municipal burdens. The revenues of the *English and Indian taxation.*

[*Sentence continued on page 462.*

[1] Compiled from the Parliamentary Return, 8th July 1880, pp. 4, 5.

[2] Customs, 20 millions; Inland revenue, 48 millions: total taxation, 68 millions. The *gross* revenue of the United Kingdom in 1880 was £81,265,055, besides £29,247,595 of local taxation; total, £110,512,650.

STATEMENT I.

ACTUAL TAXATION OF BRITISH INDIA, 1869–79.

Compiled from the Parliamentary Return dated 8th July 1880.

	1869-70.	1870-71.	1871-72.	1872-73.	1873-74.	1874-75.	1875-76.	1876-77.	1877-78.	1878-79.
	£	£	£	£	£	£	£	£	£	£
Land Revenue,	21,088,019	20,622,823	20,520,337	21,348,669	21,037,912	21,296,793	21,503,742	19,857,152	19,869,667	22,330,586
Excise,	2,253,655	2,374,465	2,369,109	2,323,788	2,286,637	2,346,143	2,493,232	2,523,045	2,457,075	2,619,349
Assessed Taxes,	1,110,224	2,072,025	825,241	580,139	20,136	2,747	510	310	86,110	900,920
Provincial Rates,	...	...	...	...	...	...	...	...	238,504	2,638,835
Customs,	2,429,185	2,610,789	2,575,990	2,653,890	2,628,495	2,678,479	2,721,389	2,483,345	2,622,296	2,326,561
Salt,	5,888,707	6,106,280	5,966,595	6,165,630	6,150,662	6,227,301	6,244,415	6,304,658	6,460,082	6,941,120
Stamps,	2,379,316	2,510,316	2,476,333	2,608,512	2,699,936	2,758,042	2,835,368	2,838,628	2,993,483	3,110,540
Total,	£35,149,106	36,296,698	34,733,605	35,680,628	34,823,778	35,309,505	35,798,656	34,097,138	34,727,217	40,867,911

Total for Ten Years ending 1879, . . . £357,394,242

Deduct Refunds, Drawbacks, and adjusting Payments, as per Parliamentary Statement, . . . 4,379,234

Gross Taxation for Ten Years ending 1879, . . £353,015,008

Yearly Average of Gross Taxation, . £35,301,500

STATEMENT II.

ACTUAL TAXATION OF BRITISH INDIA FROM 1879-80 TO 1882-83.

Compiled from the Eighteenth Parliamentary Statistical Abstract relating to British India.

	1879-80.	1880-81.	1881-82.	1882-83.	Total for the Four Years.
Land Revenue,*	£21,861,150	£21,112,995	£21,948,022	£21,876,047	£86,798,214
Salt,	7,266,413	7,115,988	7,375,620	6,177,781	27,935,802
Stamps,	3,193,739	3,250,581	3,381,372	3,379,681	13,205,373
Excise,	2,838,021	3,135,226	3,427,274	3,609,561	13,010,082
Customs,	2,280,793	2,539,612	2,361,388	1,296,119	8,477,912
Assessed Taxes,	785,318	558,720	536,829	517,811	2,398,678
Provincial Rates,	2,882,125	2,776,370	2,895,490	2,683,015	11,237,000
Total,	£41,107,559	£40,489,492	£41,925,995	£39,540,015	£163,663,061

Average actual taxation, without allowing for refunds and drawbacks, during the four years 1879–83, £40,765,765. It must be remembered, in comparing recent taxation in India with previous totals, that the value of the rupee has greatly declined, while the official conversion into pounds sterling is still made at the old nominal rate of ten rupees to the pound. The purchasing power of the taxation received in recent years is therefore less than the totals in sterling would appear to indicate.

* Excluding Land Revenue due to Irrigation.

Sentence continued from page 459.]
Mughal Empire, derived from a much smaller population than that of British India, varied, as we have seen,[1] from 42 millions *net* under Akbar in 1593 to 80 millions under Aurangzeb in 1695. The trustworthiness of these returns has been discussed in a previous chapter; and they must be taken subject to the qualifications therein indicated.

Indian taxation under the Mughals,
If we examine the items in the Mughal accounts, we find the explanation of their enormous totals. The land-tax then, as now, formed about one-half of the whole revenue. The net land revenue demand of the Mughal Empire averaged 25 millions sterling from 1593 to 1761; or 32 millions during the last century of that Empire, from 1655 to 1761. The annual *net* land revenue raised from the much larger area of British India, during the ten years ending 1879, has been 18

much heavier than now.
millions sterling (*gross,* 21 millions). But besides the land revenue there were under our predecessors not less than forty imposts of a personal character. These included taxes upon religious assemblies, upon trees, upon marriage, upon the peasant's hearth, and upon his cattle. How severe some of them were, may be judged from the poll-tax. For the

Mughal poll-tax.
purposes of this tax, the non-Muhammadan population was divided into three classes, paying respectively £4, £2, and £1 annually to the Exchequer for each adult male. The lowest of these rates, if now levied from each non-Musalmán male adult, would alone yield an amount exceeding our whole actual taxation. Yet, under the Mughals, the poll-tax was only one of forty burdens.

Summary.
We may briefly sum up the results. Under the Mughal Empire, 1593 to 1761, the existing returns of the Imperial demand averaged about 60 millions sterling a year. During the ten years ending 1879, the Imperial taxation of British India, with its far larger population, averaged 35 millions, and for the four years ending 1882-83, 40¾ millions, without allowing for refunds and drawbacks. Under the Mughal Empire, the land-tax between 1655 and 1761 averaged 32 millions. Under the British Empire, the *net* land-tax has, during the ten years ending 1879, averaged 18 millions, and 18¾ millions during the four years ending 1882-83.

Taxation of Japan.
Not only is the taxation of British India much less than that raised by the Mughal Emperors, but it compares favourably with the taxation of other Asiatic countries in our own days. The only other Empire in Asia which pretends to

[1] *Ante,* chap. xi. p. 299, etc.; table of Mughal Revenues (1593 to 1761).

a civilised government is Japan. The author has no special acquaintance with the Japanese revenues; but German statists show that over 11 millions sterling are there raised from a population of 34 million people, or deducting certain items, a taxation of about 6s. a head. In India, where we try to govern on a higher standard of efficiency, the rate of actual gross taxation averaged 3s. 8d. a head for the ten years ending 1879, and 4s. 1d. per head for the four years ending 1882–83.

If, instead of dealing with the Imperial revenues as a whole, we concentrate our survey on any one Province, we find these facts brought out in a still stronger light. To take a single instance. After a patient scrutiny of the records, it was found that, allowing for the change in the value of money, the ancient revenue of Orissa represented eight times the quantity of the staple food which our own revenue now represents.[1] The native revenue of Orissa supported a magnificent court with a crowded seraglio, swarms of priests, a large army, and a costly public worship. Under our rule, Orissa does little more than defray the local cost of protecting person and property, and of its irrigation works. In Orissa, the Rájá's share of the crops amounted, with dues, to 60 per cent., and the mildest Native Governments demanded 33 per cent. The Famine Commissioners estimate the land-tax throughout British India[2] 'at from 3 per cent. to 7 per cent. of the gross out-turn.' Ample deductions are allowed for the cost of cultivation, the risks of the season, the maintenance of the husbandman and his family. Of the balance, Government *nominally* takes one-third or a half ; but how small a proportion this bears to the crop may be seen from the returns collected by the Famine Commissioners.

[marginal notes: Taxation of a Province under the Mughals, and under the British. The land-tax. Rates per acre.]

Their figures deal with 176 out of the 199 millions of people in British India. These 176 millions cultivate 188 millions of acres, grow 331 millions sterling worth of produce, and now pay 18¾ millions of land revenue. While, therefore, they raise over £1, 15s. worth of produce per acre, they pay to Government under 2s. of land-tax per acre. Instead of thus paying 5½ per cent. as they do now, they would under the Mughal rule have been called upon to pay from 33 to 50 per cent. of the crop. The two systems, indeed, proceed

---

[1] The evidence on which these statements are based, was published in Hunter's *Orissa*, vol. i. pp. 323–329 (Smith, Elder, & Co., 1872).

[2] *Report of the Indian Famine Commission*, part ii. p. 90, as presented to Parliament, 1880.

upon entirely different principles. The Native Governments, write the Famine Commissioners, often taxed the land 'to the extent of taking from the occupier the whole of the surplus after defraying the expenses of cultivation.'[1] The British Government objects to thus 'sweeping off the whole margin of profit.'

Increase of population. What becomes of the surplus which our Government declines to take? It goes to feed an enormously increased population. The tax-gatherer now leaves so large a margin to the husbandman, that the Province of Bengal, for example, feeds three times as many mouths as it did in 1780, and has a vast surplus of produce, over and above its own wants, for exportation. 'In the majority of Native Governments,' writes the highest living authority on the question,[2] 'the revenue officer takes all he can get; and would take treble the revenue we should *Taxation in Native States.* assess, if he were strong enough to exact it. In ill-managed States, the cultivators are relentlessly squeezed: the difference between the native system and ours being, mainly, that the cultivator in a Native State is seldom or never sold up, and that he is usually treated much as a good bullock is treated, *i.e.* he is left with enough to feed and clothe him and his family, so that they may continue to work.' John Stuart Mill studied the condition of the Indian people more deeply than any other political economist, and he took an indulgent view of native institutions. His verdict upon the Mughal Government is that, 'except during the occasional accident of a humane and vigorous local administrator, the exactions had no practical limit but the inability of the peasant to pay more.'

Incidence of taxation in British India. The Famine Commission, after careful inquiries, state[3] that throughout British India the landed classes pay revenue at the rate of 5s. 6d. per head, including the land-tax for their farms, or 1s. 9d. without it. The trading classes pay 3s. 3d. per head; the artisans, 2s.—equal to four days' wages in the year; and the agricultural labourers, 1s. 8d. The whole taxation, including the Government rent for the land, averaged, as we have seen, 3s. 8d. per head during the ten years ending 1879.

---

[1] *Report of the Indian Famine Commission,* part ii. p. 90, as presented to Parliament, 1880.

[2] Report by Mr. (now Sir) Alfred Lyall, C.B., formerly Governor-General's Agent in Rájputána, afterwards Foreign Secretary to the Government of India, now Lieutenant-Governor of the North-Western Provinces and Oudh; quoted in the Despatch of the Governor-General in Council to the Secretary of State, 8th June 1880. 'Condition of India,' Blue Book, pp. 36, 37.

[3] *Report of the Famine Commission,* part ii. p. 93 (folio, 1880).

But the Famine Commissioners declare that 'any native of India who does not trade or own land, and who chooses to drink no spirituous liquor, and to use no English cloth or iron, need pay in taxation only about 7d. a year on account of the salt he consumes. On a family of three persons, the charge amounts to 1s. 9d., or about four days' wages of a labouring man and his wife.'[1]

GROSS REVENUES.—But it should always be borne in mind *Gross balance-sheet of British India.* that the actual taxation of the Indian people is one thing, and the gross revenues of India are another. As explained in a previous paragraph of this chapter, the revenues include many items not of the nature of taxation. The following table, compiled from the *Parliamentary Abstract for* 1882–83 (the latest received by the author before sending these sheets to the press), exhibits the gross imperial revenue and expenditure of India for that year, according to the system of accounts adopted at the time. For the reasons already given, it is practically impossible to analyse these gross totals in such a way as to show the actual amount raised by taxation, and the actual amount returned in protection to person and property. The actual taxation has therefore been dealt with in the two separate statements already given. It is equally impossible to compare the gross totals with those for previous years, owing to changes that have been made from time to time in the system of entering the accounts. The only profitable plan is to take some of the items, and explain their real meaning.

The list of items shows how large a portion of the gross *Analysis of Indian revenues in 1883.* revenue is not of the nature of taxation proper. Public works, including railways and irrigation and navigation canals, alone yielded in 1882–83 upwards of 12 millions sterling, or over 17 per cent. of the total. Adding the items of post-office and telegraphs, which also represent payment for work done or services supplied, the proportion would rise to over $19\frac{1}{2}$ per cent. Then the sum of $9\frac{1}{2}$ millions gross, or nearly $7\frac{1}{4}$ millions net, derived from opium, being an additional $13\frac{1}{2}$ per cent. of the gross revenue, is not a charge upon the native *Not of the nature of taxation.* taxpayer, but a contribution to the Indian exchequer by the Chinese consumer of the drug. Add to these the tributes from Feudatory States, produce of the forests, etc., and upwards

[*Sentence continued on page* 467.

[1] *Report of the Famine Commission*, part ii. p. 93 (folio, 1880).

GROSS IMPERIAL REVENUE AND EXPENDITURE OF BRITISH INDIA FOR 1882-83.

Compiled from the Eighteenth Parliamentary Abstract relating to British India.

REVENUE.		EXPENDITURE.	
Land Revenue,	£21,876,047	Land Revenue,	£3,042,491
Opium,	9,499,594	Opium,	2,282,816
Salt,	6,177,781	Salt,	449,030
Stamps,	3,379,681	Stamps,	123,398
Excise,	3,609,661	Excise,	94,431
Customs,	1,295,119	Customs,	154,982
Provincial Rates,	2,683,015	Provincial Rates,	53,455
Assessed Taxes,	517,811	Assessed Taxes,	12,883
Forest,	936,228	Forest,	567,318
Registration,	285,829	Registration,	184,501
Tributes from Native States,	689,945	Post-office,	1,194,010
Post-office,	977,797	Telegraph,	625,279
Telegraphs,	545,315	Mint,	89,280
Mint,	185,882	General Administration,	1,563,882
Law and Justice,	656,934	Law and Justice,	3,755,071
Police,	227,642	Police,	2,642,892
Marine,	222,422	Marine,	490,800
Education,	198,558	Education,	1,145,070
Medical,	56,010	Ecclesiastical,	161,477
Scientific and Minor Departments,	75,680	Medical,	692,872
Interest,	693,864	Political,	513,791
State and Guaranteed Railways Irrigation & Navigation Canals, *e.g.*, Reproductive Public Works,	10,829,661	Scientific and Minor Departments,	481,816
	1,394,439	Famine Relief and Insurance,	1,500,000
Non-productive Public Works,	839,582	Territorial and Political Pensions,	685,761
Military,	1,592,583	Civil Furlough and Absentee Allowances,	211,908
Superannuation Funds,	395,260	Superannuation Allowances and Pension,	2,203,771
Stationery and Printing,	57,858	Stationery and Printing,	507,573
Miscellaneous,	341,533	Working Expenses and Charges against Capital, Interest, etc., on Reproductive Public Works,	11,741,747
		Non-productive Public Works,	7,165,747
		Military,	17,440,250
		Interest,	4,468,132
		Refunds and Drawbacks,	316,606
		Assignments and Compensations,	1,195,087
		Exchange,	3,081,433
		Miscellaneous,	281,394
Total Revenue,	£70,125,231	Total Expenditure,	£70,621,224
		Deduct Provincial Adjustments,	1,203,626
		Net Expenditure,	£69,418,598

Sentence continued from page 465.]
of one-third of the total gross revenue is accounted for. The Revenue
whole revenue of British India of the nature of actual taxation, from
including Land Revenue, Excise, Assessed Taxes, Provincial taxation.
Rates, Customs, Salt, and Stamps, amounted in 1878 to 34¾
millions, or 3s. 7¾d. per head. In 1882–83, the gross actual
taxation of British India was upwards of 39½ millions, or
within a fraction of 4s. per head, the average for the four years
ending 1882–83 being a fraction over 4s. 1d. per head, without
allowing for deductions or drawbacks.

The land revenue, amounting to over 21¾ millions in Nature of
1882–83, forms by far the largest item. Whether it should be the land-
properly regarded as a tax, or only as rent, is a problem for tax.
political economists to settle ; but in any case, it is paid without
question, as an immemorial right of the State. It yielded in
1882–83, 31 per cent., or nearly one-third, of the gross revenue.
Of the other items of taxation, excise and stamps are
practically creations of British rule. The excise is a tax upon Excise.
intoxicating liquors and deleterious drugs, levied both on the
manufacture and on the sale, according to different systems in
different Provinces. Like the corresponding duty in England,
it is voluntarily incurred, and presses hardest upon the lowest
classes. But unlike the English excise, it can hardly be called
an elastic source of revenue, for the rate is intentionally kept so
high as to discourage consumption. No duty whatever is levied
upon tobacco. Stamps, as in England, form a complex Stamps.
item. The greater part is derived from fees on litigation, and
only a comparatively trifling amount from stamps proper on
deeds of transfer, etc.
Customs are divided into import and export duties, both Customs.
of which have been so greatly lightened in recent years,
that their permanent maintenance may be considered doubtful. Duties on exports have been altogether abolished,
with the single exception of that on rice, which brings
in from £500,000 to over £800,000 per annum. The
average for the ten years ending 1882–83 was £615,349,
but there has been a steady increase since 1878. This export
duty is levied at the rate of 3 *ánnás* a *maund*, or about 6d. per
cwt., being equivalent to an *ad valorem* rate of about 10 per
cent. The 1¼ million sterling received from customs are
practically made up of nearly half a million sterling levied on
imported liquors, and about three-quarters of a million sterling
levied on exported rice. The receipts from all other import

customs in 1882–83 were under £13,000, and those from all other exports were just over £3000; total, under £16,000, from all imports and exports, excepting imported liquors and exported rice.

Cotton Duties.

The import duty on cotton goods was finally abolished in March 1882, having been reduced in 1878, and again in 1879. Imported cotton manufactures had previously formed the most important item of the customs revenue. From 1874 to 1882 the duty on cotton goods varied from nearly a million in 1878 to over half a million in 1881–82, the average being about three-quarters of a million sterling during the nine years preceding the total abolition of the duty.

The Salt Tax.

The salt tax, which yields about 6½ millions a year, is a problem of greater difficulty. It is an impost upon an article of prime necessity, and it falls with greatest severity upon the lowest classes. On the other hand, it may be urged that it is familiar to the people, is levied in a manner which arouses no discontent; and is the only means available of spreading taxation proper over the community. The reforms of 1878 and 1882, referred to on a previous page, have equalized the incidence of the salt tax over the entire country, with the incidental result of abolishing arbitrary and vexatious customs lines. As stated on a previous page, the rate is now a uniform one of Rs. 2 per *maund*, or 5s. 5d. per cwt., throughout British India, except in Burma where the rate is 3 *ánnás* per *maund*, and in the trans-Indus tracts of the Punjab, where a special rate is levied of 8 *ánnás* per local *maund* of 103 lbs.

Indian Expenditure, 1872–1882.

GROSS EXPENDITURE.—Putting aside the cost of collection and civil administration, which explain themselves, the most important charges are the Army, Interest on Debt, Famine Relief, Loss by Exchange, and Public Works, to which may be added the complex item of Payments in England. Military

Army expenditure.

expenditure has averaged about 18 millions during the ten years ending 1882–83, and in 1882–83 was 17½ millions. Of the 17½ millions, about 13½ represent payments in India, and 4 millions payments in England. In 1877–78, the total of the

Public Debt.

Indian Public Debt (exclusive of capital invested on railways and other productive public works) was returned at over 134⅔ millions sterling, being just 13s. 6¼d. per head of the population. In 1882–83 it was returned at over 159¼ millions, or 16s. per head of the population. Part of this was of the nature of obligations or deposits not bearing interest. The charge for interest was 5 millions in 1877-78; and 4½ millions sterling in 1882-83. This low charge for interest is due, in part, to the proportion of debt which does not bear interest. The above 'Public Debt' is independent of 126⅓ millions sterling invested in railways and productive works in 1877-78; which had increased to over 134 millions thus invested in 1882-83.

In 1840, the public debt amounted to only 30 millions, Itsgrowth. and gradually rose to 52 millions in 1857. Then came the Mutiny, which added upwards of 40 millions of debt in four years. The rate of increase was again gradual, but slow, till about 1874, when famine relief conspired with public works to cause a rapid augmentation, which has continued to the present time. The most significant feature in this augmentation is the large proportion of debt contracted in England.

No charge has recently pressed harder upon the Indian ex- Famine chequer than that of Famine Relief. Apart from loss by reduced Relief. revenue, the two famines of 1874 and 1877-78 have caused a direct expenditure on charitable and relief works amounting in the aggregate to just over 14 millions. From 1878-79 to 1882-83 the expenditure on 'Famine Relief' is returned at 3½ millions (of which the greater portion was expended on Public Works, in the nature of insurance against famine, and not on actual relief); making a total of nearly 17⅔ millions during the ten years 1874 to 1883 inclusive. This amounts to an annual charge of 1¾ million sterling for 'Famine Relief.'

Loss by exchange is an item which has lately figured largely Loss by in the accounts, and is due to the circumstance that large exchange. payments in gold require to be made in England by means of the depreciated rupee. In 1869-70, the loss by exchange was more than balanced by an entry of gain by exchange on the other side of the ledger. In 1876-77, the loss amounted to a little over two millions, and in 1882-83 to over three millions sterling.

The expenditure on Public Works is provided from three Public sources—(1) the capital of private companies, with a Govern- Works ex- ment guarantee; (2) loans for the construction of railways and penditure. canals; (3) current revenue applied towards such works as are not directly remunerative. In 1877-78, the capital raised for guaranteed railways amounted to 97⅓ millions sterling, and the capital invested on State railways and other productive public works to 29 millions sterling: total, 126⅓ millions sterling on railways and productive works. In 1882-83, the capital of the guaranteed railways was reduced to 69⅔ millions Railways. sterling; the capital invested on State railways and other productive public works amounted to 64½ millions: total on railways and productive public works, 134⅛ millions sterling in 1882–83. During the interval, 35 millions sterling of capital had been transferred from the guaranteed to the State railway account, owing to the purchase of the East India line by the Government.

Local finance.

Independent of imperial finance, and likewise independent of certain sums annually transferred from the Imperial exchequer to be expended by the provincial governments, there is another Indian budget for local revenue and expenditure. This consists of an income derived mainly from cesses upon land, and expended to a great extent upon minor public works. In 1877–78, local revenue and expenditure were each returned at about 3½ millions, and in 1882–83 at about 4 millions.

Municipal finance.

Yet a third budget is that belonging to the municipalities. The three Presidency towns of Calcutta, Madras, and Bombay had in 1876–77 a total municipal income of £668,400, of which £519,322 was derived from taxation, being at the rate of 7s. per head of population. In addition, there were 894 minor municipalities, with a total population of 12,381,059. Their aggregate income was £1,246,974, of which £979,088 was derived from taxation, being at the rate of 1s. 7d. per head. In 1882–83, the total municipal revenue of the three capital towns was £1,073,715, and of the 783 minor municipalities, £1,623,522; grand total, £2,697,237. It should be remembered that these figures refer to the period before the development of municipal institutions under Lord Ripon's legislation bore fruit. In the Presidency towns, rates upon houses, etc., are the chief source of income; but in the District municipalities, excepting in Bengal and Madras, octroi duties are more relied upon. The chief items of municipal expenditure are conservancy, roads, and police.

Constitution of the army.

THE INDIAN ARMY.—The constitution of the Indian army is based upon the historical division of British India into the three Presidencies of Bengal, Madras, and Bombay. There are still three Indian armies, each composed of both European and Native troops, and each with its own Commander-in-Chief and separate staff, although the Commander-in-Chief in Bengal exercises supreme authority over the other two. There may also be said to be a fourth army, the Punjab Frontier Force, which, until 1885, was under the orders of the Lieutenant-Governor of the Province.

The Bengal army garrisons Bengal Proper and Assam, the The three Presidency armies. North-Western Provinces and Oudh, a portion of Central India and Rájputána, and the Punjab. In 1877–78 its total strength was 104,216 officers and men, of whom 63,933 were native troops. In 1882–83, the Bengal army numbered Bengal. 105,270 officers and men, of whom 66,081 were native troops. In the Bengal native army, the distinguishing feature is the presence of 6 batteries of artillery, and an exceptionally large proportion of cavalry, both of which arms are massed in the Punjab.

The Madras army extends beyond the limits of that The Presidency into Mysore, the Nizám's Dominions, the Central Madras Provinces, also to Burma across the Bay of Bengal, army. and to the Andaman convict settlements. In 1877–78, its total strength was 47,026 officers and men, of whom 34,293 were native troops. In 1882–83, the Madras army numbered 46,309 of all ranks, of whom 34,283 were natives. In the Madras native army, the distinguishing features are the large proportion of sappers and miners, the small proportion of cavalry, and the entire absence of artillery.

The Bombay army occupies Bombay Proper and Sind, The the Native States of Central India, and the outlying station Bombay army. of Aden in the Red Sea. In 1877–78, its total strength was 38,355 officers and men, of whom 26,645 were native troops. In 1882–83, the Bombay army numbered 38,897 officers and men, of whom 27,041 were natives.

The total established strength of the European and Native Total army in British India in 1877–78 (exclusive of native artificers strength; and followers) consisted of 189,597 officers and men, of 1879; whom 64,276 were Europeans, and 124,871 were native troops. The four chief arms of the service were thus composed:—(1) Artillery, 12,239 European and 901 native; (2) cavalry, 4347 European and 18,346 native; (3) engineers, 357 European (all officers) and 3239 native; (4) infantry, 45,962 European and 102,183 native. In 1882–83, the 1883. total European and Native army in British India consisted of 190,476 officers and men, of whom 63,071 were Europeans, and 127,405 were native troops. The artillery consisted of 11,329 Europeans and 1861 natives; the cavalry of 4311 Europeans and 18,375 natives, besides a bodyguard of 202 troopers; engineers, 284 Europeans (all officers) and 3251 natives; and infantry, 45,766 Europeans and 103,716 natives.

Police. POLICE.—Excluding the village watch, still maintained as a subsidiary police in many parts of the country, the regular police of all kinds in British India in 1882 consisted of a total strength of 145,421 officers and men, being an average of 1 policeman to about 6 square miles of area, or to about 1369 of the population. The total cost of maintenance was £2,378,143, of which £2,201,437 was payable from imperial or provincial revenues. The former figure gives an average cost of about £2, 15s. per square mile of area, and threepence per head of population. The average pay of each constable was Rs. 7 a month, or £8, 8s. a year.

Jails. In 1882–83, the total number of places of confinement in British India, including central and District jails and lock-ups, was 452; the total number of prisoners admitted during the year, or remaining over from the previous year, was 391,319; the daily average was 97,218. The places of transportation for all British India are the Andaman and Nicobar Islands, where there are two penal establishments, containing, in 1882, a daily average of 11,454 convicts.

Educa- PUBLIC INSTRUCTION in India is directly organized by the
tion. State, and is assisted by grants-in-aid, under careful inspection. But at no period of its history has India been without some system of popular education, independent of State organization or aid. The origin of the Deva-Nágari alphabet is lost in
In ancient antiquity, though it is generally admitted not to be of indigenous
India. invention. Inscriptions on stone and copper, the palm-leaf records of the temples, and in later days the widespread manufacture of paper, indicate not only the general knowledge, but also the common use, of the art of writing.

From the earliest times the Bráhman caste preserved, first by oral tradition, then in manuscript, a literature unrivalled in its antiquity and for the intellectual subtlety of its contents. The Muhammadan invaders introduced the profession of the historian, and attained a high degree of historical excellence, compared with European writers of the same mediæval period. Throughout every change of dynasty, vernacular instruction has been given, at least to the children of respectable classes, in
Village each large village. On the one hand, the *tols* or seminaries
schools. for teaching Sanskrit philosophy at Benares and Nadiyá recall
Sanskrit the schools of Athens and Alexandria; on the other, the
tols. importance attached to instruction in accounts reminds one of the picture which Horace has left of a Roman education.

Even at the present day, a knowledge of reading and writing, taught by the Buddhist monks, is as widely diffused throughout Burma as in many countries of Europe. Our own efforts to stimulate education have been most successful, when based upon the existing indigenous institutions.

During the early days of the East India Company's rule, the promotion of education was not recognised as a duty of Government. Even in England, at that time, education was entirely left to private, and mainly to clerical, enterprise. A State system of instruction for the whole people is an idea of the latter half of the present century. But the enlightened mind of Warren Hastings anticipated this idea by founding the Calcutta Madrasa for Muhammadan teaching (1781), and by extending his patronage alike to Hindu *pandits* and European students. Lord Wellesley's schemes of imperial dominion led to the establishment of the college of Fort William for English officials. Of the Calcutta seminaries, the Sanskrit College was founded in 1824, when Lord Amherst was Governor-General; the Medical College, by Lord William Bentinck in 1835; the Húglí Madrasa, by a wealthy native gentleman in 1836. The Sanskrit College at Benares had been established in 1791, the Agra College in 1823.

Our first efforts at education.

Calcutta Madrasa and other Colleges.

Meanwhile, the Christian missionaries made the field of vernacular education their own. Discouraged by the authorities, and under the Company liable to deportation, they not only devoted themselves with courage to their special work of evangelization, but they were also the first Europeans to study the vernacular dialects spoken by the people. Nearly two centuries ago, the Jesuits at Madura, in the extreme south, had so mastered Tamil as to leave works in that language which are still acknowledged as classical by native authors. About 1810, the Baptist mission at Serampur, above Calcutta, raised Bengali to the rank of a literary prose dialect. The interest of the missionaries in education, which has never ceased to the present day, although now comparatively overshadowed by Government activity, had two distinct aspects. They studied the vernacular, in order to preach to the people, and to translate the Bible; they also taught English, as the channel of Western knowledge.

Mission Schools.

After long and acrimonious controversy between the advocates of English and of vernacular teaching, the present system was based, in 1854, upon a comprehensive despatch sent out by Sir C. Wood (afterwards Lord Halifax). In the midst of the tumult of the Mutiny, the three Indian Universities

State system of education.

Indian universities.

were founded at Calcutta, Madras, and Bombay in 1857.[1] Schools for teaching English were by degrees established in every District; grants-in-aid were extended to the lower vernacular institutions, and to girls' schools. A Department of Public Instruction was organized in every Province, under a Director, with a staff of Inspectors. In some respects this scheme may have been in advance of the time; but it supplied a definite outline, which has gradually been filled up. A network of schools was extended over the country, graduated from the indigenous village institutions up to the highest colleges. All received some measure of pecuniary support, granted under the guarantee of regular inspection; while a series of scholarships at once stimulated efficiency, and opened a path to the university for the children of the poor.

Education Commission of 1882-83.

In 1882–83, an Education Commission, appointed by Lord Ripon's Government, endeavoured to complete the scheme inaugurated in 1854 by the Despatch of Lord Halifax. It carefully examined the condition of education in each Province, indicated defects, and laid down principles for further development. The results of its labours have been to place public instruction on a broader and more popular basis, to encourage private enterprise in teaching, to give a more adequate recognition to the indigenous schools, and to provide that the education of the people shall advance at a more equal pace along with the instruction of the higher classes. Female education and the instruction of certain backward classes of the community, such as the Muhammadans, received special attention. The general effect of the Commission's recommendations is to develop the Department of Public Instruction into a system of truly national education for India, conducted and supervised in an increasing degree by the people themselves.

Educational statistics, 1878-83.

In 1877–78, the total number of educational institutions of all sorts in British India was 66,202, attended by an aggregate of 1,877,942 pupils, showing an average of one school to every 14 square miles, and one pupil to every 100 of the population. In 1882–83, the total number of inspected schools of all classes in British India had risen to 109,216, with an aggregate of 2,790,773 scholars, showing an average of one school to every 8 square miles of area, and one pupil to every 71 of the population. Male pupils numbered 2,628,402, showing one boy at school to every 38 of the male population; and female pupils, 162,371, or one girl at school to every 610

---

[1] By Act II. of 1857 for Calcutta; by Act XXII. of 1857 for Bombay; and by Act XXVII. of 1857 for Madras.

females. These figures, however, only include State inspected or aided schools and pupils. The Census Report of 1881 returned 2,879,571 boys and 155,268 girls as under instruction throughout British India, besides 7,646,712 males and 277,207 females able to read and write, but not under instruction. The figures are evidently below the truth, and it will be remarked that the Census returns the total number of girls attending school at 5000 less than those returned as attending the State-inspected schools alone.

In 1877–78, the total expenditure upon education from all sources was £1,612,775, of which £782,240 was contributed by the provincial governments, £258,514 was derived from local rates, and £32,008 from municipal grants. These items may be said to represent State aid; while endowments yielded £37,218, subscriptions £105,853, and fees and fines £277,039. The degree in which education has been popularized, and private effort has been stimulated, may be estimated from the fact that in Bengal the voluntary payments now greatly exceed the Government grants. In 1882–83, the total educational expenditure throughout British India amounted to £2,105,653, of which £578,629 was contributed by the provincial governments, £347,376 was derived from local rates, £63,832 from municipal grants, £93,924 from subscriptions, £49,695 from Native States, £58,675 from endowments, £516,925 from fees and fines, and the remainder from other sources. *Educational finance, 1878-83.*

The three Universities of Calcutta, Madras, and Bombay were incorporated in 1857, on the model of the University of London. They are merely examining bodies, with the privilege of conferring degrees in arts, law, medicine, and civil engineering. Their constitution is composed of a Chancellor Vice-Chancellor, and Senate. The governing body, or Syndicate, consists of the Vice-Chancellor and certain members of the Senate. A fourth University, on a similar plan, but including the teaching element, and following more oriental lines, has been founded at Lahore for the Punjab. The Universities control the whole course of higher education in India by means of their examinations. The entrance examination for matriculation is open to all; but when that is passed, candidates for higher stages must enrol themselves in one or other of the affiliated colleges. *The Indian Universities. Their constitution.*

In the ten years ending 1877–78, 9686 candidates successfully passed the entrance examination at Calcutta, 6381 at Madras, and 2610 at Bombay; total, 18,610. For the ten years ending 1882–83, out of 23,226 candidates at Calcutta, 10,200 successfully passed the entrance examination; at *University statistics, 1878-1883.*

Madras, out of 28,575 candidates, 9715 passed; and at Bombay, out of 11,871 candidates, 3557 passed. Total passed entrance examination in the ten years ending 1882–83, 23,472. Many fall off at this stage, and very few proceed to the higher degrees. During the same ten years ending 1882–83, 1036 graduated B.A. and only 281 M.A. at Calcutta; 896 B.A. and 22 M.A. at Madras; 456 B.A. and 34 M.A. at Bombay: total of B.A.'s and M.A.'s in the ten years, 2725. Calcutta possesses the great majority of graduates in law and medicine, while Bombay is similarly distinguished in engineering. In 1877–78, the total expenditure on the Universities was £22,093; and in 1882–83, £21,790.

Colleges. The colleges or institutions for higher instruction may be divided into two classes,—those which teach the arts course of the Universities, and those devoted to special branches of knowledge. According to another principle, they are classified into those entirely supported by Government, and those which only receive grants-in-aid. The latter class comprises the missionary colleges. In 1877–78, the total number of colleges, including medical and engineering colleges and Muhammadan *madrasas*, was 82, attended by 8894 students. Of these, as many as 35 colleges, with 3848 students, were in Lower Bengal; and 21 colleges, with 1448 students, in Madras. In the same year, the total expenditure on the colleges was £186,162, or at the rate of £21 per student. In 1882–83, the total number of colleges, including medicine and engineering colleges and Muhammadan *madrasas*, was 96, attended by 8707 students. Of these, 34 colleges with 3754 students were in Bengal, 32 colleges with 2329 students were in Madras, and 9 colleges with 1203 students were in Bombay. In the same year, the total expenditure on colleges in British India was £173,213, or a fraction under £20 per student.

Boys' schools; The boys' schools include many varieties, which may be sub-divided either according to the character of the instruction given, or according to the proportion of Government aid which they receive. The higher schools are those in which English is not only taught, but is also used as the medium of instruction. They educate up to the standard of the entrance examination at the Universities, and generally train those candidates who seek employment in the upper grades of Government service. One of these schools, known as the *zilá* or District school, is established at the head-quarters station of every District; and many others receive grants-in-aid. The total number of high schools in 1882–83 was 530,

upper schools;

of which 492 were for males and 38 for females, the attendance
in the year comprising 68,434 males and 1165 females.

The middle schools, as their name implies, are inter- middle
mediate between the higher and the primary schools. Gene- schools;
rally speaking, they are placed in the smaller towns or larger
villages; and they provide that measure of instruction which
is recognised to be useful by the middle classes themselves.
Some of them teach English; others only the vernacular.
This class includes the *tahsílí* schools, established at the head-
quarters of every *tahsíl* or Sub-division in the North-Western
Provinces. In 1882–83, the middle schools numbered 3796,
with an attendance of 170,642 pupils. In 1877–78, the total
expenditure on both higher and middle schools was £478,250,
and in 1882–83, £491,262.

The lower or primary schools complete the series. They are primary
dotted over the whole country, and teach only the vernacular. schools.
Their extension is the best test of the success of our educational
system.

No uniformity prevails in the primary school-system through- Increase of
out the several Provinces. In Bengal, up to the last fifteen primary
years, primary instruction was neglected; but since the reforms Bengal;
inaugurated by Sir G. Campbell in 1872, by which the benefit
of the grant-in-aid rules was extended to the *páthsálás* or roadside schools, this reproach has been removed. In 1871–72,
the number of primary schools under inspection in Lower
Bengal was only 2451, attended by 64,779 pupils. By 1877–78,
the number of schools had risen to 16,042, and the number
of pupils to 360,322, being an increase of about six-fold in six
years. By March 1883, when Sir G. Campbell's reforms had
received their full development: the primary schools in Bengal
had increased to 63,897, and the pupils to 1,118,623, being
an increase of over seventeen-fold in the eleven years ending
1882–83. In 1877–78, the expenditure on primary schools
in Bengal from all sources was £78,000; towards which
Government contributed only £27,000, thus showing how
State aid stimulates private outlay in primary education. The
total expenditure in 1882–83 was returned at £318,680. This
increase, however, is more apparent than real, and results from
a large number of schools previously private being brought
under the inspection of the Education Department, and
included in its financial statements.

The North-Western Provinces owe their system of primary in North-
instruction to their great Lieutenant-Governor Mr. Thomason, Western
whose constructive talent can be traced in every branch of the Provinces;

administration. In addition to the *tahsíli* or middle schools already referred to, a scheme was drawn up for establishing *halkabandí* or primary schools in every central village (whence their name), to which the children from the surrounding hamlets might resort. The system in the North - Western Provinces has been developed by means of the educational cess added to the land revenue. Sir William Muir, during his long service in the North-Western Provinces, ending in the Lieutenant-Governorship, did much for both the primary and the higher education of the people.

in Bombay; In Bombay, the primary schools are mainly supported out of local funds raised by a cess added to the land revenue.

in Burma; In British Burma, on the other hand, primary education is still left to a great extent in the hands of the Buddhist monks, who receive little or no aid from Government. These monastic schools are only open to boys; but there are also lay teachers who admit girls to mixed classes. The local administration shows a wise disposition to avail itself of the indigenous monastic system. Government has comparatively few schools of its own in Burma, the deficiency being supplied by several missionary bodies, who obtain State aid.

in Madras. In some localities of the Madras Presidency, also, the missionaries possess a practical monopoly of primary education at the present day.

Primary education finance. In 1877–78, the amount of money expended upon lower and primary schools in British India was £406,135, or just one-fourth of the total educational budget. In 1882–83, the total expenditure on lower and primary schools throughout British India was £911,121, or a little less than one-half (£2,105,653) of the total educational expenditure of the year. Under the recommendations of the Education Commission of 1882–83, the importance assigned to primary instruction, and the proportion of the public educational funds devoted to it, will constantly tend to increase.

Girls' schools. Of late years something has been done, although not much, to extend the advantages of education to girls. In this, as in other educational matters, the missionaries have been the pioneers of progress. In a few exceptional places, such as Tinnevelli in Madras, the Khási Hills of Assam, and among the Karen tribes of Burma, female education has made real progress; for in these localities the missionaries have sufficient influence to overcome the prejudices of the people. But elsewhere, even in the large towns and among the English-speaking classes, all attempts to give a modern education to women are regarded with scarcely disguised aversion, and have obtained but slight success. Efforts were at one time made by the Bengal Government to utilize the female members of the Vishnuite sects in female education, but without permanent success. Throughout the North - Western Provinces and Oudh, with their numerous and wealthy cities, and a total female population of over 21 millions, only 8999 girls attended school in 1877–78, and 9602 in 1882–83. In Lower Bengal, the corresponding number was less than 12,000 in 1877–78, but had increased to 57,361 in 1882–83. Madras, British Burma, and in a less degree, Bombay and the Punjab, are the only Provinces that contribute to the following statistics in any tolerable proportion :—Total girls' schools throughout British India in 1877–78, 2002 ; number of pupils, 66,615 : mixed schools for boys and girls, 2955 ; pupils, 90,915 : total amount expended on girls' schools, £78,729, of which £27,000 was devoted to the 12,000 girls of Bengal. The total number of girls' schools in 1882–83 in British India was 3487, attended by 162,317 pupils. This branch of instruction will now, it is hoped, receive a further development from the recommendations of the Education Commission.

In 1877–78, the normal, technical, and industrial schools Normal numbered 155, with a total of 6864 students ; the total ex- and other special penditure was £54,260, or an average of under £8 per schools. student. In 1882–83, the number of these special institutions was 213, attended by 8078 students. Total expenditure in 1882–83, £98,571, or an average of over £12 per head. Schoolmistresses, as well as schoolmasters, are trained ; and here also the missionaries have shown themselves active in anticipating a work which Government subsequently took up.

Of schools of art, the oldest is that founded by Dr. Schools of A. Hunter at Madras in 1850, and taken in charge by the Art. Education Department in 1856. This institution, and the Art Schools at Calcutta and Bombay, founded on its model, have been successful in developing the industrial capacities of the students, and in training workmen for public employment. Their effect on native art is more doubtful, and in some cases they have tended to supersede native designs by hybrid European patterns. Museums have been established at the Provincial capitals and in other large towns.

Schools for Europeans have also attracted the attention of Schools Government. Foremost among special schools are the asylums for Euro- in the hills for the orphans of British soldiers (*e.g.* Utakámand peans. and Sanáwar), founded in memory of Sir Henry Lawrence.

Vernacu-
lar press.

Closely connected with the subject of education is the steady growth of the vernacular press, which is ever active in issuing both newspapers and books. The missionaries were the first to cast type in the vernacular languages, and to

First news-
paper.

employ native compositors. The earliest vernacular newspaper was issued in Bengali by the Baptist Mission at Serampur, in 1818. For many years the vernacular press preserved the marks of its origin, being limited almost exclusively to theo-

The theo-
logical
period.

logical controversy. The missionaries were encountered with their own weapons by the Theistic sect of the Brahma Samáj, and also by the orthodox Hindus. So late as 1850, most of the vernacular newspapers were still religious or sectarian

The politi-
cal period.

rather than political. But during the last twenty-five years, the vernacular press has gradually risen into a powerful engine of political discussion.

Statistics
of native
journalism.

The number of newspapers published in the several ver-naculars is estimated at 250 to 300, and their aggregate sale at over 250,000 copies.[1] But the circulation proper, that is, the actual number of readers, is very much larger. In Bengal, the vernacular press suffers from the competition of English newspapers, some of which are entirely owned and written by natives. In the North-Western Provinces and Punjab, from Lucknow to Lahore, about 100 newspapers are printed in Hindustání or Urdu, the vernacular of the Muhammadans throughout India. Many of them are conducted with con-siderable ability and enterprise, and may fairly be described as representative of native opinion in the large towns. The Bombay journals are about equally divided between Maráthí and Gujarátí. Those in the Maráthí language are charac-terized by the traditional independence of the race of Sivají; the Gujarátí newspapers are the organs of the Pársís, and of the trading community generally. The vernacular newspapers of Madras, printed in Támil and Telugu, are politically unim-portant, being still for the most part devoted to religion.

Books.

As regards books, or rather registered publications, in the vernacular languages, Lower Bengal takes the lead; the Punjab, Bombay, the North-Western Provinces, and Madras follow in order. In a previous chapter, the exact number of works published in the native languages of India in the various

---

[1] The above estimate must be regarded as the result of intelligent inquiry, and not as an actual enumeration. Steps are now (1885) being taken to procure accurate returns of the vernacular press. But the ephemeral existence of many native newspapers, and other features of vernacular journalism, render the undertaking not free from difficulty.

departments of literature, has been stated.[1] The following figures refer to the years 1878 and 1882-83, and comprise the whole registered publications, both in the native languages and in English. There is probably a considerable number of minor works which escape registration.

Total of registered publications in 1878, 4913. Of these, 576 were in English or European languages, 3148 in vernacular dialects of India, 516 in the classical languages of India, and 673 were bi-lingual, or in more than one language. No fewer than 2495 of them were original works, 2078 were republications, and 340 were translations. Religion engrossed 1502 of the total; poetry and the drama, 779; fiction, 182; natural science, 249; besides 43 works on philosophy or moral science. Language or grammar was the subject of 612; and law of no fewer than 249 separate works. History had only 96 books devoted to it; biography, 22; politics, 7; and travels or voyages, 2. These latter numbers, contrasted with the 1502 books on religion, indicate the working of the Indian mind.

In 1882-83, the registered publications numbered 6198, of which 655 were in English or European languages, 4208 in vernacular dialects of India, 626 in the classical languages of India, and 709 bi-lingual or in more than one language. Of the total number of published works in 1882-83, 1160 were returned as educational, and 5038 as non-educational works. Original works numbered 3146; re-publications, 2547; and translations, 505. Publications relating to religion numbered 1641; poetry and the drama, 1089; fiction, 238; natural and mathematical science, 281; philosophy and moral science, 160; history, 143; languages, 784; law, 338; and medicine, 235. Politics were represented in 1882-83 by only 11 publications, travels and voyages by only 4, while works classed as miscellaneous numbered 1231.

Book statistics, 1878.

Book statistics, 1883.

---

[1] *Ante,* chap. iv.

CHAPTER XVII.

AGRICULTURE AND PRODUCTS.

Agricul-
ture.

THE cultivation of the soil forms the occupation of the Indian people in a sense which it is difficult to realize in England. As the land-tax forms the mainstay of the imperial revenue, so the *ráyat* or cultivator constitutes the unit of the social system. The village community contains many members besides the cultivator, but they all exist for his benefit, and all are maintained from the produce of the village fields. Even in considerable towns, the traders and handicraftsmen frequently possess plots of land of their own, on which they raise sufficient grain to supply their families

The work
of almost
the whole
people.

with food. According to the returns of the general Census of 1872, the adult males directly engaged in agriculture amount to nearly 35 millions, or 56·2 per cent. of the total. To these must be added almost all the day-labourers, who number $7\frac{1}{2}$ million males, or 12·3 per cent. ; thus raising the total of persons directly supported by cultivation to 68·5 per cent. ; being more than two-thirds of the whole adult males. The Census of 1881 returned a total of 51,274,586 males as engaged in agriculture throughout British and Feudatory India. Adding to these $7\frac{1}{4}$ million of adult day-labourers, there is a total of upwards of $58\frac{1}{2}$ million persons directly supported by cultivation, or 72 per cent. of the whole male population engaged in some specified occupation.[1] The number of persons indirectly connected with agriculture is also very great. The Famine Commissioners estimate that 90 per cent. of the rural population live more or less by the tillage of the soil. India is, therefore, almost exclusively a country of peasant farmers.

---

[1] For reasons fully explained in the *Note on Indian Statistics* in the last chapter, the years ordinarily selected for population statements are the Census years 1872 and 1881 ; and for other details, 1877–78 and 1882–83. The last year for which the final Parliamentary presentment of Indian returns had been received by the author when these sheets went to press in the summer of 1885, ended on 31st March 1883.

The increase in the population has, however, developed a large landless class. The cultivated area no longer suffices to allow a plot of land for each peasant; and multitudes now find themselves ousted from the soil. They earn a poor livelihood as day-labourers; and according to the Census of 1881, comprise 7,248,491, or one-eighth of the entire adult male population. There is still enough land in India for the whole people, but the Indian peasant clings to his native District, however overcrowded. Migration or emigration has hitherto worked on too small a scale to afford a solution of the difficulty. *Landless class.*

Agriculture is carried on in the different Provinces with an infinite variety of detail. Everywhere the same perpetual assiduity is found, but the inherited experience of generations has taught the cultivators to adapt their simple methods to differing circumstances. The deltaic swamps of Bengal and Burma, the dry uplands of the Karnátik, the black-soil plains of the Deccan, the strong clays of the Punjab, the desert sand of Sind or Rájputána, require their separate modes of cultivation. In each case the Indian peasant has learned, without scientific instruction, to grow the crops best suited to the soil. His light plough, which he may be seen carrying a-field on his shoulders, makes but superficial scratches; but what the furrows lack in depth, they gain by repetition, and in the end pulverize every particle of mould. Where irrigation is necessary, native ingenuity has devised the means; although in this as in other matters connected with agriculture, a wide field remains for further development and improvement. The inundation channels in Sind, the wells in the Punjab and the Deccan, the tanks in the Karnátik, the terraces cut on every hillside, water at the present day a far larger area than is commanded by Government canals. Manure is copiously applied to the more valuable crops, whenever manure is available; its use being limited only by poverty and not by ignorance. The scientific rotation of crops is not adopted as a principle of cultivation. But in practice it is well known that a succession of exhausting crops cannot be taken in consecutive seasons from the same field, and the advantage of fallows is widely recognised. A mutation of crops takes the place of their rotation. *Various systems of agriculture. Irrigation. Manure. Rotation of crops.*

The *petite culture* of Indian husbandmen is in many respects well adapted to the soil, the climate, and the social conditions of the people. The periodicity of the seasons usually allows of two, and in some places of three, harvests in the year. For inexhaustible fertility, and for retentiveness of moisture in a dry season, no soil in the world can surpass the *regar* or ' black cotton-soil' of the Deccan. In the broad river basins, the floods annually deposit a fresh top-dressing of silt, thus superseding the necessity of manures. The burning sun and the heavy rains of the tropics combine, as in a natural forcing-house, to extract the utmost from the soil. A subsequent section will deal with possible improvements in Indian agriculture — improvements now necessary in order to support the increasing population. As the means of communication improve and blunt the edge of local scarcity, India is probably destined to compete with America as the granary of Great Britain.

Rice.

The name of rice has from time immemorial been closely associated with Indian agriculture. The rice-eating population is estimated at 67 millions, or over one-third of the whole.[1] If, however, we except the deltas of the great rivers, and the long strip of land fringing the coast, rice may be called a rare crop throughout the remainder of the peninsula. But where rice is grown, it is in an almost exclusive sense the staple crop.

Statistics of rice cultivation in different Provinces.

In British Burma, out of a total cultivated area of 2,833,520 acres, in 1877–78, as many as 2,554,853 acres, or 90 per cent., were under rice. In 1882–83, the cultivated area in British Burma had risen to 3,746,279 acres, of which 3,380,996 acres, or 90 per cent., were under rice. Independent Burma, on the other hand, grows no rice, but imports largely from British territory. For Bengal, unfortunately, no general statistics are available. But taking Rangpur as a typical District, it was there found that $1\frac{1}{2}$ million acres, out of a classified total of a little more than $1\frac{3}{4}$ million acres, or 88 per cent., were devoted to rice. Similar proportions hold good for the Province of Orissa, the deltas of the Godávarí, Kistna, and Káveri (Cauvery), and the lowlands of Travancore, Malabar, Kánara, and the Konkan. Throughout the interior of the country, except in Assam, which is agriculturally a continuation of the Bengal delta, the cultivation of rice occupies but a subordinate place. In the North-Western Provinces and Oudh, rice is grown in damp localities, or with the help of irrigation, and forms a favourite food for the upper classes; but the local supply requires to be supplemented by importation from Bengal. In Madras generally, the area under rice in 1883 amounted to about 43 per cent. of the whole food-

[1] *Report of the Indian Famine Commission*, part ii. 81 (1880).

grain area. In Bombay proper, the corresponding proportion is only 14 per cent., and in the outlying Province of Sind, 17 per cent. In the Central Provinces, the proportion rises as high as 55 per cent., but in the Punjab it falls to 3 per cent. In scarcely any of the Native States, which cover the centre of the peninsula, is rice grown to a large extent.

Rice is in fact a local crop, which can only be cultivated profitably under exceptional circumstances, although under those circumstances it returns a larger pecuniary yield than any other food-grain in India. According to the Madras system of classification, rice is a 'wet crop,' *i.e.* it demands steady irrigation. In a few favoured tracts, the requisite irrigation is supplied by local rainfall, but more commonly by the periodical overflow of the rivers, either directly or indirectly through artificial channels. It has been estimated that rice requires 36 to 40 inches of water in order to reach its full development. But more important than the total amount of water, is the period over which that amount is distributed. While the seedlings are in an early stage of growth, 2 inches of water are ample; but when the stem is strong, high floods are almost unable to drown it. In some Districts of Bengal, a long-stemmed variety of rice is grown, which will keep its head above 12 feet of water.

Throughout Bengal, there are two main harvests of rice in the year—(1) the *áus* or early crop, sown on comparatively high lands, during the spring showers, and reaped between July and September; (2) the *áman* or winter crop, sown in low-lying lands, from June to August, usually transplanted, and reaped from November to January. The latter crop comprises the finer varieties, but the former is chiefly retained by the cultivators for their own food supply. Besides these two great rice harvests of the Bengal year, there are several intermediate ones in different localities. The returns from Rangpur District specify no fewer than 295 distinct varieties of rice.[1] The average out-turn per acre in Bengal has been estimated at 15 *maunds*, or 1200 lbs., of cleaned rice. In 1877–78, when famine was raging in Southern India, the exports of rice from Calcutta (much of it to Madras) amounted to nearly 17 million cwts.

In British Burma, there is but a single harvest in the year, corresponding to the *áman* of Bengal. The grain

Methods of rice cultivation :

in Madras ;

in Bengal ;

in Burma

[1] See Hunter's *Statistical Account of Bengal*, vol. vii. pp. 234–237 (1876).

is reddish in colour, and of a coarse quality; but the average out-turn is much higher than in Bengal, reaching in some places an average of 2000 and 2500 lbs. per acre. In 1877–78, the Burmese export of rice exceeded 13 million cwts.; and in 1882–83 it exceeded 21½ million cwts., of an estimated aggregate value of over 5½ millions sterling.

Besides being practically the sole crop grown in the deltaic swamps, rice is also cultivated on all the hills of India, from Coorg to the Himálayas. The hill tribes practise one of two methods of cultivation. They either cut the mountain slopes into terraces, to which sufficient water is conveyed by an ingenious system of petty canals; or they trust to the abundant rainfall, and scatter their seeds on clearings formed by burning patches of the jungle. In both cases, rice is the staple crop, wherever the moisture permits. It figures largely in the nomadic system of hill cultivation.

Hill cultivation.

The tables on the next page show the comparative area under rice and the two great other classes of food-grains for all India. But the figures must be taken as only approximate estimates.

Area under rice.

Recent exports of wheat to Europe have drawn attention to the important place which this crop occupies in Indian agriculture. It is grown to some extent in almost every District. But, broadly speaking, it may be said that wheat does not thrive where rice does; nor, indeed, anywhere south of the Deccan. The great wheat-growing tracts of India are in the north. The North-Western Provinces in 1883 had 97 per cent. of the food-grain area under wheat, barley, and millets; and about 57 per cent. under wheat alone. In the Punjab, the proportion of wheat and barley is 61 per cent. Wheat is also largely grown in Behar, and to a less extent in the western Districts of Bengal. In the Central Provinces, wheat covers a large proportion of the food-grain area, being the chief cereal in the Districts of Hoshangabad, Narsinghpur, and Ságar. In Bombay, the corresponding proportion was only 15 per cent., and in Sind, 12 per cent. The wheat returns vary from year to year, but disclose a tendency upwards. Their significance may be learned from the fact, that in Great Britain the area under wheat is only 3 million acres, or less than one-half the amount in a single Indian Province, the Punjab. It has been estimated that the total area under wheat in India is equal to the total area under the same crop in the United States.

Wheat.

Statistics of wheat cultivation.

Out-turn of wheat.

Nor is the out-turn contemptible, averaging about 13 bushels

[*Sentence continued on page* 488.

Ratio of Area under the three Principal Classes of Indian Food-Grains.

I.

1878.

Province.	Ratio of Area under principal Food-Grains.			Total Population (British India).	Population eating Rice.
	Wheat or Barley.	Millets.	Rice.		
	Per cent.	Per cent.	Per cent.	Millions.	Millions.
Punjab, . . .	54	41	5	18¾	1
North-Western Provinces,	57	34	9	44	4
Bengal and Assam, . .	No figures available.			74	46
Central Provinces, . .	27	39	34	9¾	3
Berar, ...	17	82	1	2¾	a
Bombay, ...	7	83	10	16½	2
Madras, ...	a	67	33	31	10
Mysore, ...	a	84	16	4	1

II.

1883.

Province.	Ratio of Area under principal Food-Grains.			Total Population (British India).	Population eating Rice.
	Wheat or Barley.	Millets.	Rice.		
	Per cent.	Per cent.	Per cent.	Millions.	Millions
Punjab, ...	61	36	3	18¾	1
North-Western Provinces,	97	a	3	44	4
Bengal, ...	No figures available.			69¼	43
Assam, ...	a	a	50	4¾	3
Central Provinces, . .	45	a	55	9¾	3
Berar, ...	97	a	3	2¾	a
Bombay, ...	15	71	14	16½	2
Madras, ...	a	57	43	31	10
Mysore, ...	4	a	96	4	1

a Where a column is left blank, the separate figures are not available.

N.B.—It will be observed that in the second table, where separate figures are not available, the ratio is that which one principal class bears to the other, and not to the total food-grain area of the District. The figures for the second table are derived from the Local Administration Reports for 1883-84, except in the case of Berar and Mysore, for which the figures are for 1881-82 (Mysore) and 1882-83 (Berar). They are not, in all cases, strictly comparable with the figures in the first table, which were taken from the Famine Commissioners' Report.

Sentence continued from page 486.]

per acre in the Punjab, as compared with an average of 15½ bushels for the whole of France. The quality, also, of the grain is high enough to satisfy the demands of English millers. The price of Indian wheat in Mark Lane varies considerably from year to year; the best qualities averaging somewhat lower than Australian or Californian produce. The abolition, in 1873, of the old Indian export duty on wheat, laid the foundation of the Indo-European wheat-trade, which, since this wise measure, has attained to large dimensions. The low prices of wheat in England in 1884 gave a check to the trade—a check which is believed to be temporary.

Wheat cultivation. According to the system of classification in Upper India, wheat ranks as a *rabi* crop, being reaped at the close of the cold weather in April and May. Wherever possible, it is irrigated; and the extension of canals through the Doáb has largely contributed to the substitution of wheat for inferior cereals.

Millets. Taking India as a whole, it may be broadly affirmed that the staple food-grain is neither rice nor wheat, but millet. Excluding special rice tracts, varieties of millet are grown more extensively than any other crop, from Madras in the south, at least as far as Rájputána in the north. The two most common kinds are great millet (Sorghum vulgare), known

Chief varieties. as *joár* or *jawári* in the languages derived from the Sanskrit, as *jonna* in Telugu, and as *cholam* in Tamil; and spiked millet (Pennisetum typhoideum), called *bájra* in the north and *kambu* in the south. In Mysore and the neighbouring Districts, *ragí* (Eleusine corocana), called *náchani* in Bombay, takes the first place. According to the Madras system of classification, these millets all rank as 'dry crops,' being watered only by the local rainfall, and sown under either monsoon; farther north, they are classed with the *kharíf* or autumn harvest, as opposed to wheat.

Statistics of millet cultivation; in Madras; The following statistics show the importance of millet cultivation throughout Southern and Central India. In Madras, in 1875–76, *cholam* covered 4,610,000 acres; *ragí*, 1,636,000 acres; *varagu* or *auricalu* (Paspalum miliaceum), 1,054,000 acres; *kambu*, 2,909,000 acres; *samai* or millet proper (Panicum frumentaceum), 1,185,000,—making a total of 11,384,000 acres under 'dry crops,' being 52 per cent. of the cultivated area. The proportion was 67 per cent. of the food-grain area in 1879. In 1882–83, the area under millets and inferior cereal crops was returned at 10,942,384 acres. In the upland

region of Mysore, the proportion under 'dry crops,' chiefly in Mysore;
ragí, rises to 77 per cent. of the cultivated area, or 84 per
cent. of the food-grain area. The total under all millets, *joár*,
and *bájra* in Bombay and Sind may be taken at about 83 per
cent. ; in the Central Provinces, 39 per cent. ; in the Punjab,
41 per cent. ; and in the North-Western Provinces, 34 per cent. and other
of the total food-grain area. It should be remembered that Provinces.
these figures vary from year to year.

Indian corn is cultivated to a limited extent in all parts of Minor
the country ; barley, in the upper valley of the Ganges, through- cereals.
out the Punjab, and in the Himálayan valleys ; oats, only as
an experimental crop by Europeans. *Joár* and *ragí*, but not
bájra, are valuable as fodder for cattle.

Pulses of many sorts form important staples. In Madras, Pulses;
the area under pulses in 1875 was 2,057,000 acres, or 9 per in 1875;
cent. ; in Bombay, about 830,000 acres ; in the Punjab,
4,000,000 acres, or 21 per cent. The area under pulses in
1882–83 was returned as under :—In Madras, 1,955,946 acres, and 1883.
or 8 per cent. of the cultivated area ; in Bombay, 1,776,773
acres, or over 8 per cent. ; in the Punjab, 3,664,952 acres, or
$15\frac{1}{2}$ per cent. of the cultivated area. The principal varieties
of pulses grown, with many native names, but generically
known to Europeans as gram and *dál*, are—Cicer arietinum,
Phaseolus Mungo and P. radiatus, Dolichos biflorus, D.
sinensis and D. Lablab, Cajanus indicus, Ervum Lens, Lathyrus
sativus, and Pisum sativum.

Oil-seeds also form an important crop in all parts of the Oil-seeds;
country ; oil being universally required, according to native
custom, for application to the person, for food, and for lamps.
In recent years, the cultivation of oil-seeds has received an
extraordinary stimulus owing to their demand in Europe, especially in France. But as they can be grown after rice, etc. as
a second crop, this increase has hardly tended to diminish
the production of food-grains. The four chief varieties grown
are mustard or rape-seed, linseed, *til* or gingelly (Sesamum),
and castor-oil. Bengal and the North-Western Provinces are
at present the chief sources of supply for the foreign demand,
but gingelly is largely exported from Madras, and, to a less
extent, from Burma. Area in 1875 under oil-seeds — In in 1875 ;
Madras, about 1,200,000 acres, or nearly 6 per cent. of the
cultivated area ; in Bombay, 628,000 acres ; in the Central
Provinces, 1,358,571 acres, or nearly 9 per cent. ; in the
Punjab, 780,000 acres, or 4 per cent. Area under oil-seeds
in 1882–83—In Madras, 1,063,988 acres, or 4·7 per cent. and 1883.

of the total cultivation; in Bombay, 1,336,385 acres, or 6·1 per cent.; in the Central Provinces, 1,600,225 acres, or 11·3 per cent.; and in the Punjab, 1,039,633 acres, or 4·4 per cent. of the area under cultivation. In the year 1877–78, the total export of oil-seeds from India amounted to 12,187,020 cwts., valued at £7,360,284; in 1878–79, to 7,211,790 cwts., valued at £4,682,512; and in 1882–83, to 13,147,982 cwts., valued at £7,205,924.

Vege-
tables.
Vegetables are everywhere cultivated in garden plots for household use, and also on a larger scale in the neighbourhood of great towns. Among favourite native vegetables, the following may be mentioned :—The egg-plant, called *brinjál* or *baigan* (Solanum melongena), potatoes, cabbages, cauliflower, radishes, onions, garlic, turnips, yams, and a great variety of cucur-bitaceous plants, including Cucumis sativus, Cucurbita maxima, Lagenaria vulgaris, Trichosanthes dioica, and Benicasa cerifera. Of these, potatoes, cabbages, and turnips are of recent intro-duction. Almost all English vegetables can be raised by a careful gardener. Potatoes thrive best on the higher elevations, such as the Khásí Hills, the Nílgiris, the Mysore uplands, and the slopes of the Himálayas ; but they are also grown on the plains and even in deltaic Districts. They were first introduced into the Khásí Hills in 1830. They now constitute the prin-cipal crop in these and other highland tracts. The annual export from the Khásí Hills to Bengal and the Calcutta market is estimated at considerably over 7000 tons, valued at £50,000.

Fruits.
Among the cultivated fruits are the following :— Mango (Mangifera indica), plantain (Musa paradisiaca), pine-apple (Ananassa sativa), pomegranate (Punica Granatum), guava (Psydium Guyava), tamarind (Tamarindus indica), jack (Artocarpus integrifolia), custard-apple (Anona squamosa), *papaw* (Carica Papaya), shaddock (Citrus decumana), and several varieties of fig, melon, orange, lime, and citron. The mangoes of Bombay, of Múltán, and of Maldah in Bengal, and the oranges of the Khásí Hills enjoy a high reputation ; while the guavas of Madras and other Provinces make an excellent preserve.

Spices.
Among spices, for the preparation of curry and other hot dishes, turmeric and chillies hold the first place, and are very widely cultivated. Next in importance come ginger, coriander, aniseed, black cummin, and fenugreek. The pepper vine is confined to the Malabar coast, from Kánara to Travan-core. Cardamoms are a valuable crop in the same locality, and also in the Nepálese Himálayas. The *pán* creeper (Piper

Betle), which furnishes the 'betel-leaf,' is grown by a special caste in most parts of the country. Its cultivation requires constant care, but is highly remunerative. The areca palm, which yields the 'betel-nut,' is chiefly grown in certain favoured localities, such as the deltaic Districts of Bengal, the Konkan of Bombay, and the highlands of Southern India.

Besides 'betel-nut' (Areca Catechu), the palms of India Palms. include the cocoa-nut (Cocos nucifera), the bastard date (Phœnix sylvestris), the palmyra (Borassus flabelliformis), and the true date (Phœnix dactylifera). The cocoa-nut, which loves a sandy soil and a moist climate, is found in greatest perfection along the strip of coast-line which fringes the south-west of the peninsula, where it ranks next to rice as the staple product. The bastard date, grown largely in the country round Calcutta, and in the north-east of the Madras Presidency, supplies both the jaggery sugar of commerce, and intoxicating liquor for local consumption. Spirit is also distilled from the palmyra palm in many Districts, especially in the Bombay Presidency and in the south of Madras. The true date is almost confined to Sind.

Sugar is manufactured both from the sugar-cane and from Sugar. the bastard date-palm. The best cane is grown in the North-Western Provinces, on irrigated land. It is an expensive crop, requiring much attention, and not yielding a return within the year. The profits are proportionately large. In Bengal, the manufacture from the cane has declined during the present century; but in Jessor District, the making of date-sugar is a thriving and popular industry.[1] The preparation of sugar is almost everywhere in the hands of natives; the exceptions being a few large concerns, such as the Aska factory in the Madras District of Ganjám, the Cossipur factory in the suburbs of Calcutta, the Rosa factory at Sháhjahánpur, and the Ashta-grám factory in Mysore. These factories use sugar-cane instead of the date juice, and have received honourable notice at exhibitions in Europe.

Cotton holds a most important place among Indian agricul- Cotton. tural products. From the earliest times, cotton has been grown in sufficient quantities to meet the local demand; and in the last century there was some slight export from the country, which was carefully fostered by the East India Company. But the present importance of the crop dates The from the crisis in Lancashire caused by the American War. American War, 1862.

[1] A full account of the manufacture will be found in Hunter's *Statistical Account of Bengal*, vol. ii. pp. 280-298.

Prior to 1860, the exports of raw cotton from India used to average less than 3 millions sterling a year; but after that year they rose by leaps, until in 1866 they reached the enormous total of 37 millions. Then came the crash, caused by the restoration of peace in the United Sates; and the exports steadily fell to just under 8 millions in 1879. Since then the trade has recovered, and the total value of raw cotton exports in 1882–83 amounted to 16 millions sterling. The fact is that Indian cotton has a short staple, and is inferior to American cotton for spinning the finer qualities of yarn. But while the cotton famine was at its height, the cultivators were intelligent enough to make the most of their opportunity. The area under cotton increased enormously, and the growers managed to retain in their own hands a fair share of the profit.

Cotton Districts. The principal cotton-growing tracts are—the plains of Gujarát and Káthiáwár, whence Indian cotton has received in the Liverpool market the historic names of *Surat* and *Dholera ;* the highlands of the Deccan; and the deep valleys of the Central Provinces and Berar. The best native varieties are found in the Central Provinces and Berar, passing under the trade names of Hinganghát and Amráoti. These varieties have been successfully introduced into the Bombay District of Khándesh. Experiments with seed from New Orleans have been conducted for several years past on the Government farms in many parts of India. But it cannot be said that they have resulted in success except in the Bombay District of Dhárwár, where exotic cotton has now generally supplanted the indigenous staple.

Cotton area in Bombay; In 1875–76, the area under cotton in the Bombay Presidency, including Sind and the Native States, amounted to 4,516,587 acres, with a yield of 2,142,835 cwts. Of this total, 583,854 in 1876; acres, or 13 per cent., were sown with exotic cotton, including seed procured from the Central Provinces and also from New Orleans, with a yield of 248,767 cwts. The average yield was about 53 lbs. per acre, the highest being in Sind and Gujarát (Guzerát), and the lowest in the Southern Maráthá country. In 1875–76, the total exports were 3,887,808 cwts., from the Bombay Presidency, including the produce of the Central Provinces and the Berars, valued at £10,673,761. In 1882–83, the total area under cotton in the Bombay Presi-and 1883. dency, including Sind and the Native States, was 5,698,862 acres, yielding 3,141,421 cwts. of cleaned cotton. Of this area 796,608 acres were sown with exotic cotton, yielding an out-turn of 420,494 cwts. The exports of raw cotton from

Bombay and Sind in 1882–83, including the produce of the
Central Provinces and Berar, were 4,996,739 cwts., valued at
£13,134,693, besides cotton twist and yarn and manufactured
piece-goods to the value of £2,183,205.

In 1877–78, the area under cotton in the Central Provinces Cotton
was 837,083 acres, or under 6 per cent. of the total culti- cultivation
in Central
vated area, chiefly in the Districts of Nágpur, Wardhá, and Provinces;
Ráipur. The average yield was about 59 lbs. per acre. 1878.
The exports from the Central Provinces to Bombay, including
re-exports from Berar, were about 300,000 cwts., valued at
£672,000. In 1877–78, the area under cotton in Berar In Berar.
was 2,078,273 acres, or 32 per cent. of the total cultivated
area, chiefly in the two Districts of Akola and Amráoti. The
average yield was as high as 67 lbs. of cleaned cotton per
acre. The total export was valued at £2,354,946, almost
entirely railway-borne. In 1882–83, the area under cotton in 1883.
the Central Provinces had decreased to 612,687 acres, or
4 per cent. of the then cultivated area. In the same year,
the area under cotton in Berar was 2,139,188 acres, or 32
per cent. of the cultivated area.

In Madras, the average area under cotton is about In Madras;
1,500,000 acres, chiefly in the upland Districts of Bellary
and Karnúl, and the low plains of Kistna and Tinnevelli.
The total exports in 1876–77 were 460,000 cwts., valued
at about 1 million sterling. In 1882–83, cotton was grown
on 1,456,423 acres in Madras. In the same year, the total
value of the cotton exports from Madras, raw and manufactured, was £1,898,351. In Lower Bengal the cultivation of in Bengal;
cotton seems on the decline. The local demand has to be met
by imports from the North-Western Provinces and the bordering
hill tracts, where a short-stapled variety of cotton is extensively
cultivated. The total area under cotton in Lower Bengal
is estimated at only 162,000 acres, yielding 138,000 cwts. of
cleaned cotton. Of this, 31,000 acres are in Sáran, 28,000 in
the Chittagong Hill Tracts, and 20,000 in Cuttack. Throughout in the
N.W. Pro-
the North-Western Provinces, and also in the Punjab, sufficient vinces and
cotton is grown to meet the wants of the village weavers. Punjab.

The total export of raw cotton from Indian ports in 1878–79 Total
was 2,966,569 cwts., valued at £7,914,091, besides cotton cotton
exports;
twist and yarn to the value of £937,698, and cotton manufactures valued at £1,644,125. By 1882–83 the exports of 1878 and
raw cotton from all Indian ports had increased to 6,170,173 1883.
cwts., valued at £16,055,758; besides cotton twist and yarn
to the value of £1,874,464, and cotton manufactures valued

at £2,093,146. Total value of cotton exports in 1882–83, raw and manufactured, £20,023,368.

Cotton-cleaning. The cotton-mills of Bombay will be treated of in the next chapter under 'Manufactures.' But apart from weaving and spinning, the cotton trade has given birth to other industries, for cleaning the fibre and pressing it into bales for carriage. **1877;** In 1876–77, there were altogether 2506 steam gins for cleaning cotton in the Bombay Presidency, besides 22 in the Native States. In addition, there were 130 full-presses worked by steam power, and 183 half-presses worked by **and 1883.** manual labour. In 1882–83, there were altogether 2787 steam gins for cleaning cotton in the Bombay Presidency, 96 steam cotton presses, and 141 cotton presses worked by manual labour. The total amount of capital invested in the cotton industry in the Bombay Presidency is estimated at about £900,000. Cotton gins and presses are also numerous at the chief marts in the North-Western and Central Provinces, and Berar.

Jute. Jute ranks next to cotton as a fibre crop. The extension of its cultivation has been equally rapid, but it is more limited in area, being practically confined to Northern and Eastern **The jute area of Bengal.** Bengal. In this tract, which extends from Purniah to Goalpárá, for the most part north of the Ganges and along both banks of the Brahmaputra, jute is grown on almost every variety of soil. The chief characteristic of the cultivation is that it remains entirely under the control of the cultivator. Practically a peasant proprietor, he increases or diminishes his cultivation according to the state of the market, and keeps the profits in his own hands. The demand for jute in Europe has contributed more than any administrative measure to raise the standard of comfort throughout Eastern Bengal.

The jute plant. The plant that yields the jute of commerce is called *pát* or *koshta* by the natives, and belongs to the family of mallows (Corchorus olitorius and C. capsularis). It sometimes attains a height of 12 feet. The seed is generally sown in April, the favourite soil being *chars*, or alluvial sandbanks thrown up by the great rivers; and the plant is ready for cutting in August. When it first rises above the ground, too much water will drown it; but at a later stage, it survives heavy floods. After being cut, the stalks are tied up in bundles, and thrown **Preparation of fibre.** into standing water to steep. When rotted to such a degree that the outer coat peels off easily, the bundles are taken out of the water, and the fibre is extracted and carefully washed. It now appears as a long, soft, and silky thread; and all that remains to do is to make it up into bales for export. The final process of pressing is performed in steam-presses at the Mechancentral river marts, principally at Howrah or in the outskirts ism of jute of Calcutta. The trade is to a great extent in the hands of trade. natives. *Bepáris* or travelling hucksters go round in boats to all the little river marts, to which the jute has been brought by the cultivators. By their agency the produce is conveyed to a few great centres of trade, such as Sirájganj and Náráinganj, where it is transferred to wholesale merchants, who ship it to Calcutta by steamer or large native boats, according to the urgency of demand.

In 1872–73, when speculation was briskest, it is estimated Jute outthat about 1 million acres were under jute, distributed over 16 turn and exports, Districts, which had a total cultivable area of 23 million acres. 1873; The total export from Calcutta in that year was about 7 million cwts., valued at £4,142,548. In 1878–79, the total 1878; export of raw jute from India was 6,021,382 cwts., valued at £3,800,426, besides jute manufactures to the value of £1,098,434. In 1882–83, the total exports of raw jute from 1883. Indian ports amounted to 10,348,909 cwts., of the value of £5,846,926, besides jute manufactures, principally in the shape of gunny-bags, of the aggregate value of £1,487,831. The total number of steam jute mills in Bengal, either private property or owned by joint-stock companies, in 1882–83 was 18, affording employment to 41,263 persons.

Jute is an exhausting crop to soils without river-inundation. Aspects to This fact is well known to the cultivators, who generally the husbandman. allow jute-fields to lie fallow every third or fourth year. A fear has sometimes been expressed that the profits derived from jute may have induced the peasantry to neglect their grain crops. But the apprehension seems to be groundless. For the most part, jute is grown on flooded lands which would otherwise often lie untilled. It only covers a very small portion of the total area, even of the jute Districts, say 4 per cent. ; and the fertility of the rice-fields of Eastern Bengal is such that they could support a much denser population than at present. Jute, in short, is not a rival of rice; but a subsidiary crop, from which the cultivator makes a certain additional income in hard cash.

Indigo is one of the oldest, and, until the introduction of tea-Indigo. planting, ranked as the most important, of the Indian staples grown by European capital. In Bengal proper, its cultivation Its decline has greatly declined since the first half of this century. in Lower English indigo planters have forsaken the Districts of Húglí, Bengal. the Twenty-four Parganás, Dacca, Farídpur, Rangpur, and

Indigo.   Pabná, now dotted with the sites of ruined old factories. In
Nadiyá, Jessor, Murshidábád, and Maldah, the industry is
still carried on; but it has not recovered from the depression
and actual damage caused by the indigo riots of 1860, and
the emancipation of the peasantry by the Land Act of 1859.
Indigo of a superior quality is manufactured in Midnapur,
along the frontier of the hill tracts.

Its culti-   The cultivation on the old scale still flourishes in Behar,
vation in   from which is derived one-half of the total exports from
Behar;   Calcutta.   Complete statistics of area are not available, as
there are many small indigo concerns throughout the country
in native hands.   Some years ago, it was estimated that in
Tirhut alone there were 56 principal concerns, with 70 outworks, producing annually about 20,000 *maunds* of dye; in
Sáran, 30 principal concerns and 25 outworks, producing about
12,000 *maunds;* in Champáran, 7 large concerns, producing
also 12,000 *maunds.*[1]   The Behar Indigo Planters' Association, the responsible mouthpiece of the Behar indigo interest,
has at present (1885) 73 factories belonging to the Association in the Indigo Districts of Behar.   Under these head
factories there are 220 out-factories, most of them in charge
of European assistants.   The area under indigo cultivation in
the above concerns is approximately 250,000 acres, giving
employment to 75,900 persons, exclusive of a large staff
(Native and European) for management and supervision.   The
estimated outlay, at the rate of a little over £3 per acre, is
about £750,000 annually spent in the Districts.[2]   It has been
estimated that the total amount of money annually distributed
by the planters of Behar cannot be less than 1 million sterling.

in N.-W.   Across the border of Bengal, in the North-Western Provinces,
Provinces;   indigo is grown and manufactured to a considerable extent by
native cultivators.   In the Punjab, also, indigo is an important
native crop, especially in the Districts of Múltán, Muzaffargarh,
in Madras.   and Dera Ghází Khán.   In Madras, the total area under
indigo is about 300,000 acres, grown and manufactured entirely
by the natives, chiefly in the north-east of the Presidency,
extending along the coast from Kistna to South Arcot, and
inland to Karnúl and Cuddapah.

----

[1] The factory *maund* of indigo weighs 74 lbs. 10 oz.
[2] The author takes this opportunity of thanking Mr. E. Macnaghten,
Officiating Secretary to the Behar Indigo Planters' Association, for the foregoing figures, and for other valuable materials, referring to as late a period
as June 1885.   They have, as far as possible, been incorporated in passing
these pages through the press.

In 1877–78, the total export of indigo from all India was Indigo exports. 120,605 cwts., valued at £3,494,334; in 1878–79, 105,051 cwts., valued at £2,960,463. In 1882–83, the export of indigo was 141,041 cwts., of the value of £3,912,997.

In Bengal, indigo is usually grown on low-lying lands, with System of sandy soil, and liable to annual inundation; in Behar, on indigo-planting. comparatively high land. A common practice is for the planter to obtain from the *zamíndár* or landlord a lease of the whole village area for a term of years; and then to require the *ráyats* or cultivators to grow indigo on a certain portion of their farms every year, under a system of advances. The seed, of which an excellent kind comes from Cawnpur, is generally sown about March; and the crop is ready for gathering by the beginning of July. A second crop is sometimes obtained in September. When cut, the leaves are taken to the factory, to be steeped in large vats for about ten hours until the process of fermentation is completed. The water is then run off into a second vat, and subjected to a brisk beating, the effect of which is to separate the particles of dye and cause them to settle at the bottom. Finally, the sediment is boiled, strained, and made up into cakes for the Calcutta market. In recent years, steam has been introduced into the factories for two purposes: to maintain an equable temperature in the vats while the preliminary process of fermentation is going on, and to supersede by machinery the manual labour of beating.

In the middle of the present century, the abuses connected Indigo-planting in Bengal; with indigo-planting became a serious problem for the Indian Legislature. In some Districts, particularly in Lower Bengal, in the neighbourhood of Calcutta, indigo-planting was worked by a system of advances to the cultivators which plunged them into a state of hopeless hereditary indebtedness to the planters. The Land Law of 1859 (Act x.), by defining and improving the legal status of the cultivator throughout Bengal, gave a death-blow to this system in Districts in which it had been abused. The results on indigo-planting in several Districts around Calcutta have been described in a previous paragraph.

The system pursued in Behar had, from an early period, in Behar, been different. Instead of compelling the cultivator to give up his best lands to indigo by the pressure of hereditary indebtedness, the Behar planters to a large extent obtained lands of their own on lease, or by purchase, and cultivated at their own risk, or by hired labour. This system has, however, its own complications, and for a time gave rise to strained relations between the planters, the native landholders, and the tenants.

Behar Indigo Planters' Association.

In 1877, the Government of Bengal expressed dissatisfaction at the condition of the Indigo Districts of Behar, and proposed to issue a Commission of Inquiry. A responsible Association was, however, formed by the planters themselves, in communication with the Bengal Government, to readjust, as far as necessary, the relations between the planters, native landholders, and cultivators. The Association thus formed has been productive of much good, both by preventing the occurrence of disputes, and by arbitrating between the parties when disputes arise. In 1881, the Lieutenant-Governor of Bengal publicly thanked the Association for its 'most cordial and loyal co-operation in correcting the abuses which he had occasion to mention in 1877.' The Annual Reports from the District Officers since that year have been satisfactory. During 1884, the Secretary to the Association stated that every dispute referred to the Association had been amicably adjusted. The relations between capital and labour and land in overcrowded tracts, almost entirely dependent on the local crops raised, are, however, always apt to be strained.

Opium,

The opium of commerce is grown and manufactured in two special tracts: (1) the valley of the Ganges round Patná and Benares; and (2) a fertile table-land in Central India, corresponding to the old kingdom of Málwá, for the most part still under the rule of native chiefs, among whom Sindhia and Holkar rank

in Bengal and Málwá.

first. In Málwá, the cultivation of poppy is free, and the duty is levied as the opium passes through the British Presidency of Bombay; in Bengal, the cultivation is a Government monopoly.

in Rájputána.

Opium is also grown for local consumption throughout Rájputána, and to a very limited extent in the Punjab and the Central Provinces. Throughout the rest of India it is absolutely prohibited. In the Ganges valley, the cultivation is supervised from two agencies, with their head-quarters at Patná and Gházípur, at which two towns alone the manufacture is conducted.

Bengal out-turn; 1872; and 1883.

In the year 1872, the Bengal area under poppy was 560,000 acres; the number of chests of opium sold was 42,675; the sum realized was £6,067,701, giving a net revenue of £4,259,376. The whole of this was exported from Calcutta to China and the Straits Settlements. In 1882–83, the number of chests of Bengal opium sold was 56,400, the sum realized was £7,103,925, the net revenue being £4,821,712. The amount of opium exported from Bombay raises the average exports of opium to about 11 or 12 millions sterling, of which about 7 or 8 millions represents net profit to Government. In 1878–79, 91,200 chests of opium were exported from India, of the value of £12,993,985, of Total Indian out-turn. which £7,700,000 represented the net profit to Government. In 1882–83, 91,798 chests of Bengal and Málwá opium were exported, of the value of £11,481,379, of which £7,216,778 represented the net profit to Government.

Under the Bengal system, annual engagements are entered Bengal opium system : into by the cultivators to sow a certain quantity of land with poppy; and it is a fundamental principle that they may engage or refuse to engage, as they please. As with most other Indian industries, a pecuniary advance is made to the cultivator advances. before he commences operations, to be deducted when he delivers over the opium at the subordinate agencies. He is compelled to make over his whole produce, being paid at a fixed rate, according to quality. The best soil for poppy is high land which can be easily manured and irrigated. The cultivation requires much attention throughout. From the commencement cultiva- tion ; of the rains in June until October, the ground is prepared by repeated ploughing, weeding, and manuring. The seed is sown in the first fortnight of November, and several waterings are necessary before the plant reaches maturity in February.

After the plant has flowered, the first process is to remove manufac- ture. the petals, which are preserved, to be used afterwards as coverings for the opium-cakes. The juice is then collected during the month of March, by scarifying the capsules in the afternoon with an iron instrument, and scraping off the exudation next morning. The quality of the drug mainly depends upon the skill with which this operation is performed. In the beginning of April, the cultivators bring in their opium to the subordinate agencies, where it is examined and weighed, and the accounts are settled. The final process of preparing the drug in balls for the Chinese market is conducted at the two central agencies at Patna and Gházípur. This generally lasts until the end of July, but the balls are not dry enough to be packed in chests until October.

Tobacco is grown in every District of India for local con- Tobacco sumption. The soil and climate are favourable; but the quality of native cured tobacco is so inferior, as to scarcely find a market in Europe. The principal tobacco-growing tracts are Chief tobacco Rangpur and Tirhut in Bengal, Kaira in Bombay, the delta of areas. the Godávarí, and Coimbatore and Madura Districts in Madras. The two last-mentioned Districts supply the raw material for the well-known 'Trichinopoli cheroot,' almost the only form of Indian tobacco that finds favour with Europeans; the produce of the *lánkás* or alluvial islands in the Godávarí is manufactured into 'Coconadas.' The tobacco of Northern Bengal is largely exported to British Burma; for the Burmese, who are great smokers, do not grow sufficient for their own needs. The manufacture of tobacco in Madras, Burma, and Bengal, is now making progress under European supervision, and promises to supply an important new staple in the exports of India.

Tobacco trade; 1877;   In 1876–77, the total registered imports of tobacco into Calcutta from the inland Districts were 521,700 *maunds*, valued at £261,000, of which more than half came from the single District of Rangpur. Tobacco is also grown for export in the Chittagong Hill Tracts. The tobacco of Tirhut is chiefly exported towards the west. The total area under tobacco in that District is estimated at 40,000 acres, the best quality being grown in

and 1883. *parganá* Saressa of the Tájpur Sub-division. In 1882–83, the imports of tobacco from the inland Districts into Calcutta were 650,583 *maunds*, of an estimated value of £540,601.

Tobacco-curing.   During the past ten years, a private firm, backed by Government support, has been growing tobacco in Northern India, and manufacturing it for the European market. The scene of its operations is two abandoned stud-farms, at Gházípur in the North-Western Provinces, and at Pusa in Tirhut District, Bengal. In 1878–79, about 240 acres were cultivated with tobacco, the total crop being about 160,000 lbs. Five English or American curers were employed. Some of the produce was exported to England as 'cured leaf;' but the larger part was put upon the Indian market in the form of 'manufactured smoking mixture.' This mixture is in demand at regimental messes and canteens, and has also found its way to Australia. The enterprise may now be said to have passed beyond the stage of experiment. An essential condition of success is skilled supervision in the delicate process of tobacco-curing. Tobacco to the value of £128,330 was exported from India in 1878–79, and to the value of £117,156 in 1882–83.

Uncertainty of Indian crop statistics.   Before proceeding to crops of a special character, such as coffee, tea, and cinchona, it may be well to give a general view of the area covered by the staples of Indian agriculture. The table on the opposite page must be taken as approximate only. It represents, however, the best information available (1882–83). Its figures show various changes from the estimates in 1875, incorporated in some of the foregoing paragraphs. But it is necessary to warn the reader, that Indian agricultural returns do not always stand the test of statistical analysis. In most cases the local returns have to be accepted without the possibility of verification; alike in the preceding pages, and in this tabular statement. Steps are now being taken to secure a higher degree of trustworthiness in such returns.

APPROXIMATE AREA IN ACRES OCCUPIED BY THE PRINCIPAL CROPS IN SOME INDIAN PROVINCES IN 1877–78 AND 1882–83.

	Madras.		Bombay and Sind.		Punjab.		Central Provinces.		British Burma.		Mysore.		Berar.	
	1877–78.	1882–83.	1877–78.	1882–83.	1877–78.	1882–83.	1877–78.	1882–83.	1877–78.	1882–83.	1877 78.	1881–82.*	1877–78.	1882–83.
Rice, ...	4,600,000	5,608,751	1,707,000	1,871,315	400,000	775,367	4,550,000	4,416,054	2,555,000	3,380,996	540,000	554,752	31,000	22,827
Wheat, ...	16,000	27,051	915,000	1,626,544	7,000,000	6,734,357	3,600,000	3,619,704	...	...	11,000	21,058	525,008	746,391
Millet and inferior grains,	10,600,000	10,942,384	6,734,000	12,008,795	6,000,000	8,905,149	5,140,000	5,618,174	...	...	3 400,000	3,139,560	2,760,000	2,368,542
Pulses, ...	1,600,000	1,955,946	945,000	1,776,773	3,200,000	3,664.962							180,000	409,243
Oil-seeds, ...	800,000	1,063,988	808,000	1,336,385	800,000	1,039,633	1,360,000	1,600,225	15,000	19.339	130,000	147,464	460,000	545,030
Cotton, ...	1,000,000	1,456,423	1,420,000	2,640,748	660,000	860,631	840,000	612,687	10,000	4,740	15,000	20,893	2,080,000	2,139,188
Tobacco, ...	60,000	78,707	41,000	59,137	80,000	66,790	48,000	22,866	17,000	15,746	19,000	12,986	17,000	24,722
Indigo, ...	120,000	508,774	24,000	17,736	110,000	162,903	...	85	700	79	...	...	...	...
Sugar-cane, ...	21,000	46,216	54,000	66,310	38,000	401,045	100,000	53,938	4,0000	7,121	13,000	24,076	5,000	4,530

* No later statistics are available for Mysore than those for 1881-82, the last year in which the State was under British administration.

Coffee.

The cultivation of coffee is confined to Southern India, although attempts have been made to introduce the plant both into British Burma and into the Bengal District of Chittagong. The coffee tract may be described as a section of the landward slope of the Western Gháts, extending from Kánara in the north to Travancore in the extreme south. This tract includes almost the whole of Coorg, the Districts of Kadur and Hassan in Mysore, and the Nílgiri Hills enlarged by the recent annexation of the Wainád. Within the last few years, the cultivation has extended to the Shevaroy Hills in Salem District, and to the Palni Hills in Madura.

Coffee area.

Introduction into India.

Unlike tea, coffee was not introduced into India by European enterprise; and even to the present day its cultivation is largely conducted by natives. The Malabar coast has always enjoyed a direct commerce with Arabia, and yielded many converts to Islám. One of these converts, Bába Budan, is said to have gone on a pilgrimage to Mecca, and to have brought back with him the coffee berry, which he planted on the hill range in Mysore still called after his name. According to local tradition, this introduction of the berry happened about two centuries ago. The shrubs thus sown lived on, but the cultivation did not spread until the beginning of the present century.

The State of Mysore and the Bába Budan range also witnessed the first opening of a coffee-garden by an English planter about forty-five years ago. The success of this experiment led to the extension of coffee cultivation into the neighbouring tract of Manjarábád, also in Mysore, and into the Wainád Sub-division of the Madras District of Malabar. From 1840 to 1860, the enterprise made slow progress; but since the latter date, it has spread with great rapidity along the whole line of the Western Gháts, clearing away the primeval forest, and opening a new era of prosperity to the labouring classes.

Its progress, 1840-60.

Coffee statistics, 1878-82; area;

The following statistics relate to the years 1878 and 1882. In 1877-78, there were under coffee—in Mysore, 128,438 acres, almost confined to the two Districts of Hassan and Kadur; in Madras, 58,988 acres, chiefly in Malabar, the Nílgiris, and Salem; in Coorg, 45,150 acres: total, 232,576 acres, exclusive of Travancore. In 1881-82, the latest year for which statistics are available for Mysore, the total area under coffee cultivation in that State was 159,165 acres; in Madras (in 1882-83), 61,481 acres; and in Coorg, 48,150 acres. The average out-turn is estimated at about 5 or 6 cwts. per acre of mature plant. The total Indian exports (from Madras)

Exports.

in 1877–78 were 33,399,352 lbs., valued at £1,355,643, of Coffee exports, 1878
which about one-half was consigned to the United Kingdom.
In 1878–79, the exports amounted to 38,336,000 lbs., valued
at £1,548,481. In 1882–83, the exports amounted to to 1883.
40,768,896 lbs., but the value had slightly decreased to
£1,419,131. The decrease in value was mainly due to a fall
in prices in London, owing to an overstocked market. Nearly
two-thirds of the coffee exports in 1882–83 were to the United
Kingdom, and over one-fourth to France.

Considerable judgment is required to select a suitable site Sites for coffee-gardens;
for a coffee-garden, for the shrub will only thrive under special
circumstances, which it is not very easy to anticipate before-
hand. It is essential that the spot should be sheltered from
the full force of the monsoon, and that the rainfall, though
ample, should not be excessive. The most desirable elevation elevation;
is between 2500 and 3500 feet above sea-level. The climate
must be warm and damp, conditions which are not conducive
to the health of Europeans. Almost any kind of forest land
will do, but the deeper the upper stratum of decomposed
vegetable matter the better.

The site chosen for a garden is first cleared with the axe, clearing;
of jungle and undergrowth, but sufficient timber-trees should
be left to furnish shade. In the month of December, the
berries are sown in a nursery, which has previously been
dug, manured, weeded, and watered as carefully as a garden.
Between June and August, the seedlings are planted out in
pits dug in prepared ground at regular intervals; an operation cultiva-tion;
which demands the utmost carefulness in order that the roots
may not be injured. In the first year, weeding only is
required; in the second year, the shrubs are 'topped,' to keep
them at an average height of about three feet; in the third
year they commence to bear, but it is not until the seventh
or eighth year that the planter is rewarded by a full crop.
The season for blossoming is March and April, when the
entire shrub burgeons in a snowy expanse of flower, with a
most delicate fragrance. Gentle showers or heavy mists at
this season contribute greatly to the fecundity of the blossoms.

The crop ripens in October and November. The berries picking;
are picked by hand, and collected in baskets to be 'pulped' on pulping;
the spot. This operation is performed by means of a revolving
iron cylinder, fixed against a breastwork at such an interval that
only the 'beans' proper pass through, while the husks are
rejected. The beans are then left to ferment for about twenty-
four hours, when their saccharine covering is washed off.

Coffee;

After drying in the sun for six or eight days, they are ready to be put in bags and despatched from the garden. But before being shipped, they have yet to be prepared for the home market. This is done at large coffee-works, to be found at the western ports and in the interior of Mysore. The berries are

peeling.

here 'peeled' in an iron trough by broad iron wheels, worked by steam power; and afterwards 'winnowed,' graded, and sorted for the market.

Tea.

The cultivation of tea in India commenced within the memory of men still living, and the industry now surpasses even indigo as a field for European capital. Unlike coffee-planting, the enterprise owes its origin to the initiation of Government, and it was slow to attract the attention of the natives. Early travellers reported that the tea-plant was indigenous to the southern valleys of the Himálayas; but they were mistaken in the identity of the shrub, which was the

Home of the tea-plant, Assam.

Osyris nepalensis. The real tea (Thea viridis), a plant akin to the camellia, grows wild in Assam, being commonly found throughout the hill tracts between the valleys of the Brahma-putra and the Bárak. It there sometimes attains the dimensions of a large tree; and from this, as well as from other indications, it has been plausibly inferred that Assam is the real home of the plant, which was thence introduced at a prehistoric date into China.

Discovered 1826.

The discovery of the tea-plant growing wild in Assam is generally attributed to two brothers named Bruce, who brought back specimens of the plant and the seed, after the conquest of the Province from the Burmese in 1826. In January 1834, under the Governor-Generalship of Lord William Bentinck, a committee was appointed 'for the purpose of submitting a plan for the introduction of tea-culture into India.' In the following year, plants and seed were brought from China, and widely distributed throughout the country. Government itself

State experiments, 1834-49.

undertook the formation of experimental plantations in Upper Assam, and in the sub-Himálayan Districts of Kumáun and Garhwál in the North-Western Provinces. A party of skilled manufacturers was brought from China, and the leaf which they prepared was favourably reported upon in the London market. Forthwith private speculation took up the enterprise.

Private Companies, 1839-51.

The Assam Tea Company, still the largest, was formed in 1839, and received from the Government an extensive grant of land, with the nurseries which had been already laid out. In Kumáun, retired members of the civil and military services came forward with equal eagerness. Many fundamental mistakes as to site, soil, and methods of manufacture were made in those early days, and bitter disappointment was the chief result. But while private enterprises languished, Government steadily persevered. It retained a portion of its Assam gardens in its own hands until 1849, when the Assam Company began to emerge from their difficulties. Government also carried on the business at Kumáun, under the able management of Dr. Jameson, as late as 1855.

The real progress of tea-planting on a great scale in Assam dates from about 1851, and was greatly assisted by the promulgation of the Waste-Land Rules of 1854. By 1859 there were already 51 gardens in existence, owned by private individuals; and the enterprise had extended from its original head-quarters in Lakhimpur and Sibságar as far down the Brahmaputra as Kámrúp. In 1856 the tea-plant was discovered wild in the District of Cachar in the Bárak valley, and European capital was at once directed to that quarter. At about the same time, tea-planting was introduced into the neighbourhood of the Himálayan sanitarium of Dárjíling, among the Sikkim Himálayas. *Rapid progress, 1851–65. Cachar. Dárjíling.*

The success of these undertakings engendered a wild spirit of speculation in tea companies, both in India and at home, which reached its climax in 1865. The industry recovered but slowly from the effects of the disastrous crisis, and did not again reach a stable position until 1869. Since that date it has rapidly but steadily progressed, and has been ever opening new fields of enterprise. At the head of the Bay of Bengal in Chittagong District, side by side with coffee on the Nílgiri Hills, on the forest-clad slopes of Chutiá Nágpur, amid the low-lying jungle of the Bhután Dwárs, and even in Arakan, the energetic pioneers of tea-planting have established their industry. Different degrees of success may have rewarded them, but in few cases have they abandoned the struggle. The market for Indian tea is practically inexhaustible. There is no reason to suppose that all the suitable localities have yet been tried; and we may look forward to the day when India will not only rival, but supersede, China in her staple product. *Crisis of 1865. Subsequent history.*

The total exports of tea in 1877–78 from British Indian ports amounted to 33½ million lbs., valued at a little over 3 millions sterling. During the next five years the exports had risen to 58¼ million lbs. in 1882–83, valued at 3¾ millions sterling. The detailed figures for all India, including exports across the frontier by land, will be presently given. *Statistics of Indian tea, 1877–78 to 1882–83.*

The progress of the tea industry in the various Provinces may best be illustrated by a review of the statistics of the production in the two years 1877–78 and 1882–83.

Provincial statistics of tea, 1878. Assam.

In 1877–88, the total area taken up for tea in Assam, including both the Brahmaputra and the Bárak valleys, was 736,082 acres, of which 538,961 acres were fit for cultivation; the total number of separate estates was 1718; the total out-turn was 23,352,298 lbs., at the average rate of 286 lbs. per acre under mature plant.

Bengal.

In Bengal, the area taken up was 62,642 acres, of which 20,462 acres were under mature plant, including 18,120 acres in the single District of Dárjíling; the number of gardens was 221; the out-turn was 5,768,654 lbs., at the rate of 282 lbs. per acre under mature plant.

N.-W. Provinces.

In the North-Western Provinces there were, in 1876, 25 estates in the Districts of Kumáun and Garhwál, with an out-turn of 578,000 lbs., of which 350,000 lbs. were sold in India to Central Asian merchants; and in 1871, 19 estates in Dehra Dún, with 2024 acres under tea, and an out-turn of 297,828 lbs.

Punjab.

In the Punjab there were, in 1878, 10,046 acres under tea, almost entirely confined to Kángra District, with an out-turn of 1,113,106 lbs., or 111 lbs. per acre.

Madras.

In Madras, the area under tea on the Nílgiris was 3160 acres; the exports from the Presidency were 183,178 lbs., valued at £19,308.

Provincial statistics of tea, 1882–83.

In 1882–83, the area actually under cultivation in Assam was 178,851 acres, of which 156,707 acres were under mature, and 22,144 acres under immature plant. Besides the area already occupied with tea, some 600,000 acres have been taken up for plantation purposes, and immense tracts yet untouched are still available. The present (1884) depressed state of the tea market, due, it is said, to over-production and attention to quantity rather than to quality, has, however, for the present checked the further appropriation of land for tea.

Assam.

The total out-turn from 1017 tea estates in Assam in 1882–83 is returned at 45,472,941 lbs., of which 28,089,805 lbs. were manufactured in the Brahmaputra valley or Assam proper, and 17,383,136 lbs. in the Surmá valley Districts of Cachar and Sylhet. Average out-turn, 290 lbs. per acre of mature plant. The figures given above for 1882–83 show a larger area under plant, and a very considerable increase in out-turn, over that of any previous year. Approximate value of tea exports from Assam into Bengal, £2,232,524. In Bengal the area under tea cultivation in 1882–83 was 48,091 acres, of which 36,079 acres were under mature, and

12,012 acres under immature plant. There were also 46,093 Bengal. acres taken up for tea, but not actually under plant. The total number of plantations was 300, with an out-turn of 11,170,564 lbs., being at the rate of 309 lbs. per acre of mature plant. More than three-fourths of the Bengal tea come from Dárjíling and Jalpaigurí Districts, on the lower slopes or submontane tracts of the Himálayas. The cultivation, however, is rapidly extending in other localities, as in Chittagong, on the east coast of the Bay of Bengal, and in the elevated plateau of Chutiá Nágpur. In the Punjab, out of Punjab. 11,058 acres under tea in 1882–83, no fewer than 10,075 acres were in Kángra District. The total out-turn in 1882–83 is not returned, but may be estimated at about a million lbs. In Madras, 5337 acres were under tea in 1882–83, but the Madras. out-turn is not stated, although the exports amounted to 309,548 lbs., valued at £32,905.

The following figures exhibit the exports of tea in 1878 and Tea 1883. In 1877–78, the total export of tea by sea from British exports, India amounted to 33,656,715 lbs., valued at £3,061,867. In 1883. 1882–83 the amount was 58,233,345 lbs., valued at £3,738,842. With the exception of Madras, which exported 309,548 lbs. of tea in 1882, valued at £32,905, and Chittagong, at which an export trade in tea has sprung up, the whole exports of Indian tea are shipped from Calcutta. The bulk of the tea goes to the United Kingdom, which absorbed 53,415,603 lbs., valued at £3,389,406, from Bengal in 1882–83. The Calcutta Tea Syndicate, established a few years ago with a view to opening new markets for Indian tea, has succeeded in establishing a firm, and it is hoped an increasing trade in tea with the Australian colonies and the United States. Exports to Australia, which in 1881–82 amounted to 871,913 lbs., valued at £63,404, were forced up in 1882–83 to 2,713,268 lbs., valued at £177,167. Similarly, the exports to the United States increased from 195,686 lbs., valued at £14,675 in 1881–82, to 671,264 lbs., valued at £50,988 in 1882–83. The effect of this sudden expansion of trade, however, was to temporarily overstock the market, and shipments in some cases resulted in a loss. The trans-frontier export from the Punjab into Central Asia has steadily decreased of late years; and in 1882–83, the exports of Indian tea across the Punjab frontier was only 488,200 lbs., valued at £29,924, as against an export of 1,217,840 lbs., valued at £181,634, in 1877–78.

Excluding the figures given for Madras, the whole of the Port of Indian tea is shipped from the port of Calcutta, and shipment.

almost the whole was, till recently, sent to the United Kingdom.

Tea culti-vation.
The processes of cultivation and manufacture are very similar throughout the whole of India, with the exception that in Upper India the leaf is prepared as green tea for the markets of Central Asia. Three main varieties are recognised—Assam,

Varieties of the tea-plant.
China, and hybrid. The first is the indigenous plant, some-times attaining the dimensions of a tree; yielding a strong and high-priced tea, but difficult to rear. The China variety, originally imported from that country, is a short bushy shrub, yielding a comparatively weak tea and a small out-turn per acre. The third variety is a true hybrid, formed by crossing the two other species. It combines the qualities of both in vary-ing proportions, and is the kind most sought after by planters.

Seed.
In all cases, the plant is raised from seed, which in size and appearance resembles the hazel-nut. The seeds are sown in carefully prepared nurseries in December and January, and at first require to be kept shaded. About April, the seedlings are sufficiently grown to be transplanted, an operation which continues into July.

Sites for tea-gardens.
The site selected for a tea-garden should be well-drained and comparatively elevated land; as it is essential that water should not lodge round the roots of the plants. In Assam, which may be taken as the typical tea district, the most favourite situation is the slopes of low hills, that everywhere rise above the marshy valleys. On the summit may be seen the neat bungalow of the planter, lower down the coolie lines, while the tea bushes are studded in rows with mathematical

Soil.
precision all round the sides. The best soil is virgin forest land, rich in the decomposed vegetable matter of ages. Great pains are expended to prevent this fertile mould from being washed away by the violence of the tropical rains. In bringing new land into condition, the jungle should be cut down in December, and burned on the spot in February. The ground is then cleaned by the plough or the hoe, and marked out for the seedlings by means of stakes planted at regular intervals of about 4 feet from each other.

Work of a tea-garden;
For the first two years, the work of the planter is to keep the young shrubs clear of weeds. Afterwards, it is neces-sary to prune the luxuriance of the bushes in the cold season every year. The prunings should be buried round the roots of the plant for manure. The plants begin to come into bearing in the third year, and gradually reach their maximum

'flushes;'
yield in their tenth year. The produce consist of the 'flushes'

or successive shoots of young leaves and buds, which first
appear in the beginning of the rainy season. There are
from five to seven full flushes in the season from March to
November. The bushes are picked about every ten days by picking;
women and children, who are paid by weight on bringing their
baskets to the factory, when the operation of manufacture
forthwith begins.

The leaf is first spread out lightly on trays or mats in 'wither-
order that it may 'wither,' *i.e.* become limp and flaccid. ing;'
Under favourable conditions, this result is effected in a single
night; but sometimes the natural process has to be accelerated
by exposure to the sun or by means of artificial heat. The
next operation is known as 'rolling,' performed either by the rolling;
manual labour of coolies or by machinery. The object of
this is to twist and compress the leaf into balls, and set up
fermentation. The final stage is to arrest fermentation by drying;
drying, which may be effected in many ways, usually by the
help of machinery. The entire process of manufacture after
'withering,' does not take more than about four hours and a
half. All that now remains is to sort the tea in sieves, sorting.
according to size and quality, thus distinguishing the various
grades from Flowery Pekoe to Broken Congou, and to pack it
for shipment in the well-known tea chests.

The introduction of the quinine-yielding cinchona into Cinchona.
India is a remarkable example of success rewarding the in- Clements
defatigable exertions of a single man. When Mr. Clements Markham
Markham undertook the task of transporting the seedlings from 1860.
South America to India in 1860, cinchona had never before been
reared artificially. The experiment in arboriculture has not
only been successfully conducted, but it has proved remunerative
from a pecuniary point of view. A cheap febrifuge has been
provided for the fever-stricken population of the Indian plains,
while the surplus bark sold in Europe more than repays interest
upon the capital expended. These results have been produced
from an expenditure of about £100,000.

The head-quarters of cinchona cultivation in Southern Nílgiri
India are on the Nílgiri Hills, where Government owns four planta-
plantations, from which seeds and plants are annually tions.
distributed to the public in large quantities; and there are
already several private plantations, rivalling the Government
estates in area, and understood to be very valuable pro-
perties. The varieties of cinchona most commonly cultivated Varieties.
are C. officinalis and C. succirubra; but experiments are

being conducted with C. calisaya, C. pubescens, C. lanceolata, and C. pitayensis. Now that the success of the enterprise is secure, the Madras Government is curtailing its own operations. No fresh land is being taken up, but the plantations are kept free from weeds. The quinologist's department has been abolished, and the bark is sold in its raw state.

Spread of cinchona ; From the central establishment of the Government on the Nílgiris, cinchona has been introduced into the Palni Hills in Madura District, into the Wainád, and into the State of Travancore. The total area under cinchona in Government and private plantations in 1882–83 was 2607 acres. Plantations have also been opened by Government near in Southern India ; Merkára in Coorg, on the Bába Budan Hills in Mysore, and in Tsit-taung (Sitang) District in British Burma. Failure has attended the experiments made at Mahábaleshwar in the Bombay Presidency, and at Nongklao in the Khásí Hills, Assam.

in Bengal. But the success of the Government plantation at Dárjíling, in Northern Bengal, rivals that of the original plantation on the Nílgiris. The area has been gradually extended, and the bark is manufactured into quinine on the spot by a Government quinologist. The species mostly grown is C. succirubra, which yields a red-coloured bark, rich in its total yield of alkaloids, but comparatively poor in quinine proper. Efforts are being made to increase the cultivation of C. calisaya, which yields the more valuable bark ; but this species is difficult to propagate.

The febrifuge, as issued by the Bengal Government, is in the form of a white powder, containing the following alkaloids :—
Cinchona. Alkaloids. Quinine, cinchonidine, cinchonine, quinamine, and what is known as amorphous alkaloid. It has been authoritatively described as 'a perfectly safe and efficient substitute for quinine in all cases of ordinary intermittent fever.' It has been substituted for imported quinine, in the proportion of three-fourths to one-fourth, at all the Government dispensaries, by which measure alone an economy of more than £20,000 a year has been achieved ; and it is now eagerly sought after by private druggists from every part of the country.

Cinchona statistics, 1877–78. The following show the out-turn and financial results of the two large Government plantations in 1877–78 and in 1882–83 :—In 1877–78, the crop on the Nílgiris gave 138,808 lbs. of bark, of which 132,951 lbs. were shipped to England, and the rest supplied to the Madras and Bombay medical departments. At Dárjíling, the crop in 1877–78 amounted to 344,225 lbs.

of bark, which was all handed over to the quinologist, and yielded 5162 lbs. of the febrifuge.

In 1882–83, the four Government plantations on the Nílgiri Hills comprised a total area of 847 acres, with 765,763 full-grown plants. The total out-turn of bark (exclusive of stocks in hand) was 129,713 lbs. The quantity shipped to the home market was 62,518 lbs., realizing £9768, while 69,327 lbs. were sold locally by public auction, realizing £10,639, or an average of 3s. 1½d. per lb. The total proceeds from the Nílgiri plantations in 1882–83, including sale of seeds, plants, etc., was £20,842 ; expenditure, £8335, leaving a profit of £12,507. In the Government plantations in Dárjíling District, the area in 1882 was 2294 acres, with 4,711,168 full-grown plants. The out-turn of the year, 396,980 lbs. of dry bark, was the heaviest ever yielded. By far the greater proportion was converted locally into cinchona febrifuge by the Government quinologist, while about 42,000 lbs. of bark were forwarded to London at the request of the Secretary of State, to be there converted into various forms of febrifuge, and returned to India for trial by the Medical Department. The revenue derived from the Dárjíling sales to the public, to the medical and other departments, and from sale of seeds, plants, etc., amounted to £15,280 in 1882–83, the operations of the year resulting in a direct profit of £6628, equal to a dividend of 6½ per cent. on the capital outlay. Total profit from the Nílgiri and Dárjíling plantations in 1882–83, £19,135.

Cinchona statistics, 1882–83.

Profits of cinchona, 1882–83.

These profits, however, do not represent the whole of the gains. In Bengal alone, the cost of an equal quantity of quinine would have amounted to £40,132, while the cost of the febrifuge produced was only £6898, showing a saving of £33,234. The total saving effected since the opening of the factories up till the end of the year 1882–83, is stated to be £235,000, or more than double the cost of the plantations. Besides the Government cinchona estates, a number of private plantations have been established, covering an area of about 2500 acres, with about 2⅔ millions of full-grown plants.

Indirect profits.

Sericulture in India is a stationary, if not a declining industry. The large production in China, Japan, and the Mediterranean countries controls the European markets ; and on an average of years, the imports of raw silk into India exceed the exports. The East India Company from the first took great pains to foster the production of silk. As early as 1767, two years after the grant of the financial administration of Bengal had been conferred upon the Company, we find

Silk.

The Company's early silk-factories.

the Governor, Mr. Verelst, personally urging the *zamíndárs*, gathered at Murshidábád for the ceremony of the *Punyá*, 'to give all possible encouragement to the cultivation of mulberry.'

Italian reelers, 1769. In 1769, a colony of reelers was brought from Italy to teach the system followed in the filatures at Novi. The first silk prepared after the Italian method reached England in 1772, and Bengal silk soon became an important article of export. Similar efforts started at Madras in 1793 were abandoned after a trial of five years. The silk-worm is said to have been

Tipú's experiments, 1795. introduced into Mysore by Tipu Sultán, and for many years continued to prosper. But recently the Mysore worms have been afflicted by an epidemic ; and despite the enterprise of an Italian gentleman, who imported fresh breeds from Japan, the business has dwindled to insignificance.

Bengal factories, 1799-1833. Bengal has always been the chief seat of mulberry cultivation. When the trading operations of the Company ceased in 1833, they owned 11 head factories in that Province, each supplied by numerous filatures, to which the cultivators brought in their cocoons. The annual export of raw silk from Calcutta was then about 1 million lbs. But in those days the weaving of silk formed a large portion of the business of the factories. In 1779, Rennel wrote that at Kasímbázár alone about 400,000 lbs. weight of silk was consumed in the local European factories. In 1802, Lord Valentia describes Jangipur as 'the greatest silk station of the Company, with 600 furnaces, and giving employment to 3000 persons.' Under the new Charter of 1833, the Company's silk trade and its commerce with China were to cease. But it could not suddenly throw out of employment the numbers of people employed upon silk production, and its factories were not entirely disposed of until 1837.

Silk area of Bengal. When the Company abandoned the trade on its own account, sericulture was taken up by private enterprise, and still clings to its old head-quarters. At the present time, the cultivation of the mulberry is mainly confined to the Rájsháhí and Bardwán Divisions of Lower Bengal. This branch of agriculture, together with the rearing of the silk-worms, is conducted by the peasantry themselves, who are free to follow or abandon the business. The destination of the cocoons is twofold. They may either be sent to small native filatures, where the silk is roughly wound, and usually consumed in the hand-looms of the country ; or they may be brought to the great European factories, which generally use steam machinery, and consign their produce direct to Europe.

The exports vary considerably from year to year, being

determined partly by the local yield, and still more by the prices ruling in Europe. The following are the returns for 1877-78 and 1882-83. In 1877-78, about 1½ million lbs. of silk were exported, viz. :—Raw silk, 658,000 lbs. ; *chasan*, or the outer covering of the cocoon, 823,000 lbs. ; the aggre- gate value was £750,439. In the same year, the imports of raw silk (chiefly received at Bombay and Rangoon) were a little over 2 million lbs., valued at £678,069. By 1882-83, the imports of raw and manufactured silk had considerably exceeded the exports of the Indian production. In that year the exports of raw silk amounted to only 665,838 lbs., valued at £596,836, besides silk manufactures valued at £306,928. On the other hand, the imports of foreign silk into British Indian ports in the same year amounted to 2,386,150 lbs., valued at £1,074,156, besides 9,671,261 yards of manufactured silk, and 2989 lbs. of silk thread, valued at £977,768. Silk statistics, 1878-1883.

The cultivation of the mulberry is chiefly carried on in the Ben- gal Districts of Rájsháhí, Bográ, Maldah, Murshidábád, Bírbhum, Bardwán, and Midnapur. No complete statistics are available, but in Rájsháhí alone the area under mulberry is estimated at 80,000 acres. The mulberry grown as food for the silk-worms is not the fruit-tree with which we are familiar in England, but a comparatively small shrub. Any fairly good land that does not grow rice will grow mulberry. But the shrubs must be pre- served from floods ; and the land generally requires to be arti- ficially raised in square plots, with broad trenches between, like a chess-board. The mulberry differs from most Indian crops in being a perennial, *i.e.* it will yield its harvest of leaves for several years in succession, provided that care be taken to preserve it. It is planted between the months of November and January. Three growths of silk-worms are usually obtained in the year—in November, March, and August. Mulberry cultivation in Bengal.

Besides the silk-worm proper (Bombyx mori), fed upon the mulberry, several other species of silk-yielding worms abound in the jungles of India, and are utilized, and in some cases domesticated, by the natives. Throughout Assam, especially, an inferior silk is produced in this way, which has from time immemorial furnished the common dress of the people. These 'wild silks' are known to commerce under the generic name of *tasar* or *tusser*, but they are really the produce of several distinct varieties of worm, fed on many different trees. The worm that yields *tasar* silk in Chutiá Nágpur has been identified as the caterpillar of Antherœa paphia. When wild, it feeds indiscriminately upon the *sál* (Shorea robusta), the Jungle silks ; (*tasar*). in Bengal ;

baer (Zizyphus jujuba), and other forest trees; but in a state of semi-domestication, it is exclusively reared upon the *ásan* (Terminalia tomentosa), which grows conveniently in clumps. The cocoons are sometimes collected in the jungle, but more frequently bred from an earlier generation of jungle cocoons. The worms require constant attention while feeding, to protect them from crows and other birds. They give three crops in the year—in August, November, and May—of which the second is by far the most important.

in Central Provinces; The *tasar* silk-worm is also found and utilized throughout the Central Provinces, in the hills of the Bombay Presidency, and along the southern slopes of the Himálayas. During the past twenty years, repeated attempts have been made to raise this industry out of its precarious condition, and to introduce *tasar* silk into the European market. That the raw material abounds is certain ; but the great difficulty is to obtain it in a state which will be acceptable to European manufacturers. Native spun *tasar* thread is only fit for native hand-looms. In

in Assam. Assam, two distinct qualities of silk are made, the *eriá* and *mugá*. The former is obtained from the cocoons of Phalœna cynthia ; and the worm is fed, as the native name implies, upon the leaves of the castor-oil plant (Ricinus communis). This variety may be said to be entirely domesticated, being reared indoors. *Mugá* silk is obtained from the cocoons of Saturnia assamungis. The moth, which is remarkable for its size, is found wild in the jungle ; but the breed is so far domesticated that cocoons are brought from one part of the Province to another, and the *súm* tree is artificially propagated to supply the worms with food.

Lac. The collection of lac is in a somewhat similar position to that of *tasar* silk. The lac insect abounds on certain jungle trees in every part of the country ; and from time immemorial it has been collected by the wild tribes, in order to be worked up into lacquered ware. But European enterprise has not yet placed the industry upon a stable and an organized basis. Although lac is to be found everywhere, foreign exportation is almost entirely confined to Calcutta, which draws its supplies from the hills of Chutiá Nágpur, and in a less degree from Assam and Mírzápur in the North-Western Provinces. Lac is known to commerce both as a gum (shell-lac) and as a

Lac statistics, 1878-1883. dye. In 1878, the total exports of lac of all kinds were 104,717 cwts., valued at £362,244. In 1879, the total exports were 91,985 cwts., valued at £300,072. In 1882-83, the exports of lac of all kinds was 138,844 cwts., of the value of £699,113.

Lac (*lák*) is a cellular, resinous incrustation of a deep orange Descrip-
colour, secreted by an insect (Coccus lacca) round the branches tion of lac.
of various trees, chiefly *kúsúm* (Schleichera trijuga), *palás*
(Butea frondosa), *pipal* (Ficus religiosa), and *baer* (Zizyphus
jujuba). The principal component is resin, forming about 60
or 70 per cent., from which is manufactured the shell-lac of Shell-lac.
commerce. Lac-dye is obtained from the small cells of the Lac-dye.
incrustation, and is itself a portion of the body of the female
insect. The entire incrustation, while still adhering to the
twig, is called stick-lac. In order to obtain the largest quantity Stick-lac.
of dye, the stick-lac should be gathered before the young come
out, which happens twice in the year—in January and July.
The dye is first extracted by repeated processes of washing
and straining, while the shell-lac is worked up from what
remains in a hot and semi-liquid state.

For all articles in which a fast colour is not required, lac-dye Uses of
can never compete with the cheaper and less permanent lac-dye.
aniline dyes; while for more lasting colours, cochineal is
preferred. Lac-dye, however, is said to be superior even to
cochineal in resisting the action of human perspiration; and
it is probable that in the event of the supply of cochineal
falling off, lac-dye might be used in its stead to produce the
regimental scarlet. It has largely replaced cochineal of late
years in dyeing officers' coats; and a further extension of its use
for similar purposes seems possible. The chief establishment
in India for manufacturing lac was for long near Dorandá,
in Lohárdagá District, Chutiá Nágpur, to which stick-lac is
brought in from all the country round as far as the Central
Provinces. The annual out-turn is about 6000 cwts. of shell-
lac, made from double that quantity of raw material. In
1877–78, this factory had for a time to cease working, owing
to the depressed state of the market in Europe.

The efforts of Government to improve the native methods Model
of agriculture, by the establishment of model farms under farms.
skilled European supervision, have not been generally successful. In too many cases, the skilled agriculturists from
Europe have been gardeners rather than farmers. In other
cases, believing only in their own maxims of high cultivation
—deep ploughing, subsoil drainage, manuring, and rotation
of crops—they have despised the ancient rules of native
experience, and have not adapted their Western learning to
the circumstances of a tropical country. Nevertheless, many

valuable experiments have been made, and much information, chiefly of a negative character, has been gained.

The small success attained.   The Government model farms have been abandoned in Bengal, in Assam, and in the Punjab.   In the North-Western Provinces, the propagation of flowers, fruits, vegetables, and trees is still prosecuted (1885).   In Bombay there are (or were lately) three model farms ; and in the Central Provinces one, on which the common crops of the country are raised at a loss.   The Saidápet (Sydapet) farm, near the city of Madras, is the only establishment at which experiments have been conducted on a scale and with a perseverance sufficient to yield results of value.

Saidápet Farm.   This farm was started by a former Governor, Sir William Denison, in 1865, and has been for the past thirteen years under the able management of Mr. Robertson, Agricultural Reporter to the Madras Government.   It covered in 1884 an area of 300 acres in a ring fence, of which 139 acres were under crop, and 36 acres under timber, chiefly casuarina.   Important experiments have been made, of which some produced encouraging results, indicating the general direction in which improvements may be effected in the agricultural practice of the Presidency.   It has been proved that many of the common ' dry crops ' can be profitably cultivated for fodder at all seasons of the year.   Those most strongly recommended are yellow *cholam* (Sorghum vulgare), guinea grass (Panicum jumentosum), and horse-gram (Dolichus biflorus).   Sugar-cane and rice also yield excellent fodder, when cut green.   Attention has been given to subsoil drainage, deep ploughing, the fertilizing powers of various manures, and the proper utilization of irrigation water.

It is right to mention, however, that doubts are entertained as to whether the results of the experiments at the Madras Government Farm are equal to the outlay upon them.   [Since these pages went to press, the farming operations at Saidápet have been given up, except so far as required for the practical instruction of agricultural pupils.]   A School of Agriculture has been established at Saidápet, in connection with the model farm, with subordinate branches in the Districts, so as to diffuse as widely as possible the agricultural lessons that have been already learned.   At the end of 1882–83, the school was attended by 69 pupils.   In 1882–83, the expenditure on the farm was returned at £1083, as against receipts amounting to £559.   The expenditure on the School of Agriculture in the same year was £2484, against receipts amounting to only £33, 8s.

To many it seems doubtful whether such experiments can Is success possible? be made to yield profitable results. The *Hindu Patriot* put the case in very pithy words : 'The native cultivators have nothing to learn so far as non-scientific agriculture is concerned, and the adoption of scientific agriculture is wholly beyond their means.' If the only alternative lay between a strictly scientific and an altogether unscientific husbandry, a candid observer would have to concur in the *Hindu Patriot's* conclusion. But the choice is not thus limited. In England one little improvement takes place in one district, another small change for the better in another. Strictly scientific The problem of improved husbandry. farming trebles the produce ; a field which produces 730 lbs. of wheat without manure can be made to yield 2342 lbs. by manure. But the native of India has neither the capital nor the knowledge required to attain this result. If, therefore, the problem before him was to increase his crops threefold, even his best wishers might despair of his success. But the task before him is a much less ambitious one ; namely, to gradually increase by perhaps 10 or 20 per cent. the produce of his fields, and not by 300 per cent. at a stroke.

Wheat land in the North-Western Provinces, which now Out-turn of crops. gives only 840 lbs. an acre, yielded 1140 lbs. in the time of Akbar, and would be made to produce 1800 lbs. in East Norfolk. The average return of food-grains in India shows about 700 lbs. per acre ; in England, wheat averages over 1700 lbs. Mr. Hume, the late Secretary to the Government of India in its Department of Agriculture, declares, that ' with proper manuring and proper tillage, every acre, broadly speaking, of land in the country can be made to yield 30, 50, or 70 per cent. more of every kind of crop than it at present produces ; and with a fully corresponding increase in the profits of cultivation.'

The first impediment to better husbandry is the fewness and The three impediments: (1) Want of cattle. weakness of the cattle. ' Over a great portion of the Empire,' writes the late Secretary to the Agricultural Department in India, ' the mass of the cattle are starved for six weeks every year. The hot winds roar, every green thing has disappeared, no hot-weather forage is grown ; the last year's fodder has generally been consumed in keeping the well-bullocks on their legs during the irrigation of the spring crops ; and all the husbandman can do is just to keep his poor brutes alive on the chopped leaves of the few trees and shrubs he has access to, the roots of grass and herbs that he digs out of the edges of fields, and the like. In good years, he just succeeds ; in bad years, the weakly ones die of starvation. But then come the rains. Within the week, as though by magic, the burning sands are carpeted with rank, luscious herbage, the cattle *will* eat and over-eat; and millions die of one form or other of cattle disease, springing out of this starvation followed by sudden repletion with rank, juicy, immature herbage.' Mr. Hume estimates 'the average annual loss of cattle in India by preventable disease' at 10 million beasts, worth 7½ millions sterling. He complains that, up to the time when he wrote, no real attempt had been made to bring veterinary knowledge within reach of the people, or to organize a system of village plantations which would feed their cattle through the summer. The Department of Agriculture, as re-established under Lord Ripon's Government, has endeavoured to remedy these omissions, particularly in regard to the diffusion of veterinary knowledge. The statistics and breeds of agricultural stock will be given on a subsequent page.

(2) Want of manure. The second impediment to improved husbandry is the want of manure. If there were more stock, there would be more manure; and the absence of firewood compels the people to use up even the droppings of their cattle for fuel. Under such circumstances, agriculture ceases to be the manufacture of food, and becomes a mere spoliation of the soil. Forage crops, such as lucerne, guinea-grass, and the great stemmed millets, might furnish a large supply of cattle food per acre. Government is considering whether their cultivation could not be promoted by reducing the irrigation rates on green fodder crops. A system of village plantations would not only supply firewood, but would yield leaves and an undergrowth of fodder sufficient to tide the cattle over their six weeks' struggle for life each summer. In some Districts, Government has land of its own which it could thus plant; in others, it is only a sleeping partner in the soil. In Switzerland, the occupiers of *allmends*, or communal lands, are, at least in some cantons, compelled by law to keep up a certain number of trees. It seems a fair question whether plantations ought not in many parts of India to be made an incident of the land tenure. They would go far to solve the two fundamental difficulties of Indian agriculture—the loss of cattle, and the want of manure. The system of State Forestry at present pursued will be described in a subsequent section.

Utilization of manure. Meanwhile, the natives set an increasing value on manure. The great cities are being converted from centres of disease into sources of food-supply. For a time, caste prejudices stood in the way of utilizing the night-soil. 'Five years ago,' writes the Secretary to the Poona Municipality, 'agriculturists would not touch the *poudrette* when prepared, and could not be induced to take it away at even a nominal charge. At present, the out-turn of manure is not enough to keep pace with the demand, and the peasants buy it up from four to six months in advance.' At Amritsar, in the Punjab, 30,000 donkey-loads were sold in one year. A great margin still exists for economy, both in the towns and villages; but the husbandman is becoming more alive to the utilization of every source of manure, and his prejudices are gradually giving way under the stern pressure of facts.

The third impediment to improved agriculture in India is (3) Want the want of water. Sir J. Caird believes that if only one-third of water. of the cultivated area were irrigated, India would be secure against famine. An extension of irrigation would alone suffice to raise the food-supply annually by more than $1\frac{1}{2}$ per cent. in most years; and thus more than keep pace with the general increase of the population. Since India passed to the Crown, great progress has been made in this direction. Money has been invested by millions of pounds; 200 millions of acres are now under cultivation; and in the five British Provinces which require it most, 28 per cent. of the cultivated area, or say one-third, was in 1883 artificially supplied with water. Those Provinces are the Punjab, the North-West, Oudh, Sind, and Madras. Looking to what has of late years been done, and to what yet remains to be done by wells and petty works with the aid of loans from the State, we may still reckon on a vast increase of food from irrigation. The pecuniary and statistical aspects of irrigation will be dealt with hereafter.

Having thus summarized the three impediments to improved husbandry, it may be profitable to examine in detail the three subjects immediately connected with them, namely, the Agricultural Stock of India, Forests, and Irrigation.

Throughout the whole of India, excepting in Sind and the Agriculwestern Districts of the Punjab, horned cattle are the only tural beasts used for ploughing. The well-known humped breed stock. of cattle predominates everywhere, being divided into many varieties. Owing partly to unfavourable conditions of climate and soil, partly to the insufficiency of grazing ground, and partly to the want of selection in breeding, the general condition of the cattle is miserably poor. As cultivation advances,

Want of fodder.

the area of waste land available for grazing steadily diminishes, and the prospects of the poor beasts are becoming worse rather than better. Their only hope lies in the introduction of fodder crops as a regular stage in the agricultural course.

Famous breeds.

There are, however, some fine breeds which are carefully fostered. In Mysore, the *amrit mahál*, a breed said to have been formed by Haidar Alí for military purposes, is kept up by the local authorities. In the Madras Districts of Nellore and Karnúl, the indigenous breed has been greatly improved under the stimulus of cattle shows and prizes, founded by British officials. In the Central Provinces there is a high-class breed of trotting bullocks, in great demand for wheeled carriages. The large and handsome oxen of Gujarát (Guzerát) in Bombay, and of Hariáná in the Punjab, are excellently adapted for drawing heavy loads in a sandy soil. The statistics of live stock for various Provinces of India will be given in the form of a table on p. 523.

The worst cattle are to be found always in deltaic tracts,

Buffaloes.

but here their place is to a large extent taken by buffaloes. These last are more hardy than ordinary cattle, their character being maintained by crossing the cows with wild bulls, and their milk yields the best *ghí*, or clarified butter. In British Burma, the returns show that the total number of buffaloes is nearly equal to that of cows and bullocks. Along the valley of the Indus, and in the sandy desert which stretches

Camels.

into Rájputána, camels supersede cattle for all agricultural operations. In the Punjab, the total number of camels was 125,584 in 1883.

Horses.

The breed of horses has generally deteriorated since the demand for the native strains, for military purposes, declined upon the establishment of British supremacy. In Bengal proper, and in Madras, it may be broadly said that native breeds do not exist. The chief breeds in Bombay are those of the Deccan and of Káthiáwár, in both of which Provinces Government maintains establishments of stallions. The Punjab, however, is the chief source of remounts for our Native cavalry ; the total number of horses in that Province in 1883 being returned at 76,238, in addition to 33,773 ponies. About the beginning of the present century, a stud department was

Government studs.

organized by Government to breed horses for the use of the Bengal army. This system was abolished as extravagant and inefficient by Lord Mayo in 1871. Remounts are now obtained in the open market ; but the Government still maintains a number of stallions, including horses imported from England, or half English bred, and high-class Arabs. Excellent horses are bred by the Baluchí tribes along the western frontier.

Horse fairs are held yearly in the various Provinces of India. The principal ones in the Punjab, the part of India which furnishes the main supply of the Native cavalry remounts, are at Ráwalpindi, Dera Ghází Khán, Jhang, Dera Ismáil Khán, and Muzaffargarh. The number of horses exhibited varies greatly from year to year ; but about 5000 may be expected for sale at these five fairs. Prizes to the amount of about £1500 are awarded. The average price of remounts for the Native cavalry has risen of late years from £17 to about £22. Horse shows are also held at Sháhpur, Gujrát, Rohtak, and Jalálábád, which are ordinarily well attended and successful. In recent years, much attention has been paid in the Punjab to the breeding of mules for military purposes ; and the value of these animals has been conspicuously proved in the course of the operations in Afghánistán. In 1882–83, the Government maintained 152 donkey stallions, of which 34 were imported from Europe, 74 from Arabia, and the remainder were of various native breeds. Some of the mules bred reach the height of 15 hands. The best ponies come from Burma, Manipur (the original home of the game of polo), and Bhután.

The catching of wild elephants is now either a Government monopoly, or is conducted under strict Government supervision. The chief source of supply is the north-east frontier, especially the range of hills running between the valleys of the Brahmaputra and the Bárak. During the year 1877–78, about 260 elephants were captured in the Province of Assam, yielding £3600 to Government. Of these, 170 were captured by lessees of the privilege, and 90 by the Government *kheddá* department. In 1882–83, the number of elephants caught was 475, yielding a Government revenue of £8573. Elephants are also captured to a smaller extent in the mountains bordering Orissa ; in Mysore and Coorg, among the Western Gháts ; and in Burma, for the timber trade. They are used by Government for transport, and are eagerly bought up by native chiefs and landowners as objects of display. The wild elephant will be treated of in the subsequent chapter on Indian zoology.

Sheep and goats are commonly reared in the wilder parts of the country for the sake of their wool. Both their weight for the butcher and their yield of wool are exceedingly low. In Mysore, and at the Saidápet farm, near Madras, attempts have been made to improve the breed of sheep by

Horse fairs.

Mules.

Ponies.

Elephants.

Numbers caught, 1878 and 1883.

Sheep and goats.

Pigs.

crossing with merino rams, although without much success, except at Saidápet. Pigs of great size and most repulsive appearance are everywhere reared, but are eaten only by the lowest of out-castes.

Statistics of Live Stock.

The table on the opposite page summarizes the information collected regarding live stock in those parts of India where the statistics can be obtained with some approximation to accuracy. But they must be regarded as intelligent estimates rather than as verified returns.

Forests.

The forests of India are beginning to receive their proper share of attention, both as a source of natural wealth and as a department of the administration. Up to about twenty-

Destruction of jungle.

five years ago, the destruction of forests by timber-cutters, by charcoal-burners, and above all, by nomadic cultivation, was allowed to go on everywhere unchecked. The extension of tillage was considered as the chief care of Government, and no regard was paid to the improvident waste of jungle on all sides. But as the pressure of population on the soil became more dense, and the construction of railways increased the demand for fuel, the question of forest conservation forced itself into notice. It was recognised that the inheritance of future generations was being recklessly sacrificed. The importance of forests, as affecting the general meteorology of a country, was also being taught by bitter experience in Europe. On many grounds, therefore, it became necessary to preserve what remained of the forests in India, and to repair the mischief of previous neglect, even at considerable expense.

Growth of the Forest Department, 1844–67.

In 1844 and 1847, the subject was actively taken up by the Governments of Bombay and Madras. In 1864, Dr. Brandis was appointed Inspector-General of Forests to the Government of India; and in the following year the first Forest Act passed the Legislature (No. VII. of 1865). The regular training of candidates for the Forest Department in the schools of France and Germany dates from 1867. In the interval which has since elapsed, sound principles of forest administration have been laid down and gradually enforced. Indiscriminate timber-cutting has been prohibited; the burning of the jungle by the hill tribes has been confined within bounds; large areas have been surveyed and demarcated; plantations have been laid out; and forest conservation has become a reality in India.

From a botanical point of view, the forests may be divided

[*Sentence continued on page* 524.

Approximate Numbers of Live Stock and of certain Agricultural Implements in Six Indian Provinces in 1882-83.

	Madras.	Bombay and Sind.	Punjab.	Central Provinces.	Berar.	British Burma.
Bullocks,	3,687,782	3,344,518	} 6,121,417	} 5,356,477	} 1,540,007	917,861
Cows,	3,453,129	2,321,728				687,360
Buffaloes,	1,483,938	1,534,053	...		299,064	
Horses,	7,941	} 137,774	} 76,238	13,335	8,746	} 8,366
Ponies,	30,189		33,773	90,514	27,426	
Donkeys,	124,731	78,179	251,068	24,660	27,707	...
Elephants,	481	...	...	...	4	1,685
Camels,	50	...	125,584	59	996	...
Sheep and Goats,	8,941,813	3,470,692	3,864,013	828,592	404,006	25,782
Pigs,	254,557	...	41,161	123,439	5,515	136,353
Carts,	313,528	412,751	92,855	313,637	119,562	212,380
Ploughs,	2,013,011	1,088,357	1,803,278	892,769	109,687	356,903

Sentence continued from p. 522.]

Indian timber-trees.

into several distinct classes, determined by varying conditions of soil, climate, and rainfall. The king of Indian forest trees is the teak (Tectona grandis), which rivals the British oak as

Teak.

material for ship-building. The home of the teak is in the Bombay Gháts, Kánara, Cochin, Travancore, and the Burmese peninsula, where it flourishes under an excessive rainfall.

Sál.

Second to teak is the *sál* (Shorea robusta), which is indigenous along the lower slopes of the Himálayas from the Sutlej basin east to Assam, among the hills of Central India, and in the Eastern Gháts down to the Godávarí river. On the Himálayas of North-Western India, the distinguishing timber-tree is

Deodárq.

the *deodára* (Cedrus Deodara) ; while on the North-Eastern Himálayan frontier its place is occupied by Pinus Kasya and other trees, such as oak and chestnut, of a temperate zone.

These noble trees supply the most valuable timber, and form the chief care of the Forest Department. But they are only the aristocracy of countless species, yielding timber,

South Indian forests.

firewood, and other products of value. In the south of the peninsula, the mountain range of the Western Gháts, from Travancore northwards into Kánara, is clothed with an inexhaustible wealth of still virgin forest. Here there are three

The three forest-belts.

separate vegetations. (1) An evergreen belt on the seaward face of the mountains, where grow the stately *pún* (Calophyllum inophyllum), valuable as spars for ships, the *anjalli* or wild jack (Artocarpus hirsuta), and a variety of ebony (Diospyros Ebenum). (2) A belt of mixed forest, varying from 10 to 40 miles in width, which yields teak, blackwood (Dalbergia latifolia), and Lagerstrœmia microcarpa, and here and there continuous avenues of lofty bamboos. (3) A dry belt, extending over the central plateau, in which the vegetation declines

Sandal-tree.

in size and abundance. The precious sandal-wood (Santalum album), limited almost entirely to Mysore and Kánara, thrives best on a stony soil, with a light rainfall. In the Bombay Presidency, the chief forest areas, excluding Kánara, are to be found in the mountainous extension of the Western Gháts, known as the Sahyádri range, and in the delta of the Indus in the outlying Province of Sind.

Sind forests.

The Sind river-valley forests present many peculiar features. They are locally reported to have been formed as game preserves by the Mírs or Musálmán rulers, and are divided into convenient blocks or *belás*, fringing the entire course of the Indus. Being absolute State property, their management is embarrassed by no difficulties, excepting those caused by the uncontrollable floods of the river. They furnish abundant firewood, but little timber of value, their chief produce being *babúl* (Acacia arabica), *bahán* (Populus euphratica), and tamarisk (Tamarix dioica). In the Punjab, the principal forests of *deodára* (Cedrus Deodara) lie beyond the British frontier, in the Himálayan valleys of the great rivers; but many of them have been leased from the bordering States, in order to secure a supply of firewood and railway sleepers. On the Punjab plains, the only woods are those growing on the *rákhs* or upland plateaux which rise between the converging river basins. The chief trees found here are varieties of Prosopis, Capparis, and Salvadora; but the Forest Department is now laying out more valuable plantations of *sissu* (Dalbergia Sissoo), *baer* (Zizyphus jujuba), and *kikar*. {.marginnote}Punjab forests.

The North-Western Provinces present the Himálayan type of forest in Kumáun and Garhwál, where the characteristic trees are the *chil* (Pinus excelsa) and *chir* (Pinus longifolia), with but little *deodára*. Farther west occurs a forest-belt of *sál*, which may be said to form the continuous boundary between Nepál and British territory. Owing to the facility of water communication and the neighbourhood of the great cities of Hindustán, these *sál* forests have long ago been stripped of their valuable timber, and are but slowly recovering under the care of the Forest Department. Oudh and Northern Bengal continue the general features of the North-Western Provinces; but the hill station of Dárjíling is surrounded by a flora of the temperate zone. {.marginnote}Forests of N.-W. Provinces, of Oudh and N. Bengal.

Calcutta has, from its foundation, drawn its supply of firewood from the inexhaustible jungles of the SUNDARBANS, which have recently been placed under forest conservancy rules. This tract, extending over 5000 square miles, is a dismal swamp, half land, half sea or fresh water, overgrown by an almost impenetrable jungle of timber-trees and underwood. The most valued wood is the *sundári* (Heretiera littoralis), which is said to give its name to the tract. Assam and Chittagong, like the Malabar coast and British Burma, still possess vast areas of virgin forest, although the more accessible tracts have been ruthlessly laid waste. Beside *sál* and Pinus Kasya, the timber-trees of Assam include *nahor* or *nágeswar* (Mesua ferrea), *súm* (Artocarpus Chaplasha), and *járul* (Lagerstrœmia Flos-Reginæ). Ficus elastica, yielding the caoutchouc of commerce, was formerly common, but now the supply is chiefly brought from beyond the frontier. Plantations of teak, *tún* (Cedrela Toona), *sissu*, and Ficus elastica are {.marginnote}Sundarban forests. Assam forests.

Burmese forests. now being formed and guarded by the Forest Department. In Burma, the importance of teak exceeds that of all the other timber-trees together. Next comes iron-wood (Xylia dolabriformis), and Acacia Catechu, which yields the cutch of commerce. **Central India.** Throughout the centre of the peninsula, forests cover a very extensive area; but their value is chiefly local, as none of the rivers are navigable. Towards the east, *sál* predominates, and in the west there is some teak; but fine timber of either species is comparatively scarce. Rájputána has a beautiful tree of its own, the Anogeissus pendula, with small leaves and drooping branches.

Forest administration. 'Reserved' forests. From the administrative point of view, the Indian forests are classified as 'reserved' or as 'open.' The reserved forests are those under the immediate control of officers of the Forest Department. They are managed as the property of the State, with a single eye to their conservancy and future development as a source of national wealth. Their limits are demarcated after survey; nomadic cultivation by the hill tribes is prohibited; cattle are excluded from grazing; destructive creepers are cut down; and the hewing of timber, if permitted at all, is placed **'Open' forests.** under stringent regulations. The open forests are less carefully guarded; but in them, also, certain kinds of timber-trees **'Plantations.'** are preserved. A third class of forest lands consists of plantations, on which large sums of money are spent annually, with a view to the rearing and development of timber-trees.

Forest finance, 1873-1883. It is difficult to present, in a summary view, the entire financial aspects of the labours of the Forest Department. In 1872-73, the total area of reserved forests in India was **1873.** estimated at more than 6,000,000 acres; and the area has probably been doubled since that date. In the same year, the total forest revenue was £477,000, as compared with an expenditure of £295,000, thus showing a surplus of £182,000. **1878.** By 1877-78, the revenue had increased to £664,102, of which £160,308 was derived from British Burma, and £126,163 from Bombay. The forest exports in that year included—teak, valued at £406,652; lac and lac-dye, £362,008; caoutchouc, £89,381; and gums, £183,685.

1883. By the end of 1882-83, the total forest revenue had further increased to £963,859, of which £250,389 was derived from British Burma, £209,035 from Bombay, £101,340 from the North-Western Provinces and Oudh, £97,765 from the Central Provinces, £90,644 from Madras, £76,671 from the Punjab, £69,396 from Bengal, £24,861 from Assam, £28,704 from Berar, and £13,802 from Coorg. From each of these Provinces a surplus profit was realized over working expenses. A small forest revenue is also obtained from tracts in Ajmere and in Báluchistan, but not sufficient, up to 1883, to cover the expenses of the Department. Total forest expenditure in 1882–83, £577,726, showing a surplus of £386,133. Average forest revenue for ten years ending 1882–83, £703,424 per annum; average expenditure, £467,624; average surplus, £235,800. But the above figures fail to exhibit the true working of the Forest Department, which is gradually winning back for India the fee-simple of her forest wealth, when it was on the point of being squandered beyond the possibility of redemption.

The practice of nomadic cultivation by the hill tribes may conveniently be described in connection with forest conserva- Nomadic cultivation. tion, of which it is the most formidable enemy. In all the great virgin forests of India, in Arakan, on the north-east Its area. frontier of Assam and Chittagong, throughout the Central Provinces, and along the line of the Western Gháts, the aboriginal tribes raise their crops of rice, cotton, and millets by a system of nomadic tillage. A similar method has been found in Madagascar; and, indeed, from its simplicity and its appropriateness, it may fairly be regarded the most primitive form of agriculture followed by the human race. Known as *taungya* in Burma, *júm* on the north-east frontier, *dahya* in Central India, *kil* in the Himálayas, and *kumári* in the Western Gháts, it is practised without material differences by tribes of the most diverse origin.

The essential features of such husbandry are the burning Its varie- down of a patch of forest, and sowing the crop with little or no ties. tillage in the clearing thus formed. The tribes of the Bombay coast break up the cleared soil with a sort of hoe-pick and spade, or even with the plough; in other parts of India, the soil is merely scratched, or the seed scattered on the surface without any cultivation. In some cases, a crop is taken off the same clearing for two or even three years in succession; but more usually the tribe moves off every year to a fresh field of operations. Every variety of implement is used, from the bill-hook, used alike for hewing the jungle and for turning up the soil, to the plough. Every degree of permanence in the culti-vation may be observed, from a one-year's crop to the stage at which an aboriginal tribe, such as the Kandhs, visibly passes from nomadic husbandry to regular tillage.

To these nomad cultivators the words rhetorically used by Tacitus of the primitive Germans are strictly applicable

Forest-clearing by fire :

—*Arva per annos mutant; et superest ager.* The wanton destruction wrought by them in the forest is incalculable. In addition to the timber-trees deliberately burned down to clear the soil, the fire thus started not unfrequently runs wild through the forest, and devastates many square miles. Wherever timber has any value from the proximity of a market, the first care of the Forest Department is to prohibit these fires, and to assign heavy penalties for any infringement of its rules. The success of a year's forest operations is mainly estimated by the degree in which the reserves have been saved from the flames.

Restraints on it.

Merits of nomadic tillage.

But vast tracts of country yet remain in which it would be equally useless and impossible to place restraints upon nomad cultivation. The system yields a larger return for the same amount of labour than permanent plough-husbandry. A virgin soil, manured many inches deep with ashes, and watered by the full burst of a tropical rainfall, returns forty and fifty-fold of rice, which is the staple grain thus raised. In addition to rice, Indian corn, millet, oil-seeds, and cotton, are sometimes grown in the same clearing, the seeds being all thrown into the ground together, and each crop ripening in succession at its own season. Except to the eyes of a forest officer, a patch of nomadic tillage is a very picturesque sight. Men, women, and children all work together with a will, for the trees must be felled and burned, and the seed sown, before the monsoon breaks. Save on the western coast and the Ghâts (where the plough is occasionally used), the implement generally employed for all purposes is the *dáo* or hill-knife, which performs the office alike of axe, hoe, dibbler, and sickle.

Irrigation.

In a tropical country, where the rainfall is capricious in its incidence and variable in its amount, the proper control of the water-supply becomes one of the first cares of Government. Its expenditure on irrigation works may be regarded as an investment of the landlord's capital, by which alone the estate can be rendered profitable. Without artificial irrigation, large tracts of country would lie permanently waste, while others could only be cultivated in exceptionally favourable seasons. Irrigation is to the Indian peasant what high cultivation is to the farmer in England. It augments the produce of his fields in a proportion far larger than the mere interest upon the capital expended. It may also be regarded as an insurance against famine. When the monsoon fails for one or two seasons in succession, the cultivator of 'dry lands' has no

Its function in India,

hope; while abundant crops arc raised from the fortunate fields commanded by irrigation works. This contrast was painfully realized in Southern India during the terrible years of 1876 to 1878, the limit between famine and plenty being marked by the boundaries·of the irrigated and non-irrigated areas. It would, however, be an error to conclude that any outlay will absolutely guarantee the vast interior of the peninsula from famine. Much, indeed, can be done, and much is being done, during year by year, to store and distribute the scanty and irregular famine. water-supply of this inland plateau. But engineering possibilities are limited, not only by the expense, but by the unalterable laws of nature. A table-land, with only a moderate rainfall, and watered by few perennial streams, broken by many hill ranges, and marked out into no natural drainage basins, can never be completely protected from the vicissitudes of the Indian seasons.

Irrigation is everywhere dependent upon the two supreme Irrigation considerations of water-supply and land-level. The sandy areas. desert, which extends from the hills of Rájputána to the basin of the Indus, is as hopelessly closed to irrigation, from its almost entire absence of rainfall, as is the confused system of hill and valley in Central India, with its unmanageable levels. Farther west, in the Indus valley, irrigation becomes possible, and in no part of India has it been conducted with greater perseverance and success. The entire Province of Sind, and Sind. several of the lower Districts of the Punjab, are absolutely dependent upon the floods of the Indus. Sind has been compared to Egypt, and the Indus to the Nile; but the conditions of the Indian Province are much the less favourable of the two. In Sind, the average rainfall is barely 10 inches in the year; the soil is a thirsty sand; worst of all, the river does not run in confined banks, but wanders at its will over a wide valley. The rising of the Nile is a beneficent phenomenon, which can be depended upon with tolerable accuracy, and which the industry of countless generations has brought under control for the purposes of cultivation. The inundation of the The uncon- Indus is an uncontrollable torrent, which sometimes does as trollable much harm as good. Indus.

Broadly speaking, no crop can be grown in Sind except under Irrigation irrigation. The cultivated area of over two million acres may in Sind, be regarded as entirely dependent upon artificial water-supply, 1877–83. although not entirely on State irrigation works. The water is drawn from the river by two classes of canals—(1) inundation channels, which only fill when the Indus is in flood; and

Irrigation in Sind, (2) perennial channels, which carry off water by means of dams at all seasons of the year. The former are for the most part the work of ancient rulers of the country, or of the cultivators themselves; the latter have been constructed since the British conquest. In both cases, care .has been taken to utilize abandoned beds of the river. Irrigation in Sind is treated as an integral department of the land administration. In in 1877; 1876–77, about 900,000 acres were returned as irrigated from works for which capital and revenue accounts are kept. The chief of these are the Ghár, Eastern and Western Nárá, Sukkur (Sakhar), Phuleli, and Pinyari Canals; the total receipts were about £190,000, almost entirely credited under the head of land revenue. In the same year, about 445,000 acres were irrigated from works for which revenue accounts only are kept, yielding about £75,000 in land revenue. The total area 'usually irrigated' in Sind was returned in 1880 at about 1,800,000 acres, out of a cultivated area of 2,250,000 acres.

1883. The actual area cultivated by means of canal irrigation in Sind in 1882–83 was 1,673,293 acres, including *jagír* or revenue-free lands; the area assessed for Government revenue being 1,508,292 acres. The gross assessed revenue from all sources amounted to £294,898, and the maintenance charges to £135,118, leaving a net revenue of £159,780. The net actual receipts from productive irrigation works returned 4·25 per cent., and those from ordinary irrigation works, 12·95 per cent. on the capital outlay incurred up to the end of the year. Total capital outlay up to the end of 1882–83, £958,012, of which £623,267 had been expended on productive works, and £334,745 on ordinary irrigation works.

Irrigation in Bombay, In the Bombay Presidency, irrigation is conducted on a comparatively small scale, and mainly by private enterprise. Along the coast of the Konkan, the heavy local rainfall, and the annual flooding of the numerous small creeks, permit rice to be grown without artificial aid. In Gujarát (Guzerát) the supply is drawn from wells, and in the Deccan from tanks; but both of these are liable to fail in years of deficient rainfall. Government has now undertaken a few comprehensive schemes of irrigation in Bombay, conforming to a common type. The head of a hill valley is dammed up, so as to form an immense reservoir, and the water is then conducted over the fields by channels, in some cases of considerable length. In 1877. 1876–77, the total area in Bombay (excluding Sind) irrigated from Government works was about 180,000 acres, yielding a revenue of about £42,000. In the same year, the expenditure

on irrigation (inclusive of Sind) was £65,000 under the head
of extraordinary, and £170,000 under the head of ordinary;
total, £235,000. In 1882–83, the area irrigated by Govern- 1883.
ment works in Gujarát and the Deccan amounted to 28,735
acres from productive works, and 138,468 acres from works
not classed as productive. Total Government irrigation,
167,203 acres; yielding a revenue of £77,746, against an
expenditure of £37,171, leaving a surplus of £30,575.
Besides these Government works, irrigation is carried on to
a much larger extent in Bombay by private individuals from
tanks, ponds, and watercourses. Ordinary irrigated area in
Bombay (exclusive of Sind), 550,000 acres, out of a total
cultivated area of 22¼ million acres.

In some parts of the Punjab, irrigation is only one degree Irrigation
less necessary than in Sind, but the sources of supply are more in the
numerous. In the northern tract, under the Himálayas, and 1879–84.
in the upper valleys of the Five Rivers, water can be obtained
by digging wells from 10 to 30 feet below the surface. In the
south, towards Sind, 'inundation channels' are usual. The
upland tracts which rise between the basins of the main rivers
are now in course of being supplied by the perennial canals of
the Government. According to the returns for 1878–79, out 1879.
of a grand total of 23,523,504 acres under cultivation, 5,340,724
acres were irrigated by private individuals, and 1,808,005
acres by public 'channels;' total area under irrigation,
7,148,729 acres, or 30 per cent. of the cultivated area. The
three principal Government works in the Punjab are the
Western Jumna Canal, the Bárí Doáb Canal, and the Sirhind, The three
the main branch of which, and some of its distributaries, were great
opened in November 1882. An account of each of these works Canals.
is given in separate articles in *The Imperial Gazetteer of India*.[1]

Up to the close of 1877–78, the capital outlay on the three
great Punjab Canals was £3,645,189; the total income in
that year was £263,053, of which £171,504 was classified as
direct, and £91,549 as indirect; the total revenue charges on
works in operation were £224,316, of which £146,419 was
for maintenance, and £77,897 for interest, thus showing a
surplus of £38,737. On the Western Jumna Canal, taken
singly, the net profit was £83,112 in 1877–78.

By the end of 1883–84, the gross revenue from the Bárí Irrigation
Doáb and Western Jumna Canal, together with the Indus and in the
Sutlej Inundation Canals, amounted to £428,416, and the 1883–84.

[1] See articles JUMNA CANAL, Eastern and Western, BARI DOAB CANAL,
SIRHIND CANAL, in *The Imperial Gazetteer of India*.

Punjab Canal finance, 1884.

working expenses to £197,032, thus yielding a net revenue of £231,384, equal to a return of nearly 5 per cent. on the capital of the canals opened. This is exclusive of the Muzaffargarh Inundation Canal, which has no capital account, but which in 1882–83 yielded a return of £22,035, against working expenses amounting to £15,365, leaving a surplus of revenue over expenditure of £6670. Irrigation from the Sirhind Canal had only just commenced, but the revenue will increase in proportion to the rate of progress in constructing the distributary channels. This work, together with the completion of branch-distributaries, is being pushed on as rapidly as possible.

Punjab Canal statistics, 1884.

The capital outlay on the three great Punjab canals, exclusive of contributions by Native States towards the construction of the Sirhind Canal, amounted at the close of 1883–84 to £5,033,284, the capital expended during the latter year being £282,524. Area irrigated from Government canals in 1883–84 :—Western Jumna Canal, 472,426 acres ; Bárí Doáb Canal, 390,860 acres ; Sirhind Canal, 5030 acres ; inundation canals, 783,752 acres : total, 1,652,068 acres. The ordinary irrigated area in the Punjab, from Government works as well as by private individuals, may now be taken at about 8 million acres, out of a total cultivated area of over 23 million acres.

Irrigation in the N.-W. Provinces.

The North-Western Provinces present, in the great *doáb*, or high land between the Ganges and the Jumna, a continuation of the physical features to be found in the Punjab. The local rainfall, indeed, is heavier, but before the days of artificial irrigation almost every drought resulted in a terrible famine. It is in this tract that the British Government has been perhaps most successful in averting such calamities. In Sind, irrigation is an absolute necessity ; in Lower Bengal, it may be regarded almost as a luxury ; in the great river basins of Upper India, it serves the twofold object of averting famines caused by drought ; of introducing more valuable crops and higher methods of agriculture.

Four great canals of the Doábs, 1878-83. 1878.

Concerning private irrigation from wells in the North-Western Provinces, details are not available. The great Government works are the Ganges Canal, the Eastern Jumna Canal, the Agra Canals, and the Lower Ganges Canal.[1] Up to the close of 1877–78, the total outlay had been £5,673,401. The gross income in that year was £438,136, of which £337,842 was derived from water-rates, and £100,294 from enhanced land revenue ; the working expenses amounted to

[1] A full account of each of these works will be found under article GANGES CANAL, *The Imperial Gazetteer*, vol. iii.

£143,984, leaving £294,152 for surplus profits, or 6·77 per N.-W.P. cent. on the total capital expended on works in operation. Canals. The total area irrigated in the North-Western Provinces was 1,461,428 acres. Of this total, 415,659 acres were under wheat, and 139,375 under sugar-cane.

The total capital outlay on the four main canals just men- The four great canals, 1882-83. tioned in the North-Western Provinces up to 1882–83, was £6,499,741, of which £138,677 were expended during 1882–83.

The other canals in the N.-W. Provinces, not classed as pro- ductive works, included, in 1882–83, the following—namely, the Minor canals, N.-W.P. Dún Canal, the Rohilkhand and Bijnor Canal, the Bundelkhand irrigation works, the Cawnpur branch of the Lower Ganges Canal, and the Betwá Canal, constructed as a famine insurance work. Total capital expended on all Government canals in the North-Western Provinces up to the end of 1882–83, £6,890,769, of which £232,341 was spent during the latter year. These canals may all be considered as practically complete, with the exception of the Lower Ganges and Agra Canals, in which some of the distributaries are as yet (1884) unfinished ; and the Betwá Canal, which was under construction at the end of 1882–83.

The gross revenue of the canals in the N.-W. Provinces, Total canal revenue in N.-W.P., 1883. including water-rates, increased land revenue due to the canals, navigation charges in 1882–83, was £645,918 ; the charges against revenue amounted to £215,813, thus leaving a net revenue of £430,105, or over 6 per cent. on the total capital outlay, exclusive of the Betwá Canal. Deducting from this the interest charges for the year, which amounted to £249,601, there remained a clear profit or surplus of £180,504. The total area irrigated during 1882–83 was 1,974,175 acres, of which Irrigated area, 1883. 1,462,023 were supplied by the Ganges and Lower Ganges Canals, or their branches. Of the irrigated area, 728,385 acres were under wheat; 662,693 acres under other food crops; 316,145 acres under indigo ; 198,322 acres under sugar-cane, and 52,493 acres under cotton. Besides the canal irrigation, a vast area in the North-Western Provinces is supplied with water from wells, tanks, and miscellaneous works. The total area ordinarily irrigated in the North-Western Provinces (exclud- ing Oudh) may be estimated at 7 to 8 million acres.

No irrigation works have yet been introduced into Oudh by Irrigation in Oudh. Government. A fair local rainfall, the annual overflow of the rivers, and an abundance of low-lying swamps, combine to furnish a water-supply which is ample in all ordinary years. According to the Settlement returns, out of a total cultivated area of 8,276,174 acres, 2,957,377 acres, or 36 per cent., are irrigated by private individuals. But this figure probably includes low lands watered by natural overflow.

Irrigation in Bengal Proper.

Throughout the greater part of Bengal Proper there is scarcely any demand for artificial irrigation, but Government has undertaken to construct works in those exceptional tracts where experience has shown that drought or famine is to be feared. In the broad valleys of the Ganges and the Brahmaputra, and along the deltaic seaboard, flood is a more frequent calamity than drought; and embankments here take the place of canals. The Public Works Department in Lower Bengal has over 2000 miles of embankments under its charge, upon which £79,105 was expended in 1877–78, either as direct outlay or in advances to landowners. The wide expanse of Northern Bengal and Behar, stretching from the Himálayas to the Ganges, is also rarely visited by drought; although, when drought does come, the excessive density of the population brings the danger of famine very near. In Sáran District it has been found necessary to carry out a scheme for utilizing the discharge of the river Gandak.

Embankments.

The Orissa Canals.

The great irrigation works in Lower Bengal are two in number, and belong to two different types :—(1) In the delta of Orissa, an extensive system of canals has been constructed on the pattern of those lower down the Coromandel coast. They store up the water by means of a weir or anicut thrown across the Mahánadi river.[1] The Orissa works are intended to avert the danger of both drought and flood, and also to be useful for navigation. In average seasons, *i.e.* in five years out of six, the local rainfall is sufficient for the rice crop, which is here the sole staple of cultivation; and therefore it is not to be expected that these canals will be directly or largely remunerative. But, on the other hand, if they save the Province from a repetition of the disastrous year 1865–66, the money will not have been expended in vain. A canal, originally designed as a branch of the Orissa works, runs through Midnapur District and debouches on the Húglí.

The Son Canal.

(2) In South Behar, the flood discharge of the Son has been intercepted, after the system of engineering followed in the North-West, so as to irrigate the thirsty strip of land along the south bank of the Ganges, where distress has often been severely felt.[2] In this case, also, the expenditure must be regarded rather as an insurance fund against famine than as reproductive outlay. The works are not yet complete,

[1] See article MAHANADI, *The Imperial Gazetteer.*
[2] See article SON CANALS, *The Imperial Gazetteer.*

but the experience already gained proves that irrigation is wanted even in ordinary seasons.

Up to the close of the year 1877-78, the capital expendi- Irrigation in Bengal, 1878-83. ture on all the State irrigation works in Lower Bengal was £4,653,903; the gross income for the year was £49,477; the working expenses were £70,286, and the estimated interest on 1878. capital, at 4½ per cent., amounted to £203,971, thus showing a deficit of £224,780. The area irrigated was about 400,000 acres.

By the end of 1882-83, the total direct capital outlay Irrigation in Bengal, 1882-83. (excluding interest) on State navigation and irrigation canals in Bengal was £5,331,726; the gross income for the year was £207,444 (including the Calcutta Canals and Nadiya river works, for which capital and revenue accounts are not kept), and the working expenses £514,898, showing a deficit of £307,454. Adding to this the amount of interest on capital, which in 1882-83 amounted to £211,550, calculated at 4 per cent., the total net deficit for the year amounted to £519,004. The four chief navigation and irrigation canals, however, returned a surplus (excluding interest) of £15,527 of revenue over working expenses. The great deficit of current expenditure over current revenue occurred in the Orissa coast canals, embankments, drainage works, etc. The area irrigated from Government canals in the Lieutenant-Governorship of Bengal is about 450,000 acres. Including private works, about 1 million acres out of a total estimated area of 54½ million acres under cultivation, are irrigated in Lower Bengal.

In the Madras Presidency, and generally throughout Southern Irrigation in Madras India, facilities for irrigation assume a decisive importance in determining the character of agriculture. Crops dependent on the rainfall are distinguished as 'dry crops,' comprehending the large class of millets. Rice is grown on 'wet land,' which means land capable of being irrigated. Except on the Malabar or western coast, the local rainfall is nowhere sufficiently ample, or sufficiently steady, to secure an adequate water-supply. Everywhere else, water has to be brought to the fields from rivers, from tanks, or from wells. Of the total cultivated area of Madras, 17 per cent. was returned by the Famine Commissioners in 1878 as *assessed* as 'wet land;' or 'Dry' and 'wet' land. 5⅜ millions of acres out of an estimated cultivated area of 32 millions. But the *actual* irrigated area from all sources, including tanks and wells, was returned by the Famine Commissioners at about 7 millions of acres.

From time immemorial, the industrious population of the Petty native works. Madras Districts has made use of all the means available to store up the rainfall, and direct the river floods over their fields. The upland areas are studded with tanks, which sometimes cover square miles of ground; the rivers are crossed by innumerable anicuts or dams, by which the floods are diverted into long aqueducts. Most of these works are now the property of Government, which annually expends large sums of money in maintenance and repairs, looking for remuneration only to the augmented land revenue. The average rate of assessment is 9s. 6d. per acre on irrigated land, as compared with only 2s. 3d. per acre on unirrigated land.

Works in the Madras deltas, 1878-83. It is therefore not only the duty, but the manifest advantage, of Government to extend the facilities for irrigation in Madras, wherever the physical aspect of the country will permit. The deltas of the Godávari, the Kistna, and the Káveri (Cauvery), have within recent years been traversed by a network of canals, and thus guaranteed against risk of famine.[1] Smaller works of a similar nature have been carried out in other places; while a private company, with a Government guarantee, has undertaken the more difficult task of utilizing on a grand scale the waters of the Tungabhadra[2] amid the hills and vales of the interior. The *assessed* irrigated area in the Presidency, of **1878.** 5⅓ million acres, yielded in 1878 a land revenue of 2 millions sterling. Of this total, 1,680,178 acres, with a revenue of £739,778, were irrigated in 1878 by eight great systems, for which revenue and capital accounts were kept. The minor works consisted of about 35,000 tanks and irrigation canals, and about 1140 anicuts or dams across streams. The whole area under irrigation from public and private sources in Madras was in 1878, as already stated, about 7 million acres, out of a total cultivated area of 32 million acres.

Madras irrigation works, 1882-83. In 1882-83, the Madras irrigation scheme included seven main systems, classified as productive public works; namely, —the Godávari delta system, the Kistna delta system, the Penner (Ponnaiyár) anicut system, the Sangam anicut project (under construction), the Karnúl canal (purchased from the Madras Irrigation Company in July 1882), the Káveri delta system, and Srivaikuntham anicut system. An account of each of these works separately will be found in *The Imperial Gazetteer of India*. Irrigation and navigation works, not classified as productive, include those known as the Chedambaram tank system, the Pálár anicut system, the Pelandorai anicut system, the Madras water-supply and irriga-

---

[1] See article GODAVARI RIVER, *The Imperial Gazetteer.*
[2] See article TUNGABHADRA, *The Imperial Gazetteer.*

tion extension project, and the Buckingham Canal. There are also a number of minor irrigation and protective works, for which neither capital nor revenue accounts are kept. The area irrigated by productive public works in Madras in 1882–83 was 1,757,579 acres; and that by all other Government irrigation works, 2,615,590 acres; making a total of 4,373,169 acres.

The acquisition of the Karnúl Canal during 1882 materially raised the outlay invested in productive public works, and greatly reduced the returns yielded in former years by this class of works in Madras. The total capital outlay, direct and indirect, incurred on productive public works up to the end of 1882–83, amounted to £3,990,552. The gross revenue, including share of enhanced land revenue, amounted to £360,062; the maintenance charges, direct and indirect, was £107,197, leaving a net revenue of £252,865, equal to 6·34 per cent. on the total capital outlay up to the end of the year. If, however, the outlay on the Sangam anicut works (which had not commenced to earn revenue in 1882–83), and the purchase money for the Karnúl canal, be excluded from the account, the net returns would be 12 per cent. on the capital outlay, against 13¾ per cent. obtained during the previous year. With regard to irrigation and navigation canals not classified as productive, the capital outlay, direct and indirect, incurred up to the end of 1882–83, amounted to £988,907. The gross revenue during 1882–83, including share of land revenue debitable to these works, was £31,319; the expenditure was £27,520, leaving a net revenue of £3799, equal to 0·38 per cent. on the total capital outlay.

Madras Irrigation Finance, 1883.

In Mysore, tanks, anicuts, and wells dug in the dry beds of rivers afford the means of irrigation. Since the late disastrous famine of 1876–78, comprehensive schemes of throwing embankments across river valleys have been undertaken by Government. The whole area under irrigation from public and private sources in Mysore is ¾ of a million acres, out of a total cultivated area of 4 to 5 million acres.

Irrigation in Mysore.

In the Central Provinces, irrigation still remains a private enterprise. According to the Settlement returns, out of a total cultivated area of 13,610,503 acres, 804,378 acres, or 6 per cent., are irrigated by private individuals. The only Government work is a tank in the District of Nimár. In 1882–83, the area irrigated by private individuals was returned at 770,583 acres, and by Government works, 238 acres from the Nimár tank, out of a total of 14,165,212 acres of cultivated area.

In Central Provinces.

In British Burma, as in Lower Bengal, embankments take the

In Burma.

place of canals; and are classed as 'irrigation works' in the reports. Within the last few years, Government has spent £318,000 in Burma under this heading, to save the low rice-fields along the Irawadi from destructive inundation.

Statistics for British India, 1868 to 1883. The foregoing paragraphs have given the Provincial statistics of irrigation, so far as available. The differences in the local systems, and the variety of sources from which the outlay on irrigation works is derived, render a single generalized statement for all India misleading. Apart from private irrigation works, and certain classes of Government works, the capital expended by the Government on irrigation is returned at 19 millions sterling during the sixteen years ending 1882–83. Including 1¾ million sterling expended on the Madras Irrigation Company's works (taken over by Government), the total outlay would amount to nearly 21 millions sterling during the same period. This statement, although it altogether fails to disclose the whole expenditure on Indian irrigation, suffices to show the magnitude of the operations involved.

The following table shows the extent of cultivation and the average area irrigated in the Provinces for which the facts can be obtained. They were specially collected by the Indian Famine Commission, and published in its Report of 1880. But they must be taken as only approximate estimates. They differ from data obtained from other sources; as may be seen by comparing the figures in the table with the later ones given in the foregoing Provincial paragraphs.

ORDINARY AREA OF CULTIVATION AND OF IRRIGATION IN CERTAIN PROVINCES, AS ESTIMATED IN 1880.

Province.	Area ordinarily cultivated.	Area ordinarily irrigated.	Percentage of irrigation to cultivation.
	Acres.	Acres.	
Punjab, ...	21,000,000	5,500,000	26·2
North-Western Provinces and Oudh, . . .	36,000,000	11,500,000	32·0
Bengal, ...	54,500,000	1,000,000	1·8
Central Provinces, . .	15,500,000	770,000	5·0
Berar, ...	6,500,000	100,000	1·5
Bombay, ...	24,500,000	450,000	1·8
Sind, ...	2,250,000	1,800,000	80·0
Madras, ...	32,000,000	7,300,000	23·0
Mysore, ...	5,000,000	800,000	16·0
Total for the Provinces for which the facts were ascertained, . .	197,250,000	29,220,000	14·8

It will be seen from the preceding table that irrigation is most Distribu-
resorted to in the Provinces with the scantiest or most pre- tion of
carious rainfall. In Sind, tillage depends almost entirely on an irrigation
over India.
artificial water-supply ; and four-fifths of the cultivated area are Sind.
ascertained to be irrigated. In Northern India, the deficient Northern
rainfall of the Punjab and the high-lying *doábs*, or intermediate India.
river plains of the North-Western Provinces, also demands a
large measure of irrigation. The irrigated area, accordingly,
amounts to from over one-fourth to one-third of the whole
cultivation. In Madras, it is under one-fourth ; in Mysore, it is Southern
one-sixth ; in the Central Provinces, it is one-twentieth. But India.
the dry uplands of Bombay, the Central Provinces, and Berar, Central
where the proportion of irrigated lands sinks to about one- India.
sixtieth, undoubtedly require a larger artificial water-supply
than they possess at present. The black soil of these tracts,
however, is very retentive of moisture. To a certain extent it
stores up and husbands the rainfall. It thus lessens the necessity for irrigation. In Bengal, where the irrigated area is only Lower
1·8 per cent. of the cultivated area, the abundant rainfall and Bengal.
the inundations of the Ganges, the Brahmaputra, the Mahánadi, and of the river systems connected with these main
arteries, take the place of canals or an artificial water-supply.

FAMINES.—In any country where the population is dense Famines.
and the means of communication backward, the failure of a
harvest, whether produced by drought, by flood, by blight, by Natural
locusts, or by war, causes intense distress. Whether such calamities.
distress shall develop into famine is merely a matter of degree,
depending upon a combination of circumstances—the comparative extent of the failure, the density of the population,
the practicability of imports, the facilities for transport, the
resources of private trade, and the energy of the administration.

Drought, or a failure of the regular rainfall, is the great Causes of
cause of famine. No individual foresight, no compensating scarcity;
influences, can prevent those recurring periods of continuous
drought with which large Provinces of India are afflicted.
Even an average rainfall in any one year, if irregularly distributed, or at the wrong seasons, may affect the harvest to a
moderate degree; so also may flood or blight. The total
failure of one monsoon may result in a general scarcity. But and of real
famine proper, or widespread starvation, is usually caused by a famine.
succession of seasons of drought. The cultivators of India are
seldom dependent upon a single harvest, or upon the crops of one
year. In the event of a partial failure, they can draw for their

food-supply either upon their own grain pits or upon the stores of the village merchants. The first sufferers, and those who also suffer most in the end, are the class who live by daily wages. But small is the number that can hold out, either in capital or credit, against a second year of insufficient rainfall; and even the third season sometimes proves adverse. The great famines in India have been caused by drought, and usually by drought continued over two or three years.

Water-supply. It becomes necessary to inquire into the means of husbanding the water-supply. That supply can be derived only from three sources—(1) Local rainfall; (2) natural inundation; and (3) artificial irrigation from rivers, canals, tanks, or wells. Any of these sources may exist separately or together. In only a few parts of India can the rainfall be entirely trusted, as both sufficient in its amount and regular in its distribution. These favoured tracts include the whole strip of coast beneath the Western Ghâts, from Bombay to Cape Comorin; the greater part of the Provinces of Assam and Burma; together with the Favoured Provinces. deltaic districts at the head of the Bay of Bengal. In these Provinces the annual rainfall rarely, if ever, falls below 60 to 100 inches; artificial irrigation and famine are there alike unknown.

The irrigation area of India. The rest of the Indian peninsula may be described as liable, more or less, to drought. In Orissa, the scene of the most intense famine of recent times, the average rainfall exceeds 60 inches a year; in Sind, which has been exceptionally free from famine under British rule, the average drops to less than 10 inches. The local rainfall, therefore, is not the only element to be considered. Broadly speaking, artificial irrigation has protected, or is now in course of protecting, certain fortunate regions, such as the eastward deltas of the Madras rivers and the upper valley of the Ganges. The rest, and by far the greater portion, of the country is still exposed to famine. Meteorological science may possibly teach us to foresee what is coming.[1] But it may be doubted whether administrative efforts can do more than alleviate the calamity when once famine has declared itself. Lower Bengal and Oudh are watered by natural inundation as much as by the local rainfall; Sind derives its supplies mainly from canals filled by the floods of the Indus; the Punjab and the North-Western Provinces are dependent largely upon wells; the Deccan, with the entire south, is the land of tanks and reservoirs. But in all these Provinces, when the rainfall has failed over a series of

[1] See the chapter on Indian Meteorology at the end of this volume.

years, the canal supply must likewise fail after no long interval.
Waterworks on a scale adequate to guarantee the whole of
India from drought not only exceed the possibilities of finance;
they are also beyond the reach of engineering skill.

The first great famine of which we have any trustworthy *Summary*
record is that which devastated the lower valley of the Ganges *of Indian famines,*
in 1769-70. One-third of the population of Bengal is credibly *1770-1878.*
reported to have perished. The previous season had been
bad; and, as not uncommonly happens, the break-up of the *1769-70.*
drought was accompanied by disastrous floods. Beyond the
importation into Calcutta and Murshidábád of a few thousand
hundredweights of rice from the Districts of Bákarganj and
Chittagong, it does not appear that any public measures for
relief were taken or proposed.[1]

The next great famine was that which afflicted the Karnátik *Famines of*
from 1780 to 1783, and has been immortalized by the genius *1780-83;*
of Burke. It arose primarily from the ravages of Haidar Alí's
army. A public subscription was organized by the Madras
Government, from which sprang the 'Monegar Choultry,' a permanent Madras institution for the relief of the native poor. In
1783-84, Hindustán Proper suffered from a prolonged drought,
which stopped short at the frontier of British territory. Warren
Hastings, then Governor-General, advocated the construction
of enormous granaries, to be opened only in times of necessity.
One of these granaries or *golás,* stands to the present day in
the city of Patná, but it was never used until the scarcity of
1874. In 1790-92, Madras was again the scene of a two- *1790-92;*
years' famine, which is memorable as being the first occasion
on which the starving people were employed by Government
on relief works. Famines again occurred in Southern India
in 1802-04, 1807, 1812, 1824, 1833, 1854, and 1866. A
terrible dearth in 1838 caused great mortality in the North- *1838.*
Western Provinces.

But so little was done by the State in these calamities, that *Famines*
few administrative lessons can be learned from them. In *of 1861*
1860-61, however, a serious attempt was made to alleviate an
exceptional distress in the North-Western Provinces. About
half a million persons are estimated to have been relieved, at
an expenditure by Government of about three-quarters of a

[1] A full account of the famine of 1769-70 is given in Hunter's *Annals of
Rural Bengal,* pp. 19-55 (5th ed.). The official record of this and the
subsequent famines will be found in the *Report of the Indian Famine
Commission,* presented to Parliament 1880, part i. paras. 62-84.

and of
1866.

million sterling.   Again, in 1865-66, which will ever be known as the year of the Orissa famine, the Government attempted to organize relief works and to distribute charitable funds.   But on neither of these occasions can it be said that its efforts were successful.   In Orissa, especially, the admitted loss of one-fourth of the population proves the danger to which an isolated Province is exposed.   The people of Orissa died because they had no surplus stocks of grain of their own ; and because importation, on an adequate scale, was physically impossible by sea or land.

Famine of
1873-74.

Passing over the prolonged drought of 1868-70 in the North-Western Provinces and Rájputána, we come to the Behar scarcity of 1873-74, which first attracted the interest of England.   Warned by the failure of the rains, and watched and stimulated by the excited sympathy of the public in England, the Government carried out a costly but comprehensive scheme of relief.   By the expenditure of $6\frac{1}{2}$ millions sterling, and the importation of 1 million tons of rice, all loss of life was prevented.   The comparatively small area of distress, and the facilities of communication by rail and river, allowed of the accomplishment of this feat, which remains unparalleled in the annals of Indian famine.

Famine of
1876-78.

The famine of 1876-78 is the widest spread and the most prolonged that India has experienced.   The drought commenced in Mysore by the failure of the monsoon in 1875 ; and the fear of distress in the North-Western Provinces did not pass away until 1879.   But it will be known in history as the great famine of Southern India.   Over the entire Deccan, from Poona to Bangalore, the south-west monsoon failed to bring its usual rainfall in the summer of 1876.   In

Failure of
rain, 1876.

the autumn of the same year, the north-east monsoon proved deficient in the south-eastern Districts of the Madras Presidency.   The main food crop perished throughout an immense tract of country ; and, as the harvest of 1875 had also been short, prices rapidly rose to famine rates.   In November 1876, starvation was already at work, and Government adopted measures to keep the people alive.   The next eighteen months, until the middle of 1878, were devoted to one long

Failure of
rain, 1877.

campaign against famine.   The summer monsoon of 1877 proved a failure ; some relief was brought in October of that year by the autumn monsoon ; but all anxiety was not removed until the arrival of a normal rainfall in June 1878.

Meanwhile the drought had reached Northern India, where it found the stocks of grain already drained to meet the famine

in the south. Bengal, Assam, and Burma were the only Scarcity in
Provinces which escaped in that disastrous year. The North- Northern
Western Provinces, the Punjab, Rájputána, and the Central 1877-78.
Provinces suffered from drought throughout the summer of
1877, and, from its consequences, far into the following year.

When once famine gets ahead of relief operations, the flood Famine in
of distress bursts its embankments, and the people simply the South.
perish. Starvation and the long attendant train of famine-
diseases sweep away their hundreds of thousands. In 1876-78,
the importation of grain was left free, and within twelve months
268,000 tons were brought by land, and 166,000 tons by sea,
into the distressed Districts of Southern India.

The total expenditure of Government upon famine relief Famine
in 1876-78 may be estimated at 11 millions sterling, not expendi-
including the indirect loss of revenue, nor the amount debited 1876-78.
against the State of Mysore. For this large sum of money
there is but little to show in the shape of works constructed.
The largest number of persons in receipt of relief at one time
in Madras was 2,591,900 in September 1877; of these only
634,581 were nominally employed on works, while the rest
were gratuitously fed. From cholera alone, the deaths were Cholera.
returned at 357,430 for Madras, 58,648 for Mysore, and
57,252 for Bombay. Dr. Cornish, the Sanitary Commissioner of Madras, well illustrated the effects of the famine
by the returns of births and deaths over a series of years.
In 1876, when famine, with its companion cholera, was
already beginning to be felt, the births registered in Madras
numbered 632,113, and the deaths 680,381. In 1877, the Decrease
year of famine, the births fell to 477,447, while the deaths of birth-
rose to 1,556,312. In 1878, the results of the famine showed 1877-78.
themselves by a still further reduction of the births to
348,346, and by the still high number of 810,921 deaths. In
1879 the births recovered to 476,307, still below the average,
and the deaths diminished to 548,158. These figures are
only approximate, but they serve to show how long the results
of famine are to be traced in the vital statistics of a people.

With regard to the deaths, the Famine Commissioners thus Total
report: 'It has been estimated, and in our opinion on sub- deaths
stantial grounds, that the mortality which occurred in the famine of
Provinces under British administration during the period of 1876-78.
famine and drought extending over the years 1877 and 1878
amounted, on a population of 197 millions, to 5¼ millions in
excess of the deaths that would have occurred had the seasons
been ordinarily healthy; and the statistical returns have made

certain what has long been suspected, that starvation and distress greatly check the fecundity of the population. It is probable that from this cause the number of births during the same period has been lessened by 2 millions; the total reduction of the population would thus amount to about 7 millions. Assuming the ordinary death-roll, taken at the rate of 35 per thousand, on 190 millions of people, the abnormal mortality of the famine period may be regarded as having increased the total death-rate by about 40 per cent.'

Famine a weak check on population. But when estimated over a period of years, the effect of famine as a check upon the population is small. The Famine Commissioners calculate that, taking the famines of the past thirty years, as to which alone an estimate of any value can be made, the abnormal deaths caused by famine and its diseases have been less than 2 per thousand of the Indian population per annum. As a matter of fact, cultivation quickly extended after the famine of 1877–78, and there were in Bombay and Madras 120,000 more acres under tillage shortly after the long protracted scarcity than before it.

Famine of 1876–78 summarized. The famine of 1876–78 affected, directly, a population of 58⅓ million persons, and an area of 257,300 square miles. The average number daily employed by the State on relief works was 877,024. The average number of persons daily in receipt of gratuitous State relief was 446,641, besides private charities. Land revenue was remitted to close on 2 millions sterling. The famine lasted from 12 months in the North-Western Provinces, to 22 months in Madras. Its total cost, including both outlay and loss of revenue, is officially returned at £11,194,320.[1] A Commission was appointed to inquire into the causes of famine in India, and the means of averting or alleviating those calamities. Its report, presented to both Houses of Parliament in 1880, is replete with carefully collated facts regarding the past, and with wise suggestions for the future.

During the seven years which have elapsed since the great calamity of 1878, up to the time when these pages went to the press (June 1885), there has been no scarcity in India sufficiently intense or widespread to deserve the name of famine. Almost every season has brought a partial failure of the rains in one Province or another. But improved means of communication, and prompt measures for dealing with the distress, have prevented local scarcity from developing in any year into general famine.

[1] *Report of the Indian Famine Commission*, part i. p. 24 (1880).

CHAPTER XVIII.

MEANS OF COMMUNICATION.

THE means of communication in India may be classified Internal under four headings—(1) railways, (2) roads, (3) rivers, and communications. (4) canals.

The existing system of railway communication in India Indian dates from the administration of Lord Dalhousie. The first railways. Indian line of rail was projected in 1843 by Sir Macdonald Their Stephenson, who was afterwards active in forming the East history, 1843-71. Indian Railway Company. But this scheme was blighted by the financial panic that followed soon afterwards in England. Bombay, the city which has most benefited by railway enterprise, saw the first sod turned in 1850, and the first line of a few miles opened as far as Thána (Tanna) in 1853. The elaborate minute, drawn up by Lord Dalhousie in the latter year, substantially represents the railway map of India at the present day, although filled in by Lord Mayo's extensions of 1869 and by subsequent lines.

Lord Dalhousie's scheme consisted of well-chosen trunk Lord Dal-lines, traversing the length and breadth of the peninsula, housie's and connecting all the great cities and military cantonments. 1853. These trunk lines were to be constructed by private companies, to whom Government should guarantee a minimum of 5 per cent. interest on their capital expended, and from whom it should demand in return a certain measure of subordination. The system thus sketched out was promptly carried into execution, and by 1871 Bombay was put into direct railway communication with the sister Presidencies of Calcutta and Madras. The task remaining for Lord Mayo in 1870 was the Lord development of traffic by means of feeders, which should tap Mayo's branch the districts of production, and thus open up the entire lines, 1870. country. This task he initiated by the construction of minor State lines on a narrower gauge, and therefore at a cheaper rate, than the existing guaranteed railways.

Four classes of Indian lines.

'Guaranteed' railways.

The railways of India are now divided into four classes. In the first place, there are the railways constructed by guaranteed companies, for the most part between 1855 and 1875. These guaranteed railways, as a rule, follow the main lines of natural communication, and satisfy the first necessities of national life, both commercial and political. In the second place, there is a system of branch State lines, constructed during the last fifteen years, and some of them destined to yield fruit only in the future. The third class comprises railways worked by private companies under a system of Government concessions. The fourth class are railways within Native States.

The four systems.

(1) Guaranteed railways.

Each of these classes of railways has been constructed on a different system in regard to the method by which the capital was raised. The four systems may be briefly, although not accurately, described as follows. The guaranteed lines were constructed by companies formed in England, who raised their capital from their own shareholders under a guaranteed interest of 5 per cent. from the Government of India. Profits in excess of 5 per cent. were to be shared between the Government and the Company, but the Government reserved the right of buying up the lines at their market value after certain terms of years. The construction of guaranteed railways was carried out by the Company's staff under the supervision of Government.

(2) State railways.

(3) 'Assisted.'

The State railways were constructed from capital raised by the Government direct; and they were executed by engineers in Government employ. The 'assisted' railway companies are a more recent development. They raise their capital under a guarantee of a low interest from Government, with free grants of land, or other concessions. The guarantee is usually for a limited period; but, as presently explained, different arrangements are made in each case.

(4) Native State railways.

The Native State lines are constructed from capital found by the individual State. The execution and management of these lines have, as a rule, been conducted by a staff employed by the Government of India, or by the trunk railway companies to which they serve as feeders.

Guaranteed lines.

The guaranteed lines, including the East Indian, which was transferred to Government on 1st January 1880, the Eastern Bengal Railway similarly transferred in 1883, and the Sind, Punjab, and Delhi Railway to be taken over by Government in January 1886, comprise the following :—(1) The East Indian, running up the valley of the Ganges from Calcutta (Howrah) as far as Delhi, with a branch to Jabalpur. (2) The Eastern

Bengal Railway, traversing the richest portion of the Gangetic valley, and connected with the Northern Bengal State Railway. (3) The Great Indian Peninsula, which starts from Bombay, and sends one arm north-east to Jabalpur, with a branch to Nágpur, and another south-east to the frontier of Madras. (4) The Madras line, with its terminus at Madras city, and two arms running respectively to the Great Indian Peninsula junction at Ráichur and to Beypur on the opposite coast, with branches to Bangalore and Bellary. (5) The Oudh and Rohilkhand, with its numerous branches, connecting Lucknow with Cawnpur, Benares, Alígarh, Moradábád, Bareli, Saháranpur, and Hardwár. (6) The Bombay, Baroda, and Central India, which runs due north from Bombay through the fertile plain of Gujarát, to Ahmadábád, where it joins the Rájputána-Málwá State Railway, and ultimately connects with the East India and Sind, Punjab, and Delhi systems at Delhi and at Agra. (7) The Sind, Punjab, and Delhi, consisting of three sections, one in Lower Sind, another from Delhi to Lahore, and the third from Lahore to Múltán. (8) The South Indian (the only guaranteed line on the narrow gauge), in the extreme south, from Tinnevelli to Madras city, with branches to Arconum, Erode, Negapatam, Tuticorin, and Pondicherri.

The State lines are too numerous to be individually described. They include the extension from Lahore to Peshawar on the north-west frontier; the 'missing link,' from Múltán to Haidarábád, thus bringing the Punjab into direct connection with its natural seaport at Karáchi (opened throughout in 1878); the Rájputána-Málwá State Railway connecting Ahmadábád with Delhi, Agra, and Khándwá; and the Northern Bengal State Railway. The last-named line starts from Sára-ghát opposite the Damukdiha station of the Eastern Bengal Railway, whence it runs northwards to the foot of the Himálayas. A small 2 feet gauge railway is thence carried up to the sanitarium of Dárjíling, now within twenty-four hours' journey of Calcutta. Among other State lines, the following may be specified. The Tirhút State Railway with its various branches intersects Northern Behar, and is intended to extend to the Nepál frontier on one side, and to Assam on the other. The Dacca and Maimansingh Railway will open out Eastern Bengal; the Nágpur-Chhatísgarh Railway taps the great wheat-growing Districts of the Central Provinces. Shorter State lines or branches from the trunk railways are numerous. In British Burma, a State line runs up the Irawadi valley from Rangoon to Prome, with an extension to the frontier station of

Allan-myo. A second line up the Sittaung valley to Taung-ngu, is open for more than half its length, and the remainder is expected to be opened in 1886.

Assisted railways. Of the assisted railway companies, the principal are the Bengal and North-Western, running from the Sonpur station of the East Indian Railway to Bahraich in Oudh; the Bengal Central line from Calcutta to Khúlná bordering on the Sundarbans; the various branches of the Southern Maráthá Railway in the Deccan, of which 214 miles out of a sanctioned length of 718½ miles were open in March 1885; the Rohilkhand and Kumáun line; the Assam line to the recently-opened coal measures in Lakhimpur District; the little 2 feet gauge Dárjíling-Himálayan Railway (above mentioned); two short lines from the East Indian Railway to the shrine of Tarakeswar in Húglí District, and to Deogarh in the Santál Parganás, which are annually resorted to by large numbers of pilgrims from all parts of India. Other lines belonging to the assisted class are projected or have commenced construction. It is proposed to make on this system the Nágpur-Bengal line, which will connect the Chhatísgarh wheat plateau with the Húglí river, and thus complete an almost straight line of communication between Calcutta and Bombay. The Bhopál-Gwalior line will also be made on the assisted system; together with other lines belonging to the inner circle of communication in the interior of India.

The 'assisted' system. The principle adopted in the assisted system is for Government to guarantee a low rate of interest, or to give a guarantee for a limited period. The Company has therefore the keenest inducement to make the railway pay, as its profits, above the low guaranteed rate, depend on its own exertions, and on the economical working of the line. The Government recoups itself for the money advanced under the low guarantee before the line has begun to pay, by taking a share of the profits of the line when they exceed the guaranteed interest. This is the general principle of the assisted railways in India. But it is worked out differently in the case of almost every separate line; especially as regards the rate of interest guaranteed, and the duration or limits of the guarantee.

Native railways. Besides these there are 663½ miles of railway now (1885) opened in Native States, which have been constructed at the expense of the chiefs. The principal of these are the Baroda Railway, and the Bhaunagar-Gondal Railway in Western India, the Bhopál-Itársi line in Central India, the Jodhpur line in

Rájputána, the Nizám's Railway in Haidarábád, the Mysore Railway in Southern India, and the Rájpura-Patiála line in the Punjab. The railways passing through the States of Gwalior and Holkar are not included in this list, as they were constructed, not at the cost of the chiefs themselves, but out of the proceeds of a loan made to the Government by the Mahárájás Sindhia and Holkar, and are worked entirely by Government in connection with the Rájputána-Málwá Railway.

The two following paragraphs exhibit the railway statistics Railway of India for the years 1878 and 1885. They indicate the statistics, 1878 and progress which has been made during the seven years, since 1885; the materials for the first edition of this book were compiled.

In 1878, the total mileage open for traffic was 8215 miles, of 1878; which 6044 miles belonged to guaranteed railways, and 2171 miles to State railways; total capital expended, £115,059,434, being £95,430,863 on the former, and £19,628,591 on the latter class; number of passengers conveyed, 38,519,792; number of tons of goods and minerals, 8,171,617; number of live stock, 594,249; gross receipts, £10,404,753; gross expenses, £5,206,938; net earnings, £5,197,815, of which only £195,787 is credited to the State railways; percentage of gross expenses to gross receipts, 50·04, varying from 34·97 in the case of the East Indian main line to an average of 78·27 for all the State lines. These figures showed 1 mile of railway to every 109 square miles of area in 1878, as compared with the area of British India, or to 180 square miles, as compared with the area of the entire peninsula. The average cost of construction per mile was almost exactly £14,000. The guaranteed railways, embracing the great trunk lines throughout India, are on the 'broad gauge' of 5 feet 6 inches; the State lines follow, as a rule, the narrow or metre gauge of 3·281 feet. On 31st March 1879, the total 1879. length opened was 8545 miles; and the capital invested, 120 millions sterling.

The total extent of railways open for traffic in India on Railway the 31st March 1885 was 12,004 miles, of which 6906 statistics, miles were in the hands of companies, either guaranteed 1885. or assisted; 4434 miles were State lines, either Imperial or Provincial; and 664 miles belonged to Native States. On the same date, the extent of railway line under construction was 3555 miles, of which 963 miles were in the hands of companies, 2125 miles were under construction by the State, and 467 miles by Native States.

The capital outlay on railways and connected steamer services Railway
capital.

Railway finance, 1884. (exclusive of the Rohilkhand-Kumáun and Bareilly - Pilibhít lines), amounted on 31st December 1884 to £155,450,366. Of this sum, £105,319,144 was expended by guaranteed companies (inclusive of the cost of the East Indian Railway, which stands at £35,065,667); £42,924,898 on State railways (Imperial and Provincial); £3,423,259 on assisted companies' lines ; and £3,783,065 on Native State lines. The gross receipts during the calendar year 1884 amounted to £16,066,225, and the working expenses to £8,156,157. The net revenue amounted to £7,910,068, or 5·09 per cent. on the total capital expended up to the 31st December 1884. Of the net revenue, the East Indian Railway, including the State branches worked by the Company, contributed £2,796,414 ; the guaranteed lines, £3,397,183 ; State lines, Imperial and Provincial, £1,609,156 ; and lines in Native States, £114,812. The total number of passengers carried was 73,815,119, the receipts amounting to £5,070,754. The aggregate tonnage of goods and merchandise carried was 16,663,007 tons, the receipts from goods traffic, etc., amounting to £10,565,941.

Roads.   As the railway system of India approaches its completion, the relative importance of the roads naturally diminishes. From a military point of view, rapid communication by rail

Old military routes. has now superseded the old marching routes as completely as in any European country. Like Portsmouth in England, Bombay in India has become the national harbour for the embarkation and disembarkation of troops. On landing at Bombay, regiments proceed, after a rest, to the healthy station of Deolálí on the plateau of the Deccan, whence they can reach their ultimate destinations, however remote, by easy railway stages.

The 'Grand Trunk Road.'   The Grand Trunk Road, running up the entire valley of the Ganges from Calcutta to the north-west frontier, first planned as a highway of armies in the 16th century by the Afghán Emperor Sher Sháh, and brought to completion under the administration of Lord William Bentinck, is now for the most part untrodden by troops. The monument, erected to commemorate the opening of the military road up the Bhor Ghát to wheeled traffic from Bombay, remains unvisited by all but the most curious travellers. Railways have bridged

Bombay inland route. the widest rivers and the most formidable swamps. They have scaled, with their aerial zigzags, the barrier range of the Gháts ; and they have been carried on massive embankments over the shifting soil of the Gangetic delta.

But although the railway system now occupies the first place, both for military and commercial purposes, the actual import- ance of roads has increased rather than diminished. They do not figure in the imperial balance-sheet, nor do they strike the popular imagination; but their construction and repair constitute one of the most important duties of the District official. They promote that regularity of local communication upon which the progress of civilisation so largely depends. The substitution of the post-cart for the naked runner, and of wheeled traffic for the pack-bullock, is one of the silent revolutions effected by British rule. *Extension of roads*

The more important roads are all carefully metalled, the material almost everywhere employed being *kankar* or cal- careous limestone. In Lower Bengal and other deltaic tracts, where no kind of stone exists, bricks are roughly burnt, and then broken up to supply metal for the roads. The minor streams are crossed by permanent bridges, with foundations of stone, and not unfrequently iron girders. The larger rivers have temporary bridges of boats thrown across them during the dry season, which give place to ferries in time of flood. Avenues of trees along the roads afford shade, and material for timber. The main lines are under the charge of the Public Works Department. The maintenance of the minor roads has, by a recent administrative reform, been thrown upon the shoulders of the local authorities, who depend for their pecuniary resources upon District committees, and are often compelled to act as their own engineers. Complete statistics are not available to show the total mileage of roads in British India, or the total sum expended on their maintenance. *Road metal.* *Bridges of boats.*

Inland navigation is almost confined to the four great rivers, the Ganges, the Brahmaputra, the Indus, and the Irawadi. These flow through broad valleys, and from time immemorial have been the chief means of conveying the produce of the interior to the sea. South of the Gangetic basin, there is not a single Indian river which can be called navigable. Most of the South Indian streams, although mighty torrents in the rainy season, dwindle away to mere threads of water and stag- nant pools during the rest of the year. The Godávari and the Narbadá, whose volume of water is ample, are both obstructed by rocky rapids, which engineering skill has hitherto been unable to overcome. A total sum of $1\frac{1}{2}$ million sterling has been almost in vain expended upon the former river, with a view to improving it as a navigable highway. It is doubtful *Rivers.* *The Godá- vari works.*

whether water carriage is able to compete, as regards the more valuable staples, with communication by rail. But for cheap and bulky staples, or for slow subsidiary traffic, it is difficult to overrate the economic importance of the Indian rivers.

The Ganges.

After the East Indian Railway was fairly opened, through steamers ceased to ply upon the Ganges ; and the steam flotilla on the Indus shrank to insignificance when through communication by rail became possible between Múltán and Karáchi. On the Brahmaputra and its tributary the Bárak, and on the Irawadi, steamers still run secure from railway competition. But it is in the Gangetic delta that river navigation attains its highest development. There the population may be regarded as half amphibious. Every village can be reached by water in the rainy season, and every family keeps its boat. The main channels of the Ganges and Brahmaputra, and their larger tributaries, are navigable throughout the year. During the rainy months, road carriage is altogether superseded. All the minor streams are swollen by the rainfall on the hills and the local downpour ; while fleets of boats sail down with the produce that has accumulated in warehouses on the river banks.

The Brahmaputra.

Minor streams

River trade.

The statistics of this subject belong rather to the department of internal trade,[1] but it may be mentioned here that the number of laden boats registered in Bengal in the year 1877–78 was 401,729. These formed but a fraction of the real total. Boat-racing forms a favourite native sport in the deltaic and eastern Districts. It is conducted with great spirit and rivalry by the villagers. In some places, the day concludes with an illuminated boat procession by torchlight.

The Nadiyá rivers.

The great majority of the Bengal rivers require no attention from Government, but the network known as the three Nadiyá rivers is kept open for traffic only by close supervision. These three rivers, the Bhágiráthí, Jalangí, and Mátábhángá, are all offshoots of the Ganges, which unite to make up the head-waters of the Húglí.[2] In former times, the main volume of the Ganges was carried to the sea by one or other of these channels. But they now receive so little water as to be navigable only in the rainy season, and then with difficulty. Since the beginning of the present century, Government has undertaken the task of preventing these Húglí head-waters from

[1] Dealt with in next chapter.
[2] See article HUGLI RIVER, *The Imperial Gazetteer*, for an account of the engineering history of these rivers. It is also given in greater detail in Hunter's *Statistical Account of Bengal*, vol. ii. pp. 19-32.

further deterioration. A staff of engineers is constantly employed to watch the shifting bed, to assist the scouring action of the current, and to advertise the trading community of the depth of water from time to time. In the year 1882–83, a total sum of £11,667 was expended on this account, while an income of £18,296 was derived from tolls.

The artificial water channels of India may be divided into two classes. (1) Those confined to navigation ; (2) those constructed primarily for purposes of irrigation. Of the former class, the most important examples are to be found in the south of the peninsula. On both the Malabar and the Coromandel coasts, the strip of low land lying between the mountains and the sea affords natural facilities for the construction of an inland canal running parallel to the shore. In Malabar, the salt-water lagoons or lakes, which form so prominent a feature in the local geography, merely required to be supplemented by a few cuttings to supply continuous water communication from the port of Calicut to Cape Comorin. On the east coast, the Buckingham Canal, running north from Madras city as far as the delta of the Kistna, has recently been completed without any great engineering difficulties. In Bengal there are a few artificial canals, of old date, but of no great magnitude, in the neighbourhood of Calcutta. The principal of these form the system known as the Calcutta and Eastern Canals, which consist for the most part of natural channels artificially deepened, in order to afford a safe boat route through the Sundarbans. Up to the close of the year 1877–78, a capital of £360,332 had been expended by Government on the Calcutta Canals; the gross income in 1877–78 was £44,120 ; after deducting cost of repairs, etc., charged to revenue account, and interest at the rate of 4½ per cent., a net profit was left amounting to £8748. In 1882–83, the tolls on the Calcutta Canals realized £53,372. The Hijili Tidal Canal in Midnapur District, which cuts off a difficult corner of the Húglí river, yielded a net revenue of £3171 in the same year. In 1882–83, this canal only yielded a net profit of £446, owing to the cost of dredging operations, and the consequent closing of the canal for a portion of the year.

Most of the great irrigation works, both in Northern and Southern India, have been so constructed as to be available also for navigation. The general features of these works have been already described. So far as regards Bengal, navigation

Navigable canals.

Malabar backwaters.

Buckingham Canal.

Calcutta canals.

Hijili Canal.

Navigation on Bengal canals ;

on the Orissa Canals in 1877–78 yielded £3384, and in 1882–83, £10,847; on the Midnapur Canal, £10,692 in 1877–78, and £10,642 in 1882–83; and on the Son Canals, £5965 in 1877–78, and £3906 in 1882–83; the aggregate being considerably larger than was derived from irrigation. In Madras, boat tolls in the Godávari delta brought in £4496 in 1877–78, and £6295 in 1882–83. In the Kistna delta, tolls realized £1718 in 1877–78, and £3956 in 1882–83. The works of the Madras Irrigation Company on the Tungabhadra were not made available for navigation until 1879, and they were taken over by Government in 1882. Their navigation receipts in that year amounted to £1068.

on Madras canals.

CHAPTER XIX.

COMMERCE AND TRADE.

FROM the earliest days, India has been a trading country. Trade of
The industrial genius of her inhabitants, even more than her India.
natural wealth and her extensive seaboard, distinguished her
from other Asiatic lands. In contrast with the Arabian
peninsula on the west, with the Malayan peninsula on Ancient.
the east, or with the equally fertile empire of China, India
has always maintained an active intercourse with Europe.
Philology proves that the precious cargoes of Solomon's
merchant ships came from the ancient coast of Malabar.
The brilliant mediæval republics of Italy drew no small share
of their wealth from their Indian trade. It was the hope of
participating in this trade that stimulated Columbus to the
discovery of America, and Da Gama to the circumnavigation
of the Cape of Good Hope. Spices, drugs, dyes, and rare Mediæval.
woods; fabrics of silk and cotton; jewels, and gold and silver,
—these were the temptations which allured the first adventurers
from Europe.

The East and the West were then separated by a twelve-
month's voyage, full of hardships and perils. A successful
venture made the fortune of all concerned, but trade was a
lottery, and not far removed from piracy. Gradually, as the
native kingdoms fell, and the proud cities of mediæval India
sank into ruin, the legendary wealth of India was found to
rest upon an unstable basis. It has been reserved for our
own day to discover, by the touchstone of open trade, the real Modern.
source of her natural riches, and to substitute bales of raw
produce for boxes of curiosities. The cotton, grain, oil-seeds,
and jute of India now support a large population in England.

Before entering on the statistics of Indian trade, it is well to The
apprehend the function which commerce has now to perform modern
in India. The people have in some Provinces outgrown the trade in
food-producing powers of the soil; in many others, they are India.
pressing heavily upon these powers. Agriculture, almost their
sole industry, no longer suffices for their support. New

New industries necessary.
industries have become a necessity for their well-being. Commerce and manufactures have therefore obtained an economical importance which they never had before in India; for they represent the means of finding employment and food for the rapidly increasing population. A popular sketch of the social aspects of Indian trade will therefore be first given, before arranging in more logical sequence the facts and figures connected with its recent history and development.

Large sea-borne trade impossible under the Mughals.
A large external trade was an impossibility under the Mughal Emperors. Their capitals of Northern India, Agra and Delhi, lay more than a thousand miles from the river's mouth. But even the capitals of the seaboard Provinces were chosen for military purposes, and with small regard to the commercial capabilities of their situation. Thus, in Lower Bengal, the Muhammadans under different dynasties fixed in succession

Their capitals,
on six towns as their capital. Each of these successive capitals was on a river bank; but not one of them possessed any foreign trade, nor indeed could have been approached by an

merely royal camps.
old East Indiaman. They were simply the court and camp of the king or the viceroy for the time being. Colonies of skilful artisans settled round the palaces of the nobles to supply the luxurious fabrics of oriental life. After the prince and court had in some new caprice abandoned the city, the artisans remained, and a little settlement of weavers was often the sole surviving proof that the decaying town had once been a capital city. The exquisite muslins of Dacca and the soft silks of Murshidábád still bear witness to the days when these two places were successively the capital of Bengal. The artisans worked in their own houses. The manufactures of India were essentially domestic industries, conducted by special castes, each member of which wove at his own hereditary loom, and in his own village or homestead.

Growth of trading cities under British rule.
One of the earliest results of British rule in India was the growth of great mercantile towns. Our rule derived its origin from our commerce; and from the first, the East India Company's efforts were directed to creating centres for maritime trade. Other European nations, the Portuguese, the Dutch, the Danes, and the French, competed with us as merchants and conquerors in India, and each of them in turn attempted to found great seaports. The long Indian coast, both on the east and the west, is dotted with decaying villages which were once the busy scenes of those nations' early European trade. Of all their famous capitals in India, not one has now the

commercial importance of Cardiff or Greenock, and not one of them has a harbour which would admit at a low tide a ship drawing 20 feet.

The truth is, that it is far easier to pitch a camp and erect a palace, which, under the native dynasties, was synonymous with founding a capital, than it is to create a centre of trade. Emporia of commerce must grow of themselves, and cannot be called suddenly into existence by the fiat of the wisest autocrat. It is in this difficult enterprise, in which the Portuguese, the Dutch, the Danes, and the French had successively failed, that the British in India have succeeded. We make our appearance in the long list of races who have ruled that splendid empire, not as temple-builders like the Hindus, nor as palace and tomb builders like the Musalmáns, nor as fort-builders like the Maráthás, nor as church-builders like the Portuguese; but in the more commonplace capacity of town-builders, as a nation that had the talent for selecting sites on which great commercial cities would grow up, and who have in this way created a new industrial life for the Indian people. *The English as city-builders.*

Calcutta and Bombay, the two commercial capitals of India, are the slow products of British rule. Formerly, the industries of India were essentially domestic manufactures, each man working at his hereditary occupation, at his own loom or at his own forge. Under British rule, a new era of production has arisen in India—an era of production on a great scale, based upon the co-operation of capital and labour, in place of the small household manufactures of ancient times. To Englishmen, who have from our youth grown up in the midst of a keen commercial civilisation, it is not easy to realize the change thus implied. *A new era of production, based on co-operation and capital.*

The great industrial cities of British India are the type of this change. Under native rule, the country had reached what political economists of Mill's school called 'the stationary stage' of civilisation. The husbandmen simply raised the food-grains necessary to feed them from one harvest to another. If the food crops failed in any district, the local population had no capital and no other crops wherewith to buy food from other districts; so, in the natural and inevitable course of things, they perished. Now, the peasants of India supplement their food-supply with more profitable crops than the mere foodstuffs on which they live. They also raise an annual surplus of grain for exportation, which is available for India's own wants in time of need. Accordingly, *Growth of industrial cities.*

there is a much larger aggregate of capital in the country; that is to say, a much greater national reserve or staying power. The so-called 'stationary stage' in India has disappeared, and the Indian peasant is keenly alive to each new demand which the market of the world may make upon the industrial capabilities of his country; as the history of his trade in cotton, jute, wheat, and oil-seeds proves.

Summary of Indian exports, 1700-1885.   At the beginning of the last century, before the English became the ruling power in India, the country did not produce £1,000,000 a year of staples for exportation. During the first three-quarters of a century of our rule, the exports slowly rose to about £10,000,000 in 1834. During the half century since that date, the old inland duties and other remaining restrictions on Indian trade have been abolished. Exports have multiplied by eight-fold. In 1880, India sold to foreign nations £66,000,000 worth, and in 1884–85, upwards of £80,000,000 worth of strictly Indian produce, which the Indian husbandman had raised, and for which he was paid. In 1880, the total foreign trade of India, including both exports and imports, exceeded £122,000,000. In 1884–85, the total foreign import and export trade of India, excluding treasure and Government stores, was over £136,000,000, or including treasure and Government stores, nearly £155,000,000.

India's balance of trade.   India has more to sell to the world than she requires to buy from it. During the five years ending 1879, the staples which she exported exceeded by an annual average of over £24,000,000 the merchandise which she imported.[1] During the next five years ending 31st March 1884, the gross surplus of exports of merchandise over imports rose to 30 millions sterling per annum.[2]

About one-third of this favourable balance of trade India receives in hard cash. During the five years ending 1879, she accumulated silver and gold, exclusive of re-exports, at the rate of £7,000,000 per annum, and during the next five years ending March 1884 at the rate of £11,000,000 per annum. With another third she pays interest at low rates for the capital with which she has constructed the material framework of her industrial life, — her railways, irrigation works,

What she does with the balance.

---

[1] This calculation deals with the *gross* surplus of exports over imports, without going into the question of re-exports of foreign goods. The total 'merchandise' exported, during the five years ending 1879, averaged £63,000,000; the total 'merchandise' imported averaged £38,000,000. *Vide post*, Table at p. 562, entitled *Foreign Trade of India*.

[2] This also is the gross surplus, without deductions for re-exports.

cotton mills, coal mines, indigo factories, tea-gardens, docks, steam-navigation lines, and debt. For that capital she goes into the cheapest market in the world, London; and she remits the interest, not in cash, but in her own staples, which the borrowed capital has enabled her to bring cheaply to the seaboard. With the remaining third of her surplus exports, she pays the home charges of the Government to which she owes the peace and security that alone have rendered possible her industrial development.

The Home Charges include not only the salaries of the supervising staff in England, and the pensions of the military and civil services, who have given their life's work to India, but the munitions of war, a section of the army, including the cost of its recruitment and transport, stores for public works, and the *materiel* for constructing and working the railways. That *materiel* can be bought more cheaply in England than in India; and India's expenditure on good government is as essential an item for her industrial develop-ment, and repays her as high a profit, as the interest which she pays in England for the capital with which she has constructed her dockyards and railways. But after paying for all the Home Charges for the interest of capital raised in England for Indian railways, and other reproductive works, and for the *materiel* required for their construction and maintenance, India has still a surplus of £11,000,000 from her export trade for which she receives payment in silver and gold.

The 'Home Charges.'

India's yearly savings.

The trade of India may be considered under four heads— (1) sea-borne trade with foreign countries; (2) coasting trade; (3) frontier trade, chiefly across the northern mountains; (4) internal traffic within the limits of the Empire.

Divisions of Indian trade.

The sea-borne trade most powerfully attracts the imagina-tion, and we have the most trustworthy statistics regarding it. With an extensive seaboard, India has comparatively few ports. Calcutta monopolizes the commerce, not only of Lower Bengal, but of the entire river-systems of the Ganges and the Brahmaputra. Bombay is the sole outlet for the products of Western India, Gujarát (Guzerát), the Deccan, and the Central Provinces; Karáchi (Kurrachee) performs a similar office for the valley of the Indus; and Rangoon for that of the Irawadi. These four ports have been chosen as the termini where the main lines of railway debouch on the sea. In the south of India alone is the sea-borne trade distributed along the coast.

Sea-borne trade.

The four great ports.

The south-western side has a line of fair-weather ports, from Goa to Cochin. On the south-east there is not a safe harbour, nor a navigable river-mouth; although ships anchor off the shore at Madras, and in several other roadsteads, generally near the mouths of the rivers. A Madras harbour has, however, been under construction during several years; and, in spite of destructive cyclones and storm-waves, the work is now well advanced. Since these sheets went to press, a project has been put forward for constructing docks at Madras, to cover 25 acres, protected by groins thrown out at right angles from the beach, and by a breakwater (1885).

Of the total foreign trade of India, Calcutta and Bombay till recently controlled about 40 per cent. each. Madras had 6 per cent., Rangoon 4 per cent., and Karáchi 2 per cent., leaving a balance of only 8 per cent. for all the remaining ports of the country. In 1884–85, Bombay had 43·51 per cent. of the foreign trade; Calcutta, 36·97 per cent.; Madras, 5·43 per cent.; Rangoon, 4·67 per cent.; and Karáchi, 3·79 per cent.,

Minor ports. leaving only 5½ per cent. for the minor ports, of which the principal are—Chittagong, Maulmain, Akyab, Tuticorin, and

The two centres. Coconada. Calcutta and Bombay form the two central depôts for collection and distribution, to a degree without a parallel in other countries. The growth of their prosperity is an index of the development of Indian commerce.

Early Portuguese trade, 1500-1600. When the Portuguese, the pioneers of Eastern adventure, discovered the over-sea route to India, they were attracted to the Malabar coast, where they found wealthy cities already engaged in active commerce with Persia, Arabia, and the opposite shore of Africa. From Malabar they brought back pepper and other spices, and the cotton calicoes which took their name from Calicut. Fixing their head-quarters at Goa, they advanced northwards to Surat, the ancient port not only for Gujarát but for all Western Upper India. But with the Portuguese, the trading instinct was subordinate to the spirit of proselytism and to the ambition of territorial aggrandizement.

Dutch monopoly, 1600. The Dutch superseded them as traders, and organized a colonial system upon the basis of monopoly and forced labour, which survives in Java to this day. Last of all

English factories, 1625. came the English, planting factories at various points along the Indian coast-line, and content to live under the shadow of the native powers. Wars with the Portuguese, with the Dutch, and with the French, first taught the English their own strength; and as the Mughal Empire fell to pieces, they were compelled to become rulers in order to protect their commercial settlements. Our Indian Empire has grown out of trade; but, meanwhile, our Indian trade has grown even faster than our empire.[1]

'The Governor and Company of Merchants of London _{English} trading to the East Indies' was incorporated by Royal Charter on 31st December 1600, having been directly called into existence by the grievance of monopoly prices imposed upon pepper by the Dutch. Its first voyage was undertaken in 1601 by five ships, whose cargoes consisted of £28,742 in bullion and £6860 in goods; the latter being chiefly cloth, lead, tin, cutlery, glass, quicksilver, and Muscovy hides. Their destination was 'Atcheen in the Far East' (Sumatra). The first English factory was established at Bantam in Java, in 1603. The return cargoes, partly captured from the Portuguese, comprised raw silk, fine calicoes, indigo, cloves, and mace. The earliest English factories on the mainland of India were founded at Masulipatam in 1610, and Surat in 1612–15. In 1619, ten ships were despatched to the East by the Company, with £62,490 in precious metals and £28,508 in goods; the proceeds, brought back in a single ship, were sold for £108,887. The English made no great advance in trade during the 17th century. By the massacre of Amboyna (1623) the Dutch drove the English Company out of the Spice Islands, and the period of its great establishments (*aurangs*) for weaving had not yet commenced in India.

Early in the 18th century, our affairs improved. During the _{Our trade} twenty years ending 1728, the average annual exports from England of the East India Company were £442,350 of bullion and £92,288 of goods. The average imports were valued at £758,042, chiefly consisting of calicoes and other woven goods, raw silk, diamonds, tea, porcelain, pepper, drugs, and saltpetre. In 1772, the sales at the India House reached the total value of 3 millions sterling; the shipping owned by the Company was 61,860 tons. From 1760 onwards, the Custom House returns of trade with the East Indies are given in Macpherson's *History of Commerce*. But they are deceptive for comparative purposes, as they include the trade with China as well as with India.

In 1834, when the Company's monopoly of trade with China _{Statistics} as well as with India ceased, the exports from India were valued _{for 1834.} at £9,674,000, and the imports at £2,576,000. Shortly after

---

[1] The history of the early European settlements in India has been already dealt with in chapter xiv. pp. 356-377.

that date, trade was freed from many vexatious restrictions.
Inland duties were mostly abolished in Bengal in 1836, in
Bombay in 1838, and in Madras in 1844; the inland sugar
Inland
duties
abolished,
1836-48. duties in 1836 and the inland cotton duties in 1847. The
navigation laws were repealed in 1848. The effect of these
reforms, and the general progress of Indian commerce, may
be seen in the table below. It exhibits the foreign trade of
the country, in millions sterling, for each of the nine quinquennial periods between 1840 and 1884.

Before, however, entering on the items of Indian trade, the
method which has been adopted in dealing with them ought to
be explained. Many of those items may be regarded as agricultural productions, and as manufactures or native industries,
as well as articles of export or internal trade. In such cases
it has been deemed best to deal with them in each of these
aspects, even at the cost of repetition. Thus cotton is treated
of alike in the chapter on agriculture, and in those on trade
and on manufactures. This plan will be most convenient to
those who wish to consult the individual chapters, without the
necessity of reading the whole volume.

FOREIGN TRADE OF INDIA FOR FORTY-FIVE YEARS, CLASSIFIED
ACCORDING TO QUINQUENNIAL PERIODS, IN MILLIONS
STERLING.

PERIODS.	IMPORTS.			EXPORTS.		
	Cotton Manufactures.	Total Merchandise.	Treasure.	Raw Cotton.	Total Merchandise.	Treasure.
1840-44,	3·19	7·69	2·74	2·34	14·62	0·48
1845-49,	3·75	9·14	3·07	1·68	17·00	1·32
1850-54,	5·15	11·06	4·79	3·14	20·10	1·00
1855-59,	6·94	15·58	11·27	3·11	25·85	0·92
1860-64,	10·92	23·97	17·07	15·56	43·17	1·02
1865-69,	15·74	31·70	17·62	25·93	57·66	1·80
1870-74,	17·56	33·04	8·56	17·41	57·84	1·59
1875-79,	19·29	38·36	9·81	11·52	63·13	2·81
1880-84,	22·48	47·95	12·61	14·29	79·97	1·26
Average in millions sterling,	11·67	24·27	9·72	10·55	42·15	1·36

Steadiness
of its
growth. The preceding table shows a rapid and steady growth,
which only finds its parallel in the United Kingdom. The
exceptional imports of silver from 1855 to 1859 were required
to pay for the Mutiny; those from 1859 to 1864 represent the

price of the cotton sent to Manchester during the American war.

Before examining in detail the history of some of the chief staples of trade, it may be convenient to give in this place, as an illustration of the steady growth of Indian foreign trade, the statistics of three years, 1877-78, which was a year of inflation despite the incidence of famine in Southern India ; of 1882-83 ; and of 1884-85. In 1877-78, the total foreign sea-borne trade exceeded 126 millions sterling in value. The transactions on behalf of Government, such as stores, equipments, and munitions of war, show an import of £2,138,182, and an export of £36,615. The imports of merchandise were £39,326,003, and of treasure £17,355,460 ; total imports, £56,681,463. The exports of merchandise were £65,185,713, and of treasure £2,155,136 ; total exports, £67,340,849. *Indian trade in 1878.*

These figures exhibit an excess of exports over imports amounting to £10,659,386 ; and an excess of treasure imported to the amount of £15,200,324. By far the larger share of the trade of 1878, amounting to 61 per cent., was conducted with the United Kingdom ; next came China, with 13 per cent. ; and then the following countries in order :—France, Straits Settlements, Ceylon, Italy, United States, Mauritius, Austria, Persia, Arabia, Turkey, Egypt, Australia, Aden, East Coast of Africa. The total number of vessels that entered and cleared in 1877-78 was 12,537, with an aggregate of 5,754,379 tons, or an average of 459 tons each. Of the total tonnage, 76 per cent. was British, 7 per cent. British Indian, and 15 per cent. foreign ; American, Italian, and French being best represented in the latter class. *Excess of exports.* *India's chief customers.* *Indian shipping.*

The total value of the Indian foreign seaboard trade in 1882-83, including merchandise, treasure, Government stores, etc., exceeded 150 millions sterling, or 24 millions in excess of the total value of the trade in 1877-78. The imports of private merchandise amounted to £50,003,041, and of treasure to £13,453,157 ; total private imports, £63,456,198, or £6,774,735 above the imports of 1877-78. The exports of merchandise amounted to £83,400,865, and of treasure to £980,859 ; total exports, £84,381,724, or £17,040,875 above the exports of 1877-78. Excess of exports over imports in 1882-83 (exclusive of Government transactions), £20,925,526. The Government transactions, such as stores, equipments, munitions of war, railway plant, etc., show an import of £2,092,670, and an export of £145,458, including £61,200 of Government treasure. *Indian trade in 1882-83.*

Suez Canal trade, 1882-83.

Of the private imports, £47,172,542, or 74·3 per cent., came in 1882 *via* the Suez Canal, and £16,283,656, or 25·7 per cent., by other routes. Of the exports, £44,438,288, or 52·7 per cent., went *via* the Canal, and £39,943,436, or 47·3 per cent., by other routes. Of the total import and export private trade, aggregating £147,837,922, £91,610,830, or 61·9 per cent., passed through the Suez Canal, and £56,227,092, or 38·1 per cent., by other routes. The total number of sailing and steam vessels that entered and cleared British Indian ports from foreign countries in 1882–83, was 11,715 with an aggregate burthen of 7,071,884 tons, or an average of 513 tons each. Of the total shipping, 4257 vessels with a total of 5,366,770 tons were returned as British, 2525 with 361,189 tons as British Indian, 1834 with 1,168,293 tons as foreign, and 3099 with 175,632 tons as native craft, in 1882–83.

Indian trade in 1884-85.

The figures for 1884–85 show a steadily increasing trade. In that year, the total value of the private sea-borne foreign export and import trade was returned at over 152 millions, or 26 millions over the total sea-borne trade in 1877–78, and of 2 millions over that of 1882–83. The imports of private merchandise in 1884–85 amounted to £53,147,919, and of treasure to £13,878,841 ; total private imports, £67,026,760, or £10,345,297 in excess of the imports of 1877–78, and £3,570,562 in excess of those for 1882–83. The exports of merchandise amounted to £83,115,443, and of treasure to £1,885,679 ; total private exports, £85,001,122, or £17,660,273 over the exports of 1877–78, and of £619,398 over those for 1882–83. Excess of exports over imports in 1884–85, £17,974,362. The Government imports in the shape of stores, materials of war, railway plant, treasure, etc., amounted to £2,563,111, and the exports to £138,007.

Suez Canal trade, 1884-85.

Of the private trade, merchandise and treasure to the value of £51,605,827, or 76·99 per cent. of the imports, were, in 1884, imported *via* the Suez Canal, while £47,530,200, or 55·9 per cent. of the total exports, were exported by the same route. Of the total import and export private trade in 1884–85, £99,136,025, or 65·2 per cent., passed through the Suez Canal, and £52,891,855, or 34·8 per cent., proceeded by other routes. The total number of sailing and steam vessels that entered and cleared British Indian ports with cargoes from and to foreign countries in 1884–85, was 8222, with an aggregate burthen of 5,814,904 tons, or an average of 707 tons each.

Statistics are not yet (July 1885) available to exhibit in Distribu- detail the total value and distribution of the foreign trade of tion of Indian India in 1884–85. The figures in the following paragraphs and trade; tables refer to 1882–83, the latest year for which the final returns, as printed by command of Parliament, have been received.

Of the entire trade in 1882–83, £81,770,117, or 55·31 per in 1882-83. cent., was conducted with the United Kingdom; £17,684,973, or 11·96 per cent., with China; £7,757,818, or 5·25 per cent., with France; £5,409,804, or 3·66 per cent., with Italy; and £5,330,471, or 3·44 per cent., with the Straits Settlements; and then the following countries in order :—the United States of America, 2·89 per cent. ; Austria, 2·17 per cent. ; Australia, 2·02 per cent. ; Ceylon, 1·85 per cent. ; Egypt, 1·69 per cent. ; Belgium, 1·51 per cent. ; Persia, 1·39 per cent. ; Cape and East Coast of Africa, 1·19 per cent. ; Arabia, 1·05 per cent. ; Mauritius, 1·00 per cent. ; Turkey, 0·73 per cent. ; and Aden, 0·48 per cent.

As regards imports into India, the first thing to notice is Analysis the enormous predominance of two items—cotton goods and of Indian treasure. During the forty-five years ending 1883–84, cotton imports. goods formed 33 per cent., or exactly one-third of the total, and treasure an additional 30 per cent. Next in order come metals (copper, which is largely used by native smiths, slightly exceeding iron) ; Government stores, including munitions of war, boots, liquor, and clothing for soldiers, and railway plant; liquors, entirely for European consumption ; coal, for the use of the railways and mills ; railway plant for the guaranteed and assisted companies ; salt, provisions, machinery and mill-work, and manufactured silk. It will thus be seen that, with the exception of Manchester goods, no articles of European manufacture are in large demand for native consumption, but only for the needs of our English administration ; and few raw materials, except coal, copper, iron, mineral oil, and salt.

England's export trade to India thus mainly depends upon History of piece-goods. In the beginning of the 17th century, the cotton- industry had not been introduced into England. The small goods trade : British demand for cotton-goods or calicoes was met by circuitous importations from India itself, where cotton-weaving is an immemorial industry. In 1641, 'Manchester Man- cottons,' in imitation of Indian calicoes and chintzes, were still chester, 1641. made of wool. Cotton is said to have been first manufactured

[*Sentence continued on page* 568.

Foreign Sea-borne Trade of British India for 1882-83.

Imports.

Articles.	Quantities.		Value.
Apparel, ...	...	...	£769,752
Arms, Ammunition, etc., .	...	...	79,577
Books, Paper, and Stationery,	...	...	625,431
Coal, Coke, etc., . . tons	...	628,824	1,019,883
Cotton Twist and Yarn, . lbs.	...	49,392,375	£3,378,190
Cotton Piece-Goods and } yards Manufactures, }	...	1,642,798,990	21,431,872
Total Cotton Goods,	...	...	24,810,062
Drugs and Medicines, . .	...	...	391,673
Dyes, ...	...	...	206,640
Fruits and Vegetables, . .	...	...	211,435
Glass, and Manufactures of, .	...	...	483,743
Gums and Resins,	...	...	117,921
Hardware, Cutlery, and Plate,	...	...	791,791
Horses, ...	...	...	186,815
Ivory, ...	...	...	212,107
Jewellery and Precious Stones,	...	...	307,189
Liquors { Ale, Beer, and Porter, gals.	1,170,554		£272,323
Spirits, . . . ,,	949,169		674,969
Wines and Liqueurs, . ,,	418,169		387,322
Total Liquors, . . ,,	...	2,537,892	1,334,614
Machinery and Mill Work,	...	..	1,342,398
Metals { Iron, . . . tons	...	157,597	£1,870,494
Steel, . . . ,,	...	10,645	163,415
Brass, . . . cwts.	...	11,962	64,688
Copper, . . . ,,	...	450,098	1,938,376
Spelter, . . . ,,	...	127,383	125,669
Tin, . . . ,,	...	42,718	277,306
Lead, . . . ,,	...	73,583	101,104
Quicksilver, . . lbs.	...	354,689	37,100
Unenumerated, . .	...	...	37,834
Total Metals, . .	...	...	4,615,986
Oils, ...	...	...	1,050,897
Paints and Colours, . .	...	...	234,450
Perfumery, . . .	...	...	63,336
Porcelain and Earthenware, .	...	...	170,002
Provisions, . . .	...	...	1,087,186
Railway Plant and Rolling Stock,[1]	...	...	1,116,434
Salt, ... tons	...	338,065	515,184
Silk (raw) and Thread, . lbs.	...	2,386,150	£1,074,156
Silk Manufactures, . yards	...	9,671,261	977,768
Total Silk, . .	...	...	2,051,924
Spices, ... lbs.	...	...	510,854
Sugar, ... cwts.	...	672,672	1,086,961
Tea, ... lbs.	...	2,751,085	193,052
Tobacco, . . .	...	...	83,608
Umbrellas, ...	...	...	232,829
Wood, and Manufactures of,	...	...	99,384
Wool (raw), . . . lbs.	...	2,781,257	£68,931
Wool, Manufactures of, yards	...	6,932,779	984,873
Total Wool & Woollen Goods,	...	...	1,053,804
All Other Articles, . .	...	...	2,946,119
Total Merchandise, .	...	..	£50,003,041
Treasure, . . .	...	..	13,453,157
Total Merchandise and } Treasure, . }	...	...	£63,456,198
Government Imports,	...	...	2,092,670
Grand Total of } Imports, . }	...	...	£65,548,868

[1] Exclusive of material for East Indian and other State railways.

FOREIGN SEA-BORNE TRADE OF BRITISH INDIA FOR 1882-83.

Articles.	Quantity.		Value.	
EXPORTS.				
Coffee, . . . cwts.	...	364,008	...	£1,419,131
Coir, and Manufactures of ⎱ (excluding Cordage), ⎰ ,,	...	173,209		152,129
Cotton (raw), . . . ,,	...	6,170,173	£16,055,758	
Cotton Twist and Yarn, .	...	...	1,874,464	
Cotton Manufactures, .	...	...	2,093,146	
Total Cotton & Cotton Goods,	...	...		20,023,368
Drugs and Medicines, .	...	...	...	154,463
Indigo, ... cwts.	...	141,041	£3,912,997	
Other Dyes (except Lac), .	...	...	258,436	
Total Dyes (except Lac),	...	...		4,171,433
Rice (including Paddy), . cwts.	31,258,288		£8,476,327	
Wheat, ... ,,	14,193,763		6,088,814	
Other Grains, . . . ,,	1,165,826		319,571	
Total Grain, . . . ,,		46,617,877		14,884,712
Gums and Resins, . . ,,	...	282,416	...	356,931
Hemp, and Manufactures of,	...	...	...	44,236
Hides and Skins, . . No.	...	26,539,988	...	4,444,946
Horns, ...	...	...	...	181,785
Ivory, and Manufactures of,	...	...	...	112,469
Jewellery and Precious Stones,	. .	...	...	65,177
Jute (raw), ... cwts.	...	10,348,909	£5,846,926	
Jute, Manufactures of, ⎰ bags ⎱ yards	... ...	66,737,651 ⎱ 4,601,247 ⎰	1,487,831	
Total Jute and Jute Goods,	...	...		7,334,757
Lac (dye, shell, etc.), . . cwts.	...	138,844	...	699,113
Oils, ...	...	...	...	443,764
Opium, ...chests	...	91,798	...	11,481,379
Saltpetre, ... cwts.	...	399,565	...	388,766
Seeds, ... ,,	...	13,147,982	...	7,205,924
Silk (raw), ... lbs.	...	665,488	£596,838	
Silk, Manufactures of, .	...	...	306,928	
Total Silk and Silk Goods,	...	...		903,766
Spices. . . . . lbs.	...	20,947,105	...	417,291
Sugar, ... cwts.	...	1,428,360	...	989,009
Tea, ... lbs.	...	58,233,345	...	3,738,842
Tobacco, ...	...	...	...	117,156
Wood, and Manufactures of,	...	...	...	56,370
Wool (raw), . . . lbs.	...	26,380,327	£1,002,833	
Wool, Manufactures of, .	...	...	183,348	
Total Wool & Woollen Goods,	...	...		1,186,181
All Other Articles, . .	...	...	...	2,427,607
Total Merchandise,[1] .	...	...	...	£83,400,865
Treasure, . . .	...	...	...	980,859
Total Merchandise and ⎱ Treasure, . . ⎰	...	...	...	£84,381,724
Government Exports, .	...	...	...	145,458
GRAND TOTAL OF ⎱ EXPORTS, . ⎰	...	...		£84,527,182

[1] Viz. ⎰ Indian Produce or Manufacture, £80,598,155
      ⎱ Foreign Merchandise, . . 2,802,710

                                    £83,400,865

Sentence continued from page 565.]

Cotton introduced 1676. in England in 1676. To foster the nascent industry, a succession of statutes were passed prohibiting the wear of imported cottons; nor was it until after the inventions of Arkwright and others, and the application of steam as a motive power, had secured to Manchester the advantage of cheap production, that these protective measures were entirely removed. In the present century, Lancashire rapidly improved on her instructors.

Cotton-goods imports, 1840–83. During the five years 1840–45, the annual import of cotton manufactures into India averaged a little over £3,000,000 sterling. In each subsequent quinquennial period, there has been a steady increase, until in 1877–78 the import reached the total of £20,000,000 sterling, and in 1882–83 nearly £21,500,000, or an increase of more than seven-fold in forty-four years.

Imports of treasure. The importation of treasure is perhaps still more extraordinary, when we bear in mind that it is not consumed in the using, but remains permanently in the country. During the same period of forty-four years, the net import of treasure, deducting export, has reached the enormous aggregate of 358¾ millions sterling, or a fraction under £1, 8s. per head of the 256 million inhabitants of British and Feudatory India. By far the larger portion of this was silver; but the figures for gold, so far as they can be ascertained, are by no means inconsiderable.

Proportion of gold to silver. During the ten years ending 1875, when the normal value of silver as expressed in gold was but little disturbed, the total net imports of treasure into India amounted to just 99 millions. Of this total, 62½ millions were in silver, and 36½ millions in gold, the latter metal forming more than one-third of the whole. On separating the re-exports from the imports, the attraction of gold to India appears yet more marked. Of the total imports of gold, only 7 per cent. was re-exported, while for silver the corresponding portion was 19 per cent. Roughly speaking, it may be concluded that India then absorbed annually about 5 millions of silver, and 3 millions sterling of gold; say a total hoard of 7 to 8 millions sterling of the precious metals each year during the decade ending 1875.

Gold and silver circulation. The depreciation of silver which has since taken place has caused an increase in the import of silver, and a corresponding decrease in the export of gold. The figures since 1876 do not show the normal state of things. But even in 1877–78, when the value of silver in terms of gold touched a low point, although India drew upon its hoards of gold for export to the amount of more than 1 million sterling, she at the same time imported 1½ million, showing a net import of half a million of gold. It has been estimated that the gold circulation of India amounts to 1,620,000 of gold *mohars* (Rs. 16 to Rs. 20 each), worth about three millions sterling ; as compared with £158,000,000 of silver and £2,960,000 of copper. In addition, 10 million sovereigns are said to be hoarded in India, mainly in the Bombay Presidency, where the stamp of St. George and the Dragon is valued as a religious symbol. As already stated, the net accumulation of silver and gold in India, after allowing for re-exports, averaged 7 millions sterling during the five years ending 1879 ; and rose to an average of 11 millions sterling during the next quinquennial period ending 31st March 1884.

Turning to the exports, the changes in relative magnitude demand detailed notice. In 1877–78, raw cotton for the first time for many years fell into the second place, being surpassed by the aggregate total of food-grains. In 1882–83, raw cotton had again advanced into the first place among the exports, exceeding the value of food-grains by upwards of a million sterling. Oil-seeds show as a formidable competitor to cotton, jute nearly doubles indigo, hides and tea come close behind ; while exports of cotton manufactures exceed coffee in value by upwards of half a million. The imports of sugar, in value although not in quantity, exceed the exports ; the trade in raw silk is about equally balanced ; while spices, once the glory of Eastern trade, were exported in 1877–78, to the value of only £226,515, as compared with imports of spices of twice that value (£488,884). In 1882–83, spices were exported to nearly the same value as the imports, namely, exports £417,391, and imports £510,854.

The export of raw cotton has been subject to excessive variations. At the close of the last century, cotton was sent to England in small quantities, chiefly the produce of the Central Provinces, collected at Mírzápur and shipped at Calcutta ; or the produce of Gujarát (Guzerát) despatched from Surat. In 1805, the cotton from Surat was valued at £108,000. In the same year, only 2000 bales of East Indian cotton were imported into Great Britain. But this figure fails to show the average ; for by 1810, the corresponding number of bales had risen to 79,000, to sink again to 2000 in 1813, and to rise to 248,000 in 1818. Bombay did not begin to participate in this trade until 1825, but has now acquired the practical monopoly, since the railway diverted to the west the produce of

Analysis of Indian exports.

Export of raw cotton.

Its history 1805–34.

the Central Provinces.　In 1834, when the commerce of India was thrown open, 33,000,000 lbs. of cotton were exported.

Export of raw cotton since 1840;　Analysing the exports of cotton during the forty-five years since 1840, we find that in the first quinquennial period they averaged $2\frac{1}{3}$ millions sterling in value, and did not rise perceptibly until 1858, when they first touched 4 millions.　From that date increase was steady, even before the American exports were cut off by the war in 1861.　During the American war, India made the most of her opportunity, although quality did not keep pace with the enhanced price.　The export of raw cotton reached its highest value at $37\frac{1}{2}$ millions sterling in 1865, and its highest quantity at 803,000,000 lbs. in 1866.

and since 1865.　Thenceforth the decline has been constant, although somewhat irregular, the lowest figures both of quantity and value being those of 1878-79, when the exports amounted to 2,966,569 cwts., valued at £7,914,091.　The principal feature of the trade in 1877-78 was the comparatively small amount shipped to the United Kingdom, and the even distribution of the rest among continental ports.　Indian cotton has a short staple, which is ill-suited for the finer counts of yarn spun in the Lancashire mills.　In 1877-78, out of a total of nearly $3\frac{1}{2}$ million cwts., less than $1\frac{1}{2}$ million cwts. was consigned to England; of the remainder, France took 611,000 cwts.; Italy, 434,000; Austria, 407,000; China, 209,000; and Germany, 109,000.　The export of raw cotton in 1878-79 amounted in value to £7,914,091, and of twist and cotton goods, to £2,581,823.　In 1882-83, out of a total export of over 6 million cwts. of raw cotton, 2,865,065 cwts. were shipped to the United Kingdom, 937,934 cwts. to Italy, 764,550 cwts. to Austria, 585,766 cwts. to France, 333,708 cwts. to Belgium, 114,412 cwts. to Germany, and 364,519 cwts. to Hong-Kong.　In 1882-83, raw cotton was exported to the value of £16,055,758; cotton twist and yarn, £1,874,464 and cotton manufactures, £2,093,146.　Total cotton exports, £20,023,368.

Export of jute;　Second in importance to cotton as a raw material for British manufacture comes jute.　At the time of the London Exhibition of 1851, jute fibre was almost unknown, while attention was even then actively drawn to rhea or China grass, which remains to the present day unmanageable by any cheap process. From time immemorial, jute has been grown in the swamps of Eastern Bengal, and has been woven into coarse fabrics for bags and even clothing.　As early as 1795, Dr. Roxburgh called attention to the commercial value of the plant, which he

grew in the Botanical Gardens of Calcutta, and named 'jute,'
after the language of his Orissa gardeners; the Bengalí word
being *pát* or *koshta*. In 1828–29, the total exports of jute in 1828;
were only 364 cwts., valued at £62. From that date the trade
steadily grew, until in the quinquennial period ending 1847–48 in 1848.
the exports averaged 234,055 cwts. The Crimean war, which
cut off the supplies of Russian flax and hemp from the Forfar-
shire weavers, made the reputation of jute. Dundee forthwith
adopted the new fibre as her speciality, and the Bengal cultivators as readily set themselves to meet the demand.

Taking quinquennial periods, the export of raw jute rose Later
from an average of 969,724 cwts. in 1858–63 to 2,628,100 cwts. history,
in 1863–68, and 4,858,162 cwts. in 1868–73. The highest 1858-78;
figures reached prior to 1882 were in the year 1872–73, with
7,080,912 cwts., valued at £4,330,759. A falling off subsequently took place, partly owing to the competition of the
weaving-mills in the neighbourhood of Calcutta; but the trade
continued on a permanent basis. By far the greater bulk of
the exports is consigned to the United Kingdom, and a large
proportion direct to Dundee. In 1877–78, out of a total of
5,450,276 cwts., 4,493,483 cwts. were sent to the United
Kingdom, 845,810 cwts. to the United States, 110,983 cwts. to
'other countries,' chiefly France, which has prosperous weaving-
mills at Dunquerque.

In 1882–83, the exports of raw jute had increased to and
10,348,909 cwts. valued at £5,846,926, being considerably 1882-83.
higher both in quantity and value than the figures for any
previous year. Of this quantity 7,834,136 cwts. valued at
£4,709,299 were exported to the United Kingdom, 2,002,731
cwts. valued at £814,847 to the United States, 184,508 cwts.
valued at £116,042 to Germany, 147,644 cwts. valued at
£89,454 to Austria. Jute manufactures to the number of
60,737,654 gunny-bags, valued at £1,431,581, were exported
in 1882–83, Australia taking nearly one-third of the total
number of bags, and upwards of one-half of the total value.
Including 4,601,247 yards of gunny cloth, and 1346 cwts. of
rope and twine, the total export trade of raw and manufactured
jute amounted in 1882–83 to £7,334,757 in value.

The export of raw jute is almost monopolized by Calcutta,
although Chittagong, which is nearer the producing Districts, is
beginning to take a share in the business.

The export of grain, as already noticed, reached in 1878 a Export
higher total than that of cotton, although cotton again has of food-
taken the first place in exports. The two staple cereals are grains.

Rice.

rice and wheat. Rice is exported from British Burma, from Bengal, and from Madras. The latter Presidency usually despatches about 2½ million cwts. a year, chiefly to its own emigrant coolies in Ceylon; but in 1877–78, this trade was almost entirely checked by the famine. In that year, besides supplying the necessities of Madras, Bengal was able to send nearly 6 million cwts. to foreign ports. The Burmese rice is chiefly exported for distillation or starch; the Bengal exports are chiefly intended for food, whether in Ceylon, the Mauritius, the Straits Settlements, the West Indies, or Europe.

Burmese rice.

From the point of view of the English market, rice means almost entirely Burmese rice, which is annually exported to the amount of about 20 million cwts., valued at over 5 millions sterling. In the Indian tables, this is all entered as consigned to the United Kingdom; although, as a matter of fact, the rice fleets from Burma only call for orders at Falmouth, and are there diverted to various continental ports. Burmese rice is known in the trade as 'five parts cargo rice,' being but imperfectly husked before shipment, so that it contains about one part in five of paddy or unhusked rice. It has a thick, coarse grain, and is principally utilized for distillation or for conversion into starch.

Rice trade in 1878;

In 1877–78, the exports of rice to the United Kingdom amounted to 10,488,198 cwts., being slightly less than the average,—but about half of this total is known to be re-exported to foreign countries; the direct exports to the Continent were only 68,839 cwts. to Germany, and 20,117 to France. Siam and Cochin China supply the wants of China, but India has a practical monopoly of the European market. In 1878–79, after India had begun to recover from the famine, although prices continued to rule high, the total export of rice was 21¼ million tons, valued at 9 millions sterling (£8,978,951).

in 1882-83.

The total foreign exports of rice and paddy from British India in 1882–83 amounted to 31,258,288 cwts., valued at £8,476,327. Of the total quantity, 12,381,486 cwts., valued at £3,211,398, went to the United Kingdom, although, as explained above, a large proportion is re-exported to other European countries. The other countries largely consuming Indian rice were—the Straits Settlements, 4,092,521 cwts.; Egypt, 2,973,703 cwts.; Ceylon, 2,883,534 cwts.; Malta, 2,732,442 cwts.; Mauritius, 1,227,671 cwts.; Arabia, 832,574 cwts.; South America, 786,557 cwts.; France, 605,735 cwts. Italy, 165,662 cwts.; Germany, 124,447 cwts., etc. Of the total exports of 31,258,288 cwts., 21,330,587 cwts., or 68·2 per cent., were exported from British Burma; 7,855,151 cwts., or 25'1 per cent., from Bengal; 1,448,540 cwts. from Madras; 552,537 cwts. from Bombay; and 71,473 cwts. from Sind.

An export duty is levied on rice in India at the rate of 3 *ánnás* per *maund*, or about 6d. per cwt. A similar duty on wheat was repealed in 1873, and that trade has since conspicuously advanced. *Export duty on rice.*

In 1874–75, the export of wheat was about 1 million cwts. Forthwith it increased year by year, until in 1877–78 it exceeded 6⅓ million cwts., valued at nearly 3 millions sterling. In 1878–79, the quantity fell to 1 million cwts., valued at £520,138, owing to the general failure of the harvest in the producing Districts. But as railways open up the country, and the cultivators find a steady market in England, India may, as already mentioned, some day become a rival to America and Russia in the wheat trade of the world. The Punjab is a great and rapidly developing wheat-growing tract in India; but up till recently the supplies have chiefly come from the North-Western Provinces and Oudh, being collected at Cawnpur, and thence despatched by rail to Calcutta. As indicated below, Bombay has now taken the place of Calcutta in the exportation of wheat, the opening of the Rájputána-Málwá Railway having put Bombay in direct communication with the Punjab wheat tract. In 1877–78, out of the total of 6,340,150 cwts., Bengal exported 4,546,062 cwts., Bombay 1,159,443, and Sind 607,470. The chief countries of destination were—the United Kingdom, 5,731,349 cwts.; the Mauritius, 154,888; and France, 116,674. *Export of wheat.* *Wheat trade in 1878;*

Since 1877–78, the wheat export trade has rapidly extended, and in the year 1882–83 it stood at 14,193,763 cwts., valued at £6,088,934. Nearly one-half of the total exports, or 6,575,160 cwts., went to the United Kingdom, 3,567,712 cwts. to France, 1,458,898 cwts. to Belgium, 799,550 cwts. to Egypt, 578,246 cwts. to Holland, 176,063 cwts. to Italy, 494,098 cwts. to Gibraltar, and 163,358 cwts. to Malta. Of the total wheat, Bombay exported 6,957,752 cwts., or 49'2 per cent.; Calcutta, 4,439,405 cwts., or 31'4 per cent.; and Karáchi, 2,732,275 cwts., or 19'3 per cent., the small balance being sent from Madras and Rangoon. *in 1882-83.*

It is said that Italy is beginning to utilize the hard, white Indian wheat for the manufacture of macaroni.

Oil-seeds were freed in 1875 from their former export duty of 3 per cent. *ad valorem*. During the ten previous years, the average annual export was only about 4 million cwts.; but *Exports of oil-seeds in 1877-78.*

Oil-seeds in 1877-78. the fiscal change, coinciding with an augmented demand in Europe, has since trebled the Indian export. In 1877–78, the export of oil-seeds amounted to 12,187,020 cwts., valued at $7\frac{1}{3}$ millions sterling. Of this, Bengal contributed 7,799,220 cwts., and Bombay 3,179,475 cwts. Linseed and rape are consigned mainly to the United Kingdom, while France takes almost the entire quantity of *til* or gingelly. In 1879, the export of oil-seeds fell to $7\frac{1}{4}$ million cwts., valued at

in 1882-83. £4,682,512. In 1882–83, exports of oil-seeds had again increased to 13,147,982 cwts., valued at £7,205,924, of which 5,898,383 cwts., valued at £3,397,840, went from Bombay, and 5,592,896 cwts., valued at £2,817,140, from Bengal. The principal countries of destination were—the United Kingdom, 6,409,134 cwts.; France, 3,923,964 cwts.; Belgium, 1,001,164 cwts.; Egypt, 631,388 cwts.; Italy, 445,773 cwts.; United States, 321,688 cwts.; and Holland, 254,014. Besides oil seeds, British India exported in 1882–83, 3,644,632 gallons of expressed oil, and 201,116 cwts. of oil-cake, of the total value of £445,529.

Exports of indigo in 1877-78; In actual amount, although not in relative importance, indigo holds its own, notwithstanding the competition of aniline dyes. The export of 1877–78 amounted to 120,605 cwts. valued at £3,494,334. Of this total, Bengal sent 99,402 cwts., and Madras 16,899 cwts. In 1878–79, the export of indigo amounted to 105,051 cwts., valued at £2,960,463. In

1882-83; 1882–83, the exports of indigo amounted to 141,041 cwts., of the value of £3,912,997, of which 99,715 cwts., valued at £3,023,540, were sent from Bengal; and 33,474 cwts., valued at £763,096, from Madras. The most noticeable feature in this trade is the diminishing proportion sent direct to England

its destination, 1882-83. and the wide distribution of the remainder. In 1882–83, only 60,645 cwts. were consigned direct to the United Kingdom; 27,285 cwts., or about one-fifth, to the United States; 16,076 cwts. to Egypt, thence probably re-shipped to Europe; 15,513 cwts. to France; 8394 cwts. to Austria; 6077 cwts. to Persia; 4033 cwts. to Turkey; and 1607 cwts. to Italy.

Safflower. Of other dyes, the export of safflower has fallen off being only in demand in the United Kingdom, and as a rouge in China and Japan; the export in 1877–78 was 3698 cwts., valued at £14,881. In 1882–83, the exports of safflowe

Myro-balams. amounted to 3008 cwts., value £9203. The export of myro balams, on the other hand, was greatly stimulated by the Russo Turkish War, which interrupted the supply of valonica and galls from Asia Minor. The quantity rose from 286,350 cwts

in 1875–76 to 537,055 cwts. in 1877–78, valued in the latter
year at £230,526. In 1882–83, the exports of myrobalams
were 471,167 cwts., value £184,697. Practically the whole
is sent to the United Kingdom. Turmeric exports amounted Turmeric.
to 146,865 cwts. in 1877–78, valued at £123,766, of which the
United Kingdom took about one-half. In 1882–83, the exports
of turmeric had dropped to 63,570 cwts., valued at £37,207.
Lac-dye, like other kinds of lac, shows a depressed trade, the Lac.
exports in 1877–78 having been 9570 cwts., valued at £29,009.
In 1882–83, the exports of lac-dye had fallen to 3927 cwts.,
valued at £4610, the whole of which was sent to the United
Kingdom and the United States.

No Indian export has made such steady progress as tea, Exports of
which has multiplied more than seven-fold in the space of tea.
fifteen years. In 1867–68, the amount was only 7,811,429
lbs.; by 1872–73, it had reached 17,920,439 lbs.; in 1878–79,
without a single step of retrogression, it had further risen to
34,800,027 lbs., valued at £3,170,118; and in 1882–83, to
a total of 58,233,345 lbs., of the value of £3,738,842.
Until recently, Indian tea was practically confined to the
United Kingdom, but markets have recently been opened out
in Australia and the United States. The exports to the
United Kingdom in 1882–83 amounted to 54,108,114 lbs., to
Australia 2,772,461 lbs., and to the United States 676,507 lbs.

Indian tea has now a recognised position in the London Indian and
market, generally averaging about 4d. per lb. higher in China tea.
value than Chinese tea; but it has failed to win acceptance
in most other countries, excepting Australia. Its growing
importance as compared with Chinese tea appears from
the following figures. In 1872, the imports of Indian tea
into England were to those of Chinese tea as 1 to 9·7; in
1874, as 1 to 7·5; in 1876, as 1 to 5·6; and in 1878, as 1 to 4·7.

The exports of coffee from India are stationary, if not Coffee.
declining. The highest amount during the past fifteen years was
507,296 cwts. in 1871–72, the lowest amount 298,587 cwts. in
1877–78, valued at £1,338,499. In 1878–79, the export of
coffee was 342,268 cwts., valued at £1,548,481. The export
of coffee had slightly increased by 1882–83 to 364,008 cwts.,
but showed a decrease in value to £1,419,131.

Among manufactured goods, cotton and jute deserve notice, Export of
although by far the greater part of the produce of the Indian cotton
mills is consumed locally. The value of Indian cotton-manufac- tures,
tured goods exported in 1877–78 was £1,142,732; in 1879–80, in 1877-78;
£1,644,125; and in 1882–83, £2,093,146. The exports of

Export of cotton manufactures,

twist and yarn, spun in the Bombay mills, increased from 3 million lbs. in 1874–75 to 15½ million lbs. in 1877–78, valued at £682,058. The chief places of destination were — China, 13,762,133 lbs.; Aden, 1,181,120 lbs.; and Arabia, 393,371 lbs. The export of twist and yarn in

in 1882-83.

1878–79 was valued at £937,698. By 1882–83, the exports of twist and yarn, nearly all from Bombay, had increased to 44,859,175 lbs., value £1,874,464, chiefly to China, Japan, Java, and Aden. Indian-made piece-goods belong to two classes. Coloured goods, woven in hand-looms, are annually exported from Madras to Ceylon and the Straits, to the value of about £230,000, the quantity being about 8 million yards; while in 1877–78, grey goods from the Bombay mills were sent to Aden, Arabia, Zanzibar, and the Mekran coast, amounting to over 10 million yards, and valued at £141,509. By 1882–83, the export of grey goods from Bombay had increased to 41,799,370 yards; value £466,260.

Exports of jute manufactures.

Jute manufactures consist of gunny-bags, gunny cloth, and rope and twine, almost entirely the produce of the Calcutta mills. In these, the value of the exports tends to increase faster than the quantity, having multiplied nearly four-fold in the five years ending 1882–83. In 1877–78, the total export of jute manufactures was valued at £771,127, and in 1879–80 at

Gunny-bags, in 1877-78;

£1,098,434. Gunny-bags, for the packing of wheat, rice, and wool, were exported in that year to the number of more than 26½ millions, valued at £729,669. Of this total, £298,000 (including by far the most valuable bags) was sent to Australia, £162,000 to the Straits, £80,000 to the United States, £77,000 to Egypt, £32,000 to China, and £81,000 to other countries, which comprises a considerable quantity destined for England. In 1878–79, the export of gunny-bags had increased to 45⅓ millions. Of gunny cloth in pieces, nearly 3 million yards were exported, almost entirely to the United States; in 1878–79, these exports had increased to upwards of 4½ million yards. Of rope and twine, 4428 cwts. were exported in 1877–78, valued at £5443.

Gunny-bags, in 1882-83.

By 1882–83, the number of gunny-bags exported had increased to 66,737,654, of a value of £1,431,584, the principal countries to which they were sent being Australia, China, the Straits Settlements, and the United States. Gunny cloth to the extent of 4,601,247 yards was also exported in the same year to the value of £55,802; as were also rope and twine, 1346 cwts., valued at £1872. The total export of Indian jute manufactures in 1882–83 was valued at £1,487,831, or double the figure (£771,127) for 1877–78.

The following statistics, being taken from Indian returns, do Countries with which India trades. not in all cases show the real origin of the imports or the ultimate destination of the exports, but primarily the countries with which India has direct dealings. London still retains its pre-eminence as the first Oriental mart in the world, whither buyers come from the other countries of Europe to satisfy their wants. To London Germans come for wool, Frenchmen for jute, and all nations for rare dyes, spices, and drugs.

The opening of the Suez Canal restored to the maritime cities of the Mediterranean a share of the Eastern business which they once monopolized. But, on the other hand, the advantage of prior possession, the growing use of steamers, and the certainty of being able to obtain a return freight, all tend to favour trade with England, carried in English bottoms. As the result of these conflicting influences, the trade of India with the United Kingdom, while in actual amount it remains pretty constant, shows a relative decrease as compared with the total trade.

Taking merchandise only, the average value of English exports and imports during the two years 1867–69 amounted to slightly more than 58 millions sterling, out of a total of nearly 86 millions, being 66 per cent. Ten years later, the India's trade with England average value of English trade for 1877–79 was still 58 millions, but the total value had risen to 100 millions, and the proportion had therefore fallen to 56¾ per cent. In 1882–83, the total value of the English private imports and exports of merchandise had risen to 75¾ millions ; but the proportion to the total trade of a little less than 133½ millions (excluding Government stores and private and Government treasure) had fallen to 56·7 per cent. Next to the United Kingdom comes China, with an Indian trade of about 15¼ millions (imports and exports), or 11½ per cent. Of this, nearly 11½ millions represent opium, the only other articles which China takes from India with China. being raw cotton, cotton twist, and gunny-bags. In return, China sends silver, copper, raw silk and silk goods, sugar and tea, the balance of trade being adjusted through England. It is said that Chinese tea is now only consumed in India by natives, or sent across the frontier into Central Asia. The annual quantity imported into India is about 2½ million lbs., and the price is extremely low.

The trade with the Straits may be regarded as a branch India's trade with the Straits ; of the Chinese trade. The exports are valued at over 3½ millions sterling, of which more than a half consists of opium, the rest being principally made up by rice and gunny-bags. The imports are tin, areca-nuts, pepper, and raw silk,

with
Ceylon;

valued altogether at less than one-half of the exports. The trade with Ceylon is merely a form of coasting trade, large quantities of rice being shipped in native craft along the Madras coast to feed the Tamil coolies in that island. The imports

with
Mauritius.

are hardly a sixth of the exports in value. With Mauritius, rice is exchanged for sugar to a large amount.

India's
trade with
France;

Of European countries, France and Italy alone deserve notice beside England. In 1877–78, the Indian exports to France reached the large total of nearly 6 millions sterling, consisting chiefly of oil-seeds (rape and gingelly), indigo, cotton, silk, and coffee. The direct imports in the same year were valued at only £451,000, principally apparel and millinery, brandy and wines, and silk goods; but the same articles are also sent in considerable, although unascertained, quantities *viâ* England. In 1882–83, the exports to France amounted to £7,207,962, and the direct imports to £484,367. The

with Italy.

trade with Italy shows a steady increase; the Indian exports to Italy having risen from £1,100,000 in 1877–78 to £3,383,507 in 1882–83, and the return imports from £250,000 to £444,433. The exports are cotton, silk, oil-seeds (sesamum), and hides; the imports—corals, glass beads and false pearls, spirits and wines, and silk goods.

India's
trade
with the
United
States;

The trade with the United States comes next to that with Italy, aggregating a total for exports and imports of £4,277,560. The exports are indigo, hides, raw jute and gunny-bags, lac, saltpetre, and linseed; the imports are almost confined to mineral oils. In 1878–79, the import of ice (formerly an important item in the trade with the United States) fell off greatly, under competition from local manufacture at Calcutta and Bombay, and it has now entirely ceased; while the imports to India of American kerosene oil rose to 3 million gallons in 1878–79, and to the enormous quantity of 20 million gallons in 1882–83.

with
Australia.

The trade of India with Australia was formerly limited to the export of rice, gunny-bags, and castor-oil, and the import of copper and horses. A little coal is sent from Australia, and a little coffee from India. Hitherto Australia has preferred to drink Chinese tea; but a considerable development of trade in this and other Indian products has taken place since the Melbourne and other Colonial Exhibitions. The total exports to Australia in 1882–83 aggregated £1,088,918; return imports, £476,591.

The following tables summarize the private foreign trade of India in 1877–78 and 1882–83 :—

DISTRIBUTION OF FOREIGN TRADE OF INDIA IN 1877-78 AND 1882-83

(*Exclusive of Government Stores, and of Government and Private Treasure*).

	1877-78				1882-83			
	Imports.	Exports.	Total.	Percentage of value on grand total.	Imports.	Exports.	Total.	Percentage of value on grand total.
	£	£	£		£	£	£	
EUROPE—								
United Kingdom,	32,211,303	29,613,606	61,824,909	59·2	40,365,926	35,429,872	75,795,798	56·7
France,	451,105	5,967,002	6,418,107	6·1	484,367	7,207,962	7,692,329	5·8
Italy,	349,228	1,870,006	2,219,234	2·1	444,433	3,383,507	3,827,940	2·9
Austria,	113,078	1,465,891	1,578,969	1·5	270,395	2,602,556	2,872,951	2·1
Belgium,	119	218,706	218,825	·2	77,434	2,151,727	2,230,161	1·8
Other European countries,	48,667	975,413	964,080	1·0	135,681	2,415,945	2,551,626	1·9
Total,	33,173,500	40,950,624	73,224,124	70·1	41,779,236	53,191,569	94,970,805	71·2
AFRICA—								
Egypt,	42,461	577,752	620,213	·6	44,084	2,113,167	2,157,251	1·6
Mauritius,	642,471	1,148,217	1,790,688	1·7	882,706	592,669	1,475,375	1·1
Eastern coast ports,	217,964	281,080	499,044	·5	325,421	582,700	908,121	·7
Other African ports and islands,	3,405	157,599	161,004	·1	9,318	400,813	410,131	·3
Total,	906,301	2,164,648	3,070,949	2·9	1,261,529	3,689,349	4,950,878	3·7
AMERICA—								
United States,	279,717	1,932,727	2,212,444	2·1	934,342	3,343,218	4,277,560	3·2
Other American countries,	708	339,167	339,875	·3	4,100	418,868	422,968	·3
Total,	280,425	2,271,894	2,552,379	2·4	938,442	3,762,086	4,700,528	3·5
ASIA—								
China,	1,423,673	12,743,149	14,166,822	13·6	2,072,037	13,160,105	15,232,142	11·4
Straits Settlements,	1,079,702	2,581,736	3,661,438	3·5	1,596,692	3,638,734	5,235,426	3·9
Ceylon,	530,555	2,544,516	3,075,071	3·0	573,775	1,392,616	1,966,391	1·5
Persia,	469,507	873,193	1,342,700	1·3	573,620	1,223,878	1,797,498	1·3
Arabia,	323,692	682,934	1,006,626	·9	282,442	776,269	1,058,711	·3
Aden,	161,046	330,643	491,689	·5	69,588	575,672	645,260	·5
Other Asiatic countries,	679,393	486,843	1,166,146	1·1	379,089	901,668	1,280,757	1·0
Total,	4,667,478	20,243,014	14,910,492	23·9	5,547,243	21,668,942	27,216,185	20·4
AUSTRALASIA—								
Australia, including Tasmania and New Zealand,	298,298	455,534	753,832	·7	476,591	1,088,918	1,565,509	1·2

DISTRIBUTION OF PRINCIPAL EXPORTS OF RAW PRODUCE IN 1877-78 AND 1882-83 (*in cwts.*).

	Cotton.		Jute.		Rice.		Wheat.		Indigo.	
	1877-78.	1882-83.	1877-78.	1882-83.	1877-78.	1882-83.	1877-78.	1882-83.	1877-78.	1882-83.
United Kingdom,	1,440,000	2,865,065	4,493,483	7,834,136	10,488,198	12,381,486	5,731,349	6,575,160	51,641	60,645
France,	611,000	585,766	...	...	20,117	605,735	116,674	3,567,712	29,999	15,513
Germany,	109,000	114,412	...	184,508	68,839	124,447	...	...	...	...
Austria,	407,000	764,550	...	147,644	...	...	...	...	6,618	8,304
Italy,	434,000	937,934	...	65,528	...	165,662	...	...	1,392	1,607
United States,	...	...	845,810	2,002,731	...	...	...	...	9,832	27,285
Egypt,	...	...	...	...	...	2,973,793	...	799,550	12,417	16,076
Persia,	...	...	...	...	126,824	...	...	...	4,148	6,077
Mauritius,	...	...	...	...	1,461,931	1,227,671	154,888	64,706	...	...
China,	219,000	368,556	...	...	...	...	...	...	...	...
Straits Settlements,	...	...	...	...	1,022,431	4,092,521	...	...	...	...

The opening of the Suez Canal in 1869, while it has stimu- Trade *via* the Suez Canal. lated every department of trade into greater activity, has not materially changed its character. The use of the Canal implies steam power. In 1871–72, the first year for which statistics are available, the total number of steamers trading with India which passed through the Canal was 422, with a tonnage of 464,198. Every subsequent year shows an increase until the great fall in trade in 1878–79. In 1877–78, the number of steamers passing through the Canal was 1137, with a burthen of 1,617,839 tons, or 64 per cent. of the total steam tonnage. Although there was a considerable falling off in the two follow-ing years, the Canal trade speedily recovered itself; and in 1880–81, 1459 steamers of 2,133,872 tons passed the Canal. The highest figures hitherto reached were in 1881–82, when 1989 steamers of 2,887,988 tons passed the Canal. In the following year, 1882–83, the number of Canal steamers was 1645 of 2,585,920 tons.

As might be anticipated, the imports to India, being for the most part of small bulk and high value, first felt the advantages of this route. In 1875–76, 85 per cent. of the Growth of the Canal trade. imports from Europe and Egypt (excluding treasure) passed through the Canal, but only 29 per cent. of the exports. The export trade, however, has rapidly increased, showing that such bulky commodities as cotton, grain, oil-seeds, and jute now largely participate in the advantages of rapid transport afforded by the Canal. In 1877–78, the import trade *via* the Canal amounted to 74 per cent. of the total imports into British India, and the Canal exports to 36 per cent. of the total exports. In 1882–83, while the import trade *via* the Canal remained stationary at 74 per cent., the proportion of Canal exports had increased to 52 per cent. The proportion of both import and export trade passing through the Suez Canal has increased from 45 per cent. in 1877–78 to 61 per cent. in 1882–83. The Canal has reduced the length of the voyage from London to Calcutta by about thirty-six days. The route round the Cape was more than 11,000 miles, and occupied nearly three months; that through the Canal is less than 8000 miles, and takes from 30 to 45 days.

Sir R. Temple, when Finance Minister in 1872, drew up a Sir R. Temple on the balance of Indian trade. valuable State Paper, in which he placed in a clear light the various means by which the apparent excess of exports over imports is liquidated. His conclusions were based on special materials reaching from 1835 to 1871. They are therefore summarized here without attempting to extend them to the period which has since elapsed. The balance of trade during recent years has already been dealt with at pp. 558-9.

Indian commerce for thirty-six years.

During the thirty-six years between 1835 and 1871, the value of merchandise exported from India amounted to £1,012,000,000, say one thousand millions sterling; the value of merchandise imported into India amounted to £583,000,000, showing an excess of £429,000,000 in the exports. The value of treasure imported in the same period was £312,000,000, against £37,000,000 exported, being a net import of £275,000,000. Deducting this from the excess of merchandise exports, a balance of £154,000,000 has to be accounted for otherwise than in the ordinary operations of trade. The first item to be considered is freight. Next come all payments made in England, whether by the Indian Government or by private persons resident in India. During the thirty-six years taken, the aggregate amount of payments in England on Government account (now represented by the Secretary of State's bills) amounted to £113,000,000. These bills are drawn to meet charges due in England under such heads as civil and military pensions, interest on debt and on railway capital, military stores, etc. ; and they are bought by bankers or merchants, who require to meet their own payments in India. They operate, financially, as if treasure had been sent to India, and thus reduce the apparent balance of trade at one stroke from £154,000,000 to £41,000,000. The remaining item to be considered is the remittances to England on private account, which it is impossible to ascertain with any pretension to accuracy. In 1872, this item was estimated at £3,500,000 a year; but in former years it had been much less, and it is now probably much more. It includes such divers matters as the savings of officials, profits of trade and planting, interest on capital invested, etc. Together with freightage, it would make up the balance of £41,000,000 yet unaccounted for, and thus finally equalize and account for the balance of India's foreign trade.

The balance ; how accounted for.

Government remittances.

Private remittances.

Balance from Chinese trade.

The phenomena of the trade between India and China are to be explained on the same principles. In 1872-73, the total exports from India to China were valued at £12,074,347, to which opium alone contributed £10,529,673. The total imports from China were valued at only £1,355,171, showing an excess of £10,719,176 in exports, for which India receives no direct return from China. In this case, China pays her debt to India by the excess of her exports to England, which are there placed to the credit of India. During the twenty years between 1852 and 1871, the aggregate balance of trade in favour of China in her dealings with England amounted to £112,000,000. This amount was available to settle China's equally unfavourable balance with India, and was in fact paid by China for Indian opium, as certainly as if the opium had been sent to China *viâ* England. It is evident, therefore, that if the Chinese were to greatly increase their imports of English goods, the exchanges of India might be seriously affected.

The foreign trade of India is practically monopolized by five ports, namely, Calcutta, Bombay, Madras, Rangoon, and Karáchi; but the entire seaboard along both sides of the peninsula is thronged by native craft, which do a large coasting business. In the Gulfs of Kachchh (Cutch) and Cambay, on the Malabar coast, and in the southern Districts facing Ceylon, a large portion of the inhabitants are born sailors, conspicuous alike for their daring and for their skill in navigation. In 1873–74, which may be regarded as a normal year, the total number of vessels engaged in the coasting trade which cleared and entered was 294,374, with an aggregate of 10,379,862 tons; the total value of both coasting exports and imports was £34,890,445. Of the total number of vessels, 280,913, with 4,843,668 tons, were native craft. Bombay and Madras divided between them nearly all the native craft; while in Bengal and Burma, a large and increasing proportion of the coasting traffic is carried in British steamers. *Coasting trade. Statistics of coast trade and shipping, 1874;*

In 1877–78, the year of famine, the number of ships increased to 319,624; the tonnage to 15,732,246 tons; and the value to £67,814,446. By far the largest item was grain, of which a total of 1,137,690 tons, valued at 13 millions sterling, was thrown into the famine-stricken Districts from the seaboard. Next in importance came raw cotton and cotton goods. The trade in raw cotton in 1877–78 amounted to 387,438 cwts., valued at £957,900, much of which was merely transhipped from one port to another within the Bombay Presidency. Cotton twist and yarn in the same year amounted to 17,425,993 lbs., valued at £965,038, of which the greater part was sent from Bombay to Bengal and Madras. The total value of the exports coastwise of cotton piece-goods was £620,866, including about 24 million yards of grey goods sent from Bombay to Bengal and to Sind in nearly equal proportions, and about 2 million yards of coloured goods from Madras. Stimulated by the activity of the grain trade caused by the *in 1878. Staples of the coast trade, 1878.*

famine, the exports of gunny-bags from Calcutta coastwise rose to a total value of nearly £960,000. The trade in areca-nuts in 1877–78 amounted to nearly 44 million lbs., valued at over £500,000. Burma consumes most of these, obtaining its supplies from Bengal; while Bombay gets considerable quantities from Madras, from the Konkan and Goa, and from Bengal. Sugar (refined and unrefined) figures to the large amount of £900,000 in 1877–78, of which the greater part came from Bengal. The movements of treasure coastwise showed a total of just 5 millions sterling, being exceptionally augmented by the conveyance of silver to Burma in payment for rice supplied to Madras.

The growth and increasing importance of the coasting trade of India may be illustrated by a comparison of the statistics for 1878–79, the year after the famine, when trade may be said to have returned to its normal condition; with those for 1882–83, the latest year for which full details are available.

In 1878–79, a total of 4080 steamers, of 3,614,349 tons, entered the coast ports with cargoes, while 97,767 sailing vessels, of 2,151,673 tons, also entered with cargoes. Total number of vessels with cargoes entered, 101,847, of 5,766,022 tons. The number of vessels which cleared with cargoes in the same year, was 3981 steamers, of 3,412,546 tons, and 84,597 sailing vessels, of 1,940,196 tons. Total number of vessels cleared with cargoes, 88,578, of 5,352,742 tons. Grand total of vessels entered and cleared, 190,425, of 11,118,764 tons. The steam coasting trade is almost entirely monopolized by British or British Indian vessels. Of the 8061 steamers which entered or cleared Indian ports coastwise in 1878–79, only 46 were foreign, while not a single one was native; average tonnage of each steamer, 871 tons. Of the 182,364 sailing vessels, 177,567 were small native craft, of an average of only a little over 18 tons each; 2792 were foreign vessels, of an average burthen of 62 tons; while 2005 were British or British Indian sailing ships, of an average of 342 tons. The total value of the private coasting trade in 1878–79 was—Imports, merchandise, £21,978,011, and treasure, £3,777,852; total, £25,755,863. Exports, merchandise, £23,172,328, and treasure, £2,442,657; total, £25,614,985. Total of private imports and exports, merchandise, £45,150,339, and treasure, £6,220,509; grand total, £51,370,848. Government imports in 1878–79 comprised—stores, £436,407, and treasure, £2,644,480; total, £3,080,887. The exports comprised—

stores, £316,206, and treasure, £1,891,763; total, £2,207,969. Coasting
Grand total Government imports and exports, £5,288,556. ^{trade}

The figures of the coasting trade for 1882–83 show that In 1882–
4780 steamers with cargoes, of 5,040,898 tons, and 83.
103,203 sailing vessels, of 2,070,626 tons, entered Indian
coast ports ; while 4735 steamers, of 4,925,967 tons,
and 93,383 sailing vessels, of 1,931,639 tons, cleared during
the year. Total vessels entered and cleared with cargoes,
9515 steamers, of 9,966,865 tons; 196,587 sailing vessels,
of 4,002,265 tons; total vessels of all classes, entered
and cleared, 206,101 ; tonnage, 13,969,130. Of the 9515
coasting steamers which entered or cleared Indian ports in
1882–83, 9439 were British or British Indian, and 76 foreign,
with a total of 9,966,865 tons, or an average of 1047
tons each. Sailing vessels included—265 British, with an
average of 692 tons ; British Indian, 3060, average 118·6
tons ; foreign, 2990, average 41·4 tons ; and native craft,
190,271, average 17·5 tons. The total value of the private
coasting trade in 1882–83 was — Imports, merchandise,
£25,419,831, and treasure, £4,066,557 ; total, £29,486,388.
Exports, merchandise, £24,524,241, and treasure, £3,316,125 ;
total, £27,840,366. Total value of private imports and exports,
merchandise, £49,944,072, and treasure, £7,382,682 ; grand
total, £57,326,754. This total, however, includes £5,217,328
of re-imports, and £6,035,678 of re-exports ; grand total,
£11,253,006 representing re-exports and re-imports of the
foreign trade given in the previous section of this chapter.
The Government imports in 1882–83 comprised — stores,
£459,985, and treasure, £1,882,411 ; total, £2,342,396.
The exports comprised — stores, £358,026, and treasure,
£2,497,265 ; total, £2,855,291. Grand total of Government
imports and exports, by coasting vessels, £5,197,687.

Comparing the figures for the two years, it will be seen that Com-
the number of vessels engaged in carrying cargoes coastwise parison
increased by 15,676, and the tonnage by 2,850,366 tons, between years.
1878–79 and 1882–83. The increase was principally in the
steam traffic. Of the private trade, imports of merchandise in
the same period increased by £3,441,820, and of treasure by
£288,705; total, £3,730,525. Exports of merchandise
increased by £1,351,913, and of treasure by £873,468; total,
£2,225,381. Including both imports and exports, the value
of the merchandise carried coastwise showed an increase of
£4,793,733, and of treasure by £1,162,173; grand total
increase of private merchandise and treasure, £5,955,906.

Adding the value of Government imports and exports, the total coast-borne trade of India increased from £56,659,404 in 1878–79 to £62,524,441 in 1882–83, or by £5,865,037.

Frontier trade. FRONTIER TRADE.—Attempts have been made to register the trade which crosses the long land frontier of India on the north, stretching from Baluchistán to Independent Burma. The returns obtained for a period of five years ending 1882–83 show an annual trans-frontier landward trade averaging about $9\frac{1}{3}$ millions sterling; the yearly imports averaging about 5 millions, and the exports about $4\frac{1}{3}$ millions sterling. Of this, nearly one-half, or 44 per cent., belongs to Burma, and between one-fourth and one-third, or upwards of 28 per cent., to the Punjab and Sind. Details of this import and export trans-frontier trade for each of the five years will be found in the tables on subsequent pages. The figures, although perhaps not absolutely accurate, may be accepted as substantially correct.

Three main trade routes to Afghánistán. Three main trade routes pierce the Suláimán Mountains, across the western frontier of the Punjab and Sind. These are—(1) the Bolan Pass, which collects the trade both of Kandahár and Khelát, and debouches upon Sind at the important mart of Shikárpur, whose merchants have direct dealings with the remote cites of Central Asia ; (2) the Gomal Pass, leading from Ghazní to Dera Ismáil Khán, which is followed by the half-military, half-trading clan of Povindahs, who bring their own caravans of camels into the heart of India ; (3) the Khaibar Pass, from Kábul to Pesháwar.

Value of Afghán trade. The aggregate value of the annual trade with Afghánistán, previous to the late war, was estimated at 1 million sterling each way, or a total of 2 millions ; but it has since decreased. The figures for 1875–76, which, however, are stated to be incomplete, give the value of the imports from Afghánistán at £914,000, consisting chiefly of raw silk, dried fruits and nuts, *manjít* or madder and other dyes, *charas* (an intoxicating preparation of hemp) and other drugs, wood, and furs ; the total exports in 1875–76 were valued at £816,000, chiefly cotton goods both of native and European manufacture, Indian tea, indigo, and salt. In 1882–83, the total imports from Afghánistán and the neighbouring hill tribes into Sind and the Punjab amounted to £526,560, and the exports to £863,445 ; total, £1,390,005.

Trade with Central Asia. The Punjab also conducts a considerable business *viâ* Kashmír with Ladákh, Yarkand, and Kashgar, estimated at about 1 million sterling altogether. The chief marts on the side of

India are Amritsar and Jálandhar, from which latter place the route runs northwards past Kángra and Pálampur to Leh, where a British official has been stationed since 1867, in which year also a fair was established at Pálampur to attract the Yarkandí merchants. Merchandise is usually conveyed across the Himálayan passes on the backs of sheep and yaks ; but British enterprise has successfully taken mules as far as Leh. In 1875–76, the total imports from Kashmír were valued at £484,000, chiefly *pashmina* or shawl-wool, *charas*, raw silk, gold-dust and silver ingots, and borax ; the exports were valued at £342,000, chiefly cotton goods, food-grains, metals, salt, tea, and indigo. In 1882–83, the imports from Kashmír into the Punjab amounted to £505,335, and the exports to £349,477; total, £854,812. The whole trans-frontier landward trade of the Punjab in 1882–83 was—imports, £981,167, and exports, £1,083,920 ; grand total, £2,065,087. *Himálayan traffic;*

Farther east, the Independent State of Nepál cuts off direct intercourse with Tibet for a total length of nearly 700 miles, bordering the North-Western Provinces, Oudh, and Behar. Little trade is allowed to filter through Nepál, to and from Tibet (amounting in value in 1882–83 to £82,519 for both imports and exports); yet a very large traffic is everywhere carried on along the frontier between the Nepális and British subjects. The Nepál Government levies transit duties impartially on all commodities; but it is asserted that their fiscal tariff is not intended to be protective, and does not in fact operate as such. Markets are held at countless villages along the boundary, for the exchange of rural produce and articles of daily consumption ; and many cart tracks cross the line from our side, to lose themselves in the Nepál *tarái.* The principal trade route is that which starts from Patná, and proceeds nearly due north through Champáran District to the capital of Khatmandu ; but even this is not passable throughout for wheeled traffic. From Khatmandu, two routes branch off over the central range of the Himálayas, which both ultimately come down into the valley of the Tsanpu, or great river of Tibet. *with Nepál. Frontier marts. Nepál trade routes.*

In 1877–78, the registered trade with Nepál (which is doubtless below the truth) amounted to a total of £1,687,000, of which more than two-thirds was conducted by Bengal. The imports from Nepál were valued at £1,054,000, the principal items being food-grains and oil-seeds, cattle, timber, and horns. Other articles of import which do not figure prominently in the returns are musk, borax, *chireta*, madder, *Nepál trade values.*

Trade with Nepál;

cardamoms, *chauris* or yak-tails, ginger, *balchar* or scented grass, furs, and hawks. The Indian exports to Nepál in

1877

1877–78 were valued at £633,000, chiefly European and native piece-goods (of cotton, wool, and silk), salt, metals, raw cotton, sugar, and spices. To these may be added the miscellaneous articles which may be usually found in a pedlar's pack. In

and 1882.

1882–83, the total imports from Nepál into the North-Western Provinces, Oudh, and Bengal amounted to £1,378,175, and the exports from British India to £855,346; grand total,

Bhután.

£2,233,521. The trade with Sikkim and Bhután is at present too insignificant to require notice, although it is possible that our future entry into Tibet may lie through these States.

North-east frontier trade;

A certain amount of traffic is conducted with the hill tribes on the north-east frontier, who almost surround the Province of Assam from Bhután to Manipur. According to the returns

1877 and 1882.

for 1877–78, the total frontier trade of Assam amounts to about £100,000 a year. In 1882–83 it amounted to £115,206, £83,318 being imports, and £31,888 exports. It consists chiefly of the bartering of rice, cotton cloth, salt, and metals, for the raw cotton grown by the hill tribes, and for the caoutchouc, lac, beeswax, and other jungle produce which they collect.

Trade with Independent Burma;

The trade with Independent Burma has a special character, and it has for some years past been subject to a fairly accurate system of registration. The main route is by the Irawadi river, which is navigable by large steamers. The trade on the Sittang (Tsit-taung) is chiefly confined to the import of timber. Registration is also attempted at six land stations. The total trade

1877–78.

in 1877–78 was valued at £3,426,000, almost equally divided

Imports.

between exports and imports. The principal imports from Independent Burma into British Burma were timber (£213,000), raw cotton (£163,000), sesamum oil (£130,000), manufactured silk (£107,000), jaggery sugar (£98,000), cattle (£88,000) and ponies (£20,000), cotton goods woven from European yarn (£46,000), earth-oil (£65,000), and cutch (£41,000). Many of these articles are liable to be declared royal monopolies (although these monopolies were abolished in 1882), and consequently the figures fluctuate greatly year by year. Other imports of interest, though of smaller value, are pickled tea (£19,000) and jade (£18,000).

Exports; 1877–78.

The exports from British to Independent Burma in 1877, were rice (£435,000), cotton piece-goods (£207,000) and cotton

twist and yarn (£188,000), manufactured silk (£173,000), Trade with
ngá-pi or salted fish (£159,000), raw silk (£84,000), woollen Upper Burma,
goods (£43,000), salt (£33,000), etc. Many of these goods 1877-78.
were formerly the subjects of royal monopoly, or they competed with the products of manufactories started by the king
at Mandalay. Salt is exempted from the ordinary customs
duties at Rangoon, and pays only a transit duty of 1 per cent.
if declared for Independent Burma.[1]

Full details of the import and export trade between British Burmese
Burma and Independent Burma and the Shan States for trade, 1882-83.
1882–83 are not available. As regards totals, the imports
amounted to £2,504,135 in value, and the exports to
£1,752,299 ; total, £4,256,434.

The trade between British Burma and Siam was estimated Siam
in 1877–78 at the total value of £126,000, being £69,000 trade.
for imports from Siam, and £57,000 for exports. In 1882–83,
the trade between British Burma and Siam amounted to—
imports from Siam, £40,349, and exports, £141,958 ; total,
£182,307.

The following tables exhibit the total trans-frontier land trade
of India (1) with the different border countries and tribes, and
(2) the extent to which it is participated in by the neighbouring
British Provinces :—

TRANS-FRONTIER LANDWARD TRADE OF INDIA WITH EXTERNAL STATES FOR THE FIVE YEARS 1878–79 TO 1882–83.

FROM	Landward Imports into India.				
	1878-79.	1879-80.	1880-81.	1881-82.	1882-83.
Afghánistán and neighbouring tracts and hill tribes, .	£ 765,849	£ 611,418	£ 441,536	£ 487,852	£ 526,560
Kashmír, ...	558,537	409,744	709,272	495,949	505,335
Ladákh, ...	17,104	17,013	17,846	37,248	51,284
Tibet, ...	153,969	71,349	63,393	64,206	58,322
Nepál, ...	1,235,238	1,397,487	1,606,929	1,389,548	1,378,175
Sikkim and Bhután, . . .	24,738	61,103	43,395	35,339	33,399
N.E. States beyond the Bengal and Assam Frontier, .	36,402	47,312	53,027	64,949	81,078
Independent Burma and Shan States, ...	2,072,441	2,222,165	2,126,857	2,110,346	2,504,135
Siam, ...	35,717	80,047	41,325	39,966	40,349
Total Imports, . .	4,899,995	4,917,638	5,103,580	4,725,403	5,178,637

[1] *N.B.*—Since these pages went to the press, Independent Burma has
been incorporated into the British Empire. The above figures will
therefore soon lose their value.

TRANS-FRONTIER LANDWARD TRADE OF INDIA—(*continued*).

INTO	Landward Exports from India.				
	1878-79.	1879-80.	1880-81.	1881-82.	1882-83.
Afghánistán and neighbouring tracts and hill tribes, .	£ 897,715	£ 1,184,695	£ 1,312,677	£ 1,239,725	£ 863,445
Kashmír, ...	255,545	282,426	384,934	359,193	349,477
Ladákh, ...	8,817	15,729	31,177	35,860	32,228
Tibet, ...	14,861	20,139	18,214	21,973	24,197
Nepál, ...	805,361	859,358	923,724	869,720	855,346
Sikkim and Bhután, . . .	17,166	34,576	28,513	21,508	24,973
N.E. States beyond the Bengal and Assam Frontier, .	17,935	15,657	27,676	21,990	27,213
Independent Burma and Shan tribes, ...	1,868,092	1,813,666	1,848,819	1,613,981	1,752,299
Siam, ...	86,067	66,386	109,730	150,415	141,958
Total Exports, . .	3,971,559	4,292,632	4,685,464	4,334,365	4,071,136
GRAND TOTAL IMPORTS AND EXPORTS, ...	8,871,554	9,210,270	9,789,044	9,059,768	9,249,773

TRANS-FRONTIER LANDWARD TRADE OF INDIA FOR THE BRITISH BORDER PROVINCES FOR THE FIVE YEARS 1878–79 TO 1882–83.

INTO	Landward Imports into India.				
	1878-79.	1879-80.	1880-81.	1881-82.	1882-83.
Sind, ...	£ 249,842	£ 251,558	£ 117,475	£ 130,248	£ 119,722
Punjab, ...	1,218,269	820,591	1,071,329	912,813	981,167
N.W. Provinces and Oudh,	439,154	531,595	615,507	633,664	617,222
Bengal, ...	844,006	961,140	1,075,853	827,376	832,724
Assam, ...	40,566	50,542	55,234	70,990	83,318
British Burma, ...	2,108,158	2,302,212	2,223,977	2,150,312	2,544,484
Total Imports, . .	4,899,995	4,917,638	5,159,375	4,725,403	5,178,637

FROM	Landward Exports from India.				
	1878-79.	1879-80.	1880-81.	1881-82.	1882-83.
Sind, ...	£ 215,235	£ 403,212	£ 326,670	£ 236,910	£ 162,759
Punjab, ...	949,963	1,080,940	1,403,449	1,398,995	1,083,920
N.W. Provinces and Oudh,	203,343	296,767	339,146	280,526	279,349
Bengal, ...	628,587	614,146	629,246	629,224	618,963
Assam, ...	20,272	17,515	28,404	24,314	31,888
British Burma, ...	1,954,159	1,880,052	1,958,549	1,764,396	1,894,257
Total Exports, . .	3,971,559	4,292,632	4,685,464	4,334,365	4,071,136
GRAND TOTAL IMPORTS AND EXPORTS, ...	8,871,554	9,210,270	9,844,839	9,159,768	9,249,773

THE INTERNAL TRADE of India greatly exceeds her foreign Internal
commerce; but it is impossible to estimate its amount. On trade of
India.
the one hand, there is the wholesale business, connected with
the foreign commerce, in all its stages—the collection of
agricultural produce from a hundred thousand villages, its
accumulation at a few great central marts, and its despatch to
the seaboard. The sea-imports and manufactured articles are
distributed by the same channels, but in the reverse direction.
On the other hand, there is the interchange of commodities
of native growth and manufacture, sometimes between neighbouring Districts, but also between distant Provinces. With
unimportant exceptions, free trade is the rule throughout the
vast peninsula of India, by land as well as by sea. The
Hindus possess a natural genius for commerce, as is shown
by the daring with which they have penetrated into the heart
of Central Asia, and to the east coast of Africa. Among the
benefits which British rule has conferred upon them, is the
removal of the internal duties and other restraints which
native despotism had imposed upon trading energies.

Broadly speaking, the greater part of the internal trade Internal
remains in the hands of the natives. Europeans control the trade in
native
shipping business, and have a share in the collection of some hands.
of the more valuable staples of export, such as cotton, jute,
oil-seeds, and wheat. But the work of distribution, and the
adaptation of the supply to the demand of the consumer,
naturally fall to those who are best acquainted with native
wants. Even in the Presidency towns, most of the retail shops
are owned by natives.

The Vaisya, or trading caste of Manu, has now scarcely Trading
a separate existence; but its place is occupied by offshoots castes:
and well-marked classes. On the western coast the
Pársís, by the boldness and extent of their operations, tread
close upon the heels of the great English houses. In
the interior of the Bombay Presidency, business is mainly
divided between two classes, the Baniyás of Gujarát and the
Márwárís from Rájputána. Each of these profess a peculiar
form of religion, the former being Vishnuites of the Vallabhá-
chárya sect, the latter Jains. In the Deccan, their place is in
taken by Lingáyats from the south, who again follow their Southern
India;
own form of Hinduism, which is a species of Siva-worship.
Throughout Mysore, and in the north of Madras, Lingáyats
are also found, but along the eastern seaboard the predominating
classes of traders are the castes named Chetties and Komatis.
Many of these trading castes still claim Vaisya descent.

in Northern India.

In Bengal, however, many of the upper classes of Súdras have devoted themselves to wholesale trade; although here also the Jain Márwárís from Rájputána and the North-West occupy the front rank. Their head-quarters are in Murshidábád District, and Jain Márwárís are found throughout the valley of the Brahmaputra, as far up as the unexplored frontier of China. They penetrate everywhere among the wild tribes; and it is said that the natives of the Khási Hills are the only hillmen who do their own business of buying and selling. In the North-Western Provinces and Oudh, the traders are generically called Baniyás; and in the Punjab are found the Khatris (Kshattriyas), who have perhaps the best title of any to regard themselves as descendants of the original Vaisyas.

Trade Census; 1872 and 1881.

According to the general Census of 1872, the total number of persons throughout British India connected with commerce and trade was 3,224,000, or 5·2 per cent. of the total adult males. In 1881, throughout British and Feudatory India, 3,232,120 adult males were returned as engaged in commerce and trade, or 3·87 per cent. of the total male population engaged in some specific occupation.

Local trade of India.

THE LOCAL TRADE of India is conducted in the permanent *bázárs* of the great towns, at weekly markets in the rural villages, at annual gatherings held for religious purposes, or by means of travelling brokers and agents. The cultivator himself, who is the chief producer and also the chief customer, knows little of large cities, and expects the dealer to come to his own door. Each village has at least one resident trader, who usually combines in his own person the functions of

The village money-lender.

money-lender, grain merchant, and cloth-seller. The simple system of rural economy is entirely based upon the dealings of this man, whom it is sometimes the fashion to decry as a usurer, but who is often the one thrifty person among an improvident population. If his rate of interest is high, it is only proportionate to the risks of his business. If he sometimes makes a merciless use of his legal position, the fault rests rather with the inflexible rules of our courts, which enable him to push the cultivators to extremes not allowed under native rule. Abolish the money-lender, and the general body of cultivators would have nothing to depend upon but the harvest of the single year. The money-lender deals chiefly in grain and in specie.

In those Districts where the staples of export are largely

grown, the cultivators commonly sell their crops to travelling Travelling
brokers, who re-sell to larger dealers, and so on until the brokers.
commodities reach the hands of the agents of the great shipping houses. The wholesale trade thus rests ultimately with a
comparatively small number of persons, who have agencies, or
rather corresponding firms, at the central marts.

Buying and selling, in their aspects most characteristic of Religious
India, are to be seen not in the large cities, nor even at the fairs.
weekly markets, but at the fairs which are held periodically at
certain spots in most Districts. Religion is always the original
cause of these gatherings or *melás*, at some of which nothing
is done beyond bathing in the river, or performing pious
ceremonies. But in the majority of cases, religion merely
supplies the opportunity for secular business. Crowds of
petty traders attend, bringing the medley of articles which can
be packed into a pedlar's wallet ; and the neighbouring villagers
look forward to the occasion, to satisfy alike their curiosity
and their household wants.

The improvement in means of communication, by the con- Increase of
struction of railways and metalled roads, has directly developed internal
internal no less than foreign trade. Facilities for rapid trade.
carriage tend to equalize prices not only over large areas of
country, but also over long periods of time. As wheeled carts
supersede pack-bullocks, and as railroads supersede carts, the
whole of India will gradually become one country for the
purposes of food supply. It is by this means alone that a
guarantee can be provided against the ravages of famine.
The vicissitudes of a tropical climate will always cause local The chief
failures of the harvest, whether by drought or by flood, which safeguard
against
science indeed may learn to foresee, but which no practicable famine.
schemes of irrigation or embankment can altogether avert.
But India, as a whole, has never yet been unable in any single
year to yield sufficient food for her population. The real
problem of famine is a problem of distribution.

In former times, the inhabitants of one District might be How trade
perishing of starvation, while plenty reigned in a District acts in
famine.
but 100 miles distant. In 1866, the people of Orissa were
decimated, not so much by drought or by inundation, as by the
impossibility of transport. In 1877, the distress in Madras
was alleviated by the importation of nearly one million tons
of grain, all of which was carried inland by two lines of rail
in twelve months. Supplies were drawn, not only from the
seaboard of Bengal and Burma, but from the most remote

2 P

Provinces. In the year 1877-78, the Central Provinces exported grain to the amount of more than 300,000 tons, and the Punjab to the amount of 400,000 tons, all of which were conveyed south by rail. Trade has never known such a stimulus as was afforded on this occasion, when the carrying power proved barely equal to the strain. If the famine had happened before the opening of the railway, it would have resulted in a loss of life without parallel even in the annals of India.

Normal action of internal trade

But the utility of local trade is not to be judged of only at such a crisis. In normal seasons, it tends alike to regulate prices and to promote a higher standard of comfort. Within the last twenty-five years, the cultivators have learnt for the first time the real value of their produce. In the old days, little was grown beyond grain crops for the year's food. The slightest failure meant local distress; while a bumper harvest so depreciated the value of grain, that part of the crops was often left unreaped to rot in the fields. In 1780 and 1781, a suspension of revenue had to be granted to the District of Sylhet, because the harvest was so bountiful that it would not pay the cost of carriage to market, and consequently the farmers had no means of obtaining money. Even so late as 1873, the Collector of Rangpur reported that ' the yield of rice was considered too good by the *ráyats*, as prices were thereby kept down.' The extended cultivation of staples for export, such as cotton, jute, and oil-seeds, together with the substitution of more valuable crops for the inferior grains, is now modifying the entire system of Indian agriculture. Land is not being withdrawn from food crops to any appreciable extent, but the *ráyat* is everywhere learning to cultivate high-priced subsidiary crops which will help to pay his rent.

equalizes prices;

introduces more valuable crops.

Statistics of internal trade.

It is impossible to express in figures the precise extent of the internal trade of India. But the following statistics will serve in some measure to show both its recent development and its actual amount. They are based upon the registration returns which were collected in certain Provinces. Owing to changes in the system of registration, it is not safe to institute general comparison between different years. Inter-provincial trade statistics are now chiefly confined to railway returns and the traffic passing through certain registration centres.

Central Provinces.

In 1863-64, the external trade of the Central Provinces, both export and import, was estimated to amount to 102,000 tons, valued at £3,909,000. By 1868-69, after the opening of the Jabalpur Railway, it had increased to 209,000 tons, valued at £6,795,000. In 1877–78, the year of the famine in Southern India, the corresponding figures were 635,000 tons, and £9,373,000, showing an increase in 14 years of more than six-fold in quantity, and considerably more than two-fold in value. The comparatively small increase in value is partly to be attributed to the exclusion of opium, which merely passes through in transit from Málwá. In 1882–83, the total external trade of the Central Provinces, imports and exports, as represented by the railway-borne traffic to stations outside the Chief-Commissionership, and the registered trade with adjoining Native States, was returned at over 650,000 tons, valued at £8,451,047.

In 1874–75, the total external trade of the Punjab amounted Punjab. to about 600,000 tons, valued (but probably overvalued) at about £16,000,000. By 1877–78 it had increased to nearly 900,000 tons, valued at £17,500,000. In 1882–83, the external trade of the Punjab trans-frontier, railway borne, and boat traffic, was returned at nearly three-quarters of a million tons, of the value of 13⅔ millions. These figures show a decrease in 1882–83, as compared with 1877–78, of more than one-sixth both in weight and value. The high figures of 1877–78 are, however, accounted for by the famines in Kashmír and South India, in consequence of which there were abnormally large exports of wheat and other grains from the Punjab in both directions.

The total trade of Behar in 1877–78 was valued at Behar. £16,000,000. In 1882–83, the registered figures show that the East Indian Railway carried a total merchandise valued at over £19,000,000, to and from the 'Behar block.' But perhaps the significance of such enormous totals will become plainer if we take the case of a single mart, Patná, which may claim to be considered one of the most important centres of inland traffic in the world. Favourably situated on the Ganges, near the confluence of the Son (Soane) and the Gogra, where the principal trade route branches off to Nepál, it has become a great changing station for the transfer of goods from river to rail.

In 1876–77, the imports and exports of Patná city (ex- Trade of cluding the Government monopoly of opium, and probably Patná, omitting a good deal besides) were officially registered to a 1877. value of 7¼ millions sterling. Many articles are included twice over as exported and imported, but the imports alone amounted to more than 4 millions. Among the principal items on one side or the other may be mentioned—European piece-goods, £1,217,000 ; indigo, £789,000 ; oilseeds, £557,000 ; salt, £389,000 ; sugar, £274,000 ; food grains, £258,000 ; hides, £185,000 ; saltpetre, £156,000. In 1882–83, the East Indian Railway returns alone show a total import and export trade for Patná (excluding opium) amounting to over 5¼ millions sterling, nearly 2½ millions being imports and over 2¾ millions exports. As regards the river and road trade of Patná city, no recent statistics are available, as registration has there been abandoned for some years past.

Growth of a mart, Dongargáon.   Another example of the growth of local trade is exhibited at Dongargáon, as described in the *Report on the Trade and Resources of the Central Provinces*,—a model of what such a report should be. Dongargáon now forms the principal market for grain on the fertile plateau of Chhatísgarh, which is perhaps destined to become a regular source of wheat supply to England. Thirty years ago, it was a petty hamlet of about 20 houses, buried in wild jungle, and only distinguished from the neighbouring villages by a weekly *bázár* held on Sunday. In 1862, the enterprising agent of a Nágpur firm of native merchants settled here, and began to make purchases of grain. The number of houses has now risen to about 2000, of which the majority are tiled. Dongargáon had a resident population in 1881 of 5543. In the busy season, the concourse daily present in the *bázár* is estimated at 100,000, with 13,000 carts and 40,000 bullocks and buffaloes. Buyers come from as far west as Bombay, while the grain of all the adjoining Districts is brought here for sale.

A yearly fair, Kárágolá.   A third example of the varying methods of Indian trade may be found in the annual fair held at Kárágolá in Purniah. This fair dates from the beginning of the present century, although its site has changed from time to time. It lasts for about ten days in the month of February. During that season a little town of shops, constructed of bamboos and matting, rises on the sandy plain that stretches between the village and the bank of the Ganges. The business is entirely of a retail character, the local staples of grain, jute, and tobacco being conspicuously absent. But every article of necessity or luxury for a native household is to be bought. Cloth of all kinds, from thick English woollens to fine Dacca muslins ; iron-mongery and furniture from Monghyr ; boots, shawls, silks, and brocades from the cities of the North-West ; hand-mills, curry-stones, and lac ornaments from the hills of Chutiá Nágpur ; knives, yaks' tails, ponies, musk, and other drugs, brought down by the Nepális ; miscellaneous ware from England, such as umbrellas, matches, soap, paper, candles, buttons, etc.,—all find a ready sale. In 1876, the attendance was estimated at 40,000, and in 1881 at 30,000 persons ; and the fees upon shops levied by the landowner realized £150. Such fairs are always protected by a special body of police, and the European official in charge of the District or Sub-division is usually present.

CHAPTER XX.

ARTS AND MANUFACTURES.

Manu-
factures
of India.
INDIA may be truly described as an agricultural rather than a manufacturing country, yet it must not be inferred that she is destitute of the arts of civilised life. She has no swarming hives of industry to compare with the factory centres of Lancashire; nor any large mining population. But in all manufactures requiring manual dexterity and artistic taste, India may challenge comparison with Europe in the last century; in many of them, with England at the present day. The rival kingdoms into which the country was formerly divided, gave birth to numerous arts of luxury.

Art work. When the first European traders reached the coast of India in the 16th century, they found a civilisation both among 'Moors' and 'Gentoos' at least as highly advanced as their own. In architecture, in fabrics of cotton and silk, in goldsmith's work and jewellery, the people of India were then unsurpassed.

But while the East has stood still, as regards manufactures on a great scale, the West has advanced by gigantic strides without a parallel in the history of human progress.

English
competi-
tion.
On the one hand, the downfall of the native courts deprived the skilled workman of his chief market; while on the other, the English capitalist has enlisted in his service forces of nature against which the village artisans in vain try to compete. The tide of circumstance has compelled the Indian weaver to exchange his loom for the plough, and has crushed many of the minor handicrafts.

The tide
now
turned.
Some consolation can be found in the establishment, within the past few years, of mills fitted out by English capital with English machinery. A living portion of our own industrial activity has been transplanted to Indian soil. Manchester is growing up in miniature at Bombay, and Dundee at Calcutta. The time may yet come when India shall again clothe her people with her own cotton; she already supplies sacks from her jute for the commerce of the world.

Historically the most interesting, and still the most im- Native industries.
portant in the aggregate, of all Indian industries are the
simple crafts in every rural hamlet. The weaver, the potter, The village craftsmen.
the blacksmith, the brazier, the oil-presser, are members of a
community, as well as inheritors of a family occupation. On
the one hand, they have a secure market for their wares ; and
on the other, their employers have a guarantee that their trades
shall be well learned. The stage of civilisation below these
village industries is represented by the hill tribes, where the
weaving of clothes is done by the women of the family. An
advanced stage may be found in those villages or towns which
possess a little colony of weavers or braziers noted for some
speciality. Yet one degree higher is the case of local arts
of luxury, such as ivory-carving or the making of gold lace.

Another form of native industry owes its origin to European
interference. Many a village in Bengal and on the Coromandel Fortified weaving settle-ments.
coast still shows traces of the time when the East Indian Com-
pany and its European rivals gathered large settlements of
weavers round their little forts, and thus formed the only
industrial towns that ever existed in India. But when the
Company gave up its private trade in 1813 and 1834,
such centres of industry rapidly declined ; and the once
celebrated muslins of India have been driven out of the
market by Manchester goods.

Cotton-weaving is a very ancient industry of India. In Cotton-weaving in India,
England it dates back only a couple of centuries. Wool and
linen were England's historical staples ; but in India cotton-
weaving was practised before the time of the *Mahábhárata.*
The Greek name for cotton fabrics, *sindon,* is etymologically
the same as that of India, or Sind ; while in later days, Calicut
on the Malabar coast has given us ' calico.' Cotton cloth has
always been the single material of Indian clothing for both
men and women, except in Assam and Burma, where silk is
preferred, perhaps as a survival of an extinct trade with China.
The author of the *Periplus,* our earliest authority on the trade an indi-genous industry.
of India, enumerates a great variety of cotton fabrics among
her exports. Marco Polo, the first Christian traveller, dilates
on the ' cotton and buckram ' of Cambay. When European
adventurers found out the way to India, cotton and silk always
formed part of the rich cargoes they brought home.

The English appear to have been specially careful to fix
their earliest settlements amid weaving populations—at Surat,
at Calicut, at Masulipatam, at Húglí. In delicacy of texture,
in purity and fastness of colour, in grace of design, Indian

Causes of
its decline.
cottons may still hold their own against the world. But in the matter of cheapness, they have been unable to face the competition of Manchester. Many circumstances conspired to injure the Indian industry. In the last century, England excluded Indian cotton fabrics, not by fiscal duties, but by absolute prohibition. A change of fashion in the West Indies, on the abolition of slavery, took away the best customer left to India. Then came cheapness of production in Lancashire, due to improvements in machinery. Lastly, the high price of raw cotton during the American War, however beneficial to the cultivators, fairly broke down the local weaving trade in the cotton-growing tracts. Above all, the necessity under which England lies to export something to India to pay for her multifarious imports, has permanently given an artificial character of inflation to this branch of business.

Still a
domestic
industry.
Despite all these considerations, hand-loom weaving still holds its own with varying success in different parts of the country. Regarded as a trade, it has become unremunerative. Little is made for export, and the finer fabrics generally are dying out. The far-famed muslins of Dacca and of Arní are now well-nigh lost specialities. But as a village industry, weaving is still carried on everywhere, though it cannot be said to flourish. If Manchester piece-goods are cheaper, native piece-goods are

Supplies
three-fifths
of Indian
consumpt.
universally recognised as more durable. Comparative statistics are not available; but it may be roughly estimated that about three-fifths of the cotton cloth used is woven in the country from native thread or from imported twist.

Cotton-
weaving
in Madras,
1870;
In 1870, the Madras Board of Revenue published a valuable report on hand-loom weaving, from which the following figures are taken. The total number of looms at work in that Presidency, with its then population of 31 millions, was returned at 279,220, of which 220,015 were in villages and 59,205 in towns, showing a considerable increase upon the corresponding number in 1861, when the *mohartarfa*, or assessed tax upon looms, was abolished. The total estimated consumption of twist in 1870 was 31,422,712 lbs., being at the rate of 112 lbs. per loom. Of this amount, about one-third was imported twist, and the remainder country-made. The total value of the cotton goods woven was returned in 1870 at $3\frac{1}{2}$ millions sterling, or £12, 10s. per loom; but this was believed to be much under the truth.

The export of country-made cotton cloth from Madras in the same year, 1870, was about £220,000. By 1882–83, the export of country-made cloth from Madras had dwindled to £45,196.

In the Central Provinces, where hand-loom weaving still in Central
flourishes, and where the statistics are more trustworthy than 1878; Provinces,
in some other parts of India, the number of looms in 1877–78
was returned at 87,588, employing 145,896 weavers, with an
annual out-turn valued at £828,000. In 1882–83, there were
in the Central Provinces three large cotton mills at work, besides
143,801 looms, giving employment to 164,273 workmen, with
an out-turn valued at £858,219. In 1878–79, the export of
Indian piece-goods from the Central Provinces was valued at
£162,642. In 1882–83, it was valued at £147,773.

As regards Bengal, hand-loom weaving is generally on the in Bengal;
decline. The average consumption of piece-goods throughout
the Province is estimated at about 5s. per head, and the
returns of registered trade show that European piece-goods are
distributed from Calcutta at the rate of about 2s. 5d. per head.
In Midnapur, Nadiyá, and Bardwán, the native weavers still
hold their own, as appears from the large imports of European
twist; but in the eastern Districts, which have to balance
their large exports of jute, rice, and oil-seeds, the imports of
European cloth rise to 2s. 7d. per head.

No part of India has more cruelly felt the English com- in Bom-
petition than Bombay. But in Bombay, the introduction of bay.
steam machinery is already beginning to restore the work to
native hands. Twist from the Bombay mills is now generally
used by the hand-loom weavers of the Presidency, and is
largely exported to China. But it is in the finer fabrics
produced for export that the Bombay Districts have suffered
most. Taking Surat alone, the export by sea of piece-goods
at the beginning of the century was valued at £360,000 a
year. By 1845, the value had dropped to £67,000, rising
again to £134,000 in 1859; but in 1874, it was only £6332.

It is impossible to enumerate the many special fabrics which Special
are still produced in various parts of the country. First Indian
among these are the far-famed muslins of Dacca, which can fabrics.
still be obtained to order, although the quality is far inferior Dacca
to what it was when Dacca was the capital of a luxurious muslins.
Muhammadan court. Most of the weavers are Hindus, and
the high development which their industry has reached may
be judged from the fact that they employ no fewer than 126
distinct implements. The finest muslins are woven plain, but
patterns of coloured silk are afterwards embroidered on them
by a separate class of workmen. (For the decay of the Dacca
manufactures, and the transfer of the weaving communities to
agricultural employments, see article DACCA in *The Imperial*

Gazetteer of India.) Fine muslin is woven in small quantities at Sarail in the adjoining District of Tipperah ; and Sántipur, in Nadiyá, still retains its reputation for delicate fabrics. But with these exceptions, cotton-weaving in Bengal produces only coarse articles for common use.

Madras muslins. In Madras, the fine fabrics maintain their ground better, although the trade is nowhere flourishing. Among those deserving mention are the muslins of Arní, the cloth woven by the Nairs on the Malabar coast, the chintzes of Masulipatam, the *panjam* or '120-thread' cloth of Vizagapatam, and the blue Bangalore *salampurs* of Nellore. At Bangalore, the descendants of the cloths. old court weavers still manufacture a peculiar kind of cloth, printed in red and black with mythological designs. In the Bombay Bombay Presidency, Ahmadábád, Surat, and Broach are the fabrics. chief centres of the manufacture of printed *sáris*, for which Gujarát is celebrated ; while Poona, Yeola, Násik, and Dhárwár produce the fabrics dyed in the thread, which are much worn by the Maráthá races. Silk is often combined with cotton on the looms, and the more expensive articles are finished off with a border of silk or gold lace. Chándá and Hoshangábád are the largest weaving towns in the Central Provinces.

Indian silk- Silk-weaving is also a common industry everywhere, silk weaving : fabrics, or at least an admixture of silk with cotton, being universally affected as a mark of wealth. Throughout British Burma, and also in Assam, silk is the common material of clothing ; usually woven by the women of the household. In in Burma Burma, the bulk of the silk is imported from China, generally and Assam ; in a raw state ; but in Assam it is obtained from two or three varieties of worms, which are generally fed on jungle trees, and in Bengal. may be regarded as semi-domesticated. Bengal is the only part of India where sericulture, or the rearing of the silkworm proper on mulberry, can be said to flourish. The greater part of the silk is wound in European filatures, and exported in the raw state to Europe. The native supply is either locally consumed, or sent up the Ganges to the great cities of the North-West. A considerable quantity of raw silk, especially for Bombay consumption, is imported from China. *Tasar* silk, from the cocoons of semi-domesticated worms, does not contribute much to the supply. (*Vide ante*, pp. 511–514.)

Classes of silk As compared with cotton-weaving, the silk fabrics form a fabrics. town rather than a village industry. Silk fabrics are of two kinds—(1) those composed of pure silk, and (2) those with a cotton warp crossed by a woof of silk. Both kinds are often embroidered with gold and silver. The mixed fabrics are known as *mashru* or *sufi*, the latter word meaning 'permitted,' because the strict ceremonial law will not allow Muhammadans to wear clothing of pure silk. They are extensively woven in the Punjab and Sind, at Agra, at Haidarábád in the Deccan, and at Tanjore and Trichinopoli in Madras. Pure silk fabrics are either of simple texture, or highly ornamented in the form of *kinkhabs* or brocades. The latter are a speciality of Benares, Brocades. Murshidábád, Ahmadábád, and Trichinopoli. Their gorgeous hues and texture may be inferred from the following names :— *Shikargah,* 'hunting-ground;' *chand-tara,* 'moon and stars;' *mazchar,* 'ripples of silver;' *murgala,* 'peacock's neck.' Printed silks are woven at Surat for the wear of Pársí and Gujaráthí women.

Quite recently, mills with steam machinery have been estab- Steam silk-lished at Bombay, which weave silk fabrics for the Burmese factories. market, chiefly *lúngyís, tamains,* and *patsoes.* The silk manu-factures exported from India consist almost entirely of the handkerchiefs known as *bandannas* and *corahs,* with a small proportion of *tasar* fabrics. The trade, after a temporary period of depression, appears now to be increasing. In 1875–76, silk manufactures to the extent of 2,468,052 yards, valued at £238,000, were exported from India. In 1877–78, the export of manufactured silk had decreased to 1,481,256 yards, valued at £147,000. By 1878–79, the value of the trade had risen to £195,897 ; by 1880-81, to £250,256 ; and by 1882–83, to £306,928.

Embroidery has already been referred to in the two pre- Embroi-ceding paragraphs. The groundwork may be either silk, dery. cotton, wool, or leather. The ornament is woven in the loom, or sewn on afterwards with the needle. The well-known *choga,* which has recently come into popular use in England for dressing-gowns, is made of *patu* or camel's hair, embroidered Camel's in Kashmír, the Punjab, and Sind. The still better known hair. and more valuable Kashmír shawl, made either in Kashmír Kashmír itself or at Ludhiána, and a few other towns of the Punjab, is shawls. composed of *pashmína,* or the soft wool of the so-called shawl-goat, which is a native of the Himálayan plateaux. Muslin is embroidered with silk and gold thread at Dacca, Patná, and Delhi. Sind and Cutch (Kachchh) have special embroideries of coloured silk and gold. Leather-work is embroidered in Gujarát Leather-(Guzerát). In some of the historical capitals of the Deccan, such work. as Gulbargah and Aurangábád, velvet (*makhmal*) is gorgeously Velvet. embroidered with gold, to make canopies, umbrellas, and housings for elephants and horses, for use on State occasions.

Not only the goldsmith, but also the jeweller lends his aid
to Indian embroidery. A *chadar*, or shawl made by order of a
late Gáekwár of Baroda, is thus described by Sir G. Birdwood :
' It was composed entirely of inwrought pearls and precious
stones, disposed in an arabesque fashion, and is said to have
cost a *kror* of rupees (say 1 million sterling). Although the
richest stones were worked in it, the effect was most har-
monious. When spread out in the sun, it seemed suffused
with an iridescent bloom, as grateful to the eye as were the
exquisite forms of its arabesques.'

A jewelled shawl.

Carpets and rugs may be classified into those made of
cotton and those made of wool. The former, called *satranjis*
and *daris*, are made chiefly in Bengal and Northern India,
and appear to be an indigenous industry. They are usually
white, striped with blue, red, or chocolate, and sometimes
ornamented with squares and diamonds. The woollen or
pile carpets, known as *kalin* and *kalicha*, are those which
have recently attained so much popularity in England, by
reason of the low price at which the out-turn of the jail
manufactories can be placed on the market.

Carpets and rugs, of cotton ; of wool.

The pile carpet is indigenous to Persia and Túrkistán,
where the best are still made. The art came into India with
the Muhammadans. ' The foundation for the carpet is a
warp of strong cotton or hempen threads ; and the peculiarity
of the process consists in dexterously twisting short lengths
of coloured wool into each of the threads of the warp, so
that the two ends of the twist of wool stick out in front.
The projecting ends are then clipped to a uniform level,
and the lines of work are compacted together by striking
them with a blunt instrument ' (Birdwood). The historical
Indian seats of the industry are Kashmír, the Punjab, and
Sind ; Agra, Mírzápur, Jabalpur, Warangal in the Deccan,
Malabar and Masulipatam. Velvet carpets are also made at
Benares and Murshidábád, and silk pile carpets at Tanjore
and Salem.

Process of manu-facture.

Seats of carpet-weaving.

At the London Exhibition of 1851, the finest Indian rugs
came from Warangal, the ancient capital of the Andhra dynasty,
about 80 miles east of Haidarábád. Their characteristic
feature was the exceedingly numerous count of the stitches,
about 12,000 to the square foot. 'They were also perfectly
harmonious in colour, and the only examples in which silk was
used with an entirely satisfactory effect' (Birdwood). The
price was not less than £10 per square yard. The common
rugs, produced in enormous quantities from the jails at Lahore,

Warangal rugs.

Jabalpur, Mírzápur, Benares, and Bangalore, sell in England
at 7s. 6d. each.

Gold and silver, and jewels, both from their colour and their Gold-
intrinsic value, have always been the favourite material of smiths'
Oriental ornament. Even the hill tribes of Central India and jewellery.
the Himálayas show skill in hammering silver into brooches,
armlets, and necklets. Imitation of knotted grass and of Hill-work.
leaves seems to be the origin of the simplest and most
common form of gold ornament, the early specimens consisting of thick gold wire twisted into bracelets, etc. A second
archaic type of decoration is to be found in the chopped gold
jewellery of Gujarát (Guzerát). This is made of gold lumps,
either solid or hollow, in the form of cubes and octahedrons, Cube
strung together on red silk. Of artistic jeweller's work, the jewellery.
best known examples are those from Trichinopoli, Cuttack,
and Kashmír.

Throughout Southern India, the favourite design is that
known as *swámi*, in which the ornamentation consists of figures
of Hindu gods in high relief, either beaten out from the surface or fixed on to it by solder or screws. The Trichinopoli Trichino-
work proper, which has been to some extent corrupted to suit poli.
English taste, includes also chains of rose gold, and bracelets
of the flexible serpent pattern. The silver filigree work of
Cuttack, identical in character with that of ancient Greece Cuttack.
and of Malta at the present day, is generally done by boys,
whose sensitive fingers and keen sight enable them to put the
fine silver threads together with the necessary rapidity and
accuracy. The goldsmith's work of Kashmír is of the kind Kashmír.
known as 'parcel-gilt,' and is further distinguished by the
ruddy colour of the gold used. 'Its airy shapes and exquisite
tracery, graven through the gilding to the dead white silver
below, softening the lustre of the gold to a pearly radiance,
give a most charming effect to this refined and graceful work'
(Birdwood). The hammered *repoussé* silver work of Cutch Cutch.
(Kachchh), although now entirely naturalized, is said to be of
Dutch origin. Similar work is done at Lucknow and Dacca.

The goldsmith's art contributes largely to embroidery, as has
already been mentioned. Gold and silver thread is made by
being drawn out under the application of heat. The operation
is performed with such nicety, that 1 rupee's worth of silver
will make a thread nearly 800 yards long. Before being used
in the loom, this metallic thread is generally twisted with silk.
For the manufacture of cloth of gold (*sonári*) or cloth of silver
(*rupíri*), the wire is beaten flat, so as to form the warp to a

woof of thin silk or cotton. A third kind of metallic ornamentation is practised at Jaipur in Rájputána and Haidarábád
in the Deccan, by printing muslins with patterns of gold and
silver leaf.

Precious stones. Precious stones are lavishly used by Indian jewellers, who
care less for their purity and commercial value than for the
general effect produced by a blaze of splendour. ' But
nothing can exceed the skill, artistic feeling, and effectiveness
with which gems are used in India both in jewellery proper
and in the jewelled decoration of arms and jade' (Birdwood).
The general character may be learned from the following description of a hair-comb in the Prince of Wales' collection, made at
Jaipur : 'The setting is of emerald and ruby Jaipur enamel on
gold, surmounted by a curved row of large pearls, all on a
level, each tipped with a green glass bead. Below is a row of
small brilliants, set among the elegantly designed green and
red enamelled gold leaves which support the pearls. Then a
row of small pearls, with an enamelled scroll-work set with
brilliants between it and a third row of pearls ; below which
comes a continuous row of minute brilliants forming the lower
edge of the comb, just above the gold prongs.'

Indian iron-work. The chief duty of the village smith is, of course, to make
the agricultural implements for his fellow-villagers. But in
many towns in India, chiefly the sites of former capitals, iron-
work still attains a high degree of artistic excellence. The
manufacture of arms, whether for offence or defence, must
always be an honourable industry ; and in India it attained a
high pitch of excellence, which is not yet forgotten. The
magnetic iron-ore, found commonly in the form of sand,
yields a charcoal steel which is not surpassed by any in the
Cutlery. world. The blade of the Indian *talwár* or sword is sometimes
marvellously watered, and engraved with date and name ;
sometimes sculptured in half-relief with hunting scenes ; sometimes shaped along the edge with teeth or notches like a saw.
Matchlocks and other fire-arms are made at several towns in
the Punjab and Sind, at Monghyr in Bengal, and at Viziana-
garam in Madras.

Chain armour. Chain armour, fine as lacework, and said to be of Persian
derivation, is still manufactured in Kashmír, Rájputána, and
Cutch (Kachchh). Ahmadnagar in Bombay is famous for its
spear-heads. Both fire-arms and swords are often damascened
in gold, and covered with precious stones. In fact, the characteristic of Indian arms, as opposed to those of other Oriental
countries, is the elaborate goldwork hammered or cut upon

them, and the unsparing use of gems. Damascening on iron Dama-
and steel, known as *kuft*, is chiefly practised in Kashmír, and scened steel.
at Gujrát and Siálkot in the Punjab. The process consists
of encrusting gold upon the surface of the harder metal.
Damascening in silver, which is chiefly done upon bronze, is
known as *bidari* work, from the ruined capital of Bidar in the
Nizám's Dominions, where it is still chiefly carried on.

The village brazier, like the village smith, manufactures the Brass and copper.
necessary vessels for domestic use. Chief among these vessels
is the *lotá*, or globular bowl, universally used in ceremonial
ablutions. The form of the *lotá*, and even the style of orna- The *lotá*.
mentation, has been handed down unaltered from the earliest
times. A *lotá* now in the India Museum, which was disinterred
from a Buddhist cell in Kúlu, and must be at least fifteen
centuries old, represents Prince Siddhartha going on a high
procession. Benares enjoys the first reputation in northern Benares ware.
India for work in brass and copper, producing not only
vessels for domestic and ceremonial use, but also images and
religious emblems. In the south, Madura and Tanjore have a
similar fame; and in the west, Ahmadábád, Poona, and Násik.
At Bombay itself, large quantities of imported copper are
wrought up by native braziers.

The temple bells of India are well known for the depth and
purity of their note. In many localities the braziers have a
speciality, either for a peculiar alloy or for a particular process
of ornamentation. Silver is sometimes mixed with the brass,
and in rarer cases gold. *Bidari* work, or the damascening of *Bidari* ware.
silver upon bronze, has already been alluded to. In this case,
the metal ground is said to be an amalgam of copper, lead,
and tin, made black by dipping in a solution of sal-ammoniac,
saltpetre, salt, and blue vitriol. At Moradábád, in the North-
Western Provinces, and at Bhilwárá in Udaipur State, Rájputána, tin is soldered upon the brass, and incised through in
floriated patterns, which are marked by filling in the ground
with a black composition of lac. At Purniah in Bengal, a
variety of *bidari* ware is made of zinc and copper, damascened
with silver, the processes of which are described at length in
Hunter's *Statistical Account of Bengal*.[1] The brass or rather
bell-metal ware of Murshidábád, known as *khágrai*, has more
than a local reputation, owing to the large admixture of silver.

The demand for enormous quantities of brass-work at the Deteriora-
lowest price for the London market, is rapidly deteriorating tion of brass-
both the designs and the workmanship of the Benares articles. work.

[1] Vol. xv. pp. 355-357.

The native braziers are almost compelled to degrade their industry, when they find that the most vulgar patterns, deeply but hastily carved, command a ready sale; while their old faithful work can scarcely find an English customer, at the price necessary for production.

Indian pottery.

Next to the loom of the weaver, the potter's wheel is the characteristic emblem of an ancient civilisation. From time immemorial, the potter has formed an essential member of the Hindu village community. Pottery is made in almost every village, from the small vessels required in cooking to the large jars for storing grain, and the earthenware floats used to ferry persons across a swollen stream. But although the industry is universal, it has in few Provinces risen to the dignity of a fine art. Perfection has been reached neither in the substance, as in the porcelain of China, nor in the ornamentation, as in ancient Greece. The clay in many places works up well, but the product remains mere earthenware, and rarely receives a high finish.

Its imperfections.

In Sind and the Southern Punjab the potter's craft has risen to a high art; and here the industry is said to have been introduced by the Muhammadans. Sind pottery is of two kinds, encaustic tiles and vessels for domestic use. In both classes the colours are the same—turquoise blue, copper green, dark purple or golden brown, under an exquisitely transparent glaze. The usual ornament is a conventional flower pattern, sometimes pricked in from paper, but often painted with much freedom and grace. The tiles, evidently of the same origin as those of Persia and Turkey, are chiefly found in the ruined mosques and tombs of the old Musalmán dynasties; but the Sind industry still survives at the little towns of Saidpur and Bubri; and at Haidarábád, Karáchi, Tatta, and Hála.

Sind pottery.

Tiles.

Glazed tiles and pottery are also manufactured at Lahore and Múltán in the Punjab. Efforts have been made by the Bombay School of Art to foster this indigenous industry; but, as in other cases of European patronage, the Indian artisan loses his originality when set to copying alien models. Something, however, has been done in the right direction by reproducing the old designs from the cave temples of Ajanta and Karlí, in the pottery made at the Bombay School of Art. The Madura pottery also deserves mention, from the elegance of its form and the richness of its colour.

Punjab and Bombay pottery.

Sculpture.

The earliest Indian sculptures are found in the monasteries, *topes*, and 'rails' of ancient Buddhism. The best specimens disclose the still fresh impulse derived from Greek or Roman artists—that impulse which has been historically treated in previous chapters, pp. 112 and 170–172. With the revival of Bráhmanism, Indian sculpture degenerated. Modern Hindu statuary possesses a religious rather than an æsthetic interest.[1] But exquisite flat-carving, and perforated arabesque windows or screens in hard sandstone and marble, are still produced at Agra and Jaipur.

In the cities of Gujarát (Guzerát), and in other parts of India where the houses are built of wood, their fronts are ornamented with elaborate carving. The favourite materials are black-wood (Dalbergia latifolia), sandal-wood, and jack-wood. The supply of sandal-wood comes from the forests of the Western Gháts in Kánara and Mysore, but some of the finest carving in it is done at Surat and Ahmadábád. Examples of 17th century Indian carving indicate that the art received a powerful impulse from the Dutch along the Bombay coast. But Indian wood-carving is an art of very great antiquity. The early stone architecture of the Buddhists is evidently based, both in regard to structure and ornaments, on pre-existing wooden forms. Some of the patterns of modern Indian wood-carving are preserved from that earlier period in exquisite open carving in marble, or open lattice-work windows in hard stone. The more durable material has survived, and now tells its tale. The Burmese are also celebrated for their luxuriant wood-carving. *Wood-carving.*

Akin to wood-carving, is the inlaying of the articles known as 'Bombay boxes.' This art is known to be of modern date, having been introduced from Shiraz in Persia towards the close of the last century. It consists of binding together in geometrical patterns, strips of tin-wire, sandal-wood, ebony, ivory, and stag's horn. At Vizagapatam in Madras, similar articles are made of ivory and stag's horn, with scroll-work edged in to suit European taste. At Máinpuri, in the North-Western Provinces, wooden boxes are inlaid with brass wire. The chief seats of ivory-carving are Amritsar, Benares, Murshidábád, and Travancore, where any article can be obtained to order in ivory, from a full-sized palanquin to a lady's comb. Human figures in clay, dressed to the life, are principally made at Krishnagar in Bengal, at Lucknow, and at Poona. *Inlaying. Ivory-carving. Clay figures.*

---

[1] For Indian architecture, painting, and musical instruments, see *ante*, chap. iv.

European industries.   The preparation of tea, coffee, and indigo have been already described in connection with agriculture.   It remains to give some account of those manufactures proper, conducted by steam machinery, and under European supervision, which have rapidly sprung up in certain parts of India during the past few years.   These comprise cotton, jute, silk, and wool, and beer, paper, leather, etc.

Cotton mills, 1854-79.   The first mill for the manufacture of cotton yarn and cloth by machinery worked by steam, was opened at Bombay in 1854.   The enterprise has since expanded to vast dimensions.   In 1879, the total number of mills throughout India was 58, with about a million and a half spindles, and twelve thousand looms, giving employment to upwards of 40,000 persons

Their distribution throughout India.   —men, women, and children.   Of this total, 30 mills, or more than half, were in the island of Bombay, which now possesses a busy manufacturing quarter with tall chimney-stalks, recalling the aspect of a Lancashire town; 14 were in the cotton-growing Districts of Gujarát (Guzerát), also in the Bombay Presidency; 6 were in Calcutta and its neighbour-hood; 3 at Madras; 2 at Cawnpur in the North-Western Provinces; 1 at Nágpur in the Central Provinces; 1 at Indore, the capital of Holkar's Dominions; and 1 at Haidarábád, the residence of the Nizám.

Cotton mills, 1884: Government returns.   By 1884, the number of steam cotton mills for which returns had been received by Government had increased to 74, with 1,895,284 spindles, and 16,251 looms, giving employment to a total of 61,836 men, women, and children.   Of these, 35 were in the town and island of Bombay; 21 were in other Districts of the Bombay Presidency, chiefly Gujarát; 6 in Bengal, in the suburbs or vicinity of Calcutta; 5 in Madras, namely, 4 in Madras town, and 1 in Bellary District; 3 at Cawnpur in the North-Western Provinces; 2 in the Central Provinces, namely, at Nágpur and at Hinghanghát; and 1 each at Indore and Haidarábád in the Deccan.

Cotton mills, 1884: private returns.   Private returns of the cotton industry show a somewhat different result to that quoted above.   A carefully-compiled statement gives the figures up to the 30th June 1884 as follows:—On that date there were, in the town and island of Bombay itself, 43 cotton mills, namely, 38 in work, and 5 in course of construction, with a total paid-up capital of £4,580,430; the number of spindles was 1,251,726, and of looms (in 22 mills), 11,985; giving employment to a daily average of 36,071 men, women, and children; quantity of cotton consumed (in 36 mills) in twelve months, 1,218,490 cwts. Elsewhere in the Bombay Presidency there were 18 mills, with a total paid-up capital for 17 mills of £943,706. The number of spindles was 289,153, and of looms, in the only 12 mills which had them, 2314. Number of hands employed, 9293; quantity of cotton consumed, 235,935 cwts. There were thus, in June 1884, in the Bombay Presidency, 61 mills, either in active operation or in course of construction, with a total paid-up capital of £5,452,136, employing 45,364 hands, and consuming 1,454,475 cwts. of cotton. In the other Provinces of India there were 20 mills, namely, 6 in Bengal, 3 in the North-Western Provinces, 1 in the Central Provinces, 1 at Haidarábád, and 9 in Madras, of which 4 were under construction in June 1884. The total paid-up capital of these mills outside the Bombay Presidency was £1,414,950; number of spindles, 79,176, and of looms, 1426; number of hands employed daily, 17,472; quantity of cotton consumed during the year, 371,591 cwts. Throughout India there were thus 81 mills in June 1884, constructed at a cost of £6,867,086; with 1,520,055 spindles, and 15,725 looms, consuming 1,826,016 cwts. of cotton during the previous twelve months, and affording employment to a daily average of 62,836 men, women, and children.

The general character of the cotton industry and its progress Nágpur may be inferred from the following returns supplied by the Cotton Mill: 1882. Empress Spinning and Weaving Mills Company at Nágpur, which in 1882 had 30,000 spindles and 450 looms at work, and employed a daily average of 3137 hands. Their consumption of raw cotton up to 1880 averaged 1,707,000 lbs. a year; their out-turn has averaged 1,040,000 lbs. of yarn valued at £45,358, and 627,700 lbs. of cloth valued at £30,661. In 1882, the consumption of raw cotton at these mills was 3,796,240 lbs., with an out-turn of 1,804,530 lbs. of twist, and 1,494,945 lbs. of manufactured cloth, of a total value of £159,386.

This rapid and widespread development sufficiently proves Sound that the new industry, though still in its infancy, is being basis of carried on under wholesome conditions, and meets a real facture. the manu- demand. Checks have from time to time occurred at Bombay, caused partly by competition with European goods recklessly thrown upon the market regardless of profit, and partly by that mismanagement to which joint-stock enterprise is peculiarly exposed. But with the revival of general commerce, the

Bombay mills have always again started upon a career of renewed activity.

Cheap material.

Their advantages over the English manufacturer are manifest. The crop of raw material and the market for the manufactured article are both at their very doors, thus saving a double freight.

Cheap labour.

Labour is cheap, abundant, docile, and not liable to strike. A certain amount of prejudice exists in favour of their products,

No adulteration.

partly because of their freedom from adulteration, and partly from the patriotic pride naturally felt for a native industry. Lastly, up to March 1882, they had the slight protection of a moderate customs duty of 5 per cent. *ad valorem* (imposed for fiscal purposes solely) upon imported goods. The cotton import duties were finally abolished, together with the general import duties upon all but a few excepted articles of merchandise, such as arms and ammunition, liquors, etc., by the Indian Tariff Act, xi. of 1882.

The drawbacks.

On the other hand, they labour under not a few countervailing disadvantages. The cost of erection, including spindles and

Cost of erection.

fitting up, was said (1877) to be about three times as much in India as in England. Thus a mill containing 50,000 spindles, which in Lancashire might be set up for about £1 per spindle, or a total of £50,000, would cost at Bombay about £150,000. On this capital the initial charge for interest would be only £2500 a year in England, calculated at 5 per cent., as com-

High interest.

pared with £13,500 in India, at the rate of 9 per cent. Again, the cost of fuel, and all stores which require to be imported from England, tells greatly against the Bombay mills. Another important consideration which it is difficult to estimate in all

Short staple.

its bearings, is the quality of Indian cotton, known as 'short stapled,' which does not admit of being spun into the finer kinds of yarn. Consequently the Indian mills can only turn out the lower 'counts' of yarn, and the coarser fabrics of piece-goods, leaving English imports of the higher classes without competition.

Only coarse qualities made.

Adopting the technical language of the trade, the great bulk of the yarn spun in Indian mills consists of numbers 6, 10, and 20 mule twist. Water twist is spun in smaller quantities, generally of number 16. The maximum of either kind is number 30. The mills are capable of spinning up to 40 ; but as a matter of fact, they never attempt this number, owing partly to the inferior quality of the cotton, and partly to the carelessness of the work-people. As regards piece-goods, the kinds principally woven in the mills are those known as T cloths, domestics, sheetings, drills, and jeans, made entirely from the yarn spun in the same mills. Long-cloths, *chadars* and *dhutis*, are also manufactured ; and recently attempts have been made to turn out drawers, stockings, night-caps, and towelling. But Manchester still possesses a practical monopoly both of the higher 'counts' of yarn which are used by the hand-loom weavers, and of the superior qualities of cloth.

The Indian mills are almost without exception the property Joint-stock of joint-stock companies, the shares in which are largely taken cotton up by natives. The overlookers are skilled artisans brought mills. from England, but natives are beginning to qualify them-selves for the post. The operatives are all paid by the piece ; and, as compared with other Indian industries, the rates of wages are high. In 1877, at Bombay, boys earned from 14s. Bombay to £1 a month ; women, from 16s. to £1 ; and jobbers, from wages. £3 to £6, 10s. Several members of one family often work together, earning between them as much as £10 a month. The hours of work are from six in the morning to six at night, with an hour allowed in the middle of the day for meals and smoking. The Indian Factories Act, xi. of 1881, regulates the hours of work for children and young persons, and enforces the fencing of dangerous machinery, etc.

Besides supplying the local demand, these mills are gradually Statistics beginning to find a market in foreign countries, especially for of Bombay their twist and yarn. Between 1872–73 and 1882–83, the manu-cotton export of twist from Bombay increased from 1,802,863 lbs. factures. valued at £97,162 in 1872–73, to 21,271,059 lbs. valued at £883,665 in 1878–79, and to 42,598,400 lbs. valued at £1,705,978 in 1882–83, or an increase of twenty-four-fold in quantity and nearly eighteen-fold in value in eleven years. Within the same period, the export of grey piece-goods from Bombay increased from 4,780,834 yards valued at £75,495 in 1872–73, to 14,993,336 yards valued at £198,380 in 1878–79, and to 30,730,396 yards valued at £357,320 in 1882–83. The total foreign exports of Indian twist and yarn, and of Indian manufactured grey, white, and coloured piece-goods from all Indian ports amounted to £2,578,382 in value in 1882–83.

The above figures refer to Indian produce and manufactures only ; and are exclusive of $1\frac{1}{3}$ million sterling of re-exported British cotton manufactures. Including these re-exports, the total exports of cotton twist, yarn, and manufactures amounted to just under 4 millions in 1882–83 from all Indian ports. Sent to The twist and yarn is mostly sent to China and Japan, the China and piece-goods to the coast of Arabia and Africa. Africa.

The figures for the coasting trade show a slower growth, the total value of twist carried from port to port in 1878–79 having been £804,996, and of piece-goods (including hand-loom goods), £654,553. In 1882–83, cotton twist and yarn to the value of £896,369, and piece-goods to the value of £633,316, were exported in the coasting trade, apart from exports to foreign countries.

Future of the trade.

Mr. O'Conor, who has devoted much attention to the matter, thus summarizes his opinion regarding the future of the Indian cotton mills in his *Review of Indian Trade* for 1877–78 :—'Whether we can hope to secure an export trade or not, it is certain that there is a sufficient outlet in India itself for the manufactures of twice fifty mills; and if the industry is only judiciously managed, the manufactures of our mills must inevitably, in course of time, supersede Manchester goods of the coarser kinds in the Indian market.' The correctness of this opinion is further shown by Mr. O'Conor's *Review of Indian Trade* for 1884–85, in which he states—'The importation of the coarser kinds of twist has long been unimportant, the yarn of the Indian mills having driven it out of the market. Even the medium kinds are now diminishing, an indication that the Indian mills are beginning to make them too.'

Wool mills.

Besides cotton mills, wool-weaving by steam machinery has recently been established in India, the principal mills being the Egerton Mills in Gurdáspur District, Punjab, and the Cawnpur woollen mills in the North-Western Provinces.

Jute mills.

The jute mills of Bengal have sprung up in rivalry to Dundee, as Bombay competes with Manchester ; but in Bengal the capital for jute-manufacturing is almost entirely supplied by Europeans. The jute-mills cluster round Calcutta, and on the opposite side of the river in Howrah District. The industry has also taken root at Sirájganj, far away up the Brahmaputra, in the middle of the jute-producing country.

Number in 1882-83.

In 1882–83, the total number of jute mills in India was 21, of which 19 were in Bengal, 1 at Kolába on Bombay island, and 1 at Chittivalása in Vizagapatam District, Madras. The weaving of jute into gunny cloth is an indigenous hand-loom industry in Northern Bengal, chiefly in the Districts of Purniah and Dinájpur. The gunny is made by the semi-aboriginal tribe of Koch, Rájbansí or Páli, both for clothing and for bags ; and, as with other industries practised by non-Hindu races, the weavers are the women of the family, and not a distinct caste. The mills turn out bags, and

also cloth in pieces to a limited extent. The bags vary in Jute.
size, according to the markets for which they are intended. Varieties
The largest are the twilled wool packs sent to Australia, of gunny-
which measure 56 inches by 26½, and weigh about 10½ bags.
lbs. each. The smallest are the Hessian wheat bags for
California, measuring 36 inches by 22, and weighing only
12 ounces. The average weight may be taken to be from
2 to 2½ lbs.

The mills in Calcutta and its neighbourhood were estimated Out-turn of
in 1878 to keep about 4000 looms at work ; the total amount of Calcutta
jute mills,
raw jute worked up annually was about 1½ million cwts., which 1878 ;
yielded about 90 million bags. The 21 steam jute mills in
India in 1883 worked 6139 looms and 112,650 spindles, the and 1883.
total quantity of raw jute worked up in the year being returned
at 2,831,778 cwts. These figures are below the mark, as
certain companies and private individuals have not supplied
full information. The jute manufacturing industry afforded
employment to 47,868 men, women, and children in 1882–83.

The activity of the jute trade, and the general direction of Indian and
the exports, will be seen by comparing the figures for 1877–78 foreign
consump-
and 1882–83 in the two following paragraphs. tion.

In 1877–78, 3 million bags were brought into Calcutta from 1878,
Pabná District, being the product of the Sirájganj mills. The
total exports from Calcutta by sea and land of both power-loom
and hand-made bags numbered 80 millions in 1877-78, of which
not more than 6 millions were hand-made. The East Indian
Railway took 20 millions for the grain marts of Behar and
the North-Western Provinces (chiefly Patná and Cawnpur) ;
and 1 million went as far as Ludhiána in the Punjab. The
total exports by sea in 1877–78 exceeded 57 millions, of
which 32 millions represent interportal, and 25 millions foreign
trade. Bombay took as many as 16 millions, and British
Burma 12 millions. In fact, Calcutta supplies bagging for the
whole of India.

In 1882–83, besides the local manufactures in Calcutta, and 1883.
28,972,920 bags were imported into that city from the interior
Districts, of which 12,494,243 were power-loom and 16,478,677
hand-made. The total exports from Calcutta of power-loom
and hand-made bags numbered 123,219,477 bags. Of the
internal trade, the East Indian Railway carried 16,808,855
bags for the following marts and Districts :—Patná (3,189,970),
Cawnpur (2,583,210), Faizábád (959,455), Delhi (676,375),
Santál Parganás (623,945), Monghyr (609,875), Bírbhúm
(558,915), and Bardwán (544,355). The total internal

exports by rail, boat, and road amounted to 18,877,715 bags
The exports by sea numbered 104,341,762 bags, of which
45,018,189 represented coasting, and 59,323,573 foreign
exports.

The foreign jute trade may be given in greater detail, for
gunny-weaving is perhaps the single Indian manufacture that
Sea-borne has secured a great foreign market. The sea-borne export
exports of of jute manufactures (bags and cloth) in 1872–73 was
jute.
valued at £188,859. By 1878–79, the value had risen to
Growth of £1,098,434, and by 1882–83 to £1,487,831, or an increase
the trade. of £389,397 in four years. These figures seem to justify
Mr. O'Conor's statement in his *Review of Indian Trade* for
1878–79, that 'there is little room to doubt that in course of
time India will be able, not only to supplant the manufactures
of Dundee in the American and other foreign markets, but
to supply England herself with bags more cheaply than they
can be made in Dundee.' On the other hand, it must be
recollected that large figures, and even growing figures, do not
necessarily show that a business is remunerative. Calcutta,
like Bombay, sometimes suffers from the mismanagement incidental to joint-stock enterprises. The principal countries
which take Indian gunny-bags are :—Australia, £714,747 in
1882–83 ; Straits Settlements, £189,869 ; United States
(California), £164,405 ; China, £173,295.

Brewing.   Brewing has been established on a large scale at the hill
stations for several years. There were in 1882–83, 22 breweries
Statistics in India ; 12 in the Punjab and the North-Western Provinces,
of Indian at Mari (Murree), Simla, Solon, Kasauli, Dalhousie, Masuri
brewing,
1877–83. (Mussoorie), Náini Tál, Chakráta, and Rániíkhet ; 2 in
Bombay, at Moody Bay and at Bandorá ; 3 in Madras, at
Utakamand and Coonoor ; 4 at Bangalore in Mysore ; and 1 at
Rangoon. The total quantity of beer brewed was returned at
2,162,888 gallons in 1877, and 2,597,298 gallons in 1882–83.
The quantity imported into India in 1878–79 was 2 million
gallons by Government, and 1 million gallons on private
account. In 1882–83, the Government imports were just
under 1½ million gallons, and the private imports a little over
1 million gallons, total 2,656,788 gallons ; so that the Indian
breweries now satisfy one-half of the entire demand. Indian
brewed beer is rising in public favour, and is rapidly superseding imported beer for commissariat purposes. In 1875,
349,095 gallons of Indian beer were purchased by the
Bengal Commissariat Department ; in 1883, the quantity thus

purchased was 1,936,221 gallons, as against 1,486,234 gallons imported by Government.

At Simla, imported beer sells at over 18s. per dozen quarts, Beer while that from the local breweries can be obtained for 10s. per prices. dozen. The hops are entirely imported. An experimental hop plantation of 100 acres established by the Mahárájá of Kashmír has not yet proved a practical success ; but efforts are still being made, both in Kashmir and in India, to successfully introduce the hop plant into the country. The imports of hops show an increase from 1529 cwts. in 1875–76, to Hop 1807 cwts. in 1876–77, and 2135 cwts. in 1877–78. In imports. 1882–83, however, the import of hops had fallen to 1940 cwts. valued at £42,983.

The steam paper mills established in the neighbourhood of Paper-Calcutta and at Bombay have almost entirely destroyed the making. local manufactures of paper which once existed in many parts of the country. The hand-made article, which was strong though coarse, and formed a Muhammadan speciality, is now no longer used for official purposes.

The Government possesses a large leather factory at Cawn- Leather. pur, which turns out accoutrements, saddlery, etc., of excellent quality. Two large European firms have also established leather factories at Cawnpur. Indeed, leather hand-manufactures have long been an important local industry in Oudh and the North-Western Provinces. They are worked so cheaply as to discourage importation from England, except in the case of *articles de luxe,* and saddlery or harness for the richest classes.

Rice-husking by steam machinery is largely carried on at the Rice-ports of British Burma. husking.

CHAPTER XXI.

MINES AND MINERALS.

Mines and minerals. THE Indian peninsula, with its wide area and diversified features, supplies a great store of mineral wealth. In utilizing this wealth, English enterprise has met with many rebuffs. Capital has been expended in many cases with no result except disappointment. But the experience has not been thrown away; and mining industry, now established on a sure basis, is gradually rising into an important position.

Indian iron. In purity of ore, and in antiquity of working, the iron deposits of India rank among the first in the world. They are to be found in every part of the country, from the northern mountains of Assam and Kumáun to the extreme south of Madras. Wherever there are hills, iron is found and worked Indigenous to a greater or less extent. The indigenous methods of methods. smelting the ore, handed down unchanged through countless generations, yield a metal of the finest quality in a form well suited to native wants. But they require an extravagant supply of charcoal; and notwithstanding the cheapness of native labour, the product cannot compete in price with imported iron from England. European enterprise, attracted by the richness of the ore and the low rate of wages, has repeatedly tried to establish ironworks on a large scale. But hitherto each of these attempts has ended in failure.

Failure of English efforts, 1825; The most promising early efforts were those undertaken in Madras by Mr. Heath óf the Civil Service, the anticipator of the Bessemer process. In 1825, he founded a company which opened works at Porto Novo on the Coromandel coast, in the hills of Salem District, and at Beypur in Malabar. The iron and steel produced were of first-rate quality; and all went well so long as an unlimited supply of charcoal could be obtained in the neighbourhood of the furnaces. But when this essential condition of cheap production gradually ceased, the enterprise became unremunerative, and had to be 1880. abandoned. Within the last few years, an attempt has been made to smelt ore by means of coal, according to English methods, in the neighbourhood of Ráníganj and in Bírbhúm and Mánbhúm. Coal abounds, and also limestone as a flux; but in this case, again, the company made no profit, and has been compelled to wind up. Similar experiments in the Central Provinces and in Kumáun have met with similar results.

In 1882–83, the Bengal Government took over the works Efforts by of the suspended Barákhar Iron Company at Khenduá in Government. Mánbhúm District, and cast and pig iron is now manufactured on the spot. The iron-works are doing a considerable amount of good, as not only do they encourage the private coal companies in the neighbourhood, but they also give employment to a large number of skilled workmen. They also promise to be remunerative; and the question of the expansion of the works is (1884) under the consideration of Government. With the exception of these works, iron in India is manufactured only by peasant families of smelters, each working on a very small scale.

The initial difficulty in India is to find the three elements Difficulties of iron-working, namely, the ore, the flux, and the fuel, suffi- of Indian ciently near to each other. The second difficulty is the choking works. of the furnaces from the excessive quantity of ash in the coal.

Coal has been known to exist in India since 1774, and is Indian said to have been worked as far back as 1775. The first coal. English coal-mine was opened at Ráníganj in 1820. There are now (1885) 65 working collieries in the country, with an annual out-turn of about 1 million tons. In India, as elsewhere, coal and railway extension have gone hand in hand. Coal is comparatively worthless unless it can be brought to market by rail; and the price of coal is the chief element in determining the expenses of railway working. The history of coal in India History of is, on the whole, a record of continual progress. The first Bengal coal- mine, as already mentioned, dates from 1820; and it has been mining, worked regularly up to the present time. In 1878, its out- 1820; put was 50,000 tons. Until about 1840 no other mine was opened; but the commencement of the East Indian Railway in 1854 gave a fresh impetus to the industry, and since that 1854; date collieries have been set on foot at the rate of two or three every year. The largest number of additions was seven in 1874. From these are supplied not only the railway itself, but also the jute mills of Calcutta, and the river steamers of Lower Bengal.

In 1883, there were in all 62 working collieries in Bengal, 1883. besides 15 others, principally in the Santál Parganás, which were either closed, or were not working during the year. The

Ráníganj Sub-division, with its 50 working collieries, had an output of 603,591 tons in 1883, as compared with an average output of 547,930 tons in the previous three years. Four new mines were opened during the year. Hazáríbagh and Mánbhúm Districts contain 6 collieries, which yielded an out-turn of 559,849 tons in 1883, against an annual average for the three previous years of 502,860 tons. The East Indian Railway Company's valuable mines at Karharbárí and Srírámpur are situated within Hazáríbagh District. In 1883, these two mines yielded a total output of 308,000 tons, against an average of 274,087 in the three previous years. The total out-turn from all the working mines in Bengal in 1883 was 1,200,957 tons, against an average of 1,058,084 tons for the three previous years. In

Imported coal.

1882–83, the imports of coal into Calcutta by sea were only 74,610 tons, so that Bengal now uses locally about 94 per cent. of Indian to about 6 per cent. of foreign coal. Bombay and Madras are entirely supplied with coal from England.

Coalmining in Central Provinces;

The collieries in the Central Provinces, the only other Indian ones worked on a large scale, are limited to the supply of the Great Indian Peninsula Railway. They consist of—(1) the Warorá colliery in Chándá District, under the management of the Public Works Department; and (2) the Mohpání colliery, which has been leased to the Narbadá Coal Company.

(1) Warorá colliery;

In 1878–79, the Warorá colliery put out 43,000 tons, of which 11,000 tons consisted of slack. The gross receipts were £18,686, and the net receipts £5873, being about 8·3 per cent. on the estimated capital expenditure of £70,000. In 1883, the Government mine at Warorá yielded an out-turn of 95,738 tons, and averaged 51,376 tons in the previous three years. The profits are estimated at 4 to 6 per cent. But it is difficult to fix the sum, as the accounts are mixed up with those of the Wardhá State Railway, a branch from the Nágpur line of the Great Indian Peninsula Railway. Cost of raising coal in the Central Provinces, Rs. 2. 10. (5s. 3d.) per ton; price paid by the Railway Company for large coal, Rs. 5 (10s.) per ton. In 1877–78, the cotton mills at Nágpur took 4872 tons.

(2) Mohpání colliery.

The Mohpání colliery had an output in 1878–79 of 8900 tons, valued at £8000. In 1883, the total output from Mohpání mine was 19,281 tons, as against an average of 13,714 tons in the previous three years. Almost the whole of this was taken by the Great Indian Peninsula Railway. Extensive coal-fields have recently been discovered at Umária, within the Native State of Rewá, only 34 miles beyond the

northern boundary of the Central Provinces, which are
believed to extend into the northern portion of Jabalpur.

The principal drawback of Indian coal is its large proportion Excessive
of ash; varying from 14 to 20 per cent., as against 3 to 6 per ash of Indian
cent. in English coal. This places Indian coal measures at coals.
a great disadvantage, alike for iron-smelting and locomotive
purposes. But it has been proved that, with efficient fire-
grates and proper manipulation, 135 lbs. of Warora coal will
do the work of 100 lbs. of English coal.

The Ráníganj coal-field has been estimated at an area of 500 Ráníganj
square miles. In this 'black country' of India, which is dotted coal-field.
with tall chimney-stalks, many European companies are at work,
besides many native firms.[1] At first coal was raised from open
workings; but regular mining is now carried on, according to
the system known as 'pillar and stall.' The seams are entirely
free from gas, so that the precautions usual in England against
explosion are found unnecessary. The miners are all drawn
from the aboriginal races, chiefly Santáls and Baurís, who are
noted for their endurance and docility. Baurís work with the
pick, but Santáls will consent to use no other instrument than
the crowbar. Wages are high, and the men look well-fed,
although they waste their surplus earnings in drink.

The coal-fields of India lie almost entirely in the broad Distribu-
centre of the peninsula, between the Ganges and the Godávari. tion of coal in
South of the Godávari no carboniferous strata exist; and the India.
whole Presidency of Madras is thus compelled to depend for
its supply upon importation. North of the Ganges, the only
extensive fields are to be found in the outlying Province of Outlying
Assam. There, in the Khásí and Jaintia Hills, mines have beds in Assam,
been worked on a small scale for many years; but the aggregate of the deposits is insignificant, and the difficulties of
carriage almost insurmountable. Still farther away, in the
frontier District of Lakhimpur, a large coal-field of excellent
quality was discovered at Mákum; and a private company has
been established with a view to open out the field, by means of
a railway. The company obtained a lease of the coal-beds for
a period of twenty years, and a light railway has been constructed to the mines. Operations have not yet been carried
sufficiently far to justify any forecast as to the profitable work-

[1] For a full account of the Ráníganj coal-field, see article RANIGANJ in
The Imperial Gazetteer; and for its geological aspects, see a subsequent
chapter.

ing of these deposits. In 1883–84, the out-turn from the Mákum mines was about 450 tons a week ; but the company hopes to increase the out-turn to 3000 tons a week, which it is estimated will allow the mines to be worked at a fair profit.

Dárjíling, Punjab.

Coal is also found in the neighbourhood of Dárjíling, and in the Salt Range of the Punjab.

Apart from these outlying beds, the central coal-fields of India have been divided by Mr. Blanford, of the Geological Survey,

The four great coal-fields.

into the four following groups :—(1) The Dámodar valley, including both Ráníganj and Karharbárí, which yields at least nine-tenths of all the coal as yet produced in India, and finds a ready market at Calcutta. (2) The Chutiá Nágpur group, extending over a wide area of mountainous and difficult country, as yet but imperfectly explored. (3) The Narbadá valley, south of the Sátpura range, where actual borings have hitherto proved disappointing, except in the case of the Mohpání colliery, which is connected by a short branch with the main line of the Great Indian Peninsula Railway. (4) The Godávari valley, where coal has been traced from Nágpur southwards as far as Ellore : In this coal-field the only successful works are at Warorá.

Future of Indian coal.

Of the future of Indian coal it is difficult to speak with certainty. On the one hand, the demand is constant, and increases with the construction of every fresh mile of railway, and every new factory. On the other hand, the quality is distinctly inferior to English coal, which comes out to India at a low freight—almost at ballast rates. Ráníganj coal, which is the best of the Indian coals, can do only from one-half to two-thirds of the duty performed by the same amount of English coal. It contains a low proportion of fixed carbon, and more than three times the average percentage of ash.

Indian salt.

Salt, an article of supreme necessity to the Indian peasant, who eats no butcher's meat, except a festival goat or kid at rare intervals, is derived from three main sources, exclusive

Its three sources.

of importation from Europe.[1] (1) By evaporation from sea-water along the entire double line of seaboard from Bombay to Orissa, but especially in Gujarát and on the Coromandel coast. (2) By evaporation from inland salt lakes, of which the Sámbhar Lake in Rájputána affords the chief example. The right of working this lake was leased by Government in 1870 from the Mahárájás of Jaipur and Jodhpur, within whose territories it is situated, and who are paid a royalty upon the out-turn. (3)

---

[1] For the administrative aspects of Indian salt, see *ante*, chap. xvi. ; and for its geological aspects, *post*, chap. xxii.

By quarrying solid hills of salt in the north-east of the Punjab.
The last is the only source in which salt in India can be said
to exist as a mineral. It occurs in solid cliffs, which for extent
and purity are stated to have no rival in the world. The Salt
Range runs across the two Districts of Jehlam (Jhelum) and The Pun-
Sháhpur, from the bank of the Jehlam river to Kálábágh in jab salt
Bannu District. Similar deposits are found beyond the Indus range.
in Kohát District, where the salt is of two kinds, red and
green; and in the Hill State of Mandi bordering on Kángrá
District. The salt is found in the red marls and sandstones of
the Devonian group. In some cases it can be obtained from
open quarries; but more generally it is approached by regular
mining by pick and blasting, through wide galleries. The
principal mine is at Kheura in Jehlam (Jhelum) District, now
called after Lord Mayo. The total annual out-turn in the
Punjab is returned at about 50,000 tons, yielding an average
net revenue to Government of from £300,000 to £350,000.

In Southern India, salt made by evaporation is almost Salt supply
universally consumed. Lower Bengal, and especially Eastern of Madras
Bengal, use salt imported from Cheshire, at low rates of gal.
freight, and paying the excise duty at Calcutta or other port of
entry. In Orissa and South-Western Bengal, both imported
salt and salt made by solar evaporation are consumed; the
solar salt being alone considered pure for religious purposes or
for the priests.

India has almost a monopoly of the supply of natural Indian
saltpetre, upon which Europe largely depends for the manu- saltpetre.
facture of gunpowder. It occurs with other saline substances
as a white efflorescence upon the surface of the soil in many
parts of the country, especially in the upper valley of the
Ganges. Its preparation leaves common salt as one of the
residuary products; and fiscal restraints have accordingly
tended to limit the manufacture to the most remunerative
region, which is found in North Behar.

The system of saltpetre manufacture is simple, and is System
entirely in the hands of a special caste of natives, called of manu-
Nuniyás, who are conspicuous for their capacity of enduring facture.
hard work. As is the case with most Indian industries, they
work under a system of money advances from middle-men,
who are themselves sub-contractors under large central houses
of business. In former times, the East India Company engaged
in the manufacture on its own account; and when it gave up
its private trade, the works were taken over by European firms.

But these have in their turn retired from the business, which is now in a state of decline (almost killed in Southern India), partly owing to the general fall in price, and partly to the restrictions imposed by the salt preventive department.

Process of manu-facture.
The manufacturing season begins with the cold season in November. The presence of saltpetre in the soil is revealed by efflorescence after a heavy fall of rain. This earth is scraped together, and first placed in a large vessel, through which water is filtered. The brine is then boiled in pots, and crude saltpetre mixed with common salt is the result. The proportion of salt to saltpetre is said to be about one-sixth. The sale of this salt is prohibited under stringent penalties. The crude saltpetre is now handed over to the refiners, who work on a larger scale than the Nuniyás. It is again subjected to a process of boiling in large iron boilers of English manu-facture, and is allowed to crystallize gradually in open wooden troughs. In refining, it loses nearly one-half its weight, and is now ready for the market. In 1873, the single District of Tirhút contained 22,528 filters, and 305 refineries.

Exports of saltpetre.
The exports of saltpetre from Calcutta are fairly constant, averaging about 450,000 cwts. a year, of which one-half goes to the United Kingdom. More than two-thirds of the total comes from Behar, chiefly from the Districts of Tirhút, Sáran, and Champáran, though Patná is the railway station for despatch to Calcutta. Cawnpur, Gházípur, Allahábád, and Benares, in the North-Western Provinces, send small quantities; while a little comes from the Punjab.

Indian gold.
Although silver has ever been the currency of India in his-torical times, that metal is nowhere found in the country, nor in the adjoining States of Central Asia. Gold, on the other hand, exists in many parts of India, and probably in large quantities. The 'Ophir' of King Solomon has been identified by some scholars with the Malabar coast. However that may be, India claims to rank as a gold-producing country. Many hill streams are washed for gold, alike in the extreme south, in the central plateau, and on the north-east and north-west frontiers. Gold-washing is everywhere in India a miserable business, affording the barest livelihood; but the total amount of gold obtained cannot be insignificant.

Gold-mining in Madras.
In recent years, attention has been prominently drawn to the possibility of extracting gold from the quartz formation of Southern India, which bears many points of resemblance to

the auriferous quartz reefs of Australia. The principal localities are in the Wainád (Wynaad) Sub-division of the Nílgiri
District, and in Kolár District of Mysore. Gold-washing has
always been practised here ; and the remains of old workings
show that at some unknown period operations have been
conducted on a large scale. Since about 1870, individual
pioneers have been prospecting in this region. Crushing the
quartz by rude native methods, they proved that it contained
a larger proportion of gold than is known to give a profit in
Australia. These experiments on the southern ends of six
reefs yielded an average of 7 dwts. per ton of quartz, rising in
one case to 11 dwts. The best assay of the gold showed a
fineness of slightly over 20 carats. In 1879, Government
summoned a practical mining engineer from Australia, whose
report was eminently hopeful. He described the quartz reefs as
of great extent and thickness, and highly auriferous. One reef
in Kolár, laid bare 100 feet longitudinally, had given an average
of 1 oz. of gold per ton. In order to attract capital, Government proposed to grant mining leases at a dead rent of Rs. 5
(10s.) per acre, subject to no royalty or further tax. Several
English companies with large capital entered the field, and the
reports of their professional advisers held forth high hopes of
success. Those hopes have not, however, been yet realized.
Gold-mining in Southern India is in a depressed state; although
some of the operations again hold out promise of success (1885).

The other Indian metals comprise copper, lead, and tin. Other
Copper exists in many parts of the country in considerable metals.
quantities. The richest mines are in the lower ranges of the Copper.
Himálayas, from Dárjíling westward to Kumáun. The ore
occurs in the form of copper pyrites, often accompanied by
mundic, not in true lodes, but disseminated through the slate
and schist. The miners are almost always Nepálís, and the Nepálí
remoteness of the situation has deterred European capital. miners
The extent of abandoned workings shows that these mines
have been known and worked for many years. The best
seams show a proportion of copper slightly above the average
of Cornish ore, but the ordinary yield is not more than
about 4 per cent.

The mines resemble magnified rabbit-holes, meandering 'Rabbit-
passages being excavated through the rock with little system. hole'
The tools used are an iron hammer and chisel, with some- mines
times a small pick. After extraction, the ore is pounded,
washed, and smelted on the spot. The price obtained

for the metal is Rs. 2. 8. per 3 *sers*, or at the rate of about
10d. a pound. Copper-ore, of fair purity and extending over
Singbhúm a considerable area, also occurs in Singbhúm District of
copper. Chutiá Nágpur, where there are many deserted diggings and
heaps of scoriæ. In 1857, a company was started to reopen
the workings at these mines; but although large quantities of
ore were produced, the enterprise did not prove remunerative,
and was finally abandoned in 1864. A similar attempt to
Nellore. work the copper found in Nellore District in Madras also
ended in failure.

Lead. Lead occurs, in the form of sulphuret or galena, along
the Himálayas on the Punjab frontier, and has been worked
Tin. at one place by an English company. Tin is confined to
the Burmese peninsula. Very rich deposits, yielding about
70 per cent. of metal, occur over a large extent of country in
Mergui and Tavoy Districts of the Tenasserim Division. The
ore is washed and smelted, usually by Chinese, in a very rough
and unscientific way. Recent experiments by a European firm
tend to show that the deposits, although rich and extensive,
are not sufficiently deep to repay more elaborate processes.
Antimony. Antimony, in the form of *surmá*, largely used by the natives
as a cosmetic for the eyes, is chiefly derived from the hill
States of the Punjab. It is also found in Mysore and Burma.
The minerals of Rájputána have not yet been thoroughly
Cobalt. investigated; but they include an ore of cobalt, used for
colouring enamel.

Petroleum, Petroleum is produced chiefly in Independent Burma, but
it has also been found in British Burma, in Assam, and in
the Punjab. Near the village of Ye-nan-chaung in Upper
in Burma; Burma, on the banks of the Irawadi, there are upwards of
100 pits or wells with a depth of about 250 feet, from which
petroleum bubbles up in inexhaustible quantities. The annual
yield in 1877 was estimated at 11,000 tons, of which a considerable quantity was exported. Petroleum wells are also found
in the British Districts of Akyab, Kyauk-pyu (Kyouk-hpyu),
Pegu, and Thayet-myo, which first attracted British capital with
most promising results in 1877.

Oil-refin- Two private oil-refining companies having obtained a lease
ing in from Government, under favourable conditions, of certain
Burma. areas at Minbyin in Ramri island, Kyauk-pyu District, are
working a number of wells by means of steam boring machinery,
under the superintendence of Canadian experts, with satisfactory results. The oil when refined is of a high quality; but

the expensiveness of the machinery and costly European agency have so far proved an obstacle to the financial success of the industry. The native oil-wells are constructed and managed on much more economical principles than the English companies, and many of them yield large profits.

The principal English company, the Boronga, has (1884) Chief oil 24 wells, one of them having a depth of over 1200 feet. companies: Only 10 were at work in 1883-84, yielding an out-turn of 234,000 gallons of oil, of which 65,400 gallons was refined, and the remainder sold in a crude state, the total realizations for the year being about £6000. The Arakan Oil Company, newly started, yielded during 1883-84 an out-turn of 107,800 gallons from 5 wells out of 7 sunk by them, the deepest being 400 feet, all of which was sold on the spot in its crude state. The native wells, bored by means of locally-made tools, windlasses, and sheers, run down to a depth of 250 to 350 feet. The total out-put of the whole field, including English companies and native wells, numbering about 170 in all, during the year, was 404,325 gallons. The imports of crude oil from the Ye-nanchaung wells in Upper Burma were 968,210 gallons, most of which was taken by the Rangoon refinery, which produced 640,000 gallons of refined oil during the year.

In Assam, petroleum occurs in the neighbourhood of the in Assam; coal-fields in the south of Lakhimpur District. It was formerly worked in connection with the coal by a private European capitalist, but the enterprise failed to prove a success. A Government concession to work the oil-beds was granted to the Assam Railways and Trading Company, along with the Mákum coal-fields; but up till 1884 no attempt had been made by the company to work the oil. In the Punjab, in Punjab. petroleum is worked experimentally by the Public Works Department at two spots in Ráwal Pindí District. In 1873-74, the total yield was 2756 gallons; and in 1882-83, 5000 gallons. Petroleum is also found in Bannu District, and probably in other neighbouring Districts of the Punjab.

The commonest and also the most useful stone of India is Stone, etc. *kankar*, a nodular form of impure lime, which is found in almost every river valley, and is used from one end of the peninsula to the other for metalling the roads. Lime for building Lime. (*chunám*) is derived from two sources—(1) from burning limestone and *kankar*, and (2) from the little shells so abundantly found in the marshes, rivers, and lakes. Calcutta derives its chief supply of limestone from the quarries of the Khásí

Hills in Assam, known as 'Sylhet lime,' and from the Susuniá
quarries in Bánkurá District.   Except for occasional beds of
Kankar.   *kankar,* the lower valley of the Ganges is absolutely destitute
of stone; nor does the alluvial soil afford good materials for
Pottery.   brickmaking or fine pottery.   But a European firm has recently
established large pottery and cement works at Ráníganj in
Bardwán, which employ about 500 hands, and carry out contracts for drainage pipes and stoneware.   These works are
annually increasing in importance and value.

The centre of the peninsula, and the hill country generally,
Building-   abounds in building-stone of excellent quality, which has
stone.   been used locally from time immemorial.   Among the finest
Marble.   stones may be mentioned—the pink marble of Rájputána,
of which the historical buildings at Agra were constructed;
the trap of the Deccan; the sandstone of the Godávari
and the Narbadá; and the granite of Southern India.
Slate.   Quarries of slate are scattered through the peninsula, and
Mica and   sometimes worked by European capital.   Mica and talc are
talc.   also quarried to make ornaments.   Among the hills of Orissa
and Chutiá Nágpur, household vessels and ornaments are
skilfully carved out of an indurated variety of potstone.

Precious   Despite its legendary wealth, which is really due to the
stones.   accumulations of ages, India cannot be said to be naturally
prolific in precious stones.   Under the Muhammadan rule,
Diamonds, diamonds were a distinct source of State revenue; but at the
present day, the search for them, if carried on anywhere in
British territory, is too insignificant an occupation to have
attracted the notice of Government.   The name of Golconda
has passed into literature; but that city, once the Musalmán
capital of the Deccan, was rather the home of the diamond-
cutters than the actual source of supply.   It is believed that the
at Gol-   far-famed diamonds of Golconda actually come from the sand-
conda;   stone formation, which extends across the eastern borders of
the Nizám's Dominions into the Madras Districts of Kistna
and Godávari.   A few worthless stones are still found in this
region.
in Sam-   Sambalpur, on the upper channel of the Mahánadi river
balpur;   in the Central Provinces, is another spot once famous for
diamonds.   In the last century, a British officer was despatched
to Sambalpur by Clive to arrange for remittances home by
means of Sambalpur diamonds.   As late as 1818, a stone is
said to have been found here weighing 84 grains and valued
at £500.   The river valleys of Chutiá Nágpur are also known

to have yielded a tribute of diamonds to their Muhammadan conqueror.

At the present day, the only place where the search for diamonds is pursued as a regular industry is the Native State of Panna (Punnah) in Bundelkhand. The stones in Bun-are found by digging down through several strata of gravelly delkhand. soil, and washing the earth. Even here, however, the pursuit is understood to be unremunerative, and has failed to attract European capital.

About other gems very little information is available. The town of Cambay in Gujarát (Guzerát) is celebrated for its Carne-carving of carnelian, agate, and onyx. The stones come from lians. the neighbourhood of Ratanpur, in the State of Rájpípla. They are dug up by Bhíl miners, and subjected to a process of burning before being carved. The most valued colour for carnelians is red, but they are also found white and yellow. Lapis lazuli is found in the mountains of the north, and is freely used in the decoration of temples and tombs.

Inferior pearl fisheries are worked off the coast of Madura Pearl District in the extreme south, and in the Gulf of Cambay; fisheries. but the great majority of Indian pearls come either from Ceylon (which is also rich in other gems) or from the Persian Gulf. In the year 1700, the Dutch obtained a lease of all the pearl fisheries along the Madura coast, and sublet the right of fishing to native boatmen, of whom 700 are said to have taken licences annually at the rate of 60 *écus* per boat.

We have now sketched the physical aspects of India, its Scientific past history, and its present administration and condition branches under British rule. It remains to briefly deal with the topics of the of scientific interest connected with the country: its material framework or geology; its climatic conditions, or meteorology; its animal and vegetable products; and the health statistics of its population. Each of these subjects forms the subject of many elaborate volumes, and the adequate treatment of any one of them would demand a body of scientific coadjutors not available to the author of this work. But some account of them may be useful for administrative purposes.

The following pages are offered, not for the instruction of Scope specialists, but to the general reader who wishes to study of the India in all its various aspects. In previous sections, the chapters. author has not hesitated to repeat himself when dealing with Indian products, such as opium, cotton, and salt; first from the administrative and then from the economic point of view. For he believes that such repetitions are convenient to many who desire a view of the subject under each head.   In like manner, the following sections will not shrink from repetitions, in referring to certain productions, such as coal, iron, or forests, in their scientific aspects.

CHAPTER XXII.

GEOLOGY OF INDIA.

FOR geological purposes British India may be mapped out into the four geographical divisions of—the Himálayan region, the Indo-Gangetic plain, Peninsular India, and Burma.[1]

THE HIMÁLAYAN REGION.—The geology of this tract is more Ilimá-complex and less fully known than that of the Peninsular layas. area. Until the ground has been carefully gone over by the Geological Survey, many points must remain doubtful; and large areas of the Himálayas (Nepál and Bhután) are still inaccessible to Europeans. The oldest rock of the Himálayas is a gneiss, differing in character from the gneiss of the Penin- Gneiss, sula, and from that of Assam and Burma. The Himálayan gneiss is usually white and grey, its felspar orthoclase and albite; it contains much mica and mica schist, and is more uniform in character than the gneiss of the Peninsula. The latter is usually pink, its felspar being orthoclase and oligoclase; it contains little mica schist, but often has quartzite and hornblendic rock. Hornblende occurs in the syenitic gneiss of the Northern Himálayan (or Ladákh) range.

The Central Himálayan region may be described as con- Central sisting of two gneissic axes, with a trough or synclinal valley gneissic between them, in which fossiliferous beds have been deposited axes. and are now preserved. The gneiss of the southern or main axis (the 'central gneiss' of Dr. Stoliczka) is the oldest; that of the northern or Ladákh axis comes next in age. The gneiss of the Ladákh axis is generally syenitic, or is that variety of the Himálayan gneiss already described as containing hornblende. It is probably an extremely altered condition of ordinary marine sediment. The gneiss of the central axis is the ordinary kind; it is penetrated by granite, which ranges along some of the highest peaks. Between these two gneissic

---

[1] This section is based upon the official *Manual of the Geology of India*, by Messrs. H. B. Medlicott and W. T. Blanford, 2 vols., Government Press, Calcutta, 1879. Mr. W. Topley, of the English Geological Survey, conducted the preliminary condensation.

axes occurs the basin-shaped valley, or the Hundes and Zanskar synclinal. In this valley, fossiliferous rocks are preserved, giving representatives of the Silurian, Carboniferous, Triassic, Jurassic, and Cretaceous formations. All these seem there to have followed each other without important breaks or unconformities; but after the deposition of the Cretaceous rocks of the Himálayan region, important changes appear to have taken place in its physical geography. The Nummulitic (Eocene) strata were laid down on the eroded edges of some of the older beds, and in a long trough within the Silurian gneiss of the Ladákh axis.

Lower Himá layas.

On the south of this true Himálayan region there is a band of country known as the Lower Himálaya, in which the beds are often greatly disturbed, and even completely inverted, over great areas; the old gneiss apparently overlying the sedimentary rocks. This Lower Himálayan region is about 50 miles wide, and consists of irregular ridges, varying from 5000 to 8000 feet in height, and sometimes reaching 12,000 feet. Resting upon the gneiss, but often through inversion apparently underlying it, in the neighbourhood of Simla, is a series of unfossiliferous beds (schists, quartzites, sandstones, shales, limestones, etc.) known in descending order as the Krol, Infra-Krol, Blaini, and Infra-Blaini beds. In the Krol beds is

Krol limestone.

a massive limestone (Krol limestone) probably representing the limestone of the Pir Panjál range, which is most likely of Carboniferous age. The Blaini and Infra-Blaini beds are probably Silurian.

Sub-Himá-layas.

The Lower Himálayan range ends at the Sutlej valley, west of which the continuation of the central range is followed immediately by the third or sub-Himálayan range. This occurs almost always on the south of the Lower Himálayas, and is composed of later Tertiary rocks (Siwáliks, etc.), which stretch parallel with the main chain. Generally, the sub-Himálayas consist of two ranges, separated by a broad, flat valley (dún or 'doon'); the southern slope, overlooking the great Indo-Gangetic plain, is usually the steepest. Below Náini Tál and Dárjíling (Darjeeling), the sub-Himálayan range is wanting; on the Bhután frontier the whole range is occasionally absent, and the great alluvial plain slopes up to the base of the Lower Himálayan region.

Siwálik beds.

It is within the sub-Himálayan range that the famous Siwálik beds occur, long known for their vast stores of extinct mammalia. Of about the same age are the Manchhar beds of Sind, which also contain a rich mammalian fauna. The Lower Manchhars probably correspond to the Náhan beds, the lowest of the Siwáliks ; they rest upon the Gaj beds, which are probably Upper Miocene. From this it would seem that the lowest Siwáliks are not older than Upper Miocene. The higher Siwálik beds are considered by Mr. W. T. Blanford to be Pliocene, and to this later period he also refers the mammalian beds of Pikermi in Greece. These have a large number of fossils in common with the Siwáliks; but they contain, at their base, a marine band with Pliocene shells. The Manchhar and Siwálik beds are chiefly of fresh-water origin.

The Salt Range in the north-west of the Punjab has, in Salt addition to its economic value, a special geological importance. Range. Representatives of most of the great European formations of Silurian and later epochs are found in it; and throughout the vast length of time represented by these formations there is here no direct evidence of any important break in succession, or unconformity. The lowest beds (salt marl, probably Silurian) and the highest (Siwáliks) are found through the range. But the others cannot be traced continuously throughout ; some occur well developed in one place, some in another. All the principal fossiliferous beds of the Jurassic, Triassic, and Carboniferous formations are confined to the western part of the range.

THE INDO-GANGETIC PLAIN covers an area of about 300,000 Indo-square miles, and varies in width from 90 to nearly 300 Gangetic miles. It rises very gradually from the sea at either end. The Plain. lowest point of the watershed between the Punjab rivers and the Ganges is about 924 feet above sea-level. This point, by a line measured down the valley, but not following the winding of the river, is about 1050 miles from the mouth of the Ganges and 850 miles from the mouth of the Indus, so that the average inclination of the plain, from the central watershed to the Its slope sea, averages only about 1 foot per mile. It generally exceeds to the sea. this near the watershed ; but there is here no ridge of high ground between the Indus and the Ganges, and a very trifling change of level would often turn the upper waters of one river into the other. It is not unlikely that such changes have in past time occurred. Towards the sea, the slope becomes almost imperceptible.

There is no evidence that the Indo-Gangetic plain existed as Its geo-such in pre-Tertiary times. The alluvial deposits made known logical age. by the boring at Calcutta, have already been described in

Its alluvial deposits. sufficient detail.[1] They prove a gradual depression of the area through the later Tertiary times. There are peat and forest beds, which must have grown quietly at the surface, alternating with deposits of gravel, sand, and clay. The thickness of the delta deposit is unknown; 481 feet was proved at the bore hole, but probably this represents only a very small part of the deposit. Outside the delta, in the Bay of Bengal, is a deep depression known as the 'swatch of no ground'; all around it the soundings give only 5 to 10 fathoms, but they very rapidly deepen to over 300 fathoms. The sediment seems to be carried away from this hole by the set of the currents; so that it has remained free from silt whilst the neighbouring sea-bottom has gradually been filled up. If so, the thickness of the alluvium is at least 1800 feet, and may be much more.

Its geological history. The Indo-Gangetic plain dates back to Eocene times; the origin of the Himálayas may be referred to the same period. Numerous minor disturbances occurred in the area which is now Northern India during Palæozoic and Secondary times, but the great disturbance which has resulted in the formation of the existing chain of the Himálayas took place after the deposition of the Eocene beds. Disturbances even greater in amount occurred after the deposition of the Pliocene beds. The Eocenes of the sub-Himálayan range were deposited upon uncontorted Palæozoic rocks, but the whole has since been violently contorted and disturbed. There are some indications that the disturbing forces were more severe to the eastward during middle Tertiary times, and that the main action to the westward was of later date. It seems highly probable that the elevation of the mountain ranges and the depression of the Indo-Gangetic plain were closely related. This view gains some support from a glance at the map, where we see that the curves of the great mountain chains are strictly followed by those of the great alluvial plain. Probably both are due to almost contemporary movements of the earth's crust; these movements, though now of greatly diminished intensity, have not wholly ceased. The alluvial deposits prove depressions to have occurred in quite recent geological times; and within the Himálayan region earthquakes are still common, whilst in Peninsular India they are rare.

Peninsular India. PENINSULAR INDIA.—The oldest rocks here consist of gneiss, in three tracts :—throughout a very large part of Bengal and

[1] *Vide ante*, chap. i. p. 26.

Madras, extending to Ceylon; among the Aravalli ranges; and in Bundelkhand. Of these formations, the gneiss of Bundelkhand is known to be the oldest, because the oldest Transition rocks rest upon it; whereas the same Transition rocks are altered and intersected by granitic dykes which proceed from the gneiss of the other tracts. The Transition rocks are of great but unknown age. The Vindhyan rocks which succeed them are of very old Palæozoic age, perhaps pre-Silurian. Yet long before the earliest Vindhyan rocks were laid down, the Transition rocks had been altered and contorted. In more recent times there have been local disturbances, and large faults have in places been found; but the greater part of the Peninsular rocks are only slightly disturbed, and the most recent of the great and widespread earth movements of this region date back to pre-Vindhyan times.

The Vindhyan series are generally sharply marked off from Vindhyan older rocks; although in the Godávari valley there is no rocks. well-defined line between these and the Transition rocks. The Vindhyan beds are divided into two groups. The Lower Lower, with an estimated thickness of only 2000 feet, or slightly Vindh- more, cover a large area,—extending, with but little change yans. of character, from the Son (Soane) valley in one direction to Cuddapah, and in a diverging line to near Bijápur—in each case a distance of over 700 miles. The Upper Vindhyans Upper cover a much smaller area, but attain a thickness of about Vindh- 12,000 feet. The Vindhyans are well-stratified beds of sand- yans. stone and shale, with some limestones. As yet they have yielded no trace of fossils, and their exact age is consequently unknown. So far as the evidence goes, it appears probable that they are of very ancient Palæozoic age, perhaps pre-Silurian. The total absence of fossils is a remarkable fact, and one for which it is difficult to account, as the beds are for the most part quite unaltered. Even if they are entirely of fresh-water origin, we should expect that some traces of life from the waters or neighbouring land would be found.

The Gondwána series is in many respects the most interest- Gondwána ing and important of the Indian Peninsula. The beds are series. almost entirely of fresh-water origin. Many sub-divisions have been made, but here we need only note the main division into two great groups:—Lower Gondwánas, 13,000 feet thick; Upper Gondwánas, 11,000 feet thick. The series is mainly confined to the area of country between the Narbadá and the Son (Soane) on the north, and the Kistna (Krishna) on the south ; but the western part of this region is in great part covered by newer beds. The lowest Gondwánas are very constant in character, wherever they are found ; the upper numbers of the lower division show more variation, and this divergence of character in different Districts becomes more marked in the Upper Gondwána series. Disturbances have occurred in the lower series before the formation of the upper.

Gondwána fossils. The Gondwána beds contain fossils which are of very great interest. In large part these consist of plants which grew near the margins of the old rivers, were carried down by floods, and deposited in the alluvial plains, deltas, and estuarine areas of the old Gondwána period. So vast was the time occupied by the deposition of the Gondwána beds, that great changes in physical geography and in the vegetation repeatedly occurred. The plants of the Lower Gondwánas consist chiefly of acrogens (Equisetaceæ and ferns) and gymnogens (cycads and conifers), the former being the more abundant. The same classes of plants occur in the Upper Gondwánas ; but there the proportions are reversed, the conifers, and still more the cycads, being more numerous than the ferns, whilst the Equisetaceæ are but sparingly found. But even within the limits of the Lower Gondwána series there are great diversities of vegetation, three distinct floras occurring in the three great divisions of that formation. In many respects the flora of the Pánchet group. highest of these three divisions (the Pánchet group) is more nearly related to that of the Upper Gondwánas than it is to the other Lower Gondwána floras.

Tálcher group. One of the most interesting facts in the history of the Gondwána series is the occurrence near the base (in the Tálcher group) of large striated boulders in a fine mud or silt, the boulders in one place resting upon rock (of Vindhyan age) which is also striated. There seems good reason for believing that these beds are the result of ice-action. They probably nearly coincide in age with the Permian beds of Western Europe, in which Professor Ramsay long since discovered evidence of glaciation. But the remarkable fact is that this old ice-action occurred within the tropics, and probably at no very great height above the sea.

Dámodar series and coal-fields. The Dámodar series, the middle division of the Lower Gondwánas, is the chief source of coal in Peninsular India, yielding more of that mineral than all other formations taken together. The Karharbári group is the only other coal-bearing formation of any value. The Dámodars are 8400 feet thick in the Ráníganj coal-field, and about 10,000 feet thick in the Sátpura basin. They consist of three divisions; coal occurs in the upper and lower, ironstone (without coal) in the middle division. The Ráníganj coal-field is the most important in India. So far as yet known, it covers an area of about 500 square miles, running about 18 miles from north to south, and about 39 miles from east to west; but it extends farther to the east under the laterite and alluvium. It is traversed by the Dámodar river, and also the road from Calcutta to Benares and by the East Indian Railway. From its situation and importance, this coal-field is better known than any other in India. Much has been learnt concerning it since the last examination by the Geological Survey, especially from the recent reports by Mr. H. Bauermann. *Ráníganj coal-field.*

The upper or Ráníganj series has eleven seams, with a total thickness of 120 feet, in the eastern district, and thirteen seams, 100 feet thick, in the western district. The average thickness of the seams worked is from 12 to 18 feet, but occasionally a seam reaches a great thickness—20 to 80 feet. The lower or Barákhar series (2000 feet thick) contains four seams, of a total thickness of 69 feet. Compared with English coals, those of this coal-field are of a poor quality; they contain much ash, and are generally non-coking. The seams of the lower series are the best, and some of these at Sánktoria, near the Barákhar river, are fairly good for coke and gas. *Ráníganj coal-seams.* *Barákhar seams.*

The best coal in India is in the small coal-field at Karharbári. The beds here are lower in the series than those of the Ráníganj field; they belong to the upper part of the Tálcher group, the lowest of the Gondwána series. The Karharbári coal-beds cover an area of about 11 square miles; and have three seams, varying from 9 to 33 feet thick. The lowest seam is the best, and it is nearly as good as English steam coal. This coal-field, now largely worked, is the property of the East Indian Railway, which is thus supplied with fuel at a cheaper rate than any other railway in the world. Indian coal usually contains phosphoric acid, which greatly lessens its value for iron-smelting.[1] *Karharbári coal-field.*

The Dámodar series, which, as we have seen, is the chief source of coal in India, is also one of the most important *Dámodar iron-stone.*

---

[1] The economic aspects of Indian coal have been dealt with in the chapter on Mines and Minerals. For full accounts of the Indian coal-fields, see articles RANIGANJ, KARHARBARI, etc., in *The Imperial Gazetteer of India.*

sources of iron. The ore occurs in the middle division, coal in the highest and lowest. The ore is partly a clay ironstone, like that occurring in the coal-measures of England, partly an oxide of iron or hæmatite. It generally contains phosphorus, which prevents its use in the preparation of the finer qualities of steel. A similar difficulty attends the use of the Cléveland ore of North Yorkshire. Experiments have been in progress for years in search of a process which shall, in an economical manner, obtain iron from Cleveland ore free from phosphorus, latterly, it is hoped, with some success. If this be so, India will be a great gainer. Excellent iron-ore occurs in the metamorphic rocks south of the Dámodar river. Laterite (see below) is sometimes used as ore. It is very earthy, with a low percentage of metal; but it contains only a comparatively small proportion of phosphorus.[1]

Kankar. The want of limestone for flux, within easy reach, is generally a great drawback as regards iron-smelting in India. *Kankar* or *ghutin* (concretionary carbonate of lime) is collected for this purpose from the river beds and alluvial deposits. It sometimes contains as much as 70 per cent. of carbonate of lime; but generally the proportion is much less, and the fluxing value proportionally diminished. The real difficulty in India is to find the ore, the fuel, and the flux, in sufficiently close proximity to yield a profit.

Deccan trap. The enormous mass of basaltic rock known as the Deccan trap, is of great importance in the geological structure of the Indian Peninsula. It now covers an area of about 200,000 square miles, and probably extended in former times over a much wider area. Where thickest, the traps are at least 6000 feet in depth. They form the most striking physical features of the country, many of the most prominent hill ranges being the denuded edges of the basaltic flows. The great volcanic outbursts which produced this trap commenced in the Cretaceous period, and lasted into the Eocene period.

Laterite ; Laterite is a ferruginous and argillaceous rock, varying from 30 to 200 feet thick, which often occurs over the trap area, but is also found in other tracts. As a rule, it makes rather barren land; it is highly porous, and the rain rapidly sinks into it. Laterite may be roughly divided into two kinds, high-level; high-level and low-level laterite. The former, which covers a large area of the high basaltic plains, is believed by Mr. R. B.

[1] For the economic aspects of Indian iron, see chapter on Mines and Minerals.

Foote to be very frequently the product of decomposition of
the trap, and to have been thus formed in the place where it
is now found. Sometimes the high-level laterite overlies
gneiss or other rocks; and in these cases it has probably
been transported. The low-level laterite is generally more low-level.
sandy in character, and is often associated with gravels. In
most cases this has clearly been carried down to its present
position, probably largely by sub-aerial action, aided by rains
and streams. Possibly in some cases it has been spread out
along the coasts by marine action. The low-level laterite
fringes the coast of the Peninsula, from near Bombay on the
west and Orissa on the east, to Cape Comorin. It is not
continuous throughout these regions; and it is of very varying
width and elevation. The age of the high-level laterite is
unknown. Its formation probably extended throughout a long
period of time, much of which must be of very ancient
date; for the laterite, together with the underlying basalt, has
suffered extensive denudation.

As regards gems, the geologist comes to the same con- Precious
clusion as the economist, viz. that the precious stones stones.
of ancient India were the product of forced labour, and
that the search for them in our days can scarcely repay the
working expenses.

BRITISH BURMA.—The geological structure of Burma com- Burma :
prises three sections—western, middle, and eastern, nearly its three
corresponding to the Divisions of Arakan, Pegu, and Tenas- sections.
serim.

The geological groups met with in Arakan and Pegu are, Pegu and
in the ascending order, as follow. The crystalline rocks of Arakan.
Taung-ngu; age undetermined, comprising beds of different
ages. Axial or Arakan group, occupying the northern part of
Arakan range; age probably Triassic. Nummulitic group,
including the entire range of Arakan; age Eocene or early
Tertiary. Pegu group, occupying the whole of the country
east of the Irawadi to the Sittaung river; age Miocene or
middle Tertiary. Fossil-wood group, most largely developed
in eastern Prome, in which fossil-wood, in the form of silicified
trunks of trees, some of them 30 to 40 feet long, is plentifully
present; age probably Pliocene or newer Tertiary. Lastly, the
Alluvium group, comprising older alluvial deposits in places
where the river channels are excavated, and newer alluvial

deposits thrown down on the surface by the Irawadi and other rivers.

Tenas-
serim.   In geological structure, Tenasserim is entirely distinct from Pegu and Arakan; the groups in ascending order are as follow. The crystalline rocks; age uncertain. Mergui group, largely developed in Mergui District; age perhaps Silurian. Maulmain group, well seen near Maulmain and Amherst; age lower Carboniferous. Tenasserim group, embracing the various coalfields in the southern part of the Tenasserim Division; age doubtful, but probably Tertiary.

CHAPTER XXIII.

METEOROLOGY OF INDIA.

THE great peninsula of India, with its lofty mountain ranges Meteoro-
and its extensive seaboard, exposed to the first violence of logy of
India.
the winds of two oceans, forms an exceptionally valuable and
interesting field for the study of meteorological phenomena.
But the Department of Government which deals with these
phenomena has had to contend with many obstacles; and it
is only within the last few years that trustworthy statistics have
been obtained from a complete system of registration stations.
Every year, however, is now adding to our knowledge of the
meteorology of the country, and supplying authentic materials
for purposes of comparison and induction.

METEOROLOGICAL GEOGRAPHY.—After the general description Meteoro-
of the country given at the beginning of this volume, it is only logical
Geography
necessary to sketch very briefly the meteorological geography
of India. The following paragraphs are condensed from
an interesting account in the official *Report on the Meteorology
of India* (for 1883), by Mr. H. F. Blanford. Mr. Blanford's
volume on the *Meteorology of India*, being the second part of
The Indian Meteorologist's Vade-Mecum (Government Press,
Calcutta, 1877), should be in the hands of every student.
The great mountain ranges of the HIMALAYAS and the SULAI-
MANS, which form the northern and north-western boundaries of
India, have been fully described.[1] From the gorge of the Indus
to that of the Dihong (Bráhmaputra), a distance of 1400 miles,
the Himálayas form an unbroken watershed, the northern flank Himá-
of which is drained by the upper valleys of these two rivers; layas.
while the Sutlej (Satlaj), starting from the southern foot of the
Kailás peak, breaks through the watershed, dividing it into
two very unequal portions, that to the north-west being the
smaller. The average elevation of the higher Himálayas may
be taken at not less than 19,000 feet, and therefore equal to

[1] *Vide ante,* chap. i. pp. 3–10; also articles HIMALAYAS and SULAIMAN
MOUNTAINS, *The Imperial Gazetteer of India.*

the height of the lower half of the atmosphere; indeed, few
of the passes are under 16,000 or 17,000 feet. Across this
mountain barrier there appears to be a constant flow of air,
more active in the day-time than at night, northwards to the
arid plateau of Tibet. There is no reason to believe that any
transfer of air takes place across the Himálayas in a southerly
direction; unless, indeed, in those elevated regions of the
atmosphere which lie beyond the sphere of observation. But
a nocturnal flow of cooled air, from the southern slopes, is
felt as a strong wind where the rivers debouch on the plains,
more especially in the early morning hours. This current
probably contributes to lower the mean temperature of the belt
of plain country which fringes the mountain zone.

Himá-layan air-currents.

The Eastern Himálayas present many points of contrast
with the western parts of the range. The slopes of the Sikkim
and Bhután Hills, where not denuded for the purposes of cultivation, are clothed with an almost impenetrable forest, which
at the lower levels abounds in figs, rattans, and representatives
of a tropical humid climate. At higher levels they are covered
with oaks, chestnuts, magnolias, pines, etc., of the most
luxuriant growth.

Eastern Himá-layas.

In the Western Himálayas, on the other hand, the spurs of
the outer ranges are more sparsely clad with forest, especially
on their western faces; and naked precipitous crags are of
constant occurrence. The vegetation of the lower and warmer
valleys, and of the fringing belt (the Tarái), is comparatively
thin, and such as characterizes a warm but dry region. Pines
of several species form a conspicuous feature of the landscape
at lower levels. It is chiefly the outer ranges that exhibit
these contrasted features; and they depend partly on the
difference of latitude, but mainly on that of rainfall. In
Sikkim and Bhután this is abnormally copious, and is discharged full on the face of the range. As the chain recedes
to the north-west, the greater is the distance to be traversed
by the vapour-bearing winds in reaching it, and the more
easterly is their direction. For such winds, whether coming
from the Bay of Bengal (apparently their principal source) or
from the Arabian Sea, turn on reaching the Gangetic valley,
and blow more or less parallel to its axis and that of the
mountain range.

Western Himá-layas.

Vapour-bearing winds.

The country on either side of the Suláimán range is
characteristically arid. Dry winds from the desert tracts of
Persia and Baluchistán predominate throughout the year.
The scanty cultivation on the hills is dependent on the

Punjab frontier.

winter snows, or the rare showers which reach them from the eastward, or the supply of the larger local streams. The lower plains would be uninhabitable but for the fertilizing irrigation furnished by the great river that traverses them.

At the foot of the great Himálayan barrier, and separating it from the more ancient land which now forms the highlands of the peninsula, a broad plain, for the most part alluvial, stretches Indus from sea to sea. On the west, in the dry region, this is plain occupied partly by the alluvial deposits of the Indus and its tributaries; partly by the saline swamps of Kachchh (Cutch), and the rolling sands and rocky surface of the desert of Jaisalmer The great (Jeysulmere) and Bikáner; and partly by the more fertile Indian desert. tracts to the eastward. Over the greater part of this region rain is of rare occurrence; and not infrequently more than a year passes by without a drop falling on the parched surface. On its eastern margin, however, in the neighbourhood of the Aravalli Hills, and again in the Northern Punjab, rain is more frequent, occurring both in the south-west monsoon, and also at the opposite season in the cold weather. As far north as Sirsa and Múltán, the average rainfall does not much exceed 7 inches.

The alluvial plain of the Punjab passes into that of the Gangetic Gangetic valley without visible interruption. Up or down this plain. plain, at opposite seasons, sweep the monsoon winds, in a direction at right angles to that of their nominal course; and in this way the vapour brought by winds from the Bay of Bengal, is discharged as snow and rain on the peaks and hill-sides of the Western Himálayas. Nearly the whole surface is under cultivation; and it ranks among the most productive as well as the most densely populated regions of the world. The rainfall diminishes from 100 inches at the south-east corner of the Gangetic delta to less than 30 inches at Agra and Delhi, and there is an average difference of from 15 to 25 inches between the northern and southern borders of the plain.

Eastward from the Bengal delta, two alluvial plains stretch Eastern up between the hills that connect the Himálayan system with Bengal. that of the Burmese peninsula. The first is that of Assam and the Bráhmaputra, long and narrow, bordered on the north by the Himálayas, on the south by the lower plateau of the Gáro, Khási, and Nágá Hills. The second, or Sylhet and Cachar valley, is chiefly occupied by swamps and *jhíls*, and separates the Gáro, Khási, and Nágá Hills from those of Tipperah and the Lushái country. The climate of both these plains is damp and equable, and the rainfall is prolonged and generally heavy, especially on the southern slopes of the hills. A meteorological peculiarity of some interest has been noticed, more especially at the stations of Sibságar and Silchár, viz. the great range of the diurnal variation of barometric pressure, particularly during the cool months of the year. It is the more striking, since at Rúrki, Lahore, and other stations near the foot of the Himálayas, this range is less than on the open plains.

Central table-land. The highlands of the peninsula are cut off from the Himálayan ranges by the Indo-Gangetic plain. They are divided into two unequal parts, by an almost continuous chain Sátpura range. of hills, loosely known as the Sátpura range, running across the country from west-by-south to east-by-north, just south of the Tropic of Cancer. This chain may be regarded as a single feature, forming the principal watershed of the peninsula. The waters to the north of it drain chiefly into the Narbadá (Nerbudda) and the Ganges; those to the south, into the Tápti, the Godávari, the Mahánadi, and smaller streams. In a meteorological point of view, this central chain of hills is of much importance. Acting together with the two parallel valleys of the Narbadá and Tápti, which drain the flanks of its western half, it gives a more decided easterly and westerly direction to the winds of this part of India, and condenses a tolerably copious rainfall during the south-west moonsoon.

Málwá plateau. Separated from this chain by the valley of the Narbadá on the west, and that of the Son (Soane) on the east, the plateau of Málwá and Baghelkhand occupies the space intervening between these valleys and the Gangetic plain. On the western Aravalli range. edge of the plateau are the ARAVALLI HILLS, which run from near Ahmadábád up to the neighbourhood of Delhi, and include one hill, Mount Abú, over 5000 feet in height. This range exerts an important influence on the direction of the wind, and also on the rainfall. At Ajmere, an old-established meteorological station at the eastern foot of the range, the wind is predominantly south-west. Both here and at Mount Abú the south-west monsoon rains are a regular phenomenon; which can hardly be said of the region of scanty and uncertain rainfall which extends from the western foot of the range and merges in the Bikáner desert.

Southern plateau. The peninsula south of the Sátpura range consists chiefly of the triangular plateau of the Deccan, terminating abruptly on the west in the Sahyádri range (Western Ghâts), and shelving to the east (Eastern Gháts). This plateau is swept by the south-west monsoon after it has surmounted the western barrier of the Gháts. The rainfall is consequently light at Poona and places similarly situated under the lee of the range, and but moderate over the more easterly parts of the plateau. The rains, however, are prolonged to the north of the Sátpuras three or four weeks later than in Southern India, since they are brought there by the easterly winds which blow from the Bay of Bengal in October and the early part of November; when the re-curved southerly wind ceases to blow up the Gangetic valley, and sets towards the Karnátik. This was formerly thought to be the north-east monsoon, and is still so spoken of by some writers; but the rainy wind is really a diversion of the south-west monsoon.

At the junction of the Eastern and Western Gháts rises the Anamalai bold triangular plateau of the Nílgiris, and to the south of Hills. them come the Anamalais, Palnis (Pulneys), and Travancore Hills. These ranges are separated from the Nílgiris by a broad depression or pass known as the Pálghát gap, some 25 miles wide; the highest point of which is about 1500 feet above the sea. This gap affords a passage to the winds, which elsewhere are barred by the chain of the Western Gháts. The country to the east of the gap receives the rainfall of the south-west monsoon; and during the north-east monsoon, ships passing Beypur meet with a stronger wind from the land than is felt elsewhere on the Malabar coast. According to Captain Newbold, the Pálghát gap 'affords an outlet to those furious storms from the eastward which sweep the Bay of Bengal, and, after traversing the peninsula, burst forth through it to the neighbouring sea.'

In the coast-strip of low country which fringes the peninsula Southern below the Western Gháts, the rainfall is heavy, the climate warm coast-strips. and damp, the vegetation dense and tropical. The steep slopes of the Gháts, where they have not been artificially cleared, are also thickly clothed with forest.

Ceylon should, for meteorological purposes, be included Meteoro- in this survey. The country both south and west of the logy of Ceylon. hills which occupy the south centre of the island is very rugged down to the coast. The rainfall is here frequent and Rainy heavy; and the temperature being high and equable, the south-west region. vegetation is dense and very luxuriant, such as is characteristic of islands in tropical seas, and also of the coast of Travancore. The plains on the east coast are drier, and both in climate Drier east and vegetation bear much resemblance to those of the Karnátik. coast.

When the south-west monsoon is blowing in May and June, and discharging torrents of rain on the forest-clad spurs and slopes that face to windward, the contrast presented by the eastward face of the same hills is very striking, and the two phases of climate are sharply demarcated. Newara Eliya (7000 feet), day after day, and even week after week, lies under a dense canopy of cloud, which shrouds all the higher peaks, and pours down in almost incessant rain. But let the traveller leave the station by the Badulla road, and cross over the main range at a distance of two or three miles from Newara Eliya. As he begins the descent towards Wilson's bungalow, he emerges on a panorama of the grassy downs of the lower hills, bathed in dazzling sunshine; while on the ridge above he sees the cloud-masses ever rolling across from the west, and dissolving away in the drier air to leeward. Hence the east and west coasts of Ceylon are as strongly contrasted in climate as those of the southern extremity of the Indian peninsula.

The contrast.

British Burma.

In British Burma, the western face of the Arakan Yoma hills, like that of the Indian Western Gháts, is exposed to the full force of the south-west monsoon, and receives a very heavy rainfall. At Sandoway, this amounts to an annual mean of 212 inches. It diminishes to the northwards; but even at Chittagong, it amounts to 104½ inches annually.

Upper Burma.

The country around Ava, as well as the hill country of North Burma, is the seat of occasional severe earthquakes, one of which destroyed Ava city in 1839. The general meridianal direction of the ranges and valleys determines the direction of the prevailing surface winds; subject, however, to many local modifications. But it would appear, from Dr. Anderson's observations of the movement of the upper clouds, that throughout the year there is, with but slight interruption, a steady upper current from the south-west, such as has been already noticed over the Himálayas. The rainfall in the lower part of the Irawadi valley, viz. the delta and the neighbouring part of the Province of Pegu, is very heavy, about 190 inches; the climate is warm and equable at all seasons. But higher up the valley, and especially north of the Pegu frontier, the country is drier, and is characterized by a less luxuriant vegetation, and by a retarded and more scanty rainfall of about 56 inches.

Observatories.

OBSERVATORIES.—Up to the year 1883, meteorological observatories had been established at 125 stations in India (including British Burma, the Andamans, and Nepál). These observatories are situated at all elevations, from the highest, LEH (11,502 feet above mean sea-level) and CHAKRATA (7051 feet), to SAGAR ISLAND, 25 feet, and NEGAPATAM, only 15 feet above mean sea-level.

OBSERVATIONS.—The observations taken at Indian meteoro- Observalogical stations record — (1) temperature of solar and of tions. nocturnal radiation, (2) air temperature, (3) atmospheric pressure, (4) direction and velocity of the wind, (5) humidity, (6) cloud proportion, and (7) rainfall. For full information on each of these subjects, the reader is referred to the valuable and deeply interesting reports of Mr. F. Blanford and Mr. Eliot, printed at the Government Press, Calcutta, and available to all inquirers at the India Office, London.

SOLAR RADIATION.—Although, theoretically, differences in Solar the height above ground of the registering thermometer produce radiation. little difference in the amount of radiation from the ground, yet the nature of the surface forms an important feature, the action of which differs very considerably in different parts of India, and interferes with an exact comparison of results obtained from different stations. Thus, the radiation from the parched, heated, and bare surface of the soil in the North-Western Provinces in May, must be considerably greater than from the moist grass-covered surface of the soil at the coast stations of Bengal and Western India in the same month.

The following figures are obtained from Bengal stations Returns. where the instruments are believed to be accurate and comparable. The yearly average maximum equilibrium temperatures of compared sun thermometers *in vacuo*, varied in these stations from 121·5° F. at Dárjíling (much the lowest average) and 131·3° at Goálpárá (the next lowest), to 145·6° at Bardwán and 147·4° at Cuttack. The excess of the above over the corresponding maximum shade temperatures was :— at Dárjíling, 59·1°; at Goálpárá, 48·4°; at Bardwán, 57°; and at Cuttack, 55·8°.

TEMPERATURE OF THE AIR.—From the average annual mean Temperatemperatures of 117 stations (derived from the means of three ture of the or more years), the following figures are taken. In the two air. following stations in this list, the average mean yearly tem- Mean perature was over 82° F. :—Trichinopoli, 82·1°; Vizagapatam, yearly tempera. 82·8°. Both of these stations are in the Madras Presidency. The tures. next highest means are returned by Madras, 82°; Madura (also in Madras), 81·9°; Negapatam, 81·6°; Masulipatam, 81·3°; Karnúl, 81·2°; Sironcha, 81°; Cuttack, 80·7°; Bellary and Salem,

80·4° ; Port Blair, 80·3° ; Bikáner, 80° ; False Point, 79·3° ; Goa, 79·9° ; Cochin, 79·6° ; Ságar Island, 78·6° ; Deesa, 79·9° ; and Calcutta, 77·8°. The mean annual temperature of Bombay is

Hill stations.

79·7°. The lowest means are obtained at the hill stations of Dárjíling, 51·8° ; Simla, 55° ; Murree, 56·1° ; and Chakráta, 56·3°. Between these and the next coolest stations is a gap, Masuri (Mussoorie) following with 59·2°, Ráníkhet with 60·2°, Pachmarhi with 68·7°, and Ráwal Pindi with a yearly mean of 69·3°. The highest mean monthly temperatures given are :— 94·7° at Jhánsí, in May ; 94·4° at Múltán, in June ; 93·7° at

Monthly temperatures.

Lahore, Delhi, and Agra, in June. The lowest monthly means are returned by the four coldest hill stations mentioned above, the figures being :—Murree—January 39°, February 39·4° ; Simla — January 40·4°, February 41·4° ; Chakráta — January 42·3°, February 43·4° ; Dárjíling — January 39·4°, February 41·2°. The mean temperature at Leh in January is 17·1°, and in December 23·1° F.

Atmospheric pressure.

ATMOSPHERIC PRESSURE.—The Meteorological Report for 1883 contains a table showing the annual mean pressure at 111 stations, corrected (except in the case of Madras) to the Calcutta standard, which reads 0·011 inch higher than that of Kew. From that table the following figures are obtained. The mean yearly pressure in inches at the highest stations is : —22·944 at Dárjíling, 23·224 at Chakráta, 23·275 at Simla, 24·059 at Ráníkhet, 26·392 at Pachmarhi, and 26·924 at Bangalore. The greatest annual mean pressures returned are : —29·889 at Cochin, 29·845 at Negapatam, 29·840 at Madras, and 29·821 at Bombay. These pressures are not reduced to the level of the sea.

Wind.

WIND.—The general directions of the wind in different parts of the peninsula have already been noticed in the introductory portion of this chapter describing the meteorological geography of the country.

Humidity.

HUMIDITY.—The humidity figures given in the Report for 1877 are, according to Mr. Eliot, the Officiating Meteorological Reporter to the Government of India, not generally intercomparable, as the mean relative humidity is deduced from a varying number of daily observations.

Cloud proportion.

CLOUD PROPORTION.—The Report for 1883 gives the averages of estimated cloud proportion for 113 stations in India, an overcast sky being represented by 10 and a clear sky by 0. Some of the extreme figures follow. The average annual proportion of clouded sky is represented at Sibságar by 7·19 ; at Merkára by 6·68 ; at Dárjíling by 6·44 ; at Trichinopoli by

6·04; at Coimbatore by 5·19; at Salem by 4·66. The lowest proportions recorded are :— for Jhánsí, 1·20; Hyderábád (Sind), 1·69; Múltán, 1·66; Dera Ismáil Khán, 2·04; Ságar (Saugor), in the Central Provinces, 2·43.

RAINFALL.—The average annual rainfall at 435 stations is Rainfall. recorded in the Meteorological Report for 1883, from which the following figures were derived.

In the Punjab, the highest average fall (124·91 inches) is at The Dharmsála, which is situated on the face of the hills, and Punjab. exposed to the full force of the monsoon; the next highest recorded is little more than half that amount, or 71·24 inches, at Simla. The lowest average falls in the Punjab are :—5·88 inches at Muzaffargarh, 7·07 at Múltán, 7·03 at Dera Ghází Khán, and 8·46 at Dera Ismáil Khán. All these stations are protected by the Suláimán range from the monsoon.

In Rájputána and Central India the minimum is 12·07 Rájputána inches at Pachbadra, and the maximum, 63·21, at Mount Abú, and Central India. the highest point in this part of India.

In the North-Western Provinces the heaviest rainfalls are North-at Masuri (94·72 inches), Naini Tál (91·17), and Dehra (74·91), Western Provinces. all of which lie high; the minimum average fall is 25·28 at Muttra, the next lowest figures being 26·06 at Alígarh, 25·66 at Agra, and 25·70 at Bulandshahr—all stations on the plains.

In Oudh, the maximum rainfall is at Bahraich, 43·48 inches; Oudh. and the minimum at Rái Bareli, 32·18 inches.

The following stations of Bengal have an average rainfall of Bengal. more than 100 inches :—Baxa, 220·91; Jalpáigurí, 129·21; Mongpú, 128·43; Dárjíling, 120·85; and Kuch Behár, 130·89—all at the base of the hills; Noákhálí, 111·75; Demagiri, 112·97; Cox's Bazaar, 141·60; and Chittagong, 104·58, all near the north-east corner of the Bay of Bengal. The lowest averages are returned by Keunjhar, 32·61 inches; Buxar, 39·04; Chhapra, 39·15; and Gáyá, 40·29. The average rainfall throughout Bengal is 67 inches.

Assam possesses in Cherra Poonjee (Chárá Punjí) the Assam. station with the largest rainfall in the world. Former returns gave the fall at 368 inches; later and fuller returns at 481·80 inches. A total fall of 805 inches was reported in 1861, of which 366 were assigned to the single month of July. In 1850, Dr. Hooker registered 30 inches in twenty-four hours, and returned the fall from June to November of that year at 530 inches. In the four days 9th to 12th September 1877, 56·19 inches were registered. The cause of this extraordinary rainfall is noticed in the chapter on Physical Geography. The following stations in Assam have also a very high average rainfall:— Silchár, 118·85 ; Sylhet, 156·12 ; Dibrugarh, 113·53 ; and Turá, 123·80. The lowest recorded averages in Assam are at Samaguting (52·58 inches) and Gauháti (69·26 inches), both on the northern side of the hills separating Cachar from Assam.

Central Provinces.　In the Central Provinces, the highest average falls are at Pachmarhi, 77·85 inches, and Bálághát, 65·92 ; lowest averages, Khandwá, 33·29 inches, and Arvi, 35·09 inches.

Bombay.　In Bombay, two stations on the Gháts are recorded as having an average rainfall of over 250 inches, viz. :—Malcolmpet (Mahábleshwar), 258·49 ; and Baura (Fort), 255·28. Next in order come Matherán, with 245·24 inches ; Lonauli, with 165·13 ; Honawár, 138·08 ; and Igatpuri, Kárwár, Vingúrla, and Ratnágiri, with 124·19, 116·03, 110·89, and 104·55 inches respectively. The lowest average rainfalls recorded in Bombay are :—18·82 inches at Mandargi ; 20·97 at Dhulia ; and 21·41 at Gokak. The average rainfall in Bombay is 67 inches.

Sind.　In Sind, the average rainfall is very low, varying from 16·17 inches at Nagar, and 11·09 at Umárkot, to 4·65 at Shikárpur, and 4·33 at Jacobábád.

Madras.　In Madras, the highest local averages recorded are :—132·87 inches at Mangalore ; 129·68 at Cannanore ; 128·21 at Merkára ; 125·66 at Tellicherri ; 115·04 at Calicut ; and 115·02 at Cochin—all on the west coast. The lightest falls recorded are : —at Bellary, 17·64 ; Tuticorin (sheltered by the Gháts), 19·44 ; Guti (Gooty), 21·79 ; and Coimbatore, 21·34. All these stations lie low. The average fall at the stations on the east coast is about 41 inches. A fair average rainfall for Madras Presidency is 44 inches.

British Burma.　The rainfall along the coast of British Burma is heavy, as might be expected, the following averages being recorded :— Sandoway, 212·03 inches ; Tavoy, 197·02 ; Akyab, 197·61 ; Maulmain, 189·37 ; Kyauk-pyu, 174·79. The smallest rainfall is at Thayet-myo (47·37) and Prome (53·00), sheltered by the Yoma range.

Port Blair.　The rainfall at Port Blair and Nancowry is also heavy, the averages being returned as 118·38 and 108·91 inches respectively.

Sun-spot cycles.　SUN-SPOT CYCLES.—These alleged cycles have formed the subject of several separate papers, and the results were popularly summed up in a joint article by Mr. Norman

Lockyer and the present author in the *Nineteenth Century* for November 1877. It will therefore suffice here to state the views of the 'Indian Meteorological Department on the intricate questions involved. The following are the inferences which the meteorology of India appears to suggest, if not to establish. There is a tendency at the minimum sun-spot periods to prolonged excessive pressure over India, and at the maximum sun-spot periods to an unusual development of the winter rains, and to the occurrence of abnormally heavy snowfall over the Himálayan region (to a greater extent probably in the Western than the Eastern Himálayas). This appears also to be usually followed by a weak south-west monsoon. The characteristics of a weak monsoon are, great irregularity in the distribution of the rainfall over the whole of India, and the occurrence of heavy local rainfalls, which tend, by a law of rainfall and of air-motion, to recur over the same limited areas. The irregularity of rainfall distribution is often shown by the persistence of dry land winds and the prolonged absence of rain over considerable areas. These areas of drought and famine are partly marked off by nature, depending to a certain extent on the geographical features and position of the district. Thus, the rains are more likely to fall below the amount necessary for cultivation in the dry region of the Deccan or in Upper India, than over the Malabar coast area or the Province of Bengal.

CHAPTER XXIV.

ZOOLOGY AND BOTANY OF INDIA.

Mammals. WILD ANIMALS.—First among the wild animals of India must
be mentioned the lion (Felis leo), which is recorded to have
been not uncommon within historical times in Hindustán
Lion. Proper and the Punjab. The lion is now confined to the *Gir*, or
rocky hill-desert and forest of Káthiáwár. A peculiar variety
is there found, marked by the almost total absence of a mane;
but whether this variety deserves to be classed as a distinct
species, naturalists have not yet determined. The lion has
now almost entirely disappeared; and the official Gazetteer of
Káthiáwár states that there are now (1884) probably not more
than ten or a dozen lions and lionesses left in the whole *Gir*
forest tract. They are strictly preserved. The former extent
of the lion's range, or the degree to which its presence impressed the imagination, may be inferred from the common
personal names, Sinh or Singh, Sher, and Haidar, which all
signify 'lion.' Sher, however, is also applied to the tiger.
Tiger. The characteristic beast of prey in India is the tiger (Felis
tigris), which is found in every part of the country from the
slopes of the Himálayas to the Sundarban swamps. Sir Joseph
Fayrer, the highest living authority on this subject, believes
that 12 feet is the maximum length of the tiger, when measured
from nose to tip of tail immediately after death. The advance
of cultivation, even more than the incessant attacks of sportsmen, has gradually caused the tiger to become a rare animal
in large tracts of country; but it is scarcely probable that he
ever will be exterminated from India. The malarious *tarái*
fringing the Himálayas, the uninhabitable swamps of the
Gangetic delta, and the wide jungles of the central plateau,
are at present the chief home of the tiger. His favourite
food appears to be deer, antelope, and wild hog. When
these abound, he does not attack domestic cattle. Indeed,
the natives of certain Districts consider the tiger as in
some sort their protector, for he saves their crops from
destruction by the wild animals on which he feeds. But when

once he develops a taste for human blood, then the slaughter which he works becomes truly formidable.

The confirmed man-eater, generally an old beast, disabled from overtaking his usual prey, seems to accumulate his tale of victims in sheer cruelty rather than for food. A single tiger is known to have killed 108 people in three years. Another killed an average of about 80 persons per annum. A third caused 13 villages to be abandoned, and 250 square miles of land to be thrown out of cultivation. A fourth, so lately as 1869, killed 127 people, and stopped a public road for many weeks, until the opportune arrival of an English sportsman, who killed him. Such cases are, of course, exceptional, and generally refer to a past period, but they explain the super-stitious awe with which the tiger is regarded by the natives. ^{Man-eating Tiger.}

The favourite mode of shooting the tiger is from the back of elephants, or from elevated platforms (*macháns*) of boughs in the jungle. In Central India and Bombay, tigers are shot on foot. In Assam, they are sometimes speared from boats, and in the Himálayas they are said to be ensnared by bird-lime. Rewards are given by Government to native *shikáris* for the heads of tigers varying in time and place according to the need. In 1877, 819 persons and 16,137 cattle were reported to have been killed by tigers. On the other side of the account, 1579 tigers were destroyed by native hunters, and £3777 paid in rewards ; besides the slaughter by English sportsmen. In 1882, no fewer than 895 persons and 16,517 cattle were returned as killed by tigers. The sum of £4800 was paid during the year to native *shikáris* for the destruction of 1726 tigers.

The leopard or panther (Felis pardus) is far more common than the tiger in all parts of India, and at least equally de-structive to life. The greatest length of the Indian leopard is about 7 feet 6 inches. A black variety, as beautiful as it is rare, is sometimes found in the extreme south of the Indian peninsula, and also in Java. The cheetah or hunting leopard (Felis jubata) must be carefully distinguished from the leopard proper. This animal appears to be a native only of the Deccan, where it is trained for hunting the antelope. In some respects it approaches the dog more nearly than the cat tribe. Its limbs are long, its hair rough, and its claws blunt and only partially retractile. The speed with which it bounds upon its prey, when loosed from the cart, exceeds the swiftness of any other wild mammal. If it misses its first attack, it scarcely ever attempts to follow, but returns to its master. Among ^{Leopard.} ^{Cheetah.}

Other species. other species of the family Felidæ found in India may be mentioned the ounce or snow leopard (F. unica), the clouded tiger (F. macroscelis), the marbled tiger cat (F. marmorata), the jungle cat (F. chaus), and the common viverrine cat (F. viverrina).

Wolf. Wolves (Canis lupus) abound throughout the open country, but are rare in the wooded districts. Their favourite prey is sheep, but they are also said to run down antelopes and hares, or rather catch them by lying in ambush. Instances of their attacking man are not uncommon ; and in 1882, 278 persons, principally children, besides 8661 cattle, were reported to have been killed by wolves. In 1827, upwards of 30 children were carried off by wolves in a single *pargana* or fiscal division ; and the story of Romulus and Remus has had its counterpart in India within recent times. The Indian wolf has a dingy reddish-white fur, some of the hairs being tipped with black. By some naturalists it is regarded as a distinct species, under the name of Canis pallipes. Three distinct varieties, the white, the red, and the black wolf, are found in the Tibetan Himálayas.

Fox. The Indian fox (Vulpes bengalensis) is comparatively rare ; but the jackal (Canis aureus) abounds everywhere, making

Jackal. night hideous by its never-to-be-forgotten yells. The jackal, and not the fox, is usually the animal hunted by the packs of hounds kept by Europeans.

Dog. The wild dog or *dhole* is found in very many of the wilder jungles of India, including Assam and British Burma. Its characteristic is that it hunts in packs, sometimes containing 30 dogs, and does not give tongue. When once a pack of wild dogs has put up any animal, whether deer or tiger, that animal's doom is sealed. They do not leave it for days, and finally bring it to bay, or run it down exhausted. These wild dogs have sometimes been half domesticated, and trained to hunt for the use of man. A peculiar variety of wild dog exists in the Karen Hills of Burma, thus described from a specimen in confinement. It was black and white, as hairy as a Skye-terrier, and as large as a medium-sized spaniel. It had an invariable habit of digging a hole in the ground, into which it crawled backwards, remaining there all day with only its nose and ferrety eyes visible. Among other dogs of India are the pariah, which is merely a mongrel, run wild and half-starved ; the poligar dog, an immense creature peculiar to the south ; the greyhound, used for coursing ; and the mastiff of Tibet and Bhután.

The striped hyæna (Hyæna striata) is common, being found wherever the wolf is absent. Like the wolf, it is very destructive both to the flocks and to children.

Of bears, the common black or sloth bear (Ursus labiatus) is common throughout India wherever rocky hills and forests occur. It is distinguished by a white horse-shoe mark on its breast. Its food consists of ants, honey, and fruit. When disturbed it will attack man, and it is a dangerous antagonist, for it always strikes at the face. The Himálayan or Tibetan sun-bear (Ursus tibetanus) is found along the north, from the Punjab to Assam. During the summer it remains high up in the mountains, near the limit of snow, but in the winter it descends to 5000 feet, and even lower. Its congener, the Malayan sun-bear (Helarctos malayanus), is found in British Burma, where also there is a smaller species (Helarctos euryspilus), and a very large animal reported to be as big as the American grizzly. There were 114 persons returned as killed by bears in 1882.

The elephant (Elephas indicus) is found in many parts of India, though not in the north-west. Contrary to what might be anticipated from its size and from the habits of its African cousin, the Indian elephant is now, at any rate, an inhabitant, not of the plains, but of the hills; and even on the hills it is usually found among the higher ridges and plateaux, and not in the valleys. From the peninsula of India the elephant has been gradually exterminated, being only found now in the primæval forests of Coorg, Mysore, and Travancore, and in the Tributary States of Orissa. It still exists in considerable numbers along the *tarái* or submontane fringe of the Himálayas. The main source of supply at the present time is the confused mass of hills which forms the north-east boundary of British India, from Assam to Burma. Two varieties are there distinguished, the *gunda* or tusker, and the *makna* or *hine*, which has no tusks.

The reports of the height of the elephant, like those of its intelligence, seem to be exaggerated. The maximum is probably 12 feet. If hunted, the elephant must be attacked on foot, and the sport is therefore dangerous, especially as the animal has but few parts vulnerable to a bullet. The regular mode of catching elephants is by means of a *kheda* or gigantic stockade, into which a wild herd is driven, then starved into submission, and tamed by animals already domesticated. The practice of capturing them in pitfalls is discouraged as cruel and wasteful. Elephants now form a Government monopoly throughout India. The shooting of them is prohibited, except when they become dangerous to man or destructive to the crops; and the right of capturing them is only leased out upon conditions.

Elephant Preserva- tion Act.   A special law, under the title of 'The Elephants Pre-servation Act' (No. VI. of 1879), regulates this licensing system. Whoever kills, captures, or injures an elephant, or attempts to do so, without a licence, is punishable by a fine of 500 rupees for the first offence; and by a similar fine, together with six months' imprisonment, for a second offence. In the year 1877–78, a total of 264 elephants were captured in the Province of Assam, yielding to Government a revenue of £3600. In 1882–83, 475 elephants were captured in Assam, yielding a revenue to Government of £8573. In the season of 1873–74, no less than 53 elephants were captured at one time by Mr. Sanderson, formerly the superintendent of the Kheda Department in Mysore, who has made a special study of the Indian elephant, as Sir S. Baker has of the same animal in Ceylon. Although the supply is decreasing, elephants con-tinue to be in great demand. Their chief use is in the timber trade, and for Government transport. They are also bought up by native chiefs at high prices for ostentation. Sixty persons were reported as killed by elephants in 1882.

The Rhin- oceros.   Of the rhinoceros, four distinct varieties are enumerated, two with a single, and two with a double horn. The most familiar is the Rhinoceros unicornis, commonly found in the Brahma-putra valley and its wide swamps. It has but one horn, and is covered with massive folds of naked skin. It sometimes attains a height of 6 feet; its horn, which is much prized by the natives for medicinal purposes, seldom exceeds 14 inches in length. It frequents swampy, shady spots, and wallows in mud like a pig. The traditional antipathy of the rhinoceros to the elephant seems to be mythical. The Javan rhinoceros (R. sondaicus) is found in the Sundarbans. It also has but one horn, and mainly differs from the foregoing in being smaller, and having less prominent 'shields.' The Sumatran rhinoceros (R. sumatrensis) is found from Chittagong south-wards through Burma. It has two horns and a bristly coat. The hairy-eared rhinoceros (R. lasiotis) is known from a specimen captured at Chittagong, and sent to the Zoological Gardens, London. Two are at Calcutta.

The wild Hog.   The wild hog (Sus scrofa, *var.* indica) is well known as affording the most exciting sport in the world—'pig-sticking.' It frequents cultivated localities, and is the most mischievous enemy which the husbandman has to guard against ; doing more damage than elephants, tigers, leopards, deer, and antelope, all put together. A rare animal, called the pigmy hog (Porculia salvania), exists in the *tarái* of Nepál and Sikkim, and has been shot in Assam. Its height is only 10 inches, and its weight does not exceed 12 lbs.

The wild ass (Equus onager) is confined to the sandy The wild deserts of Sind and Kachchh (Cutch), where, from its speed Ass. and timidity, it is almost unapproachable.

Many wild species of the sheep and goat tribe are to be Sheep and found in the Himálayan ranges. The Ovis ammon and O. Goats. poli are Tibetan rather than Indian species. The *urial* and the *shapu* are kindred species of wild sheep, found respectively in Ladákh and the Suláimán range. The former comes down to 2000 feet above the sea, the latter is never seen at altitudes lower than 12,000 feet. The *barhal*, or blue wild sheep, and the *markhor* and *tahr* (both wild goats) also inhabit the Himálayas. A variety of the ibex is also found there, as well as in the highest ranges of Southern India. The *sarau* (Nemorhædus rubidus), allied to the chamois, has a wide range in the mountains of the north, from the Himálayas to Assam and Burma.

The antelope tribe is represented by comparatively few Antelopes. species, as compared with the great number found in Africa. The antelope proper (Antilope cervicapra), the ' black buck ' of sportsmen, is very generally distributed. Its special habitat is salt plains, as on the coast-line of Gujarát (Guzerát) and Orissa, where herds of 50 does may be seen, accompanied by a single buck. The doe is of a light fawn colour, and has no horns. The colour of the buck is a deep brown-black above, sharply marked off from the white of the belly. His spiral horns, twisted for three or four or more turns like a corkscrew, often reach the length of 30 inches. The flesh is dry and unsavoury, but is permitted meat for Hindus, even of the Bráhman caste. The four-horned antelope (Tetraceros quadricornis) and the gazelle (Gazella bennettii) are also found in India. The *chiru* (Pantholops hodgsoni) is confined to the Himálayan plateaux.

The *nílgái* or blue cow (Portax pictus) is also widely dis- Nílgái. tributed, but specially abounds in Hindustán Proper and Gujarát. As with the antelope, the male alone has the dark blue colour. The *nílgái* is held peculiarly sacred by Hindus, from its fancied kinship to the cow, and on this account its destructive inroads upon the crops are tolerated.

The king of the deer tribe is the *sámbhar* or *gerau* (Cervus Deer.

aristotelis), erroneously called 'elk' by sportsmen. It is found on the forest-clad hills in all parts of the country. It is of a deep-brown colour, with hair on its neck almost like a mane ; and it stands nearly 5 feet high, with spreading antlers nearly 3 feet in length. Next in size is the swamp deer or *bára - singha*, signifying 'twelve points' (Cervus duvaucelli), which is common in Lower Bengal and Assam. The *chitál* or spotted deer (Cervus axis) is generally admitted to be the most beautiful inhabitant of the Indian jungles. Other species include the hog deer (Cervus porcinus), the barking deer or muntjac (Cervulus muntijac), and the so-called mouse deer (Tragulus meminna). The musk deer (Moschus moschiferus) is confined to Tibet.

The Bison.   The ox tribe is represented in India by some of its noblest species. The *gaur* (Bos gaurus), the 'bison' of sportsmen, is found in all the hill jungles of the country, in the Western Gháts, in Central India, in Assam, and in British Burma. This animal sometimes attains the height of 20 hands (close on 7 feet), measuring from the hump above the shoulder. Its short curved horns and skull are enormously massive. Its colour is dark chestnut, or coffee-brown. From the difficult nature of its habitat, and from the ferocity with which it charges an enemy, the pursuit of the bison is no less dangerous and no less exciting than that of the tiger or the elephant. Akin to the *gaur*, though not identical, are the *gayál* or *mithún* (Bos frontalis), confined to the hills of the north-east frontier, where it is domesticated for sacrificial purposes by the aboriginal tribes ; and the *tsine* or *banting* (Bos sondaicus), found in Burma.

The Buffalo.   The wild buffalo (Bubalus arni) differs from the tame buffalo only in being larger and more fierce. The finest specimens come from Assam and Burma. The horns of the bull are thicker than those of the cow, but the horns of the cow are larger. A head has been known to measure 13 feet 6 inches in circumference, and 6 feet 6 inches between the tips. The greatest height is 6 feet. The colour is a slaty black ; the hide is immensely thick, with scanty hairs. Alone perhaps of all wild animals in India, the buffalo will charge unprovoked. Even tame buffaloes seem to have an inveterate dislike to Europeans.

Rat tribe.   The rat and mouse family is only too numerous. Conspicuous in it is the loathsome bandicoot (Mus bandicota), which sometimes measures 2 feet in length, including its tail, and weighs 3 lbs. It burrows under houses, and is very destructive to plants, fruit, and even poultry. More interesting is the tree rat (Mus arboreus), a native of Bengal, about 7 inches long, which makes its nest in cocoa-nut palms and bamboos. The voles or field mice (genus Arvicola) occasionally multiply so exceedingly as to seriously diminish the out-turn of the local harvest, and to require special measures for their destruction.

The ornithology of India, although it is not considered so rich in specimens of gorgeous and variegated plumage as that of other tropical regions, contains many splendid and curious varieties. Some are clothed in nature's gay attire, others distinguished by strength, size, and fierceness. The parrot tribe is the most remarkable for beauty. So various are the species, that no attempt is made here even to enumerate them, but the reader is referred for details to the scientific works on the subject.[1]

Among birds of prey four vultures are found, including the common scavengers (Gyps indicus and G. bengalensis). The eagles comprise many species, but none to surpass the golden eagle of Europe. Of falcons, there are the peregrine (Falco peregrinus), the *shain* (Falco peregrinator), and the *lagar* (Falco jugger), which are all trained by the natives for hawking; of hawks, the *shikara* (Astur badius), the sparrow hawk (Accipiter nisus), and the crested goshawk (Astur trivirgatus). Kingfishers of various kinds, and herons are sought for their plumage. No bird is more popular with natives than the *maina* (Acridotheres tristis), a member of the starling family, which lives contentedly in a cage, and can be taught to pronounce words, especially the name of the god Krishna.

Waterfowl are especially numerous. Of game-birds, the floriken (Sypheotides auritus) is valued as much for its rarity as for the delicacy of its flesh. Snipe (Gallinago scolopacina, etc.) abound at certain seasons, in such numbers that one gun has been known to make a bag of 100 brace in a day. Pigeons, partridges, quail, plover, duck, teal, sheldrake, widgeon—all of many varieties—complete the list of small game. The red jungle fowl (Gallus ferrugineus), supposed to be the ancestor of our own poultry, is not good eating; and the same may be said of the peacock (Pavo cristatus), except when young. The pheasant does not occur in India Proper; but a white variety is found in Burma, and several beautiful species (conspicuously the *manaul*) abound in the Himálayas.

Birds.

Birds of prey.

Game birds.

---

[1] Especially those of Jerdon, Gould, Hume, and Marshall.

Reptiles.　The serpent tribe in India is numerous; they swarm in the gardens, and intrude into the dwellings of the inhabitants, especially during the rainy season. Most are comparatively The harmless, but the bite of others is speedily fatal.[1] The cobra 'cobra.' di capello—the name given to it by the Portuguese, from the appearance of a hood which it produces by the expanded skin about the neck—is the most dreaded (Naja tripudians). It seldom exceeds 3 or 4 feet in length, and is about an inch and a quarter thick, with a small head, covered on the forepart with large smooth scales; it is of a pale brown colour above, and the belly is of a bluish-white tinged with pale brown or yellow. The Russellian snake (Daboia Russellii), about 4 feet in length, is of a pale yellowish-brown, beautifully variegated with large oval spots of deep brown, with a white edging. Its bite is extremely fatal. Itinerant showmen carry about these serpents, and cause them to assume a dancing motion for the amusement of the spectators. They give out that they render snakes harmless by the use of charms or music—in reality, by extracting the venomous fangs. But, judging from the frequent accidents, they sometimes seem to dispense with this precaution. All the salt-water snakes in India are poisonous, while the fresh-water forms are innocuous.

Deaths from snake-bite.　Sir Joseph Fayrer has demonstrated that none of the reputed antidotes will cure the bite of the cobra, if the snake is full-grown, and if its poison fang is full and be not interfered with by clothing. The most hopeful remedy in all cases of snake-bite is the injection of ammonia. The loss of life from this cause in India is painful to contemplate. But the extermination of snakes is attended with great difficulty, from the great number of the species, the character of the country, the rapid undergrowth of jungle, and the scruples of the people. Something, however, is being effected by the Statistics, offer of rewards. In 1877, a total of 16,777 persons are 1877; reported to have been killed by snakes, as compared with only 819 by tigers. In the same year, rewards to the amount of £811 were given for the destruction of 127,295 snakes. In and 1882. 1882, a total of 19,519 persons are reported to have been killed by snakes, as compared with 2606 by tigers, leopards, and all other wild beasts. A sum of £1487 was paid in 1882 for the destruction of 322,421 venomous reptiles.

Crocodile.　The other reptiles include two varieties of crocodile (C.

[1] Sir Joseph Fayrer's *Thanatophidia* is the standard work on Indian snakes. Vincent Richards' *Landmarks of Snake Poison Literature* is an excellent compendium.

porosus and C. biporcatus) and the garial (Gavialis gangeticus). Scorpions also abound.

All the waters of India—the sea, the rivers, and the tanks— Fishes. swarm with a great variety of fishes,[1] which are caught in every conceivable way, and furnish a considerable proportion of the food of the poorer classes. They are eaten fresh, or as nearly fresh as may be; for the art of curing them is not generally practised, owing to the exigencies of the salt monopoly. In Burma, the favourite relish of *nga-pi* is prepared from fish. At Goálandá, at the junction of the Bráhmaputra with the Ganges, and along the Madras coast, establishments have been established for salting fish in bond. The indiscriminate slaughter of fry, and the obstacles opposed by irrigation dams to breeding fish, are said to be causing a sensible diminution in the supply in certain rivers. Measures of conservancy have been suggested; but their execution is attended with great difficulty, owing to the habits and the necessities of the poorer population.

Among Indian fishes, the Cyprinidæ or carp family and the Siluridæ or cat-fishes are best represented. From the angler's point of view, by far the finest fish is the *mahsir*, found in all hill streams, whether in Assam, the Punjab, or the south. One has been caught weighing 60 lbs., which gave play for more than seven hours. Though called the salmon of India, the *mahsir* is really a species of barbel. One of the richest and most delicious of Indian fishes is the *hilsá*, which tastes and looks like a sort of fat white salmon. It is caught in immense quantities in the rivers of the Bengal delta, and forms a staple article of food in Calcutta. The Bombay and Madras markets are still better supplied by a variety of delicate fishes. But the enhanced price of this important article of native diet throughout the country, the decreased supply, and the ever-increasing fineness of the meshes of the nets employed in catching the fry, are matters of grave concern alike to the Government and to the poorer classes of the population.

In this connection may be mentioned the *susu* or Gangetic Dolphin. dolphin (Platanista gangetica); a mammal often erroneously called a porpoise. Both the structure and habits of this animal are very singular. It measures from 6 to 12 feet in

---

[1] The latest standard works on Indian fishes and their economic aspects are the Reports and official volume by Dr. Francis Day, late Inspector-General of Fisheries to the Government of India; available to all inquirers, at the India Office, London.

length, and in colour is sooty-black. Its head is globular, with a long, narrow, spoon-shaped snout. Its eyes are rudimentary, like those of the mole; and its ear-orifices are no bigger than pin-holes. Its dentition, also, is altogether abnormal. It frequents the Ganges and Indus from their mouths right up to their tributaries within the hills. A specimen has been taken at least 1000 miles above Calcutta. Ordinarily its movements are slow, for it wallows in the muddy bed of the river, and only at intervals comes to the surface to blow. The *susu* belongs to the order *Cetacea ;* and inquiries have recently been directed to the point whether its blubber might not be utilized in commerce.

Insects.

The insect tribes in India may be truly said to be innumerable; nor has anything like a complete classification been given of them in the most scientific treatises. The heat and the rains give incredible activity to noxious or troublesome insects, and to others of a more showy class, whose large wings surpass in brilliancy the most splendid colours of art. Stinging musquitoes are innumerable, with moths and ants of the most destructive habits, and other insects equally noxious and disagreeable. Amongst those which are useful are the

Locusts.

bee, the silkworm, and the insect that produces lac. Clouds of locusts occasionally appear, which leave no trace of green behind them, and give the country over which they pass the appearance of a desert. Dr. Buchanan saw a mass of these insects in his journey from Madras to the Mysore territory, about 3 miles in length, like a long narrow red cloud near the horizon, and making a noise somewhat resembling that of a cataract. Their size was about that of a man's finger, and their colour reddish. They are swept north by the wind till they strike upon the outer ranges of the Himálayas.

Indian flora.

FLORA.[1]—Unlike other large geographical areas, India is remarkable for having no distinctive botanical features peculiar to itself. It differs conspicuously in this respect

[1] For a general sketch of the flora of India, recourse must still be had to the introductory essay to the *Flora Indica,* published by Hooker & Thomson in 1855. The *Flora of British India,* the preparation of which is in progress at Kew, will comprise descriptions of all the species known to science up to the date of publication. It will form a great national work on the botany of India. For the following paragraphs on the flora, written by Mr. W. T. T. Dyer of Kew, the author is indebted to the courtesy of Messrs. A. & C. Black, publishers of the *Encyclopædia Britannica.*

from such countries as Australia or South Africa. Its vegetation is in point of fact of a composite character, and is constituted by the meeting and blending of the various floras adjoining,—of those of Persia and the south-eastern Mediterranean area to the north-west, of Siberia to the north, of China to the east, and of Malaya to the south-east. Space does not admit of a minute discussion of the local features peculiar to separate districts; but regarded broadly, four tolerably distinct types present themselves: namely, the Himálayan, the North-Western, the Assamese or Malayan, and the Western India type.

The upper levels of the Himálayas slope northwards Upper gradually to the Tibetan uplands, over which the Siberian Himálayas. temperate vegetation ranges. This is part of the great temperate flora which, with locally individualized species but often with identical genera, extends over the whole of the temperate zone of the northern hemisphere. In the Western Himálayas, this upland flora is marked by a strong admixture of European species, such as the columbine (Aquilegia) and hawthorn (Cratægus oxyacantha). These disappear rapidly eastward, and are scarcely found beyond Kumáun.

The base of the Himálayas is occupied by a narrow belt Lower forming an extreme north-western extension of the Malayan Himálayas. type described below. Above that, there is a rich temperate flora which in the eastern chain may be regarded as forming an extension of that of Northern China, gradually assuming westwards more and more of a European type. Magnolia, Aucuba, Abelia, and Skimmia may be mentioned as examples of Chinese genera found in the Eastern Himálayas, and the tea-tree grows wild in Assam. The same coniferous trees are common to both parts of the range. Pinus longifolia extends to the Hindu-Kush; P. excelsa is found universally except in Sikkim, and has its European analogue in P. Peuce, found in the mountains of Greece. Abies Smithiana extends into Afghánistán; Abies Webbiana forms dense forests at altitudes of 8000 to 12,000 feet, and ranges from Bhután to Kashmír; several junipers and the common yew (Taxus baccata) also occur. The deodar (Cedrus Deodara), which is indigenous to the mountains of Afghánistán and the north-west Himálayas, is nearly allied to the Atlantic cedar and to the cedar of Lebanon, a variety of which has recently been found in Cyprus. Another instance of the connection of the Western Himálayan flora with that of Europe is the holm oak (Quercus Ilex), so characteristic of the Mediterranean region.

North-
west.

The north-western area is best marked in Sind and the Punjab, where the climate is very dry (rainfall under 15 inches), and where the soil, though fertile, is wholly dependent on irrigation for its cultivation. The low-scattered jungle contains such characteristic species as Capparis aphylla, Acacia arabica (*babúl*), Populus euphratica (the 'willows' of Ps. cxxxvii. 2), Salvadora persica (erroneously identified by Royle with the mustard of Matt. xiii. 31), tamarisk, Zizyphus, Lotus, etc. The dry flora extends somewhat in a south-east direction, and then blends insensibly with that of the western peninsula; some species representing it are found in the upper Gangetic plain, and a few are widely distributed in dry parts of the country.

Assam and
Malayan
peninsula.

This area is described by Sir Joseph Hooker as comprising 'the flora of the perennially humid regions of India, as of the whole Malayan peninsula, the upper Assam valley, the Khási mountains, the forests of the base of the Himálayas from the Brahmaputra to Nepál, of the Malabar coast, and of Ceylon.'

Western
India.

The Western India type is difficult to characterize, and is intermediate between the two just preceding. It occupies a comparatively dry area, with a rainfall under 75 inches. In respect to positive affinities, Sir Joseph Hooker has pointed out some relations with the flora of tropical Africa as evidenced by the prevalence of such genera as Grewia and Impatiens, and the absence, common to both countries, of oaks and pines which abound in the Malayan archipelago. The annual vegetation which springs up in the rainy season includes numerous genera, such as Sida and Indigofera, which are largely represented both in Africa and Hindustán. Palms also in both countries are scanty, the most notable in Southern India being the wild date (Phœnix sylvestris); Borassus and the cocoa-nut are cultivated. The forests, although occasionally very dense, as in the Western Gháts, are usually drier and more open than those of the Malayan type, and are often scrubby. The most important timber-trees are the *tún* (Cedrela Toona), *sál* (Shorea robusta), the present area of which forms two belts separated by the Gangetic plain; satin-wood (Chloroxylon Swietenia), common in the drier parts of the peninsula; sandal-wood, especially characteristic of Mysore; iron-wood (Mesua ferrea), and teak (Tectona grandis).

CHAPTER XXV.

VITAL STATISTICS OF INDIA.

THE vital statistics of India[1] are derived from five chief Five sources. Of these, the first or European army consists of sources of foreigners under special medical conditions, and subject to health returns. the disturbing influence of ' invaliding.' The second, or native army; the third, or jail population; and the fourth, or police; are all composed of natives, but of natives under special conditions as regards food, discipline, or labour. It is dangerous to generalize from returns thus obtained, with regard to the health statistics of the ordinary population of India. For that

[1] The literature of Indian health statistics and medical aid may be divided into eight chief classes :—(1) Separate treatises by a series of medical observers, dating from the latter part of the 18th century and continuing up to the present time. (2) Official special Reports of the Medical Boards of Bengal, Madras, and Bombay on the great outbreak of cholera in 1817 ; the Medico-Topographical Reports (1825-40) of the chief stations of the Madras Presidency, by the Medical Board of that Presidency. (3) The Transactions of the Medical Physical Society of Calcutta (1823-39), and of Bombay (1837-76) ; the Indian Annals of Medical Science (Calcutta) from 1853-80 ; other medical journals at different periods in the three Presidencies. (4) Reports on the Medical Education of the Natives of India, commencing with vernacular medical schools in Calcutta and Bombay (1820-30), developing (1835-57) into the Medical Colleges of Bengal, Madras, and Bombay, and extending into medical schools at Haidarábád (Deccan), Nágpur, Agra, Lahore, Balrampur (Oudh), Patná, Dacca, Poona, Ahmadábád. (5) Reports on Vital Statistics by the various Medical Boards, Medical Departments, and Inspectors-General of Hospitals; since 1827 these assume a prominent place. (6) The Annual Reports of the Sanitary Commissioner with the Government of India, since 1874, and of the Sanitary Commissioners to the local Governments ; the Annual Reports of the Inspectors-General of Jails, of the Inspectors-General of Police, and of the health officers to municipal bodies in the various Presidencies and Provinces. (7) Reports by special Committees or Commissions, such as those on the Bardwán fever, on the cattle-plague in Bengal, the Orissa famine of 1866, the Madras famine of 1878, etc. (8) Annual Reports of the public hospitals, dispensaries, and other medical charities. The author has been unable to test all the dates in this footnote ; but he reproduces some of them, unverified, from a memorandum supplied to him by Dr. Morehead, formerly of Bombay.

population, however, a system of registration exists, and this system forms the fifth source of our data on the subject.

Registra-
tion of
general
population.
Why
untrust-
worthy.

In certain Provinces, registration is carried out with some degree of efficiency. But the natives shrink from publicity touching the details of their life. They could only be forced to give uniform and absolutely trustworthy returns of births, deaths, marriages, sex, and age by a stringent legislation, and a costly administrative mechanism, from which the Government wisely abstains. In municipalities, however, registration furnishes a fairly accurate account of the vital statistics of the urban population. For the rural Districts, special areas in some Provinces were selected for statistical supervision ; and this has been now gradually extended, with the exception of certain exceptionally situated tracts, to practically the whole population. But the results obtained are still necessarily imperfect.

The
Census.

The Census operations, conducted under special legislation, will furnish a general picture of the Indian people every ten years. But the complete details have, up to the present time of writing, been obtained only for the two Censuses of 1871 and 1881. The chief results of the Census of 1881 are given in chapter ii., and in Appendices I. to X. at the end of this volume.

Sources of
error.

In treating of the public health of India, therefore, three points must always be borne in mind. The data are obtained either, first, from limited classes under special medical conditions ; or second, from limited areas under special statistical supervision ; or third, from a general system of registration spread over the whole country, but which has hitherto failed to yield trustworthy results. General averages from such sources, struck for the entire population, can only be accepted as estimates based upon the best information at present available.

Death-rate
in India.

Subject to the above remarks, it may be stated that the evidence goes to show an annual death-rate of 32·57 per thousand in India. During the famine of 1877–78, the death-rate in Madras was ascertained to be equal to an annual rate of 53·2 per thousand. In 1877, the death-rate among the European troops in India was 12·71 per thousand, being the lowest recorded up to that year; in the native army, 13·38 per thousand ; in the public jails, 61·95 per thousand, rising to 176 per thousand in the Madras prisons, which were flooded by the famine-stricken population. In 1883, the death-rate returns of European troops in India showed a mortality of

10·88 per thousand, the lowest recorded in any year for which full returns have been compiled. In the native army in 1883 the mortality on the total strength was 11·76 per thousand, or including men absent from their regiments, 14·31 per thousand, being about one-half the average rates for 1877–81. The jail mortality also showed a satisfactory reduction, the death-rate having fallen to 33·64 per cent.

The returns of births, as given hereafter for each Province, are too untrustworthy to allow of an attempt to calculate the birth-rate for the whole country. The average duration of life in India is, on slender foundation, estimated at $30\frac{3}{4}$ years. Instead of attempting generalizations, which, although interesting to the speculative statist, might mislead the actuary and be perverted into an unsound basis for induction, the following paragraphs are confined to the returns as furnished for the separate Provinces; together with the health statistics of the European troops, the native army, and the jail population. The following paragraphs are condensed from the Reports of the Sanitary Commissioner with the Government of India, for 1877 and 1883. *Average duration of life.*

In Bengal, the system of collecting statistics over specially selected areas has been abolished, and an attempt is being made to obtain returns equally from the whole Province. The registration of deaths in 1877 showed a ratio of 17·96 per thousand (varying in different Districts from 36 down to 8), which, according to the Sanitary Commissioner, 'must be very much under the truth.' The mortality in towns (where the registration is less incomplete) was returned at 32·49 per thousand, compared with 17·39 in the rural circles. Of the total death-rate, 20·24 per thousand was among males, and only 15·69 among females, 'a discrepancy which must be due in the main to defective registration.' The birth-rate, which averaged 10·20 per thousand for the whole Province, varied, according to the returns, from 35 in Patná to only 6 per thousand in Bardwán and Bákarganj Districts. The male births were returned in 1877 as exceeding the female births in the proportion of 118 to 100. *Vital statistics of Bengal in 1877.*

Registration of vital statistics in Bengal is still very imperfect, and it is only with regard to deaths that any attempt is made at a general registration. The total number of deaths returned in 1883 as occurring among a population under registration of 66,163,884, was 1,245,676, or at the rate of $18\frac{1}{2}$ per thousand (varying in different Districts from a maximum of 36 down to a minimum of 10 per thousand). The defective character of the registration is shown by the fact that the *Vital statistics of Bengal in 1883.*

death-rate among the males was 20·59 per thousand, and among the females 17·08 per thousand, showing an apparent increase of over 18 per cent. of male over female deaths. It is also exhibited in a comparison of the mortality in towns and rural circles. In 96 towns in Bengal where registration is necessarily under closer control, the death-rate amounted to 27·28 per thousand, while in 552 rural registration circles it was only 18·49. Compulsory birth registration in Bengal is only enforced in 46 towns and municipalities, with a population of 1,685,159. These returned a total birth-rate of 22·08 per thousand in 1883 ; but that this is below the truth is exhibited by the fact that the deaths exceeded the births in the ratio of 7·87 per thousand, as well as by the fact that the registered male births in towns exceeded the female births by 14 per cent. The following figures show the causes of the registered deaths in 1883, and the ratio they bear to the general mortality :—Fevers, 13·81 per thousand ; cholera, 1·36 ; small-pox, 0·14 ; bowel complaints, 0·83 ; injuries, 0·35 ; all other causes, 2·30 per thousand.

Vital statistics of Madras in 1877. In the Madras Presidency, both births and deaths were much affected in 1877 by the famine which desolated that part of the country, and registration was conducted under special difficulties. Though many defects are consequently apparent, the Sanitary Commissioner is of opinion 'that the relative intensity of the famine in different circles is fairly represented by the mortuary registration.' The general registered death-rate was 53·2 per thousand ; and in Madras city, 116·7 per thousand (*see* article MADRAS PRESIDENCY, *The Imperial Gazetteer of India*). Among males, the rate is given as 58·4, and among females 48·06 per thousand, 'which points to imperfections in the record of female deaths.' The following figures show the causes under which the deaths of 1877 in Madras were classified :—Cholera, 12·2 per thousand ; small-pox, 3·02 ; fevers, 16·06 ; bowel complaints, 4·5 ; injuries, 0·5 ; all other causes, 16·8 per thousand. The number of registered deaths in 1876 was 23·34, and in 1875, 21·1 per thousand. The famine resulted in a marked reduction in the birth-rate, the ratio for 1877 being only 16·3, or less than that of 1876 by more than 5 per thousand. For every 100 female births, 107 male births were registered. In the nine Districts where the famine was most severe, the birth-rate was only 12 per thousand, whereas in the eight where the people suffered less, the rate was 20 per thousand. Excess of deaths over births in Madras Presidency in 1877, according to the above figures, 36·9 per thousand of the population. The registration of births and deaths was not compulsory in Madras in 1877.

Registration of vital statistics is still very imperfect in Madras, although better than in the Bengal Districts. The total number of deaths returned in 1883 as occurring among a population under registration of 28,503,100, was 541,930, or at the rate of 19·0 per thousand (varying in the several Districts from a maximum of 38·6 to a minimum of 11·8 per thousand), the rate of male deaths being 19·7, and of female deaths 18·3 per thousand. The urban death-rate in 76 towns, with a population of 1,696,075, was 24·9 per thousand, as against 18·6 per thousand in 153 rural registration circles, with a total population of 26,839,745. The total number of births registered in 1883 was 791,774, or 27·7 per thousand, a larger number and ratio than in any year since 1869, when registration was first commenced. The excess of male over female births is less in proportion in Madras than in any other Province of India, the ratio being 104·6 males to 100 females. The death-rate from different causes in 1883 was returned as follows :—Fevers, 7·1 per thousand ; cholera, 1·2 ; small-pox, 1·3 ; bowel complaints, 0·7 ; injuries, 0·4 ; all other causes, 8·0 per thousand. Excess of births over deaths registered in 1883, 8·7 per thousand of population. *Vital statistics of Madras in 1883.*

In the Bombay Presidency, famine affected the death-rate in 1877, and the year was also more than usually unhealthy, cholera and small-pox being both epidemic. The mortality, according to the returns, was at the rate of 38·76 per thousand. In the famine-stricken Districts the mortality was 55·09, compared with 25·71 per thousand in 1876. The following figures show the causes of the deaths registered in 1877 :—Cholera, 2·53 ; small-pox, 1·69 ; fevers, 20·79 ; bowel complaints, 3·72 ; injuries, 0·46 ; all other causes, 8·55 per thousand. The birth-rate in 1877 was 19·26 per thousand (varying from 29 to 6), or 2·09 per thousand less than the rate for 1876—'a result which is for the most part ascribed to the effects of famine ; but also, in great measure, to neglect in registration.' For every 100 female births, 111 male births were registered. Excess of deaths over births in Bombay Presidency in 1877, 19·54 per thousand of the population. *Vital statistics of Bombay in 1877.*

Registration shows better results in the Bombay Presidency than in Madras or Bengal, but in the Sind Districts it is still very imperfect, and the returns from these lower the average for the entire Presidency. The total number of deaths returned in 1883 was 420,198, or 25·53 per thousand of the *Vital statistics of Bombay in 1883.*

total population (varying from 41·97 per thousand in Khándesh to 9·19 in the Upper Sind Frontier District), the ratio of male deaths being 26·02, and of female deaths 25·02 per thousand. The male deaths registered were 111·06, for every 100 female deaths. The urban death-rate in 62 towns and municipalities, with a total population of 2,105,756, was 29·61 per thousand, as against 24·94 per thousand in 223 rural registration circles, with a population of 14,348,658. The ratio of mortality due to different causes was returned as follows :—Fevers, 16·21 per thousand ; cholera, 2·31 ; small-pox, 0·81 ; bowel complaints, 2·14; injuries, 0·36 ; all other causes, 3·70. The number of births registered during the year was 501,801, giving a rate of 30·50 per thousand of the population, which would be considerably higher but for defective returns from Sind. Throughout the entire Presidency, 109·22 male births were registered for every 100 female. The excess of the registered births over the deaths was at the rate of 4·97 per thousand of the population.

Vital statistics of North-Western Provinces and Oudh in 1877. The North-Western Provinces and Oudh together returned a death-rate in 1877 of 19·67 per thousand, varying from 29 to 12 per thousand. For Oudh alone, the rate was 17·1 ; and for the North-Western Provinces alone, 20·6. The mortality in the towns of the amalgamated Province was 29·43, compared with 18·99 in the rural circles ; and of the total death-rate, 21·06 was among males, and 18·12 among females. The registration of births, which in 1877 was confined to the municipalities, showed an average rate of 39·22 per thousand, varying from 70 at Urai to 14 at Dehra. Excess of births over deaths, 10·27 per thousand of the population.

Vital statistics of North-Western Provinces and Oudh in 1883. Considerable improvement in registration of vital statistics in the North-Western Provinces and Oudh has been effected since 1877, and birth as well as death registration is now carried on throughout the entire Lieutenant-Governorship. The statistics, however, still bear internal evidence that at the best they are only approximately accurate. The total number of deaths returned in 1883 (a year of improved health, accompanied by plenty and cheapness of food) was 1,216,297, or at the rate of 27·57 per thousand of the population, the lowest for any year since 1877 (varying from 48·33 to 17·49 per thousand), the rate of male deaths being 28·49, and of female deaths 26·58 per thousand, the excess of male over female deaths being on an average 15·88 per cent. The urban death-rate in 103 towns and municipalities, with a total population of 2,756,493, was 35·32 per thousand, as against 27·05 per thousand in 1044 rural registration circles, with a population of 41,351,376. The ratio of mortality due to different causes was returned as follows :—Fevers,18·82 per thousand ; cholera, 0·41 ; small-pox, 3·14 ; bowel complaints, 1·51 ; injuries, 0·48 ; all other causes, 3·21 per thousand. The mortality from small-pox was unusually high during the year. The average birth-rate in 1883 was 40·84 per thousand, the highest on record since 1879, when the general registration of births was first intro-duced into these Provinces, and the highest in any of the Provinces of India in 1883. The birth-rates in the various Districts ranged from 58·24 per thousand in Lálitpur to 20·39 per thousand in Dehra Dun. Throughout the Lieutenant-Governorship as a whole, 111·81 boys were born for every 100 girls. Except in the malaria-infested Tarái, the registered births exceeded the deaths in every District, the total excess of births over deaths being at the ratio of 13·27 per thousand of the population.

In the Punjab, the death-rate for 1877 was recorded as 20 per thousand, and the same rate applies to both males and females taken separately. The District average varies from 27 per thousand in Lahore to 8 in Kohát on the frontier. In the towns, the mean mortality was 33 per thousand, varying between a maximum of 52 (in the town of Delhi) and a minimum of 12 (in Kohát). In 1877, births were registered only in the municipal towns of the Punjab, and the results showed a birth-rate of 31·86 per thousand. Excess of births over deaths, 5 per thousand of the population. *Vital statistics of the Punjab in 1877.*

In 1883, the total number of deaths returned in the Punjab was 475,741, or at the rate of 25·25 per thousand of the population (varying in the several Districts from 35 to 16 per thousand), the rate of male deaths being 25·13, and of female deaths 25·39 per thousand. The urban mortality in 1883, in 49 towns and municipalities, with a population (excluding that of four hill sanitaria) of 1,310,383, was at the rate of 30 per thousand, as against 25 per thousand in 397 rural registration circles, with a population of 17,512,378. The ratio of mortality due to different causes was returned as follows :—Fevers, 16·25 per thousand ; cholera, 0·01 ; small-pox, 0·64; bowel complaints, 0·77 ; injuries, 0·28 ; all other causes, 7·29 per thousand. The average birth-rate during the year was 39 per thousand throughout the Punjab as compared with an average of 41 in municipal towns. Throughout the Punjab as a whole, 115·14 boys were born for every 100 girls, or an excess of 15·14 per cent. of male over female births. The excess of *Vital statistics of the Punjab in 1883.*

births over deaths was at the rate of 14 per thousand of the general population. The year, however, was an exceptionally healthy one, and the mortality from the chief diseases was less than in any year since 1877.

Vital statistics of the Central Provinces in 1877. In the Central Provinces and in Berar, the registration of births and deaths is more general, and the results obtained approach nearer to accuracy than in any of the other Provinces of India. The recorded death-rate in the Central Provinces in 1877 was 23·91 per thousand, varying from 38 in Mandlá to only 18 in Nágpur District. Among males the death-rate was 25·66, and among females 22·11 per thousand. In the towns, the rate was 35·86 per thousand. In 1877, the total number of births registered in the Central Provinces show a rate of 39·26 per thousand ; varying from a maximum of 45 per thousand in Biláspur to a minimum of 31 in Nágpur. The proportion of male births recorded was 111 for every 100 female births. Excess of registered births over deaths in the Central Provinces in 1877, 15·35 per thousand of the population.

Vital statistics of the Central Provinces in 1883. In 1883, the total number of deaths returned in the Central Provinces, among a population of 8,817,185 under registration, was 304,763, or an average rate of 34·56 per thousand (varying in the several Districts from 48·84 to 26·13), the rate of male deaths being 35·83, and of female deaths 33·28 per thousand, the excess of male over female deaths being 9 per cent. The urban mortality in 1883, in 74 towns and municipalities, with a total population of 757,092, was at the rate of 35·56 per thousand, as compared with 34·48 per thousand in 94 rural registration centres, with a population cf 8,060,093. The ratio of mortality due to different causes was as follows :—Fevers, 19·86 per thousand ; cholera, 1·84 ; small-pox, 0·53 ; bowel complaints, 3·02 ; injuries, 0·52 ; all other causes, 8·79 per thousand. Total number of births regis-tered, 357,864, or at the average rate of 40·59 per thousand, varying in the several Districts from 54·29 to 34·15. Male births preponderated over female births by 7·61 per cent. The excess of registered births over deaths was at the rate of 6·03 per thousand of the population.

Vital statistics of Berar in 1877. In Berar, the general registered death-rate was returned in 1877 at 28·1 per thousand. In the towns alone the mortality was 31·4 per thousand. The birth-rate shown by the returns of 1877 was 39·5 per thousand, varying from 47 in Akola to 35 in Wún District. The number of male births recorded was 109 for every 100 female births. Excess of births over deaths in Berar in 1877, 11·40 per thousand of the population.

The year 1883 was a particularly unhealthy one in Berar, owing, it is supposed, to abnormally heavy rainfall ; and a severe epidemic of cholera largely raised the mortality returns. The total number of deaths returned during the year was 135,081, or at the rate of 51·3 per thousand of the population (varying in the several Districts from 65·7 to 39·3 per thousand) ; the rate of male deaths was 51·4, and of female deaths 51·3 per thousand, the excess of male over female deaths being 7 per cent. The urban death-rate in 11 towns and municipalities, with a population of 138,378, was 53·2 per thousand, as against 51·3 per thousand in 134 rural registration circles, with a population of 2,491,640. The ratio of mortality due to different causes was as follows :—Fevers, 20·3 per thousand ; cholera, 10·6 ; small-pox, 1·5 ; bowel complaints, 7·2 ; injuries, 0·4 ; all other causes, 11·3 per thousand. The average birth-rate in 1883 was 40·3 per thousand, varying from 43·2 to 37·8 per thousand, the male births exceeding the female by 6·5 per cent. Owing to the cholera epidemic, and general unhealthiness of Berar in 1883, the registered deaths exceeded the births in that year in the ratio of 11 per thousand of the population.

Vital statistics of Berar in 1883.

In Assam, the system of registration in 1877 was that formerly in vogue in Bengal, of which this Province until recently formed part. The returns were taken over certain selected areas, and the results were quite untrustworthy. The death-rate, as ascertained from these returns, was only 10·9 per thousand, varying in the several Districts from 29 to 5 per thousand. The births recorded in the selected areas were at the rate of 20 per thousand, ranging from 34 to 10 per thousand. The figures show an excess of deaths over births in Assam in 1877 of 4·9 per thousand of the population.

Vital statistics of Assam in 1877.

Compulsory registration throughout the whole of Assam, with the exception of certain hill tracts, was not introduced till the latter half of 1882 ; and the results, as might be expected, do not even approximate to accuracy. In 1883, the total number of deaths registered was returned at 122,932, or an average of 27·14 per thousand of the population (varying in the several Districts from 41·89 to 16·27 per thousand), the rate of male deaths being 28·34, and of female deaths 25·89 per thousand. Excess of male over female registered deaths, 16 per cent. In 21 towns and municipalities, with a total population of 99,202, the average death-rate was

Vital statistics of Assam in 1883.

30·07 per thousand, as against 27·08 per thousand in 657 rural registration circles, with a population numbering 4,428,732. The ratio of mortality due to different causes was as follows :— Fevers, 14·90 per thousand ; cholera, 3·29 ; small-pox, 1·36 ; bowel complaints, 3·19 ; injuries, 0·27 ; other causes, 4·12 per thousand. The average birth-rate in 1883 was 23·91 per thousand, those of the males exceeding the females by nearly 10 per cent. Excess of registered deaths over births, 3·23 per thousand of the population.

Vital statistics of British Burma in 1877.   In British Burma, registration is shown to be even more defective than in the worst Provinces of India. The average death-rate, according to the returns in 1877, was 17·44 per thousand, the rate for males being 18, and for females 16 per thousand. In Myanaung the deaths were returned at 119, and at Maulmain at less than 13 per thousand. In the towns the mortality was 34 per thousand, compared with 15 in the rural circles. The birth returns showed a rate of only 21 per thousand ; 'and this general average,' to use the words of the Report in 1877, 'is made up of such extremes that no reliance can be placed on the figures.' In one place the birth-rate was no less than 115 per thousand, in another it was as low as 5. Excess of registered births over deaths in British Burma in 1877, 4 per thousand of the population.

Vital statistics of British Burma in 1883.   No improvement in registration in British Burma seems to have been effected up to 1883. Indeed, in that year the death-rate had fallen below the figures returned for 1877. In 1883, the total registered deaths numbered 53,583, or a rate of 14·67 per thousand of the population under registration (varying in the several Districts from 21·42 to 9·22), the male deaths being returned at 15·37, and the female deaths at 13·86 per thousand. The excess of registered male deaths over female deaths was 27 per cent. In 20 towns and municipalities, with a total population of 425,775, the registered death-rate was 25·50 per thousand, against 13·24 per thousand in 823 rural registration circles, with a population numbering 3,227,854. The ratio of mortality due to different causes was as follows :—Fevers, 7·19 per thousand ; cholera, 0·60 ; small-pox, 0·19 ; bowel complaints, 0·76 ; injuries, 0·17 ; other causes, 5·76. The birth-rate of the Province was returned at 23 per thousand, ranging in the several Districts from 31·65 to 16·60. The registered male births exceeded those of the females by 6 per cent. The registered births exceeded the deaths in the ratio of 8·0 per thousand of the population. A revised scheme of

registration for British Burma is now (1884) under considera
tion, the adoption of which it is hoped will result in more
accurate statistics.

After what has been stated in the introductory paragraph of Danger of
this section, it is manifest that the figures quoted from the using these
statistics.
Reports of the Sanitary Commissioner with the Government
of India are of little or no value for the purpose of establishing
the comparative healthiness or unhealthiness of the different
portions of the country. To construct a comparative table out
of the provincial returns would be misleading, if any attempt
were made to use it for actuarial purposes. But the tables on
the four following pages may be interesting as showing the
defects and uncertainties of Vital Statistics in India, as well as
the progress towards accuracy which has been effected between
1877 and 1883 in registering births and deaths among the
general population. The wide variations in both the birth and
death rates for various Districts usually arise from different
degrees of imperfection in the registration.

HEALTH OF THE EUROPEAN ARMY.—The sanitary statistics Health
of the army in India are, in every way, more trustworthy than of the
European
those obtained for the general population; and as they have Army;
been regularly collected on a uniform system for a number of
years, it is possible to draw valuable inferences.

The sanitary history of the European Army during 1877 its general
was more favourable than in any previous year for which the statistics
in 1877,
statistics are on record. The total strength of the European Army in India in 1877 was returned at 57,260 men; the
admissions into hospital numbered 71,992 (1257 per thousand
of average strength); daily sick, 3196 (56 per thousand); deaths,
728 (12·71 per thousand). The averages for the five years
1871–1875 were as follows:—admissions into hospital, 1394
per thousand; daily sick, 57; deaths, 17·62 per thousand.
'Not only,' writes the Sanitary Commissioner, 'do the results
compare favourably with the averages of the five years 1871 to
1875, but, what is deserving of special notice, the admission-
rate and death-rate are the lowest which have yet (1877) been
attained.'

In 1883, the total strength of the European Army in India and 1883.
was 55,525; the average admission into hospital being at
the rate of 1336 per thousand; daily sick, 63 per thousand;
while the deaths were 10·88 per thousand, the lowest on

[*Sentence continued on page* 680.

BIRTH-RATE AMONG GENERAL POPULATION IN INDIAN PROVINCES IN 1877.

PROVINCE.	Population under Registration.	RATIO OF BIRTHS PER 1000 OF POPULATION.			Number of Males born to every 100 Females born.	Excess of Births over Deaths per 1000 of Population.	Excess of Deaths over Births per 1000 of Population.
		Maximum for any one District.	Minimum for any one District.	Mean for the Province.			
Bengal,	58,281,453	35	6	18·20	118	·07	...
North-Western Provinces,[1]	2,231,534	70	14	39·22	117	10·27	...
Punjab,	3,022,071	51	12	31·86	111	5·00	...
Central Provinces,	7,408,074	45	31	39·26	111	15·35	...
Berar,	2,184,945	47	35	39·50	109	11·40	...
British Burma,	2,934,981	115	5	21·07	105	4·00	...
Assam,	120,821	34	10	20·90	123	...	4·9
Madras Presidency,[2]	29,209,542	36	5	16·30	107	...	36·9
Bombay Presidency,[2]	16,181,741	29	6	19·26	111	...	19·54

BENGAL PRESIDENCY. (brackets the first seven provinces)

[1] Births were not registered in Oudh in 1877.

[2] It should be remembered, as already stated, that the averages in Madras, and to a less degree in Bombay, were powerfully influenced by the Famine (1877). The average death-rate in 1876 was 23·34 per thousand in Madras, and 21·81 per thousand in Bombay. The birth-rate in 1876 in Madras was 21·6 per thousand ; and in Bombay, 21·35.

DEATH-RATE AMONG GENERAL POPULATION IN INDIAN PROVINCES IN 1877.

Province		Population under Registration.	Area in Square Miles.	Average Population per Square Mile.	Ratio of Deaths per 1000 of Population in Districts.			Death-rate per 1000.	
					Maximum.	Minimum.	Mean.	Male.	Female.
BENGAL PRESIDENCY.	Bengal,	59,993,332	144,614	415	36	8	17·96	20·24	15·69
	North-Western Provinces and Oudh,	42,724,741	104,402	409	29	12	19·67	21·06	18·12
	Punjab,	17,487,125	104,975	166	27	8	20·00	20·00	20·00
	Central Provinces,	7,408,074	65,162	113	38	18	23·91	25·66	22·11
	Berar,	2,184,945	16,227	134	34	20	28·10	[1]	[1]
	British Burma,	2,934,981	88,283	33	119	11	17·44	18·47	16·33
	Assam,	3,805,364	27,319	131	29	5	10·90	6·30	4·60
Madras Presidency,		29,209,542	138,318	222	119	[2]17	53·20	[2]58·40	48·06
Bombay Presidency,		16,181,741	124,196	130	101	[2]8	38·76	[2]41·32	36·01

[1] Not given by Sanitary Commissioner.

[2] It should be remembered, as already stated, that the averages in Madras, and in a lesser degree in Bombay, were powerfully influenced by the Famine (1877). The average death-rate in 1876 was 23·34 per thousand in Madras, and 21·81 per thousand in Bombay. The birth-rate in 1876 in Madras was 21·6 per thousand; and in Bombay, 21·35.

BIRTH-RATE AMONG GENERAL POPULATION IN INDIAN PROVINCES IN 1883.

Province.	Population under Registration.	Ratio of Births per 1000 of Population.			Number of Males born to every 100 Females born.	Excess of Births over Deaths per 1000 of Population.	Excess of Deaths over Births per 1000 of Population.
		Maximum for any one District.	Minimum for any one District.	Mean for the Province.			
Bengal (46 Municipalities and Towns),	1,685,159	49·17	6·40	22·08	114·00	...	7·87
North-Western Provinces and Oudh,	44,107,869	58·24	20·39	40·84	111·81	13·27	...
Punjab,	18,842,264	53·32	10·04	39·00	115·14	14·00	...
Central Provinces,	8,817,185	54·29	34·15	40·59	107·61	6·03	...
Berar,	2,630,018	43·20	37·80	40·30	106·50	...	11·00
British Burma,	3,653,629	31·65	16·60	22·92	106·00	8·00	...
Assam,	4,527,934	59·13	13·28	23·91	109·73	...	3·23
Madras Presidency,	28,503,100	40·90	13·70	27·70	104·60	8·70	...
Bombay Presidency,	16,454,414	44·09	15·92	30·50	109·22	4·97	...

BENGAL PRESIDENCY. (bracket grouping rows Bengal through Assam)

DEATH-RATE AMONG GENERAL POPULATION IN INDIAN PROVINCES IN 1883.

PROVINCE.	Population under Registration.	Area in Square Miles.	Average Population per Square Mile.	RATIO OF DEATHS PER 1000 OF POPULATION IN DISTRICTS.			DEATH-RATE PER 1000.	
				Maximum.	Minimum.	Mean.	Male.	Female.
Bengal,	66,163,884	144,863	457	36·07	9·93	18·82	20·59	17·08
North-Western Provinces and Oudh,	44,107,869	106,104	416	48·33	17·49	27·57	28·49	26·58
Punjab,	18,842,264	107,989	175	35·00	16·00	25·25	25·13	25·39
Central Provinces,	8,817,185	71,245	124	48·84	26·13	34·56	35·83	33·28
Berar,	2,630,018	16,062	164	65·70	39·30	51·30	51·40	51·30
British Burma,	3,653,629	75,087	49	21·42	9·22	14·67	15·37	13·86
Assam,	4,527,934	¹27,666	¹162	41·89	16·27	27·14	28·34	25·89
Madras Presidency,	28,593,100	139,900	221	38·60	11·80	19·00	19·70	18·30
Bombay Presidency,	16,454,414	123,860	133	41·97	9·19	25·53	26·02	25·02

(BENGAL PRESIDENCY.)

¹ Exclusive of the Khási and Jaintia Hills, and of Tura station in the Gáro Hills.

Sentence continued from page 675.]
record since 1870. The loss from invaliding was 33 per thousand, making a total loss from all causes of 44 per thousand of average strength, or about 12 per thousand below the average of thirteen previous years. The ratio of loss due to invaliding in 1883 was about 4 per cent. below the average. In 1883, the death-rate in the Bengal Army was as low as 11·21 per thousand. In Madras, the death-rate in 1883 was as low as 10·19 per thousand, the lowest in the three Presidencies. Rate of mortality in the Bombay Army in 1883, 10·50 per thousand of average strength.

Nine chief causes of sickness.   In all three Presidencies, the same diseases form the nine chief causes of sickness, with slight variations in the order in which they occur.   These nine were :—malarial fevers, venereal diseases, wounds and accidents, abscess and ulcer, respiratory diseases, rheumatism, diarrhœa, hepatitis, and dysentery. They are here given in the order of their frequency (1883) in Bengal. Malarial fevers, which stood first in both Bengal and Bombay (486 and 436 admissions per 1000 respectively), were replaced at the top of the list in Madras by venereal diseases (289 admissions per 1000); respiratory diseases and rheumatism, which took the fifth and sixth places in Bengal, were seventh and ninth in Madras, and fourth and sixth in Bombay ; whereas dysentery and hepatitis, which came fifth and eighth in Madras, came ninth and eighth in Bengal, and occupied the same position in Bombay. The arrangement of the diseases in all three Presidencies accorded generally, to a remarkable extent, with the experience of previous years ; and the year 1883 may be taken as a typical one. Total admissions into hospital from all causes, 1336 per 1000 in all India. In the Bengal Army, the average admissions were 1463 per 1000 ; in Madras, 1013 ; and in Bombay, 1249 per 1000.

The chief causes of mortality.   The six principal causes of deaths in Bengal in 1877 were in the order of their frequency : enteric fever, apoplexy, hepatitis, cholera, remittent and continued fevers, and dysentery. In all three Presidencies, the six forms of disease which contributed most to the death-rate were the same.   The total death-rate from these six diseases were—in Bengal, 6·60 out of a total mortality of 11·21 per 1000 ; in Madras, 6·47 out of a total mortality of 10·19 per 1000 ; and in Bombay, 5·39 out of a total of 10·50 per 1000. Enteric fever headed the list of the chief causes of death in all three Presidencies ; Madras having the highest ratio (2·86 per 1000 followed by Bengal (2·52 per 1000), and Bombay (1·55 per 1000).

Cholera was not prevalent during 1883, and added but little to the army mortality throughout India. The experience of a number of years goes to show that enteric fever is in the main a disease of young soldiers new to India, the majority of sufferers being men in their first or second year. With reference to the great prevalence of venereal diseases in the European Army, it is stated that 'the working of the lock hospitals in all three Presidencies during 1877 must be pronounced to have been more or less a failure;' and in 1883 the admission rate into military hospitals for venereal diseases was reported to be only a fraction lower in protected than in unprotected stations.

Out of a total, in 1883, of 604 deaths in the European British Causes of Army in India, 133 were due to enteric fever, 26 to other fevers, invaliding. 51 to cholera, 63 to hepatitis, 61 to apoplexy, 38 to phthisis, 37 to diseases of the respiratory organs, 17 to heart disease, and 23 to dysentery and diarrhœa.

The following tables show—(1) the health-statistics of the European troops throughout all India, for a series of years ending 1883; and (2) the sickness, mortality, and invaliding among those troops in 1883, arranged separately under the three Presidencies :—

DEATH-RATE AMONG EUROPEAN TROOPS IN INDIA, 1871–1883.

PERIOD.	Strength.	RATIO PER 1000 OF AVERAGE STRENGTH.				
		Admissions into Hospital.	Daily Sick.	Deaths.	Invaliding.	TOTAL LOSS.
1871 to 1875 (average), .	58,432	1394	57	17·62	43·09	61
1876, . .	57,858	1361	56	15·32	38·90	54
1877, . .	57,260	1257	55	12·71	42·25	55
1878, . .	56,475	1651	68	21·46	45	66
1879, . .	49,582	1977	78	24·28	49	73
1880, . .	51,796	1789	74	24·85	26	51
1881, . .	58,728	1605	70	16·86	38	55
1882, . .	57,269	1445	65	12·07	33	45
1883, . .	55,525	1336	63	10·88	33	44
Average, .	56,666	1492	63	17·43	40	57

SICKNESS, MORTALITY, AND INVALIDING AMONG EUROPEAN
TROOPS IN THE THREE PRESIDENCIES DURING 1883.

PRESIDENCY.	Average Strength.	RATIO PER 1000 OF AVERAGE STRENGTH.				
		Admissions into Hospital.	Daily Sick.	Deaths.	Invaliding.	TOTAL LOSS.
Bengal, . .	34,079	1463	66	11·21	31	42·21
Madras, . .	10,498	1013	59	10·19	33	43·19
Bombay, . .	10,948	1249	57	10·50	38	48·50

Health of the Native Army, in 1877 and 1883,   HEALTH OF THE NATIVE ARMY.—The sickness and mortality in 1877 in the regular Native Armies of Bengal, Madras, and Bombay, the Central India Regiments, Punjab Frontier Field Force, and Haidarábád Contingent, are shown by the following figures :—average strength of troops (present with regiments), 113,966; admissions into hospital, 1030 per thousand; daily sick, 32 ; deaths from cholera, 1·53 ; deaths from all causes, 10·90, or, including men dying while absent from their regiments, 13·38 per thousand.   In 1883, the total average strength of the Native Army of India (present with regiments) was 114,830 ; admissions into hospital, 923 per thousand ; average daily sick, 31; deaths from cholera, 1·15 per thousand ; deaths from all causes, 11·76 per thousand of actual regimental strength, or 14·31 per thousand, including deaths among absentees.   Malarial fevers are the chief cause of admission into hospital; wounds and accidents come next; followed by dysentery, diarrhœa, and enteric fever.   The mortality amounted to 27·28 per cent. of the total treated, the lowest since 1877.   Respiratory diseases were the cause of the largest mortality, namely, 3·91 per thousand, followed by fevers, 1·41 ; and by cholera, 1·15 per thousand.

of Bengal ;   In the Bengal Native Army, the death-rate in 1883 was 10·55 per thousand, a lower ratio than for any one year since 1877, when it was 10·32 per thousand.   In the Central India Regiments, the mortality was as low as 7·89 per thousand in 1883, compared with 9·71 in 1877, and with 11·10, the average of the ten years preceding 1877.   In the Punjab Frontier Force, the death-rate, including deaths among absentees, was 23·35 per thousand in 1883, and excluding absentees, 21·46 ; while in 1877 the rate was 12·26 per thousand.   Altogether, the Sanitary Commissioner reports that the health of the

Native Army in Bengal is very satisfactory, and that there is still a tendency towards diminishing mortality in normal years.

In the Madras Native Army, the regimental mortality, in- of Madras; cluding deaths among absentees, was 14·36 per thousand in 1877, and 12·51 per thousand in 1883. Excluding deaths of absentees, the ratio was 11·80 per thousand in 1877, and 10·76 per thousand in 1883. Besides garrisoning its own Province, the Madras Army supplies troops for British Burma and the Andaman and Nicobar islands, as also to certain Districts in the Central Provinces, and to Cuttack District in Orissa.

In the Bombay Native Army, the death-rate, including of Bombay. deaths among absentees, in 1877 was 12·96 per thousand, varying from 11·65 for regiments in the northern Division of Bombay, to 18·81 for those in the Konkan. In 1883, the rate of mortality, including deaths among absentees, was 14·96 per thousand; excluding absentees, the rate among those actually serving with their regiments was 12·81 per thousand.

The returns for the Haidarábád Contingent, both for 1877 Haidár- and 1883, are more favourable than those for any other portion ábád Con- of the Native Army. The admissions into hospital in 1877 were tingent. only 806 per thousand; daily sick, 26; and mortality (including deaths among absentees), 9·61 per thousand. The number of deaths from cholera, however (4·43 per thousand), was much above that recorded in any other part of the Native Army. In 1883, the admissions into hospital had fallen to an average of 572 per thousand, the daily sick-rate to 20 per thousand, and the mortality to 7·59 per thousand.

The sickness and mortality in the Regular Native Army Results in and other forces in 1877 and 1883 are compared in the the three following tables:— Presi- dencies compared.

SICKNESS AND MORTALITY AMONG NATIVE TROOPS IN 1877.

PRESIDENCY, ETC.	Deaths per 1000, including Deaths among Absentees.	Average Strength (present with Regiments).	RATIO PER 1000.			
			Admissions into Hospital.	Daily Sick.	Deaths from Cholera.	Deaths from all Causes.
Bengal Native Army, . .	13·63	39,649	1096	33	·35	10·32
Madras ,, ,, . .	14·36	28,304	860	28	2·79	11·80
Bombay ,, ,, . .	12·96	23,388	1074	33	1·93	10·90
Central India Regiments, .	10·59	5,046	810	25	·79	9·71
Punjab Frontier Field Force,	14·55	10,359	1403	41	...	12·26
Haidarábád Contingent, .	9·61	7,220	806	26	4·43	9·42
India, . .	13·38	113,966	1030	32	·53	10·90

SICKNESS AND MORTALITY AMONG NATIVE TROOPS IN 1883.

PRESIDENCY, ETC.	Deaths per 1000, including Deaths among Absentees.	Average Strength (present with Regiments).	RATIO PER 1000.			
			Admissions into Hospital.	Daily Sick.	Deaths from Cholera.	Deaths from all Causes.
Bengal Native Army, .	13·98	40,932	985	32	0·56	10·55
Madras ,, ,, .	12·51	27,703	737	27	2·92	10·76
Bombay ,, ,, .	14·96	23,576	994	35	0·47	12·81
Central India Regiments, .	10·16	5,197	595	19	0·39	7·89
Punjab Frontier Field Force,	23·35	10,438	1,419	45	0·00	21·46
Haidarábád Contingent, .	9·31	6,983	572	20	2·15	7·59
India, . .	14·31	114,830	923	31	1·15	11·76

Health of the jail population.   HEALTH OF THE JAIL POPULATION.—The Report of the Sanitary Commissioner with the Government of India for 1877, was the first which included the vital statistics of the jails of all three Presidencies. 'The year 1877, to which it refers,' says the Sanitary Commissioner, 'is particularly unfortunate for commencing this change, as, owing to famine and distress over great portion of both Madras and Bombay, the number of prisoners in those parts was suddenly increased far beyond all precedent; the new prisoners were, in large proportion, received in a low state of health, consequent on continued privation; the jails having such large and unexpected calls for accommodation on them, were, as a rule, greatly overcrowded, and the sickness and mortality, as was to be expected, have been lamentably in excess of former years.'

General statistics, 1877.   The average number of prisoners throughout India in 1877 was returned at 110,147; admissions into hospital numbered 1017 per thousand; daily sick, 36 per thousand; average death-rate, 61·95 per thousand. The months of October and November gave the highest admission rate, 97; and the month of November the highest death-rate, 9·18. Dysentery, diarrhœa, and cholera were the main causes of mortality, the three together accounting for 33·61 out of the total of 61·95 per thousand. 'There are no previous figures with which these general results of 1877 can be compared; they deserve attention as the first collection of statistics regarding the sickness and mortality among the prisoners of all India, a collection which cannot fail in a few years to contribute very valuable

information.' The returns for the Bengal Presidency were very Returns
favourable, the mortality being 31·88 per thousand, as com- for the
three Pre-
pared with 37·51 in 1876, 33·65 in 1875, and 46·09, the sidencies,
average for the ten-year period, 1864–73. In the Madras Pre- in 1877;
sidency, the returns showed a mortality of 176·01, while the
ratio for the Bombay Presidency was 54·37 per thousand.
The causes of these high figures have already been indicated.
In only 17 of the 34 jails in the Madras Presidency was the
death-rate under 100 per thousand; in the others it varied
much, rising to 200, 300, 500, and in one (Coimbatore District
Jail) to 657 per thousand. And in Bombay Presidency,
where similar causes were at work, though in a minor degree,
the mortality, 54·37 per thousand, was double what it had
been for years.

Although 1877 was an abnormal year, especially in Madras in 1883.
and Bombay, owing to the causes stated above, the returns for
1883 show a great improvement in the vital statistics of Indian
jails over those of the previous five years. The average prison
population in India in 1883 was 88,174, as against 112,670 in
the previous five years; the admissions into hospital were
996 per thousand, as compared with an average of 1189 in
1877–81; average daily sick, 36 per thousand in 1883, as
compared with 44·9 per thousand in 1877–81. The cholera
mortality was in the ratio of 2·28 per thousand in 1883, against
an annual average of 4·48 for the previous five years; deaths
from dysentery and diarrhœa showed a ratio of 10·64 per
thousand in 1883, against 24·97 per thousand in the years
1877–81; while the deaths from all causes were 31·37 per
thousand in 1883, as against 63·01 per thousand in the five
years 1877–81. The heaviest jail mortality in 1883 was in
the Central Provinces (70·97 per thousand), Bengal (52·21
per thousand), and Assam (43·12 per thousand), while the
lowest ratio was reached in Berar, with only 8·49 deaths per
thousand.

The following tables condense the health statistics of the
Indian jails in 1877 and in 1883 :—

[SICKNESS

Sickness and Mortality in Indian Jails, 1877.

Province.	Average Strength.	Admissions into Hospital.	Daily Sick.	Cholera.	Bowel Complaints.	Atrophy and Anæmia.	All Causes.
		Ratio per 1000 of Average Strength.			Deaths.		
Bengal Proper, . .	17,862	1276	39	8·29	18·98	3·42	49·66
North-Western Provinces,[1]	21,668	535	21	1·43	5·45	1·89	19·71
Oudh,[1]	6,726	504	16	...	2·08	1·19	10·56
Punjab, ...	12,129	1504	37	·08	10·64	1·07	33·80
Central Provinces, . .	3,484	907	37	·29	12·92	12·92	45·06
Berar, ...	963	937	26	...	1·04	5·19	15·58
Assam, ...	1,261	1382	40	11·10	23·00	2·38	56·30
British Burma, . . .	4,686	844	38	19·63	18·56	4·27	56·76
Madras,[2]	20,328	967	40	26·12	85·15	24·50	176·01
Bombay,[2]	11,531	935	27	3·64	26·19	8·67	54·37
Andamans, . . .	9,039	1687	76	...	5·20	7·19	34·30

[1] These, although now under one Local Government, are shown separately for comparison with former years. The favourable results in Oudh are worthy of attention.

[2] It should be remembered that the mortality in the Madras and Bombay Jails in 1877 was greatly increased by the reception of starving prisoners during the famine.

Sickness and Mortality in Indian Jails, 1883.

Province.	Average Strength.	Admissions into Hospital.	Daily Sick.	Cholera.	Bowel Complaints.	Atrophy and Anæmia.	All Causes.
		Ratio per 1000 of Average Strength.			Deaths.		
Bengal Proper, . . .	14,288	1498	50	4·27	23·44	2·94	52·21
North-Western Provinces and Oudh, . .	22,924	563	23	2·18	4·32	1·48	19·76
Punjab, ...	12,128	951	27	...	6·18	1·24	29·11
Central Provinces, . .	3,875	919	36	2·84	46·71	4·13	70·97
Berar, ...	1,060	558	14	...	1·89	...	8·49
Assam, ...	1,206	2125	56	5·80	16·58	3·32	43·12
British Burma, . . .	5,149	1159	39	7·96	7·96	1·55	28·94
Madras, ...	7,666	861	32	1·96	12·78	2·61	29·87
Bombay, ...	7,806	734	27	2·05	6·79	1·67	34·33
Andamans, . . .	11,511	1454	67	...	2·87	·69	19·63

APPENDICES.

APPENDIX I.—AREA, TOWNS AND VILLAGES, HOUSES, POPULATION, ETC. OF BRITISH INDIA IN 1881.

(Compiled from the Tabular Statements appended to the Imperial Census Report.)

Provinces.	Area in square miles.	Towns, Villages, Manzais, etc.	Occupied Houses.	Population.			Average Number of—				
				Males.	Females.	Total Population.	Persons per square mile.	Villages, etc., per 100 square miles.	Persons per village.	Houses per square mile.	Persons per house.
Government of Madras,	141,001	52,648	5,711,325	15,421,043	15,749,588	31,170,631	221	37	592	46	5.5
" of Bombay, with Sind,	124,122	24,598	2,822,741	8,497,718	7,956,696	16,454,414	133	20	669	29	5.8
Lieutenant-Governorship of Bengal,[1]	193,198	264,765	11,036,774	34,625,591	34,911,270	69,536,861	360	137	263	60	6.3
" of the Punjab,	106,632	34,334	2,706,914	10,210,053	8,640,384	18,850,437	177	32	549	33	6.9
" of the North-Western Provinces, Chief-Commissionership of Oudh,	106,111	105,421	6,866,503	22,912,556	21,195,313	44,107,869	416	99	418	65	6.4
" of Central Provinces,	84,445	34,612	2,336,976	4,959,435	4,879,356	9,838,791	117	41	284	30	4.2
" of Assam,	46,341	22,408	859,388	2,503,703	2,377,723	4,881,426	105	48	218	19	5.6
Commissionership of Berar,	17,711	5,585	466,027	1,380,492	1,292,181	2,672,673	151	32	479	28	5.7
" of Ajmere,	2,711	739	64,118	248,844	211,878	460,722	170	27	623	32	7.2
" of Coorg,	1,583	503	22,357	100,439	77,863	178,302	113	32	354	16	7.9
Chief-Commissionership of British Burma,	87,220	15,857	677,362	1,991,005	1,745,766	3,736,771	43	18	236	8	5.5
TOTAL OF BRITISH INDIA,	911,075	561,460	33,570,485	102,850,879	99,038,018	201,888,897	222	62	360	37	6.0

1 The area returned for Bengal includes 5976 square miles of unsurveyed and half-submerged Sundarbans. The figures for Bengal also include 36,634 square miles of area, and 2,845,405 of population, belonging to Native States superintended directly by the Provincial Government.

2 X

APPENDIX II.—TOWNS AND VILLAGES IN BRITISH INDIA, CLASSIFIED ACCORDING TO POPULATION, IN 1881.

(Compiled from the Imperial Census Report.)

Provinces.	With less than 200 Inhabitants.	From 200 to 500 Inhabitants.	From 500 to 1000 Inhabitants.	From 1000 to 2000 Inhabitants.	From 2000 to 3000 Inhabitants.	From 3000 to 5000 Inhabitants.	From 5000 to 10,000 Inhabitants.	From 10,000 to 15,000 Inhabitants.	From 15,000 to 20,000 Inhabitants.	From 20,000 to 50,000 Inhabitants.	Upwards or 50,000 Inhabitants.	Total Number of Villages and Towns.
Government of Madras, . . .	21,559	14,067	9,379	5,042	1,291	813	404	48	15	21	9	52,648
,, of Bombay and Sind, .	7,067	8,534	5,471	2,464	545	319	132	39	8	13	6	24,598
Lieutenant-Governorship of Bengal, .	165,263	67,307	23,561	6,994	1,058	340	146	49	14	22	11	264,765
,, ,, of the Punjab,	11,937	11,879	6,348	2,954	693	349	115	20	8	13	8	34,324
,, ,, of the North-Western Provinces,	46,096	34,817	16,690	5,941	1,099	483	192	51	20	18	14	105,421
Chief-Commissionership of Oudh,	19,077	11,233	3,379	693	121	61	32	7	3	3	3	34,612
,, ,, of the Central Provinces, .	14,469	5,285	1,290	326	35	7	4	3	...	...	...	22,408
Chief-Commissionership of Assam,[1]	2,225	1,883	962	356	72	53	24	6	2	2	...	5,585
Commissionership of Berar,	271	244	125	51	16	11	4	...	1	2	...	739
,, of Ajmere,[2] ,, of Coorg,[2]	234	149	99	16	3	1	1	...	...	...	...	503
Chief-Commissionership of British Burma, .	9,963	4,886	819	142	19	8	10	2	4	2	2	15,857
TOTAL FOR BRITISH INDIA, .	298,161	160,284	68,123	24,979	4,952	2,445	1,064	225	75	96	53	561,460

[1] The details and the total of villages in Assam differ by 989 villages in the Gáro and Nágá Hills, which were not classified according to population.

[2] Details available for only 725 villages.

APPENDIX III.—CULTIVATED, CULTIVABLE, AND UNCULTIVABLE AREA, LAND REVENUE, ETC., IN 1881.

IN PROVINCES FOR WHICH RETURNS EXIST.

(*Compiled from the Provincial Census Reports.*)

PROVINCES.	Total Area Assessed and Unassessed in square miles.	GOVERNMENT ASSESSED AREA IN SQUARE MILES.				Total Government Land Revenue, including Cesses and Local Rates levied on Land.	Total Rental paid by Cultivators, including Cesses and Rates.	Average incidence of Government Revenue per Cultivated Acre.	Average incidence of Rent per Cultivated Acre.
		Total.	Cultivated.	Cultivable.	Un-cultivable.				
						£	£	s. d.	s. d.
Government of Madras, . . .	140,821	59,094	38,753	13,223	7,118	5,130,003	6,716,181	4 $1\frac{1}{4}$	5 $0\frac{5}{8}$
Government of Bombay, . . .	117,757	63,692	51,015	12,677	No returns.	3,602,097	No returns.	1 $10\frac{3}{4}$	...
Lieutenant-Governorship of Bengal, .	150,588	No returns.	No returns.	No returns.	No returns.	4,441,784	13,489,196	No returns.	
Lieut.-Governorship of the Punjab, .	107,010	97,662	32,467	34,261	30,934	2,302,359	4,879,054	2 0	4 $4\frac{1}{3}$
Lieutenant-Governorship of the N.-Western Provinces and Oudh,	106,111	95,981	52,056	19,266	24,659	6,573,536	11,647,767	3 $11\frac{1}{8}$	6 $8\frac{5}{8}$
Chief-Commissionership of the Central Provinces, . . .	84,445	64,121	24,462	20,163	19,496	647,345	1,326,024	0 $9\frac{7}{8}$	1 $8\frac{7}{8}$
Chief-Commissionership of Assam (exclusive of hill tracts), . .	27,666	6,714	6,714	No returns.	No returns.	383,543	No returns.	1 $9\frac{1}{2}$	...
Commissionership of Berar, . .	17,714	12,702	10,069	1,773	860	677,317	No returns.	2 $1\frac{1}{3}$	...
Commissionership of Coorg, . .	1,583	285	186	99	No returns.	36,058	36,058	6 $0\frac{3}{4}$	6 $0\frac{3}{4}$
Commissionership of Ajmere, . .	2,711	1,766	910	36	820	40,933	No returns.	2 0	No rets.
Chief-Commissionership of British Burma, ...	87,220	5,443	5,400	43	No returns.	703,237	No returns.	4 $0\frac{5}{8}$	...
TOTAL, . . .	843,626[1]	407,460	222,032	101,541	83,887	24,538,212	38,094,280	2 $9\frac{1}{4}$[2]	...

[1] The areas in this column are in some cases only approximate to those given in the general table of area and population of British India.
[2] This average is exclusive of Bengal, for which Province no details of cultivated, cultivable, and uncultivable area are available.

APPENDIX IV.—POPULATION OF BRITISH INDIA, CLASSIFIED ACCORDING TO SEX AND AGE, IN 1881.

(Compiled from the Tables of the Imperial Census Report.)

PROVINCES.	MALES.				FEMALES.				BOTH SEXES.			
	Boys under 15.	Male Adults 15 and upwards.	Age unspecified.	Total Males.	Girls under 15.	Female Adults 15 and upwards.	Age unspecified.	Total Females.	Children under 15.	Adults 15 and upwards.	Age unspecified.	Grand Total.
Government of Madras, .	5,886,087	9,040,879	494,077	15,421,043	5,761,831	9,527,603	460,154	15,749,588	11,647,918	18,568,482	954,231	31,170,651
Government of Bombay, .	3,371,089	5,126,629	..	8,497,718	3,065,956	4,890,740	..	7,956,696	6,437,045	10,017,369	..	16,454,414
Lieut.-Governorship of Bengal,[1]	14,229,149	20,271,425	125,017	34,625,591	13,420,629	21,382,277	108,364	34,911,270	27,649,778	41,653,702	233,381	69,536,861
Lt.-Governorship of the Punjab,	3,928,578	6,274,254	7,221	10,210,053	3,314,052	5,326,176	756	8,640,384	7,242,630	11,600,430	7,377	18,850,437
Lt.-Governorship of the North-Western Provinces and Oudh,	8,735,283	14,177,273	..	22,912,556	7,651,764	13,543,549	..	21,195,313	16,387,047	27,720,822	...	44,107,869
Chief-Commissionership of the Central Provinces, .	2,053,909	2,905,326	200	4,959,435	1,949,987	2,929,182	187	4,879,356	4,003,896	5,834,508	387	9,838,791
Chief-Commissionership of Assam	1,011,010	1,401,303	91,390	2,503,703	938,905	1,349,172	89,646	2,377,723	1,949,915	2,750,475	181,036	4,881,426
Commissionership of Berar, .	513,382	867,110	..	1,380,492	497,496	794,685	..	1,292,181	1,010,878	1,661,795	..	2,672,673
Commissionership of Ajmere, .	89,033	159,811	..	248,844	75,472	136,406	..	211,878	164,505	296,217	..	460,722
Commissionership of Coorg, .	30,986	69,453	..	100,439	28,911	48,952	..	77,863	59,897	118,405	..	178,302
Chief-Com. of British Burma, .	776,890	1,214,115	..	1,991,005	734,526	1,011,240	..	1,745,766	1,511,416	2,225,355	..	3,736,771
TOTAL, .	40,625,396	61,507,578	717,905	102,850,879	37,439,529	60,939,982	658,507	99,038,018	78,064,925	122,447,560	1,376,412	201,883,897

1 Including Native States superintended directly by the Bengal Provincial Government.

APPENDIX V.—POPULATION OF BRITISH INDIA, CLASSIFIED ACCORDING TO RELIGION, IN 1881.

(Compiled from the Tables of the Imperial Census Report.)

Provinces.	Hindus.	Muhammadans.	Aboriginal Tribes.	Buddhists.	Christians.	Sikhs.	Jains.	Satnámis.	Kabírpanthis.	Nat-Worshippers.	Pársís.	Jews.	Bráhmos.	Kumbhipathias.	Unspecified and Others.	Total of all Religions.
Government of Madras,	28,497,678	1,933,561	...	1,535	711,080	...	24,973	...	...	...	143	30	132	...	1499	31,170,631
Government of Bombay,	12,308,582	3,021,131	562,678	...	138,317	127,100	216,224	...	...	...	72,065	7,952	...	...	365	16,454,414
Lieutenant - Governorship of Bengal,[1].	45,452,806	21,704,724	2,055,822	155,809	128,135	549	1,609	...	...	...	156	1,059	788	...	35,404	69,536,861
Lieutenant - Governorship of the Punjab,	7,130,528	10,525,150	...	2,864	33,420	1,121,004	35,826	...	...	...	462	...	...	...	1,183	18,850,437
Lieutenant - Governorship of the North-Western Provinces, Chief-Commissionership of Oudh.	38,055,394	5,922,886	...	102	47,664	3,644	799,957	...	...	...	114	101	6	...	...	44,107,869
Chief-Commissionership of the Central Provinces,	7,317,830	275,773	1,533,599	17	11,949	97	45,718	358,161	294,474	...	399	63	7	692	12	9,838,791
Chief-Commissionership of Assam,	3,062,148	1,317,022	488,251	6,563	7,093	14	158	...	...	...	242	...	177	...	...	4,881,426
Commissionership of Berar,	2,425,654	187,555	37,338	1	1,335	525	20,020	...	...	...	75	3	...	...	...	2,672,673
Commissionership of Ajmere,	376,029	57,809	...	...	2,225	182	24,308	...	...	...	21	94	...	...	...	460,722
Commissionership of Coorg,	162,489	12,541	...	...	3,152	...	99	...	...	...	...	...	...	...	...	178,302
Chief - Commissionership of British Burma,	88,177	168,881	...	3,251,584	84,219	...	5	...	...	143,581	83	204	37	...	...	3,736,771
TOTAL FOR BRITISH INDIA,	144,875,315	45,127,033	4,677,688	3,418,476	1,168,589	1,253,115	448,897	358,161	294,474	143,581	73,760	9,506	1,147	692	38,463	201,888,897

1 Including Native States superintended directly by the Bengal Provincial Government.

APPENDIX VI.—ASIATIC NON-INDIAN POPULATION OF BRITISH INDIA, CLASSIFIED ACCORDING TO BIRTH-PLACE, IN 1881.

(*Compiled from the Tables in the Imperial Census Report.*)

Provinces.	Afghanistán.	Arabia.	Baluchistán.	China.	Nepál.	Upper Burma.	Armenia.	Bhután.	Ceylon.	Japan.	Java.	Persia.	Siam.	Straits Settlements.	Tibet.	Turkey in Asia.	Other Asiatic Countries, and unspecified. 1216
Government of Madras,	127	498	114	81	330	4	...	...	2332	9	4	31	15	390	3	72	
Government of Bombay,	7,265	4,626	57,312	285	105	...	...	...	70	...	15	2,672	12	130	1	215	
Lieutenant-Governorship of Bengal,	834	354	...	825	85,011	98	11	3,549	77	8	...	313	3	175	1,090	...	
Lieutenant - Governorship of the Punjab,	112,712	196	1,478	97	2,660	...	...	30	18	5	1	63	2	10	706	...	
Lieut.-Governorship of the North-Western Provinces and Oudh,	1,140	223	1	28	39,490	...	4	17	71	3	...	65	...	...	956	16	
Chief - Commissionership of the Central Provinces,	225	20	17	27	66	...	...	...	12	...	...	7	...	7	...	...	
Chief-Commissionership of Assam,	58	1	2	13	6,395	...	...	1,367	1	...	...	1	...	4	...	2	
Commissionership of Berar,	90	14	...	1	5	...	...	1	...	...	...	3	...	...	...	5	
Commissionership of Ajmere,	106	24	...	...	17	...	...	...	1	...	...	...	...	...	...	...	
Commissionership of Coorg,	17	...	...	4	1	...	...	...	14	...	1	...	...	...	...	...	
Chief-Commissionership of British Burma,	24	77	...	11,314	60	334,737	2	...	82	11	...	69	2,509	1,140	...	...	
TOTAL,	122,598	6,033	58,924	12,675	134,140	334,839	17	4,964	2678	36	21	3,224	2,541	1,856	2,756	310	1216

Grand total of Asiatic non-Indians residing in British India, 688,828.

APPENDIX VII.—NON-ASIATIC POPULATION OF BRITISH INDIA, CLASSIFIED ACCORDING TO BIRTH-PLACE, IN 1881.

(Compiled from the Tables of the Imperial Census Report.)

Provinces.	United Kingdom	Africa	America	Australia	Austria	Bavaria	Belgium	Denmark	France	Germany	Greece	Holland	Iceland	Ionian Isles	Italy	Malta	Norway	Portugal	Prussia	Roumania	Russia	Spain	Sweden	Switzerland	Turkey in Europe	Other European Countries, and unspecified
Government of Madras	5,883	786	142	35	13		46	26	382	146	4	23		4	59	15	10	59	6		20	9	28	35	6	
,, of Bombay	13,772	1775	286	94	81		50	1	123	194	49	1			72	11	3	20	13		45	6	15	5		
Lieutenant-Governorship of Bengal	10,583	315	397	113	133		53	49	216	306	61	27	5		158	22	82	23		24	94	29	131	30	250	
Lieutenant-Governorship of the Punjab	17,590	23	99	11	8	1	3	2	42	73	2	2			8	8		8			1	14	4	1	15	
Lieutenant-Governorship of the North-Western Provinces and Oudh	20,184	183	195	56	7		1		48	64	58	2	3		44	10		2	5			8	1	9	68	
Chief-Commissionership of the Central Provinces	2,774	6	26	10		1			24	5	2	2			9			5	6		12		8	1		
Chief-Commissionership of Assam	795	6	26	14			3	1	8	5					2	1	1	1					1			
Commissionership of Berar	97	5	6				1		1	3							1							1		
Commissionership of Ajmere	872	4	9	3			1		4	6					3			8								
Commissionership of Coorg	134	1	2	1					8	10					2											
Chief-Commissionership of British Burma	5,346	18	143	18	52		12	44	85	337	19	21			388	35	260	7			26	12	148	3	13	
TOTAL, .	78,030	3122	1331	355	294	2	170	123	941	1149	195	78	8	4	745	102	357	133	30	24	198	78	336	85	352	541

Grand total non-Asiatic population of British India, 88,783. This table is reproduced from the Imperial Census Report. But by comparing it with other materials, it evidently leaves a considerable number of the non-Asiatic population of India unaccounted for (probably the British troops). The table showing the Christian population according to race and sect returns the total of British-born and other Europeans in India at 142,612.

APPENDIX VIII.—LIST OF THE 149 TOWNS IN BRITISH INDIA OF WHICH THE POPULATION
EXCEEDS 20,000, IN 1881.

(*Compiled from the Table in the Imperial Census Report.*)

NAME OF TOWN.	PROVINCE.	DISTRICT.	POPULATION.
1. Bombay City and Island, . .	Bombay, . . .	... ...	773,196
2. Calcutta City, ...	Bengal, . . .	... ...	433,219
3. Calcutta Suburbs, . . .	Bengal, . . .	... ...	251,439
Total, . .	. . . . .	. . . .	684,658
4. South Suburban, . . .	Bengal, . . .	24 Parganás, . .	51,658
5. North Suburban, . . .	Bengal, . . .	24 Parganás, . .	29,982
Grand total of Calcutta and suburbs,	. . . . . .	. . . .	766,298
6. Madras City, ...	Madras, . . .	... ...	405,848
7. Lucknow, ...	Oudh, . . .	Lucknow, . . .	261,303
8. Benares, ...	N.-W. Provinces, .	Benares, . . .	199,700
9. Delhi, ...	Punjab, . . .	Delhi, . . .	173,393
10. Patná, ...	Bengal, . . .	Patná, . . .	170,654
11. Agra, ...	N.-W. Provinces, .	Agra, . . .	160,203
12. Bangalore, ...	Mysore, . . .	Bangalore, . .	155,857
13. Amritsar, ...	Punjab, . . .	Amritsar, . . .	151,896
14. Cawnpur, ...	N.-W. Provinces, .	Cawnpur, . . .	151,444
15. Lahore, ...	Punjab, . . .	Lahore, . . .	149,369
16. Allahábád, ...	N.-W. Provinces, .	Allahábád, . .	148,547
17. Rangoon, ...	British Burma, .	Rangoon, . . .	134,176
18. Poona, ...	Bombay, . . .	Poona, . . .	129,751
19. Ahmadábád, ...	Bombay, . . .	Ahmadábád, . .	127,651
20. Bareilly (Bareli), . . .	N.-W. Provinces, .	Bareilly, . . .	113,417
21. Surat, ...	Bombay, . . .	Surat, . . .	109,844
22. Howrah, ...	Bengal, . . .	Howrah, . . .	105,206
23. Meerut, ...	N.-W. Provinces, .	Meerut, . . .	99,565
24. Nágpur, ...	Central Provinces, .	Nágpur, . . .	98,299
25. Trichinopoli, . . .	Madras, . . .	Trichinopoli, . .	84,449
26. Pesháwar, ...	Punjab, . . .	Pesháwar, . .	79,982
27. Dacca, ...	Bengal, . . .	Dacca, . . .	79,076
28. Gayá, ...	Bengal, . . .	Gayá, . . .	76,415
29. Jabalpur, ...	Central Provinces, .	Jabalpur, . . .	75,705
30. Sháhjahánpur, . . .	N.-W. Provinces, .	Sháhjahánpur, .	74,830
31. Madura, ...	Madras, . . .	Madura, . . .	73,807
32. Karáchí, ...	Sind, . . .	Karáchí, . . .	73,560
33. Múltán, ...	Punjab, . . .	Múltán, . . .	68,674
34. Bhágalpur, ...	Bengal, . . .	Bhágalpur, . .	68,238
35. Ambála, ...	Punjab, . . .	Ambála, . . .	67,463
36. Moradábád, ...	N.-W. Provinces, .	Moradábád, . .	67,387
37. Darbhanga, ...	Bengal, . . .	Darbhanga, . .	65,955
38. Farukhábád.	N.-W. Provinces, .	Farukhábád, . .	62,437
39. Koil (Alígarh), . . .	N.-W. Provinces, .	Alígarh, . . .	61,730
40. Sholápur, ...	Bombay, . . .	Sholápur, . . .	61,281
41. Saháranpur, ...	N.-W. Provinces, .	Saháranpur, . .	59,194
42. Gorakhpur, ...	N.-W. Provinces, .	Gorakhpur, . .	57,922
43. Calicut, ...	Madras, . . .	Malabar, . . .	57,385
44. Mírzapur, ...	N.-W. Provinces, .	Mírzapur, . . .	56,378
45. Faizábád, ...	Oudh, . . .	Faizábád, . . .	55,570
46. Monghyr, ...	Bengal, . . .	Monghyr, . . .	55,372
47. Tanjore, ...	Madras, . . .	Tanjore, . . .	54,745
48. Negapatam, ...	Madras, . . .	Tanjore, . . .	53,855
49. Bellary, ...	Madras, . . .	Bellary, . . .	53,460
50. Maulmain, ...	British Burma, .	Maulmain, . .	53,107
51. Ráwal Pindi, . . .	Punjab, . . .	Ráwal Pindi, . .	52,975
52. Jálandhar, ...	Punjab, . . .	Jálandhar, . .	52,119
53. Chaprá, ...	Bengal, . . .	Sáran, . . .	51,670
54. Khampti, ...	Central Provinces, .	Nágpur, . . .	50,987
55. Salem, ...	Madras, . . .	Salem, . . .	50,667
56. Combaconum, . . .	Madras, . . .	Tanjore, . . .	50,098
57. Behar, ...	Bengal, . . .	Patná, . . .	48,968
58. Ajmere, ...	Rájputána, . .	Ajmere, . . .	48,735
59. Haidarábád, ...	Sind, . . .	Haidarábád, . .	48,153
60. Muttra, ...	N.-W. Provinces, .	Muttra, . . .	47,483
61. Siálkot, ...	Punjab, . . .	Siálkot, . . .	45,762
62. Ságar (Saugor) . . .	Central Provinces, .	Ságar, . . .	44,416
63. Ludhiána, ...	Punjab, . . .	Ludhiána, . . .	44,163
64. Cuddalore, ...	Madras, . . .	South Arcot, .	43,545
65. Arrah, ...	Bengal, . . .	Shahábád, . .	42,998
66. Jaunpur, ...	N.-W. Provinces, .	Jaunpur, . . .	42,845
67. Cuttack, ...	Bengal, . . .	Cuttack, . . .	42,656
68. Shikárpur, ...	Sind, . . .	Shikárpur, . .	42,496
69. Muzaffarpur, . . .	Bengal, . . .	Muzaffarpur, . .	42,460
70. Murshidábád, . . .	Bengal, . . .	Murshidábád, . .	39,231
71. Firozpur, ...	Punjab, . . .	Firozpur, . . .	39,570

LIST OF 149 TOWNS IN BRITISH INDIA OF WHICH THE POPULATION EXCEEDS 20,000—*continued.*

NAME OF TOWN.	PROVINCE.	DISTRICT.	POPULATION.
74. Ahmadnagar,	Bombay,	Ahmadnagar,	37,492
75. Vellore,	Madras,	North Arcot,	37,491
76. Broach,	Bombay,	Broach,	37,281
77. Conjevaram,	Madras,	Chengalpat,	37,275
78. Hubli,	Bombay,	Dhárwár,	36,677
79. Pálghát,	Madras,	Malabar,	36,339
80. Amroha,	N.-W. Provinces,	Moradábád,	36,145
81. Bandar (Masulipatam),	Madras,	Kistna,	35,056
82. Etawah,	N.-W. Provinces,	Etawah,	34,721
83. Bardwán,	Bengal,	Bardwán,	34,080
84. Akyab,	British Burma,	Akyab,	33,989
85. Bhiwání,	Punjab,	Hissár,	33,762
86. Budaun,	N.-W. Provinces,	Budaun,	33,680
87. Midnapur,	Bengal,	Midnapur,	33,560
88. Gházípur,	N.-W. Provinces,	Ghazípur,	32,885
89. Belgáum,	Bombay,	Belgáum,	32,697
90. Mangalore,	Madras,	S. Kánara.	32,099
91. Húglí and Chinsura,	Bengal,	Húglí,	31,177
92. Agarpárá,	Bengal,	24 Parganás,	30,317
93. Vizagapatam,	Madras,	Vizagapatam,	30,291
94. Burhanpur,	Central Provinces,	Nimár,	30,017
95. Pilíbhít,	N.-W. Provinces,	Pilíbhít,	29,721
96. Sántipur,	Bengal,	Nadiyá,	29,687
97. Satára,	Bombay,	Satára,	29,028
98. Bandá,	N.-W. Provinces,	Bandá,	28,974
99. Coconada,	Madras,	Godávari,	28,856
100. Prome,	British Burma,	Prome,	28,813
101. Nadiád,	Bombay,	Kaira,	28,304
102. Bassein,	British Burma,	Bassein,	28,147
103. Chandausi,	N.-W. Provinces,	Moradábád,	27,521
104. Nellore,	Madras,	Nellore,	27,505
105. Krishnagar,	Bengal,	Nadiyá,	27,477
106. Sukkur,	Sind,	Shikárpur,	27,389
107. Dhárwár,	Bombay,	Dhárwár,	27,191
108. Khurjá,	N.-W. Provinces,	Bulandshahr,	27,190
109. Násik,	Bombay,	Násik,	27,070
110. Ellichpur,	Berar,	Ellichpur,	26,728
111. Tellicherri,	Madras,	Malabar,	26,410
112. Cannanore,	Madras,	Malabar,	26,386
113. Hathrás,	N.-W. Provinces,	Alígarh,	25,656
114. Serampur,	Bengal,	Húglí,	25,559
115. Ellore,	Madras,	Godávari,	25,092
116. Hájípur,	Bengal,	Muzaffarpur,	25,078
117. Pánipat,	Punjab,	Karnál,	25,022
118. Ráipur,	Central Provinces,	Ráipur,	24,948
119. Rájáhmahendri (Rajahmundry),	Madras,	Godávari,	24,555
120. Batála,	Punjab,	Gurdaspur,	24,281
121. Rewárí,	Punjab,	Gurgáon,	23,972
122. Berhampur,	Bengal,	Murshidábád,	23,605
123. Berhampur,	Madras,	Ganjám,	23,599
124. Amráoti,	Berár,	Amráoti,	23,550
125. Tinnevelli,	Madras,	Tinnevelli,	23,221
126. Karnál,	Punjab,	Karnál,	23,133
127. Mayavaram,	Madras,	Tanjore,	23,044
128. Gujránwála,	Punjab,	Gujránwála,	22,884
129. Vizianágaram,	Madras,	Vizagapatam,	22,577
130. Adoni,	Madras,	Bellary,	22,441
131. Dera Ghází Khán,	Punjab,	D. G. Khán,	22,309
132. Dera Ismáil Khán,	Punjab,	D. I. Khán,	22,164
133. Deoband,	N.-W. Provinces,	Saharanpur,	22,116
134. Purí,	Bengal,	Purí,	22,095
135. Naihátí,	Bengal,	24 Parganás,	21,533
136. Brindában,	N.-W. Provinces,	Muttra,	21,467
137. Sambhál,	N.-W. Provinces,	Moradábád,	21,373
138. Hoshiarpur,	Punjab,	Hoshiarpur,	21,363
139. Fatehpur,	N.-W. Provinces,	Fatehpur,	21,328
140. Nasírábád,	Ajmere,	Ajmere,	21,320
141. Bettiah,	Bengal,	Champáran,	21,263
142. Jehlam (Jhelum),	Punjab,	Jehlam,	21,107
143. Sirájganj,	Bengal,	Pabná,	21,037
144. Chittagong,	Bengal,	Chittagong,	20,969
145. Nagína,	N.-W. Provinces,	Bijnaur,	20,503
146. Karnúl (Kurnool),	Madras,	Karnúl,	20,329
147. Balasor,	Bengal,	Balasor,	20,265
148. Mainpurí,	N.-W. Provinces,	Mainpurí,	20,236
149. Pánroti,	Madras,	S. Arcot,	20,172

Population of 56 towns with above 50,000 inhabitants,			6,591,810
Population of 93 towns between 20,000 and 30,000,			2,794,935
Total population of 149 largest towns			9,386,745

APPENDIX IX.—POPULATION OF BRITISH INDIA, CLASSIFIED ACCORDING TO EDUCATION, IN 1881.

(Compiled from the Table in the Imperial Census Report.)

| | ALL RELIGIONS. | | | | | | HINDUS. | | | | | |
| | Male. | | | Female. | | | Male. | | | Female. | | |
PROVINCES.	Under Instruction.	Able to Read and Write, but not under Instruction.	Total Male Population.	Under Instruction.	Able to Read and Write, but not under Instruction.	Total Female Population.	Under Instruction.	Able to Read and Write, but not under Instruction.	Total Male Hindus.	Under Instruction.	Able to Read and Write, but not under Instruction.	Total Female Hindus.
Government of Madras,	519,823	1,535,790	15,421,043	39,104	94,571	15,749,588	449,034	1,363,866	14,104,951	22,113	65,536	14,592,727
,, of Bombay,	271,469	672,895	8,497,718	18,460	32,648	7,956,696	199,765	485,851	6,291,598	6,331	9,937	6,016,984
Lieut.-Governorship of Bengal,	1,009,999	1,991,583	34,625,591	35,760	61,449	34,911,270	753,267	1,546,140	22,578,544	21,295	38,460	22,874,262
,, of the Punjab,	157,623	482,129	10,210,053	6,101	8,407	8,640,384	76,000	325,069	3,883,915	913	1,973	3,246,613
Lieut.-Governorship of the North-Western Provinces and Oudh,	299,225	1,033,458	22,912,556	9,771	21,590	21,195,313	232,055	879,182	19,813,098	3,298	10,874	18,240,296
Chief-Commissionership of the Central Provinces,	76,849	157,023	4,959,435	3,171	4,187	4,879,356	63,475	130,271	3,700,467	1,794	1,941	3,617,363
Chief-Commissionership of Assam,	33,376	79,644	2,503,703	1,068	1,786	2,377,723	24,333	62,626	1,580,458	482	982	1,481,650
Commissionership of Berar,	27,347	57,827	1,380,492	356	789	1,292,181	23,659	50,623	1,252,541	221	445	1,173,113
,, of Ajmere,	5,697	24,486	248,844	245	963	211,878	3,427	14,131	202,226	86	450	173,803
,, of Coorg,	4,268	8,839	100,439	431	356	77,863	3,817	6,982	90,705	333	145	71,784
Chief-Commissionership of British Burma,	215,237	701,828	1,991,005	31,056	31,740	1,745,766	1,369	15,300	73,929	227	365	14,248
	2,620,913	6,745,502	102,850,879	145,523	258,486	99,038,018	1,830,201	4,880,041	73,572,432	57,993	131,108	71,302,883

APPENDIX IX.—POPULATION OF BRITISH INDIA, CLASSIFIED ACCORDING TO EDUCATION, IN 1881—*continued.*

Provinces.	Muhammadans — Male: Under Instruction.	Muhammadans — Male: Able to Read and Write, but not under Instruction.	Muhammadans — Male: Total Male Muhammadans.	Muhammadans — Female: Under Instruction.	Muhammadans — Female: Able to Read and Write, but not under Instruction.*	Muhammadans — Female: Total Female Muhammadans.	Christians — Male: Under Instruction.	Christians — Male: Able to Read and Write, but not under Instruction.	Christians — Male: Total Male Christians.	Christians — Female: Under Instruction.	Christians — Female: Able to Read and Write, but not under Instruction.	Christians — Female: Total Female Christians.
Government of Madras,	42,656	110,897	952,388	4,353	8,121	981,173	27,020	57,176	349,082	12,592	20,784	361,998
,, of Bombay,	36,477	71,889	1,612,154	3,526	4,586	1,408,977	7,723	23,943	81,190	3,999	6,935	57,127
Lieut.-Governorship of Bengal,	244,158	415,666	10,855,771	8,241	11,747	10,848,953	7,498	20,149	67,715	5,295	10,322	60,420
Lieut.-Governorship of the Punjab,	68,551	95,816	5,639,845	3,224	2,399	4,885,305	2,254	17,874	25,044	1,629	3,550	8,376
of the North-Western Provinces and Oudh,	57,850	116,763	3,022,445	2,428	3,474	2,900,441	5,632	19,988	31,208	3,958	7,030	16,456
Chief-Commissionership of the Central Provinces,	6,752	12,720	140,611	451	667	135,162	972	4,213	7,170	645	1,327	4,779
Chief-Commissionership of Assam,	7,614	14,397	673,189	89	205	643,833	441	1,549	4,088	306	492	3,005
Commissionership of Berar,	2,760	3,859	97,230	85	117	90,325	78	424	772	38	182	563
,, of Ajmere,	777	1,853	31,999	41	55	25,810	154	1,110	1,551	106	329	674
of Coorg,	305	1,112	7,880	35	30	4,661	144	716	1,775	62	177	1,377
Chief-Commissionership of British Burma,	5,711	22,121	110,731	1,161	1,094	58,150	6,260	17,024	46,419	2,951	5,212	37,800
	473,611	867,003	23,144,243	23,634	32,495	21,982,790	58,176	164,166	616,014	31,491	56,340	552,575

APPENDIX IX.—POPULATION OF BRITISH INDIA, CLASSIFIED ACCORDING TO EDUCATION, IN 1881—*continued.*

PROVINCES.	BUDDHISTS.						SIKHS.					
	Male.			Female.			Male.			Female.		
	Under Instruction.	Able to Read and Write, but not under Instruction.	Total Male Buddhists.	Under Instruction.	Able to Read and Write, but not under Instruction.	Total Female Buddhists.	Under Instruction.	Able to Read and Write, but not under Instruction.	Total Male Sikhs.	Under Instruction.	Able to Read and Write, but not under Instruction.	Total Female Sikhs.
Government of Madras,	38	239	864	...	...	671	...	...	...	...	...	...
„ of Bombay,	...	...	...	...	...	...	6,093	21,396	67,613	206	345	59,487
Lieut.-Governorship of Bengal,	1,696	5,172	78,555	96	193	77,254	20	90	304	1	3	245
„ of the Punjab,	33	196	1,359	...	...	1,505	9,458	35,976	639,460	305	435	481,544
Lieut.-Governorship of the North-Western Provinces and Oudh,	9	17	61	...	...	42	283	818	2,776	3	13	868
Chief-Commissionership of the Central Provinces,	1	3	10	...	...	7	4	20	59	...	...	38
Chief-Commissionership of Assam,	247	535	3,863	...	54	2,700	1	2	5	...	...	9
Commissionership of Berar,	...	1	1	...	...	...	5	53	305	...	1	220
„ of Ajmere,	...	...	...	...	...	...	15	39	115	...	1	67
Chief-Commissionership of Coorg, „ of British Burma,	199,836	644,742	1,686,263	26,094	24,816	1,565,321	...	...	...	...	...	...
	201,860	650,905	1,770,976	26,190	25,063	1,647,500	15,879	58,394	710,637	515	798	542,478

APPENDIX IX.—POPULATION OF BRITISH INDIA, CLASSIFIED ACCORDING TO EDUCATION, IN 1881—*continued.*

PROVINCES.	JAINS.						PARSIS.					
	Male.			Female.			Male.			Female.		
	Under Instruction.	Able to Read and Write, but not under Instruction.	Total Male Jains.	Under Instruction.	Able to Read and Write, but not under Instruction.	Total Female Jains.	Under Instruction.	Able to Read and Write, but not under Instruction.	Total Male Pársis.	Under Instruction.	Able to Read and Write, but not under Instruction.	Total Female Pársis.
Government of Madras,	1,023	3,483	12,761	31	96	12,212	19	56	87	4	17	56
,, of Bombay,	11,680	49,288	118,350	261	546	97,874	8,463	18,350	36,744	3,950	9,878	35,321
Lieut.-Governorship of Bengal,	138	716	1,174	10	11	435	22	75	117	7	20	39
,, of the Punjab,	1,283	7,034	19,047	19	19	16,779	41	148	312	11	24	150
Lieut.-Governorship of the North-Western Provinces and Oudh,	3,371	16,582	42,819	74	172	37,138	11	70	88	3	11	26
Chief-Commissionership of the Central Provinces,	2,007	6,809	23,570	190	104	22,148	35	177	265	10	47	134
Chief-Commissionership of Assam,	9	133	145	...	...	13	...	...	...	...	...	...
Commissionership of Berar,	821	2,749	10,752	6	7	9,268	22	92	157	6	36	85
,, of Ajmere,	1,313	7,286	12,846	10	114	11,462	1	37	51	1	6	24
,, of Coorg,	1	17	66	...	...	33	1	12	13	1	4	8
Chief-Commissionership of British Burma,	...	3	3	...	2	2	7	34	56	3	8	27
	21,646	94,100	241,533	601	1,071	207,364	8,622	19,051	37,890	3,996	10,051	35,870

APPENDIX IX.—POPULATION OF BRITISH INDIA, CLASSIFIED ACCORDING TO EDUCATION, IN 1881—*continued.*

| PROVINCES. | ALL OTHERS, including Kabírpanthis, Satnámís, Kumbhipathiás, Jews, Nat-worshippers, Bráhmos, Aboriginal Tribes, and unspecified. | | | | | |
| | Male. | | | Female. | | |
	Under Instruction.	Able to Read and Write, but not under Instruction.	Total Male 'Others.'	Under Instruction.	Able to Read and Write, but not under Instruction.	Total Female 'Others.'
Government of Madras, . .	33	73	910	11	17	751
„ of Bombay,. .	1,268	2,178	290,069	277	421	280,926
Lieut.-Governorship of Bengal, .	3,200	3,575	1,043,411	815	693	1,049,662
„ of the North-Western Provinces and Oudh, .	3	16	1,071	...	7	112
Chief - Commissionership of the Central Provinces, . .	14	38	61	7	16	46
Chief-Commissionership of Assam, .	3,603	2,810	1,087,283	81	101	1,099,725
Commissionership of Berar, . .	731	492	241,955	191	53	246,473
„ of Ajmere, . .	2	26	18,734	...	1	18,607
„ of Coorg, . .	10	30	56	1	8	38
Chief-Commissionership of British Burma, .	2,054	2,604	73,604	620	243	70,218
	10,918	11,842	2,757,154	2,003	1,560	2,766,558

(Compiled from the Tables in the Provincial Census Reports.)

PROVINCES.	HINDUS.			MUHAMMADANS.					CHRISTIANS.			ABORIGINAL TRIBES.	MISCELLANEOUS.[1]	GRAND TOTAL.
	Bráhmans.	Rájputs.	Other Castes.	Sunnís.	Shíahs.	Wahábís, Faráizís.	Unspecified.		Natives.	Eurasians.	British Born and other Europeans.			
Madras,	1,122,070	207,465	27,168,143	1,758,375	44,378	1,102	129,706		564,904	21,892	125,184	...	28,312	31,170,631
Bombay,	664,411	196,906	11,447,265	2,940,764	78,531	178	1,653		111,823	2,893	23,601	562,678	423,706	16,454,414
Bengal,	2,754,100	1,409,354	41,289,352	20,964,657	262,293	2,144	475,630		86,366	14,705	27,124	2,055,822	195,374	69,536,861
Punjab,	809,081	652,181	5,669,266	10,320,022	95,655	2,414	107,059		3,823	1,821	27,776	...	1,161,339	18,850,437
N.-W. Provinces and Oudh,	4,655,204	3,027,400	30,370,790	5,752,056	170,547	28	255		13,255	7,726	26,683	...	83,925	44,107,869
Central Provinces,	332,207	221,849	6,765,774	259,608	6,772	186	9,207		5,558	1,230	5,161	1,533,599	699,640	9,838,791
Assam,	119,075	10,541	2,932,532	1,308,712	6,377	1,340	593		5,462	1,631	...	488,251	6,912	4,881,426
Berar,	65,754	46,148	2,313,752	185,686	1,360	39	470		579	542	214	37,338	20,791	2,672,673
Ajmere,	22,388	15,876	337,765	57,262	547	...	...		799	196	1,230	...	24,659	460,722
Coorg,	2,445	480	159,564	12,540	1	...	...		2,637	287	228	...	120	178,302
British Burma,	...	...	88,177	150,821	11,287	1,249	5,524		71,355	4,998	7,866	...	3,395,494	3,736,771
TOTAL FOR BRITISH INDIA,	10,546,735	5,788,200	128,540,380	43,710,503	677,748	8,680	730,102		865,601	57,921	245,067	4,677,688	6,040,272	201,888,897

[1] Includes Buddhists, Jains, Pársís, Satnámís, Kabírpanthís, Jews, Bráhmos, etc.

N.B.—The figures given in this table are compiled direct from the Provincial Census Reports. It will be observed that in regard to the Christian population, some of the figures differ from those given in previous tables from the Imperial Census Report. The difference probably arises from the 'unspecified' columns being in some cases included as 'Europeans' in the Provincial Census Reports. The total of Christians agrees with the special returns of Christians within British India compiled for chapter ix. of this volume.

INDEX.

——o——

A

Companies, 374-376 ; Swedish Company (1731 A.D.), 376 ; causes of failure of foreign European Companies, and of English success in India, 376, 377 ; European traders in India in 1872 and 1881, 377.

Everest, Mount, peak of the Himálayas, and highest measured mountain in the world, 5.

Everest, Rev. Mr., calculations regarding silt discharge of Ganges, 27.

Exchange, Loss by, 469.

Excise administration, distilleries, rice-beer, opium, *gánjá, charas*, 454, 455 ; 467 ; expenditure and income of British India, 465-470.

Excommunication from caste privileges, 199, 200.

Executive Council of the Governor-General, 432.

Export trade of India, its origin and growth, analysis and principal staples of, 567 ; 569-580 ; distribution of exports to different countries, 569, 580 ; coasting trade, 584-586.

External sources of the ancient history of India, 163.

F

Fa-Hian, Chinese Buddhist pilgrim of the 5th century A.D., 155.

Famine relief expenditure, 469.

Famines, 539-544 ; causes of scarcity and of real famine, 539 ; means of husbanding the water-supply, 540 ; irrigation area, 540, 541 ; summary of Indian famines, 541, 542 ; the great famine of 1876-78, its causes, 542, 543 ; famine expenditure, 543 ; mortality from disease and starvation, 543, 544 ; famine a weak check on population, 544.

Faulmann, *Buch der Schrift*, quoted, 103 (footnote).

Fauna of India, 10.—*See* also ZOOLOGY, 652-662.

Female education, 478, 479.

Feræ Naturæ of India.—*See* ZOOLOGY AND BOTANY.

Ferdousi, Persian poet and historian in the days of Mahmúd of Ghazní, 275.

Fergusson, Mr. James, Paper in the *Journal of the Royal Asiatic Society for April* 1880, quoted, 147 (footnote) ; *Tree and Serpent Worship*, quoted, 185 (footnote 4) ; 204 (footnote 1) ; *History of Architecture*, 304 (footnotes).

Fetish-worship in Hinduism, 205, 206.

Feudatory India, the thirteen groups of Native States, 43 ; population, 45.

Filatures.—*See* SILK.

Final Struggles of the French in India, by Colonel Malleson, 379 (footnote).

Finances and taxation of India, obscurities and changes in system of account, 457-465 ; taxation of British India, 459-461 ; taxation under the Mughals and under the British, 462, 463 ; taxation in Native States, 464 ; incidence of taxation in British India, 464, 465.

Firishta's *Rise of the Muhammadan Power in India*, Colonel Briggs' translation, quoted, 271 (footnote) ; 287 (footnote 2) ; 291 (footnotes).

Firozshahr, Battle of, 411.

First Buddhist Council (543 B.C.), 143.

Fíruz Tughlak, the third king of the Tughlak dynasty (1351-88 A.D.), his great canals and public works, 285.

Fishes, 661, 662.

Fitch, Newberry, and Leedes, the first English traders in India (1583 A.D.), 364.

Flint weapons of ancient India, 53.

Flora of India, 662-664.

Food-grains, Export of, 571-573.

Forde, Colonel, recapture of Masulipatam from the French (1759), 385.

Foreign trade of India, its gradual growth, 561-581 ; returns of foreign trade (1840-84), 562-564 ; staples of import and export sea-borne trade (1882-83), 565-581.

Forest Department, Growth of, and its administration, 522-528 ; Forest Conservancy statistics, 526, 527 ; 'open' and 'reserved' forests, 526.

Forests of the Himálayas, 8 ; in Southern and South-Western India, 38-40 ; in Sind and Punjab, 524, 525 ; North-Western Provinces, 525 ; Sundarbans, 525 ; Assam and Burma, 525, 526.—*See* also FOREST DEPARTMENT, *ut supra*.

Fortified weaving settlements of the East India Company, 599.

Fourth Buddhist Council (40 A.D.), 147.

Fo-wei-kian-king, Chinese translation from the Sanskrit of the 'dying instructions of Buddha,' 141 and footnote.

Fox, The Indian, 654.

France, India's foreign trade with, 578, 579.

French East India Companies, and the present French possessions in India, 372 ; French and English in the Karnátik, the first French war (1746-48), 378 ; capture of Madras by the French (1746), and its restoration to the English (1748), 379 ; French influence in India (1798-1800), and intrigues with Tipú Sultán and the Nizám of Haidar-ábád, 394, 395.

Frobisher's, Davis', Hudson's, and Baffin's

2 Z

3 A

For Product Safety Concerns and Information please contact our EU representative GPSR@taylorandfrancis.com Taylor & Francis Verlag GmbH, Kaufingerstraße 24, 80331 München, Germany

Printed and bound by CPI Group (UK) Ltd, Croydon, CR0 4YY
11/04/2025
01844009-0009